W9-BSN-617

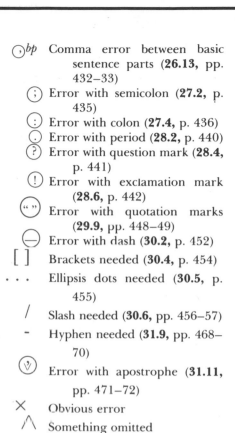

⊙*bp*   Comma error between basic sentence parts (**26.13**, pp. 432–33)

(;)   Error with semicolon (**27.2**, p. 435)

(:)   Error with colon (**27.4**, p. 436)

(.)   Error with period (**28.2**, p. 440)

(?)   Error with question mark (**28.4**, p. 441)

(!)   Error with exclamation mark (**28.6**, p. 442)

(" ")   Error with quotation marks (**29.9**, pp. 448–49)

(—)   Error with dash (**30.2**, p. 452)

[ ]   Brackets needed (**30.4**, p. 454)

· · ·   Ellipsis dots needed (**30.5**, p. 455)

/   Slash needed (**30.6**, pp. 456–57)

-   Hyphen needed (**31.9**, pp. 468–70)

(ᵛ)   Error with apostrophe (**31.11**, pp. 471–72)

×   Obvious error

∧   Something omitted

⊓⊔   Transpose these two elements

ABBREVIATIONS FOR CHAPTER TITLES

WRITING

A COLLEGE
HANDBOOK

Second Edition

James A. W. Heffernan

Dartmouth College

John E. Lincoln

WRITING

A COLLEGE HANDBOOK

Second Edition

W · W · NORTON & COMPANY
NEW YORK   LONDON

Copyright © 1986, 1982 by W. W. Norton & Company, Inc.
All rights reserved.
Printed in the United States of America.

The text of this book is composed in Baskerville, with display
type set in Baskerville. Composition and manufacturing by
The Maple-Vail Book Manufacturing Group.

Library of Congress Cataloging in Publication Data

Atheneum: Reynolds Price, excerpted from *Permanent Errors*. Copyright © 1970
Reynolds Price. Reprinted with the permission of Atheneum Publishers,
Inc.

Columbia University: Eugene Raskin, from "Walls and Barriers." Reprinted by
permission from the *Columbia University Forum*. Copyright © 1957 by The
Trustees of Columbia University in the City of New York. All rights reserved.

Curtis Brown Literary Agency. Fred Hoyle: Excerpt from THE NATURE OF THE
UNIVERSE by Fred Hoyle. Reprinted by permission of Curtis Brown, Ltd.
Copyright © 1960 by Fred Hoyle.

Annie Dillard: from *Sight Into Insight, Pilgrim at Tinker Creek*. Reprinted by permission of the author and her agent, Blanche C. Gregory, Inc. Copyright ©
1974 by Annie Dillard.

Dissent: X. J. Kennedy, from "Who Killed King Kong?" Reprinted by permission.

Oscar Handlin: from *Race and Nationality in American Life*. Copyright Oscar Handlin 1957, renewed 1985. Reprinted by permission.

Harper & Row: Gwendolyn Brooks: first stanza from "a song in the front yard"
(p. 12) in THE WORLD OF GWENDOLYN BROOKS by Gwendolyn Brooks.
Copyright 1945 by Gwendolyn Brooks Blakely. Erich Fromm: specified ex-
cerpt adapted from pp. 57–58 in THE HEART OF MAN by Erich Fromm,
Volume XII of RELIGIOUS PERSPECTIVES, planned and edited by Ruth
Nanda Anshen. Copyright © 1964 by Erich Fromm.

Holt, Rinheart and Winston: From "New Hampshire" from *The Poetry of Robert Frost*
edited by Edward Connery Lathem. Copyright 1923, © 1969 by Holt, Rinehart and Winston. Copyright 1951 by Robert Frost. Reprinted by permission of Holt, Rinehart and Winston, Publishers.

Houghton Mifflin: Definition of "cool." © 1980 by Houghton Mifflin Company.
Reprinted by permission from *The American Heritage Dictionary of the English
Language*. From *The Education of Henry Adams* by Henry Adams. Copyright
1946 by Charles F. Adams. Reprinted by permission of Houghton Mifflin
Company.

Since this page cannot legibly accommodate all the copyright notices, p. 663 con-
stitutes an extension of the copyright page.

ISBN 0-393-95499-4

W. W. Norton & Company, Inc., 500 Fifth Avenue, New York, N.Y. 10110
W. W. Norton & Company Ltd., 37 Great Russell Street, London WC1B 3NU

2 3 4 5 6 7 8 9 0

CONTENTS

I.
WRITING ESSAYS

II.
WRITING SENTENCES

III.

PUNCTUATION AND MECHANICS

IV.

THE RESEARCH PAPER

PREFACE TO THE SECOND EDITION

The first edition of this book set out to demonstrate that good writing is not simply the absence of grammatical error but the presence of rhetorical power. Though this second edition differs in a number of ways from the first, the leading aim of the book remains unchanged. While identifying the mistakes commonly made in student writing and showing how to correct them, it focuses on what student writers can do rather than on what they cannot or should not do. Above all, it seeks to explain and illustrate the various ways in which students can generate rhetorically effective prose.

Since many teachers like to start by introducing students to the writing process as a whole, Part I, "Writing Essays," begins with a five-chapter overview of that process. Users of the first edition will find that this new overview is at once more systematic and more thorough than the original one. While the original three-chapter overview gave short shrift to the important task of formulating a thesis and did not treat revising at all, the new overview gives special attention to both tasks, and it integrates them within a fully coherent guide to the writing process in five basic steps: pre-writing, discovering a thesis, organizing the first draft, revising (making large-scale changes), and editing (making small adjustments and corrections).

After five chapters on the writing process as a whole, chapters 6–10 of Part I treat special aspects of the process. Description, narration, methods of exposition, strategies of argumentation, and techniques of persuasion are all explained in more detail and with more examples than the first edition provided. Part I also devotes one chapter each to the writing of paragraphs and the choosing of words, and it ends with a chapter on how to turn reading into writing: how to use reading matter as a source of stimulation, as an object of analysis or interpretation, or as a model to be imitated.

Part II, "Writing Sentences," takes a fundamentally positive approach to sentence construction. This second edition treats sentence errors more thoroughly and precisely than the first one did, and our reference system—which has also been revised and improved—makes it easy to find specific advice on error correction. But since this book was written to be read as well as consulted, most of the chapters in Part II begin by explaining and illustrating the rhetorical impact of a particular construction when it is correctly and effectively used. Before we attack the misplaced modifier, for instance, we show what a well-placed modifier can do; and before we identify the wrong ways of joining independent clauses (the run-on sentence and the comma splice), we show what coordination can do. Using lively examples from student essays as well as from the work of leading writers, we consistently aim to show students how they can exploit the rich, vital, and inexhaustible resources of the English language. Our chief aim in the whole of Part II, in fact, is summed up by the title of the new chapter that ends Part II: "Invigorating Your Style."

The emphasis on rhetorical effect in Part II is reinforced by the exercises. Instead of merely calling for the correction of errors, many of them ask students to expand or combine short sentences, to finish sentences that we start for them, or to imitate complete sentences. The exercises will therefore help students to increase the variety of constructions they actually use and the variety of rhetorical effects they can achieve.

Part III, "Punctuation and Mechanics," is meant for reference. Teachers familiar with the first edition will find that what was once a single chapter has now been broken up into seven chapters (chapters 26–32), and that many points which were previously grouped together in long sections are now treated separately in short, readily accessible sections with their own headings. As a result, teachers and students alike will find specific advice on problems in punctuation—especially on problems with the comma—much easier to find.

Part IV, "The Research Paper," provides a detailed guide to the preparation and writing of a research paper. Users of the first edition will find that material originally presented in just two large chapters (one on preparing the paper, the other on writing it) has now been divided into five smaller ones. These new chapters define more sharply the steps involved in a research paper: preparing it, writing it, documenting it, and preparing the final copy. After one chapter on each of these steps, a final chapter is given to the sample research paper.

We begin Part IV by noting that a research paper may furnish an analytical argument about its topic or an explanatory survey of it; then we trace the developments of a particular argumentative paper from beginning to end. We explain not only how to use a library, take notes, cite sources, and avoid plagiarism, but also how to plan and organize the paper, how to keep quotations under control, how to make them serve an argument or an explanatory survey rather than take it over completely. We also thoroughly explain the new MLA style of parenthetical citation, and we show how it is used in a wholly new sample research paper: an argumentative paper on the vexing problem of how to make college possible for truly needy students. (A sample survey-type research paper appears in Appendix 1.)

Two Glossaries—one on usage and the other on grammatical terms—are followed in this new edition by four appendices. For teachers who prefer that students cite sources with notes rather than parentheses, the first appendix explains the MLA note style and shows how it is used in a sample paper, "Options for Working Mothers." Appendix 2 explains and illustrates with a few examples the APA method of parenthetical citation. Appendix 3 is a brief introduction to writing with a word processor as well as to computer programs that help students find errors and weaknesses in their writing. Finally, appendix 4 moves "Beyond Freshman English" into the various kinds of writing that students have to do for other courses and other purposes. With apt illustrations, the chapter shows how to write an examination essay, a résumé and covering letter for a job application, a business letter, a letter of protest, and a personal statement for an application to a school of law, medicine, business, or graduate studies. Appendix 4 tries to demonstrate, in fact, that the ability to write well can have a real and lasting effect upon a student's life.

Many teachers may find that this book by itself serves all the needs of a beginning composition course. To help you in various ways, however, we have prepared a number of supplements. For students who need intensive work on the sentence, we have revised *Writing—A College Workbook,* which offers brief instruction and extensive exercises on every aspect of sentence structure treated in parts II and III of the *Handbook.* To assist you in identifying the problems of individual students, we have provided a revised set of diagnostic tests. Finally, for your own use, we have revised our instructor's manual. This provides not only the answers to the exercises in the *Handbook* and the *Workbook* but also a number of suggestions on how to use the *Handbook* in a composition course.

JAMES A. W. HEFFERNAN
JOHN E. LINCOLN

ACKNOWLEDGMENTS

We have incurred many debts in the preparation of this book, and we are happy to acknowledge them here. It began as *The Dartmouth Guide to Writing*, by John E. Lincoln—a book of lessons and exercises issued by Dartmouth College for its students under a grant from the Lilly Foundation.

For help with the second edition, we are grateful, first of all, to the many teachers who took time to respond to our publisher's questionnaire; to Barbara Weaver, Anderson College; and to a small group of teachers who acted as on-going consultants on the entire manuscript: Diane DeLuca, Windward Community College; Michael Hennessy, Southwest Texas State University; Philip Keith, St. Cloud University; William T. Liston, Ball State University; William Martin, Armstrong State College; Rosemary O'Donoghue, Western New England College; and Craig Waddell, Rensselaer Polytechnic Institute.

In addition, we acknowledge our continuing debt to those teachers who used the preliminary edition of part of this book with their freshman-composition students during the fall of 1978 and told us how it worked. They are Joseph Adams, Northern Virginia Community College; Virginia Bothun, Willamette University; Kenneth Davis and Michael C. Tourjee, University of Kentucky; Elsie Deal, Edinboro State College; Pauline Glover, University of Tennessee; Tom Miles, West Virginia University; Patricia Moody, Syracuse University; S. F. Murray, Old Dominion University; Maureen Potts, University of Texas; Delma E. Presley, Georgia Southern College; Malinda Snow, Georgia State University (who also read the entire manuscript in a later draft); William Walsh, California State University—Northridge; Gregory Waters and Danny Rendleman, University of Michigan; Linda Wells, University of Wisconsin; Karl Zender, University of California—Davis; and Sander Zulauf, County College of Morris.

We are also indebted to many others for various kinds of help and advice: to William Cook, James Epperson, Robert Fogelin, G. Christian Jernstedt, John Lanzetta, Chauncey Loomis, Priscilla Sears, Rosalie O'Connell, Karen Pelz, Brenda Silver, William M. Smith, and Henry Terrie, all of Dartmouth College; to Joel Broadkin and Leslie Freeman, of the New York Institute of Technology; and to Harry Brent, Rutgers University, Camden College of Arts and Sciences; Alma G. Bryant, University of South Florida; Michael Cartwright, California State College—Bakersfield; Lynne Constantine, James Madison University; the late Gregory Cowan, Texas A & M University; Hubert M. English, Jr., University of Michigan; John J. Fenstermaker, Florida State University; Barbara Munson Goff, Cook College of Rutgers University; S. J. Hanna, Mary Washington College; James Hartman, University of Kansas; Joan E. Hartman, College of Staten Island, City University of New York; Francis Hubbard, University of Wisconsin—Milwaukee; Naomi Jacobs, University of Missouri—Columbia; Mildred A. Kalish, Suffolk County Community College; C. H. Knoblauch, Columbia University; James MacKillop, Onondaga Community College; Stephen R. Mandell, Drexel University; John C. Mellon, University of Illinois Chicago Circle Campus; Susan Miller, University of Wisconsin—Milwaukee; James Murphy, California State University—Hayward; Karen Ogden, University of Manitoba; Andrew Parkin, University of British Columbia; Kenneth Roe, Shasta College; Ann Sharp, Furman University; Craig B. Snow, University of Arizona; Ken M. Symes, Western Washington State College; Keith A. Tandy, Moorhead State University; Mary Thysell, University of Waterloo; and Harvey S. Wiener, La Guardia Community College. We both thank George Savvides, Charles Rice, Donald Murray, Charles Moran of the University of Massachusetts, and Ron Fortune, Illinois State University.

We must record here, too, our indebtedness to the many students who have contributed examples of what they do in their writing—in particular, Mitch Arion, Barbara Clark, Natica Lyons, Sarah Watson, Bart Naylor, Tony Fenwick, Erica Berl, Lisa Miles, James Mann, Timothy Boyle, Ken Oshima, Qiao Xing, David Lenrow, Sherri Hughes, Rick Kurihara, Daphne Bien, Scott Jaynes, Adam Usadi, Steven Arkowitz, Susanmarie Harrington, and David Leitao. Thanks are due as well to Michael Freeman and Lois Krieger, who gave us their expert advice on the use of library resources for research, and also to those who generously supplied us with material for appendix 4: Frances R. Hall of Dartmouth Medical School, Robert Sokol and Kenneth Shewmaker of Dartmouth College, and Andrew Vouras of the New England Telephone Company. We also thank Jay Wright and Barbara Cunningham of the Dartmouth College English Department, who kindly helped us with the photocopying of material for this edition.

In addition, we wish to thank present and former members of our publisher's staff for their signal contributions. Ethelbert Nevin II and John E. Neill each played a part in persuading us to write the book, and John W. N. Francis played a crucial role in helping us to develop the first edition. Esther Jacobson, who copyedited the first edition, and Marian Johnson, who copyedited the second, not only saved us from many errors but decisively helped us to clarify the organization of the book. We also owe thanks to Barry Wade, James Jordan, John Hawkins, Sarah Wolbach, Nancy Dale Muldoon, Diane O'Connor, Nancy K. Palmquist, Rachel Teplow, and Carol Stiles, whose aid has been invaluable. Lastly and resoundingly, we thank John Benedict, whose editorial zeal and wholehearted cooperation have been just as indispensable to the completion of the second edition as they were to the first.

We also wish to acknowledge our debt to the following books and articles: Monroe Beardsley, *Thinking Straight*, 4th ed. (New York: Prentice-Hall, 1975); N. R. Cattell, *The New English Grammar* (Cambridge, MA: MIT Press, 1969); Elaine Chaika, "Grammars and Teaching," *College English* 39 (March 1978), 770–83; Francis Christensen, "A Generative Rhetoric of the Sentence," "Notes toward a New Rhetoric," and "A Generative Rhetoric of the Paragraph," in *The Sentence and the Paragraph* (Urbana, IL: NCTE, 1966); Harry H. Crosby and George F. Estey, *College Writing: The Rhetorical Imperative* (New York: Harper & Row, 1968); George O. Curme, *English Grammar* (New York: Barnes and Noble, 1947); Bergen and Cornelia Evans, *A Dictionary of Contemporary American Usage* (New York: Random House, 1957); Charles Fillmore, "The Case for Case," in *Universals in Linguistic Theory*, ed. Emmon Bach and Robert T. Harms (New York: Holt, Rinehart and Winston, 1968); Linda S. Flower and John R. Hayes, "Problem Solving Strategies and the Writing Process," *College English* 39 (December 1977), 449–61; W. Nelson Francis, *The Structure of American English* (New York: Ronald, 1958); Robert J. Geist, *An Introduction to Transformational Grammar* (New York: Macmillan, 1971); William E. Gruber, " 'Servile Copying' and the Teaching of English Composition," *College English* 39 (December 1977), 491–97; A. S. Hornby, *A Guide to Patterns and Usage in English* (London: Oxford University Press, 1954); Darrell Huff, *How to Lie with Statistics* (New York: W. W. Norton & Company, 1954); Roderick A. Jacobs and Peter S. Rosenbaum, *En-*

glish *Transformational Grammar* (Waltham, MA: Blaisdell, 1968); Otto Jespersen, *Essentials of English Grammar* (London: George Allen & Unwin, 1959); James L. Kinneavy, *A Theory of Discourse* (New York: W. W. Norton and Company, 1980); John C. Mellon, *Transformational Sentence Combining* (Urbana, IL: NCTE, 1969); Donald Murray, *A Writer Teaches Writing: A Practical Method of Teaching Composition* (Boston: Houghton Mifflin, 1968), and also various essays and lectures; Frank O'Hare, *Sentence Combining* (Urbana, IL: NCTE, 1973), and *Sentencecraft* (Lexington, MA: Ginn, 1975); Mina Shaughnessy, *Errors and Expectations: A Guide for the Teacher of Basic Writing* (New York: Oxford University Press, 1977); Harry Shaw, *Errors in English and Ways to Correct Them* (New York: Barnes and Noble, 1970); the *MLA Handbook for Writers of Research Papers* (New York: Modern Language Association, 1984); and the *Publication Manual of the American Psychological Association,* 3rd ed. (Washington, D.C.: American Psychological Association, 1983).

Lastly, we thank our spouses, Nancy Heffernan and Mary Lincoln, who contributed to the preparation of this book in ways too numerous to mention, and we thank our children—Andrew and Virginia Heffernan, and Chris, Peter, and Brian Lincoln—for supplying both vivid samples of their own writing and their own special brand of encouragement.

J.A.W.H.
J.E.L.

WRITING

A COLLEGE HANDBOOK

Second Edition

INTRODUCTION

Talking and Writing

Talking is something most of us seem to do naturally. We learn to talk almost automatically, first imitating the words we hear and then imitating the ways in which people around us put them together. Well before we learn how to put words on paper, we unconsciously learn how to use them in speech.

But no one learns to write automatically. You cannot write even a single letter of the alphabet without a conscious effort of mind and hand, and to get beyond the single letter, you must be shown how to form words, how to put words together into sentences, and how to punctuate those sentences.

Writing, then, is a means of communication you must consciously learn. And part of what makes it hard to learn is that written words usually have to express your meaning in your absence, have to "speak" all by themselves. When you speak face to face with a listener, you can communicate in many different ways. You can raise or lower the pitch or volume of your voice to emphasize a point; you can grin, frown, wink, or shrug; you can use your hands to shape out a meaning when you don't quite have the words to do it; you can even make your silence mean something. But in writing you have to communicate without facial expressions, gestures, or body English of any kind. You have to speak with words and punctuation alone.

Furthermore, writing is a solitary act. When you talk, you normally talk to someone who talks back, who raises questions, who lets you know whether or not you are making yourself clear. But when you write, you work alone. Even if you are writing a letter to a friend, he or she will not suddenly materialize to prod or prompt you into speech, to help you fill in the gaps that so often occur when you try to tell a story or give an explanation off the top of your head. To write well, you have to anticipate the reactions of a reader you cannot see or hear.

But writing does have one big advantage over speaking. It gives you time to think, to try out your ideas on paper, to choose your words, to read what you have written, to rethink, revise, and rearrange it, and, most importantly, to consider its effect on a reader. Writing gives you time to find the best possible way of stating what you mean. And the more you study the craft of writing, the better you will use your writing time.

Standard English

This book aims to help you write effectively in English. But since there are many kinds of English, you should know which kind this book aims to teach—and why.

The language called "English" is used in many parts of the world. It is spoken not only in England but also in the British West Indies and in countries that were once British colonies—such as Canada, the United States, Australia, India, and Nigeria. These are all "English-speaking" countries, but they have different ways of using English. Sometimes, for instance, they have different words for the same thing:

>   truck [U.S.] = lorry [Great Britain]
>   pond [U.S.] = billabong [Australia]

Sometimes they have different ways of spelling or pronouncing the same word:

>   labor [U.S.] = labour [Great Britain and Canada]
>   recognize [U.S.] = recognise [Great Britain and Canada]
>   laugh: pronounced "laff" in the U.S., "lahff" in Great Britain
>   paint: pronounced "paynt" in the U.S., "pint" in Australia
>   check [U.S.] = cheque [Great Britain and Canada]

Sometimes they use different grammatical forms:

>   The jury has reached a verdict. [U.S.]
>   The jury have reached a verdict. [all other English-speaking countries]

Probably you have already noticed differences such as these. Even if you have never traveled abroad, you have probably heard British or Australian speech. When you did, you could undoubtedly tell after just a few words that what you were hearing was different from any kind of English commonly spoken in North America. The reason for the difference is that a living language never stands still. Like the people who speak it and the world they speak it in, it changes. And if English-speaking peoples live far enough apart, the English they use will change in divergent ways. That is why English sounds different in different parts of the world.

Just as English varies from one country to another, it also varies from one region of a country to another, and from one cultural or ethnic group to another. Consider these statements:

> She'll say I be talkin
> She'll say I am talking.
>
> They ain't got no ponies; they got big horses: I rode one, real big uns.
> They don't have any ponies; they have big horses. I rode one, a really big one.
>
> I have three brother and two sister.
> I have three brothers and two sisters.

These statements illustrate four dialects—four kinds of English used in North America. The first statement in each pair illustrates a regional or ethnic dialect; the second illustrates Standard English. Each of these dialects has its own distinctive character and rules. But of them all, Standard English is the only one normally taught in schools and colleges, the only one normally required in business and the professions, and the only one widely used in writing—especially in print. Why does Standard English enjoy this privilege? Is it always better than any other kind? And if you were raised to speak an ethnic or regional dialect, must you stop speaking that dialect in order to learn the Standard one?

There is no easy answer to the first of those three questions. But the answer to the second one is no. Standard English is not always better than any other kind. In a spoken exchange, it can sometimes be less expressive—and therefore less effective—than a regional or ethnic dialect. Compare, for instance, the original version of a regional proverb with the Standard version:

> Them as has, gets; them as ain't, gets took.
> Those who have, get; those who do not have, get taken.

These two statements strike the ear in different ways. While the first has the expressive vitality of regional speech, the second—the Standard version—sounds comparatively stiff. The original packs more punch.

Part of what makes the original version so effective is the tradition that stands behind it, and because of that tradition, the answer to the third question we raised is also no. A regional or ethnic dialect is not just a way of speaking; it is the living record of a shared heritage and shared concerns. For this reason, no one who speaks such a dialect should be forced to give it up.

But if many people can learn more than one language, most people can learn more than one dialect, and whatever the dialect you were raised to speak, you can and should learn to write Standard English. Whether or not it is better than any other dialect for purposes of speech, it is what you will normally be expected to use in your writing. During college, it is what teachers will expect you to use in essays, exams, reports, and research papers. After college, it is what others will expect you to use in anything you write for business or professional purposes. For all of these reasons, Standard English is what this book aims to help you learn.

Grammar and Rhetoric

The grammar of a language is the set of rules by which its sentences are made. You started learning the rules of English grammar as soon as you started to talk. Well before you learned how to write, you could have said which of these two statements made sense:

> *Eggs breakfast fried I two for had.
> I had two fried eggs for breakfast.

The words in each statement are the same, but you can readily see that only the second arrangement makes sense. You instinctively know that some ways of arranging the seven words are acceptable and others are not. You may not be able to say just why the word order in the first arrangement is wrong, but you know that it is.

Good writing requires a working knowledge of grammar, a refinement of the basic or instinctive knowledge you already have. But good writing is more than the act of obeying grammatical rules. It is also the art of using rhetoric—of arranging words, phrases, sentences, and paragraphs in such a way as to engage and sustain the reader's attention.

The power of rhetoric can sometimes be felt in a single sentence. Patrick Henry said, "Give me liberty, or give me death." Franklin D. Roosevelt said, "The only thing we have to fear is fear itself." General George S. Patton said to his troops after a battle, "You have been baptized in fire and blood and have come out steel." Martin Luther King, Jr., said to a crowd of civil-rights demonstrators, "I have a dream." As these examples help to show, the sen-

---

*From this point on, nonstandard constructions in this book are marked with a star, except in chapter 17, where sentence fragments are clearly identified in other ways. We also use asterisks to mark misspelled words in drafts of student essays.

tence is at once the basic unit of writing and the basic source of its rhetorical effects. A good sentence not only takes its place with other sentences but also makes a place for itself, striking the reader with its own special clarity and force. One aim of this book, therefore, is to help you maximize the rhetorical impact of every sentence you write.

Yet you do not normally write single sentences in isolation. You write them in sequence, and rhetoric is the art of making that sequence effective—of moving from one sentence to another in a paragraph, and from one paragraph to another in an essay. It is the art of sustaining continuity while continually moving ahead, of developing a description, a narrative, an explanation, or an argument in such a way as to take the reader with you from beginning to end. The ultimate aim of this book, therefore, is to explain the rhetoric of the writing process as a whole.

Using This Book

You can use this book in one of two ways: as a textbook for a course in composition, or as a reference guide to help you with a large variety of writing tasks in college and afterward.

If you are using this book in a composition course, your teacher will undoubtedly assign certain chapters or sections to the whole class. In addition, after seeing what you individually have written, your teacher will probably assign certain sections and exercises specifically chosen to meet your needs. But since you may want to use this book on your own as well, you should know how it is organized.

We have divided this book into four main parts. Part I, "Writing Essays," first guides you through the whole writing process from pre-writing to proofreading your final draft. Then it treats particular kinds of writing, such as exposition and persuasion, and particular parts of the writing process, such as paragraphing and choosing words. Part II, "Writing Sentences," is designed chiefly to explain and illustrate the variety of ways you can use sentence structure. We explain the things you can't or normally shouldn't do, such as writing sentence fragments and misplacing modifiers. But we emphasize the things you can and should do, such as varying your sentence patterns, using modifiers of all kinds, organizing your sentences by means of coordination and subordination, enhancing coordination with parallelism, controlling emphasis by the way you arrange your words, and invigorating your style.† Part III, "Punctuation and Mechanics," explains the rules of punctuation as

†To illustrate various constructions, we often quote other writers, and we often italicize certain words in their sentences to stress particular points. In all such cases, the italics are ours, not the writers'.

well as spelling and the use of mechanical conventions such as capitals and italics. Part IV, "The Research Paper," explains how to prepare, write, and document a library research paper.

At the end of the book are two alphabetical glossaries. The Glossary of Usage explains many of the words or phrases that writers find troublesome or confusing; the Glossary of Terms defines the terms that are commonly used in discussions of writing. Although the terms we use are printed in **boldface type** in the text and defined where they first appear, you may find this glossary an additional aid.

Finally, the book includes four appendices designed to serve special needs. Appendix 1 explains how to cite sources in a research paper with footnotes or endnotes. Appendix 2 explains how to cite sources in the APA parenthetical style. Appendix 3 briefly explains how to write with a word processor. And Appendix 4 explains writing in the world "beyond Freshman English," where you will have to compose such things as essay exams, personal statements for applications to professional schools, and covering letters for job applications.

Since this book is designed for ready reference as well as for steady reading, we have tried to make it as easy as possible for you to locate specific advice on every subject we cover. If you are seeking information on your own, the best places for you to start looking are the summary on the back endpapers—which shows you the layout of the entire *Handbook* in chart form—and the table of contents at the beginning of the book. Both the summary and the contents list every major topic, so all you need to do is turn to the appropriate page. If you can't find the topic you want in either the summary or the table of contents, go to the index, which lists all topics alphabetically and gives the page numbers for each one.

In skimming through the book, you will notice various abbreviations and symbols (such as *mod* and *//*). These are explained in the two alphabetical lists on the front endpapers: "Abbreviations for Chapter Titles" and "Symbols for Revision." In these lists, each abbreviation and symbol is followed by a chapter title or a brief explanation, along with a reference to the appropriate part of the text.

The abbreviations and symbols are intended for use by your instructor in marking your papers. If, for example, you see *mod* or $(//)$ on your paper, you can look for it on the front-endpaper lists. There you'll find that *mod* refers you to the "Modifiers" chapter and that $(//)$ refers you to the section explaining how to correct faulty parallelism.

Alternatively, your instructor may refer you to a specific topic by using one of the section numbers, which are listed on the back endpapers and in the table of contents. That is, instead of writing ⃝// on your paper, your instructor may write **14.4,** which refers to chapter 14, section 4, where we deal with faulty parallelism. Smaller points are treated in lettered subsections such as **22.2A,** "Forming the Active Voice."

One other feature of this book that will help you find specific topics quickly is the reference box in the upper margin of each page. Inside the box is the appropriate section number (e.g., **14.4**); above the box is the chapter abbreviation (e.g., *coor/pc*); and underneath the box, whenever it is needed for reference, is the revision symbol (e.g., ⃝//). We hope these reference devices will help you find information conveniently both during your composition course and afterward.

I

WRITING ESSAYS

1

PRE-WRITING

Sometimes the hardest part of writing is getting started. Looking at a sheet of blank white paper is like looking at a snow-covered car on an icy winter morning and wondering if the engine will turn over. When the car doesn't start, of course, there are certain simple things you can do—like calling somebody to come and recharge the battery. But what happens when the mind doesn't start? Where do you get a brain recharged?

Inspiration is a mysterious process, and no one can say just when and how it will strike. But it strikes those who work for it much more often than those who simply wait for it. So how do you work for inspiration? How do you create the conditions under which the words will begin to flow? To that question this book has no single, simple answer. Creating an essay is an intensely personal process, and you will finally have to choose the method that works best for you. But it's important to have a method of some kind, to know what to do while waiting for inspiration. Here are our suggestions.

1.1 Give Yourself Time to Make Discoveries

For most writers, composing is neither all work nor all inspiration. It's a process of moving back and forth from one to the other, from concentration to relaxation, from pushing ideas to playing with them, and then making discoveries. You need time to make the process work well, but time alone will not make your discoveries for you. You have to earn the magic moments of inspiration by periods of conscious and concentrated effort.

At the start, therefore, you should think about your work schedule. Few writers can work productively for more than four hours without a break. If you try to exceed your limit, you may find yourself slowing down or running dry or going around in circles, stuck in the groove because you're too weary to think straight. The smart way to write a paper is to proceed in stages, to set yourself short-term goals to be reached in periods of well-focused concentration.

So whether you are choosing a topic yourself or trying to decide what to do with a topic assigned by your teacher, you should start by giving yourself a couple of days to discover ideas and test them out. Some ideas need seedtime. They bloom in your conscious mind only after they have taken root in your subconscious. But like seedlings, they must be watered and fertilized in order to grow. This chapter aims not only to help you find ideas but also to make them grow.

1.2 Writing on Unassigned Topics

If you're free to choose your own topic, try any one of the following methods of discovery:

1. Write nonstop for twenty minutes. Write a letter to a friend that begins, "The reason I like/dislike writing (or any other activity) is . . ." Write without stopping. Don't worry about spelling, punctuation, grammar, or even making sense; just write whatever comes to mind. After twenty minutes, read what you have written, and underline anything you find interesting, even surprising. Now write about this point for ten minutes without stopping. When finished, you may find that you have come upon a topic you want to develop into a full-scale essay.

2. Examine a conflict. Since the richest moments of experience are often born out of conflict, suppose you recall a time when you were made or asked to do something you did not want to do. When and where did it happen? How did you feel about having to act against your will? How did you feel about the person who asked you to do so? What did you learn from the episode? Raising questions like these—and trying to answer them—will help you think more about the experience until you discover the point you want to explore in depth.

3. Spy on people. Have you noticed the way some people (including you, perhaps) behave at rock concerts, at movies, in shopping centers, in department stores, in supermarkets, in classrooms, in restaurants, on sidewalks, on beaches, at parties? Does anything they do, say, or wear strike you as funny or strange or irritating? If so, why? And if you had the power to change their behavior, what would you do?

4. Choose a topic you want to know more about. Tap your curiosity. Investigate a subject that interests you. As you learn about it, you will find yourself increasingly eager to share your new knowledge with others—especially if the subject is one you have wondered about for some time. Look for the unexpected. Surprises ill interest your readers as much as they interest you.

5. Share your expertise. Help others learn how to do something you do well. You may be an expert photographer, carpenter, guitar player, computer operator, cartoonist, salesclerk, or actor. What advice could you give others who would like to acquire your skill? What should they be prepared to do and sacrifice? What characteristics do they need to have? What obstacles will confront them? What kind of regimen should they follow?

EXERCISE 1   Writing about Your Own Writing Experience

Follow the instructions given above in item 1, but start with these words: "I like writing because . . ." or "I dislike writing because . . ."

EXERCISE 2   Exploring a Moment of Conflict

Recall a time in your life when you felt bullied, cheated, or deceived. When, where, and how did it happen? How did you feel about yourself? How did you feel about the other person? What did you learn from this experience? As you consider these questions, write about them for ten minutes without stopping.

EXERCISE 3   Writing about People

After rereading item 3 above, write nonstop for ten minutes about a person or group that amuses or annoys you. Write as fast as you can. Don't worry about grammar, spelling, or punctuation. Just get your thoughts and description down.

EXERCISE 4   Asking Questions

After rereading item 4 above, jot down as many questions as you can about a subject you would like to investigate.

EXERCISE 5   Exploring Your Favorite Subject

Explain what puzzles or fascinates you most about your favorite subject. Write for ten minutes.

1.3 Make an Assigned Topic Your Own

When a topic is assigned, find a way to make it your own. Most of the writing you do in college will be on assigned topics. The way to get started on an assigned topic is to discover its connection with what you already know, with your own interests and experience.

Suppose you are asked to write about the free enterprise system. Your first thought may be of huge corporations: Du Pont, IBM, General Motors, Chrysler, AT&T. But big firms like these are far outnumbered by small ones such as pizza parlors, taxicab companies, barbershops, hairdressing salons, and drug stores. Lee Iacocca is a businessman; but so is the street vendor selling leather belts or costume jewelry at a busy intersection, and so is the ten-year-old behind a lemonade stand on a hot summer afternoon. If you've ever had a job, you've had the chance to see how someone else runs a business. If you've participated in Junior Achievement, you've helped to run a company yourself. And if you've ever sold anything of your own, whether goods or services (such as lawn-mowing or babysitting), then you know what it means to run your own business, however small. Finally, if at different times you've worked for someone else and for yourself, you have firsthand experience of the difference between the predictability of a set wage and the unpredictability of profit, between security and risk, between earnings that are guaranteed but limited and earnings that are unguaranteed but limitless. Personal experience, then, can be just what you need to find your way into a topic.

Consider what two different students did with two different topics assigned to them. Asked to write about the free enterprise system, Virginia decided to explain how she and a few other girls organized a summer playgroup when they were only nine-years-old and how their profits rose to nearly three hundred dollars each in the fourth summer of their operation. Asked to write about sports, Tim decided to concentrate on hockey because he had played it for years and especially because the whole experience of scoring goals fascinated him. Beginning in section 1.5, we will show how each of these students moved from a topic to a thesis, and we will trace the development of Tim's essay right up to its final version.

EXERCISE 6 **Making a Topic Your Own**

Describe a personal experience that you might use to make a point about any one of the following topics:

families	the selective service system	free enterprise
computers	crime	music
education	sports	transportation
farming	housing	

1.4   Cut the Topic Down to a Size You Can Manage

One of the biggest obstacles to the success of a short essay is an oversize topic. If you try to write eight hundred words on the free enterprise system, you will probably find that you have room for only commonplace generalizations about it: big businesses don't pay their fair share of taxes; company executives are overpaid; workers are underpaid; the whole system takes from the many and gives to the fortunate few. When you fill up a paper with generalizations like these, you leave yourself no room to think and discover or to use your own experience. Also, you bore your readers by telling them what they have already heard many times before.

If you can define a particular topic in terms of your own experience, you have already begun reducing it to a manageable size. But even as you connect it to your own experience, you should try to isolate and identify a piece of it, to make your topic as precise and specific as possible. Here are some examples:

GENERAL	SPECIFIC	MORE SPECIFIC
sports	hockey	scoring goals
medical care	artificial organs	artificial hearts
computers	word processing	spelling-checker programs
working women	working mothers	working mothers with small children
elections	role of TV in elections	role of TV in election of John F. Kennedy
nuclear power	nuclear waste	disposal of nuclear waste
television	television commercials	women in TV commercials
music	singing	singing in a group
pollution	acid rain	effects of acid rain on trees
immigration	illegal aliens	employment of illegal aliens
free enterprise	small business	running a playgroup
transportation	owning a car	maintaining an engine

EXERCISE 7   Cutting a Topic Down to Size

Take any one of the topics listed in exercise 6 and make it as specific as possible.

> EXAMPLE
> crime   shoplifting   punishment of shoplifters

1.5 Ask Questions

Once you have chosen a topic and cut it down to manageable size, you can open it up with questions. Journalists commonly dig up information by asking what? who? when? where? how? why? If you think of your topic not as an object but as an action, you can ask these questions to help you generate an essay. What happened? Who made it happen or was affected by it? When and where did it happen? How did it happen? Why was it made to happen? Finally, you can ask, What effect did it have?

Not all of these questions will work for every topic. If you're writing about an earthquake or some other natural disaster, for instance, you may not be able to say who caused it without invoking the mysterious hand of Providence. But every one of these questions can be tried with any topic as a way of opening up its possibilities and generating further questions. Consider the questions raised by Tim, the hockey player, as he thought about scoring goals in hockey games:

What happens when I score a goal? What are the parts of the process? What goes through my mind as the puck goes past the goalie? What do I see? What do I feel? What do I hear?

Who besides me gets into the action? What about my teammates? What about the goalie? What about the coach? What about the crowd?

When and *where* do I score goals? How often? What is the moment of scoring like? Where am I when the puck goes into the net? What is the scene that surrounds me?

How do I score? Do I plan the shot, or is it just a lucky accident every time? How is my body positioned? Am I stopped or moving, hunched over or standing up straight?

Why do I love to score? Is it because I want to do my best for the team? Or because I love to hear the cheers of the crowd? Or because the coach will think I'm terrific? Or does it have something to do with just getting that puck past the goalie?

What effect does my scoring have? What does it do to the crowd? What does it do to my teammates? What does it immediately do for me?

The crucial thing about this stage of the pre-writing process is to hit your topic with every question you can think of. You probably won't get around to answering all of the questions you raise, and some of them may not even have answers. But the more questions you raise, the more deeply you will penetrate the world of your topic. Use the basic questions to generate others, to liberate your curiosity.

EXERCISE 8   Asking Questions

Using each of the question categories illustrated above, ask at least twelve questions about the topic you defined in exercise 7.

1.6   Choose a Basic Question to Help You Define a Key Problem or Conflict

All of the questions you ask can help you generate material, and a good deal of this material may find its way into your essay. But just as you need to define your topic as specifically as possible, you also need a basic question to help you define the key problem or conflict you will try to resolve. For Virginia, who had helped to organize a summer playgroup, the key question was *How?* How did she and her friends—as young as they all were—manage to run such a highly successful business? For Tim, the key question was *Why?* Why did he love scoring goals so much? Was it because scoring served the team—or because it served his own ego?

Obviously, different ways of defining a key conflict or problem will lead to different kinds of essays. The choice of a *How* question commits the writer to a search for practical means, for what has been done to achieve a particular result or could be done to solve a specific problem. The choice of a *Why* question commits the writer to a search for reasons, for motives or purposes.

To focus on one basic question is also to see its relation to others. When Tim decided to concentrate on why he loved scoring, he knew that he would also have to say something about how he scored, about what he felt when it happened, about the people involved, about the scene and the moment of the shot, and about its effects. But he decided to make all of these other points secondary, to use them in answering the question *Why?* In choosing this question, he was taking a decisive step forward. He now had not only a specific topic, but also a definite purpose.

EXERCISE 9   Choosing a Basic Question and Defining a Conflict

Pick one of the questions you wrote down for exercise 8 and say what conflict or problem it raises. Then make a list of the other questions that may help you resolve the conflict or problem.

1.7   Get Reactions to Your Question

One of the hardest things about writing is that you normally have to do it alone. Before you begin to write, therefore, find someone you can talk to about the basic question you plan to explore. If you already have some idea of how you might answer the question, your listener may give you a different answer. Hearing it will make you more sensitive to the complexity of your subject, more skillful in anticipating possible misunderstandings or objections to your point of view, and therefore more effective in explaining or defending it.

EXERCISE 10   Getting Responses

Explain to someone else the basic question you hope to explore and also—if you can—your own ideas about how to answer it. Then (1) record his or her response in writing and (2) comment on the response.

1.8   Use Analogies

An analogy answers the question "What's it like?" Because analogies let you translate abstract ideas or feelings into concrete terms, they can open your eyes to a whole new way of looking at your topic. One student writing on families found the key to her essay when she imagined her own fatherless family as a picture puzzle broken up and left without all of its pieces. Another student compared job hunting in a tight market to looking for an unlocked window in a locked-up house. And a third student compared getting a college education to wandering through a supermarket, trying to stick with a definite plan (a shopping list of required or carefully chosen courses) and yet now and then being tempted into impulse buying: taking a course because it just looks good or has a catchy name.

Thinking up analogies is a purposeful kind of play in which you let your imagination go. Don't worry about going too far; if the analogy won't work, you'll find out soon enough. You're not yet formally writing. You're still trying out ideas, and anything goes.

EXERCISE 11   Using Analogies

Think of an analogy to express the basic problem or conflict you defined in exercise 10.

1.9   Work with a Nugget

As you think about your topic, do you find yourself struck by a single word, phrase, idea, or example connected with it? If so, that may be a nugget for you, a rich source of further ideas. A single phrase can sometimes start a whole train of ideas that can be worked into your paper. In Tim's case, the nugget was "freeze-frame." Once it came to his mind, it summoned up for him the moment of scoring, the instant when everything in a game of lightning speed and perpetual motion came—or seemed to come—to a sudden halt. You'll see what he did with this nugget in the next chapter.

Exercise 12   Working with a Nugget

Write for five minutes on any suggestive word, phrase, idea, or example connected with your topic.

1.10 Read with a Purpose

Whether you've been assigned a topic or have chosen your own, one good way of exploring the topic is to read about it. You may not even have to go to the library. In the nearest newspaper or magazine you will find articles on a variety of subjects—articles that can help you choose your topic, define it, enrich it, or enlarge it. Reading gives you not only a point of departure but also a continuous supply of information. Suppose you are writing about television. It will help you to know that according to David Sohn (in "A Nation of Videots"), "the average American watches about 1200 hours of TV each year, yet reads books for only five hours per year." It will also help you to know that Robert Lewis Shayon finds TV "a lollipop trap—a pattern of prime-time entertainment programming planned, produced, and directed primarily at the twelve- to seventeen-year-old viewer" ("Consumers, Commercials, and Men about Town"). Facts and quotations like these generate questions. Why do people let TV take over so much of their time? How are children and teenagers presented on TV?

Reading in order to write is a special kind of reading, and we discuss it fully later in the book. (See chapter 10, pp. 196–223.) But the following chapter concerns the next stage in the process of writing: freewriting your way to a thesis.

Exercise 13   Reading with a Purpose

From any printed source available to you—a book, a magazine, or a newspaper—take a single interesting fact or opinion, and write about it for ten minutes.

2

FREEWRITING YOUR WAY TO A THESIS

If you have followed all or even some of the suggestions made in the previous chapter, you may now have in mind not only a specific topic but also an answer to your basic question. If so, you may be ready to formulate a **thesis:** a specific statement about your topic, a precise declaration of what you will aim to show in your essay as a whole. The student writing on families, for instance, found that she had discovered her thesis as soon as she thought of using puzzle pieces to explain her fatherless family. She would aim, she decided, to show how love, understanding, and mutual commitment reorganized the remaining pieces.

If you can now formulate a statement such as this about your own topic, you may not need the present chapter. But you will probably find that a well-defined thesis does not always emerge in the pre-writing stage. Even after you have cut down your topic, formulated questions, played with possible analogies, and worked with a nugget, you may still feel uncertain of your aim, unable to see or to say just exactly what your essay will show. If that is the case, you can do one of two things: (1) you can start writing with a tentative or provisional statement of thesis, knowing you may change it later on; (2) you can use **directed freewriting** to discover a thesis.

2.1 Directed Freewriting

Directed freewriting is writing that seeks the answer to a specific question but ignores all other constraints. It works best when fully energized by the pre-writing process—by questions, analogies, and nuggets—but it need not have any particular order or form. In freewriting, you don't have to worry about an introduction or conclusion, about paragraphing, about spelling, or even about completing all of your sentences. Just plunge in and seek an answer to your basic question—as Tim did in this piece of freewriting:

> Why score? For glory? For the good of the team? Maybe. But mainly I love the mind trip, the personal high I get from it—the feeling inside. *Especialy in hockey. The strange thing is, I know I'm going to score before I shoot. It's like getting up when the phone rings because I somehow *know* it's for me. I don't try and *analize why I know—I just *know.* A *wonderfull sensation. And that's what comes to me when I get ready to shoot. Peace. I relax and don't even consciously try to shoot, the shot just happens. Often I can't even remember looking at the puck, I'm so relaxed at this point I might not have. The feeling at this point is one of perfection. Everything is going right and I'm not even trying to do anything. Of course not every shot is like this, otherwise right now I'd be at the Bruins training camp on my way to hockey stardom instead of writing this. But since every shot is *not* perfect, and most of them end up looking like a third grader's and feeling like my body was working against itself, arms flailing one way and legs slipping the other, the ones that are perfect give me a wonderful sense of what the game should be like. And then there's the freeze-frame. Often I can't remember looking at the puck when I shoot, but I can always see it go into the goal. No matter how fast it goes or how far away I'm shooting from, I can always see the puck hitting the twine at the back of the net. And at that moment I see the whole world in a freeze-frame. I see where every other player is standing I even see the expressions of a face or two in the crowd. When the freeze-frame ends, the sense of power strikes. I realize then that the goalie tried his hardest but couldn't stop my shot. I was better than he was. For any human being in an intensely competitive situation that's a major high. Then the crowd begins to cheer, furthering the high. This is why I love to score goals. I don't want to sound selfish, and in all honesty I don't think I'm a selfish player. I don't try and hog the glory, and after a second or two of power trip, I come back to earth. But for that single moment I'm on top of the world looking down on it, and it's all mine.

This passage shows what you can do with freewriting. Writing at high speed, liberated from the need to worry about spelling or grammar or punctuation or paragraphing or organization, free from everything but the intense desire to re-create in words the experience of scoring, Tim discovered his thesis: he loved scoring because it gave him the sensation of power.

*Misspelled words in Tim's writing are marked with asterisks.

For one more example of what you can discover while freewriting, consider Virginia's account of her experience running a playgroup:

> The idea: a summer playgroup for little kids, a kind of neighborhood day camp. But how could we start it? How could we organize it? How could we make it succeed? Made schedules and lists and estimated profits. Thought of possible customers, possible partners. So exciting! Called Megan, because she was my best friend, and Jennifer, because she was reliable, and Karen, because she was a good organizer. Reactions from them: some excitement, a lot of doubt. But none in my mind. Of course that soon changed. *Very discouraged* when people turned us down. The Velezes: "Our kids have other things to do in the summer." The Moors: "I'd love to, but you kids are only nine." I *hated* rejection. Decided on a three week program, 3 mornings a week from 9 to 12. Karen called a few people, but not Megan or Jennifer. They made signs for the library and the supermarket bulletin board. I remember arguments. Arguing over daily schedules, arguing over who was doing what and who was going to do what, and wondering about things like whether we could get sued if some kid got hurt. Worrying. Felt sometimes that we were just going to be wasting our summer. Got more rejections and almost gave the whole thing up. Finally, the first day. Four kids showed up: Lynne, Beth, Corby, Topher. One for each of us. A cute gang. We made lunch, sang songs, ran around, played games. What responsibility! What fun! Mom, of course, was inside, but we were outside in the backyard, and the four of us—four 9-year-olds—had a whole *business* going. We were earning money—75¢ an hour each—and loving it. No teachers or parents telling us what to do. We were in charge. Profits for that first summer: $15.00. "Not worth it," said Jennifer. OK, she was out. And right then we started planning for next summer. Next year we'd make real money! And we did. The summer I was 10 we got Anna to replace Jennifer because Anna was a lot of fun and a good babysitter. Megan was treasurer. We all had jobs, we were experienced now, we decided to be organized. And we were, sort of. This time we ran 5 mornings a week for two weeks. We had about 8 kids. Some fights between Anna and Karen rubbed off a bit on the kids. Melania joined us for a few days at the end, but that led to more fights over money when we split the take and she said she wasn't getting enough. Anyway, I made $50.00 that summer. Not bad for a 10 year old! *3rd year*—much more enthusiasm! Parents had spread the word. We were responsible, trustworthy, fun. Mothers went to shop or work or whatever from 9 to 12 and left their kids with us. This time about 12 kids for same period—2 weeks. Had lots of activities, including field trips. Melania a full time partner now. All hard workers. Anna and Karen at my house *early* to set up tables, games, and toys. Megan spent *hours* on money matters. Mel advertised and planned. I did a bit of everything and talked to parents. Some field

trips this time too, but things got sticky when the wildlife museum charged us admission. We needed more money. Anna and I told the parents we had to raise our rates, another $1.00 a week for field trips. *Great mistake*, lost 2 customers and some credibility. Still, I made $125 that summer. *4th summer*. Wonderful! We hardly had to advertise at all. They called us. We had *so many* kids. Some days as many as 25! We had to turn people away. Karen had quit because we weren't really friends anymore. I kind of wished she was there to wallow in our success. The kids loved us—it was a great year. Megan kept the books like a pro. Anna was a ball of energy. I talked to the parents. Mel made sure everything was perfect, and this time it was! We each made close to $300.00 that year.

Obviously, this is not a systematic guide to running a successful business. It's a free-form account of how the author and her friends managed to overcome all the problems they faced in starting a particular business and making it go from one summer to the next. What Virginia discovered in writing this passage was the answer to her basic question about how they made the playgroup succeed. The answer would become her thesis: in spite of the rejections, the miscalculations, the squabbles, and the partners who quit, she and her friends made their playgroup succeed by resolutely persisting from one summer to the next.

EXERCISE 1   Directed Freewriting

Using as much as possible of the material you developed in the pre-writing exercises of chapter 1, write without stopping for one full hour on the problem or conflict you defined in exercise 9. Concentrate on finding an answer, a solution, an explanation that satisfies you. *Do not worry about anything else.*

After freewriting for an hour, give yourself a break. Get away from your desk for a while, and think about anything *but* your topic. You need to relax your brain before moving on to the next step—which will be to formulate a thesis from the freewritten material you have just produced.

2.2   Formulating a Thesis

The thesis should be a one-sentence declaration of what you will aim to show in your essay as a whole. Formulating a statement of thesis takes time and careful thought, but a well-wrought thesis will lead the way to a well-wrought essay. This section explains how to find the germ of your thesis in your freewritten material, and then how to construct the thesis itself.

If the process of freewriting has taken you into the heart of your topic, you have probably managed to set down on paper at least one thing that you did not consciously know when you started writing. When you return to your desk, therefore, the first thing you should do is to read what you have written and underline the most important point you discovered. If you aren't sure just where that point is, your instructor may be able to help you find it.

Tim found his most important point in one set of words that jumped out at him as he read: *When the freeze-frame ends, the sense of power strikes.* There, he felt, was the answer to the question he had started with—the question *Why do I love scoring goals?*

Turning this underlined set of words into a statement of thesis took a little more thought. If the underlined words held the answer to the question *Why?,* Tim needed a statement that took the form of an answer, a statement that hinged on the word *because.* What he first came up with was this:

> I love scoring goals because it gives me a sense of power.

Now he had a clear, definite, one-sentence answer to his basic question. But looking again at his freewritten material, he saw that his statement of thesis lacked something. It failed to indicate that the power trip lasted only "a second or two." So he added a qualifying word:

> I love scoring goals because it momentarily gives me a sense of power.

The addition of *momentarily* made the statement more precise. But Tim still felt something missing. His statement made no reference to any other reasons for his love of scoring, and therefore failed to indicate the unique importance of this one. He solved the problem by starting off with *Though:*

> Though many things make me want to score goals, I love scoring most of all because it momentarily gives me a sense of power.

This kind of statement not only announces the main point of the essay to come. By ranking that point above others, it also begins the work of organizing the essay. Thus it provides exactly what the writer needs for his first draft: a clear sense of direction.

How do you know when a thesis is ready? How do you know when to stop tinkering with it and start using it to organize your essay? Only you can answer this question for certain. But as a general rule, your thesis is ready when (1) it makes a precise, restricted, organized assertion about your topic, and (2) it clearly reveals your attitude toward the topic.

2.3 Finding Your Tone

Your attitude toward the topic determines the **tone** of your essay. Will you be earnest or playful? Will you be authoritative or speculative? Will you be skeptical or committed? Will you be confident or troubled? Tim's thesis, for instance, shows him to be confident, open, candid, not at all afraid to say that a sense of power excites him. The tone of the thesis thus announces the tone of the essay to come, the kind of feeling it will express. (For a full discussion of tone, see section 4.2.)

2.4   Sample Theses on a Variety of Topics

Different topics, of course, will bring forth different kinds of theses. But whatever the topic, a good thesis seldom comes quickly. It usually results from a succession of tries. The following examples—all but one from student essays—show what a succession of tries can produce:

1. TOPIC: a fatherless family
   THESIS: Though my father's leaving turned the perfect family picture into a puzzle and though he took some of the pieces with him, a combination of love, understanding, and mutual commitment helped us to put the remaining pieces back together.
   TONE: sensitive, determined, brave

2. TOPIC: women in TV commercials
   THESIS: Though television shows often glamorize women, TV commercials typically present them as housewives in distress so they can be rescued by the sponsor's product.
   TONE: skeptical, shrewd, unimpressed by the quick fix

3. TOPIC: social competition in a small community
   THESIS: Though the five clans of the Shinnecook Indian Tribe sometimes envy and resent each other, they stand together against outsiders because they know that unity alone will keep their land from being lost.
   TONE: sincere, sympathetic, respectful

4. TOPIC: maintaining a car engine
   THESIS: Car owners who want to save money can maintain their own engines by periodically changing the oil, checking other fluids, replacing the spark plugs and the distributor parts, correcting the engine timing, and adjusting the idle speed on the carburetor.
   TONE: authoritative, considerate, reassuring

5. TOPIC: disposing of nuclear waste
   THESIS: To solve the problem of what to do with nuclear waste, the government should turn it into souvenir gift items and sell them to the American public.
   TONE: mocking, irreverent, ironical

6. TOPIC: running a summer playgroup
   THESIS: In spite of the rejections we met at first, the fights we

had among ourselves, and the fact that some girls quit along the way, we built our summer playgroup into a highly profitable business by sheer persistence.

TONE: candid, enthusiastic, self-assured

In the three chapters that follow, we will now and then refer to the essays that grew out of these various theses. But from this point on, we will illustrate the writing process chiefly by focusing on the development of just one essay—Tim's.

EXERCISE 2   Formulating a Thesis

First, underline the most important point you discovered about your topic in the process of freewriting. Second, using this point, write at least three versions of a sentence that could serve as a thesis for the essay you plan to write. Third, say which version you think is best—and why. Finally, describe the tone of this version in a few words.

3

ORGANIZING YOUR
FIRST DRAFT

If you have managed by now to formulate a statement of thesis that satisfies you, you have already started to organize your first draft. You have given yourself a sense of direction by identifying your most important point. With this point firmly in mind, you can draw other points from the material you have produced in the pre-writing and freewriting stages and arrange those points in such a way as to serve, support, and develop your thesis.

3.1 Listing and Arranging Your Points

An outline will help you to see the relations among all of your points before you start your first draft. But before you make an outline, you should make a list—in any order—of all the points you have identified up to now. Tim did this simply by rereading his free-written material and then jotting down the various points that he connected with scoring goals:

1. help the team	8. see puck going into goal
2. gain glory	9. see players and crowd
3. take mind trip	10. feel sense of power
4. feel relaxed	11. do better than goalie
5. know I'm going to score	12. hear crowd cheering
6. move smoothly, not awkwardly	13. come back to earth after
7. see world in freeze-frame	second or two

This, of course, is just a random list. But the advantage of making such a list before you make your outline is that it puts before you all of the points you have developed so far. You can then do what Tim did: underline the most important ones.

4. feel relaxed
7. see world in freeze-frame
10. feel sense of power

Your next task is to decide on the order or arrangement of your major points. To decide that, you must know what arrangements are possible and which are better than others for your particular topic. The most common arrangements are as follows.

3.1A   Chronological Order

This arrangement of points follows the order of events in time. It is normally the best order to use in explaining a process, such as tuning up a car engine or making a cake, and is also commonly used in narrating or storytelling, especially in first-person narratives. (For more on narration, see section 6.2; for more on explaining a process, see section 6.10.)

3.1B   Spatial Order

Spatial arrangement follows the order of objects in space, and for this reason it works particularly well in descriptive writing. Using it in an essay or passage about a house, for instance, you might first describe the outside and then the inside, or first describe the kitchen and then the living room. You can also use it on a large scale, moving from small to great (a house, a block, a whole city) or great to small. (For more on descriptive writing, see section 6.1.)

3.1C   Cause and Effect Order

Cause and effect order allows you to explain one point as the reason for another, or one point as the result or consequence of another. Either way, this kind of order generates strong continuity in the treatment of any topic because it is based on a logical connection. (For more on cause and effect, see section 6.3.)

3.1D   Climactic Order

When you order your writing climactically, you arrange points in order of ascending importance, rising from least important to most important. Climactic order sometimes corresponds to chronological order. In Virginia's piece of freewriting on the summer playgroup, for instance, the point she makes at the end about the great success of the final summer is more important than the setbacks of the earlier summers, which she treats earlier. But in the essay she finally wrote, she used climactic order throughout, treating all of the setbacks and problems of various summers (the rejections, the fights, the quittings) before showing how she and her friends over-came those problems through persistence.

3.1E Oppositional Order

Oppositional order opposes one point to another. It is often used at the start of a persuasive essay, when the writer first describes a particular opinion or argument and then proceeds to show what is wrong with it. (For more on this technique, see section 7.7.) You can also use oppositional order to compare and contrast two things, as shown in section 6.7, or just to highlight their differences.

Considering these alternatives, Tim decided on a combination of arrangements. He would start with oppositional order, citing first of all "Common reasons for wanting to score goals" and then mov-ing to "My reasons for wanting to score goals." After that, he would use climactic order for his major points, building up from the sense of relaxation through the freeze-frame effect— the sense of height-ened awareness—to what for him was the most important reason for wanting to score: the sense of power.

EXERCISE 1   Making a List

Make a random list of all the points in your freewritten material and of any other points from the pre-writing process that do not appear in this material. Then underline the points that you think will be most important for the development of your thesis.

EXERCISE 2   Arranging Your Major Points

Arrange your major points in the order that seems best for the develop-ment of your thesis. Then explain why you chose the order you did.

3.2   Making an Outline to Plan Your Connections

After deciding how to arrange your major points, you must decide what to do with the minor ones—or more specifically, how to con-nect them to the major ones. The best way to plan your connections is to make an outline, which may be either a vertical list with head-ings and indented subheadings, or a tree diagram.

3.2A Outlining with a Vertical List

To outline your material with a vertical list, write your thesis at the head of the page and use headings and indented subheadings:

THESIS: Though many things make me want to score goals, I love scoring most of all because it momentarily gives me a sense of power.

    I. Common reasons for wanting to score goals
      A. Help team
      B. Gain glory
      C. Hear cheers of crowd
   II. My reasons for wanting to score goals
      A. Feel relaxed
        1. Know I'm going to score a goal
        2. Move smoothly, not awkwardly
        3. Get relief from pressure to do well
      B. See world in freeze-frame
        1. See puck going into goal
        2. See other players and crowd
      C. Feel momentary sense of power
        1. Do better than goalie
        2. Take ultimate mind trip
        3. Return to earth after a moment

Besides listing points in order of rising importance, this outline groups them under headings that show their relation to each other and to the thesis. Points that were at first jotted down in a random list have now become the skeleton of an essay.

3.2B Outlining with a Tree Diagram

A tree diagram is so called because it spreads out like the branches of a tree reflected in water, as shown on p. 33. The main advantage of a tree diagram is that it lets you see your ideas branching out organically, as you think. A vertical list is a clear-cut way of laying out all of your points *after* you have decided which to include and how to arrange them. But that is exactly what a tree diagram helps you decide. Because the tree is open-ended, you can make it grow by asking questions and adding more points. You don't have to confine yourself to the points you have already listed.

As Tim studied the first tree diagram (the one on p. 33), he discovered the need for more branches. When he asked himself, for instance, whether he had actually put down all the common reasons for wanting to score goals, he realized that he ought to mention pleasing the coach: a figure he had forgotten about, even though the coach did turn up in response to his original *Who* question. Then Tim made more branches grow from the other headings. He

THESIS: **Though many things make me want to score goals, I love scoring most of all because it momentarily gives me a sense of power.**

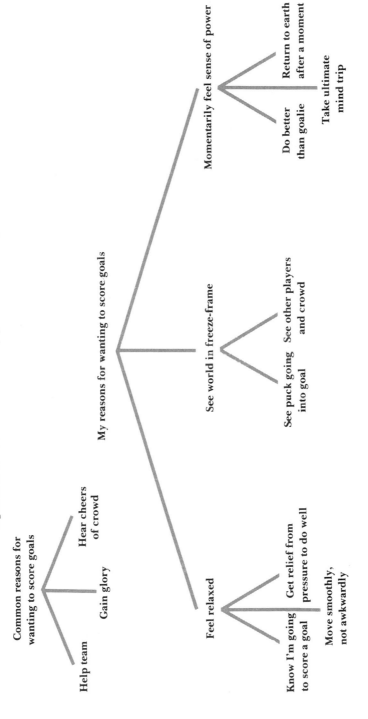

My reasons for wanting to score goals

Common reasons for wanting to score goals

Help team

Gain glory

Hear cheers of crowd

Feel relaxed

Know I'm going to score a goal

Move smoothly, not awkwardly

Get relief from pressure to do well

See world in freeze-frame

See puck going into goal

See other players and crowd

Momentarily feel sense of power

Do better than goalie

Return to earth after a moment

Take ultimate mind trip

THESIS: Though many things make me want to score goals, I love scoring most of all because it momentarily gives me a sense of power.

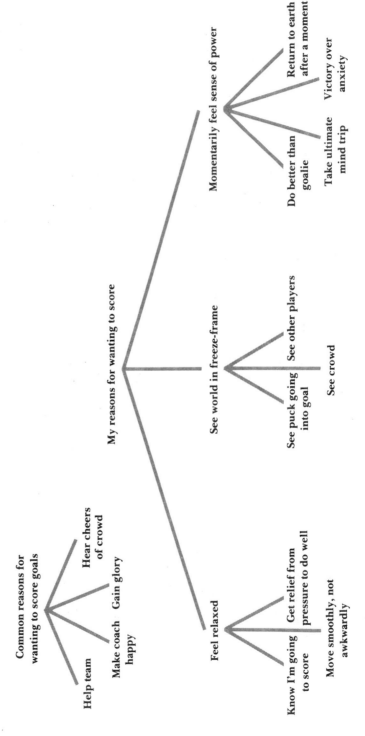

Common reasons for wanting to score goals
- Help team
- Make coach happy
- Gain glory
- Hear cheers of crowd

My reasons for wanting to score

Feel relaxed
- Know I'm going to score
- Get relief from pressure to do well
- Move smoothly, not awkwardly

See world in freeze-frame
- See puck going into goal
- See other players
- See crowd

Momentarily feel sense of power
- Do better than goalie
- Return to earth after a moment
- Take ultimate mind trip
- Victory over anxiety

realized that his sense of relaxation came partly from relief at the momentary lifting of pressure; he decided to separate his description of the crowd from his description of the players; and he saw how to reinforce his final point about power by adding "victory over anxiety"—something that "relief from pressure" had suggested to him. The result is the enlarged tree diagram on p. 34.

Because a tree diagram remains open-ended, it can be modified further as you write. Its great advantage is that *throughout the writing process,* you can use it not just as a record of your thoughts, but as a means of thinking.

EXERCISE 3   Outlining with a Tree Diagram

Following the example shown on p. 33, use a tree diagram to arrange all of your points. Then add whatever branches you think are needed.

EXERCISE 4   Outlining with a Vertical List

Using a vertical list with headings and subheadings, arrange your points in such a way as to clarify their relation to your thesis and to each other, and put them in an order that you think will best support the thesis.

3.3   Thinking about Your Readers

Once you have made an outline, you may feel ready to start writing your first draft and unwilling to think about anything else before doing so. But sooner or later, you will have to think about your readers. If you would rather do that *after* you have written your first draft, you can skip to section 3.4 and return to this section later. We have put this section here because you may want to start thinking about your readers now.

To think about your readers is, more precisely, to think about one reader in particular: your teacher. Since most of what you write in college will be read by a teacher, the question uppermost in your mind is likely to be "What does the teacher want?" Essentially, the teacher wants the kind of consideration that all good writers show for their readers. To learn how to write with such consideration, ask yourself these four questions:

1. How much do your readers know about the topic? If you underestimate their knowledge, you will bore them by telling them things they already know; if you overestimate their knowledge, you may confuse them with unfamiliar terms or incomplete explanations. Try to tell your readers only as much as they need to know in order to understand you.

How much do they need to know? When you write for a teacher, you are writing for someone who probably knows more than you do about a certain subject. But no teacher knows everything about every subject, or even everything about any subject. If you are analyzing a novel or play for a teacher of literature, for instance, you can assume that your teacher knows the plot, but not that he or she has memorized every word of the complete text. If you quote the words of a particular character, you should say who the character is; if you analyze a particular scene or episode, you should explain the circumstances surrounding it and the details that fill it out. The need to explain may be still greater when you are writing about a subject in technical terms. In a lab report written for a chemistry teacher, you can use a word like *fractionation* in full confidence that your reader will understand it. But if you want to use the word in describing a chemistry experiment for your English teacher, you will have to explain what it means.

When writing for general readers, you can assume no more than general information. The wider your audience, the smaller the body of knowledge you can take for granted. If you are writing about hockey, you can assume that most readers will understand what you mean by words such as *goalie* and *defenseman;* if you're writing about boating, you can assume a general knowledge of such things as sails, rudders, and masts. But you can't expect nonsailors to know the meaning of *luff* or the nautical meaning of *sheet.* Likewise, if you are writing about high-fidelity components, you can take for granted a general knowledge of what turntables, amplifiers, and speakers do, but you cannot assume that everyone will know the specialized meanings of *wow* and *flutter.* You need to explain such terms.

2. How do your readers feel about the topics? If you want to show that anyone can learn how to tune up an engine, you first have to realize that many people may feel there are far too many technical details to master—and far too many chances of botching the job altogether. Likewise, if you want to defend gun-control legislation to a readership that may include hunters and target shooters, you will have to show them that you understand the attractions of hunting and target shooting before you explain the danger of guns in irresponsible hands. To be effective, in other words, you must demonstrate that you understand and respect the feelings of all your readers.

3. How do your readers expect you to treat the topic? Another way of asking this question is, How does your teacher expect you to treat the topic? But the classroom is not the only place where writers work under instructions. Professional writers—especially journalists—often work under instructions from editors who tell them not only what to write about but also how to treat it. When you get a writing assignment, therefore, you should find out as much as you can about the approach you are expected to take.

In part that approach will depend on the rules of the game, the conditions under which you are writing. If your chemistry professor asks for a lab report, you are expected to record what the experiment showed, not what you felt when you performed it. But if your English teacher asks for an account of a personal experience and you decide to describe your first lab experiment, you will include your feelings, since for this assignment you are expected to describe what you felt. Students are sometimes confused because they get conflicting advice about whether or not to start sentences with *I,* or whether to use *I* at all. The advice is conflicting because different readers have conflicting expectations. If the reader expects you to make personal experience a part of your essay, you should feel free to use *I,* just as Tim does in his essay on scoring goals. If the reader expects you simply to report facts and conclusions, you should avoid *I.*

Most of the time, however, readers expect something between the personal and the impersonal, something between "I feel" and "it is." If you use *I* in every sentence, you will soon seem to be floating in a cloud of self-absorption; if you never use *I,* you may begin to sound like an impersonal machine. Most readers want objective truth, but they also want to feel that the words they read have been produced by a human being.

4. How long is the finished essay supposed to be? Often, in college and afterward, you will be assigned a minimum or a maximum number of words or pages for your essay. Aim to make your first draft half again as long as the minimum. When you revise, you will probably find many words and even an idea or two that you want to cut out. But if you have written only the minimum number of words, you won't be free to cut any of them. Writing more than you will finally want gives you the chance to produce a finished essay in which every word will truly count.

Thinking about your readers—imagining them as *listeners* to what you are saying—will help to guide you as you write. You may even find that you can put your readers into the title of your essay just to focus your attention on their needs. The student who wrote an essay on engine maintenance in a Freshman English course called it "The English Professor's Guide to Engine Maintenance."

EXERCISE 5   Thinking about What Your Readers Know

Assuming that your readers have no special knowledge of any topic, say what you think they probably know about yours, and indicate which terms or aspects of your topic require special explanation.

EXERCISE 6 Thinking about What Your Readers Feel or Believe

Assume you are writing an essay on your favorite topic for a publication aimed at college students. Name three different kinds of reaction that you think the topic itself would provoke.

With your readers in mind, with freewritten material in hand, with a thesis, an outline, and some idea of the tone you will use, you are now ready to write your first draft. The rest of this chapter will show you how to do so: how to introduce your essay, how to turn your outline headings into paragraphs that will make up the middle or body of your essay, and how to conclude it.

3.4 Introducing Your Essay

The introduction comes first for the reader, but not necessarily first for the writer. Since you can't write a good introduction until you know what you're introducing, you may want to plunge immediately into the middle of your draft, write your way to a conclusion, and only then write your introduction. But whenever you write it, this section may help you.

To write a good introduction, think first of all about what strikes you when you start reading anything. What kind of opening bores you? What kind of opening seizes your interest and makes you want to read on? The better you understand that, the better your introductions will be.

In a sense, the introduction to an essay actually begins with its title, for that is the first thing your reader will see. The title should be short but also specific. The more specific it is, the more firmly it will guide both you and your reader. Compare the titles on the left with those on the right:

College	Where College Fails Us
Maple Syrup	The Grades of Maple Syrup
Lawyers	When Lawyers Help Villains
First-Year Students	How First-Year Students Manage Money

While the titles on the left merely identify a general topic, those on the right make the topic specific and pointed, and a title such as "Where College Fails Us" clearly indicates what the writer aims to show. With that advantage in mind, Tim decided to call his essay "Why I Love Scoring Goals."

Capitalizing on the good impression made by an effective title, a good introduction captures the reader's attention and guides it to the writer's thesis. You can achieve both of these ends by any one of the following means:

1. Lead up to an explicit statement of your thesis:

> The town dump of Whitemud, Saskatchewan, could only have been a few years old when I knew it, for the village was born in 1913 and I left there in 1919. But I remember the dump better than I remember most things in that town, better than I remember most of the people. I spent more time with it, for one thing; it had more poetry and excitement in it than people did.
>
> —Wallace Stegner, "The Town Dump"

Stegner captures our attention with an opening sentence about a town dump. His second sentence makes us wonder *why* he remembers such a place. The third sentence answers that question by stating the provocative thesis of Stegner's essay: the town dump had more poetry and excitement than people did.

2. Lead up to a question that points to your thesis:

> There are more than thirty-three million investors in the United States today. Most of them are losers. Not only do they lose their money; they lose their self-confidence, their security, and the chance they had at one time to use their money to make a killing in the market. Yet the fact is that to get the money needed to invest in the market, most of these people had to be fairly successful in their chosen career. As doctors or lawyers, for example, many of them had demonstrated an ability to think clearly, to make plans for the future, and to carry them out. Why then, employing the same intelligence, do they go wrong when they try to make money in the market?   —Richard Ney, *Making It in the Market*

Ney opens with a startling observation and guides us to a provocative question. Asking a sharply worded question is always a powerful way to end an introductory paragraph. It tells us that the writer is seeking answers, and it invites us to share in the search.

3. Move from a personal story or particular example to a thesis of general significance:

> When I was six or seven years old, growing up in Pittsburgh, I used to take a penny of my own and hide it for someone else to find. It was a curious compulsion; sadly, I've never been seized by it since. For some reason I always "hid" the penny along the same stretch of sidewalk up the street. I'd cradle it at the roots of a maple, say, or in a hole left by a chipped-off piece of sidewalk. Then I'd take a piece of chalk and, starting at either end of the block, draw huge arrows leading up to the penny from both directions. After I learned to write I labeled the arrows "SURPRISE AHEAD" or "MONEY THIS WAY." I was greatly excited, during all this arrow-drawing, at the thought of the first lucky passerby who would receive in this way, regardless of merit, a free gift from the universe. But I never lurked about. I'd go straight home and not give the

matter another thought, until, some months later, I would be gripped by the impulse to hide another penny.

There are lots of things to see, unwrapped gifts and free surprises. The world is fairly studded and strewn with pennies cast broadside from a generous hand. But—and this is the point—who gets excited by a mere penny? If you follow one arrow, if you crouch motionless on a bank to watch a tremulous ripple thrill on the water, and are rewarded by the sight of a muskrat kit paddling from its den, will you count that sight a chip of copper only, and go your rueful way? It is very dire poverty indeed for a man to be so malnourished and fatigued that he won't stoop to pick up a penny. But if you cultivate a healthy poverty and simplicity, so that finding a penny will make your day, then, since the world is in fact planted in pennies, you have with your poverty bought a lifetime of days. What you see is what you get.

—Annie Dillard, "Pilgrim at Tinker Creek"

This two-paragraph introduction moves from the particular to the general. The first paragraph captures our attention with a personal story about the author's childhood; the second guides us from the personal excitement of hiding little surprises to the universal idea that all of nature is planted with them.

4. Move from a generalization to a specific thesis based on a particular case:

Sociologists study the family because it is the basic unit of society. As a Chinese student who lived with an American family for six months, I had the opportunity to compare this family with my own in China. In so doing, I learned that the differences between the two countries are mainly created within the family. Though I was raised to tell my parents everything and to depend on others, each member of the American family had a private life, and the children were trained to be independent, to refuse help even when they needed it. The differences between my family and the American one help to explain why Eastern and Western cultures have such different attitudes toward privacy, dependence, and independence.   —College student

5. Challenge a widespread assumption or stereotype:

The case *for* college has been accepted without question for more than a generation. All high school graduates ought to go, says Conventional Wisdom and statistical evidence, because college will help them earn more money, become "better" people, and learn to be more responsible citizens than those who don't go.

But college has never been able to work its magic for everyone. And now that close to half our high school graduates are attending, those who don't fit the pattern are becoming more numerous, and more obvious. College graduates are selling shoes and driving taxis;

college students sabotage each other's experiments and forge letters of recommendation in the intense competition for admission to graduate school. Others find no stimulation in their studies, and drop out—often encouraged by college administrators.
—Caroline Bird," Where College Fails Us"

The picture-perfect family includes a mother and father who are forever in love, three wonderful children, and perhaps a dog who can often be found on the living room couch even though he is not allowed in the living room. But many families today are less than picture perfect, and mine is one of them. When my father walked out eight years ago, he turned the picture into a puzzle and took some of the pieces with him. Since that time, however, a combination of love, understanding, and mutual commitment has helped us to put the other pieces back together.   —College student

6. To introduce an argument on a controversial subject, explain the position you aim to oppose. (See section 7.7A, pp. 133–34, "Making Concessions.")

After considering these alternatives, Tim decided to start with a broad generalization about scoring goals and then narrow the focus to what he had learned from his own experience in ice hockey. To write the introduction, he combined material from Part I of his outline with his statement of thesis:

Anyone who plays on a team dreams of scoring goals. Why? Most people probably think that players long to score for the good of the team, or to make the coach happy, or to gain some glory: the cheers of the crowd, the smile of a cheerleader, and perhaps a headline in the school newspaper. But none of these things can fully explain the special *excitment of scoring, or more *specificly, the "high" I get from scoring in ice hockey. Though many things make me want to score, I love it most of all because it momentarily gives me a sense of power.

As this and the other examples show, nearly all good introductions have three things in common: (1) they catch the reader's attention; (2) they lead up to a thesis; and (3) they turn on some kind of opposition. Challenging popular notions and vague ideas, they question, probe, and expose. Whether revealing the simple excitement of a penny surprise, attacking the idea that college is good for everyone, asking why intelligent people lose money in the stock market, or explaining why a hockey player loves to make goals, a good introduction rumples the bed of our assumptions and wakes us up.

EXERCISE 7   **Using Personal Experience in an Introduction**

Use the story of a personal experience to introduce a general thesis about human nature or growing up.

EXERCISE 8   **Leading Up to a Question**

Write an introductory paragraph that leads up to a question about the basic problem or conflict you aim to resolve in your essay.

EXERCISE 9   **Leading Up to Your Thesis**

Using any of the methods exemplified above, write an introduction that ends with a statement of your thesis.

3.5   Shaping the Middle of Your Essay

Whether you write your introduction before or after the rest of your essay, you will at some point have to shape the largest part—the middle. To do so, you must turn your outline into paragraphs.

3.5A   Using Your Outline and Making It Grow

Shaping the middle of your essay calls for both invention and control. You need to follow your outline, but you should not be tyrannized by it. As you write, you will not only generate words, phrases, clauses, and sentences; you will think of new evidence, new strategies, even new points to be supported in their own right. If you write down everything that comes to mind, you will simply be freewriting again. But if you close your mind to new ideas, you may be putting the body of your essay into a straightjacket. You need to do your shaping with a flexible hand.

So what do you do with a brand-new idea that comes to you as you write? Is it a gift or a distraction? Will it be an asset to the essay or a digression that will waste your time and energy? Sometimes it can be hard to decide which. If the idea obviously supports the point you are developing in a particular paragraph, you can take it up right away. If it doesn't, and if you are using a tree diagram, see whether the new idea can be grafted onto a branch of the tree, for use later on. You can thus make your outline grow even as you follow its guidance.

3.5B   Thinking in Paragraphs

To write a sentence is to work with words, phrases, and clauses; to write a paragraph is to work with sentences. Paragraphing is a deliberate act, the act of thinking about the connections and the differences between one sentence and another. To think this way is to think in paragraph form—the form that all good writing customarily assumes.

One way to think in paragraphs is to use each of the headings in your outline as a paragraph starter. Following the revised tree diagram shown on p. 34, Tim had already used the items clustered under the first heading—"Common reasons for wanting to score goals"—in his introductory paragraph. Reading from left to right across the diagram, he then turned to the items clustered under "Feel relaxed" for his next paragraph. Here is what he wrote:

> Scoring brings me a sense of relaxation. It begins even before I shoot, because even then I can see the puck going into a goal. I don't try to visualize the goal. The picture just flashes into my mind. The feeling is both *exhilerating and frustrating. When I see the picture a peacefulness fills me. I become relaxed and don't even consciously try to shoot. The shot just happens. Often I cannot remember looking at the puck, and I am so relaxed I might not have. The feeling at this point is one of perfection. Unfortunately not every shot is like this, nor can every shot be made perfect. If I try to consciously *vizualise a goal, the shot feels forced. My body works against me rather than with me. When I unconsciously "see" a goal, I will always score, but if the effort to "see" a goal is conscious, I will not. This lack of conscious control is disturbing. I feel as if fate is controlling my shot and I can do nothing about it. I cannot make a goal happen. It happens almost by itself.
>
> Scoring also gives me relief from pressure. In a competitive situation, players experience intense pressure to play to the best of their ability. Their parents, friends, schoolmates, teammates, and above all their coach expect a strong performance. So when I score, I feel a sense of relief. I have met the demands placed on me, and I can relax—for a moment anyway.

This is what Tim did in his first draft with the items clustered under "Feel relaxed" in the tree diagram. But Tim did not follow his outline slavishly; he modified it as he wrote. First, while developing the points about foreknowledge and perfection, he discovered a new point: making a perfect shot is "disturbing" because he feels as if fate is controlling him. Second, he wrote two paragraphs on relaxation instead of the one forecast by his diagram. Possibly because he felt the first paragraph was getting too long—especially with the new point added—he decided to treat "Get relief from pressure to do well" in a paragraph of its own. He then wrote two more paragraphs—one for each of the other two headings:

> This moment of relaxation heightens my awareness of the world around me. Though I often cannot remember looking at the puck, I can always see it slide into the goal. No matter how fast the shot or how far away it was taken from, I can always see the puck hitting the twine at the back of the net. At this instant I see the world in a freeze-frame. Every other player seems caught, as if someone had

suddenly stopped a fast-moving film. I can see the goalie down on the ice, the defensemen, the wingers cheering with their sticks in the air. Sometimes I can even catch the expressions of a face or two in the crowd.

In this frozen moment, the sense of power strikes. As I look at the goalie stretched out on the ice, I can see that he tried with every inch of his body to stop the puck, but couldn't because I shot it past him. For anyone driven by the urge to compete, this is a moment of pure triumph. *The ultimate mind trip. I have two victories now—one over the goalie, and one over the anxiety inside me, the fear that I will disappoint others. The crowd seems to cheer for me alone: not for the team or the coach or the school, but just for me. In that moment the world is mine.

Working from his outline and modifying it as he writes, Tim has now drafted the middle of his paper. Since this is only the first draft, it is not yet all it should be, and Tim has some revisions to make, as we will see in the next chapter. But by turning the headings of his outline into paragraphs, he has already created the building blocks of which his essay will be made. (For a detailed discussion of paragraphing, see chapter 8.)

Exercise 10   Drafting the Middle

Using your outline as a guide, write one paragraph for each of its headings. If you find that a particular heading generates more or less than one paragraph, feel free to modify the outline. Remember that this is only a first draft.

3.6   Ending Your Essay

The ending of your essay is your last chance to clarify and emphasize your main point or to specify its implications. To end an essay effectively, do any one of the following things:

1. Make the implications of your thesis explicit:

> We have found that violence on prime-time network TV cultivates exaggerated assumptions about the threat of danger in the real world. Fear is a universal emotion, and easy to exploit. The exaggerated sense of risk and insecurity may lead to increasing demands for protection, and to increasing pressure for the use of force by established authority. Instead of threatening the social order, television may have become our chief instrument of social control.
> —George Gerbner and Larry Gross, "The Scary World of TV's Heavy Viewer"

This ending is spare. It does not retrace all the steps of the argument that came before it or cite all the evidence supporting the authors' main point. It simply restates that point in the first sentence, and then connects it with the increased demand for protection. This point in turn leads to the explicit statement of what has already been said implicitly: television may have become our chief instrument of social control.

2. Reaffirm your thesis in terms that widen its significance:

> Poetry is seldom useful, but always memorable. I think I learned more from the town dump than I learned from school: more about people, more about how life is lived, not elsewhere but here, not in other times but now. If I were a sociologist anxious to study in detail the life of any community, I would go very early to its refuse piles. For a community may be as well judged by what it throws away—what it has to throw away and what it chooses to—as by any other evidence. For whole civilizations we have sometimes no more of the poetry and little more of the history than this.
> —Wallace Stegner, "The Town Dump"

Stegner's explanation of the poetry and excitement he found in a particular town dump leads in the end to a wide-ranging generalization: that all communities and even all civilizations may be judged by what they discard.

3. Recommend a specific course of action:

> The physically handicapped have the liabilities of a minority group. Shouldn't they be given the rights of a minority group? The answer is affirmative. It is time the action was also.
> —Nancy Weinberg, "Disability Isn't Beautiful"

4. Answer a question posed by the introduction:

Norman Cousins begins "The Right to Die" with an introductory paragraph that leads to a question: "Does an individual have the obligation to go on living even when the beauty and meaning and power of life have gone?" He ends the essay as follows:

> Death is not the greatest loss in life. The greatest loss is what dies inside us while we live. The unbearable tragedy is to live without dignity or sensitivity.

5. Reaffirm your thesis with a final telling example:

To end an essay on the amount of garbage produced by New York City, Katie Kelley tells what she saw and heard at Fresh Kills, a Staten Island dumping site:

> "It sure has changed out here," one worker, who has been at Fresh Kills for years, told me. "Why, there used to be fresh natural

springs over there." He gestured out over the hundreds of acres of garbage. Natural crab beds once flourished in the area. Now they, too, are gone, buried under tons of garbage.   —"Garbage"

The final paragraph clinches the point of the whole essay. Instead of summarizing her principal points or restating her main one, the writer makes us see the quantity of garbage we produce and its smothering effect. The picture of the springs and crab beds buried under tons of garbage is far more effective than any final abstract statement about garbage could be.

As these examples show, you can end an essay in a variety of ways. You can answer a question, recommend a course of action, restate the main point of your essay, reaffirm your thesis in terms that widen its significance, or reaffirm it with one final example. But in any case, your final paragraph is your final chance to drive your main point home. Whatever else it does, it should leave the reader with a clear understanding of what you have been trying to show or to do in the essay as a whole.

After considering these alternatives, Tim decided to end by reaffirming his thesis in terms that widened its significance. Here is what he wrote:

> When the cheers subside, I lose my empire and become just another player again, reabsorbed by the game. But every time the moment of triumph comes, I learn once more why scoring excites me so much. On or off the hockey rink or the playing field, life is frustrating. We miss shots; we reel from body checks; and sometimes we fall flat on our faces. To score is for one shining moment to conquer all frustration. Anxiety has been banished, and we rule the world. Ultimately, it is not for the team or the school or the coach that I love to score. It is for myself.

EXERCISE 11   Ending an Essay

First, turn to p. 96 and put a card or small sheet of paper over paragraph 6. Then turn to p. 95 and read the first five paragraphs of the essay titled "Why Videotapes Won't Kill Movie Theatres." Finally—without looking at paragraph 6—furnish your own concluding paragraph for this essay.

EXERCISE 12   Comparing Endings

Read paragraph 6 on p. 96 and compare it with your own concluding paragraph. Then explain what each ending does and how well it works.

EXERCISE 13   Ending your Own Essay

Write a paragraph to conclude the essay you have been writing in this chapter.

4

REVISING YOUR FIRST DRAFT

If you have taken the steps explained in chapters 1 to 3, you now have in hand the first draft of your essay. Two more stages of work remain: revising and editing.

Literally, **revising** means "looking again," and it can be hard to look again. Tired, pressed for time, or bored with writing your essay, you may want just to be rid of it—to get it to your reader as a way of getting it off your desk and off your mind. But you should try to keep it on your mind a little longer. If you don't take another look at your essay, you cannot clearly see what its effect on the reader will be. An unrevised piece of writing is like an uninspected machine. Neither one is likely to work very well.

So how do you make a piece of writing work well? Just what does revising involve? Many students think it simply means making corrections—eliminating errors in spelling, grammar, punctuation, and usage. But that is small-scale revising, or what we in this book call **editing.** The kind of revising we treat in this chapter is large-scale. It involves looking again at the whole substance of your first draft, at its tone, at its general aim and method, at the relation between its thesis and the paragraphs that make it up.

Looking at the whole of your draft in this way does not mean overlooking individual sentences or even individual words, for a single word can sometimes clarify the transition between one paragraph and another, or the relation between a paragraph and your thesis. But the first principle of revising is this: *try to solve big problems before turning to small ones.* If you try to solve both at the same time, you may find yourself laboring over a particular sentence and then deciding to rewrite or cut out altogether the whole paragraph that contains it. We therefore suggest that you revise and edit your draft in two successive stages, and for that reason, we treat revising in this chapter and editing in the next.

Revising means looking again at your work with the reader firmly in mind. If you skipped "Thinking about Your Readers" in the previous chapter (section 3.3, pp. 35–38), now is the time to read it. If you did read it, you might well reread it now. Effective revision of your writing demands constant attention to the needs and expectations of those you are writing for.

In college the kinds of revisions you make will largely depend on the expectations of one reader in particular: your teacher. If your teacher has asked to see your first draft and has returned it with specific suggestions for improvement, you should of course heed those suggestions. But not every essay you submit in college will be returned with a request for revision. Some will simply be returned with a final grade. Eventually, therefore, you will have to learn how to revise and edit your essays *before* you submit them, how to see for yourself what they need. To that end, this and the following chapter may help.

4.1 Developing Your Texture—Using Generalizations and Specifics

Texture is something good writers create by interweaving general ideas with specific details. As you reread your own writing, therefore, you should alternately ask yourself two questions: (1) What piece of detail could I use to illustrate the general point I've just made? (2) What general point can I derive from the specific thing I've just mentioned? If the writing itself fails to answer these questions, it probably needs some work. Writing that lacks specific detail will strike the reader as thin, abstract, and empty, like a big square box made of clear plastic. Writing that lacks generalizations will seem unfocused and undefined, like a newspaper without headlines. But the combination of generalizations and specifics will help you develop your texture.

If you want to know just what generalizations and specifics are, here are some examples of each:

1. GENERALIZATION: Free enterprise combines high risk with the possibility of high rewards.
   SPECIFIC EXAMPLE: To start my own summertime lawn-care service, I had to lay out all my savings—nearly two thousand dollars—on a used pickup, a used mower, a new fertilizer spreader, and a couple of big rakes. But by the end of the summer, I had

cleared almost four thousand dollars, and I sold the pickup for fifteen hundred.

2. GENERALIZATION: Even here and now in the United States, public school students can be legally subjected to cruel and unusual punishment.
SPECIFIC EXAMPLE: In 1977, the U.S. Supreme Court ruled that a junior high school principal in Dade County, Florida, committed no crime when he hit a student more than twenty times with a wooden paddle while two assistant principals held the student's arms and legs. The student's offense was leaving the stage of the school auditorium less promptly than he should have.

3. GENERALIZATION: Laughter takes many different forms.
SPECIFIC DETAIL: The nervous giggle, the cackle, the chuckle, and the guffaw are just a few of its variations.

4. GENERALIZATION: In his first year as a pop musician, he had a hard time.
SPECIFIC DETAIL: He could not afford heat or hot water in his apartment, so he had to warm himself with heavy blankets and go to a public bathhouse for his showers.

Used in combination, generalizations and specifics act like road signs for the reader. Just as a well-marked road has general signs to say where you are headed (NORTH, WEST) and specific signs to say what's just ahead (BUMP, CURVE, CROSSROAD), so a good piece of writing has general signs to say where the writer is headed and specific ones to keep the readers' eyes on the road, to hold their attention. As you revise your writing, therefore, you can improve it by doing two things:

1. Add specifics to make generalizations vivid and tangible:

> Religion has always been a major cause of persecution. An extreme example would be World War II, where religion was used in a discriminatory fashion.   —Student essay, first draft

> REVISED: Religion has always been a major cause of persecution. During World War II, the German Nazis sent millions of men, women, and children to death in concentration camps simply because they were Jews.

2. Add generalizations to explain the significance of specific statements:

> As the team members dressed for the first day of practice, they said nothing to each other but "What's your name?" and "Where are you from?" Most of them dressed as fast as they could and finished the job while running out onto the field. One player said

to me, "All of these guys are so much bigger than I am that I wonder if I've even got a chance of playing."

—Student essay, first draft

REVISED: On the first day of practice, competitiveness made us all tense and wary. While dressing we said nothing to each other but "What's your name?" and "Where are you from?" Most of the players dressed as fast as they could and finished the job while running out onto the field. They each wanted to be first. Everyone seemed to be looking at the rest of the team and measuring himself against the others. One player said to me, "All of these guys are so much bigger than I am that I wonder if I've even got a chance of playing."

EXERCISE 1   **Recognizing Generalizations and Specifics**

1. Identify the ways in which the writer of the following passage moves between general or abstract points and specific details.

Boys are wild animals, rich in the treasures of sense, but the New England boy had a wider range of emotions than boys of more equable climates. He felt his nature crudely, as it was meant. To the boy Henry Adams, summer was drunken. Among senses, smell was the strongest—smell of hot pine-woods and sweet-fern in the scorching summer noon; of new-mown hay; of ploughed earth; of box hedges; of peaches, lilacs, syringas; of stables, barns, cowyards; of salt water and low tide on the marshes; nothing came amiss. Next to smell came taste, and the children knew the taste of everything they saw or touched, from pennyroyal and flagroot to the shell of a pignut and the letters of a spelling book—the taste of A-B, AB, suddenly revived the boy's tongue sixty years afterwards. Light, line, and color as sensual pleasures came later and were as crude as the rest. The New England light is glare, and the atmosphere harshens color. The boy was a full man before he ever knew what was meant by atmosphere; his idea of pleasure in light was the blaze of a New England sun. His idea of color was a peony, with the dew of early morning on its petals. The intense blue of the sea, as he saw it a mile or two away, from the Quincy hills; the cumuli in a June afternoon sky; the strong reds and greens and purples of colored prints and children's picture-books, as the American colors then ran; these were ideals. The opposites or antipathies were the cold grays of November evenings, and the thick, muddy thaws of Boston winter. With such standards, the Bostonian could not but develop a double nature. Life was a double thing. After a January blizzard, the boy who could look with pleasure into the violent snow-glare of the cold white sunshine, with its intense light and shade, scarcely knew what was meant by tone. He could reach it only by education.

Winter and summer, then, were two hostile lives, and bred two separate natures. Winter was always the effort to live; summer was

tropical license. Whether the children rolled in the grass, or waded in the brook, or swam in the salt ocean, or sailed in the bay, or fished for smelts in the creeks, or netted minnows in the salt-marshes,
35 or took to the pine-woods and the granite quarries, or chased muskrats and hunted snapping-turtles in the swamps, or mushrooms or nuts on the autumn hills, summer and country were always sensual living, while winter was always compulsory learning. Summer was the multiplicity of nature; winter was school.

      —Henry Adams, *The Education of Henry Adams*

2. Discuss the alternation between generalizations and specific details in the first five paragraphs of Eugene Raskin's "Walls and Barriers," pp. 208–10.

EXERCISE 2   Furnishing Specifics

Add specific details or examples to the following generalization:

    The sudden cry of "Fire!" panicked everyone in the store.

EXERCISE 3   Furnishing Generalizations

Suppose you are writing a booklet to be used in recruiting young people for the U.S. Army. What *attractive* generalization about the army could you make on the basis of the following details?

    After completing basic training in obedience, each private is assigned to an advanced training unit, where he learns a particular specialty such as mechanics, radio operation, or infantry tactics. Privates who learn their specialties exceptionally well have the chance to become noncommissioned officers (NCOs) after training in leadership and supervisory skills.

EXERCISE 4   Revising with Specifics

Add specific details or examples to any passage in your first draft that leans too heavily on generalizations.

EXERCISE 5   Revising with Generalizations

Add one or more generalizations to any passage in your first draft that is not sufficiently clear in its overall significance.

4.2 Reconsidering Your Tone

When you hear someone speak, the first thing you are likely to notice is the tone of the speaker's voice. Is it loud or soft? friendly or hostile? sincere or sarcastic? The tone of the speaker's voice usually tells you something about how to interpret what he or she is saying. For instance, read these two questions out loud:

Would you mind putting out that cigarette?
Would you *mind* putting out that cigarette?

The words of both questions are exactly the same. Only the tone is different. The first question is polite; the second is insistent.

Obviously, it is harder to "hear" tone in the written word than in the spoken word. Aside from *italics* and **bold print** and exclamation points (!!!), all of which should be sparingly used, there is not much in writing that corresponds to the different ways we can make words sound in speech. Nevertheless, writers do have ways of conveying tone—of expressing an attitude toward their subject, their audience, or both.

In most of the essays you produce for college courses, you should write with straightforward sincerity: the kind of tone you commonly use in speaking to classmates and teachers. But particular subjects sometimes call for particular tones. Consider these two passages:

1. Anyone who knows that my husband Richard was one of the 53 American hostages in Iran for 444 days wouldn't be surprised to know that I still have nightmares.

But my nightmares aren't over what might have happened in Iran.

My nightmares are over what did happen four years earlier—right here in America—in a fast-food restaurant in Annandale, Va., where our 19-year-old son, Richard Jr., worked part time.

One Friday night in March he didn't come home from work. That was unlike Rick. He was a happy and responsible young man. He loved his family, told us wherever he was going and never gave us reason to worry.

The next morning, I went to the restaurant. I was told by police that my oldest son, my firstborn, had been murdered, shot in the back of the head, executed, blown away.

A robber had hidden in the restroom past closing time. He was given all the available cash without resistance, but then he herded all four remaining employees of the Roy Rogers Family Restaurant (and one of their relatives) into the back freezer and made them all lie face down on the floor. They offered no resistance. None. But he emptied his handgun into the back of their heads. In case that wasn't enough, he reloaded and did it again. And then a third time.

—Dorothea Morefield,
"Gun Control California Style: A Victim Fights"

2. Sitting down on our family's lop-sided sofa, I turned on the TV by remote control. After clicking my way through sitcoms, commercials, and movies, I settled on the 24-hour cable news channel, where the topic of the hour was the question of what America could do with its nuclear waste. I soon switched channels again, but the

question lurked in the back of my brain as I watched two *Laverne and Shirley* reruns and half of a *Three's Company* episode. All at once, during a commercial break in *Three's Company,* the answer came to me: marketing! To solve the problem of nuclear waste, the government should turn it into souvenir gift items and sell them to the American public.

For purposes of marketing, nuclear waste could assume any number of forms. It could be molded, for instance, into the shapes of the fifty states, or put into bottles with labels such as "100% Pure Nuclear Waste from Oklahoma." Made into shavings, it could be placed into a transparent plastic bubble filled with water and containing a miniature city. When the bubble was shaken, an atomic snowfall would rain down upon the tiny city. This would make a great novelty item and, in addition, the water would help filter out some of the more harmful gamma rays.

Of course it would take massive sales to reduce the vast amount of radioactive by-products now sitting in various dumps around the nation. But if a talented advertising agency took on the account, I believe it could start a run on nuclear gifts that would rival the Cabbage Patch Doll craze of 1983. Furthermore, because the supply of nuclear waste may be limited, advertisers could legitimately claim that nuclear souvenirs would someday become collectors' items. It's quite possible, in fact, that a radioactive bubble on the living room coffee table would become the ultimate status symbol.

—College student

These two passages both deal with dangerous items: handguns and nuclear waste. But they differ drastically in tone. While the first one breathes a mood of burning indignation, the second voices mockery. Playfully assuming that Americans can be persuaded to buy anything, the writer pretends to show how our horror of nuclear waste can be turned into an avid desire for it.

Not everything you read or write will have a tone as distinctive as those you find in these two passages. But every piece of writing has a tone of some kind, and the effectiveness of the writing partly depends on how well that tone is introduced and maintained. As you read your first draft, therefore, you should listen for the point at which you start to hear your own voice—the voice of a human being rather than a word processor. Does the voice sound cool, detached, and skeptical? Does it sound enraged, vulnerable, defiant, enthusiastic, urgent, or frightened? Does it sound sober, judicious, sensitive, authoritative, or simply sensible? Does it sound irreverent, playful, or carefree? Whatever the tone you hear in your writing, listen for one you like. If you like the sound of a certain passage, you may have found the tone that will work best for the finished paper, and you should try to make the paper as a whole consistent with it.

A consistent tone not only helps to define a piece of writing for the reader, but also reinforces the feelings you bring to the writing process. Just as boredom or uncertainty can inhibit you in your writing, a strong feeling or decisive attitude toward your subject can drive you along. See, for instance, how a sheer fascination with the varieties and paradoxes of laughter drives the author of the following passage:

> Laughter comes in assorted shapes and forms. The nervous giggle, the cackle, the chuckle, and the guffaw are just a few of its many and strange variations. One friend of mine is known for a laugh that convulses anyone who hears it. Another friend laughs without making a sound, but her whole body shakes and heaves so violently that I sometimes wonder if she'll come out of the laugh alive. Still another friend laughs so hard that his face wrinkles up like a raisin, his eyes squinch shut, and tears well out of the corners and trickle down his face. Why, I wonder, should laughter lead to tears? Why do we speak of "laughing to death"?
>
> —College student

Tone depends partly on the kind of diction you use—the formality or informality of your words. If you aren't sure at this point just what your level of diction is or what you want it to be, see section 9.1, pp. 170–74. For a discussion of how to catch the tone in what you read, see section 10.2A, pp. 202–6. And for examples of how a statement of thesis can express a particular tone, see section 2.3, pp. 26–27.

EXERCISE 6   Reconsidering Tone

Read the passage below and then do the following: (1) say whether or not the author expresses a consistent attitude toward honesty in speechmaking; (2) if you find his attitude inconsistent, identify the inconsistencies, and then revise the passage to make its tone consistent.

> As Patrick Henry once delivered fiery speeches that roused American colonists to revolution in the 1770s, so Martin Luther King, Jr., inspired many Americans during the 1960s. Many people in this period struggled to bring blacks and whites together, but no one expressed the ideal of integration more movingly than King when he stood in front of the Lincoln Memorial and declared to the thousands of people gathered there, "I have a dream." King spoke straight from the heart. He didn't hide his feelings, as politicians often do. Of course the reason they hide their feelings is that they can't get elected any other way. That's the problem with straightforward speaking; it doesn't win elections. But I still like to hear an honest speech now and then. It's refreshing.

EXERCISE 7   Reconsidering the Tone of Your Draft

Describe the tone of the passage you like best in your first draft, and then explain whether or not this tone persists in the draft as a whole. If it doesn't, make the necessary changes.

4.3   Reconsidering Your Aim

While rereading your draft, you should reconsider your aim. In a narrow and specific sense, you express your aim by your statement of thesis, the assertion of what you intend to show or explain in the essay as a whole. But in a broader sense, your aim depends on the relation between your writing and three other elements: you, your reader, and the world outside you both. Given these three elements, an essay may have any one of three aims:

1. If the writing chiefly concerns you, it is **self-expressive.** It aims not so much to affect the reader or to explain the outside world as to express your personal thoughts, feelings, and experiences.

2. If the writing seeks primarily to affect the reader, its aim is **persuasive;** it tries to make the reader believe something.

3. If the writing points to the world, including the world of other writings (books, poems, essays), its aim is **referential** or **expository;** it refers to something independent of you and your reader alike and seeks to explain it.

Any one of these aims can of course interact with another, and frequently does. Though Dorothea Morefield begins by expressing a deeply personal rage, her ultimate aim is to persuade us that handguns should be outlawed. You too may have more than one aim. But the better you understand your aims and the relation between them, the more effective your revising will be. When Tim Boyle reread the first draft of "Why I Love Scoring Goals" with the help of his instructor's comments (see below, section 4.5), he could see that his draft was purely expressive, solely the product of his personal feelings. The comments helped him see that what he had discovered about his own love of scoring might go beyond himself. So he decided to give his thesis a referential edge, to make it include all players. He revised it this way:

> ORIGINAL VERSION: Though many things make me want to score goals, I love scoring most of all because it momentarily gives me a sense of power.
> REVISED VERSION: Though many things make players want to score goals, my own experience in ice hockey leads me to think that we

love scoring most of all because it momentarily gives us a sense of power.

Switching from "me" and "I" to "players" and "we," Tim adjusted the focus of his thesis. But he did not abandon his expressive aim. On the contrary, he decided to explain why all players love to score by analyzing his own motives for scoring. In the next section, you will see what further revisions flowed from Tim's restatement of his aim.

Different aims, of course, call for different methods. If your aim is referential or expository, you will find methods of exposition treated in chapter 6 (pp. 82–110). If your aim is persuasive, you will find methods of persuasion treated in chapter 7 (pp. 111–43).

EXERCISE 8   **Reconsidering Your Aims**

Do four things: (1) state the primary aim of your first draft—whether expressive, referential, or persuasive—and also its secondary aim, if any; (2) if there is more than one aim, explain the relation between them; (3) say whether or not you want to adjust your aims; (4) revise your draft to make it serve your aims as well as possible.

4.4   Reconsidering Your Structure

The structure of an essay is the order of its major parts, the way its chief points have been arranged and connected with each other. In a well-structured essay, an introduction leads to a middle, and the middle in turn flows to a conclusion. The fluidity of this structure depends on three things: unity, continuity, and progression.

An essay has **unity** when all of its points serve to develop, illustrate, or reinforce its thesis. (A unified essay may also contain points that qualify or even oppose the thesis, but if so, they must be subordinated to the points that support it.) An essay has **continuity** when the reader can see a line of thought connecting each of its points from beginning to end. And an essay has **progression** when each new paragraph adds something new to the points already made.

To judge the unity, continuity, and progression of your first draft, consider these questions:

1. Does your statement of thesis express the main point you now want to make? If you followed our suggestions in chapter 2, you formulated a thesis before writing your first draft. But in the process of writing that draft, you may have discovered a new way of looking at your topic or even changed your mind entirely about it. Suppose, for instance, that you set out to show from your own experience the advantages of owning and running a small business, but then found yourself dwelling on the disadvantages—the risk, the worries, the long hours, the hassle of bill-collecting—and concluding that you would never again repeat the experience. To unify your draft, you would first have to reformulate your statement of thesis. You could then make the essay show how and why you came to dislike running your own business.

Most of the time, however, you can bridge the gap between your statement of thesis and your draft by modifying the thesis rather than by wholly reformulating it. When Tim discovered that his own experience with scoring might have more than personal significance, he simply made the small changes shown on p. 55- 56.

When Jim—another student—decided that he wanted not just to explain engine maintenance but to persuade his readers that they could do it themselves, he dropped the technical terms from his thesis and focused instead on the learning process. Compare his original thesis with the revision:

> ORIGINAL VERSION: Car owners who want to save money can maintain their own engines by periodically changing the oil, checking other fluids, replacing the spark plugs and the distributor parts, correcting the engine timing, and adjusting the idle speed on the carburetor.
>
> REVISED VERSION: Car owners who want to save money can maintain their own engines by periodically performing a few small tasks that can be easily learned.

Unlike the original version, which is dauntingly crowded with technical terms, the revised version begins the work of persuading nonmechanical readers that engine maintenance is something they can actually do for themselves. Jim could then introduce and explain the technical terms one by one, so that readers could absorb them gradually.

2. Does your introduction announce your thesis or clearly point to it? A good introduction leads up to your thesis either directly, by stating it, or indirectly, by pointing toward it. As we have said already, a good introduction need not end with a statement of thesis; it can end with a question to be answered or with a problem to be solved by your thesis. But if the introduction fails to indicate your thesis in any way, it is misdirecting the reader and thereby weakening the unity of your draft. So whether or not you reformulate your thesis at this point, you must be sure your introduction leads up to it.

3. Can you find or state the main point of each paragraph? With each paragraph you should be able to do one of two things: find within it a sentence that expresses its main point, or state that point in a sentence. If you can't do either, the paragraph lacks unity and must either be split up, reconstructed, or both. (For detailed discussion of how to revise a drastically disorganized paragraph, see section 8.6, pp. 160–64.)

4. Does the main point of each paragraph help to support and advance the thesis? If the main point of any paragraph departs from the topic or works against the thesis, you should first try to decide whether the material in that paragraph belongs in your essay at all. If you're writing about the problems of running a lawn-care service, for instance, you might well include a paragraph on the crankiness of Mr. Galloway, who could always find grass cuttings on his driveway or wheel ruts in his lawn or something else to complain about. But a paragraph on the oddities of Mr. Galloway's house—even if it's a haunted Victorian mansion—does nothing to help your thesis along. Such a paragraph is simply irrelevant and should be cut out altogether.

If the main point of a paragraph *is* relevant to the topic and yet works against the thesis, you have a tougher problem. To cut the paragraph altogether is to run the risk of oversimplifying your essay. But to keep it in without violating the unity of your essay, you must either change your thesis or reorganize the paragraph so that the point working against your thesis is subordinated to a point working for it. Section 4.5 below shows how Tim Boyle managed this kind of reorganization with one of his paragraphs.

5. From the second paragraph on, is the first sentence of each paragraph clearly connected to the last sentence of the one before? A well-structured essay has not only unity but also continuity, an unbroken line of development from one point to the next. The line breaks when the opening sentence of a new paragraph has no connection with the closing sentence of the one before it, and the line fades when a new paragraph begins by simply saying, "Another point to consider is X."

You can often generate continuity by improving the transition between one paragraph and the next, as explained in section 8.8. If you can't solve the problem that way, consider rearranging your paragraphs—that is, rearranging the order of your major points. (For advice on arranging main points see section 3.1, pp. 29–31.)

6. Does the main point of each new paragraph move beyond the main point of the one before it? Each new paragraph in your draft should move beyond the previous one by revealing something new about the topic. If a new paragraph simply repeats the point made by the one before, your progression falters. To keep the essay moving, you should either cut the repetitive paragraph altogether or

see whether a rearrangement of your points would offset the repetitive effect.

7. Does the conclusion reaffirm the thesis? The conclusion should
reaffirm the thesis in some way, explicitly or implicitly. If it fails to
do so, or to answer the question posed in the introduction, the
reader will finish your essay without a clear understanding of your
main point, and the essay as a whole will seem unfocused or unfinished.

If you've changed your thesis during the revising process, you
will of course need to change your conclusion as well. The conclusion should reaffirm what you now regard as the main point of
your essay.

4.5 Revising in Action

The foregoing suggestions, we hope, will help you to see what kind
of revisions your first draft needs and how to make them. But to
understand the process of revision more clearly, you need to see it
in action. So consider once more the first draft of Tim's essay—this
time with his instructor's comments on it. (The paragraphs are
numbered to facilitate reference in our own comments afterward,
and the instructor is commenting only on large-scale matters at this
stage, not on small-scale errors such as misspellings. Those will be
corrected later.)

[1] Anyone who plays on a team dreams of

scoring. Why? Most people probably think that

players long to score for the good of the team,

or to make the coach happy, or to gain some

glory: the cheers of the crowd, the smile of

a cheerleader, and perhaps a headline in the

school newspaper. But none of these things can

fully explain the special excitement of scoring,

or more specifically, the "high" I get from   *Good*

scoring in ice hockey. Though many things   *introduction*

make me want to score goals, I love scoring   *and*
                                                    statement
most of all because it momentarily gives me

a sense of power.   *of thesis.*

Transition? What's the connection between this point and your thesis— or the end of your first ¶?

What's the main point of this ¶? It seems to have two competing points: 1) scoring relaxes you, 2) scoring disturbs you.

Is this the best transition you can think of?

[2] Scoring brings me a sense of relaxation. It begins even before I shoot, because even then I can see the puck going into the goal. The picture just flashes into my mind. The feeling is both *exhilerating and frustrating. When I see the picture a peacefulness fills me. I become relaxed and don't even consciously try to shoot. The shot just happens. Often I cannot remember looking at the puck, and I am so relaxed I might not have. The feeling at this point is one of perfection. Unfortunately not every shot is like this, nor can every shot be made perfect. If I try to consciously *visualise a goal, the shot feels forced. My body works against me rather than with me. When I unconsciously "see" a goal, I will always score, but if the effort to "see" a goal is conscious, I will not. This lack of conscious control is disturbing. I feel as if fate is controlling my shot and I can do nothing about it. I cannot make a goal happen. It happens almost by itself.

[3] Scoring also gives me relief from pressure. In a competitive situation, players experience intense pressure to play to the best of their ability. Their parents, friends, schoolmates, teammates, and above all their coach expect a strong performance. So when

I score, I feel a sense of relief. I have met the demands placed on me, <u>and I can relax--for a moment anyway.</u>

Here, you simply repeat the point already made. You seem to be going in circles.

[4] This moment of relaxation heightens my awareness of the world around me. Though I often cannot remember looking at the puck, I can always see it slide into the goal. No matter how fast the shot or how far away it was taken from, I can always see the puck hitting the twine at the back of the net. At this instant I see the world in a freeze-frame. Every other player seems caught, as if someone had suddenly stopped a fast-moving film. I can see the goalie down on the ice, the defensemen, the wingers cheering with their sticks in the air. Sometimes I can even catch the expressions of a face or two in the crowd.

[5] In this frozen moment, the sense of power strikes. As I look at the goalie stretched out on the ice, I can see that he tried with every inch of his body to stop the puck, but he couldn't because I shot it past him. For anyone driven by the urge to compete, this is a moment of pure triumph. *The ultimate mind trip. I have two *victroies now--one over the goalie, and one over the *anxeity inside me, the fear that I will *disapoint others. The crowd seems to cheer for me alone: not for

Good -- The tone is confident -- even exultant. It comes through strongly here.

the team or the coach or the school, but just for me. In that moment, the world is mine.

[6] When the cheers subside, I lose my empire and become just another player again, reabsorbed by the game. But every time the moment of triumph comes, I learn once more why scoring excites me so much. On or off the hockey rink or the playing field, life is frustrating. We miss shots; we reel from body checks; we sometimes fall flat on our faces. To score is for one shining moment to conquer all frustration. Anxiety has been banished, and we rule the world. Ultimately, it is not for the team or the school or the coach that I love to score, but for myself.

Very good— But since you use "we" in this ¶, couldn't you broaden your thesis and approach elsewhere to make this more than just an essay of self-expression?

On the whole, Tim found the comments encouraging. The teacher liked his introduction, his statement of thesis, his self-expressive aim, his tone of candid confidence, and his conclusion. But the question about his self-expressive aim and the comments on the middle paragraphs showed that Tim still had work to do.

First, the question about his aim led him to revise his thesis in the way already noted. He then revised his introduction to fit the revised thesis:

> Anyone who plays on a team dreams of scoring goals. Why? Most people probably think players long to score for the good of the team, or to make the coach happy, or to gain some glory: the cheers of the crowd, the smile of a cheerleader, and perhaps a headline in the school newspaper. But none of these things can fully explain the special excitement of scoring, the "high" we players get from it. Though many things make us want to score goals, my own ex-

perience in ice hockey leads me to think that we love scoring most of all because it momentarily gives us a sense of power.

This revision of the introductory paragraph made it fit the newly formulated statement of thesis. But something more was needed to bridge the gap between the end of this paragraph and the beginning of the second, between "a sense of power" and "a sense of relaxation." Tim saw that he would have to either improve the transition between paragraphs 1 and 2 or rearrange his major points.

As for paragraph 2 itself, his teacher's comment made him see that it had not one main point but two competing points: (1) scoring relaxes me because I feel the shot will be perfect; (2) scoring disturbs me because I have no control over it. Coming at the end of the second paragraph, this second point seemed to push aside the first, and even seemed to undercut the thesis. If scoring made him feel manipulated by "fate," how could it end up giving him a sense of power?

Two more problems turned up in paragraph 3. Besides the comment on the weak transitional "also" at the beginning, the comment made at the end showed him something he had completely overlooked: the similarity between the end of paragraph 3 and the beginning of paragraph 2. By simply rounding back to the point that scoring brings relaxation, the draft had become repetitive and circular. It lacked progression.

How could he solve all these problems? Where could he begin? As a rule of thumb, the best way to start solving structural problems in an essay is to reconsider the structure of the essay as a whole—or more precisely, the arrangement of its major points. It makes no sense to reconstruct a particular paragraph before you've definitely decided where that paragraph should go.

In light of the basic principle that big problems should be solved first, Tim decided to see what would happen if he reversed the order of paragraphs 2 and 3. With paragraph 3 *before* paragraph 2, he noticed, one problem suddenly disappeared: he no longer had a weak transition between the two. The echo or doubling-back effect that he got with the former arrangement became instead a link:

> END OF ¶ 2. (formerly 3) . . . I have met the demands placed on me, and I can relax—for a moment anyway.
> ¶ 3. (formerly 2) Scoring brings me a sense of relaxation.

He now had continuity, but he needed progression. What could he do with the point about relaxation? As he reread paragraph 3 in light of the new arrangement, it occurred to him that he could use **cause and effect** here (see section 6.11, pp. 105–8). He could move from the effect of relaxation to its original cause:

END OF ¶ 2. . . . I have met the demands placed on me, and I can relax—for a moment anyway.

¶ 3. Strangely enough, the relaxation begins even before I shoot. It originates from a kind of *forknowledge, a feeling that I am *definately going to score, a *wierd hunch that everything I do will turn out perfectly.

With this new beginning of paragraph 3 before him, Tim had in hand the main point of the paragraph as a whole: the relaxation comes from a foreknowledge that makes him feel confident. But to unify the paragraph and to insure that it supported his thesis, he had to do something about the other point—the one about his feeling disturbed by a lack of conscious control. He solved the problem this way:

¶ 3. Strangely enough, the relaxation begins even before I shoot. It originates from a kind of *forknowledge, a feeling that I am *definately going to score, a *wierd hunch that everything I do will turn out perfectly. The feeling is both frustrating and *exhilerating. On one hand, it bothers me that I can't control these moments of perfection. I can't control my shot. I feel instead that fate controls me. On the other hand, I feel all my usual awkwardness slip away. No longer working against me, with arms flailing one way and legs slipping the other, my body works totally for me. I am so confident of my special power that I can see the puck sliding into the goal even before my stick touches it.

This revised version not only unifies the paragraph but also makes it clearly support the thesis of the essay as a whole. The point about being disturbed—the counter-point that worked against the thesis in the original paragraph—is now subordinated to a point that works for it. Tim has moved the counter-point from the end of the paragraph to the middle, so that he can end by reaffirming his main point, which is that a foreknowledge of scoring makes him feel confidently relaxed. He has also shrewdly managed to work into the last sentence the key word of his thesis: *power*.

At the same time, Tim has added specific detail. Even though he has compressed the paragraph to sharpen the focus on its main point, he has injected a phrase about arms and legs to illustrate his "usual awkwardness." Interestingly enough, he first used this detail in freewriting, dropped it in his draft, and then found a place for it in his revision.

Three other tasks remained. First of all, to insure continuity between the new paragraph 3 and the old paragraph 4, he had to revise the opening of paragraph 4. He did so by once again using cause and effect, treating the mood of relaxation as a cause of heightened awareness:

> END OF ¶ 3. I have met the demands placed on me, and I can re-
> lax—for a moment anyway.
> ¶ 4. The effect of this mood is a heightened awareness of the scor-
> ing moment. No matter how fast the shot or how far away it was
> taken from, I can always see the puck hitting the twine at the back
> of the net. At this instant I see the world in a freeze-frame. . . .

That revision took care of the continuity between paragraphs 3
and 4. But Tim still had to bridge the gap between his introductory
paragraph and the one that would now follow it—the one about
relief from pressure. He solved the problem by using reverse chronological order, moving backward in time.

> END OF ¶ 1. . . . we love it most of all because it momentarily gives
> us a sense of power.
> ¶ 2. Before the sense of power comes a sense of relief.

He could then leave the rest of the paragraph as it was.
Finally, since Tim had changed his thesis, he had to revise his
conclusion, which would now include all players, not just himself:

> When the cheers subside, I lose my empire and become just an-
> other player again, reabsorbed by the game. But every time the
> moment of triumph comes, I learn once more why scoring excites
> me so much, and why, I believe, it so much excites anyone who
> scores. On or off the hockey rink or the playing field, life is frus-
> trating. We miss shots; we reel from body checks; we sometimes
> fall flat on our faces. To score is for one shining moment to con-
> quer all frustration. Anxiety has been banished, and we rule the
> world. Ultimately, it is not for our teams or our schools or our
> coaches that we players love to score, but for ourselves.

Since no two different drafts will ever present the same set of
problems, the revisions Tim made in his draft can merely suggest
what you might do with yours. Nevertheless, the specific things Tim
did clearly illustrate a general point worth repeating. <u>The key to
effective revision is to look again at the whole of your draft and
think big.</u> Think not about commas or misspelled words but about
the texture of your writing, about its tone, about its aim, and finally
about its structure—the relation between the thesis and the paragraphs that are meant to support and develop it. You may find that
you have to restate your thesis completely, rearrange your paragraphs drastically, or rewrite them extensively. But if you fully revise your draft, the result should be a definite improvement. (For
the final version of Tim's essay, see pp. 79–81.)

EXERCISE 9   Reworking Your Structure

Following the suggestions made in section 4.4 and the example shown just above, rework the structure of your own draft to give it unity, continuity, and progression. Feel free also to make any further changes in texture, tone, and aim that you think will improve your draft. But do not worry now about correcting errors in spelling, grammar, or punctuation. Those can wait.

5

EDITING YOUR ESSAY

Editing is the final stage of writing. After you have drafted your essay and revised it—that is, looked again at its thesis, texture, tone, aim, overall structure, and paragraphing—you need to look closely at its individual sentences and words. Even at this "final" stage, of course, new ideas may come to you. You may see new ways of developing your thesis, illustrating one of your major points, or substantiating one of your arguments. But eventually you must turn your focus from large units to small ones, from the substance and structure of your essay as a whole to the energy and structure of your sentences, to your punctuation, diction, and spelling. This chapter is designed to take you through those final steps—right up to the final copy of your essay.

5.1 Making Your Sentences Rhetorically Effective

Good writing is made of sentences that are not just grammatically correct but also rhetorically effective: vigorous, concise, emphatic, well-balanced, and varied. To achieve these effects with your own sentences, consider the following suggestions:

1. Use subordination to break the monotony of short, simple sentences and to emphasize your main points. Writing made chiefly of short, simple sentences soon becomes monotonous:

> Some working women find special ways to cope with resistance from their husbands. Take my mother's situation. She is a teacher. My father is a fine old Southern gentleman. He is opposed to her

teaching. He was raised on old-fashioned beliefs. He thinks men should work and women should stay at home. He wouldn't object to her job if the family needed a second income. We don't need it. But my mother likes her job and won't give it up. So they've solved the problem by making an agreement. He buys the necessities, and she buys the luxuries.

Too many short, simple sentences make this passage dull and featureless, with no emphasis on any point in particular. You can stress the main points in a passage like this by using subordination—that is, by combining short sentences in such a way as to show which points outrank others:

> REVISED: Some working women find special ways to cope with resistance from their husbands. Take my mother, who teaches. My father, a fine old Southern gentleman, opposes her teaching because he was raised to believe that men should work and women should stay at home unless the family needed a second income. Though our family doesn't need a second income, my mother likes her job and won't give it up. To solve the problem, they've agreed that he buys the necessities, and she buys the luxuries.

By combining short sentences and using subordination, this passage clearly emphasizes the writer's main points: (1) my father is opposed to my mother's teaching; (2) she likes her job and won't give it up; (3) they've agreed that he buys the necessities, and she buys the luxuries. (For a full discussion of subordination, see chapter 15.)

2. Vary the length and construction of your sentences. Sentences of any length and any construction soon become monotonous if they are too much alike. To combat monotony, vary your sentences. Practice alternating between simple and complex structures, between long sentences and short ones. Compare these two passages:

> a. Ultimately, it is not for our teams, our schools, or our coaches that we players love to score, but for ourselves.
> b. Ultimately, it is not for our teams, our schools, or our coaches that we players love to score. It is for ourselves.

The contrast between a long, complex sentence and a short, simple one sharpens the impact of the final point. (For more explanation of how to vary your sentences, see section 25.1.)

3. Activate Your Verbs. Wherever possible, replace forms of the verb *be*—forms such as *is, are, was, were, has been,* and *had been*—with verbs that denote action. Compare these two sentences:

a. On or off the hockey rink or the playing field, life is frustrating.
b. On or off the hockey rink or the playing field, life breeds frustration.

The change of *is* to *breeds* energizes the sentence. (For more on this effect, see section 25.2.)

Activating your verbs also means changing the passive voice to the active voice whenever there is no good reason for keeping the passive. Compare these two sentences:

a. In modern Japanese families, all of the husband's salary is taken by the wife, and all household expenditures are managed by her.
b. In modern Japanese families, the wife takes all of the husband's salary and manages all household expenditures.

The change from the passive to the active voice tightens and invigorates the sentence. (For more on the advantages of the active voice, see section 22.3.)

4. Use parallel construction to enhance the coordination of two or more items. Compare these passages:

a. To score is for one shining moment to conquer all frustration. Anxiety has been banished, and we rule the world.
b. To score is for one shining moment to conquer all frustration, to banish anxiety, and to rule the world.

Since the three effects of scoring are coordinate—that is, equal in importance—the second sentence puts all three of them in the same form. (For more on parallel construction, see chapter 14.)

5. Cut out any words you don't need. Sentences work best when they carry no more words than they need. Compare these two sentences:

a. There are many things that make me laugh.
b. Many things make me laugh.

The second version is both leaner and livelier than the first. (For a full discussion of how to eliminate wordiness from your sentences, see section 9.11.)

6. Break up and reorganize any sentence so tangled that it cannot be understood on the first reading:

*Due to the progress in military weaponry over the years, there has been an increased passivity in mankind that such advancements bring as wars are easier to fight resulting in a total loss of honor in fighting.

Making Your Sentences Rhetorically Effective **69**

Revised: Since progress in military weaponry over the years has made mankind more passive and wars easier to fight, fighting has lost all honor.

(To learn how to straighten out tangled sentences, see section 16.2.)

5.2 Checking Your Choice of Words

As you edit your essay, look for the following:

1. Words too high or too low for your level of diction. In general, you should choose your words from the middle level of diction. If you find a piece of slang or a word that sounds overly formal, consider whether it suits your subject and your audience. (See section 9.1.)

2. Words that don't say precisely what you mean. If you don't think that a particular word says exactly what you mean, it may have the wrong denotation (section 9.3) or the wrong connotation (section 9.4). In either case, you may be able to find a better word with the help of a dictionary (section 9.2).

3. Overuse of abstract or general words. The overuse of abstract words (such as *peace, freedom,* and *democracy*) and general words (such as *animals, plants,* and *humans*) can make your meaning hard to grasp. To make your meaning vivid and tangible, use concrete and specific words (section 9.5) and figurative language (section 9.6) whenever you can.

4. Jargon, euphemisms, and pretentious words. Jargon is technical terminology—words and phrases such as *feedback* and *upward mobility.* Jargon belongs in specialized essays but not in essays on subjects of general interest. Euphemisms such as *harvest* (when the meaning is *kill*) veil the truth instead of stating it openly. Pretentious words such as *utilization* (when the meaning is *use*) make sentences sound heavy and stiff. For all such words you should find plain, simple, straightforward substitutes whenever possible. (See sections 9.10–9.11.)

5. Clichés. Clichés are worn-out phrases like *last but not least, busy as a bee,* and *at this point in time.* Whenever you can, replace them with single words (such as *finally, industrious,* and *now*) or other phrases. (See section 9.8.)

5.3 Checking Your Grammar

Since errors in grammar and punctuation can be hard to spot, your teacher may have noted them for you before asking you to prepare the final version of your paper. But you can learn to spot some errors yourself by watching for the following things as you read through your draft; reading it *aloud* will increase your chances of spotting them. If you recognize in your own writing one of the errors listed here, you will find detailed advice on how to correct it in the designated section or chapter of Part II.

1. The sentence fragment

> For anyone driven by the urge to compete, this is a moment of pure triumph. *The ultimate mind trip.

The second "sentence" is actually a sentence fragment—part of a sentence punctuated as a whole one. To correct this kind of error, see chapter 17.

2. The dangling modifier

> *After exercising, a swim was taken.

After exercising is a modifier, a part of a sentence that is supposed to describe or qualify some other part. But since nothing else in this sentence tells us *who* did the exercising, the modifier has nothing to describe or qualify. It just dangles. To correct this kind of error, see section 12.20.

3. The run-on (fused) sentence

> *The quake struck without warning in minutes it leveled half the town.

This is really two sentences written as if they were one, with no punctuation at all to mark the end of the first sentence *(warning)* or the beginning of the second *(in minutes)*. To correct this kind of error, see section 13.8.

4. The misplaced modifier

> *Yoko Ono talked about her husband, John Lennon, who was killed in an interview with Barbara Walters.

The writer means to say that Yoko Ono talked about her husband in an interview with Barbara Walters. But because the modifier—*in an interview with Barbara Walters*—is misplaced, the sentence seems to say that Lennon was killed in the interview. To correct this kind of error, see sections 12.16–12.19.

5. Unclear reference of pronouns

> *When I took the Walkman back to the store, they told me I couldn't get a refund.

Who are *they*? The sentence doesn't tell us. When you use a pronoun—a word such as *they, he, she,* or *it*—the reader must be able to see clearly what it stands for. Otherwise the reference of the pronoun is unclear. To correct this error, see section 18.4.

6 Faulty shifts in pronoun reference

> *No one should be forced into a career that they believe is not right for them.

They and *them* are pronouns standing for *no one,* their antecedent. But since the writer shifts from the singular *(no one)* to the plural *(they* and *them),* the pronouns do not agree with their antecedent. To correct this kind of error, see section 18.8.

7. Incorrect pronoun case forms

> *Frank and me run five miles every day.

Me should be *I* because it serves as part of the subject of the verb *run.* To correct this kind of error, see sections 18.9–18.12.

8. Faulty agreement of subject and verb

> *Everyone like a good time.

The verb *like* needs an *-s* on the end because the subject —*Everyone*—is third-person singular. To correct errors of this kind, see chapter 19.

9. Faulty tense shifts

> *The novel describes the adventures of two immigrant families who enter the United States at New York, withstand the stresses of culture shock, and traveled to the Dakota Territory to make their fortune.

After using three present-tense verbs *(describes, enter,* and *withstand),* the writer shifts to a past-tense verb *(traveled)* with no good .reason for doing so. To correct this kind of error, see sections 21.4 and 21.5.

5.4   Checking Your Punctuation

Like errors in grammar, errors in punctuation can be hard to spot, and you may need your teacher's help to find them. But you can learn to spot some of them by watching for the following things, and you can learn how to correct these errors by turning to the designated section of Part III, "Punctuation and Mechanics."

1. Misused commas. In general, commas should not be used—

a. Right after conjunctions (section 26.2):

> *We walked all over town, but, we couldn't find the record store.

b. To set off any part of a sentence that is essential to its meaning (section 26.6):

*All students, caught cheating, will be expelled.

c. To separate the basic parts of a sentence (section 26.13):

*Poisonous gas from a pesticide factory in India, killed more than two thousand people in 1984.

d. Between independent clauses (section 13.7):

*Karen blinked, she couldn't believe her eyes.

Unlike errors a–c, this one cannot be corrected by a simple removal of the comma. See "Comma Splices," section 13.7.

2. Mispunctuated quotations.

*We are all worms," said Churchill, "but I do believe that I am a glowworm".

Quotation marks are needed before *We* in this sentence, and the closing quotation marks should go *after* the period, not before. For detailed guidance on punctuating quotations, see chapter 29.

5.5 Checking Your Spelling, Capitalization, and Apostrophes

Most writers misspell from two to five words in a five hundred–word draft, and they also make occasional errors in capitalization and the use of apostrophes. To correct these errors in your own writing, look for the following:

1. Your own spelling demons. Spelling demons are the words you have trouble spelling correctly. To identify them in the first essay you submit, you may need your teacher's comments, which could look like this:

```
        Strangely enough, the relaxation begins even

        before I shoot.  It originates from a kind of

sp.     forknowledge, a feeling that I am definately      sp.

        going to score, a wierd hunch that everything      sp.

        I do will turn out perfectly.
```

To find the correct spelling of the words marked *sp.,* see the list in section 31.8 or look them up in a dictionary. Then make an analytical list of the misspelled words as explained in section 31.1:

MISSPELLED	CORRECTLY SPELLED	ERROR
definately	definitely	nat/nit
forknowledge	foreknowledge	for/fore
wierd	weird	ie/ei

Then correct the misspelled words in your text, either by rewriting the words neatly or—if your teacher wishes—by rewriting the whole sentence in which they occur:

> It originates from a kind of foreknowledge, a feeling that I am definitely going to score, a weird hunch that everything I do will turn out perfectly.

For detailed discussion of spelling errors, see sections 31.1–31.8.

2. Words with apostrophes. Apostrophes should be used to indicate the possessive of nouns *(the boy's bicycle, the boys' bicycles)* but generally not to form the plural of nouns *(the two boys)*, or to indicate the possessive of any pronoun *(its* shape; the house was *theirs)*. If you aren't sure that you are using an apostrophe correctly, see section 31.10.

3. Names and titles. Titles should be capitalized as explained in section 32.3, and names of particular persons (Thomas Jefferson), places (Montreal), things (the Statue of Liberty), and events (World War II) should be capitalized as explained in section 32.1.

EXERCISE 1 Proofreading

Correct the spelling and add, move, or delete apostrophes as necessary in the following passage.

EXAMPLE
line 2: sports editor

My job hunt took me to Boston for an interview with Ernie Roberts, the senior sports editer of the *Boston Globe.* At 11 oclock Wensday morning I walked into the Sports Department, wide-eyed with excitment. I was hopeing to spot the writer's who's faces were fa-
5 miliar to me from the pictures printed beside there bylines. I wasn't disapointed. Both Ray Fitzgerald and Bud Collins were in site. Ernie was'nt in his office, but another man who shared the space told me to grab a seat and wait. After about ten minutes, Ernie bustled in. He apoligized for being late and explained we would have to
10 talk fast because he had an apointment in Cambridge. Then he asked me to tell him about myself. As I spoke, he grabed a cigar from his desk and began pufing. He looked happy smoking. Evry so often he would take the cigar out of his mouth, study the burning end, smile, and then take another puff. After I finished speak-
15 ing, they're was a long silense. He explained, firmly and finaly, that my inexperience was going to be more of a handicap than I had realised. He advised me to get a job with a small local paper and

possibly register for night course's in journalism. It was sound advise and helpfull to hear. I thanked him for seeing me and left.
20 Maybe someday I'll have the experiance and the credentials to apply their for a job.

5.6 Preparing Your Final Copy

If your teacher has special instructions about the format of your
final copy, you should of course respect them. But otherwise you
can follow the format illustrated by the final copy of Tim's essay on
pp. 79–81. To follow the format, do as follows:

1. Use a typewriter, word processor, or pen. (For guidance on writing with a word processor, see Appendix 3, pp. 645–50.) If you
   wish to write by hand and your teacher accepts handwritten work,
   write legibly and neatly with a dark-ink pen on standard-size white
   paper (8½ by 11 inches) with lines at least ⅜ of an inch apart.
   Do not use sheets torn from a spiral binder.
2. If you type, use a fresh, black ribbon with clean type on medium-
   weight typing paper of standard size. If you write with a word
   processor, you may use standard-size fanfold computer paper
   (*not* spread sheets), but separate the sheets and remove the per-
   forated strips before submitting your essay.
3. If you are not required to use a separate title page, follow the
   format shown in the first example on p. 77. Otherwise follow the
   second example on p. 77, and repeat the title on the first page
   of your text, as shown on p. 78.
4. After the first page of text, give your last name and the page
   number in the upper right corner, as shown on p. 78.
5. Leave a margin of one inch on each side and at the bottom of
   each page, and indent the first word of each paragraph five spaces
   from the left margin.
6. Whether you use a pen, a typewriter, or a word processor, double-space your lines and write only on one side of each sheet.
7. For safety's sake, make a carbon or photocopy of your essay before you submit it.

5.7 Proofreading and Submitting Your Essay

Before submitting your essay, check the manuscript to be sure
everything looks and reads as it should. You must see exactly what
is there—nothing more, nothing less. This is not so easy as it seems.
The mind has a way of making us believe something is on a page
when it isn't, and you may find it hard to look at words and phrases
as collections of letters rather than units of meaning. Yet you must
proofread if you are to spot mistakes in spelling and punctuation,
omissions, and unwanted repetition. Here's what to do:

1. Reread the final copy early on the day it is due. You may spot something you overlooked when writing it out.
2. Pause to examine the spelling of words that could be troublesome, making yourself see the letters and checking in your dictionary when you have the slightest doubt.
3. Check the hyphenation of divided words, again using your dictionary if necessary.
4. Make corrections neatly. If there are more than five on a page, redo the entire page.

EXERCISE 2   Proofreading

To find out how well you can see what is written on a page, compare the items in each of the following entries. If any item in a series is different from the others, describe the difference.

1. xxxxxx   xxxxxx   xxxxxx   xxxxxx   xxxxxxx
2. $+ + + + +^{\circ\circ\circ} + +$ $+ + + +^{\circ\circ\circ} + +$ $+ + - +^{\circ\circ\circ} + +$
3. /////,,,xyxxy   /////,,xyxxy   /////,,,xyxxy   /////,,,xyxxy
4. 777000066611   777000066611   777000066611

EXERCISE 3   Proofreading

Check your ability to spot a misspelling. The first word in each entry is spelled correctly. If all of the others in the series are spelled correctly, write *Correct*. If any of the others is misspelled, describe the error.

1. description   description   description   description   description
2. ambivalence   ambivalence   ambivalance   ambivalence
3. rigidity   rigidity   rigidity   rigidity   rigididy
4. occurred   occured   occurred   occurred   occurred
5. refractory   refractory   refractory   refactory   refractory

EXERCISE 4   Proofreading

We have deliberately mutilated this passage from Mark Twain's "Advice to Youth" so that it contains three misspellings, a sentence fragment, and a comma splice. Find the errors and correct them.

> You want to be very careful about lying, otherwise you are nearly sure to get caught. Once caught, you can never again be, in the eyes of the good and the pure, what you were before. Many a young person has injured himself pernamently through a single clumsy
> 5 and ill-finished lie. The result of carelessness born of incomplete training. Some authorities hold that the young ought not to lie at all. That, of course, is puting it rather stronger than necessary; still, while I cannot go quite so far as that, I do maintane, and I believe I am right, that the young ought to be temperate in the use of this
> 10 great art until practice and experience shall give them that confidence, elegance, and precision which alone can make the accomplishment graceful and profitable.

5.8 The Essay Ready to Hand In

Format with title on first page of text

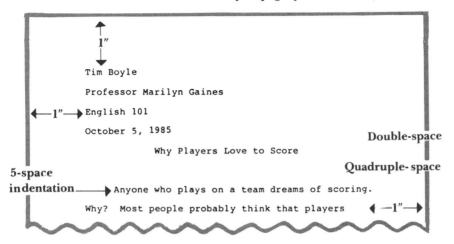

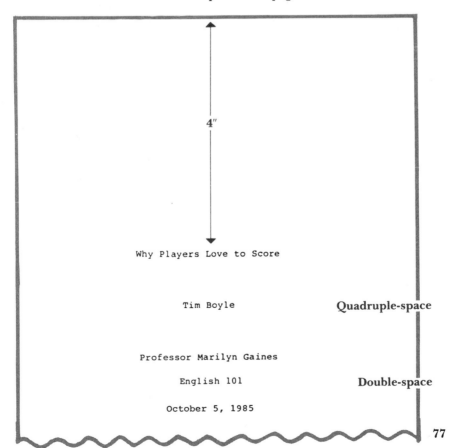

Format with separate title page

First page of text following separate title page—note repetition of title

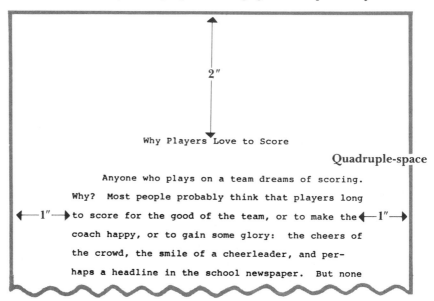

2″

Why Players Love to Score

Quadruple-space

Anyone who plays on a team dreams of scoring.
Why? Most people probably think that players long
←1″→ to score for the good of the team, or to make the ←1″→
coach happy, or to gain some glory: the cheers of
the crowd, the smile of a cheerleader, and perhaps a headline in the school newspaper. But none

Second and succeeding pages of text

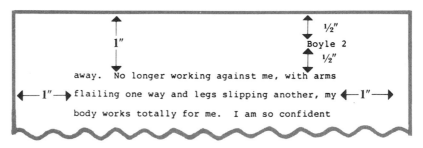

1″   ½″
          Boyle 2
          ½″

away. No longer working against me, with arms
←1″→ flailing one way and legs slipping another, my ←1″→
body works totally for me. I am so confident

Why Players Love to Score

Anyone who plays on a team dreams of scoring. Why?
Most people probably think that players long to score for
the good of the team, or to make the coach happy, or to gain
some glory: the cheers of the crowd, the smile of a
cheerleader, and perhaps a headline in the school newspaper.
But none of these things can fully explain the special
excitement of scoring or, more specifically, the "high" we
players get from it. Though many things make us want to
score, my own experience in ice hockey leads me to think
that we love it most of all because it momentarily gives us
a sense of power.

Before the sense of power comes a sense of relief. In
a competitive situation, players feel intense pressure to do
their best. Their parents, friends, schoolmates, teammates,
and above all their coaches expect a strong performance. So
when I score, I feel a sense of relief. I have met the
demands placed on me, and I can relax--for a moment anyway.

Strangely enough, the relaxation begins even before I
shoot. It originates from a kind of foreknowledge, a
feeling that I am definitely going to score, a weird hunch
that everything I do will turn out perfectly. The feeling

both frustrates and exhilarates me. On one hand, it bothers me that I can´t control these moments of perfection, that I can´t control my shot. I feel instead that fate controls me. On the other hand, I feel all my usual awkwardness slip away. No longer working against me, with arms flailing one way and legs slipping another, my body works totally for me. I am so confident of my special power that I can see the puck sliding into the goal even before my stick touches it.

The effect of this mood is heightened awareness of the scoring moment. No matter how fast the shot or how far away it is taken from, I can always see the puck hitting the twine at the back of the net. At this instant I see the world in a freeze-frame. Every other player seems caught, as if someone had suddenly stopped a fast-moving film. I can see the goalie down on the ice, the defensemen, the wingers cheering with their sticks in the air. Sometimes I can even catch the expressions of a face or two in the crowd: a pair of eyes lit up with joy, a wide-open grinning mouth.

In this frozen moment, the sense of power strikes. As I look at the goalie stretched out on the ice, I can see that he tried with every inch of his body to stop the puck, but he couldn´t. I shot it past him. For anyone driven by the urge to compete, this is a moment of pure triumph, the ultimate mind trip. I have two victories now--one over the goalie, and one over the anxiety inside me, the fear that I will disappoint others. The crowd seems to cheer for me alone: not for the team or the coach or the school, but just for me. In that moment the world is mine.

When the cheers subside, I lose my empire and become just another player again, reabsorbed by the game. But every time the moment of triumph comes, I learn once more why scoring excites me so much, and why, I believe, it so much excites anyone who scores. On or off the hockey rink or the playing field, life breeds frustration. We miss shots; we reel from body checks; we sometimes fall flat on our faces. To score is for one shining moment to conquer all frustration, to banish all anxiety, to rule the world. Ultimately, it is not for our teams or our schools or our coaches that we players love to score. It is for ourselves.

6

DESCRIPTION, NARRATION, AND EXPOSITION

Description, narration, and exposition are all strategies of development, ways of achieving the aim you set for yourself when you sit down to write. Suppose that your aim is self-expressive, and that you specifically intend to express the fear you experienced on a particular night. How do you convey that feeling? Do you describe what you saw and heard? Do you tell the story of how you came to be so frightened? **Description** and storytelling—more often called **narration**—are both strategies of development, and you can use them both together to achieve your aim.

But the same strategies may also be used for other aims. If your aim is referential, if you are not so much bent on expressing what you feel as on explaining something outside yourself, you might well use description or narration to help you do so. To explain, for instance, how to buy a good used car, you might describe the kind of car that a smart buyer looks for, or tell the story of how a foolish buyer wound up with a lemon. You can also use one or more means of **exposition,** such as comparing a good used car with a bad one, or classifying used cars according to their reliability. Finally, if your aim is to persuade the reader, you may use any one or all of the strategies just mentioned, together with the strategy most commonly used to persuade: **argument.**

This chapter and the next consider in turn each of the four major writing strategies. This chapter treats description, narration, and exposition—the art of explaining. Chapter 7 (pp. 111–43) treats the art of persuasion, with special emphasis on argumentation. Most writing combines at least two of these strategies, and we will show you some ways of combining them as we proceed. But first we explain each strategy by itself.

6.1 Description

Description is writing about the way persons, animals, or things appear. It normally takes one of three forms.

6.1A Informative Description

An informative description simply enables the reader to identify an object. While explaining how to change a spark plug, the author of the passage given on p. 103 describes the electrode as "the small open square of metal that sticks up out of the threaded tube at one end of the spark plug." That brief description enables the reader to recognize the electrode and thus to check it for signs of wear.

6.1B Analytical or Technical Description

An analytical or technical description enables the reader to understand the structure of an object. Consider this passage:

> The panda's "thumb" is not, anatomically, a finger at all. It is constructed from a bone called the radial sesamoid, normally a small component of the wrist. In pandas, the radial sesamoid is greatly enlarged and elongated until it almost equals the metapoidal bones of the true digits in length. The radial sesamoid underlies a pad on the panda's forepaw; the five digits form the framework of another pad, the palmar. A shallow furrow separates the two pads and serves as a channelway for bamboo stalks.   —Stephen Jay Gould,
> *The Panda's Thumb*

Gould is describing the peculiar structure of the panda's paw. His language is precise, objective, technical *(radial sesamoid, metapoidal bones)*, and above all analytical. He focuses not on the furry surface of the panda's paw but on the framework of "thumb" and finger bones that underlie it. This analytical description serves an argumentative aim. Gould wants to show that the panda—which long ago had nothing but five fingers in its paw—gradually developed its radial sesamoid to do the work of an opposable thumb, to operate like a human thumb in grasping the bamboo stalks that pandas love to eat. Analytically described, the panda's paw helps Gould to substantiate the theory of evolution.

6.1C Evocative Description

Evocative description re-creates the impression made by an object:

> The coyote is a long, slim, sick, and sorry-looking skeleton, with a grey wolf-skin stretched over it, a tolerably bushy tail that forever sags down with a despairing expression of forsakenness and misery, a furtive and evil eye, and a long, sharp face, with slightly lifted lip and exposed teeth. —Mark Twain

Twain's words evoke both the visual effect of the coyote and the feeling that its appearance excites. Vividly describing the coyote as a long, slim skeleton, Twain writes of its skin, its tail, its eye, its face, its slightly lifted lip, and its exposed teeth. All of these details work together to help us see the coyote as a whole. At the same time, he reinforces their effect by explicitly judging the character of the beast: *sick, sorry-looking, evil*.

Evocative description can appeal not just to the eye but to all the other senses:

> The heat of summer was mellow and produced sweet scents which lay in the air so damp and rich you could almost taste them. Mornings smelled of purple wisteria, afternoons of the wild roses which tumbled over stone fences, and evenings of honeysuckle. . . .
>
> In the heat of mid-afternoon the women would draw the blinds, spread blankets on the floor for coolness and nap, while in the fields the cattle herded together in the shade of spreading trees to escape the sun. Afternoons were absolutely still, yet filled with sounds.
>
> Bees buzzed in the clover. Far away over the fields the chug of an ancient steam-powered threshing machine could be faintly heard. Birds rustled under the tin of the porch roof.
> —Russell Baker, *Growing Up*

Baker's descriptive language appeals to the senses of smell, touch, taste, and especially of hearing. In the last paragraph, *buzzed* and *chug* are onomatopoeic—that is, they actually sound like what they mean.

A good evocative description may include abstract terms such as *sick* and *evil*, which appear in the Twain passage above. But whatever else it does, evocative description should always appeal to one or more of the senses. Only then can it re-create the impression that a person or object makes.

Compare these two descriptions:

> 1. I couldn't stand Palatka. It was poor, seedy, smelly, and ugly, and the weather was always bad. I couldn't relate to the people either. My stay there was a nightmare.

2. Situated on the banks of the St. Johns River, Palatka was surrounded by dense tropical foliage in limitless swamps. It was always hot, and it rained daily. The town's main street, made of bricks, was called Lemon Street. Weeds grew out of the spaces between the bricks and out of the cracks in the sidewalks and at the bottom of the concrete buildings, so that to a stranger the vegetation appeared to be strangling the town. There was a paper mill in town. It supplied most of the blacks and poorer whites with employment. Each morning at six they were summoned to work by a whistle that woke the entire area. Shortly thereafter Palatka was blanketed by a lavender haze and filled with a terrible stench. —Pat Jordan, *A False Spring*

In the first version, the writer gets between us and the town. He talks about his own feelings instead of showing us why and how the town affected him as it did. In the second version—which is what Jordan actually wrote—the descriptive details set the town before us. With phrases such as *dense tropical foliage in limitless swamps,* Jordan makes us feel its general steaminess, then offers a close-up of weeds poking up between the bricks and through the cracks in the sidewalks. He goes on to appeal to the ear with *a whistle,* to the eye with *a lavender haze,* and to the nose with *a terrible stench.* All of these descriptive details work together to convey a general impression of Palatka. Nowhere does the writer say that Palatka is a dreary and decaying town, but every one of his details shows us that it is.

EXERCISE 1   Informative Description

Using just a sentence or two, describe any unusual object that you know well in such a way that it could be recognized by someone seeing it for the first time.

EXERCISE 2   Analytical or Technical Description

Describe in a paragraph any one of the following in such a way that the reader can understand its structure or design:

a bicycle	a tire jack
a surfboard	the human foot
a solar house	the keystone arch
a rifle	the human hand
a trumpet	a tree

EXERCISE 3   Evocative Description

Write a one-paragraph description in which you re-create the impression that a particular person or particular animal has made on you.

EXERCISE 4 Evocative Description

Using Pat Jordan's paragraph on Palatka as a model, write an evocative description of the neighborhood in which you grew up, or (if you moved around during childhood) of the neighborhood you remember most vividly. Assume that the reader has never seen this place, and describe as many sights, sounds, and smells as possible.

6.2 Narration

6.2A Narrating Events in Chronological Order

Narration or storytelling is writing about a succession of events. The simplest kind of narration follows chronological order: the order in which the narrated events actually occurred or could have occurred. Consider this account of an incident that helped to provoke the Boston Massacre in 1770:

> On Friday, March 2, a Boston ropemaker named William Green, busy with his fellows braiding fibers on an outdoor "ropewalk" or ropemaking machine, called to Patrick Walker, a soldier of the Twenty-ninth [Regiment] who was passing by, and asked if he wanted work. "Yes," Walker replied. "Then go and clean my shithouse," was Green's response. The soldier answered him in similar terms, and when Green threatened him, he departed, swearing to return with some of his regimental mates. Return he did with no less than forty soldiers, led by a big Negro drummer.
> —Page Smith, *A New Age Now Begins*

Here the writer reports events as they followed one another in time, and his use of dialogue—of Green's actual words—makes this moment in American history come vividly alive.

EXERCISE 5 Narrating

Using chronological order, give a brief narration of a fight or quarrel you have seen or been involved in. Concentrate on how the fight or quarrel got started.

6.2B Narrating Events out of Chronological Order

A short narrative can often follow chronological order with good results. But strict adherence to chronological order in an extended narrative can lead to a boring, meaningless string of "and thens." To clarify the meaning of a sequence of events, the writer may need to depart from chronological order, moving backward to explain the cause of a particular event or jumping forward to identify its ultimate effect. Consider this example:

In June 1964 . . . two Italian fishing boats, working in tandem with a crew of 18, were dragging their nets along the bottom of the Adriatic. Toward dawn, as they pulled up the nets after a long trawl, the fishermen realized their catch was unusually heavy. . . . When they finally swung the nets inboard they saw an ungainly, prehistoric-looking figure missing both feet. It was, in fact, a 500-pound Greek statue covered with nearly 2,000 years of sea encrustations.

In November 1977, this life-size bronze fetched the highest known price ever paid for a statue—$3.9 million. The work is attributed to the fourth century B.C. Greek artist Lysippus. . . . Professor Paolo Moreno of Rome University, author of two books on Lysippus, identifies the statue as the portrait of a young athlete after victory and suggests that it may have been plundered by ancient Romans from Mount Olympus. The ship bearing the statue was probably sunk in a storm and there may well have been other treasures on board. Pliny the Elder tells us Lysippus made more than 1,500 works, all of them bronze, but it was doubted that any of the originals had survived—until this one surfaced.

The fishermen stealthily unloaded the barnacle-covered masterpiece in Fano, near Rimini, and took it to the captain's house, where it was put on a kitchen table and propped up against a wall.

—Bryan Rosten, "Smuggled!"

The first paragraph tells the story of how a statue was discovered in June 1964. To explain what makes the story important, the writer flashes forward to 1977, when the statue was sold for nearly four million dollars. Then he flashes back to ancient times, when the statue was lost. After these forward and backward flashes, he returns to the original story in the third paragraph.

EXERCISE 6   **Using Flashbacks and Flash-forwards**

Using at least one flashback and one flash-forward, tell the story of one of the following:

> your first day on a full-time job
> your first day in college
> your first meeting with someone who later became important in your life
> the first time you felt that you were doing something wrong

6.2C   Combining Description and Narration

Description and narration commonly go hand in hand. In his description of Palatka (p. 85), Pat Jordan tells us what happened there each morning: the whistle summoned workers at six, and soon the town was blanketed with haze. Conversely, this piece of narrative includes a good deal of description:

I spent my first month in town with my mouth hanging open. The sharp-dressed young "cats" who hung on the corners and in the poolrooms, bars and restaurants, and who obviously didn't work anywhere, completely entranced me. I couldn't get over marveling at how their hair was straight and shiny like white men's hair; Ella told me this was called a "conk." I had never tasted a sip of liquor, never even smoked a cigarette, and here I saw little black children, ten and twelve years old, shooting craps, playing cards, fighting, getting grown-ups to put a penny or a nickel on their number for them, things like that. And these children threw around swear words I'd never heard before, even, and slang expressions that were just as new to me, such as "stud" and "cat" and "chick" and "cool" and "hip." Every night as I lay in bed I turned these new words over in my mind. It was shocking to me that in town, especially after dark, you'd occasionally see a white girl and a Negro man strolling arm in arm along the sidewalk, and mixed couples drinking in the neon-lighted bars—not slipping off to some dark corner, as in Lansing. I wrote Wilfred and Philbert about that, too.

I wanted to find a job myself, to surprise Ella. One afternoon, something told me to go inside a poolroom whose window I was looking through. I had looked through that window many times. I wasn't yearning to play pool; in fact, I had never held a cue stick. But I was drawn by the sight of the cool-looking "cats" standing around inside, bending over the big, green, felt-topped tables, making bets and shooting the bright-colored balls into the holes. As I stared though the window this particular afternoon, something made me decide to venture inside and talk to a dark, stubby, conk-headed fellow who racked up balls for the pool-players, whom I'd heard called "Shorty." One day he had come outside and seen me standing there and said "Hi, Red," so that made me figure he was friendly.

As inconspicuously as I could, I slipped inside the door and around the side of the poolroom, avoiding people, and on to the back, where Shorty was filling an aluminum can with the powder that pool players dust on their hands. He looked up at me. Later on, Shorty would enjoy teasing me about how with that first glance he knew my whole story. "Man, that cat still *smelled* country!" he'd say, laughing. "Cat's legs was so long and his pants so short his knees showed—an' his head looked like a briar patch!"

But that afternoon Shorty didn't let it show in his face how "country" I appeared when I told him I'd appreciate it if he'd tell me how could somebody go about getting a job like his.

"If you mean racking up balls," said Shorty, "I don't know of no pool joints around here needing anybody. You mean you just want any slave you can find?" A "slave" meant work, a job.

He asked what kind of work I had done. I told him that I'd washed restaurant dishes in Mason, Michigan. He nearly dropped the powder can. "My homeboy! Man, gimme some skin! I'm from Lansing!"

I never told Shorty—and he never suspected—that he was about ten years older than I. He took us to be about the same age. At first I would have been embarrassed to tell him, later I just never bothered. Shorty had dropped out of first-year high school in Lansing, lived a while with an uncle and aunt in Detroit, and had spent the last six years living with his cousin in Roxbury. But when I mentioned the names of Lansing people and places, he remembered many, and pretty soon we sounded as if we had been raised in the same block. I could sense Shorty's genuine gladness, and I don't have to say how lucky I felt to find a friend as hip as he obviously was. —Malcolm X, *The Autobiography of Malcolm X*

Besides the dialogue we have already seen in the piece of narration by Page Smith, this story of how Malcolm X struck up a friendship with Shorty (who soon got him a job as a shoeshine boy) includes descriptions of young "cats," of little black children, of the poolroom where Malcolm met Shorty, and of Shorty himself. The combination of description and narration enables Malcolm X to fulfill his aim, which is essentially to express his own feelings: his initial amazement at the behavior of city blacks, his eagerness to find a job, and his pleasure in meeting Shorty.

EXERCISE 7   **Narrating Events in and out of Chronological Order**

This exercise has two parts. First, tell in strict chronological order the story of the most memorable trip you have taken. Then retell the story in nonchronological order, starting not with the beginning but with the part of the trip you remember best. Then work backward and forward from that point.

EXERCISE 8   **Using Description in Narration**

Use as much description as possible to expand the second version of the narrative you wrote for exercise 5.

6.3   Exposition

Exposition is writing with a referential aim. It seeks to explain someone or something in the world outside the writer. But since there are many different ways of explaining, the following sections treat each of them separately.

6.4   Using Narration and Description to Explain

Just as you can use narration and description to enrich each other, you can also use either one or both to help explain something. Suppose, for instance, you wanted to explain the relation between

American colonists and the British army in the years before the outbreak of revolution. The story of the British soldier and the Boston ropemaker would help you to show how strained the relation sometimes was.

Of course you may not happen to know many stories about the American Revolution. But you do know something about your own experience, and telling the story of a personal experience can be an effective way of launching an expository essay. Annie Dillard's introduction to her essay on seeing (see above, p. 39–40) provides one example of how personal narration can lead to exposition. Here is another example:

> When I was a little girl, my mother told me to wait for the light to turn green before I crossed the street and to cross always at the corner. This I did. Indeed, I was positive as a very young child that I would get mashed like a potato if I even so much as stepped a foot off the sidewalk while the light burned red. I followed my mother's advice until I realized that she herself jaywalked constantly, dodging in and out of moving traffic—and pulling me with her. So after a while I followed her example and not her advice.
>
> My father told me never to cheat or steal and I remember my intense humiliation the day, only 6 years old, I received a public spanking for swiping three dimes from the windowsill where they had been left by a visiting uncle. Yet my father pushed me under the turnstile to get into the subway and got me into the movies for half fare, way after I was old enough to pay full price. And my mother continually brought home reams of stationery and other supplies lifted from the offices where she worked.
>
> Both my parents exacted severe punishment for lying and yet I knew, in time, that they lied to me and to each other and to others when, presumably, they felt the occasion warranted it.
>
> And this was just part of the story. But hypocrisy about sex, about race relations, about religion, took me a longer time to see. I was out of high school before that picture began to pull together. Understanding didn't devastate me because I had begun to absorb the knowledge little by little, through the years. By the time I was 18 or 19 I guess I was both old enough to understand and strong enough to face what I saw. And [I] could face it because I learned my parents were not unusual. Most everybody's parents were the same. And we, my friends and I, did come to take it for granted. Parents were that way. Older people were that way. The word for what we found out about our parents' generation was hypocrisy. And most of us accepted it as part of life—as the way things were.   —Lynn Minton, "Double Vision"

The writer starts with personal experience and guides us from there to the main point of her essay. The first paragraph shows how the mother ignored her own advice about jaywalking, the second how both parents ignored the father's advice about stealing, the third how both ignored their own rule against lying. Successively, these personal experiences lead to the main point of the essay: hypocrisy is a fact of life.

EXERCISE 9   Using a Story to Make a Point

Tell a personal story that could be used to illustrate a general point about the experience of growing up. Then state the point itself.

6.5   Using Examples to Explain

One of the simplest means of explaining anything is to give an example. As the previous section shows, you can sometimes use an entire story to illustrate or exemplify a point. But examples can also be stated briefly, as shown in this passage:

> Anyone who reads [ancient Greek stories] with attention discovers that even the most nonsensical take place in a world which is essentially rational and matter-of-fact. Hercules, whose life was one long combat against preposterous monsters, is always said to have had his home in the city of Thebes. The exact spot where Aphrodite was born of the foam could be visited by any ancient tourist; it was just offshore from the island of Cythera. The winged steed Pegasus, after skimming the air all day, went every night to a comfortable stable in Corinth A familiar local habitation gave reality to all the mythical beings.   —Edith Hamilton, *Mythology*

This passage makes the point that the heroes of Greek mythology were said to have lived in real places. The first and last sentences state this point plainly. Between those two sentences are three examples: Hercules lived in Thebes; Aphrodite was born near Cythera; Pegasus was stabled in Corinth.

EXERCISE 10   Stating a Point

Each of the following passages offers one or more examples to explain or illustrate a point. State the point in a single short sentence.

1. A hockey player rushing up ice travels at more than twenty-five miles an hour; a slap shot hurls a frozen rubber disc toward a goalie at one hundred miles an hour. Everything that happens in hockey—passing, stickhandling, checking, shooting—happens fast.
   —Jeff Greenfield, "The Iceman Arriveth"

2. Curiosity is as clear and definite as any of our urges. We wonder what is in a sealed telegram or in a letter in which someone else is absorbed, or what is being said in the telephone booth or in low conversation.
   —James Harvey Robinson, *The Mind in the Making*

EXERCISE 11   Using Examples

Develop the following point by adding a series of short examples to illustrate it.

> Some of the most important things we need to know have to be learned outside a classroom.

6.6   Using Analogy to Explain

The first question we commonly ask about anything new and strange is "What's it like?" We ask the question because the only way we can understand what we don't know is by seeing its relation to what we do know. An **analogy** helps the reader to understand something vast, remote, abstract, or specialized by comparing it to something compact, familiar, concrete, or ordinary. Here is a brief example:

> The surface of the earth is like the skin of an orange, which cannot be spread out flat unless it is torn into strips. That is why flat maps of the whole earth always distort its appearance.

The first sentence uses an analogy to explain the point made in the second. Though a single analogy seldom extends to the length of a whole essay, it can be developed well beyond a single sentence, as in this explanation of how the universe expands:

> My nonmathematical friends often tell me that they find it difficult to picture this expansion. Short of using a lot of mathematics I cannot do better than use the analogy of a balloon with a large number of dots marked on its surface. If the balloon is blown up, the distances between the dots increase in the same way as the distances between the galaxies. Here I should give a warning that this analogy must not be taken too strictly. There are several important respects in which it is definitely misleading. For example, the dots on the surface of a balloon would themselves increase in size as the balloon was being blown up. This is not the case for the galaxies, for their internal gravitational fields are sufficiently strong to prevent any such expansion. A further weakness of our analogy is that the surface of an ordinary balloon is two dimensional—that is to say, the points of its surface can be described by two co-ordinates; for example, by latitude and longitude. In the case of the Universe we must think of the surface as possessing a third dimension. This is not as difficult as it may sound. We are all familiar with pictures in perspective—pictures in which artists have represented three-dimensional scenes on two-dimensional canvases. So it is not really a difficult conception to imagine the three dimensions of space as being confined to the surface of a balloon. But then what does the radius of the balloon represent, and what does it mean to say that the balloon is being blown up? The answer to this is that the radius

of the balloon is a measure of time, and the passage of time has the effect of blowing up the balloon. This will give you a very rough, but useful, idea of the sort of theory investigated by the mathematician. —Fred Hoyle, *The Nature of the Universe*

If you have ever seen what happens to the design on a balloon when it is blown up, you should readily understand this analogy. It is not perfect—no analogy ever is—but it does give you a rough idea of how the universe expands, a way of picturing that expansion in your mind. For the explanation of any unfamiliar subject, analogy is an enormously useful tool.

However, you should beware of arguing by analogy, of assuming that because two things are alike in some respects they are also alike in others. In some ways the expansion of the universe resembles the blowing up of a balloon. But you cannot conclude from this resemblance that the universe will eventually reach a breaking point and pop. (For more on this point, see "Arguing by Analogy," section 7.5C, p. 128.)

EXERCISE 12   Using Analogy

Explain the problems of choosing and pursuing a career by comparing this process to driving on the interstate highway system.

6.7   Using Comparison and Contrast to Explain

While an analogy involves two things of different kinds, such as an orange and the whole earth, **comparison and contrast** normally involve two things of the same kind: two cities, two schools, two games, two means of transportation. An analogy brings out the similarities between two things that we normally think of as entirely different. But most of the time, writers use comparison and contrast to explain the differences between two things that we normally think of as similar, to explain what is distinctive about each of them. Consider this passage:

> You see things vacationing on a motorcycle in a way that is completely different from any other. In a car you're always in a compartment, and because you're used to it you don't realize that through that car window everything you see is just more TV. You're a passive observer and it is all moving by you boringly in a frame.
>
> On a cycle the frame is gone. You're completely in contact with it all. You're *in* the scene, not just watching it anymore, and the sense of presence is overwhelming. That concrete whizzing by five inches below your foot is the real thing, the same stuff you walk on, it's right there, so blurred you can't focus on it, yet you can put your foot down and touch it anytime, and the whole thing,

dne

6.7

the whole experience, is never removed from immediate con-
sciousness.

—Robert Pirsig, *Zen and the Art of Motorcycle Maintenance*

Since cars and motorcycles are both in the same class—motor vehicles—and since both are familiar, the writer need not point to
their obvious similarities. Instead, he contrasts the two, and the
contrast reveals what is distinctive about riding a motorcycle: the
sense of direct, unframed, participatory contact with the outside
world. Pirsig does note the similarity between looking through the
window of a car and watching TV, but this resemblance simply
exposes the passivity of riding in a car, and thus sharpens the contrast between that and the activity of riding on a motorcycle.

6.7A   Block Structure and Alternating Structure

You can organize a comparison and contrast in either of two ways:
in blocks or in regular alternation. In a block-structured comparison and contrast, each of the two things considered gets a block of
sentences or an entire paragraph to itself. Pirsig, for instance, devotes most of his first paragraph to traveling by car and all of his
second to traveling by motorcycle. But you can also compare and
contrast two things by alternating back and forth between them.
Consider this paragraph:

> Videotaped films offer many advantages over the celluloid kind.
> For one thing, they are often cheaper. If three or more people
> want to see a movie, they can usually rent a cassette version and a
> videotape machine for less than it would cost them all to go to a
> theater. Second, movie theaters offer nothing like the range of choice
> that videotapes provide. While the moviegoer has to take whatever
> the local theater happens to be playing, the videotape viewer can
> choose from hundreds of films, including foreign or X-rated items
> that will probably never find their way onto a local screen. Third,
> while movies are shown only at fixed times, videotapes can be seen
> whenever the viewer wants to see them, and just as often as he or
> she likes. Finally, videotapes allow the viewer a kind of privacy and
> comfort that no public movie theater can possibly furnish. The vi-
> deotape viewer need not strain to hear a film over the buzz of the
> talkers sitting behind or to see it over the heads of the people sitting
> in front. Instead, he or she can enjoy it with just a few close friends
> at home.

Here the writer moves back and forth between the two things,
treating them both under a succession of categories: cost, range of
choice, timing, and privacy. Subordinating words such as *while* and
transitional words such as *instead* help to mark the contrast between
moviegoing and videotape viewing and serve to guide the reader

from one to the other. Furthermore, the writer uses comparison and contrast for a definite purpose: to explain the special attraction of videotape cassettes.

6.7B Writing an Essay of Comparison and Contrast

Because alternating structure continually reminds the reader that two things are being compared and contrasted, it can work well for the length of a paragraph. But steady alternation can become monotonous. For this reason, an essay that makes extensive use of comparison and contrast should combine alternation with block structure. The following essay not only illustrates this combination, but also shows how to introduce, sustain, and conclude a comparison and contrast.

Why Videotapes Won't Kill Movie Theaters

[1] In the late forties and early fifties, when television first invaded American homes, self-appointed prophets grimly predicted the death of the movie theater. How could it possibly compete with TV? Why would people go out and pay to see what they could get for nothing in their own homes? In recent years, the same kind of questions have been asked about videotape cassettes. Can movie theaters survive them? Can they compete with the more than five thousand commercial free movies now available for home-viewing on videotape? The answer is yes, decisively. In 1984, movie theater ticket sales in the United States and Canada reached an all-time high of four billion dollars. The question, then, is not *whether* movie theaters can survive this latest threat, but *why* they are doing so.

[2] To see what they are up against, consider the advantages of videotape. First, it's frequently cheaper. If three or more people want to see a movie, they can usually rent a videocassette and recorder for less than it would cost them all to go to a theater, and if they happen to own a VCR, they can rent a cassette for less than the price of a single admission. Second, movie theaters offer nothing like the range of choice that videotapes provide. While the moviegoer has to take whatever the local theater happens to be showing, the videotape viewer can choose from hundreds of films, including foreign or X-rated items that will probably never find their way onto a local screen. Third, while movies are shown at fixed times only, videotapes can be seen whenever the viewer wants to see them, and just as often as he or she likes. Finally, videotapes allow the viewer a kind of privacy and comfort that no public movie theater can possibly furnish. The videotape viewer need not strain to hear a film over the buzz of the talkers sitting behind or to see it over the heads of the people sitting in front. Instead, he or she can enjoy it alone or with just a few close friends at home.

[3] Given all these advantages, why haven't videotapes already put movie theaters out of business? Why are theaters selling more

tickets than ever before? Part of the answer is restlessness. Movie theaters offer us what no form of home entertainment—no matter how technologically sophisticated—will ever be able to provide: a chance to get out of the house, to get away from the kids, to leave behind the crumb-speckled carpet and the peeling wallpaper and the dirty dishes piled up in the sink. The fact that most people can make delicious dinners in the privacy of their own kitchens has not yet killed the restaurant business. Whatever we can eat, do, or see at home, all of us need an occasional night out.

[4] Movie theaters give us not only a night out but also a social experience. By forsaking the privacy of home, we escape its isolation. We go out to the movies in order to laugh, cry, and cheer with other people. Not every movie is like *The Rocky Horror Picture Show,* which invites us to dress up and act out the film ourselves, but all movies shown in theaters do invite and excite a communal response. They make us feel part of a group.

[5] Besides getting us out of the house and into the company of others, movie theaters provide a visual experience far surpassing what videocassettes now offer. To the eye, a videotaped movie has two major drawbacks: scan lines and severe reduction. Television makes a video image by breaking down the subject into thousands of bits which are then transmitted across the screen in horizontal scan lines. These are always visible, especially at close range, and enlarging the screen simply enlarges the lines. Much more noticeable than scan lines, however, is contraction. Though older movies were made for near-square screens that are roughly proportional to those of television sets, the big, spectacular, wide-screen movies of recent years simply cannot fit on a TV screen. Lopping tops of heads and bottoms of legs, reducing long shots to medium shots and close-ups, cutting away material on either side of the central image, the videocassette literally shows only part of the movie. It cannot duplicate the original.

[6] For all of these reasons, I believe that movie theaters will survive the impact of videocassettes and video machines just as well as they have survived the impact of television. Nothing to be seen now on any television screen—no matter how big—equals the clarity, magnitude, and breadth of detail to be seen on the wide screen of a movie theater showing a good 35-millimeter print. Combined with the purely social attraction of moviegoing, this visual advantage will—for the time being anyway—keep movie theaters very much alive.

This essay shows how comparison and contrast can be used to explain the main point of an entire essay. In the introductory paragraph, the author clearly states his purpose, which is to show why movie theaters have successfully competed with videotaped films. To explain this point, the author compares and contrasts the two kinds of film, using alternating structure to show the advantages of videotape (paragraph 2), then shifting to block structure for the social advantages of moviegoing (paragraphs 3 and 4) and the visual disadvantages of video viewing (paragraph 5). Since paragraph 5 also shows—by implication—the visual superiority of movie theater films, it nicely leads to the concluding paragraph 6, where the author summarizes the special advantages of moviegoing and thus completes his answer to the question originally raised.

EXERCISE 13   Comparing and Contrasting with Block Structure

Taking as a model the two paragraphs by Pirsig given on pp. 93–94, use block structure to compare and contrast the two items in any one of the following pairs:

college / high school
good teaching / bad teaching
crime / terrorism
law / custom
typing / writing with a word processor
living with one's parents / living on one's own
pop rock / heavy metal

EXERCISE 14   Comparing and Contrasting with Alternating Structure

Taking as a model the indented paragraph on p. 94, use alternating structure to compare and contrast the two items in any one of the following pairs:

any small town / any large city
watching a movie / seeing a play
cycling / motorcycling
sculpting / painting
astronomy / astrology

EXERCISE 15   Using Comparison and Contrast to Explain a Point

Using comparison and contrast, write an essay that explains any one of the following:

1. why custom is sometimes more powerful than law
2. why growing up in a small town is better than growing up in a city, or vice versa
3. why video games are better than board games, or vice versa
4. why living on one's own is better than living with one's parents, or vice versa
5. why plays are more lifelike than movies, or vice versa
6. why running one's own business is better than working for someone else, or vice versa

6.8   Using Definition to Explain

A definition explains a word or phrase. Defining a word can take up an entire essay, as shown in "What is Photography" (pp. 109–

10). But most definitions are brief, taking no more than a sentence.

Definitions come in many different forms. The least effective is the one that students most commonly use: quoting the dictionary ("Webster defines *freedom* as . . ."). Instead of quoting the dictionary, you can use one or more of the methods listed next.

1. Defining by synonym. A synonym is a word or phrase that means approximately the same thing as the word you are defining:

> *Apathetic* means "indifferent."
> *Prevaricate* means "lie."
> *Clandestinely* means "secretly."

The form of the synonym must correspond to the form of the word being defined. *Apathetic* means not "indifference," but "indifferent"; "Prevaricate" means not "lying," but "lie."

2. Defining by comparison, contrast, or analogy. You can define a word by comparing, contrasting, or likening it to another word:

> The *plover* is a bird that lives on the shore, like the sandpiper. But the plover is usually fatter, and unlike the sandpiper, it has a short, hard-tipped bill.
>
> While burglary is the stealing of property from a place, *robbery* is the stealing of property from a person.
>
> A *lien* on a piece of property is like a leash on a dog. It's a way of legally attaching the property to someone who has a claim against the property owner.

3. Defining by function. If the word denotes a person or object, you can define it by saying what the person or object does:

> An *orthopedist* treats bone diseases.
>
> An *ombudsman* defends an individual in a conflict with an institution.

4. Defining by analysis. You can define a word by naming the class of the person or thing it denotes and then giving one or more distinctive features:

	CLASS	FEATURE
An *orthopedist* is	a doctor	who specializes in bones.
A *plover* is	a bird	that lives on the shore.
A *skylight* is	a window	set in the roof of a building.

5. Defining by example. You can define a word by giving examples after naming the class of the person or thing it denotes:

> A *crustacean* is a shelled creature such as a lobster, a shrimp, or a crab.

A *planet* is a heavenly sphere such as Jupiter, Mercury, Mars, or Earth.

6. Defining by etymology. Etymology is the study of the roots of words. You can sometimes define a word by giving its root meaning and thus showing where it came from:

> *Intuition* comes from the Latin words *in* (meaning "in" or "into") and *tueri* (meaning "look" or "gaze"). Literally, therefore, it means a "looking inward."

A definition may use more than one of these methods, especially if it runs to a paragraph or longer. Here, for instance, is a definition of *interferon:*

> Interferon is a large hormone-like protein produced by the cells of all vertebrate animals. It was discovered in 1957 in Britain by virologists Alick Isaacs and Jean Lindenmann during their investigation of a curious phenomenon: people are almost never infected by more than one virus at a time. Seeking an explanation, the researchers infected cells from chick embryos with influenza virus. What they found was a substance that protected the chick cells from both the flu and other viruses. Because it interfered with the infection process, it was dubbed interferon. —*Time*, November 6, 1978

This definition combines analysis with comparison and with etymology of a sort—a little digging into the origin of the word. Interferon is a protein; that is its class. It is compared to hormones—described as "hormone-like"—and its name is said to have come from the word *interfere*.

You may want to use a word in a special or restricted sense. If so, you should clearly explain to your reader just what you mean by it. *Webster's New Collegiate Dictionary* defines *diagram* as "a line drawing made for mathematical or scientific purposes." But Kenneth Clark defines *diagram* somewhat differently—in order to explain how it functions in art:

> By "diagram" I mean a rational statement in a visible form, involving measurements, and usually done with an ulterior motive. The theorem of Pythagoras is proved by a diagram. Leonardo's drawings of light striking a sphere are diagrams; but the works of Mondrian, although made up of straight lines, are not diagrams, because they are not done in order to prove or measure some experience, but to please the eye.
> —Kenneth Clark, "The Blot and the Diagram"

Strikingly enough, Clark defines *diagram* not as a drawing but as a "statement in a visible form," a way of proving or showing something. Then he gives examples of what a diagram is and what it is not. This definition is more than an incidental piece of clarification. It turns out to be essential to Clark's essay.

EXERCISE 16   Defining

Using at least two of the methods just described, define one of the following words.

conservative	honky
suburbanite	rape
bigotry	sexism
feminist	holograph
ecology	neurotic
terrorist	gringo
hypocrite	amoeba

6.9   Explaining by Analyzing—Classification and Division

Probably you have been asked more than once to analyze a particular topic or problem. But just what does *analyze* mean? Essentially, analyzing a subject means breaking it into parts small enough to handle. If you are asked to analyze American democracy, for instance, you can start by defining it as a system of government in which the people rule. But in order to talk about "the people," you must separate them into categories or groups: voters and nonvoters, elected officials and appointed officials, presidents, governors, representatives, mayors, sheriffs, school-board members, and the like. In so doing, you are using classification and division.

Classification is the arrangement of objects, people, or ideas with shared characteristics into classes or groups. Whenever you speak of professors, sophomores, women, men, joggers, jocks, or grinds, you are grouping individuals together as a class because of one or more things they have in common. You can do the same with individual objects or ideas. You can classify motorcycles, cars, and trucks as "motor vehicles"; apples, pears, and oranges as "fruits"; monarchy, democracy, and dictatorship as "political systems." Classification is a way of imposing order on the hundreds of individual persons and things we have around us. We place these in general categories, just as we place ice cream, salt, coffee, chicken, cereal, milk, peanuts, tomatoes, eggs, lettuce, and Coke in one big shopping bag and speak of everything inside as "groceries."

Classification goes hand in hand with **division,** which is the act of cutting up one big group into several subgroups. If, for instance, you divide the class of drinks called "fruit juices" into fresh, frozen, canned, and powdered, you have identified four different subclasses of fruit juice. But instead of dividing the juices according to their forms, you could divide them according to their flavors: apple, orange, grapefruit, lemon, and so on. How you divide and classify depends on your purpose. When you come home with a bag of groceries, you commonly divide and classify them at first into just two groups: those that need refrigeration and those that don't.

In everyday living, then, everyone has to classify and divide in order to cope with a world of individual objects and people. And what is true in everyday living is also true in writing. Whenever you write about a group of people, objects, or ideas, you need a system of classifying and dividing them. Consider how the student author of this essay uses classification and division to explain Japanese society.

Insiders and Outsiders in Japanese Society

[1] Many things about Japanese society puzzle Americans. But hardest of all for Americans to understand is the Japanese devotion to groups. Unlike Americans, the Japanese do not usually think of themselves as independent individuals. They act as members of a community, of a company, or at the very least of a family, which is the minimum social unit. Whatever the group, its very existence depends on the basic difference between insiders and outsiders. Understanding that difference is the key to understanding Japanese society as a whole, and the Japanese family in particular.

[2] The first thing to be understood about *insiders* and *outsiders* is that these are relative terms. Japanese society cannot be imagined as a tight little circle of insiders surrounded by a great big ring of outsiders. It is rather a world of bubbles. In each bubble is a group of people who think of each other as insiders and who look upon all the other people in all the other bubbles as outsiders. No one can be absolutely classified as either an insider or an outsider. To be inside one bubble is, inevitably, to be outside all the others.

[3] The system is complicated because one big bubble may sometimes contain many small ones. A big company, for instance, may include many departments or sections, and each of those sections is a bubble of insiders who work together closely, see each other often, and think of all other company workers as outsiders. Yet as soon as the insiders of a particular section think of their whole company in relation to a competitor, everyone who works for the company becomes an insider, and the outsiders are those who work for the competition.

[4] The opposition between insiders and outsiders becomes still more evident when we turn from Japanese companies to Japanese families. The Japanese family does not merge with other families, or with society at large. While American families often entertain large numbers of casual acquaintances, Japanese families seldom

open their doors to anyone but insiders: family members or relatives. On the rare occasions when a close friend of the family is invited, he or she thereby becomes an insider—in effect, one of the family. Everyone else remains an outsider, and is literally kept outside the family home.

[5] The opposition between insiders and outsiders also explains why the actual structure of the Japanese family differs so much from the way it appears to the outside world, especially to Americans. Most Americans think the typical Japanese family is totally ruled by the husband, with the wife no more than a servant. In fact, the modern Japanese family is ruled by the wife. It is she who takes all of her husband's salary, oversees all household repairs and expenditures, and supervises the education of the children. Inside the family, she has absolute authority.

[6] Yet as soon as the family confronts an outsider, the husband plays the ruler. A perfect example of this switch is what happens when a Japanese family goes out to eat. Before the family leaves the house, the wife gives the husband enough cash to pay the bill. When the family members sit down in the restaurant, the wife decides what the children will eat and often what her husband will eat as well, overruling him if she finds his choices too expensive. But as soon as the waiter arrives, the husband orders for the entire family as if he had made all the choices himself. In so doing, he represents the family for the eyes of an outsider, and so long as those eyes are watching, he is in charge. When he finishes paying the check with the money that his wife has allowed him, she and the children bow to him and say, "Thank you for a good meal, Father."

[7] To understand Japanese society, then, one must understand both the power of the group and the distinction between insiders and outsiders. Since all members of a group are insiders, they can act as individuals among themselves, arguing with each other until they agree or until one of them—the wife in the case of a family group—decides for all. But to outsiders they present a united front. Once they turn from confronting each other to confronting the outside world, insiders cease to be individuals and become part of a group which determines what their public roles will be.
—Rick Kurihara

Throughout this essay, the writer uses classification and division to explain Japanese society. The basic distinction between insiders and outsiders allows him to divide and classify all individuals in relation to groups, and thus to explain how group mentality in Japan governs individual action.

This essay also shows how different means of exposition can be made to work together. Besides classifying and dividing, the author compares and contrasts Japanese society with American society in paragraphs 1 and 4, uses the analogy of bubbles to explain Japanese groups in paragraphs 2 and 3, and illustrates Japanese family life with an example in paragraph 6.

EXERCISE 17   Using Classification and Division to Explain Yourself

Write an essay in which you (1) name any group to which you belong; (2) explain what the members of the group have in common; (3) divide the group into two or more subgroups; (4) explain each of the subgroups; (5) explain whether or not you belong to any one of them; (6) explain what this analysis reveals about you.

6.10 Explaining a Process

A **process** is a sequence of actions or events that lead or are supposed to lead to a predictable result. The transformation of a caterpillar into a butterfly is a process; so is fixing a flat tire, removing an appendix, frying an egg, knitting a sweater, or writing an essay.

The way you explain a process depends on your purpose. If you want to teach someone else how to do it, you must be careful to give every step, as in this explanation of how to replace spark plugs:

> Spark plugs should be replaced every ten thousand miles because worn plugs cause poor combustion in the cylinders, and the result is a rough-running engine. To replace worn plugs, you need three tools that you can buy at any automotive parts store: a ratchet wrench with a short extension handle, a spark plug socket, and a spark plug gauge.
>
> The most important thing to know about spark plugs is that you have to remove and replace them *one at a time*. If you take them all out at once, you will have to disconnect all of their wires at the same time, and you will probably not remember which plugs they came from. Since each plug has its own wire and since the car will not run if the wires are mixed up, you should never have more than one wire disconnected at any one time.
>
> The owner's manual for your car will tell you where the spark plugs are. Once you have located them, you must do five things with each plug in turn. First, disconnect the wire attached to it. Second, with the spark plug socket placed over the plug and the ratchet wrench in the socket, remove the plug by turning the wrench counterclockwise. Third, use the spark plug gauge to measure the size of the little gap in the electrode—the small open square of metal that sticks up out of the threaded tube at one end of the spark plug. If the gap is too big, the electrode is worn, and the plug must be replaced. Fourth, insert the old plug or a new one by turning it clockwise with your fingers until it sticks, and then using the wrench to turn it a quarter of a circle more. Fifth and finally, reconnect the wire that belongs to that particular plug.
>
> —Jim Robb

This is a **teaching** explanation. It moves step by step, taking nothing for granted, and even anticipates possible missteps: *never have more than one wire disconnected at any one time.* The author also takes care to describe the *electrode* for readers who may not know what it is.

If you wish only to help your reader understand a process rather than perform it, your explanation need not cover all the steps. For example, here is an explanation of how a caterpillar becomes a butterfly:

> In contact with the proper food on leaving the egg, the caterpillar begins to eat immediately and continues until it has increased its weight hundreds of times. On each of the first three segments of the body is a pair of short legs ending in a sharp claw. These legs correspond to the six legs of the adult insect. In addition, the caterpillar has up to ten short, fleshy feet called prolegs, which are shed before it changes form. The insect passes its pupal stage incased in comparatively rigid integuments [layers] that form a chrysalis.
>
> Most butterfly chrysalides remain naked, unlike those of the moth, which have a protective cocoon. Breathing goes on through an air opening while the complete adult, or imago, develops. Wings, legs, proboscis, even the pigment in the scales, form in the tight prison of the chrysalis.
>
> At maturity, the chrysalis splits its covering and wriggles out as an imago, or perfect insect. Hanging from a leaf or rock, it forces blood, or haemolymph, into the veins of its wet wings, straightening them to their normal span. Soon the wings are dry, and the insect flies into a life of nectar drinking and courtship.
>
> —"Butterfly," *Funk & Wagnalls New Encyclopedia*

This is a **reporting** explanation. The writer describes the stages through which the insect passes, but does not explain everything about its transformation. We are not told, for instance, how the wings, legs, and proboscis form, only when and where they form. The writer is trying to help us understand an overall process—not to teach us how to become butterflies ourselves.

These two kinds of explanation differ in form as well as in purpose. The teaching explanation uses the imperative mood to give a series of commands: *disconnect, remove, insert,* and so on. The reporting explanation uses the indicative mood to describe a series of actions: *the chrysalis splits its covering and wriggles out,* the imago *forces blood . . . into the veins of its wet wings,* and *the insect flies* (For a full discussion of the imperative and indicative moods, see sections 23.1–23.3, pp. 400–401.)

EXERCISE 18   Composing a Teaching Explanation

Write a teaching explanation of any simple process that you know well and that can be taught in writing—such as changing a tire, making a bed, frying an egg, or getting from one place to another. When you have finished, see if someone else can actually perform the process by following your instructions.

EXERCISE 19   Composing a Reporting Explanation

Write a reporting explanation of any process you know well, such as climbing a cliff, painting a picture, making a clay pot, taking or developing a good photograph. If you use any specialized terms, be sure to define them as you go along.

6.11 Explaining Cause and Effect

Since any situation or event can provoke questions about its causes, its effects, or both, one good way of explaining anything is to raise such questions. Why do so many parents want their children to get a college education? Why did the Germans accept Hitler as their leader? Why did hundreds of American men, women, and children commit suicide in Guyana in November 1978? You can develop an essay by considering the answer to a question of this kind. Or you can consider the effects of a situation or event. What would happen if an atomic bomb were dropped on New York City? What would you do if you were placed in solitary confinement for thirty days? What is the effect of coeducation on college life?

When you attempt to determine the cause of a situation or event, you often construct a **hypothesis**—that is, a possible explanation of why it happened. Finding a baseball bat in your bed, for instance, you might hypothesize that your room had been visited by a practical joker while you were out, and you might even be able to guess who the joker was. In writing, you can likewise construct a hypothesis to explain a situation or event.

But whether or not you construct a hypothesis, questions about why something happens—or has happened—can often generate a whole essay. Consider this one:

An Ugly New Footprint in the Sand

[1] There were strangers on our beach yesterday, for the first time in a month. A new footprint on our sand is nearly as rare as in *Robinson Crusoe*. We are at the very edge of the Atlantic; half a mile out in front of us is a coral reef, and then nothing but 3,000 miles of ocean to West Africa. It is a wild and lonely beach, with the same surf beating on it as when Columbus came by. And yet the beach is polluted.

[2] Oil tankers over the horizon have fouled it more than legions of picnickers could. The oil comes ashore in floating patches that stain the coral black and gray. It has blighted the rock crabs and the crayfish and has coated the delicate whorls of the conch shells

with black goo. And it has congealed upon itself, littering the beach with globes of tar that resemble the cannonballs of a deserted battlefield. The islanders, as they go beachcombing for the treasures the sea has washed up for centuries, now wear old shoes to protect their feet from the oil that washes up too.

[3] You have to try to get away from pollution to realize how bad it really is. We have known for the last few years how bad our cities are. Now there is no longer an escape. If there is oil on this island far out in the Atlantic, there is oil on nearly every other island.

[4] It is still early here. The air is still clear over the island, but it won't be when they build the airstrip they are talking about. The water out over the reef is still blue and green, but it is dirtier than it was a few years ago. And if the land is not despoiled, it is only because there are not yet enough people here to despoil it. There will be. And so for the moment on this island we are witnesses to the beginning, as it were, of the pollution of our environment.

[5] When you watch a bird over the beach or a fish along the reef you realize how ill-adapted man is to this environment anyway. Physically there is nothing he can do that some other creature cannot do better. Only his neocortex, the "thinking cap" on top of his brain, has enabled him to invent and construct artificial aids to accomplish what he couldn't do by himself. He cannot fly, so he has developed airplanes that can go faster than birds. He is slower than the horse, so he invented the wheel and the internal combustion engine. Even in his ancestral element, the sea, he is clumsy and short of breath. Without his brain, his artificial aids, his technology, he would have been unable to cope with, even survive in, his environment. But only after so many centuries is his brain dimly realizing that while he has managed to control his environment, he has so far been unable to protect it.

[6] Perhaps he simply is not far enough up the evolutionary ladder to survive on this planet for very much longer. To take only two of his inefficient physical functions, he is so far unable to control either his body wastes or his population. Man is a natural polluter, and his invention of the bathroom and the incinerator has, it now becomes evident, only postponed the problem. On this island we burn our papers, bury our tin cans and dump our garbage in the bay. It is not very efficient and perhaps not even very civilized. Yet so long as there are only a few people here, it has no ill effects. But when the inevitable wave of population sweeps out from the mainland, the islanders will face the problem of their own pollution just as the New Yorker does today.

[7] Man's sexual construction is perhaps the biggest accident of his physical makeup: it is only now becoming obvious—when it may well be too late—that it would have been better if he required artificial aid to *have* children, rather than to *avoid* having them.

[8] Until the pollution of our deserted beach, it seemed simple to blame everything on the "population explosion." If the population of this island, for example, could be stabilized at a couple of

hundred, there would be very little problem with the environment in this secluded area. There would be no pollution of the environment if there were not too many people using it. And so if we concentrate on winning the war against overpopulation, we can save the earth for mankind.

[9] But the oil on the beach belies this too-easy assumption. Those tankers are not out there because too many Chinese and Indians are being born every minute. They are not even out there because there are too many Americans and Europeans. They are delivering their oil, and cleaning their tanks at sea and sending the residue up onto the beaches of the Atlantic and Pacific, in order to fuel the technology of mankind—and the factories and the power plants, the vehicles and the engines that have enabled mankind to survive on his planet are now spoiling the planet for life.

[10] The fishermen on this island are perfectly right in preferring the outboard motor to the sail. Their livelihood is involved, and the motor, for all its fouling smell, has helped increase the fisherman's catch so that he can now afford to dispense with the far more obnoxious outdoor privy. But the danger of technology is in its escalation, and there has already been a small amount of escalation here. You can see the motor oil slicks around the town dock. Electric generators can be heard over the sound of surf. And while there are only about two dozen automobiles for the ten miles of road, already there is a wrecked jeep rusting in the harbor waters where it was dumped and abandoned. The escalation of technological pollution is coming here just as surely as it came to the mainland cities that are now shrouded by fly ash.

[11] If the oil is killing the life along the coral heads, what must it not be doing to the phytoplankton at sea which provide 70 percent of the oxygen we breathe? The lesson of our fouled beach is that we may not even have realized how late it is already. Mankind, because of his technology, may require far more space per person on this globe than we had even thought, but it is more than a matter of a certain number of square yards per person. There is instead a delicate balance of nature in which many square miles of ocean and vegetation and clean air are needed to sustain only a relatively few human beings. We may find, as soon as the end of this century, that the final despoliation of our environment has been signaled not by starvation but by people choking to death. The technology—the machine—will then indeed have had its ultimate, mindless, all-unintended triumph over man, by destroying the atmosphere he lives in just as surely as you can pinch off a diver's breathing tube.

[12] Sitting on a lonely but spoiled beach, it is hard to imagine but possible to believe. —A. B. C. Whipple

Whipple introduces his essay by reporting that the wild and lonely beach on a remote island in the Atlantic has been polluted. In paragraph 2, he then proceeds to identify the cause of the pollution—

oil tankers—and the visible effects that this pollution has already had: stained coral, blighted shellfish, and globes of tar on the beach.

Having shown what pollution has already done to one beach, he considers its probable effects on other beaches (paragraph 3), its future effects on the remote island (paragraph 4), and then its deeper causes: man's incompatibility with the environment (paragraph 5), his natural tendency to pollute the earth (paragraph 6), and his failure to control the population (paragraphs 7 and 8).

At this point, however, Whipple's quest for the causes of pollution takes a revealing turn. Rejecting the "too-easy assumption" that pollution ultimately springs from overpopulation, he points his finger instead at man's obsession with the machine (paragraphs 9 and 10). Having moved from immediate causes to deeper causes, and from lesser causes to greater ones, he comes at last to technology, the most important cause of all. He has arranged his six paragraphs on the causes of pollution (paragraphs 5–10) in climactic order–that is, in ascending order of importance.

He ends his essay by returning to effects in the last two paragraphs (11 and 12). But since he has already explained what pollution has done and will do to the island, he now explains what its long-range effect may be for the entire earth: mankind choking to death for lack of oxygen.

This essay shows, then, where the pursuit of causes and effects can lead. Starting with the here and now—the pollution of a particular beach in the present—the author moves to immediate causes and short-range effects, and thence by degrees to the ultimate cause and the possibly ultimate effect. By analyzing the causes and effects of pollution, he shows just how much our way of life promotes it and how dangerous it may become.

EXERCISE 20   **Explaining Cause and Effect**

Do either one of the following:

1. Write an essay explaining why star college athletes are usually better known and more popular than top students, and show what effects this situation has on college life.
2. Write an essay explaining the causes and effects of littering.

6.12 Combining Methods of Exposition

When you are learning to write, you will find it useful to practice the various methods of exposition separately. But good writing usually combines several of them, as in the following essay:

What is Photography?

[1] Most of us think of the camera as an instrument of precision. It catches a scene in an instant, a gesture in a second, an expression in a moment, recording these with absolute fidelity for ever and ever—or so the advertisements would have us believe. But if the camera takes the picture, we have reason to ask whether photography can be an art, whether it actually requires anything more creative than the clicking of a shutter. Such questions bring us to the fundamental query: What is photography?

[2] The answer has as many sides as a professional photographer can find in a face. To the beginner, it is simple and pedestrian: photography is a succession of petty details. First, he or she must choose and buy a camera from the seemingly infinite variety of models available; then decide on film, whether color or black and white; then learn how to load and wind, how to set the shutter, the exposure meter, and the lens for proper light and focus in each photograph; then snap the pictures, one by one, have them developed, and *finally* see the results. Some of the more ingenious new cameras have eliminated one or more of these steps, but for most beginners, this succession of petty, troublesome details is what photography is all about.

[3] For all this trouble, in fact, the beginner and the ordinary amateur see the purpose of photography as primarily a matter of record. More observant than the human eye, they think, more tenacious than the human memory, the camera remembers baby as mother never could, meticulously transcribing every wrinkle of his little jowls and every bubble of his drool for the doubtful immortality of a family album. In this seizing of an instant, there seems to be scarcely more creativity (and possibly less) than is required of a Xerox machine. The beginner seldom thinks that photography is an art.

[4] And yet an art is precisely what photography can be—an art with its own rules, distinct from photo-copying and equally distinct from movie-making. For movie-making is an art compounded of many arts: writing, acting, and most especially editing—what Alfred Hitchcock simply calls "the putting together of pieces of film." But what Lessing said of poetry and painting may also be said of cinema and photography. Cinema is the movement of many pictures, and like poetry is essentially temporal, recreating the flow of time. Photography is the freezing of movement, and like painting is essentially spatial. It stops time.

[5] I speak, therefore, only of the individual picture—of the movement captured in time. And here we must remember that the camera is an instrument. The camera will not take a picture for us, any more than the carpenter's hammer will nail up a house for him. It is nothing more or less than a tool. When I was in Europe during the past summer, I bought in Paris a camera that func-

tioned beautifully. But I was something less than a master of my newly acquired device. When I expected to get the facade of the Paris Opera House I caught a piece of fire hydrant; when I expected to capture the unforgettable brilliance of the Côte d'Azur I got a patch of gray and unidentifiable coastline; when I sought to record the lights of Florence reflected one evening on the River Arno I got nothing.

[6] In part these were the blunders of a beginner, untutored in the technical subtleties of focus and exposure. But fundamentally they were failures in the discipline of form, shape, and arrangement that only a carefully ordered perspective can produce. Immanuel Kant is unintelligible to me most of the time, but I know what he means when he says that the eye creates what it sees. There is no such thing as a purely objective scene or landscape; there is only an odd collection of colors and forms, blended into a unified whole by the cohesive vision of the observer. It is he or she who creates the scene from his or her particular viewpoint, who fixes the relation between light and shadow, background and foreground, angle and curve.

[7] It is this, and only this, that makes of photography a creative art. Its instruments are admittedly more precise and more sophisticated than those of the painter, and they save a good deal of labor. But they can render no more than is actually seen or felt through the eye of the photographer himself, who catches with creative vision a moment of pain, fear, hatred, comedy, or pure beauty of form and light. Such captures are the products not of luck but of design, and in this the photographer is one with the artist of canvas and brush.

To begin with, the whole essay is a piece of definition—an attempt to define *photography*. But the writer uses a variety of methods to develop the definition. In paragraph 2, he explains the process of taking a photograph; in paragraph 3, he compares the camera to the human eye and memory; in paragraph 4, he classifies photography and painting as spatial arts, distinguishing them from the temporal arts, such as movie-making and poetry; in paragraph 5, he cites personal experience and several examples to show that the camera is only a tool; in paragraph 6, using cause and effect, he explains why the pictures he took were failures; and in paragraph 7, he uses comparison again to clinch the point that photography is a creative art.

EXERCISE 21   Combining Methods of Exposition

Using at least three of the methods of exposition we have discussed, explain a subject you know well—surfboarding, stamp collecting, auto repairing, rock climbing, jazz, fishing, architecture, or whatever.

7

PERSUASION

Persuasion is the art of getting other people to do something or to believe something without compelling them to do so. You cannot persuade with violence or with threats —with a knife, a gun, or a fist; those are the weapons of compulsion. But you can persuade with a speech, a picture, a tone of voice, a pat on the back, a tear, or a piece of writing.

Only the last of these, of course, is normally available to the writer. Magazine ads often combine picture and text to persuade us that a certain kind of toothpaste will make the teeth sexier or that a certain kind of soap will get the body cleaner, but unless you are an advertising copywriter, you normally have to persuade your readers with the written word alone. You must therefore be more than usually sensitive to their needs.

One of the first things those readers will want to know is what you want them to do or believe. You may have good reason for not telling them immediately, especially if your topic is controversial. You may not even be sure, as you plunge into a topic, just what your own point of view is. But sooner or later you must declare it: you must state a definite opinion or recommend a specific course of action. And to win approval of that opinion or recommendation, you must appeal to the feelings of your readers, to their reason, or to both.

Advertising often makes a simple, straightforward appeal to the feelings. Over a big color picture of a farming family gathered around a tractor, a recent insurance ad proclaims:

**There are people more famous we insure.
But none more important.**

Under the picture the ad continues:

> For over a hundred years, we've tried to keep personal insurance from becoming too impersonal.
> When you do business with ———, it's with one of our independent agents. So when you have a question about auto, health, home or life insurance, you deal with someone who is close to you and your situation.
> You can easily find an independent ——— agent in the Yellow Pages.
> ——— is one of the world's largest insurance companies, a size that doesn't diminish our big concern for the individual.

As in many ads, picture and text together seek to persuade readers that the advertiser cares about each of them. The means of persuasion are essentially emotional. With the family picture reinforcing the point, the reader is told that the company deals in "personal insurance," that the company agent will be "someone who is close to you and your situation." The tone is warm and reassuring; the statement is the verbal equivalent of a friendly handshake. The ad offers no evidence that the company cares about individuals. It simply tries to make you feel that the company cares.

Since feelings play a part in the formation of almost every opinion, you need to understand as well as you can the feelings of your readers. But you can seldom persuade readers by appealing to their feelings alone. If you respect their intelligence, you will also appeal to their minds. And to do that, you must construct an argument.

7.1 What Is an Argument?

We commonly think of an argument as a quarrel—a shouting match in which tempers flare and necks turn red. But strictly speaking, an argument is not a quarrel at all. It is simply a rational means of persuasion. It differs from exposition in that it seeks to convince, not just to explain, and it differs from emotional persuasion in that it seeks to convince by appealing to the mind. To see these differences more clearly, consider the following three passages:

> 1. The bear population of Maine is 7,000 to 10,000 animals, and the annual "harvest," or kill, averages 930. State wildlife biologists estimate that the number killed falls short by 120 of the "allowable harvest," i.e., "the harvest level that takes only the annual increase and does not affect the population size."
> —Jonathan Evan Maslow, "Stalking the Black Bear"

2. Every year, bloodthirsty hunters go into the Maine woods and ruthlessly shoot to death hundreds of bears. The hunters care nothing for the suffering they cause, for the blood they spill, or for the harm they do to creatures who have done no harm to them. Hunters kill for a thrill, and that is all they care about. No one seems to care anything for the bears.

3. Though some people may think hunting is nothing more than wholesale and wanton destruction of living creatures, hunters actually help to ensure the health and survival of wildlife. Take bear-hunting in Maine as a case in point. Out of the 7,000 to 10,000 bears that roam the Maine woods, hunters kill an average of 930 a year. State wildlife biologists estimate that this is 120 fewer than the annual population increase. If the bear population were allowed to grow unchecked, it would increase well over 1,000 a year, and the food available for any one bear would correspondingly decrease. By killing an average of 930 bears a year, hunters keep the annual increase down, and therefore help to ensure an adequate food supply for the bear population as a whole.

These three passages concern the same topic, but they treat it in fundamentally different ways. The first is **exposition;** it calmly explains the relation between the number of bears born and the number killed in Maine each year. The second is **emotional persuasion;** it tries to make the reader feel outrage at hunters and pity for bears. The third is **argument;** it tries to prove that hunting is beneficial to wildlife.

Consider first the difference between passage 2 and passage 3. Passage 2 relies on words like *bloodthirsty* to stir the reader's feelings; passage 3 relies on facts, figures, and authoritative estimates to gain the reader's agreement. Side by side, the two passages reveal the fundamental difference between emotional persuasion and argument. Purely emotional persuasion may well appeal to a reader who already tends to feel the way the writer does, but it is unlikely to change an opponent's mind. Words like *bloodthirsty* will simply antagonize the reader who likes to hunt. On the other hand, the argument of passage 3 is thought-provoking rather than antagonizing. It won't persuade all readers, but it will give even fervent conservationists something to think about. To combat such an argument effectively, conservationists would have to challenge its facts, figures, and estimates in a manner such as this:

4. Hunting advocates try to justify the killing of bears by arguing that it limits the annual increase in the bear population and thereby helps to ensure an adequate food supply for the bears that remain. But this argument rests on the assumption that wildlife

biologists can reliably estimate the size of the population increase, which is said to be 120 more than the number of bears killed each year. Can we be sure it is? If estimates of the bear population range from 7,000 to 10,000, how can we accurately calculate the annual increase in that population? Do we even know how many bears die each year of natural causes? If we don't know that, we cannot determine what the net annual increase in the bear population would be in the absence of hunters. And even if we knew this figure exactly, it would not tell us just how well an unregulated bear population would manage to feed itself. Without hunters threatening them, bears might well become more venturesome and thus more successful in their quest for food. We can hardly be certain, therefore, that bears are better off with hunters than they would be without them.

This is an argument designed to combat the argument made in passage 3. Like passage 2, it aims to convince the reader that bear-hunting is unjustified. But unlike passage 2, it does not appeal to the reader's feelings. It does not try to stir pity for bears or outrage at hunters. Instead, it calmly exposes the weaknesses in the pro-hunting argument, and thus appeals to the reader's mind.

Just as argument differs from emotional persuasion, so also does it differ from exposition. In exposition, every statement is offered as a matter of accepted fact. In argument, only some statements are offered as matters of fact, and these are given as reasons to make us believe assertions or claims. For example, the assertion in passage 3 that "hunters actually help to ensure the health and survival of wildlife" is disputable and needs defending. Instead of assuming that we will believe it, the writer must give us reasons for doing so.

In argument, then, one or more statements are claims in need of defending, and statements of fact are introduced to defend them. The claims to be defended may concern what is happening ("Hunters help wildlife"), or what should happen ("Hunters should be appreciated").

In practice, writers often straddle the line between exposition and argument. The essay on photography (pp. 109–10), for instance, stands somewhere between defining photography and arguing that it should be considered an art. Likewise, the argument for bear-hunting includes an explanation of what the bear population is and how it grows each year. But the distinction between exposition and argument is nonetheless important. In your own writing, you need to know when to explain, when to argue, and when to move from one to the other.

7.2 Combining General Claims and Specific Evidence

Effective arguments combine general claims with specific evidence. The general claim or proposition is essential because it tells the reader what you are arguing for, what you want him or her to believe: solar power can solve the energy crisis; presidents should have longer terms; parents should share equally the responsibility for raising their children. But unless the reader is ready to accept your general claim at once, you will need to support it with specific facts. Compare these three arguments—all written by first-term college freshmen:

1. My feeling is that all people are equal. Neither sex is superior to the other. In the times of today, men and women both have an equal opportunity for education. They can pursue any career that they are qualified for. Schools are now getting away from trying to make certain things for boys and vice versa. Children are growing up as equals.

2. Male athletes are stronger, faster, and tougher than their female counterparts. The men's record for the hundred-yard dash is about a full second faster than the women's. World records for the mile, marathon, high jump, discus, and all other track and field sports are much better on the male side than the female side. In tennis, a top male pro will always beat a top woman pro, and the same applies to swimming, skiing, basketball, hockey, and countless other sports.

3. There are differences between men and women, but none that make either sex inferior. Athletic performance is a case in point. A major study by a West German doctor has shown that because of different skeletal leverage in men and women, muscles of identical strength will produce about 5 percent greater apparent strength in men. In sports such as running and mountaineering, however, women show greater endurance and resistance to stress. Several years ago, when I assisted a friend running the Boston marathon, I noticed that although many of the male runners were literally collapsing at the finish or at least in need of help, the women rarely needed any help at all.

These three arguments reveal opposing points of view. While writers 1 and 3 claim that the sexes are equal, writer 2 claims that they are not. But these three writers differ in more than their objectives. They differ also in their argumentative methods.

Writer 1 makes general claims that are not supported by specific and relevant facts. The statement about equal opportunity in education—even if the reader accepts it as fact—does not necessarily support the claim that "all people are equal." The fact that women *may* attend colleges and professional schools does not prove that they do indeed attend such schools in the same numbers as men do or that they perform as well as men once they get there. Writer 2 is considerably more effective because, to begin with, his objective is much more specific. Instead of saying simply that men and women are equal or unequal, he limits the argument to athletics; and instead of saying simply that men are better athletes than women, he contends that they are "stronger, faster, and tougher," and then proceeds to cite specific evidence for this point.

Of course the evidence is not entirely convincing. By itself, the fact that the fastest male can outrun the fastest female does not really prove that men are generally faster than women, nor do the other world records cited answer this objection. Nevertheless, this writer does give the reader something to chew on. Instead of dealing in unsupported claims, he offers specific facts as evidence.

The writer of passage 3 does likewise. Though there is hardly enough evidence here to prove that the sexes are equal, this claim for their equality is much better supported—and hence more convincing—than that of the first passage.

7.3 Logic—Induction and Deduction

Though all effective arguments combine one or more general claims with one or more specific facts, successful argumentation requires a basic understanding of **logic.** Logic is the art of drawing **inferences** or conclusions. Whether you realize it or not, you make inferences every day. If, for instance, you accidentally slide your finger along the edge of a piece of paper and then discover a thin line of dark red on the fingertip, you will probably infer that you have cut yourself. That is a logical inference because it is based on a credible set of assumptions (the edge of a paper can be sharp enough to cut; a dark red line on the fingertip is more likely to be blood than anything else) and a known fact (you have indeed run that fingertip along the paper's edge). Likewise, if every student you met on a given day happened to be suffering from the flu, you might infer that a flu epidemic had struck your school. That would be a generalization based on a number of specific observations.

If we all make inferences every day, why do we need logic? Why do we need rules of inference? We need them because it is all too easy to make mistakes in drawing inferences, and arguments based on mistaken inferences are like buildings resting on cracked foundations. At best they will totter; at worst they will fall.

Without logic to rein us in, we commonly jump to conclusions.

How often have you heard two or three people complain about a proposal, and then concluded that everyone dislikes it? How often have you seen a particular person do something odd or offensive and then concluded, "That's the way all (men / women / Yankees / Southerners / Jews / Blacks / Honkies / Chicanos) are"? If you are sensible enough to avoid such obvious mistakes in inference as those, you may nonetheless fall into more subtle traps. Suppose you were with the police at Berkeley in 1964 when they entered the office of President Emeritus Robert Gordon Sproul to remove student demonstrators who had broken into it during the Free Speech Movement. After the demonstrators were taken out, police found papers strewn all over the floor of Sproul's office. Surely, they thought, this was the work of the demonstrators. But in fact it wasn't. The papers had been strewn about by Sproul himself, who often liked to do his work on the floor.

To avoid subtle as well as obvious traps in the construction of your own arguments, you need to know something about the two basic kinds of inference: induction and deduction. To see the difference between the two, compare the following passages:

1. Nuclear power plants are fundamentally unsafe. The history of nuclear power is a list of major accidents and near catastrophes. At Windscale, England, in 1957, a fire and a partial meltdown of a nuclear core spread radioactivity across miles of pastureland, and thousands of gallons of contaminated cows' milk had to be dumped. In 1966 another partial meltdown occurred at Unit One of the Fermi plant near Detroit. In 1970 fifty thousand gallons of radioactive water and steam escaped from the reactor vessel of the huge Commonwealth Edison plant near Chicago. At Browns Ferry, Alabama, in 1975, a single candle started a fire at a nuclear power plant that burned for seven hours, caused 150 million dollars' worth of damage and loss to the plant, and—according to some experts—very nearly caused a catastrophic release of radiation. Even after the Rasmussen report supposedly analyzed everything that could go wrong with a nuclear reactor, a malfunctioning water gauge led to yet another near meltdown, at Three Mile Island, Pennsylvania, in 1979. Taken together, all of these accidents show that the risks we run in operating nuclear power plants are intolerably high.

2. In spite of the widespread fear and resistance they often generate, nuclear power plants are fundamentally safe. From 1972 to 1975, a thorough study of nuclear power plants was made at a cost of four million dollars under the supervision of Norman Rasmussen, professor of nuclear engineering at M.I.T. Given the time, money, and expertise devoted to this study, its results must be reliable. And in fact they are not only reliable; they are also reassuring. After examining, identifying, and—with com-

Logic—Induction and Deduction **117**

puter analysis—establishing the risk of every possible accident that could release radiation from a nuclear power plant, the Rasmussen study concluded that in any given year the odds against a single death from a nuclear plant accident are five billion to one. Obviously, therefore, nuclear power plants are at least as safe as anything on earth can be.†

These two arguments not only represent different sides in the current debate about nuclear power; they also illustrate different methods of argumentation. The method of the first argument is inductive; the method of the second is deductive. We consider each method in turn.

7.3A Induction—Using Examples

Induction is the act of drawing a generalization from particular examples. In a perfect induction, all the particulars covered by the generalization have been individually surveyed. If you checked the age of every student at a particular high school, for instance, and found that each one was older than twelve and yet younger than twenty, you could conclude that they were all teenagers, and that would be a perfectly induced generalization. But perfect induction is rare because writers do not usually have the means or the time to survey all of the particulars covered by their generalizations. Instead, they draw *probable* generalizations from a small number of examples—more precisely, from representative examples of the group they are generalizing about.

Thus, to persuade the reader that nuclear power plants are unsafe, the author of argument 1 cites five major accidents that have occurred at such plants since 1957. These examples do not prove that all nuclear power plants are unsafe, but they make this generalization probable, and therefore credible. Likewise, the author of the following paragraphs uses inductive argument to persuade us that words used about women typically represent them as passive:

> One indication of women's passive role is the fact that they are often identified as something to eat. What's more passive than a plate of food? Last spring I saw an announcement advertising the Indiana University English Department picnic. It read "Good Food! Delicious Women!" The publicity committee was probably jumped on by local feminists, but it's nothing new to look on women as

† All the information in these two arguments comes from the unofficial public manuscript of a television program entitled "Incident at Browns Ferry," produced by WGBH, Boston, for NOVA, printed in Robert Fogelin, *Understanding Arguments* (New York: Harcourt Brace Jovanovich, 1978), 191–208.

"delectable morsels." Even women compliment each other with "You look good enough to eat," or "You have a peaches and cream complexion." Modern slang constantly comes up with new terms, but some of the old standbys for women are *cute tomato, dish, peach, sharp cookie, cheese cake, honey, sugar,* and *sweetie-pie.* A man may occasionally be addressed as *honey* or described as a *hunk of meat,* but certainly men are not laid out on a buffet and labeled as women are.

Women's passivity is also shown in the comparisons made to plants. For example, to *deflower* a woman is to take away her virginity. A girl can be described as a *clinging vine,* a *shrinking violet,* or a *wall flower.* On the other hand, men are too active to be thought of as plants. The only time we make the comparison is when insulting a man we say he is like a woman by calling him a *pansy.*
—Alleen Nilsen, "Sexism in English: A Feminist View"

These two paragraphs help to support the generalization that words used for women identify them with passive objects. The paragraphs each work in two stages. The opening sentence—the topic sentence—introduces a general category of passive objects: food in the first paragraph, plants in the second. Then each paragraph goes on to show that specific items in the category are far more often associated with women than with men. Taken together, the general categories and the specific examples work inductively to make the generalization probable.

EXERCISE 1   **Using Induction**

This exercise has three parts: (1) write a one-sentence generalization about any one of the groups listed below; (2) make a list of examples that could be used to support the generalization; (3) use this material to write a brief inductive argument.
Here are the groups:

TV commercials	comedians
rock songs	joggers
summer jobs	English teachers
charter flights	surfers
pets	motorcyclists

7.3B   Induction—Advantages and Disadvantages

The chief advantage of an inductive argument lies in the cumulative impact of successive examples. Because of this impact, an inductive argument can sometimes feel powerfully persuasive, and argument 1 may feel that way to you. But would it persuade anyone who is not already opposed to nuclear power plants? Would it bring any new supporters to the no-nuke side, or merely bolster the morale of the old ones? To answer questions like these about an inductive argument, you must not only weigh the impact of its examples but also consider their number and their relevance to the conclusion.

Consider first the number of examples cited in argument 1 (p. 117). Given all the nuclear power plants throughout the world, is a record of five accidents in twenty-two years really intolerable? One problem with induction is that whenever you use it, you are playing a numbers game. Unless your examples add up to a majority of the members of a given class (the class of all nuclear power plants in this instance), any generalization you make about the whole class will be vulnerable. The skeptic will always be able to say something like, "These are only isolated cases. How can you say that all or even most nuclear power plants are accident prone?"

Another problem with induction is that its effectiveness depends on the relevance of the examples cited. The accidents mentioned in argument 1 were costly, but since none of them killed or even injured anyone, why must we conclude that nuclear power plants are fatally dangerous? To justify that conclusion, the writer would have to show that each accident was nearly fatal to one or more persons. Just saying they were nearly fatal does not make them so, and if we are asked to believe that a particular accident was nearly fatal because unnamed experts say it was, then argument 1 is making the same kind of assumption made by argument 2: that experts are reliable. So the relevance of the examples cited in an inductive argument may not always be obvious or easy to establish.

7.3C Deduction—Using Premises

At this point, you may begin to see the special advantages of **deductive** argument, which depends not on the accumulation of examples but rather on the strength of two or more **premises**—points that the writer assumes or takes for granted. A perfect deduction—sometimes called a scientific deduction—is based on premises that are absolutely certain and indisputable. Suppose you discover a bowl of clear liquid that may or may not be fresh water. If you expose it to a temperature of 32 degrees Fahrenheit (at or near sea level) and find that it remains unfrozen, you can deduce with absolute certainty that the liquid is not fresh water. To reach this conclusion, you have combined a major premise with a minor one, a well-established fact about fresh water in general with a particular fact about a particular bowl of liquid. The resulting set of statements is called a syllogism, and looks like this:

MAJOR PREMISE: All fresh water freezes at 32 degrees Fahrenheit.
MINOR PREMISE: Liquid X did not freeze at 32 degrees Fahrenheit.
CONCLUSION: Liquid X is not fresh water.

As this example shows, strict deduction is not so much an instrument of persuasion as a means of demonstration. If each of the premises is a matter of indisputable fact, and if the conclusion is validly drawn (see section 7.3D), then the conclusion is also a matter of fact. No reasonable person can doubt its truth. Strict deduction, then, aims not so much to persuade as to reveal or explain.

To move from strict deduction to the kind of deduction that aims to persuade is to move from certainty to probability. Persuasive deduction rests on one or more premises that are merely probable, assumptions that the writer takes for granted but that are not beyond dispute. For example, argument 2 (pp. 117–18) is based on the assumption that a three-year, four-million-dollar study led by an M.I.T. professor of nuclear engineering is fully capable of determining just how dangerous nuclear power plants are. But unlike the premise that fresh water freezes at 32 degrees Fahrenheit, the assumption that a particular study is reliable can be doubted, and so can an argument based on this assumption. The persuasiveness of the argument depends on just how probable—that is, just how credible—the assumption is. If put into the form of a syllogism, argument 2 might look like this:

> MAJOR PREMISE: Any prolonged, expensive study that is supervised by a recognized expert in the field being studied is probably reliable.
> MINOR PREMISE: The Rasmussen study of nuclear power plants took three years, cost four million dollars, and was supervised by an M.I.T. professor of nuclear engineering.
> CONCLUSION: The findings of the study are probably reliable.

The minor premise is offered as a statement of fact, a statement there is no reason to doubt. But since the major premise—the basic assumption—is merely probable, that is all the conclusion can be.

Nevertheless, writers who want to persuade their readers do not always qualify their assumptions or conclusions with words such as "probable." Disguising probabilities as certainties, they sometimes use words like *must*, as in argument 2: "Given the time, money, and expertise devoted to this study, its results must be reliable." This is just one of the things that distinguishes the persuasive use of deduction from a formal syllogism. Another difference is that persuasive writing seldom includes all of the statements that a formal syllogism would require. The major premise given above, for instance, is nowhere explicitly stated in argument 2; it is merely implied. Furthermore, persuasive writing often links deductive arguments together. In the latter part of argument 2, the conclusion to one syllogism becomes the major premise of another:

> MAJOR PREMISE (from first syllogism): The Rasmussen study is probably reliable.

MINOR PREMISE: The study found that nuclear power plants are fundamentally safe.
CONCLUSION: In all probability, therefore, such plants are safe.

Once again, the argument actually made looks different from the syllogism because the writer wants to sound as persuasive as possible. So instead of concluding that nuclear power plants are "in all probability" safe, the writer says: "Obviously, therefore, nuclear power plants are at least as safe as anything on earth can be." But the problem with converting probability into certainty is that not all readers will buy the conversion. If the argument you make doesn't necessarily lead to an absolutely certain conclusion, be wary of claiming that it does. The more carefully your conclusion is worded, the more credible it will be.

7.3D   Validity and Truth

A deductive argument must have a validly drawn conclusion. A conclusion is **valid** when it follows necessarily from the premises— the one or more assumptions and the one or more statements of fact that the argument makes. Argument 2 assumes that the Rasmussen study is reliable and states what the study found: odds of five billion to one against a single death from a nuclear plant accident in any one year. If the assumption is credible and the statement of fact true, it necessarily follows that the annual odds against a fatal accident in a nuclear power plant are in fact five billion to one. That is a valid conclusion because it remains within the scope of the premises. If you tried to conclude that the annual odds against *any* accident in a nuclear power plant are five billion to one, your conclusion would be invalid because it would go beyond the scope of the premises, moving from one kind of accident to all kinds of accidents. A valid conclusion is one that stays within the boundaries defined by the premises. (For more on invalid conclusions, see "Arguing by Association," p. 127).

Since validity involves merely the internal consistency of an argument, a conclusion that is validly drawn is not necessarily true. To be true, it must be drawn from one or more credible assumptions and one or more true statements of fact. If you are arguing against nuclear power plants and you state that lives were lost in the 1979 accident at Three Mile Island, your argument will be unsound because the statement is false. A conclusion validly drawn from premises that are questionable or false is like a route carefully followed in strict obedience to a faulty compass. The route is only as good as the compass that determines it, and the conclusion is only as true as the premises that stand behind it.

EXERCISE 2   Using Deduction

Write a syllogism and then a short deductive argument based on the syllogism to defend or attack either one of the following points:

1. All college students should be required to study at least one foreign language.
2. No one convicted of a nonviolent crime should be sent to prison.

7.3E   Placing Your Conclusion

Whether the argument is inductive or deductive, the conclusion may sometimes be stated right at the beginning. If you want to prove inductively that nuclear power plants are unsafe, you can start by saying so, and then cite examples to support the point. If you want to prove deductively that nuclear power plants are safe, you can start by saying so, and then show how this conclusion is deduced. You may think that a conclusion should always come at the end of an argument, but in practice, a writer usually has some notion of the conclusion before he or she finds the examples or constructs the premises that are meant to prove it. In inductive reasoning especially, the conclusion often comes first. The writer begins with a claim and then gives examples to back it up.

However you reach your conclusion, where you put it is finally a matter of rhetorical choice. When you put it at the beginning, you tell the reader clearly what you intend to prove. When you put it at the end, you underscore the point that your assertion is a conclusion—the consequence of the facts or assumptions previously set out. In an inductive argument about current academic standards (chapter 10, exercise 1, pp. 200–202), Alston Chase gives a number of examples before he sets out his conclusion, and because of the way the examples build up to it, the conclusion strikes with telling effect. But in any case, an argument that runs to more than a paragraph should normally end with an explicit statement of its conclusion, even if it also starts with one. Otherwise the reader may forget the point you are trying to prove.

7.3F   Combining Induction and Deduction

The main advantage of a deductive argument is that if its assumptions are credible, its statements of fact true, and its conclusion validly drawn, it must be accepted by any reasonable person. But meeting those three conditions can be hard. Just how do you establish a credible assumption about any subject worth arguing over? You may have to defend your assumption by using induction. To show that the Rasmussen study is reliable, for instance, you may have to cite other studies that confirm its findings. Alternatively, you may choose to work from a different assumption—the assumption, for example, that any large-scale enterprise which has functioned for more than twenty years without causing a single fatal accident is fundamentally safe. But to build a convincing argument from this assumption, you will probably have to show that nuclear power plants have caused neither fatal nor nearly fatal accidents. And here you will have to cite examples; you will have to show that accidents like those at Browns Ferry and Three Mile Island have posed no real threat to human life and—on the contrary—have demonstrated the effectiveness of safety systems.

Or consider again the inductive argument. If you want to convince your reader that nuclear power plants are fundamentally dangerous, you must do more than cite a list of nearly fatal accidents. You must also use deduction. You have to define what you mean by "nearly fatal," and in this case, to define is to assume. Also, you have to assume that anything which has caused an accident nearly fatal to thousands (though not actually fatal to anyone) is intolerably dangerous. From those two assumptions, and from the list of facts you can cite about particular accidents, you may then deduce that nuclear power plants are intolerably dangerous.

Assumptions and examples are equally important for almost any argument you may want to make. There is probably no such thing as a perfectly convincing argument on any controversial subject; if there were, the controversy would end. But even on controversial subjects, some arguments are more effective than others. We have already said that effective arguments combine general claims and specific evidence. Another way of putting this is to say that effective arguments usually combine deduction and induction, carefully stated assumptions and apt examples. Consider the way this paragraph uses both:

> The Fortune 500 Company corporate executive directs a company whose sales in 1975 averaged almost $1.75 billion, whose assets totaled $1.33 billion, and which provided employment for almost 29,000 people. This executive directs the firm in a manner that allows it to earn an 11.6 percent return on its total investment. Such a rate of return is not guaranteed simply because a corporation is large. The opportunities to lose money are many; the managements of 28 of the 500 largest industrial corporations managed to show a loss in the recovery year of 1975. It is possible, moreover, to lose big: Singer reported a loss of $451.9 million in that year, and Chrysler $259.5 million. A chief executive who heads a management team that can avoid such losses and constantly succeed in earning a profit is obviously very valuable to the shareholders of a corporation. He is valuable not only to his employers but also to

other corporations; thus his own firm pays him handsomely to retain his services.

—Robert Thomas, "Is Corporate Executive Compensation Excessive?"

This passage is part of an essay which aims to show that chief executives of large corporations deserve the extremely high salaries they get. To support this point, the writer uses a deduction that may be stated in the following simplified form:

MAJOR PREMISE (ASSUMPTION): Any chief executive who enables a large corporation to avoid losses and earn profits regularly is very valuable.

MINOR PREMISE (FACT): The Fortune 500 Company corporate executive directs a huge company in such a way that it earns 11.6 percent return on its total investment.

CONCLUSION: The Fortune 500 corporate executive is very valuable.

By itself, this deductive argument is fairly persuasive. But to make it more so, the writer defends his basic assumption with an inductive argument, with specific examples about the danger of losses that large corporations face. If twenty-eight of the five hundred largest industrial corporations showed a loss in the recovery year of 1975, and if two of those companies lost hundreds of millions of dollars each, then the risk of loss is considerable, and a chief executive who makes a profit instead of a loss is indeed very valuable. This induction supports the major premise of the writer's deductive argument.

EXERCISE 3   Combining Deduction and Induction

Use induction to support the deductive argument you made for exercise 2.

7.4   Spotting Assumptions

Though nearly all arguments rest on one or more assumptions, the assumptions are not always stated. Sometimes they are merely implied. To understand the arguments of others and, more important, to make your own arguments as effective as possible, you need to know how to spot assumptions.

Two things make them hard to spot. One is that they often look like self-evident facts, and the other is that they are sometimes not stated at all. Take for instance the statement made about bears in passage 3 on p. 113: "If the bear population were allowed to grow unchecked, it would increase by well over 1,000 a year. . . ." Though this looks like a statement of fact, it is actually an estimate based on an unstated assumption. The writer assumes that the annual increase in the bear population can be *reliably* estimated—even though the total bear population may range from seven thousand to ten thousand. That kind of assumption cannot be taken at face value. It needs explaining.

Now see if you can spot the assumption in this argument:

> Infants born with severe handicaps should be allowed to die rather than forced to endure lives of pain, privation, and constant dependence. An infant born with spina bifida, for instance, has a lesion in the spinal column that usually causes an accumulation of spinal fluid within the brain and thereby leads to mental retardation. In addition, some doctors predict that children born with spina bifida will never walk and will suffer gradually worsening problems of the bowels and bladder. In at least one well-publicized case—that of Baby Jane Doe on Long Island—the doctor in charge also predicted that the child would have a life of constant pain. For all these reasons, infants born with handicaps such as spina bifida should be allowed to die.

This argument looks convincing until one considers the unstated assumption on which it is based: by examining a newborn child, a doctor can predict just what kind of life the child will have. But is such a prediction reliable? As a matter of fact, hundreds of infants born with spina bifida have been successfully treated by Dr. David McLone, chief of neurosurgery at Children's Memorial Hospital in Chicago, and he has already shown that such children can grow up to be bright, productive, fundamentally independent adults. Furthermore, to say that handicapped infants should be "allowed" to die is to assume that no one bears any responsibility for their deaths. But in fact the responsibility belongs to those who withhold treatment, and who in some cases deny the child the bare necessities of life: food and water.

For more advice on how to analyze an argument, see the next section and section 10.2E, "Judging the Supporting Points in an Essay," pp. 214–17.

Exercise 4 Spotting Assumptions

Identify the assumption made in the following passage, and explain why you think it is or is not justified.

> A woman's career threatens a marriage because it makes the woman financially independent of her husband. When a married woman depends on her husband for support, she is strongly motivated to stay with him. She knows that divorce would probably lead to a sharp reduction in her allowance and style of living, that she might have to move into smaller living quarters and give up many of the comforts and benefits she enjoys while married. But if she

has her own career, she can comfortably support herself, so she has no need for her husband. A two-career marriage, therefore, is far more likely to end in divorce than a marriage in which only the husband works.

7.5 Avoiding Fallacies *fal*

To make a deductive argument sound, you must avoid **fallacies**—unsound or illogical ways of arguing. In the following sections, we illustrate and describe the most common of them.

7.5A Arguing by Association

It is well known that Senator Blank is a critic of the Chilean government. We also know that Latin American Marxists are critics of the Chilean government. It is clear, therefore, that Senator Blank has Marxist tendencies.

Here a deductive argument is misused to promote guilt by association. Because deductive argument leads to a necessary conclusion, politicians and other public figures sometimes use it to compel belief, to make you think that what they say must be true. But the conclusion to this argument does not follow from its premises and is therefore invalid. Only if we assume that *all* critics of the Chilean government are Marxist must we conclude that any one critic of that government is. It may well be true that Senator Blank and Latin American Marxists share an opposition to the Chilean government, but this does not mean that they share anything else. (In formal logic, this kind of error is called the fallacy of the "undistributed middle.")

7.5B Assuming What Is to Be Proved

Women and men make up the human race. In this sense they are alike. They have feelings, expressed and unexpressed, due to their various upbringings in our society. People have challenged men's superiority because women have begun to fend for themselves and to seek a larger role in society. They are better able to cope with the difficulties of social acceptance and equality than men are because they have been allowed to express their feelings in the past. Men have it a bit harder. They have to learn to accept themselves as feeling human beings and to deal openly with their emotions instead of repressing them.

Men and women are emotional and intellectual equals. Neither sex is superior to the other.   —College freshman

The writer clearly wants us to believe that men and women are equal. Yet nowhere does the passage give us reasons for believing this statement. On the contrary, the passage seems to say that men and women differ, that women are much more willing to release their feelings than men are. It is fairly obvious that equality of status can exist between people who do different things—carpentry and plumbing, for instance—but that is not the kind of difference in question here. The emotional and intellectual equality that concerns the writer is not at all self-evident, and it is not proved by the statement that men and women both "make up the human race." On the whole, then, the writer takes for granted what needs to be defended, or assumes what is to be proved.

7.5C   Arguing by Analogy

> A college has no right to fire a popular teacher. To do so is like throwing out of office a public official who has just been reelected by a majority of the voters. Colleges that fire popular teachers violate the basic principles of democracy.

The problem with this argument is that a college is not a democracy. While teachers and college administrators like to know what students think of teachers—just as public officials like to know what voters think of them—teaching is not an elective office. Students do not elect teachers, and therefore they cannot reelect them. The argument is faulty because it rests on analogy: because it wrongly assumes that two things alike in some respects are alike in all.

Now here you may have a question. Since we have already said (pp. 92–93) that you can use analogy to explain, why are we now saying that you can't use it to argue? The answer is that explanation and argument are two different things—even though they may sometimes look very much alike.

If you wanted to explain what teachers do, you might well compare them to public officials. Like public officials, teachers must be able to speak effectively before various groups and must also be sensitive to the needs of individuals—whether constituents or students. But since no analogy presents a perfect likeness between two things, you cannot use analogy to *prove* that such a likeness exists.

7.5D   Arguing *Ad Hominem*

> A furor about the American funeral customs . . . has been created by Jessica Mitford's book *The American Way of Death*. [Pertinent here] are some facts about Jessica Mitford Treuhaft, which were reported in the November 5, 1963 issue of *National Review*. Several people "under oath before legally constituted agencies of both fed-

eral and state governments" have identified Jessica Mitford as a member of the Communist party. In fact, according to the *National Review*, both Mr. and Mrs. Treuhaft have a long record of Communist activities.

Jessica Mitford's Communist connections are pertinent because they place her book in perspective as part of the left-wing drive against private enterprise in general and—in this case—against Christian funeral customs in particular.

—Rev. Irving E. Howard, review of Jessica Mitford's
The American Way of Death

Jessica Mitford's book argues that funeral directors are greedy and exploitative. But instead of answering the argument itself, Irving Howard attacks the maker of the argument, labeling her a Communist and hence an enemy of free enterprise and Christianity. This is an example of argument *ad hominem* ("to the man,"—i.e., "to the person"), argument focused not on a point but on the person who made the point. It will convince those who believe that all evil in America is traceable to Communists, but it will not convince many others. The only rational way to prove that funeral directors are not exploitative is to cite evidence to the contrary.

7.5E Arguing *Post Hoc, Ergo Propter Hoc*

Up until 1976, when Republican Gerald Ford left the White House, the U.S. enjoyed the friendship and support of Iran. Many Americans lived and worked there, and Iran supplied us with much of our oil. But scarcely two years after Democrat Jimmy Carter became president, the Shah of Iran was driven out of his own country, and Americans were driven out after him. Clearly, then, the Democrats caused us to lose one of our most valuable allies in the Middle East.

This is the kind of argument you read and hear during political campaigns. It is based on the assumption called *post hoc, ergo propter hoc* ("after this, therefore because of it"): if X happened after Y, it must have happened because of Y. But *after* does not necessarily mean *because of*. If it did, the revolution in Iran could just as well be seen as the result of the Watergate scandal, the making of *Star Wars*, or your own birth—all of which occurred before the change in Iran.

7.5F Arguing off the Point

Anyone faced with a mugger has the right to kill the mugger on the spot. As everyone knows, the U.S. Constitution gives all American citizens the right to bear arms. Furthermore, there is far too much crime in the streets and subways of our major cities. No one is safe anymore. Drastic action is needed.

The writer wants to prove that victims or would-be victims of muggers have the right to kill them on the spot. But the statements following the first sentence do not prove the writer's point because they are irrelevant to it. The constitutional right to bear arms does not confer the right to kill, and the fact that many crimes have been committed does not justify summary execution as a response to any one of them. The writer is ignoring the question at issue, which is whether or not each and every threat of robbery—armed or un-armed, life-threatening or not—can justify immediate killing.

7.5G   Vagueness

Keating won by a landslide, so it is obvious that everyone in the state supports his plan to reduce the deficit in the state budget. Regardless of complaints about what his plan will do to housing for the elderly and other state-supported welfare programs, Keating's plan is clearly what the people want.

Here the problem is vagueness. What is a "landslide," and who are "the people"? Though a "landslide" victory can mean just about anything from a substantial majority of the vote to 100 percent of it, this writer wants "landslide" to mean 100 percent of it. But even if Keating captured every single one of the votes, the writer cannot conclude that everyone in the state supports Keating's plan, for "everyone" includes nonvoters as well as all voters. And who are "the people"? Though they are actually just the people who sup-port Keating's program, the writer wants to identify them with all the people in the state. Because neither "landslide" nor "the peo-ple" necessarily includes everyone in the state, the writer cannot validly conclude that everyone in the state supports Keating's plan.

7.5H   Arguing from Authority

Arguing from authority is not necessarily fallacious. If a specialist in the study of alcohol says that a driver with a blood alcohol con-tent (BAC) of .05 percent is twice as likely to have an accident as a driver who is perfectly sober, the expert's statement could certainly help to support the argument that drivers with a BAC of .05 or more should be arrested. But authority alone does not guarantee truth. If the alcohol expert says that teenagers should not be al-lowed to drive until they are eighteen, he has stepped outside his field of expertise, and his opinion is worth no more than anyone else's.

Arguing from authority requires special caution because even experts speaking within the fields of their expertise may not always be fully reliable, especially when they are making predictions and estimates rather than stating facts. If some doctors predict that infants born with spina bifida are irrevocably doomed to lives of misery and dependence, we have the right to ask why they make this prediction and whether other doctors agree. Likewise, given the number of accidents that have occurred at nuclear power plants, we can also ask whether anyone—even an M.I.T. professor of nuclear engineering—can accurately predict what the likelihood of a fatal accident in such a plant is.

To judge the value of an authoritative opinion, then, you should ask three questions: (1) Is the authority speaking on a matter in his or her own field of special expertise? (2) Who is the authority? Is he or she an unnamed "doctor" or someone with an identity, like Dr. David McLone of the Children's Memorial Hospital in Chicago? (3) Given the facts available on a given question, can any expert—no matter how distinguished—answer it with certainty?

EXERCISE 5 Spotting, Explaining, and Eliminating Fallacies

Identify and explain the fallacy in each of the following statements. Then, if you can, eliminate the fallacy by revising the statement.

> EXAMPLE
> Since 1968, when a federal gun control act made it illegal to order a handgun by mail, the crime rate has risen substantially. So any attempt to regulate guns simply aggravates crime.
> FALLACY: *Post hoc, ergo propter hoc.*
> EXPLANATION: This statement does not prove that the gun control act *caused* the increase in the crime rate, even though the increase followed the act. What the first sentence does show is that gun control laws are sometimes ineffectual. So a more workable version of the statement would look like this:
> REVISION: Since 1968, when a federal gun control act made it illegal to order a handgun by mail, the crime rate has risen substantially. Gun control laws, therefore, do not necessarily reduce crime.

1. Robert McNamara, former Secretary of Defense, opposes the so-called "Star Wars" defense system because he thinks it is technologically impossible to build an impenetrable shield against Soviet missiles. But the Soviets also oppose the "Star Wars" defense system. So McNamara unwittingly supports the Soviets.
2. The national speed limit of 55 miles per hour should be raised to at least 70 miles per hour on all interstate highways. Imposing a speed limit of 55 miles per hour is like setting a curfew that would require everyone to be off the streets and in their homes by ten o'clock every night. Grown-up people should be able to decide these matters for themselves.
3. On December 7, 1941, shortly after the United States government re-

ceived Japanese envoys who had come to discuss peace, the Japanese bombed the U.S. naval base in Pearl Harbor. That event plainly shows that a willingness to discuss peace simply encourages the enemy to attack.

4. The only way to make the tax law truly fair is to cancel all deductions and exemptions. Everyone knows that the government squanders a large part of our tax dollar on expensive and unnecessary trips for legislators and their spouses, on lavish official parties, and on military equipment for which the Pentagon is grossly overcharged. Something must be done to stop the waste in government spending.

5. Since government tests have determined that cigarette smoking is dangerous, Congress should pass a law banning the sale of cigarettes altogether.

7.6 Using Argumentative Words

Certain words signal an argument. *Therefore,* for instance, tells the reader that you are drawing a conclusion, that you are offering one statement as a reason for believing another:

> Hunters keep the growth of the bear population down and *therefore* help to ensure an adequate food supply for the bear population as a whole.

When you use a word like *therefore,* you are making an argumentative connection, and the reader will hold you responsible for it. If you introduce the word simply to fill the gap between two sentences, you are using it irresponsibly:

> Many college students have serious problems during their freshman year. *Therefore,* high school graduates should work for a year or two before starting college.

The word *Therefore* asks us to take one statement as a reason for believing another. But is the first statement in this passage a reason for believing the second? Would the problems of freshmen be eliminated if they came to college with a year or two of work behind them? There is no clear connection between these two statements, and filling the gap with *Therefore* is like trying to bridge a river with a six-inch stick. Before you connect two statements with an argumentative word, be sure that one statement actually does follow from the other.

Argumentative words include *for, since, because, so, consequently, therefore, hence* and *accordingly.* Some of these words, such as *since, for,* and *because,* may be used not only to argue but also to explain:

> To ARGUE: American businesses should be allowed to stay in South Africa *because* they help to raise the standard of living for black people there.

To EXPLAIN: President Carter opposed U.S. participation in the Moscow Olympics *because* he wanted to protest the Soviet invasion of Afghanistan.

7.7 Reckoning with the Opposition

Persuasive writing never appears in a vacuum. It springs not only from the desire to share a particular belief, but also from the recognition that others hold a contrary belief, that conflicting claims compete for public support—like rival products in the marketplace or rival candidates in a political campaign. If there is no room for disagreement, there is no need for persuasion. No reasonable writer would set out to argue the need for a reliable water supply because no reasonable person could doubt the need for it. But the very fact that a writer sets out to persuade means that there *is* room for disagreement on the topic chosen, that there is opposition to the writer's point of view.

How do you deal with the opposition in a persuasive essay? To ignore it entirely is to risk antagonizing the reader or provoking objections that may undermine your argument. To argue effectively, you must first reckon with the opposition, and thereby anticipate objections. You can do this in one of two ways—by making concessions, or by fairly and honestly defining the position you plan to oppose.

7.7A Making Concessions

A concession is a point granted to the other side: an expression of concern for the feelings of those who may disagree with you, of respect for the reasons that prompt them to do so, or of clear-cut agreement with them on one or more aspects of the topic in dispute. To see the difference an opening concession can make, compare these two introductory paragraphs—both written by college freshmen:

1. No one should be admitted to college without a personal interview. What can admissions people tell from a piece of paper? They can't really tell anything. Only when they see a student face to face can they decide what kind of a person he is.
2. An admissions officer can tell some things from a piece of paper. He can tell how well a person writes and what he is interested in, factors which go a long way toward determining if a student is capable of using the college resources to the fullest extent possible. However, there are things that an application cannot bring forth, things that can only be seen in a personal meeting. The way a person talks, the way he thinks about and answers questions on the spot, the way he reacts to certain pieces of informa-

tion, are all important aspects of a person which cannot be found on a written piece of paper.

Both of these writers are arguing in support of the same point, that no one should be admitted to college without a personal interview by an admissions officer. But the first writer makes no concessions to the other side. He simply dismisses the idea that anything can be learned about an applicant from a piece of paper. The second writer concedes or admits that certain things can be learned from a written application, and then proceeds to show that certain other things can be learned only from an interview. The transitional word *However* marks the shift from concession to assertion. (For more on transitional words, see pp. 158–60.)

Starting with concession is a good way to overcome the reader's resistance to an unpopular argument, to gain a hearing for even the most controversial point of view. Consider, for instance, how this writer opens an argument for test-tube babies:

> The mere mention of "test-tube babies" triggers instant repugnance in most of us. Visions arise, from Aldous Huxley's *Brave New World,* of moving assembly lines of glassware out of which babies are decanted at each terminus by a detached and impersonal technician. Procreation thus becomes reproduction in the full factory-like connotation of that word. And as we conjure up the distasteful (at the least) scene, words like *mechanization* and *dehumanization* reverberate through our neuronal networks.
>
> Nevertheless, despite the offense to our sensibilities provoked by even the thought of artificial wombs, there is a valid case to be made for test-tube babies in the full Huxleyan image—not mass-produced on an assembly line, perhaps, but nevertheless wholly and "artificially" grown in a scientifically monitored environment without ever being carried in the uterus of a human mother. Such a case can be made (which does not mean that I personally advocate it) on the basis not merely of bizarre and exotic speculations but of purely humane, down-to-earth considerations having to do with the health of individual babies.
>
> —Albert Rosenfeld, "The Case for Test-Tube Babies"

Here the writer begins with a whole paragraph of concession. Before he can effectively defend the growing of babies outside the womb, he must recognize that many people are horrified at the idea. Only then can he hope to gain a reasonable hearing for it. Once more a transitional word—*Nevertheless*—marks the shift from concession to assertion.

7.7B Defining the Position You Will Oppose

To begin with a concession is to express sympathetic concern for those you plan to disagree with, or even partial agreement with them. But if you see no reason for sympathetic concern or room for partial agreement, you can nonetheless begin your essay by fairly defining the position you aim to oppose, by letting the reader know that you understand and respect the views of your adversary.

One of the biggest obstacles to effective persuasion is contempt for the opposing view. Consider these opening paragraphs of a newspaper column advocating gun control:

> Logic, common sense and public opinion are on the side of gun control, but America's firearms fanatics are insufferably relentless. Now, for pete's sake, they want their own political party.
> With their own blind, the gun lovers can offer us candidates promising not a chicken in every pot, but a pistol in every pocket. And carnage in every home. Someone else to vote against.
> —Richard J. Roth, "Despite Evidence and Reason,
> Pro-Gun Talk Won't Go Away"

To describe the opponents of gun control as "firearms fanatics" who promise "a pistol in every pocket" and "carnage in every home" is to antagonize any reader who is not already on the writer's side. This is not persuasive writing; it is a slapdash mix of invective and gross exaggeration. It will rouse the antigun faithful, but it is unlikely to make any converts.

A far more effective way to introduce an argument against a particular position is to state the position in the terms used by its advocates—if possible by quoting or paraphrasing their words. Here, for instance, is Robert Thomas' introduction to his essay defending the high salaries paid to top corporate executives (see above, p. 124):

> Ralph Nader stands at the end of a long line of critics who assail the high incomes of top corporate executives. Nader and his associates suggest that "in the absence of judicial limitations, excessive remuneration has become the norm." They observe that the average top executive in each of the fifty largest industrial corporations earns more salary in a year than many of the corporate employees earn in a lifetime. Salaries are only part (albeit the major part) of the compensation the top executives receive. Bonuses, lavish retirements, stock options, and stock ownership combine to swell the incomes of corporate chief executives by another 50 to 75 percent of the executives' direct remunerations. Nader and his associates conclude that the top corporate executives receive "staggeringly large salaries and stock options."

Before Thomas begins to defend the high salaries of corporate executives, he allows Ralph Nader—a leading consumer activist— to have his say. He does not call Nader an anticorporate nut who wants to cut executive salaries to the poverty level. Instead, quoting and paraphrasing the very words of Nader and his associates, he respectfully explains why this group finds the salaries of top executives "excessive." By thus defining his adversary's position, Thomas earns the right to a respectful hearing for his own.

EXERCISE 6   Using Concession

Rewrite the following argument in one of two ways: (1) support the writer's point of view but add one or more concessive sentences at the beginning, or (2) argue against the writer's point of view by first making a concession to it and then defending the other side. Whichever you choose to do, be sure to use a transitional word between your concession and the main point you are making.

> Regional expressions are a hindrance to communication. Each part of the country has adopted many which cannot be found anywhere else. For instance, New England is the only part of the U.S. where you can order a "frappe" in a drugstore or ice cream parlor. Try ordering a frappe in Nebraska and see what kind of reaction you will get. The purpose of language is to make communication possible. By separating regions of the country from each other, nonstandardized forms of expression defeat this purpose.
>
> —College freshman

EXERCISE 7   Defining a Position You Oppose

Choose from a newspaper, magazine, or any other printed source an essay written to defend a position that you oppose. Then, using Thomas' introduction as a guide, write a paragraph defining this position as respectfully as possible.

7.8   Composing an Argumentative Essay

To show you how to reckon with the opposition and how to combine induction and deduction, we have already quoted portions of an essay by Robert Thomas (see above, pp. 124, 135). So that you can now see all the techniques of argumentation in action, here is the whole of Thomas' essay:

Is Corporate Executive Compensation Excessive?

[1] Ralph Nader stands at the end of a long line of critics who assail the high incomes of top corporate executives. Nader and his associates suggest that "in the absence of judicial limitations, excessive remuneration has become the norm." They observe that the average top executive in each of the fifty largest industrial corporations earns more salary in a year than many of the corporate employees earn in a lifetime. Salaries are only part (albeit the major part) of the compensation the top executives receive. Bonuses, lavish retirements, stock options, and stock ownership combine to swell the incomes of corporate chief executives by another 50 to 75 per-

cent of the executives' direct remunerations. Nader and his associates conclude that the top corporate executives receive "staggeringly large salaries and stock options."

[2] Those who criticize the level of compensation that corporate executives receive are critical of any persons who are, or who become, rich. The top executives of our major corporations *do* become rich. *Fortune* magazine, in a survey of the chief executives of the 500 largest industrial corporations, discovered that the median income in 1976 was $209,000 a year and that when only the 100 largest corporations were considered, the median salary was $344,000 a year.

[3] Most Americans, however, do not consider becoming rich to be a crime. Indeed, the opposite is true. Achieving wealth reflects a high level of performance in providing through the market what the economy desires.

[4] Nader and his coauthors recognize this admiration for performance and attack the level of executive compensation on other grounds. They suggest that the chief corporate executives are not entrepreneurs who risk their own capital in the search for profits, but functionaries who perform essentially the same tasks as government employees. The chief corporate executives "serve as the bureaucrats of private industry."

[5] The difference between industry and government is that the boards of directors of large corporations allegedly are more lax in discharging their responsibilities to their shareholders (by constraining excessive executive salaries) than the members of the Congress of the United States and the various elected officials of state and local governments who serve as the watchdogs for the public interest. The managements of large corporations take advantage of this laxness to request and receive excessive compensation. Moreover, this is not an isolated phenomenon confined to an occasional corporation. Nader reports that it "has become the norm."

[6] In response, consider first who a chief corporate executive is, and examine the responsibilities a chief corporate executive must discharge. The typical top executive in each of the 500 largest industrial corporations is a white Protestant male aged sixty. He got his top position at age fifty-five; he averages between fifty-five and sixty-four hours a week on the job, takes three weeks of vacation each year,and earns a salary of $209,000 a year. He has attended graduate school, and he has worked for more than two companies during his business career. He owns less than $500,000 worth of stock in the company for which he works, and during the past decade he has seen his salary rise less rapidly, in percentage terms, than the salaries of his employees. In short, he is well prepared, experienced, hardworking, and beyond middle age.

[7] Two things distinguish each of these 500 persons from several thousand others who have similar qualities. First, each is paid more. Second, each has been chosen as the person responsible for his company's present and future.

[8] The Fortune 500 Company corporate executive directs a company whose sales in 1975 averaged almost $1.75 billion, whose assets totaled $1.33 billion, and which provided employment for almost 29,000 people. This executive directs the firm in a manner that allows it to earn an 11.6 percent return on its total investment. Such a rate of return is not guaranteed simply because a corporation is large. The opportunities to lose money are many; the managements of 28 of the 500 largest industrial corporations managed to show a loss in the recovery year of 1975. It is possible, moreover, to lose big: Singer reported a loss of $451.9 million in that year, and Chrysler $259.5 million. A chief executive who heads a management team that can avoid such losses and constantly succeed in earning a profit is obviously very valuable to the shareholders of a corporation. He is valuable not only to his employers but also to other corporations; thus his own firm pays him handsomely to retain his services.

[9] Many pages of our national magazines devoted to business news—*Business Week, Forbes, Fortune*—report the movements of business executives from one firm to another. These shifts are induced by substantial increases in salary, often, according to one publication, of 30 percent or more. Some excellently managed corporations, such as IBM, General Motors, Procter and Gamble, and Xerox, are known in industry as "executive breeders." Xerox admitted in its 1976 proxy statement that its management was increasingly becoming "a target for other corporations seeking talented executives," and it proposed a new incentive plan for its executives. This request for increased executive compensation was not self-serving on the part of Xerox's management; it stemmed in part from the prior move of twelve Xerox executives to a rival copier manufacturer.

[10] The high salaries and fringe benefits that talented executives in large corporations receive stem not from laxness on the part of the boards of directors but, rather, from the boards' vigilance. Corporations must pay their executives, as well as any other employees, what they could earn by working for a rival firm, or lose them. Competition among corporations for the best people sets the level of executive compensation. If one person is to be placed in charge of a billion dollars in shareholder assets, which can easily be lost through mismanagement, even the $766,085 a year that the highest-paid corporate executive in the United States receives might not appear excessive to shareholders, especially if that salary is what it takes to get the services of the best available person.

[11] There are many examples of corporations that are well rewarded for paying the price necessary to get the best person to remedy a bad situation. In one recent case, a firm that once tried to produce computers, and whose stock had sold for as high as $173 a share, fell on hard times; in 1973 it lost $119 million on sales of $177 million and had $300 million in long-term debts. A new chief executive, who by 1976 had made the firm profitable

once again, received $200,000 a year, performance incentives that earned him another $400,000, and stock options that made him a millionaire on paper. Clearly the compensation this executive received meets the Nader criterion for being "excessive." Yet, the Bank of America thought it was a worthwhile investment to guarantee his salary in an attempt, which proved successful, to ensure the eventual repayment of the large loans it had made to the firm. Individual shareholders also applauded the move; as a result of the executive's efforts, the value of a share has increased from $2 to over $21. In this one instance, the efforts of the new chief executive succeeded in increasing the market value of the company ten times.

[12] A talented executive is highly paid because he is very productive. He earns for his firm additional net revenue at least equal in value to his compensation. If he did not, his firm would let him go. If his firm does not pay him what he is worth to others, it will lose him to a rival. The same holds true for any other valuable input in our economy and accounts as well for the high incomes received by talented persons in other fields.

[13] Consider, for a moment, the salaries paid to entertainers. The fastest way to become a millionaire is not to become a corporate executive, but to become a big rock 'n' roll star or a superstar in professional sports. In 1973, for example, there were an estimated fifty music performers earning between $1 million and $6 million a year. These thirty-five persons and fifteen groups made, annually, between three and seven times the salary paid to America's highest-paid executive. While the musicians performed, that highest-paid executive directed, and was responsible for, a company that employed 376,000 persons, had sales of over $11 billion and assets of over $10 billion, and earned almost $400 million in profits. Rock stars, moreover, earn their fortunes sooner than business executives; most start their careers as teenage idols; few have their best earning years after thirty. The average chief executive in each of the 500 largest industrial corporations does not attain that degree of success until the age of fifty-five.

[14] Or, examine the compensation paid to the superstars in professional sports. The most interesting stories on sports pages now are not reports of games but stories about the fabulous salaries received by star athletes: $3 million to Julius Erving, $1.5 million each to O.J. Simpson and Pele, $500,000 to Kareem Abdul-Jabbar, $450,000 each to Tiny Archibald and Joe Namath, $400,000 to Catfish Hunter, $360,000 to Bob Lanier, $325,000 to Bill Bradley, $302,000 to Spencer Haywood, $250,000 to John Havlicek, $237,000 to Rick Barry, $230,000 to Tom Seaver, and $225,000 to Dick Allen. More names from golf, hockey, and tennis could easily be added to the list. The reported incomes of these superstars are probably understated, since they exclude payments for endorsements and the like. These people, furthermore, work only part of the year, while the average chief executive has a forty-nine-week season.

[15] When considered in the light of the compensation paid to

extremely talented persons in other areas, the rewards earned by corporate executives do not appear excessive. A competitive economy ensures that highly productive persons command high rewards.

Here you see the stages of a well-organized argumentative essay. First of all, Thomas begins by describing at some length the position he plans to oppose. He reports not only what Nader and his associates think of high salaries, but also why they find the salaries excessive: as the "bureaucrats of private industry," chief corporate executives deserve no more than government bureaucrats. Only after thus defining the case against high salaries does Thomas set out to justify them.

Paragraphs 6–12 develop four arguments. First, using a number of specific details, Thomas shows that the typical top executive in one of the five hundred largest industrial corporations is "well prepared, experienced, hardworking, and beyond middle age." Second, using induction and deduction (as explained above, in section 7.3F), Thomas shows why a profit-generating chief executive is so valuable. Third, he explains how competition for the most effective managers drives up the cost of keeping them in any one company. Fourth, using illustrative induction (a single example standing for "many"), he shows how the high salary paid to one executive was amply justified by what he did for the market value of the company, which increased ten times under his management.

In the final paragraphs of his essay, Thomas uses induction as well as comparison and contrast to clinch his argument that top corporate executives are not overpaid. By induction, he shows that rock stars generally earn well over one million dollars a year and that superstars in professional sports generally earn well over two hundred thousand dollars. By comparison and contrast, he shows that high-earning rock stars are generally much younger than high-earning corporate executives, that high-earning athletes work less than the executives, and that both of these other groups earn considerably more.

The concluding paragraph is an implied piece of deduction based on a major premise and a minor premise that have each been inductively established—the first through a survey of various highly paid persons, and the second through a survey of executives:

> MAJOR PREMISE: A competitive economy ensures that highly productive persons command high rewards.
> MINOR PREMISE: Corporate executives are highly productive persons.
> CONCLUSION: Corporate executives command high rewards.

EXERCISE 8 Composing an Argumentative Essay

Using the following facts and any others that you may be able to gather from printed sources, compose an argumentative essay that defends or attacks the need for more gun-control laws. Whichever side you take, your essay must include all of the facts given below, and it should rely chiefly on rational argument, not emotional appeal.

1. Lincoln, McKinley, and John F. Kennedy were all killed by guns. No American president has ever been stabbed or clubbed to death.
2. Article II of the United States Bill of Rights says, "A well-regulated militia being necessary to the security of a free state, the right of the people to keep and bear arms shall not be infringed."
3. There are now almost 200 million guns in the United States, and 50 million of those are handguns.
4. According to FBI statistics (as of 1981), 70 percent of the people who are killed or wounded by gunfire are shot by relatives, acquaintances, or themselves.
5. Rifle and shotgun barrels can be sawed off with a fifty-nine-cent hacksaw blade, and the resulting weapons are more lethal than most handguns.
6. John F. Kennedy, assassinated by rifle shots in 1963, was a member of the National Rifle Association who strongly believed in the citizens' right to bear arms.
7. Theodore Roosevelt, who was wounded by a pistol shot in the chest while making a speech, recovered from the wound and afterward joined the National Rifle Association, which he staunchly supported.
8. Guns are used in 250,000 crimes each year, and 20,000 of those are homicides.
9. A 1968 report by the National Commission on the Causes and Prevention of Violence says that for every burglar stopped by a gun, four gun owners or members of their families are killed in firearm accidents.
10. Hunters kill an estimated 200 million birds and 50 million other animals each year.
11. Public opinion polls show that 70 percent of Americans favor gun registration and slightly over 50 percent favor an absolute ban.
12. The worst mass murder on record in the city of Buffalo during this century was committed with a knife and hatchet.
13. John Wilkes Booth used a Saturday Night Special (a Derringer pistol) to assassinate Lincoln.
14. McKinley was also assassinated with a pistol.
15. Together with the federal gun control act of 1968, many state laws already regulate ownership of handguns. In the states of New York and Massachusetts, for instance, persons convicted of carrying unlicensed handguns—regardless of what they are carried for—must go to jail for a year.
16. Statistics indicate that 995 handgun owners out of 1,000 are safe, responsible, law-abiding citizens.

17. One advocate of national gun controls has proposed that every gun sold in the country—whether handgun, rifle, or shotgun—should be registered, that the buyer's criminal and psychiatric record should be investigated before the gun is handed over, and that every gun sold should be test-fired so that the spent shell and slug can be kept in police ballistic files along with buyer's name, photograph, and fingerprints.

7.9 Appealing to the Emotions

A working knowledge of argumentative technique is an indispensable tool for the writer who wants to persuade. But readers are seldom persuaded by rational arguments alone. For this reason the writer should try to understand the reader's feelings and appeal to them.

To see how an appeal to the feelings can reinforce an argument that is fundamentally rational, consider the final paragraphs of Stephen Jay Gould's *Mismeasure of Man*. In the book as a whole, Gould demonstrates that biological determinism has no basis in fact. He shows that no racial, ethnic, or even mental characteristics of anyone's parents can determine what he or she will become, that intelligence cannot be reliably measured by intelligence tests, and therefore that laws requiring the sterilization of children born to allegedly feebleminded parents are scientifically unjustified. After making this argument by strictly rational means, Gould ends his book by citing the case of Doris Buck, whose fifty-two-year-old mother had been tested at a mental age of seven, and who was sterilized under a Virginia law in 1928:

> She later married Matthew Figgins, a plumber. But Doris Buck was never informed. "They told me," she recalled, "that the operation was for an appendix and rupture." So she and Matthew Figgins tried to conceive a child. They consulted physicians at three hospitals throughout her child-bearing years; no one recognized that her Fallopian tubes had been severed. Last year [1979], Doris Buck Figgins discovered the cause of her lifelong sadness.
>
> One might invoke an unfeeling calculus and say that Doris Buck's disappointment ranks as nothing compared with millions of dead in wars to support the designs of madmen or the conceits of rulers. But can one measure the pain of a single dream unfulfilled, the hope of a defenceless woman snatched by public power in the name of an ideology advanced to purify a race? May Doris Buck's simple and eloquent testimony stand for millions of deaths and disappointments and help us to remember that the Sabbath was made for man, not man for the Sabbath: "I broke down and cried. My husband and me wanted children desperately. We were crazy about them. I never knew what they'd done to me."

Given at the very end of a strictly rational, analytic, and mathematically supported argument, the story and the words of Doris Buck powerfully appeal to our emotions. They move us to see that biological determinism is not just scientifically unjustified, but unconscionably cruel.

EXERCISE 9 Reinforcing an Argument with Emotional Appeal

To reinforce the argument you made in exercise 8, use a personal experience or a particular example that will stir the reader's feelings.

8

WRITING
PARAGRAPHS

Effective essays are made with paragraphs, blocks of sentences that help the reader follow the stages of the writer's thought. Though a paragraph is commonly part of an essay, it can and sometimes does serve as an essay in its own right, and the writing of one-paragraph essays will give you small-scale practice in organization. You can sometimes learn a good deal about organization by writing a single sentence, and you can learn even more by writing a single paragraph. What you learn is the complex art of separating and connecting at the same time, of dividing groups of words into sentences and yet relating those sentences to one another, of drawing a continuous line of thought through a succession of full stops. For that reason, much of this chapter deals with the single paragraph as a self-contained unit.

But just as you learn how to relate the separate sentences of a paragraph, so also you should learn how to relate the separate paragraphs of an essay. Since most essays consist of more than one paragraph, you must know how to move from one paragraph to another as well as from one sentence to the next. So this chapter shows you how to do both.

8.1 Why Use Paragraphs? ¶

A paragraph is usually a block of sentences set off by spacing or indentation at the beginning. Paragraphs come in many shapes and sizes—from the slim one-sentence models made to fit the narrow columns of a newspaper to the wide, many-sentenced model made for the pages of a book. What do they all have in common? Perhaps we could better begin by asking what paragraphs are for. Why do writers break up essays into blocks of sentences instead of just running all the sentences together?

Part of the answer is that an essay is like a long stairway. Unless it is interrupted now and then as if by a landing, a place to stop before continuing, the reader may get confused. New paragraphs usually begin where the writer's thought turns, just as landings often come where a stairway turns. Without such turning points clearly marked by new paragraphs, here is what you have:

> [At one time the migrants] had set forth in tribes. They wandered across the steppe or edged out of the forests down to the plains with wives and children and cattle in the long columns of all their possessions. Home was where they were and movement did not disrupt the usual order of their ways. It was quite otherwise in human experience when some among the Europeans of the sixteenth and seventeenth centuries migrated. Often it was a man alone, an individual, who went, one who in going left home, that is, cut himself apart from the associations and attachments that until then had given meaning to his life. Some inner restlessness or external compulsion sent such wanderers away solitary on a personal quest to which they gave various names, such as fortune or salvation. They were a diverse group. There were priests who had brooded over the problem of a world in eternity and made the startling discovery that a holy mission summoned them away. There were noblemen in the great courts who stared out beyond the formal lines of the garden and saw the vision of new empires to be won. There were young men without places who depended on daring and their swords and were willing to soldier for their fortunes. There were clerks in the countinghouses, impatient of the endless rows of digits, who thought why should they not reach out for the wealth that set their masters high? There were journeymen without employment and servants without situations and peasants without land and many others whom war or pestilence displaced who dreamed in desperation of an alternative to home. Through the eighteenth century their numbers grew and, even more, through the nineteenth. They had various destinations. The receding ships left them at the edge of an impenetrable wilderness; they moved up the river and the dark jungle closed in behind them; they came over the pass and the jagged forest shut off the sight of the land they had left behind. They had wandered indeed alone into the strangeness.

This passage is taxing to read. Because no indentations signal the end of one sequence of thought and the beginning of another, we have trouble following the progression of thought in the passage as a whole. But see what happens when it is broken up into paragraphs, as it actually was by the author:

[At one time the migrants] had set forth in tribes. They wandered across the steppe or edged out of the forests down to the plains with wives and children and cattle in the long columns of all their possessions. Home was where they were and movement did not disrupt the usual order of their ways.

It was quite otherwise in human experience when some among the Europeans of the sixteenth and seventeenth centuries migrated. Often it was a man alone, an individual, who went, one who in going left home, that is, cut himself apart from the associations and attachments that until then had given meaning to his life. Some inner restlessness or external compulsion sent such wanderers away solitary on a personal quest to which they gave various names, such as fortune or salvation.

They were a diverse group. There were priests who had brooded over the problem of a world in eternity and made the startling discovery that a holy mission summoned them away. There were noblemen in the great courts who stared out beyond the formal lines of the garden and saw the vision of new empires to be won. There were young men without places who depended on daring and their swords and were willing to soldier for their fortunes. There were clerks in the countinghouses, impatient of the endless rows of digits, who thought why should they not reach out for the wealth that set their masters high? There were journeymen without employment and servants without situations and peasants without land and many others whom war or pestilence displaced who dreamed in desperation of an alternative to home. Through the eighteenth century their numbers grew and, even more, through the nineteenth.

They had various destinations. The receding ships left them at the edge of an impenetrable wilderness; they moved up the river and the dark jungle closed in behind them; they came over the pass and the jagged forest shut off the sight of the land they had left behind. They had wandered indeed alone into the strangeness.

—Oscar Handlin, *Race and Nationality in American Life*

Now the turns of thought are clearly marked. The first paragraph describes the movement of tribes, who carried their "home" with them. In contrast ("It was quite otherwise"), the second describes the movement of individuals, who cut themselves off from "home." The third paragraph then describes the various kinds of individuals who moved away ("They were a diverse group"), and the fourth describes their destinations. Each new paragraph marks a new stage in the development of the writer's thought and the reader's understanding.

EXERCISE 1   **Dividing a Passage into Paragraphs**

In the following passage from Loren Eiseley's "Man of the Future," we have deliberately run the author's original three paragraphs into one. Divide the passage into what you think were Eiseley's original three paragraphs, and state the main point of each.

> There are days when I find myself unduly pessimistic about the future of man. Indeed, I will confess that there have been occasions when I swore I would never again make the study of time a profession. My walls are lined with books expounding its mysteries; my
> 5 hands have been split and rubbed raw with grubbing into the quicklime of its waste bins and hidden crevices. I have stared so much at death that I can recognize the lingering personalities in the faces of skulls and feel accompanying affinities and repulsions. One such skull lies in the lockers of a great metropolitan museum.
> 10 It is labeled simply: Strandlooper, South Africa. I have never looked longer into any human face than I have upon the features of that skull. I come there often, drawn in spite of myself. It is a face that would lend reality to the fantastic tales of our childhood. There is a hint of Wells' *Time Machine* folk in it—those pathetic, childlike
> 15 people whom Wells pictures as haunting earth's autumnal cities in the far future of the dying planet. Yet this skull has not been spirited back to us through future eras by a time machine. It is a thing, instead, of the millennial past. It is a caricature of modern man, not by reason of its primitiveness but, startlingly, because of a mod-
> 20 ernity outreaching his own. It constitutes, in fact, a mysterious prophecy and warning. For at the very moment in which students of humanity have been sketching their concept of the man of the future, that being has already come, and lived, and passed away.

EXERCISE 2 Building Paragraphs

In the following passage from a student's essay about a character in a short story, some of the paragraphs are too short. Combine them so that each new paragraph marks a turn in the writer's thought.

> Humble Jewett reveals his love of natural beauty in several ways.
> When he and Amarantha reach the crest of the hill, he kneels down and prays to the Creator. He is moved to worship by the sight of the sunlight lining the distant treetops.
> 5 He has a similar reaction later in the story as he is walking to Wyker's house. He is so awestruck by the splendor of the sunset that he doesn't notice the wound in his leg.
> The sight of human beauty also casts a spell. He wants to kiss Amarantha, yet he holds back, restrained by her loveliness. It's as
> 10 if he chooses to keep such radiant beauty pure, within his sight but beyond his reach.

You have seen that paragraphing helps to mark the turns in a writer's thought. What else does it do? What other purpose does paragraph structure have? One way of answering these questions is to consider a set of sentences desperately in need of paragraph structure:

My life has been a very satisfying one so far. I've faced many challenges and attained some of the goals I've set. I am one of five children. I have two older sisters and two younger brothers. My father was a successful chef. He had a college degree in electrical
5 engineering, but chose to study cooking instead. He traveled in Europe and worked with many different chefs. He had a great influence on all of our lives. He showed me what determination and hard work could do for a person My mother was a good mother. She guided me in a very practical way. I was able to learn and grow
10 under their supervision. At times, it's hard to attain confidence in some situations, but I think of my parents and continue on. I enjoy knitting and making things for others and I also love to cook. Preparing economical meals is a constant challenge. I like to read a lot. I also enjoy watching my son grow up. Children are a tremendous
15 challenge. I read to him and try to let him be as creative as possible. I have also helped my husband go through his last year of college. It was a proud moment for me to watch him walk up and get his degree. I enjoyed working with him and learning as he did. You really get a good feeling when you've helped someone. Your re-
20 wards are twofold. Helping others is my main goal in life. I enjoy people. So far, my life has been satisfactory to me. I've got future goals set to attain. I've got lots of hard work ahead of me. I just look forward to going day by day and getting further toward my one goal of a college education with a challenging job.

—College student

The only thing that makes this set of sentences a "paragraph" is the indentation at the beginning. Every sentence here makes sense in itself, but reading these sentences one after the other is like trying to keep up with a kangaroo. The writer moves in short, sudden leaps, and the reader never knows where she will land next. She goes from goals and challenges to sisters and brothers, from parents to knitting and cooking, from helping others to helping herself. What point is she trying to make? She herself seems unsure. To reorganize a jumble like this, she must think about the connections and the differences between her sentences. Only then can she write a paragraph that makes sense.

We will return to this paragraph and go to work on it after we have examined the three basic elements of paragraph structure: unity, emphasis, and coherence.

8.2   Unity   ¶ *u*

In general, a unified paragraph is a sequence of sentences that are all clearly related to a topic sentence. The **topic sentence** states the main point of the paragraph. At times this sentence may be simply implicit rather than openly stated, but usually it is explicit. It often appears at the beginning of the paragraph.

There are two basic ways of relating the other sentences of the paragraph to the topic sentence. The first is by treating the other sentences as items in a list; the second is by treating them as links in a chain.

8.2A   Using List Structure

Consider the following paragraph:

> This is the essence of the religious spirit the sense of power, beauty, greatness, truth infinitely beyond one's own reach, but infinitely to be aspired to. It invests men with a pride in a purpose and with humility in accomplishment. It is the source of all true tolerance, for in its light all men see other men as they see themselves, as being capable of being more than they are, and yet falling short, inevitably, of what they can imagine human opportunities to be. It is the supporter of human dignity and pride and the dissolver of vanity. And it is the very creator of the scientific spirit; for without the aspiration to understand and control the miracle of life, no man would have sweated in a laboratory or tortured his brain in the exquisite search after truth.
>
> —Dorothy Thompson, "The Education of the Heart"

This paragraph opens with a topic sentence about the religious spirit. Then comes a list of sentences, each beginning with *It* and all referring to *the religious spirit,* defining and commenting on it. You can clearly see the list structure of the paragraph when the sentences beginning with *It* are separated and printed one below the other:

> TOPIC SENTENCE: This is the essence of the religious spirit—the sense of power, beauty, greatness, truth infinitely beyond one's own reach, but infinitely to be aspired to.

> SUPPORTING SENTENCES:
> 1. It invests men with a pride in a purpose and with humility in accomplishment.
> 2. It is the source of all true tolerance, for in its light all men see other men as they see themselves, as being capable of being more than they are, and yet falling short, inevitably, of what they can imagine human opportunities to be.
> 3. It is the supporter of human dignity and pride and the dissolver of vanity.
> 4. And it is the very creator of the scientific spirit; for without the aspiration to understand and control the miracle of life, no man would have sweated in a laboratory or tortured his brain in the exquisite search after truth.

Another example of list structure is one of the paragraphs by Oscar Handlin quoted on p. 146:

TOPIC SENTENCE: They were a diverse group.

SUPPORTING SENTENCES:
1. There were priests who had brooded over the problem of a world in eternity and made the startling discovery that a holy mission summoned them away.
2. There were noblemen in the great courts who stared out beyond the formal lines of the garden and saw the vision of new empires to be won.
3. There were young men without places who depended on daring and their swords and were willing to soldier for their fortunes.
4. There were clerks in the countinghouses, impatient of the end-less rows of digits, who thought why should they not reach out for the wealth that set their masters high?
5. There were journeymen without employment and servants with-out situations and peasants without land and many others whom war or pestilence displaced who dreamed in desperation of an alternative to home.

Here the topic sentence about the *diverse group* is followed by a list of sentences identifying the members of the group. Once again, all the sentences in the list follow the same basic pattern, this time taking the form *There were . . . who . . .* Only the last sentence in the paragraph *(Through the eighteenth century their numbers grew and, even more, through the nineteenth)* departs from the pattern to make a statement about all of the migrants. The pattern itself admits variety, with different constructions between *There were* and *who*. But the pattern also ensures that every sentence up to the last marches in step with the paragraph as a whole.

You can also use list structure in a paragraph of comparison and contrast. In the next example, a topic sentence about law and medicine is followed by a list of contrasts between them:

TOPIC SENTENCE: Though law and medicine are both demanding professions, medicine is more demanding than law.

SUPPORTING SENTENCES:
1. For one thing, it takes three years to earn a law degree, but four to earn an M.D., and still more years to become a fully qualified practitioner.
2. [Sentence pair] Second, lawyers always know in advance when they are scheduled to appear in court. But a doctor may be sud-denly called upon at any hour of the day or night.
3. Finally, while a lawyer's mistake can mean the loss of a case, a doctor's mistake can mean the loss of a life.

Here again, all the sentences in the list refer to the key terms in the topic sentence: *medicine* and *law*. As long as every sentence or sentence pair describes a contrast between these two, and as long as the contrast shows that medicine is more demanding than law, the paragraph will be unified. Note too that in a list-structure paragraph, you can strengthen the order of sentences by using sequence tags: *For one thing, Second,* and *Finally*.

EXERCISE 3   Using List Structure

Using list structure, develop the following paragraph by adding at least three more sentences.

TOPIC SENTENCE: Some students are infuriatingly well-organized.

SUPPORTING SENTENCES:
1. They always get their assignments done on time.
2. When the professor calls on them, they always have the right answer.

EXERCISE 4   Using List Structure

Using list structure and sequence tags, develop one of the following paragraphs by adding at least three more contrasts. The contrasts may be presented in single sentences or sentence pairs.

TOPIC SENTENCE: It is better for students to work for a year between high school and college than to go directly from one to the other.

SUPPORTING SENTENCES:
1. For one thing, a year's earnings will pay much more of a student's college expenses than a summer's earnings will.

TOPIC SENTENCE: It is better for students to go directly from high school to college than to interrupt their education with a year of work.

SUPPORTING SENTENCES:
1. For one thing, students who drop out of school for a year often forget how to study. But students who stay in school can improve their studies from one year to the next.

8.2B   Using Chain Structure

Another way of unifying the sentences in a paragraph is to use chain structure. As long as the meaning of each new sentence is linked to that of the sentence before it, the paragraph will hold together. Consider this one:

> The process of learning is essential to our lives. All higher animals seek it deliberately. They are inquisitive and they experiment.

> An experiment is a sort of harmless trial run of some action which we shall have to make in the real world; and this, whether it is made in the laboratory by scientists or by fox-cubs outside their earth. The scientist experiments and the cub plays; both are learning to correct their errors of judgment in a setting in which errors are not fatal. Perhaps this is what gives them both their air of happiness and freedom in these activities.
>
> — Jacob Bronowski, *The Common Sense of Science*

The sentences in this paragraph are like the links in a chain:

TOPIC SENTENCE: The process of learning is essential to our lives.
A. All higher animals seek it deliberately.
  B. They are inquisitive and they experiment.
    C. An experiment is a sort of harmless trial run of some action which we shall have to make in the real world; and this, whether it is made in the laboratory by scientists or by fox-cubs outside their earth.
    D. The scientist experiments and the cub plays; both are learning to correct their errors of judgment in a setting in which errors are not fatal.
    E. Perhaps this is what gives them both their air of happiness and freedom in these activities.

As the lines in the diagram indicate, only the second sentence is directly linked to the topic sentence; each of the others is linked to the one just before it, and would make no sense if it came right after the topic sentence. There are no connecting lines between sentence B and the topic sentence, for example. The link between the first and last sentences of this paragraph is indirect, a result of all the direct links between the intermediate sentences.

For the writer, the advantage of chain structure is that each sentence tends to suggest or generate the next one. The idea of the process of learning leads to the idea of learners *(All higher animals); animals* leads to a comment on what they do *(experiment); experiment* leads to a definition of that term. While a list-structure paragraph stands still, piling up detail to describe its subject or support its point, the chain-structure paragraph shows thought in motion, making associations and discoveries. When you use chain structure, you are not free to forget about the topic sentence entirely, but you are free to experiment, to pursue the trail opened up by your own sentences, and even to discover something you did not foresee when you wrote the topic sentence. When Bronowski started this paragraph with a sentence about the process of learning, did he expect to end it with a sentence about happiness and freedom?

Note too how the sentences are linked together. In sentence A, the pronoun *it* refers to *The process of learning* in the sentence just before. In sentence B, *They* refers to *All higher animals* in sentence A. In sentence C, *experiment* is repeated from sentence B, but has been turned from a verb into a noun, to serve as the subject of the new sentence. Thus the sentences move with both continuity and progression.

EXERCISE 5   Using Chain Structure

Using chain structure, develop the following paragraph by adding at least three more sentences to it. Be sure that each new sentence is linked to the one before it.

> TOPIC SENTENCE: In the next hundred years, the exploration of outer space will undoubtedly change man's relation to the earth.

> A. Earth will be just one of many places where man may choose to live.

8.2C   Combining List Structure and Chain Structure

The following paragraph by a college freshman shows how list structure and chain structure can work together:

> Going home for the Christmas vacation gave me the chance to see my life at college in a new light. At home, relatives and friends asked me how I liked the school and my classmates. I answered most of their questions with one-word responses, but I also questioned myself. Had I made any real friends? Did I like the campus atmosphere? Did I enjoy my courses as well as learn from them? As I thought about these questions, I realized that every one of them had a two-sided answer. I had picked up many acquaintances, but I could not yet call anyone my friend. I liked the general atmosphere of the campus, but disliked its conservative air. I enjoyed my courses, but felt many self-doubts. I had to admit to myself that I had no settled opinion about anything at college. I was still finding my way.

Basically, this paragraph uses a chain structure with two lists attached to it—a list of questions and a list of answers:

TOPIC SENTENCE: Going home for the Christmas vacation gave me the chance to see my life at college in a new light.

A. At home, relatives and friends asked me how I liked the school and my classmates.

   B. I answered most of their questions with one-word responses, but I also questioned myself.

   1. Had I made any real friends?

   2. Did I like the campus atmosphere?

   3. Did I enjoy my courses as well as learn from them?

      C. As I thought about these questions, I realized that every one of them had a two-sided answer.

      1. I had picked up many acquaintances, but I could not yet call anyone my friend.

      2. I liked the general atmosphere of the campus, but disliked its conservative air.

      3. I enjoyed my courses, but felt many self-doubts.

         D. I had to admit to myself that I had no settled opinion about anything at college.

         E. I was still finding my way.

Our explanation of list and chain structure does not apply to all paragraphs, or even all effective paragraphs. A one-sentence paragraph obviously has neither list nor chain structure, and even in paragraphs of many sentences, it is sometimes hard to see either one. But while you will occasionally need to use other ways of organizing paragraphs, the great advantage of these two kinds of structure is that they can help you to generate sentences as well as to keep them together.

EXERCISE 6   Using List and Chain Structure Together

Expand one of the following paragraphs by using a combination of list and chain structure.

TOPIC SENTENCE: Co-ed colleges are better than single-sex colleges.
1. A. For one thing, they promote day-to-day contact between sexes.
   B. This helps young men and women to see each other as human beings—not simply as dates.
2. A. Second, . . .

TOPIC SENTENCE: Single-sex colleges are better than co-ed colleges.
1. A. First of all, they are much more likely to promote a serious atmosphere for work.

B. It is hard for students to work seriously with members of the opposite sex around.

2. A. Second, . . .

8.3 Emphasis

Whether you are using list structure, chain structure, or a combination of both, you need to emphasize the main point of your paragraph. A paragraph without emphasis is baffling: we don't know how to look at it or what to make of it. Emphasis darkens certain lines, makes certain features stand out, and thus helps to define the character of a paragraph as a whole.

How do you emphasize your main point? You can of course underline or italicize it, but aside from these typographical methods (which should be used sparingly), the two most important ways of emphasizing a point are repetition and arrangement.

8.3A   Using Repetition for Emphasis

You may have been told that you should never repeat a word or phrase when you write, that you should scour your brain or your thesaurus for synonyms to avoid using a word or phrase again. That is nonsense. If repetition gets out of control, it will soon become monotonous and boring. But selective repetition can be highly useful.

What is selective repetition? Consider the following paragraphs:

> As a student begins his last year of high school, he may start to wonder what college or university is right for him. He will usually apply to several schools for admission. At ——— College, the student actually exchanges information on himself through his application and other forms and interviews for information about the school. It is through a fair admissions process that ——— College and her candidates for entrance learn a lot about each other. This fair exchange of ideas and insight in the admissions process can be seen through the college's application for admission, the guidance counselor forms, and the alumni interview.   —College freshman

> To me the interview comes as close as possible to being the quintessence of proper admissions procedure. It is a well-known secret (to use a paradox) that one can study for the achievement tests and the S.A.T. From personal experience I also know that schools "pad" grades and that students can receive marvelous grades without one iota of knowledge in a subject. One cannot, however, "fudge" an interview. One can buy a new suit and put on false airs, but 999 times out of 1,000 the interviewer can easily unmask the fraud and can thus reveal the true person.   —College freshman

Both of these paragraphs use repetition, but only one of them uses it selectively. In the first paragraph, repetition gets out of control. The writer uses *admission* twice, *admissions process* twice, *information* twice, *application* twice, *fair* twice, *exchanges* and *exchange*, *interviews* and *interview*. We can understand that the paragraph concerns the process of applying for admission to a college, but with so many words repeated, we cannot tell which word is more important than the others, or what particular point about the admissions process is being made. Using too much repetition is like underlining every word in a sentence or shouting every word of a speech. When everything is emphasized, nothing is.

The other writer makes repetition work by using it sparingly. *Grades* appears once too often, but the only word conspicuously repeated is the key term *interview,* which appears twice, along with *interviewer,* used once. This selective repetition keeps the eye of the reader on the writer's main point.

EXERCISE 7   Using Selective Repetition

Write a paragraph based on the topic sentence "Clothes tell more about the wearer than most people realize." Use selective repetition to emphasize the main point.

8.3B   Using Arrangement for Emphasis

You can emphasize a word by putting it at the beginning or the end of a sentence. Likewise, you can emphasize a point by putting it at the beginning or the end of a paragraph. That is why the first sentence of a paragraph is a good place to state your main point and the last sentence a good place to restate it.

The opening sentence of a paragraph always draws special attention. If you open with a topic sentence that clearly signals where the paragraph is headed, you have already begun to emphasize your main point. After the first sentence, the reader's attention moves toward the ends of the sentences and the end of the paragraph as a whole. In the paragraph on law and medicine (p. 150) the writer emphasizes the main point—that medicine is more demanding than law—by placing it at the end of each sentence or sentence pair:

> TOPIC SENTENCE: Though law and medicine are both demanding professions, medicine is more demanding than law.
> 1. For one thing, it takes three years to earn a law degree, but four to earn an M.D., and still more years to become a fully qualified practitioner.

To see what a difference arrangement makes, consider these two ways to arrange the pair of sentences coming next in the paragraph on law and medicine:

A doctor may be suddenly called upon at any hour of the day or night. But lawyers always know in advance when they are scheduled to appear in court.

Lawyers always know in advance when they are scheduled to appear in court. But a doctor may be suddenly called upon at any hour of the day or night.

In any pair of sentences linked by a transitional *But,* the second sentence has the emphasis.

Still another way of emphasizing a point is to repeat it at the end of the paragraph:

... a doctor's mistake can mean the loss of a life. All things considered, therefore, medicine is a more demanding profession than law.

8.4 Coherence ¶ *coh*

Coherence is the verbal thread that ties each new sentence in a paragraph to the one before it. When a paragraph is coherent, the reader can see a continuous line of thought passing from one sentence to the next. When a paragraph is incoherent, the sentences are discontinuous, and readers may lose their way. This is why effective paragraphs have coherence as well as unity.

To see the difference between coherence and unity, compare the following brief passages:

1. The process of learning is essential to our lives. All higher animals seek it deliberately. They are inquisitive and they experiment. An experiment is a sort of harmless trial run of some action which we shall have to make in the real world; ...

2. I enjoy watching my son grow up. Children are a tremendous challenge. I read to him and try to let him be as creative as possible.

Both passages are unified. All sentences in passage 1 refer to the process of learning, and all sentences in passage 2 refer to child-rearing. But though both passages are unified, only the first is fully coherent. Only the first—as we have already seen on p. 152—ties each new sentence to the one before it.

In the second passage, the thread of coherence breaks. While *Children* in the second sentence clearly recalls *my son* in the first, with the writer moving from the particular to the general term, the third sentence abruptly returns to the particular. To understand what *him* refers to, we have to jump back over the general sentence about *Children* to the particular sentence about *my son.* So the line of connection is broken.

EXERCISE 8   **Providing Coherence**

Rearrange the following sentences to make a coherent passage.

> I enjoy watching my son grow up. Children are a tremendous challenge. I read to him and try to let him be as creative as possible.

8.5   Using Transitional Words within Paragraphs
trans wp

Transitional words and phrases enhance the coherence of a paragraph by signaling one of the following relations between one sentence and another:

1. Time

> Technology makes life easier for everyone. *A hundred years ago* a man would have to take a horse-drawn carriage to deliver his produce to market. *Now* he can drive a truck.   —College freshman

Other words that signal time are *previously, earlier, in the past, before, at present, nowadays, meanwhile, later, in the future, eventually.*

2. Addition

> Different as they were—in background, in personality, in underlying aspiration—[Grant and Lee] had much in common. Under everything else, they were marvelous fighters. *Furthermore,* their fighting qualities were really very much alike.
> —Bruce Catton, *A Stillness at Appomattox*

Other words that signal addition are *besides, moreover, in addition.*

3. Contrast or conflict

> At many universities across the country, more than half the students in each entering class plan on entering "med" school. *But* there just aren't enough spaces for them.   —College freshman

Other words that indicate contrast or conflict are *nevertheless, however, conversely, on the other hand, still, otherwise, in contrast, unfortunately.*

4. Cause and effect

> The world of religion and philosophy was shocked recently when Henry P. Van Dusen and his wife ended their lives by their own hand. Dr. Van Dusen had been president of Union Theological Seminary; for more than a quarter-century he had been one of the luminous names in Protestant theology. He enjoyed world status as a spiritual leader. News of the self-inflicted deaths of the Van Dusens,

therefore, was profoundly disturbing to all those who attach a moral stigma to suicide and regard it as a violation of God's laws.

—Norman Cousins, "The Right to Die"

Other words that indicate cause and effect are *hence, as a result, consequently, accordingly.* Don't use *thus* to mean *therefore; thus* means *in that manner.*

5. Comparison

Geniuses have an uncanny power to defy physical handicaps. John Milton was blind when he wrote the greatest of English epics, *Paradise Lost. Likewise,* Beethoven was deaf when he composed some of his greatest symphonies.

Another word that indicates comparison is *similarly.*

6. Numerical order

Churchill had many reasons for cooperating with Stalin during the Second World War. *For one,* Stalin was battling the Germans on the Eastern front and thus reducing German pressure on England. *Second,* Russia had power, and in the face of German aggression, England needed powerful allies. *Finally,* Churchill's hatred of Hitler consumed all other feelings. Though Stalin made him uneasy, Churchill said once that to destroy Hitler, he would have made a pact with the devil himself.

Among words that indicate numerical order are *first, second, third; in the first place, in the second place, in the third place; to begin with, next, finally.* But use these words and phrases sparingly. A succession of numbered sentences soon becomes boring.

7. Spatial order

The once-a-year sale had apparently drawn just about everyone in town to Gerry's department store. *At left,* the three-acre parking lot was jammed with cars, motorcycles, and pickup trucks. *At right,* a line of people stretched down Main Street for six blocks.

Other words that indicate spatial order are *nearby, in the distance, below, above, in back, in front.*

EXERCISE 9 Making Transitions within Paragraphs

At one or more points in each of the following passages a transitional word or phrase is missing. Find the points and insert suitable transitions.

The group that led the campaign against gay rights in Florida held the belief that homosexuality is immoral and that, once allowed in an area, it would lead to a breakdown of the values of a society. Homosexuality has existed throughout the past. Some of the world's greatest geniuses have professed to be homosexuals. These men have made great contributions to society. Whether one agrees that their practices were immoral or not, one must respect the contributions of men such as Michelangelo and Tchaikovsky. —College freshman

2. Higher education in America has recently hit a new low. In liberal-arts colleges, the abolition of many or even all specific requirements for graduation has left students to find their own way, which is too often a closed alley. Allowed to take any courses they want, many students concentrate on just one subject or specialized skill. They graduate with narrow minds.

3. Revolution and moderation seldom go hand in hand. In the early years of the French revolution, the moderate Girondists were outmaneuvered by the bloodthirsty Jacobins, who launched a reign of terror. Within months after the moderate Mensheviks launched the Russian revolution of 1917, the radical Bolsheviks seized power and established a government of ruthless repression.

4. In the seventeenth century, a voyage across the Atlantic took more than two months. A supersonic plane does the trip in three hours.

8.6 Paragraphing in Action—Rearranging Sentences

Now that you have seen how good paragraphs are put together, let's return to the one that needs major reconstruction—the one by the college freshman who is also a wife and mother:

[1] My life has been a very satisfying one so far. [2] I've faced many challenges and attained some of the goals I've set. [3] I am one of five children. [4] I have two older sisters and two younger brothers. [5] My father was a successful chef. [6] He had a college degree in electrical engineering, but chose to study cooking instead. [7] He traveled in Europe and worked with many different chefs. [8] He had a great influence on all of our lives. [9] He showed me what determination and hard work could do for a person. [10] My mother was a good mother. [11] She guided me in a very practical way. [12] I was able to learn and grow under their supervision. [13] At times, it's hard to attain confidence in some situations, but I think of my parents and continue on. [14] I enjoy knitting and making things for others and I also love to cook. [15] Preparing economical meals is a constant challenge. [16] I like to read a lot. [17] I also enjoy watching my son grow up. [18] Children are a tremendous challenge. [19] I read to him and try to let him be as creative as possible. [20] I have also helped my husband go through his last year of college. [21] It was a proud moment for me to watch him walk up and get his degree. [22] I enjoyed working with him and learning as he did. [23] You really get a good feeling when you've helped someone. [24] Your rewards are twofold. [25] Helping others is my main goal in life. [26] I enjoy people. [27] So far,

my life has been satisfactory to me. [28] I've got future goals set to attain. [29] I've got lots of hard work ahead of me. [30] I just look forward to going day by day and getting further toward my one goal of a college education with a challenging job.

Rereading these sentences in the light of what you know about paragraph structure, you may see that there is matter here for at least two paragraphs: one on the writer's childhood and the influence of her parents, the other on her life and goals as a wife, mother, and college student. This division in the material becomes obvious if you examine the links between the sentences. The first sentence looks like a topic sentence, and the second is connected to it, but the third sentence has nothing to do with *challenges* and *goals*, and not until sentence 15 does either of those words appear again. Sentences 3–13 are really a detour from the road that the first two sentences open up, and therefore need to be taken out and reorganized under a topic sentence of their own.

Sentences 3–13 can be used to make a paragraph because they all concern the same topic—the writer's childhood and her parents. But to develop a paragraph from these sentences, the writer will first have to identify one of them as a topic sentence, a sentence that states the main point of the whole group. A likely candidate is sentence 12: *I was able to learn and grow under their supervision.* To make this sentence work at the beginning of the paragraph, the writer will have to change *their* to *my parents'.* She will then have the start of a paragraph:

I was able to learn and grow under my parents' supervision.

Now see how this topic sentence can help the writer organize the other sentences in the 3–13 group:

TOPIC SENTENCE: I was able to learn and grow under my parents' supervision.

3. I am one of five children.
4. I have two older sisters and two younger brothers.
5. My father was a successful chef.
6. He had a college degree in electrical engineering, but chose to study cooking instead.
7. He traveled in Europe and worked with many different chefs.
8. He had a great influence on all of our lives.
9. He showed me what determination and hard work could do for a person.
10. My mother was a good mother.
11. She guided me in a very practical way.
13. At times, it's hard to attain confidence in some situations, but I think of my parents and continue on.

There are still some problems here. The topic sentence forecasts a discussion of the writer's parents, but sentences 3 and 4 concern her brothers and sisters. Though the brothers and sisters are obviously related to the writer's parents, they are not connected with her parents' supervision of her, or—except in the phrase *our lives* (sentence 8)—with their influence on her. When sentences 3 and 4 are cut out, you actually begin to see a paragraph taking shape:

> I was able to learn and grow under | my parents' | supervision.
> 5. My ⟨father⟩ was a successful chef.

The writer now has a definite link between the topic sentence and the one that follows it. In fact, she has the beginnings of a paragraph combining list structure and chain structure:

> TOPIC SENTENCE: I was able to learn and grow under my parents' supervision. [formerly sentence 12]
>
> 1. A. My father had a great influence on my life. [8, with *all of our lives* changed to *my life*]
>   B. He showed me what determination and hard work could do for a person. [9]
>   C. He had a college degree in electrical engineering, but chose to study cooking instead. [6]
>   D. He traveled in Europe and worked with many different chefs. [7]
>   E. He was a successful chef. [5]
> 2. A. My mother was a good mother. [10]
>   B. She guided me in a very practical way. [11]
>
> CONCLUDING SENTENCE: At times, it's hard to attain confidence in some situations, but I think of my parents and continue on. [13]

This is now a paragraph: a sequence of sentences that are all related to the topic sentence. The words *parents* in the topic sentence leads to a list of two basic sentences, one about the father and one about the mother, and each of the two sentences in the list leads to its own chain of related sentences. *My father* in sentence 1A is linked to *He* in sentence 1B, and *hard work* in sentence 1B is linked to *study cooking* in sentence 1C. In turn, *study cooking* leads to *worked with many different chefs* in sentence 1D, which then leads to *successful chef* in sentence 1E. The second sentence in the list, the one about the mother, leads to just one other sentence (2B), and the paragraph concludes with an echo of its topic sentence, a restatement of its main idea.

With the basic structure of the paragraph established, the writer can improve it further by adding transitional words and combining some of the sentences. Both of these steps will strengthen the connections between the sentences, and in addition, the sentence combining will break the monotony of too many short, simple constructions. In the following revision, the new words are italicized:

> Topic Sentence: I was able to learn and grow under my parents' supervision.
>
> 1. A. My father had a great influence on me *because* he showed me what determination and hard work could do for a person.
>   B. He had a college degree in electrical engineering, but chose to study cooking instead, traveling in Europe and working with many different chefs.
>   C. He *thus became* a successful chef *himself.*
> 2. A. My mother was a good mother *who* guided me in a very practical way.
>
> Concluding Sentence: At times, it's hard to attain confidence in some situations, but I think of my parents and continue on.

There is still room for development in this paragraph. To balance the chain of sentences about the father, the writer might say more about the mother, explaining how she gave guidance and what she taught. Specific statements here would enrich the paragraph and clarify the meaning of the topic sentence.

Shaping the rest of the original passage into paragraph form is harder. For one thing, there is no obvious topic sentence. Nearly all of the other sentences concern the writer's challenges and goals, but no one sentence on this subject covers the rest in the way that sentence 12 covers sentences 5–13. The writer speaks of past goals in sentences 1–2, 20–24, and 27, of present challenges and satisfactions in sentences 14–19 and 26, and of future goals in sentences 28–30. Most revealingly, she does not seem to know whether her main goal is helping others (sentence 25) or helping herself (sentence 30), or what the relation between those two goals might be. Before she can write a coherent paragraph on her goals, she will have to do some more thinking and decide just what they are.

For paragraphing is inseparable from thinking. You can study the way other writers put sentences together, and you can learn some of the ways by which sentences are connected, but you cannot get from someone else a knowledge of your own thoughts and attitudes—a sense of your own direction. The principles of paragraph structure cannot lead you to that. But they can help you to find your direction and to compose unified, coherent paragraphs once you have clarified your thoughts.

EXERCISE 10   Expanding a Paragraph

Expand the final version of the paragraph given on p. 163 by inserting at least two sentences about the mother after sentence 2. A.

EXERCISE 11   Forming a Paragraph

Choose a topic sentence from the following list and rearrange the remaining sentences to complete a paragraph, combining them and adding words where necessary.

1. The burglary was discovered.
2. The Watergate scandal showed how extensive political corruption can be.
3. High officials at the White House tried to block a full investigation of the burglary and thereby incriminated themselves.
4. In the presidential campaign of 1972, men working for the reelection of the president tried to burglarize a building in order to get information about their political rivals.
5. For the first time in history, the president of the United States was forced to resign in disgrace.
6. Investigators discovered wrongdoing by the president himself.

EXERCISE 12   Forming a Paragraph

Choose a topic sentence from the following list and rearrange the remaining sentences to complete a paragraph, combining them and adding words where necessary.

1. The announcement of this principle led scientists in the United States and Great Britain to test and prove it by various devices.
2. The zoetrope was a cylinder covered with images.
3. According to this principle, the human eye retains an image for a fraction of a second longer than the image is present.
4. The principle was announced in 1824 by a British scholar named Peter Mark Roget.
5. One of these was a toy known as a zoetrope.
6. These simple applications of Roget's principle eventually led to the development of the motion picture.
7. Motion pictures originated from the discovery of the principle known as the persistence of vision.
8. Another device was a small book of drawings that seemed to move when flipped by the thumb.
9. The motion picture is actually a rapid succession of still pictures put together by the persistence of vision in the eye.
10. The images merged into a single picture when the cylinder was rapidly spun.

8.7 Leading Up to the Main Point

We have so far been looking at the paragraph that states its main point in the opening sentence. But there are often good reasons for delaying the main point, holding it back until after the first sentence or even saving it to the very end. Here are two alternatives to the "main point" opening.

8.7A The Concessive Opening

If you are writing an argumentative paragraph on a controversial topic, any position you take will probably meet resistance from some of your readers. You cannot defend or attack such things as abortion, capital punishment, gun control, the legalization of pot, or the lowering of the drinking age without stirring objections. In an argumentative paragraph, therefore, it is good strategy to begin by recognizing those objections, by letting readers on the other side know that you understand their point of view. You thus increase the chances that they will come to understand yours. (For a full discussion of this point, see section 7.7A.)

8.7B Putting the Main Point at the End

Put the main point at the end if you want to present it as a conclusion to the paragraph as a whole:

> Comparisons of men and women often involve physical ability. Why can't a woman lift as much as Vassily Alexyov? Where is the woman who can throw a ball like Joe Namath? But women too can tell of their superstars. Didn't Billy Jean King beat Bobby Riggs in a game of tennis? Does anyone skate more beautifully than Peggy Fleming? When all games have been played and all contests completed, a standoff appears. Men excel in some sports and women in others. There seem to be no superiorities in the battle of the sexes.　　　　　—College freshman

The writer begins with a general indication of what the paragraph will do—compare men and women physically. But not until the last three sentences does he plainly state his main point: men and women are equally successful in athletics. By saving this point to the end of the paragraph, the writer clearly indicates that it is a conclusion.

EXERCISE 13　Ending a Paragraph with a Conclusion

The final sentence of the following paragraph has been deleted. In place of the missing sentence, write a sentence of your own that could serve as a conclusion.

Although Oberlin admitted women in 1837, and Elmira Female College was founded in 1855, American higher education remained a virtually all-male affair until after the Civil War. Not only were women thought generally incapable of intellectual self-discipline and rigor, but the attempt to impose it on them was thought debilitating to both mind and body. (This may not have been wholly delusory, given the character of nineteenth-century academic life.) The men who controlled job opportunities had no interest in hiring women in any but menial roles, and men looking for wives were also unlikely to be impressed by a girl's educational qualifications. . . .

—Christopher Jencks and David Riesman, *The Academic Revolution*

8.8 Making Transitions between Paragraphs
trans bp

A good essay is more than a collection of separate paragraphs. It is made up of connected paragraphs, paragraphs linked to each other not only by the logic of what they have to say but by transitions between them. Much of what you already know about linking sentences within paragraphs can also be used to link paragraphs to each other. Here are three ways to do so.

1. Use a transitional word or phrase:

Boston today can still provide a fairly stimulating atmosphere for the banker, the broker, for doctors and lawyers. "Open end" investments prosper, the fish come in at the dock, the wool market continues, and workers are employed in the shoe factories in the nearby towns. For the engineer, the physicist, the industrial designer, for all the highly trained specialists of the electronic age, Boston and its area are of seemingly unlimited promise. Sleek, well-designed factories and research centers pop up everywhere; the companies plead, in the Sunday papers, for more chemists, more engineers, and humbly relate the executive benefits of salary and pension and advancement they are prepared to offer.

But otherwise, for the artist, the architect, the composer, the writer, the philosopher, the historian, for those humane pursuits for which the town was once noted and even for the delights of entertainment, for dancing, acting, cooking, Boston is a bewildering place. . . .   —Elizabeth Hardwick, "Boston: The Lost Ideal"

The single word *But* nicely marks the transition from a paragraph about the attractions of Boston to one about what it lacks. (Transitional words and phrases are listed and discussed on pp. 158–60.)

2. Start a new paragraph by answering one or more questions raised in the one before:

Married or single, working or not working today, women must begin to think in terms of a basic choice: Public role and private role—which is the more important? In an emergency which would you sacrifice? If your child was sick or unhappy, would you leave him in someone else's care, as a man must do? If your husband's job took him to another country, would you give up a promising career to go with him? Would you go far away from friends and relatives for your career?

However important, responsible and fulfilling a woman's work may be, the answer is quite predictable. Most women put their families first. And few will think them wrong. This is the choice women have been brought up to make and men have been taught to expect. It is the unusual woman, the woman wholly committed to her career or an impersonal goal, on whom criticism descends.

—Margaret Mead, "Women: A House Divided"

The first paragraph poses several questions stating choices women must make, and the second paragraph supplies an answer to those questions: *Most women put their families first.* The question-and-answer form makes the transition automatically, with no need for transitional words.

3. Start a new paragraph by echoing a key word or recalling a key idea from the one before:

There are days when I find myself unduly pessimistic about the future of man. Indeed, I will confess that there have been occasions when I swore I would never again make the study of time a profession. My walls are lined with books expounding its mysteries; my hands have been split and rubbed raw with grubbing into the quicklime of its waste bins and hidden crevices. I have stared so much at death that I can recognize the lingering personalities in the faces of skulls and feel accompanying affinities and repulsions.

One such skull lies in the lockers of a great metropolitan museum. It is labeled simply: Strandlooper, South Africa. I have never looked longer into any human face than I have upon the features of that skull. I come there often, drawn in spite of myself. It is a face that would lend reality to the fantastic tales of our childhood. There is a hint of Wells' *Time Machine* folk in it—those pathetic, childlike people whom Wells pictures as haunting earth's autumnal cities in the far future of the dying planet.

—Loren Eiseley, "Man of the Future"

Here the repetition of *skull* at the beginning of the second paragraph links the two paragraphs together and marks the transition

Making Transitions between Paragraphs **167**

from a general discussion of death to some thoughts about a particular skull.

You can also link paragraphs by means of a key idea, as Margaret Mead does in her essay "Women: A House Divided":

> . . . This is the choice women have been brought up to make and men have been taught to expect. It is the unusual woman, the woman wholly committed to her career or an impersonal goal, on whom criticism descends.
>
> Up to the present the dilemma is one most women have managed to avoid. One way of doing it has been by defining their work as an adjunct to their personal lives. Even today, when over one third of the women living in husband-wife homes—about 15 million married women—are working, this remains true. The kinds of positions women hold and the money they are paid are, at least in part, a reflection of women's own definitions of the place of work in their lives and of the reciprocal belief among men that giving a woman a career job is a high risk.

A *dilemma* is a difficult choice, and though *dilemma* itself does not appear in the previous paragraph, it echoes the sense of the key word *choice,* which does. It also supplies a shade of meaning that is important to Mead's discussion and that the neutral word *choice* does not have.

An effective paragraph, then, is a group of sentences that usually has both internal and external connections. Internally, the paragraph must be unified and coherent, with sentences that have some topic in common, and with a line of thought leading from one sentence to the next. Externally, a paragraph that is part of an essay should look back to what has preceded it even as it breaks new ground. Thus it will serve to guide the reader from one point to another.

EXERCISE 14   Making Transitions between Paragraphs

1. In the following passage, one or more words at the beginning of the second paragraph have been deleted. Use a transitional word or phrase to clarify the shift between the two paragraphs.

   > As children growing up in a small town, my brother and I were the only ones whose father was "different." He couldn't sing the national anthem or remember the words of the Pledge of Allegiance and found it difficult to comprehend the intricacies of football and baseball.
   >
   > . . . he was a very special parent. On rainy days he was always waiting for us at the school door, rubbers in hand; if we were ill he was there to take us home. He worked in town and was available to take us to music and dancing lessons or on little drives. When I was

a small child he planted beside my window a beautiful oak tree that grew to be taller than our home.

—Janet Heller, "About Morris Heller,"
The New York Times, May 7, 1976

2. In the following passage, we have deleted the first sentence of the second paragraph and the first two sentences of the third. For each of those paragraphs write one or two opening sentences to clarify the transition from one paragraph to the next.

> Outside, in our childhood summers—the war. The summers of 1939 to '45. I was six and finally twelve; and the war was three thousand miles to the right where London, Warsaw, Cologne crouched huge, immortal under nights of bombs or, farther, to the left where our men (among them three cousins of mine) crawled over dead friends from foxhole to foxhole towards Tokyo or, terribly, where there were children (our age, our size) starving, fleeing, trapped, stripped, abandoned.
>
> . . . A shot would ring in the midst of our play, freezing us in the knowledge that here at last were the first Storm Troopers till we thought and looked—Mrs. Hightower's Ford. And any plane passing overhead after dark seemed pregnant with black chutes ready to blossom. There were hints that war was nearer than it seemed—swastikaed subs off Hatteras or the German sailor's tattered corpse washed up at Virginia Beach with a Norfolk movie ticket in his pocket.
>
> . . . Our deadly threats were polio, being hit by a car, drowning in pure chlorine if we swam after eating. No shot was fired for a hundred miles. (Fort Bragg—a hundred miles.) We had excess food to shame us at every meal, excess clothes to fling about us in the heat of play. . . .
>
> —Reynolds Price, *Permanent Errors*

9

CHOOSING WORDS

To speak or to write is to choose words. In speaking and in the early stages of writing, you often choose them unconsciously. But to write effectively, you must choose them consciously. You must think about the words you use, their shades of meaning, and their effect on your readers. That is what this chapter aims to help you do.

9.1 Choosing Levels of Diction *d*

Good writing is made of words that suit its subject and its expected audience. As you write, you constantly need to make choices among words that have similar meanings but different effects on people. The words you choose are called your **diction,** and the choices you make establish your **level of diction**—that is, your level of formality. This may be high, low, in the middle, or mixed.

9.1A Middle Level

To see how the middle level of diction is set and maintained, consider this passage from an essay written for a college course:

> Fears based on ignorance can sometimes be conquered by scientific
> fact. In 1938 a radio program called *War of the Worlds* actually ter-

rified large numbers of Americans by pretending to report that the earth was being invaded by men from Mars. But as we now know from unmanned exploration of Mars itself, the idea that "Martians" could invade the earth is ——.

As is right for a piece on a serious subject aimed at an intelligent and somewhat critical audience (the instructor), this passage is formal rather than casual in tone. Words such as *conquered, invaded,* and *exploration* establish a level of diction that is clearly above the colloquial. But the diction is not highly formal; this passage comes from a term paper, not a State of the Union address. It is written at the middle level of diction, the normal level for most college and professional writing, the level consistent with Standard English (as defined on pp. 4–6).

What, then, should the last word be? Here are some words that would fit the meaning of the passage. Choose one:

insupportable
preposterous
incredible
ludicrous
groundless
absurd
silly
false
crazy
loony
bull

A quick glance down the list should make you see that these eleven words descend through several levels of diction, from the stately, many-syllabled formality of *insupportable* through the informality of *crazy* to the outright slanginess of *bull*. If you chose a word from the middle of the list—*ludicrous, groundless, absurd, silly* or *false*—you chose sensibly, for these words are all at the middle level of diction, and can fit into most contexts without seeming either coarse or pretentious, too low or too high. Slang words like *loony* and *bull* may be all right in conversation, but they do not suit a formal discussion of human fears, and the odds are they will not suit the audience either. So why not *insupportable,* from the top of the list? This word is impressively long, but its very length makes it carry more weight than most sentences can bear, and seasoned writers do not use long words just to impress their readers. In this case, the meaning of *insupportable* can readily be conveyed by a shorter word such as *groundless.*

As you move toward the middle of the list, choosing becomes harder. The words from *ludicrous* to *false,* all from the middle level of diction, differ not so much in formality as in the shades of their meaning, which are discussed below in section 9.3 (p. 178).

9.1B   High or Formal Level

Though the middle level of diction is the one to use in most of your college and professional writing, some occasions call for high formality. Consider this passage:

> We dare not forget today that we are the heirs of that first revolution. Let the word go forth from this time and place, to friend and foe alike, that the torch has been passed to a new generation of Americans—born in this century, tempered by war, disciplined by a hard and bitter peace, proud of our ancient heritage, and unwilling to witness or permit the slow undoing of those human rights to which this Nation has always been committed, and to which we are committed today at home and around the world.
> —John F. Kennedy, Inaugural Address

Kennedy's language is marked by stately words: *heirs, generation, heritage, witness.* He is delivering a presidential speech on a ceremonial occasion, and that requires language of high formality.

9.1C   Informal or Low Level

On the other hand, readers sometimes expect a writer to use slang—in sports reporting, for example:

> Baker led off the ninth with a scorcher into the right-field corner, and took second when Bailey bobbled the ball. Muzio caught Lehmann looking at a slider on the outside corner, but Tetrazzini clouted the next delivery into the upper deck. In the bottom of the inning Tom Stewart retired the Sox in order to ice the win.

9.1D   Mixed Levels—Pro and Con

The passages in 9.1B and 9.1C show the extremes, and ordinarily you should steer a middle course. But even when you are choosing most of your words from the middle level of diction, you may occasionally need a highly formal word, or—on the other hand—a piece of slang:

> In Moulmein, in Lower Burma, I was hated by large numbers of people—the only time in my life that I have been important enough for this to happen to me. I was sub-divisional police officer of the town, and in an aimless, petty kind of way anti-European feeling was very bitter. No one had the guts to raise a riot, but if a Euro-

pean woman went through the bazaars alone somebody would probably spit betel juice over her dress.

—George Orwell, "Shooting an Elephant"

Guts is slang, but it is not hard to see why Orwell chose to use it in this passage of otherwise middle-level diction. Unlike the passage on the Martians, this one involves violent feelings. *Guts* therefore seems right here; it has bite and pungency. These qualities are reinforced by the word *spit,* which is not quite slang, but works together with *guts* to define and vivify the abstract phrase *anti-European feeling.*

One reason the slang is effective here is that Orwell has used it sparingly and with a specific purpose in mind. If you overuse slang, your writing will begin to sound like this:

> When I got out of high school I figured I wouldn't start college right off because books were giving me bad vibes at the time and I wanted to get my head together first.

Just as bad is a sentence that suddenly lurches into slang with no good reason for doing so:

> When I finished high school, I decided not to enter college immediately because academic work was giving me bad vibes.

In formal writing, therefore, use slang sparingly, or not at all:

> When I finished high school, I decided not to enter college immediately because I just couldn't stomach any more academic work.

The verb *stomach* has plenty of force; you could also use *swallow* or simply *take.* None of these words is slang, but each of them gives most readers a stronger and more specific sense of the writer's feelings than does *bad vibes.* The more you write, the more you will find variety and power within the middle range of diction.

EXERCISE 1   Making Diction Consistent

Some of the following sentences are marred by slang. Rewrite each sentence in which you think the diction is not consistently what it should be. If any entry is acceptable as it stands, write *No change needed.*

EXAMPLE
After learning that she had caught pneumonia, Emily decided not to make the scene at David's party.
REVISED: After learning that she had caught pneumonia, Emily decided not to attend [or "not to go to"] David's party.

1. My sister wants to become a commercial-airline pilot because she has a thing about planes.
2. Grover White has been a loyal alumnus of Cowbell College because of all the pals he made there.

3. Because I messed up the midterm examination in European history, I may fail the course.
4. The variety of courses offered at Wintergreen University enables most students to enroll in classes that turn them on.
5. The best thing about taking a long run on a hot day is the feel of a cool shower afterward.
6. Employees with legitimate gripes about the working conditions in the plant should speak with their supervisor.
7. Since Jack sometimes drives recklessly, I get uptight whenever he gives me a ride.
8. Successful students have a knack for being on the ball at the right times.
9. To leave school before you have learned how to read and write is to shortchange yourself and blow your chance of entering a rewarding profession.
10. Peeved by his insults, she poured a glass of orange juice over his head.

EXERCISE 2   Making Diction Consistent

Revise the following passage to eliminate any unjustified slang or excessive formality in its diction.

> While I'm complaining, let me mention another gripe about New York. It's impossible to get a haircut here! When I inhabited a house in the town of Rye, I had a terrific barber, a person who, every month or so, would give me a straightforward trim for $3.50, a
> 5 price which was reasonable in my opinion. He always cut my tresses exactly as I wanted him to, and he never suggested that a different style would be more beneficial. I like simple haircuts but have yet to get one in the five months I've been attending Columbia University, which is right here in New York City. It is my considered opin-
> 10 ion that all of the barbers left town years ago, to be replaced by hair stylists, as they label themselves, men who use scissors on a man's locks in the way bad sculptors use their mitts to put soft clay into some kind of shape. If I present a request for a simple trim, these bums spray my head with water, comb my hair in every direction
> 15 but the right one, grab tufts, and start hacking. They try to layer it in ways only a high-priced fashion model could ever want; and they leave the sideburns raw, claiming that's how men of taste want them. Then they plug in their damned hair dryers and blow up the mess they've made. In conclusion, they have the effrontery to submit a
> 20 bill for a monetary sum in excess of $10. You can't win.

9.2   Using the Dictionary

You learn what words mean and how to use them by reading and listening to others speak. You can also learn about words by using a good dictionary—the indispensable tool of a good writer.

Abridged dictionaries suitable for college use include *The Ameri-*

can *Heritage Dictionary of the English Language, Funk and Wagnalls Standard College Dictionary, Webster's Ninth New Collegiate Dictionary, Webster's New World Dictionary of the American Language,* the *Oxford American Dictionary,* and *The Random House College Dictionary.* In addition, your college library probably has one or more of the major unabridged dictionaries—*The Random House Dictionary of the English Language,* The *Oxford English Dictionary,* and *Webster's Third New International Dictionary of the English Language.*

Words are useless, even dangerous, if you don't know what they mean or how they are used. To show you just what a dictionary can tell you about a word—even about a word you use often—here is a sample entry from *The American Heritage Dictionary:*

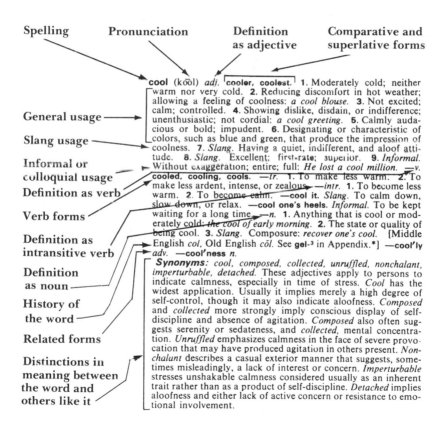

1. Spelling, syllable division, pronunciation. You already know how to spell and pronounce a one-syllable word like *cool,* but what about a longer word, such as *government?* The definition of this word begins "**gov-ern-ment** (gŭv′ərn-mənt)." With the word broken into three syllables, you can tell where to divide it when you need to hyphenate it at the end of a line. The version of the word in parentheses tells you to pronounce it with the accent on the first syllable (gŭv′). Here the word is spelled phonetically—that is, according to the way it sounds. The pronunciation key at the beginning of the dictionary (and at the bottom of each page) explains that ŭ sounds like the *u* in *cut* and ə sounds like the *e* in *item*.

2. Parts of speech. Like many other words, *cool* can be used in various ways. The abbreviation *adj.* tells you that it is being defined first as an adjective; the entry then goes on to explain what it means when used as a verb (—*v.*) and as a noun (—*n.*). The definition of *cool* as an adjective is given first because that is the way the word is most often used.

3. Forms. For certain parts of speech several forms of the word are given. For example, *adj.* is followed by *cooler* and *coolest,* the comparative and superlative forms of the adjective *cool.* Similarly, —*v.* is followed by the main forms of the verb *cool:* the past participle, *cooled;* the present participle, *cooling;* and the third-person singular for the present tense, *cools.*

4. Definitions. When a word can function in various ways (as adjective or verb, for instance), a separate set of numbered definitions is given for each. Some dictionaries begin with the earliest meaning of the word and then proceed in order to the latest ones, but most dictionaries—like the *American Heritage*—simply begin with the central, commonest meaning of the word, whether or not it is also the earliest. Some definitions are accompanied by examples: *a cool blouse, a cool greeting.*

5. Usage labels. Usage labels help you decide whether the word is suitable for the level of diction you have chosen. Here are the most common of the many possibilities:

WORD	LABEL	MEANING
cool	Informal *or* Colloquial	entire, full
cool	Slang	composure
yclept	Archaic *or* Obsolete	named, called
calculate	Regional *or* Dialect	think, suppose
nowheres	Nonstandard	nowhere

All of these labels identify words or uses of words that are not part of current Standard English. You will also find labels indicating words that are ethnically or technically specialized and will therefore have to be explained for most readers:

WORD	LABEL	MEANING
ganef	Yiddish	thief, rascal
gamophylous	Botany	having united leaves

Most of the time you need usage labels to find out not whether a word is specialized but rather what its level of diction is. As the preceding examples show, the level of diction is often set by the sense in which a word is used. *Cool* is informal only when used to mean "full" ("a cool million"), and slang only when used to mean certain other things, such as "first-rate" ("Jack is a cool guy") or "composure" ("Don't blow your cool").

6. Transitive and intransitive use of the verb. A verb may be transitive (*tr.*), intransitive (*intr.*), or both. After —*tr.* in the sample entry are definitions for *cool* as a transitive verb, one that acts on a direct object (as in "The icy stream cooled the beer"). Under —*intr.* are definitions of *cool* as an intransitive verb, a verb without a direct object (as in "The beer cooled slowly"). Sometimes the abbreviations *v.t.* and *v.i.* are used instead.

7. Etymology. The etymology of the word being defined—its history or derivation—is given in brackets: [ ]. Some dictionaries put it at the beginning of the entry. In our sample it comes near the end of the first part; there we learn that *cool* can be traced to the Old English word *cōl*. "See **gel-**[3] in Appendix" means that under the heading **gel-**[3] in the Appendix to the dictionary (which is now published separately from the dictionary itself), you can find still older roots for the word *cool* in a prehistoric group of languages known as Indo-European. The etymology of a word sometimes includes definitions of its roots. If you look up *calculate*, for instance, you will find that it comes from the Latin word *calculus*, which means "a small stone." (The ancient Romans used small stones for reckoning.)

8. Related forms. A related form is a variation on the form of the word being defined. For *cool,* the related forms include the adverb *coolly* (note the spelling) and the noun *coolness.* Sometimes these related forms have separate entries of their own.

9. Synonyms. To write well, you must know the exact meanings of the words you use so that you can distinguish between those that have similar meanings. In a standard dictionary, entries for some words include definitions of synonyms. To find more synonyms, consult a book like *Webster's New Dictionary of Synonyms.* (A thesaurus provides lists of synonyms, but does not usually define them.)

w

EXERCISE 3   Using New Words

Look up each of the following words in your dictionary, and then write a sentence containing it.

1. ingenuous
2. clandestine
3. diffident
4. flagrant
5. assiduous

6. slake
7. mordant
8. salacious
9. spry
10. venal

9.3   Choosing Words for Their Denotation

The **denotation** of a word is the specific person, object, sensation, idea, action, or condition it signifies or names. Consider again the final sentence about fear of an invasion from outer space:

> But as we now know from unmanned exploration of Mars itself, the idea that "Martians" could invade the earth is ———.

We have said that the blank should be filled with a word from the middle level of diction—from the group of words falling between high formality and slang. But within this category are to be found all of the following: *ludicrous, groundless, absurd, silly, false.* How do you know which of these synonyms to choose? Just as the sky has different shades of blue, synonyms have different shades of meaning. To choose the right word for your purposes, you must know what each one means. From a good dictionary you can learn the following:

Ludicrous means "worthy of scornful laughter."

Groundless means "unsupported by evidence." A *groundless* belief is not necessarily *silly, absurd,* or *ludicrous,* or even *false.* It simply has no basis in what is known.

Absurd means "irrational" or "nonsensical" but not "frivolous"; deadly serious people can sometimes have absurd ideas.

Silly means "frivolous," "foolish," or "thoughtless."

False means "not true." A statement may be *false* without being either *silly, ludicrous,* or *absurd.* It would be *absurd* to say that the first president of the United States was King George III, but merely *false* to say that the first president was Thomas Jefferson.

Learning just what every word denotes is not easy. A good dictionary will give you some help; beyond the dictionary, you must rely on your own experience of the way different words are used in what you read. Whatever else you do, you should develop the habit of discriminating between words, of looking for the shades of difference between words with similar meanings. Then you will know exactly how you want to describe the idea that Martians could invade the earth. Only you can make that final choice. No one else can do it for you.

EXERCISE 4 Choosing Words for Their Denotation

Using a good dictionary where necessary, answer each of the following questions.

> EXAMPLE
> Should you use *fatal* or *deadly* to describe a weapon?
> ANSWER: deadly

1. If your meaning is "annoy continually," should you use *bother* or *harass?*
2. If your meaning is "defy," should you use *flaunt* or *flout?*
3. Should you use *toady* or *flatterer* to mean "someone who lavishly praises another for material gain"?
4. Would you rather be tried by an *uninterested* or a *disinterested* jury?
5. If your meaning is "disapprove strongly," should you use *criticize* or *denounce?*

9.4 Choosing Words for Their Connotation

The **connotation** of a word is the feeling, attitude, or set of associations it conveys. To choose the word that best suits your needs in any given context, you must know how connotation can affect the meaning of a word.

Take for instance *house* and *home.* Both of these denote the same thing: a dwelling place or residence. But their connotations differ sharply. *House* connotes little more than it denotes—a place where people can live—while *home* normally connotes family affection, memories of childhood, and a reassuring sense of welcome.

Precisely because they involve feelings, the connotations of a word are sometimes too personal and variable to be defined. The connotations of *steak,* for instance, will be different for a vegetarian and for a Texas cattleman. Yet many words do have widely accepted connotations, and these determine the electrical charge of a word—positive or negative, favorable or unfavorable, generous or harsh.

Compare the adjectives in each of the following sentences:

> He is ambitious; she is pushy.
> He is tough-minded; she is ruthless.
> He is foresighted; she is calculating.
> He is firm; she is stubborn.
> He is self-respecting; she is egotistical.
> He is persistent; she is nagging.

Each pair of adjectives in these sentences is joined by denotation but split by connotation. The words describing "him" are generous, making him seem ideally suited for high responsibility in business or government. The words describing "her" are loaded with negative connotations, making her seem all but disqualified for any responsibility at all. Loaded language appeals only to readers who themselves are already loaded with the prejudices of the writer. If you want to persuade readers who have various views, you should try to choose words with connotations that are fair to your subject. This does not mean that you must never describe anyone in terms like *pushy, stubborn,* or *ruthless;* it means only that before you use such words, you must be sure your subject deserves them.

EXERCISE 5   Recognizing Connotations

Following are groups of three words alike in denotation but unlike in connotations. Arrange the words so that the one with the most favorable connotation is first and the one with the least favorable connotation is last. If you have trouble arranging them, your dictionary may help you.

EXAMPLE
pushy   ambitious   aggressive
ambitious, aggressive, pushy

1. frugal   stingy   thrifty
2. scent   stench   odor
3. corpulent   fat   plump
4. call   scream   yell
5. firmly   harshly   sternly
6. prejudiced   partial   bigoted
7. slender   emaciated   skinny
8. retreat   flee   depart
9. mistake   blunder   error
10. dull   stupid   unintelligent
11. question   interrogate   ask

EXERCISE 6   Choosing Words by Connotation

Replace the italicized word in each sentence with a word of similar denotation but more favorable connotation.

EXAMPLE
After I showed him my receipt, the store owner admitted his *blunder.*
error

1. Joe's decision to go skydiving reflects his *foolhardy* nature.
2. My uncle *reviled* me for treading on the flowers in his garden.
3. He has a *perverse* way of holding an umbrella.
4. The manager's *timidity* in discussing wages with employees is well known.
5. Professor Branch likes to *ridicule* his lab assistants about their rate of work.
6. Harold has been *shirking* his work at the laboratory.
7. Professor Whimple addressed Benwick in a *harsh* manner.
8. After dieting for a month, Flora has begun to look *skinny.*

9. His *negligent* approach to his studies may lead to disaster.
10. The downing of the airliner was a *barbarous* act.

9.5 Choosing Specific and Concrete Words *vag*

Words range in meaning from the most general to the most specific. If you want to identify something named Fido that runs, barks, and wags its tail, you can call it a *creature,* an *animal,* a *dog,* a *hound,* or a *basset.* Each of the words in this series is more specific than the one before, and each of them has its use:

> Fido is the most lovable *creature* I know.
> Fido is the only *animal* I have ever liked.
> Fido is one of our three *dogs.*
> Fido is the fastest *hound* I've ever seen.
> We have three hounds: a dachshund named Willy, a greyhound named Mick, and a *basset* named Fido.

Almost everything can be classified in several different ways, with words ranging from the very general to the very specific. If someone moves, for instance, you can write that she *moves,* or more specifically that she *walks,* or still more specifically that she *struts.* The range from general to specific may be illustrated as follows:

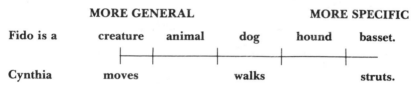

A **concrete** word names something you can see, touch, taste, smell, or hear. Examples are *fingernail, strawberry, sandpaper, smoke, whisper,* or *scream.* An **abstract** word names a feeling *(love),* a state of being *(misery),* an idea *(democracy),* a theory *(evolution),* a field of study *(biology),* or a class of things too broad to be visualized *(creature, plant, organism).* Abstract words sum up the total effect of many particular, concrete things. If you see two people smiling, kissing, and hugging, for instance, you may sum up those concrete actions in the abstract word *love.*

Almost any kind of writing benefits from the power of concrete, specific words. Notice how they are used in this paragraph written by a first-term college freshman:

> She spent several summer segments of her life waitressing at the Wharf by the Madison Beach Hotel, which had a commanding view of Long Island Sound. The restaurant, known for its fine food and friendly service, was a magnet for townies and summer tourists

alike. This clientele included the regulars, elderly who vacationed at the hotel, golfers from the club just up the street, day-trippers, and summer residents. Their common possession was the ability to try the patience of even the most efficient waitress, and she was no exception. Were it not for the lucrative financial rewards, personal challenge, and a chance to gain perspective on the business world and a range of people and problems, she would have stayed only one season. Waitressing was exhausting both mentally and physically for her. She succumbed to the pressure of time and had difficulty retaining her poise. Even so, she did manage to find humor in the sometimes slapstick disasters and near disasters which occur in every restaurant: spilled drinks, broken dishware, and head-on collisions.

This is certainly not a perfect paragraph. Aside from wordy phrases like *summer segments* instead of *summers* and *lucrative financial rewards* instead of *money*, it uses too many abstract or general words—words like *life, challenge, world, people, problems, mentally,* and *physically*. But there are many specific words here as well, beginning with the name of a specific restaurant and ending with a list of specific disasters. Indeed, the final sentence is perhaps the most effective of all. It connects the general word *humor* with the specific word *disasters*, and in turn connects *disasters* with a series of words that are vividly concrete: *spilled drinks, broken dishware,* and *head-on collisions*.

EXERCISE 7 Recognizing General and Specific Words

Following are groups of three words. Arrange the words in order, from the most general to the most specific.

EXAMPLE
walk   go   strut
go, walk, strut

1. sofa   property   furniture
2. poodle   animal   dog
3. whale   creature   mammal
4. dwelling   shelter   cottage
5. pitcher   athlete   ballplayer
6. automobile   Chevrolet   vehicle
7. run   move   sprint
8. meat   pork   food
9. literature   novel   book
10. pain   problem   toothache

EXERCISE 8 Using Concrete Words

For each of the following abstract words, give three concrete words that might be connected with it.

EXAMPLE
love
kiss, smile, hug

1. anger
2. suffering
3. friendship
4. fear
5. contact

EXERCISE 9 Using Specific and Concrete Words

Replace the italicized word in each sentence with a word or phrase that is more specific, more concrete, or both.

EXAMPLE
Janet *spoke* to Tom.
whispered

1 Believing she could win with a strong finish, Harriet *ran* to the finish line.
2. In that climate people who fail to wear hats on a sunny day soon feel *uncomfortable.*
3. Cricket is becoming a popular *activity* in Canada.
4. After George III read a copy of the *paper,* he ordered his generals to suppress the rebellion.
5. I *looked* at the wad of five-dollar bills lying in the gutter.
6. During the race there were three *accidents.*
7. *Defects* in the pavement make driving difficult.
8. On a steaming hot day, nothing tastes so good as a *drink.*
9. On my first day of highway jogging, I stumbled over an *obstruction* and fell flat on my face.
10. Eight hours of heavy lifting made my *body* ache.

9.6 Using Words Figuratively—Simile and Metaphor *fig*

Figurative language enables you to compare something abstract or unfamiliar with something concrete or familiar or both, and thus to make your meaning vividly clear. Consider the following sentences:

1. Boston is like Philadelphia; it lives on its past.
2. My grandmother's house is older than my parents' house.
3. After the mole devoured its prey, it sank into the earth as a submarine sinks into the water.   —Konrad Z. Lorenz, adapted
4. I was put into the game and stuck to my man like glue.
                                                              —College freshman

5. A sleeping child gives me the impression of a traveler in a very far country. —Ralph Waldo Emerson
6. The guide shooed his charges back along the gravel path as if they were chickens, which was what they sounded like.
—Margaret Atwood
7. What does education often do? It makes a straight-cut ditch of a free, meandering brook. —Henry David Thoreau
8. Every muscle in my body ached and cried for mercy.
—College freshman

The first two sentences make ordinary comparisons between two things of the same kind: two cities, two houses. The rest of the sentences make figurative comparisons between two dissimilar things, such as a mole and a submarine.

Figurative comparisons help us visualize the unfamiliar and the abstract. By comparing a mole to a submarine, Lorenz shows readers who may never have seen a mole how quickly and effortlessly it can burrow into the ground. Likewise, by comparing education to ditch-digging, Thoreau makes us see what this abstract process often does. Figurative language gives the reader something to look at, touch, or listen to: a submarine, a traveler, a ditch, a cry, a flock of chickens.

Sentences 3–8 all make figurative comparisons. But you may have noticed a difference in the way those comparisons are made. In sentences 3–6, the writer says that one thing is like another, acts as another does, or gives the impression of another. This type of comparison is called a **simile.** In sentences 7 and 8, the writer says or implies that one thing is another: that education is a ditch-digger, a child's mind is a meandering brook, a muscle is a crying victim. Such a comparison, which is a compressed or intensified version of the simile, is called a **metaphor.**

How do you know when to use a simile and when to use a metaphor? The preceding examples can help to show you. See what happens, for instance, when sentence 3 is changed from a simile to a metaphor:

> SIMILE: After the mole devoured its prey, it sank into the earth as a submarine sinks into the water.
> METAPHOR: After the mole devoured its prey, it was a submarine sinking into the water.

Here the metaphor doesn't work because the earth is not mentioned. The reader cannot readily imagine what the mole was actually doing, and therefore cannot make sense out of the comparison. Now see what happens when sentence 7 is changed from a metaphor to a simile:

METAPHOR: Every muscle in my body ached and cried for mercy.
SIMILE: Every muscle in my body ached and was like a victim crying for mercy.

Here the simile breaks the flow of the sentence. Since the reader can easily imagine who might be crying for mercy, you don't need to specify *victim*. Using the shortcut of the metaphor, you can go straight to *cried*. When the reader cannot imagine a missing element, you have to mention it, and you will probably need a simile. But when the reader can supply the missing element, there is no need to mention it, and you can take full advantage of the intensity and compression that a metaphor provides.

EXERCISE 10   Using Figurative Language

In each of the following sentences, an abstract word or phrase is italicized. Change it to a simile or metaphor.

EXAMPLE
Life is *something to be organized.*
REVISED: Life is like a lump of clay; it is our task to mold it.

1. Travel books are *descriptions* of far-off places.
2. Entering a roomful of strange people is *frightening*.
3. The first week of college is *confusing*.
4. The fat man *moved awkwardly* across the street.
5. The child accepted the story *trustingly*.

9.7   Avoiding Mixed Metaphor   *mix met*

A mixed metaphor is a set of two or more metaphors that do not mesh:

> *When the proposal was made, he smelled a rat, and he set out to nip it in the bud.
> *If we cannot get the deficit under control, the ship of state may soon come to the end of the road.

In the first example, a rat turns into a bud; in the second, a ship turns into something traveling a road. To correct a mixed metaphor, make your metaphors consistent:

> REVISED: When the proposal was made, he smelled a rat, and he set out to trap it.
> REVISED: If we cannot get the deficit under control, the ship of state may soon capsize.

Avoiding Mixed Metaphor   **185**

9.8   Avoiding Clichés   *cli*

Clichés are the old coins of language. Often figures of speech like *busy as a bee,* they once made a striking impression but have since been rubbed smooth by repeated handling. While it is almost impossible to avoid clichés altogether, especially in a rough draft, a proliferation of them will make your writing sound like this:

> *Last but not least,* and *in the final analysis,* we must *face up* to the *pressing dangers* that beset us *at this point in time* and for the *foreseeable future.* We cannot *point with pride* at our *sterling achievements;* we can only *view with alarm* the possibility of a *nuclear holocaust.*

An occasional cliché may slip by unnoticed. But a string of them will make your writing seem stale and second-hand, as if you were incapable of expressing any ideas of your own. You should therefore watch closely for clichés as you reread what you have written. When you spot a cliché, you can sometimes reanimate it by giving it a new twist, as in *Halfway up the ladder of success, she found several rungs missing.* But if you can't give it a new twist, replace the cliché with a carefully chosen word or phrase:

> **At this point in time,* the national debt exceeds one trillion dollars.
> REVISED: The national debt *now* exceeds one trillion dollars.

> **In rural areas doctors are *few and far between.*
> REVISED: In rural areas doctors are *scarce.*

> **Busy as a bee,* the cobbler worked from dawn to sundown every day.
> REVISED: The *industrious* cobbler worked from dawn to sundown every day.

> **Jerry's proposal *hit the nail on the head.*
> REVISED: Jerry's proposal *solved all of our problems.*

EXERCISE 11   Replacing Clichés

Replace every cliché in the following sentences with a well-chosen word or phrase. If a sentence has no cliché, write *Acceptable.*

EXAMPLE
There ought to be a law against sneezing in a movie theatre.
REVISED: People shouldn't sneeze in a movie theatre.

1. The Dean's report sent shock waves through the administration.
2. The North and South simply could not see eye to eye on the question of slavery.
3. After the party, we chewed the fat until the wee hours of the morning.
4. Plotkin's resignation came like a bolt out of the blue.
5. In the final analysis, I decided to take the job.

9.9 Using Idioms

An idiom is an expression that cannot be explained by any rule of grammar but that native speakers of a language customarily use. In English such an expression commonly includes a preposition that varies according to the words that precede or follow it:

> bored *with* television
> tired *of* television
> dependent *on* others
> independent *of* others
> conform *to* the rules
> cooperate *with* the rules
> agree *with* the professor
> agree *to* the change
> agree *on* the terms

No general rule can explain why a particular expression requires one preposition rather than another. If *bored with television* is correct, you might expect that *tired with television* would be correct also, but it is not—simply because custom puts *of* after *tired.*

Though the use of a particular preposition often reflects no more than idiomatic custom, some phrases undergo a change in meaning when the preposition is changed. To differ *with* someone means to disagree with him or her; to differ *from* someone means to be unlike the person in one or more respects. (On this point and on the difference between *compare with* and *compare to,* see the Glossary of Usage.)

If you aren't sure what preposition to use in a particular phrase, check a good dictionary or ask your teacher. (Some dictionaries provide sample sentences containing idioms. One of the best is the *Oxford Advanced Learner's Dictionary of Current English* by A. S. Hornby. Written for students of English as a second language, it contains considerable guidance in the use of prepositions with various nouns, verbs, and adjectives.)

EXERCISE 12 **Choosing Prepositions**

Fill each blank with an appropriate preposition.

EXAMPLE
Some people always complain _____ the weather _____ anyone who will listen.
ANSWER: about, to

1. The first game shattered the coach's confidence _____ Harrelson's ability to pass.
2. The information came _____ an unimpeachable source _____ access _____ the president.

3. Solomon barged ———— the office and insisted ———— speaking ————
the dean ———— once.
4. John demanded to know what happened ———— the children who had
fallen ———— the bridge when it collapsed ———— the river.
5. Crane's disgust ———— her country's racial policies and her hatred ————
its rulers drove her ———— self-imposed exile.

9.10 Avoiding Jargon, Pretentious Words, and Euphemisms

Jargon, pretentious words, and euphemisms can muffle the impact
of a sentence or choke the flow of its meaning. For this reason, you
should generally avoid all three.

9.10A Jargon *jarg*

Jargon is technical terminology. Technical terms belong in writings
on specialized subjects, but they seldom suit essays on subjects of
general interest, especially when ordinary words can be used in
their place. Consider these examples:

> When I asked my parents if I could use the car, the *feedback* was
> *negative.*
> TRANSLATION: When I asked my parents if I could use the car, the
> answer was no. [or] When I asked my parents if I could use the car,
> they said no.

> The student-faculty *interface* has deteriorated since last year.
> TRANSLATION: Student-faculty relations have deteriorated since last
> year.

> Determined to look *upwardly mobile,* the Browns *appropriated* almost
> all of their *limited resources* for a new Mercedes.
> TRANSLATION: Determined to look ambitious, the Browns spent
> almost all they had on a new Mercedes.

> I had no chance to *input* my views.
> TRANSLATION: I had no chance to say what I thought.

If you are writing on a specialized subject for general readers, you
can either explain the technical terms—as is done with *electrode* on
p. 103—or use them in such a way as to make their meanings reasonably clear:

> If we became free of disease, we would make a much better run of
> it for the last decade or so, but might still terminate on about the
> same schedule as now. We may be like the genetically different
> lines of mice . . . programmed to die after a predetermined num-
> ber of days clocked by their genomes. If this is the way it is, some

of us will continue to wear out and come unhinged in the sixth decade, and some much later, depending on genetic timetables.
—Lewis Thomas, "The Long Habit"

The technical term *genomes* is surrounded by words and phrases anyone would know: *die, clocked, wear out, come unhinged.* Even if you have never seen the word *genomes* before, you can figure out roughly what it means here: something inside you, probably having to do with your genes, that may determine how long you are going to live.

9.10B   Pretentious Words   *pret*

Pretentious words and phrases are too long and high-flown for the meaning they actually deliver. Substitute simpler words wherever possible:

> Were it not for the *lucrative financial rewards,* she would have *tendered her resignation.*
> TRANSLATION: Were it not for the money, she would have quit her job.

> *Large-size passenger vehicles utilize excessive quantities of fuel.*
> TRANSLATION: Big cars use too much gas.

> After one bite of the *nongenuine* hamburger, I threw it into the garbage.
> TRANSLATION: After one bite of the fake hamburger, I threw it into the garbage.

9.10C   Euphemisms   *euph*

A *euphemism* is a word or expression that takes the sting out of an unpleasant reality. A euphemism for *dead* is *departed;* a euphemism for the MX missile is *peacekeeper;* euphemisms for *kill* include *eliminate* and *harvest.* Since euphemisms veil the truth instead of stating it openly, you should use them only when plainer words would needlessly hurt the feelings of those you are writing for or about.

If you are writing about people with physical defects, for instance, you may wish to call them *disabled* or *handicapped* rather than *crippled, maimed,* or *club-footed.* A word like *disabled* shows consideration for the feelings of the disabled people themselves. But euphemisms should never be used to hide the truth or to spare the feelings of those who have done wrong. George Orwell gives some telling examples:

> Defenseless villages are bombarded from the air, the inhabitants driven out into the countryside, the cattle machine-gunned, the huts set on fire with incendiary bullets: this is called *pacification.*

Millions of peasants are robbed of their farms and sent trudging along the roads with no more than they can carry: this is called *transfer of population* or *rectification of frontiers*. People are imprisoned for years without trial, or shot in the back of the neck or sent to die of scurvy in Arctic lumber camps: this is called *elimination of unreliable elements*.   —"Politics and the English Language"

Pacification means "bringing peace," but the words that tell what really happened speak of war and destruction. The greater the outrage, the greater the need to hide it with a euphemism.

No absolute rule can tell you that a particular euphemism is right or wrong. You must exercise your own judgment. Irresponsible writers make free use of euphemisms to withhold vital but unpleasant facts. Honest and responsible writers use euphemisms only when plain words might needlessly offend or upset the reader. Good writing is the art of being at once truthful and tactful.

EXERCISE 13   Translating Jargon, Pretentious Words, and Euphemisms into Plain English

The following sentences are disfigured by jargon, euphemisms, or pretentious words. Using your dictionary if necessary, translate each sentence into plain English.

EXAMPLE
The very thought of flying made her paranoid.
TRANSLATION: The very thought of flying frightened her.

1. He was so surprised that he could not verbalize anything.
2. She utilized the telephone continuously.
3. The closing of the factory impacted negatively on the whole town.
4. While waiting in line at the bookstore, I interacted with a couple of sophomores.
5. Maine hunters harvest about 10 percent of the bear population every year.
6. The chief motivating factor for the attack was a desire for revenge.
7. Nonsupportive articulations often discourage grade-school children.
8. After just one week on the job, I was told that my services would no longer be required.
9. Before making her decision, the coach invited input from all members of the team.
10. The defective toys led to a barrage of negative feedback from dissatisfied customers.

9.11 Avoiding Wordiness *wdy*

Wordiness is verbal fat: words and phrases that add nothing but extra weight to sentences that could and should be leaner. To help you cut away the fat, here is one general technique and several specific ones.

9.11A   Identifying the Most Important Words

If you can't figure out how to improve a sentence that sounds wordy, do these two things: (1) Underline the most important words. (2) Make a sentence out of them, using a minimum of linking words. Here is an example:

> It is a matter of the gravest possible importance to the health of anyone with a history of a problem with disease of the heart that he or she should avoid the sort of foods with a high percentage of saturated fats.

1. It is a matter of the gravest possible importance to the health of anyone with a history of a problem with disease of the heart that he or she should avoid the sort of foods with a high percentage of saturated fats.
2. Anyone with a history of heart disease should avoid saturated fats.

9.11B   Avoiding Specific Sources of Wordiness

1. Do not repeat a word unless you need it again for clarity or emphasis:

> a. During their tour of Ottawa, *they saw* the Parliament Buildings and *they saw* the National Art Center.
> REVISED: During their tour of Ottawa, *they saw* the Parliament buildings and the National Art Center.

> b. Of all the different *topics* of controversy, from politics to religion to environmental *questions,* nothing appears to get people so inflamed as those *questions* dealing with sex.
> REVISED: Of all the different *topics* of controversy, from politics to religion to the environment, nothing appears to get people so inflamed as the *topic* of sex.

The revised version cuts out the repetition of *questions,* a word that merely repeats the meaning of *topics.* But for clarity, *topic* is repeated just once, at the end of the sentence.

> c. A college experience that piles *option* on *option* and *stimulation* on *stimulation* merely adds to the contemporary nightmare.
> —Caroline Bird

Here repetition emphasizes the sheer bewildering quantity of things that the college experience may offer. (See also "Using Repetition for Emphasis," section 8.3A, pp. 155–56.)

2. Avoid redundancy—using two or more words that mean essentially the same thing:

a. The defendant was accused of six *illegal crimes.*
REVISED: The defendant was accused of six *crimes.*

b. She spent several *summer segments of her life* waitressing at the Wharf by the Madison Beach Hotel.
REVISED: She spent several *summers* waitressing at the Wharf by the Madison Beach Hotel.

3. In general, avoid starting sentences with *There is, There are,* or *There were:*

a. *There are* many women who want to work.
REVISED: Many women want to work.

b. *There were* repeated interruptions of the meeting.
REVISED: The meeting was repeatedly interrupted.

Occasionally, however, *There is, There are,* or *There were* can be used with good effect to open a paragraph ("There are two reasons for acting now") or to line up the sentences in a list-structure paragraph (see p. 149).

4. Avoid cluttering sentences with nouns:

a. The *contribution* of the *alumni* to the *college* will be in *relation* to their *understanding* of its *goals.*
REVISED: The *alumni* will contribute to the *college* if they understand its *goals.*

b. The *reason* for his *decision* to visit *Spain* was his *desire* to see a *bullfight.*
REVISED: He decided to visit *Spain* because he wanted to see a *bullfight.* [or] He went to *Spain* to see a *bullfight.*

5. Wherever possible, get rid of adjective clauses like *who are, which was,* and *that had been:*

a. Students *who are* in the band have to practice four times a week.
REVISED: Students in the band have to practice four times a week.

b. At the flea market she bought a jewel box *which was* made with tiny seashells.
REVISED: At the flea market she bought a jewel box made with tiny seashells.

c. For many years the country was ruled by a man *who had been* appointed by himself as dictator of the country.
REVISED: For many years the country was ruled by a self-appointed dictator.

6. Replace prepositional phrases with single adjectives or adverbs:

  a. She answered *in an angry way.*
  REVISED: She answered *angrily.*

  b. We are in need *of players with intelligence.*
  REVISED: We need *intelligent players.*

  c. They were *in a state of noticeable confusion.*
  REVISED: They were *noticeably confused.*

  d. He is a leader *of honesty and ability.*
  REVISED: He is an *able, honest leader.*

7. Avoid *to be* in sentences like the following:

  a. Tired from the long day of paddling, Ken found the portage *to be* burdensome.   —First-term college freshman
  REVISED: Tired from the long day of paddling, Ken found the portage burdensome.

  b. Shakespeare is considered *to be* the greatest of all English playwrights.
  REVISED: Shakespeare is considered the greatest of all English playwrights.

8. When possible, avoid *the fact that:*

  The fact that Namath appeared in the stands nearly caused a riot.
  REVISED: Namath's appearance in the stands nearly caused a riot.

9. Avoid verbal detours:

  a. *It is very important for* speakers *to have the ability to* hold the attention of the people *that they are speaking to.*
  REVISED: Speakers must be able to hold the attention of their listeners.

  b. When we try to understand what God is, our first problem is *that of nonencounter at the level of vision.*
  REVISED: When we try to understand God, our first problem is that we cannot see him.

EXERCISE 14 Making Sentences Concise

The following sentences are wordy. Without dropping anything essential to their meaning, make each of them more concise.

  EXAMPLE
  The chipmunk who was hiding in the stone wall put his head out warily.
  REVISED: The chipmunk hiding in the stone wall put his head out warily.

  1. The kitchen in the old farmhouse has a stove that is wood-burning.
  2. In Homer's *Odyssey,* the hero is threatened by a giant who has only one eye.

3. There are two reasons that I have for not going to St. Louis: the first is that I have to write an essay for my English class; the second is that I cannot afford a bus ticket.

4. There is one good trait which Mary has and that is generosity.

5. The fact that the president arrived in Moscow was reported today in the *New York Times*.

6. The only differences between the two cars are those of size and weight.

7. The reason for her attack on the book is her hatred of obscenity.

8. Carpenters are working to replace the shingles that have been damaged by fire.

9. The general ordered his troops to advance forward quickly.

10. I have never read a biography of the life of Mackenzie King.

11. She sang in a charming way.

12. The teacher tried without any success to bring her students around to accepting the proposition that the moon was made of green cheese.

EXERCISE 15   Revising an Early Draft

The following passage illustrates weaknesses of wording common in many early drafts. Write an improved version, which should be considerably shorter and better than the original.

A Life of Resistance

Black Boy is an autobiographical account of the childhood of Richard Wright. In the autobiography Wright describes how all the odds were stacked against him from his birth until the day many years later when he headed north to Chicago. The book portrays
5 his struggle for success against these seemingly insurmountable odds, and the story illustrates in particular how his strong sense of justice allowed him to succeed. This sense of justice is shown partly in the way he responded when others tried to control his actions and behavior. Whenever someone tried to control him, his response
10 depended on how he assessed the fairness of what they wanted him to do.

Richard would not agree to submit to a punishment he felt he did not deserve. Richard had encounters with this kind of punishment while he was living with his grandmother and one of his aunts.
15 Her name was Aunt Addie, and she was mean to Richard, and she was a teacher at a church school. His aunt was continually trying to prove to the other students that she didn't favor Richard, who was her nephew. She tried to prove this by constantly punishing Richard for things he had not done. Finally she pushed him to the limit
20 when she started attempting to punish him at home for things he had not even done at school. Richard assured her that he had not done the things she was accusing him of doing. This assurance only made her furious, angry. She threatened him and warned him she would beat him physically. Then Richard grabbed a kitchen knife
25 to defend himself. He told Aunt Addie that he was not guilty of doing the things she said he had done. He said he would not accept

her abusiveness just because she wanted to prove something to the other kids at school.

When Aunt Addie saw the knife, she became even more angry, and she told Richard he was crazy. However, from that point in time onward, she stopped accusing Richard of every little thing, and, in fact, she started ignoring him totally. She said he was a lost cause. Richard found that being on his aunt's lost cause list was quite enjoyable, and he was glad that he had defied her by not accepting the punishment that he felt, with his sense of justice, he did not deserve.

10

READING IN ORDER
TO WRITE

Up to this point, we have shown you various ways of writing from your own knowledge and experience. We have shown you how to make the most of your inner resources, how to develop what you know or what you remember into a finished essay. But no one can write for long on the strength of inner resources alone. Here and there, we have already suggested that one of the best ways to get an idea for an essay or to enrich the ideas you already have is to read. This chapter is designed to amplify those earlier suggestions by showing you how to make the most of your reading when you sit down to write.

Reading generates writing in three basic ways. For a start, anything you read can stimulate a reaction—fascination, outrage, sympathy, bafflement, even just plain boredom. And as soon as you begin to **react** to a piece of writing, you can begin to think and write about that reaction. In turn, the act of thinking and writing about your reaction can lead you to think and write about what prompted it: to **analyze** what you have read, to explain, amplify, attack, defend, or evaluate the writer's facts, ideas, opinions, or arguments. Finally, any piece of writing that you enjoy reading can show you something about how to write. It can give you something to **imitate.**

This chapter will consider each of these ways of reading in order to write. We concentrate on the reading of nonfictional prose rather than literature, and we focus sharply on the reading of argumentative prose, but much of what we say can be applied to anything you read.

10.1 Subjective Response—Getting Down Your First Reaction

One way to get started writing about anything you read is to write about the way it feels to *you*. Do you like or dislike it? Why? Is it easy to understand or hard? Does it answer a question you've sometimes wondered about or tell you something you've never thought about before? Does it leave you with further questions? And how do you feel about the author?

These are all questions that call for personal, subjective answers. As soon as you get the answers down on paper, you are beginning to write as well as to think about what you have read. You don't have to justify or explain your reactions to anyone else, or even use complete sentences. At this point, you're writing only for yourself.

As an example, here is a short passage from Carl L. Becker's *Modern History*, followed by one student's subjective reaction:

> Students often say to me: "I don't know any history; I think it would be a good thing to learn some." What they seem to mean is that they have never had a "course" in history, or have never read Gibbon's *Decline and Fall of the Roman Empire*, or Mr. Rhodes's *History of the United States from the Compromise of 1850*, or other books similar to these. But they are greatly mistaken if they think they "don't know any history." Every man, woman, and child knows some history, enough at least to stumble along in the world.
>
> Suppose, for example, that you had awakened this morning totally unable to remember anything—all your other faculties working properly, but memory entirely gone. You would be in a bad way indeed! You wouldn't know who you were, or where; what you had done yesterday, or what you intended or other people expected you to do today. What could you do in that case? Wander about helplessly, seeing and hearing things, taking them in as altogether new, not at all knowing what they might mean in relation either to the past or the future. You would have to discover your little world all over again, much as you discovered it in childhood; you would have to "re-orient" yourself and get a new running start. In short, you would be a lost soul because you had ceased to have any knowledge of history, the history of your personal doings and associations in the past.
>
> For history is no more than things said and done in the past. It is as simple as that; and we might as well omit the word "past," since everything said and done is already in the past as soon as it is said or done. Done, but not done *with*. We have to remember many things said and done in order to live our lives intelligently; and so far as we remember things said and done we have a knowledge of history, for that is what historical knowledge is—*memory of things said and done*. Thus everyone has some knowledge of history, and it is quite essential that everyone should have, since it is only by

remembering something of the past that we can anticipate something of the future. Please note that I do not say *predict* the future. We cannot predict the future, but we can *anticipate* it—we can look forward to it and in some sense prepare for it. Now if memory of some things said and done is necessary, it seems that memory of more things ought to be better. The more we remember of things said and done (if they be the right things for our purpose), the better we can manage our affairs today, and the more intelligently we can prepare for what is coming to us tomorrow and next year and all our lives.

Student reaction:

> OK, OK. Knowledge and understanding of history is helpful and important. But not all *that* important. True it would be hard living every day without knowing what was said and done in the past but this could be an advantage.
> We've learned a great deal socially through history that has proved beneficial but at times it seems history has not proved helpful. So maybe *no* knowledge of history could be an advantage. If we suddenly awakened and had no memory at all I believe many problems could be solved in social relations. We wouldn't have knowledge of some of the evil or great things one minority had done, and so we wouldn't look at any one group above or below the others. We would have no knowledge of the feuds and wars that may have existed and possibly still exist between nations and minorities. Present and past discrimination and prejudice would be forgotten. Now I'm not saying this would make the world one giant, laughing, and incredibly happy place but I believe it would make the value of life much greater. Doubtless that people would still become angered with each other, but it would be for a reason of their own, not because of some hate he or his ancestors may have for that person's minority. The world would now not be divided among nations and minorities but by the quality of the people.

Something exciting happens here. Carl Becker's argument that we cannot live without history has prompted this student to take the opposite view: that we could live better without it because we would then be free of the prejudices and racial hostilities that our knowledge of the past gives us. The student does not have the whole truth, but neither does Becker. The point is that a few minutes of reading, and perhaps fifteen minutes of writing, have given the student a topic to think further about. Without Becker's essay, this student might never have thought and written about history as he did. Reading Becker has put him in touch with his own ideas.

If he wants to state those ideas persuasively, of course, he will need to do more work. He will not only have to smooth out his sentences; he may also have to sharpen his main point. Does he really want to say that *all* history is better forgotten? Or does he believe that we should not let our knowledge of the past tie our hands as we try to shape the future? Can he find examples to support his belief? Thinking about his point may bring him to a more persuasive as well as more polished formulation of it.

But polishing a personal reaction does not mean depersonalizing it. Here is the first part of a published essay in which the writer states her personal reaction to a book:

> There's a book out called *Is There Life after High School?* It's a fairly silly book, maybe because the subject matter is the kind that only hurts when you think. Its thesis—that most people never get over the social triumphs or humiliations of high school—is not novel. Still, I read it with the respectful attention a serious hypochondriac accords the lowliest "dear doctor" column. I don't know about most people, but for me, forgiving my parents for real and imagined derelections has been easy compared to forgiving myself for being a teenage reject.
>
> Victims of high school trauma—which seems to have afflicted a disproportionate number of writers, including Ralph Keyes, the author of this book—tend to embrace the ugly duckling myth of adolescent social relations: the "innies" (Keyes's term) are good-looking, athletic mediocrities who will never amount to much, while the "outies" are intelligent, sensitive, creative individuals who will do great things in an effort to make up for their early defeats. . . . In contrast, the ex-prom queens and kings he interviews slink through life, hiding their pasts lest someone call them "dumb jock" or "cheerleader type," perpetually wondering what to do for an encore.
>
> If only it were that simple. There may really be high schools where life approximates an Archie comic, but even in the Fifties, my large (5000 students), semisuburban (Queens, New York), heterogeneous high school was not one of them. The students' social life was fragmented along ethnic and class lines; there was no universally recognized, schoolwide social hierarchy. Being an athlete or a cheerleader or a student officer didn't mean much. Belonging to an illegal sorority or fraternity meant more, at least in some circles, but many socially active students chose not to join. The most popular kids were not necessarily the best looking or the best dressed or the most snobbish or the least studious. In retrospect, it seems to me that they were popular for much more honorable reasons. They were attuned to other people, aware of subtle social nuances. They projected an inviting sexual warmth. Far from being slavish followers of fashion, they were self-confident enough to set fashions. They suggested, initiated, led. Above all—this was their main appeal for me—they knew how to have a good time.
>
> —Ellen Willis, "Memoirs of a Non-Prom Queen"

This writer's account of a book she has read is both objective and subjective. Objectively, she mentions its thesis—its main point—in her first paragraph, and she goes on in the next one to describe its contents. But the rest of her discussion is personal. She is judging this book about the effects of high school in the light of what she personally observed when *she* was in high school, of what she saw not just in herself but in others—especially in those who were popular.

Another way of turning a subjective response into a finished essay is to begin with a personal experience that *introduces* one of the basic themes in the book you are writing about. Here, for instance, are the opening paragraphs of a student essay on the theme of solitude in Thoreau's *Walden:*

> The whirling snow and howling wind seemed determined to destroy me for trespassing on the sacred heights of Mount Washington in the middle of the winter. Spindrift poured down the Northern Gully like water from a faucet, but the screaming blasts of bone-chilling wind took my mind off the snow. With a cloud cover sitting on the mountaintop like a mother hen on her egg, I could see hardly anything of the steep, huge, icy headwall on which I perched. As I pressed upward, my modern steel ice tools seemed no more than thumbtacks. My arms felt like enormous sponges—full and heavy, yet also powerless. My calves burned, my feet froze, and my legs trembled like a mouse before a lion. The climb seemed endless. No rope bound me to anyone else; my climbing partner had turned back hours ago. There was only me and a wild, white, screaming world of perils. I have never in my life felt such solitude, and at the same time such freedom from loneliness.
>
> To experience this kind of solitude is to understand one of the most important things that Thoreau discovered at Walden Pond. In *Walden,* Thoreau observes that many people fear or dislike solitude, that they cannot understand how he could bear to live alone for two years. To answer this question, Thoreau reveals in his book the difference between solitude and loneliness. While these two states may seem inseparable, Thoreau shows that they can be entirely independent.

This student responds to *Walden* by recalling a personal experience of solitude. In turn, the personal experience provides him with a way into Thoreau's book. It leads him to a thesis—a statement about the meaning of the book—and thus to the germ of an essay about it.

EXERCISE 1   Expressing a Subjective Response

This exercise has three parts. (1) Read the following and record your immediate personal reaction to it—without worrying about sentence structure or form. (2) Compare Chase's description of college to your own experience of it. (3) Use your personal experience of college to introduce a statement of thesis about the meaning or value of Chase's comments.

During the last ten years most colleges have dropped mandatory courses in essay writing and foreign languages and have weakened distribution requirements in the three basic areas of social science, natural science, and the humanities. During this period the number of electives taken at the major private liberal arts colleges has increased from 29 to 35 percent.

Curriculum committees, often with students on them, and college faculties routinely add new courses to the curriculum regardless of academic value, including courses in wood shop, photography, soap opera, roller coasting, political internship, and backpacking! Thus, each year the course catalogues become thicker with fashionable offerings of little or no academic value. Even the Harvard catalogue has doubled in thickness in the last twenty years and now contains over 2600 listings. And it is still growing.

Giving "extensions" on papers and "incompletes" in courses has become a national epidemic. At Yale, according to a recent report by Associate Dean Martin Griffin, 22 percent of all students took at least one "incomplete" in the fall term of 1977. Most disturbing is the trend: while only 6 percent of the freshmen took "incompletes" that term, 20 percent of the sophomores, 33 percent of the juniors, and 31 percent of the seniors took at least one. Evidently the Yale experience teaches the rewards of procrastination.

Grade inflation is also epidemic. At Harvard, where one must assume resistance to this is greater than average, 85 percent of the class of 1977 graduated with honors, as compared with 39 percent for the class of 1957. Also, according to a recent report of the Harvard administration, 85 percent of all grades given there last year were B-minus or higher (compared with 70 percent in 1965–1966). . . .

Many colleges delete from a student's transcript any failing grade. At Unity College in Maine, for instance, this is known as "nonpunitive grading." The idea is that successes, not failures, be recorded.

Many colleges have committees, or "courts," often with students on them and sometimes without any faculty, that are empowered to overrule a professor on matters relating to giving grades, changing grades, granting extensions, incompletes, or dropping courses. Often these committees automatically find in favor of the student.

Minority programs have affected academic quality. At some schools the average SAT score of the disadvantaged students is nearly 200 points lower than that of other students (the national average for minorities is 100 points lower than that for non-minority students). Faced with that dispartiy of achievement in the classroom, the professor, feeling pressure from the minorities and suffering from white guilt, usually gives passing grades to minority students even if they are failing. But if failing students are given C's, those students who would normally have earned D's and C's will have to be given B's and A's, or else . . . the professor [will] simply throw up his hands and give all students A's.

50 As these examples suggest, America's colleges and universities
have grievously failed to maintain minimum academic standards.
For surely such standards require colleges to certify that students
have taken courses in a range of subjects which a consensus of
scholars believes are important and intellectually respectable; that
55 the work done is of a certain quality and students have been sufficiently challenged to gain new confidence in their abilities and
awareness of their weaknesses; that course policies recognize learning as a function of time, where taking twice as long to master a
subject means learning half as much; and that students have mas-
60 tered certain fundamental skills such as reading, writing, compu-
tation, and speaking a foreign language.

—Alston Chase, "Skipping through College"

10.2 Analytical Response

10.2A Catching the Tone

Earlier, we discussed the ways in which you can convey a particular
tone of voice in your own writing. (See sections 2.3, pp. 26–27, and
4.2, pp. 51–55.) But tone is also part of what you experience
when you read the writing of someone else. It affects the way you
"take" what you read—the way you feel about it and hence the way
you interpret it. When Carl Becker writes "Students often say to
me," he reveals that he is probably a teacher, but we might also
guess that from his lecture-room tone: "Please note that I do not
say *predict* the future." Politely but firmly, he is treating us as students, carefully guiding us through his explanation. The tone tells
us that he straightforwardly means what he says, so that we can
take his words at face value.

But now consider this essay:

Why I Want a Wife

I belong to that classification of people known as wives. I am A
Wife. And, not altogether incidentally, I am a mother.

Not too long ago a male friend of mine appeared on the scene
fresh from a recent divorce. He had one child, who is, of course,
with his ex-wife. He is looking for another wife. As I thought about
him while I was ironing one evening, it suddenly occurred to me
that I, too, would like to have a wife. Why do I want a wife?

I would like to go back to school so that I can become economi-
cally independent, support myself, and, if need be, support those
dependent upon me. I want a wife who will work and send me to
school. And while I am going to school I want a wife to take care
of my children. I want a wife to keep track of the children's doctor
and dentist appointments. And to keep track of mine, too. I want

a wife to make sure my children eat properly and are kept clean. I want a wife who is a good nurturant attendant to my children, who arranges for their schooling, makes sure that they have an adequate social life with their peers, takes them to the park, the zoo, etc. I want a wife who takes care of the children when they are sick, a wife who arranges to be around when the children need special care, because, of course, I cannot miss classes at school. My wife must arrange to lose time at work and not lose the job. It may mean a small cut in my wife's income from time to time, but I guess I can tolerate that. Needless to say, my wife will arrange and pay for the care of the children while my wife is working.

I want a wife who will take care of *my* physical needs. I want a wife who will keep my house clean. A wife who will pick up after my children, a wife who will pick up after me. I want a wife who will keep my clothes clean, ironed, mended, replaced when need be, and who will see to it that my personal things are kept in their proper place so that I can find what I need the minute I need it. I want a wife who cooks the meals, a wife who is a *good* cook. I want a wife who will plan the menus, do the necessary grocery shopping, prepare the meals, serve them pleasantly, and then do the cleaning up while I do my studying. I want a wife who will care for me when I am sick and sympathize with my pain and loss of time from school. I want a wife to go along when our family takes a vacation so that someone can continue to care for me and my children when I need a rest and change of scene.

I want a wife who will not bother me with rambling complaints about a wife's duties. But I want a wife who will listen to me when I feel the need to explain a rather difficult point I have come across in my course of studies. And I want a wife who will type my papers for me when I have written them.

I want a wife who will take care of the details of my social life. When my wife and I are invited out by my friends, I want a wife who will take care of the babysitting arrangements. When I meet people at school that I like and want to entertain, I want a wife who will have the house clean, will prepare a special meal, serve it to me and my friends, and not interrupt when I talk about things that interest me and my friends. I want a wife who will have arranged that the children are fed and ready for bed before my guests arrive so that the children do not bother us. I want a wife who takes care of the needs of my guests so that they feel comfortable, who makes sure that they have an ashtray, that they are passed the hors d'oeuvres, that they are offered a second helping of the food, that their wine glasses are replenished when necessary, that their coffee is served to them as they like it. And I want a wife who knows that sometimes I need a night out by myself.

I want a wife who is sensitive to my sexual needs, a wife who makes love passionately and eagerly when I feel like it, a wife who makes sure that I am satisfied. And, of course, I want a wife who will not demand sexual attention when I am not in the mood for it.

I want a wife who assumes the complete responsibility for birth control, because I do not want more children. I want a wife who will remain sexually faithful to me so that I do not have to clutter up my intellectual life with jealousies. And I want a wife who understands that *my* sexual needs may entail more than strict adherence to monogamy. I must, after all, be able to relate to people as fully as possible.

If, by chance, I find another person more suitable as a wife than the wife I already have, I want the liberty to replace my present wife with another one. Naturally, I will expect a fresh, new life; my wife will take the children and be solely responsible for them so that I am left free.

When I am through with school and have a job, I want my wife to quit working and remain at home so that my wife can more fully and completely take care of a wife's duties.

My God, who *wouldn't* want a wife?

—Judy Syfers

On the surface, the writer's tone is direct, decisive, and assertive. She leaves no doubt about what she wants. Yet the second paragraph tells us that we can't take this essay at face value. A writer who calls herself "A Wife" and who also declares that she *wants* a wife must be playing some kind of game.

We soon discover that she is masquerading as a wife-hunting man: the kind of man who expects his wife to put him through school, satisfy all of his needs, serve him and his children in every possible way, and demand nothing in return. The real purpose of the masquerade becomes clear when we consider the sheer extravagance of these requirements. What the writer actually wants is to expose the egotism and insensitivity of men who think of wives as all-purpose servants.

When a writer expresses an attitude in such a way as to make us see it as ridiculous or revolting, he or she is being **ironic.** If you hear someone say in the midst of a raging downpour that the weather is "beautiful," you know that the word is being used ironically, that the speaker really means the weather is horrible. And just as the gap between word and situation signals irony in speech, the gap between tone and content signals irony in writing. If a writer sounds direct and decisive in stating demands that are grossly inconsiderate, or earnest and sincere in proposing something crazy, silly, or wildly inconsistent, you can be fairly certain that he or she is being ironic.

Now consider the tone in this passage:

Home for Christmas my first year in college, I spoke to my best friend from high school. Elizabeth and I stayed on the phone for 45 minutes, but we had nothing very much to say to each other. After the conversation, I was upset. I remember wanting to tell my mother, who asked what the matter was, about the weirdness of discovering that this woman and I, who had talked every school day for five years, no longer had anything in common. All I could do was cry.

Except for a brief, awkward visit to my house a month later when my father died, a church wedding where Elizabeth married a man I'd gone out with in seventh grade, and two short stopovers in southern New Jersey, I don't remember ever seeing or speaking to her again.

We used to spend hours talking about our relationships with boys. We never discussed our relationship with each other. Except for the few minutes with my mother, who told me she thought Elizabeth and I never had anything in common, and my once making a distinction between acquaintances and friends, I'd never spoken about what I considered a real friendship.

Many people have expressed agreement with Cicero that "friendship can only exist between good men." I'm not one of them. As a 30-year-old woman who has had friends since grade school, I have been very concerned with those friendships. Yet only in the last few years have such relationships been acknowledged as being as important as they've always been.

It was always commonplace for girls in my high school to spend a great deal of time together. It was also commonplace for a girl to spend Saturdays with another girl listening to Johnny Mathis albums, trying on clothes to find something that fit right, or babysitting and then having the evening that was planned together usurped by some boy calling up for a date. When this happened to me, I felt betrayed. I never said anything. It didn't occur to me that this wasn't the natural order of things. I didn't know anyone who complained, nor do I remember anyone who ever turned down a boy because she'd already made plans with a girl.

—Susan Lee, "Friendship, Feminism, and Betrayal"

Here the tone is neither didactic nor ironically assertive. The writer is neither telling us plainly what we ought to think ("Please note . . .") nor pretending to say the opposite of what she really means. Instead, her tone is confiding. As candidly as possible, she is striving to recall the conflicts she experienced in her adolescent friendships with other women.

EXERCISE 2 Recognizing Tone

Read the following passage and then briefly describe (1) the author's attitude toward his audience, (2) his tone, and (3) his intention.

Being told I would be expected to talk here, I inquired what sort of talk I ought to make. They said it should be something suitable to youth—something didactic, instructive, or something in the nature of good advice. Very well. I have a few things in my mind which I have often longed to say for the instruction of the young;

for it is in one's tender early years that such things will best take root and be most enduring and most valuable. First, then, I will say to you, my young friends—and I say it beseechingly, urgingly—

Always obey your parents, when they are present. This is the best policy in the long run, because if you don't they will make you. Most parents think they know better than you do, and you can generally make more by humoring that superstition than you can by acting on your own better judgment.

Be respectful to your superiors, if you have any, also to strangers, and sometimes to others. If a person offend you, and you are in doubt as to whether it was intentional or not, do not resort to extreme measures; simply watch your chance and hit him with a brick. That will be sufficient. If you shall find that he had not intended any offense, come out frankly and confess yourself in the wrong when you struck him; acknowledge it like a man and say you didn't mean to. Yes, always avoid violence; in this age of charity and kindliness, the time has gone by for such things. Leave dynamite to the low and unrefined.   —Mark Twain, "Advice to Youth"

10.2B   Finding the Writer's Main Point

The first place to look for a writer's main point is the first sentence you read. Consider this paragraph:

> People feel safer behind some kind of physical barrier. If a social situation is in any way threatening, then there is an immediate urge to set up such a barricade. For a tiny child faced with a stranger, the problem is usually solved by hiding behind its mother's body and peeping out at the intruder to see what he or she will do next. If the mother's body is not available, then a chair or some other piece of solid furniture will do. If the stranger insists on coming closer, then the peeping face must be hidden too. If the insensitive intruder continues to approach despite these obvious signals of fear, then there is nothing for it but to scream or flee.
> —Desmond Morris, *Manwatching: A Field Guide to Human Behavior*

The first sentence of this paragraph states its main point: "People feel safer behind some kind of physical barrier." Every other sentence is a specific illustration of this general point. The behavior of "people" is illustrated by the actions of the tiny child; the "physical barrier" is illustrated by the mother's body and the chair or other piece of solid furniture.

Though the first sentence is the first place to look for the writer's main point, you will often have to look further. For example:

> The movement has many faces: from sweet ladies handing out red roses and right-to-life cookbooks, to demonstrators brandish-

ing bottled fetuses and hoodlums attacking medical clinics. It has many voices as well: from righteous ministers preaching the sanctity of unborn souls, to editorials raising the specter of the holocaust, to crowds screaming "murderer" at elected officials who take a different position.

This is the anti-abortion movement, a cause that refuses to yield. Six years ago, the U.S. Supreme Court ruled that the right to have an abortion is beyond the reach of government. Since then, public-opinion polls have consistently shown that a majority of Americans favor making abortion a matter for patient and doctor to decide. Despite these developments, the subject is more politically explosive today than ever before. Opposition to abortion has become the most implacable, and perhaps the nastiest, public-issue campaign in at least a half century.

      —Roger M. Williams, "The Power of Fetal Politics"

The first paragraph speaks of a "movement." But since no sentence in this paragraph tells us openly what the movement is, we are driven onward to the next paragraph. Here we find out what the movement is, and here also we find the writer's main point about it: "Opposition to abortion has become the most implacable, and perhaps the nastiest, public-issue campaign in at least a half century."

So how do you know this is the main point? How do you know the writer isn't mainly interested in the Supreme Court ruling or the results of public-opinion polls—both of which are mentioned in the second paragraph? The answer is that only the last sentence in the second paragraph contains, so to speak, all the other sentences in both paragraphs. Each of the other sentences specifically shows that the anti-abortion movement is either nasty or implacable. The Supreme Court ruling and the public-opinion polls are cited simply to show how implacable the movement is, how stubbornly it resists the judgments of both the Supreme Court and the court of public opinion.

Sometimes no one single sentence states the writer's main point. Consider this passage:

> I once choked a chicken to death. It was my only barefaced, not to say barehanded, confrontation with death and the killer in me and happened on my grandparents' farm. I couldn't have been more than nine or ten and no firearms were included or necessary. I was on my knees and the chicken fluttered its outstretched wings with the last of the outraged protest. I gripped, beyond release, above its swollen crop, its beak gaping, translucent eyelids sliding up and down. . . . My grandfather, who was widely traveled and world-wise, in his eighties then, and had just started using a cane from earlier times, came tapping at that moment around the corner of the chicken coop and saw what I was doing and started gag-

ging at the hideousness of it, did a quick assisted spin away and never again, hours later nor for the rest of his life, for that matter, ever mentioned the homicidal incident to me. Keeping his silence, he seemed to understand; and yet whenever I'm invaded by the incident, the point of it seems to be his turning away from me.

—Larry Woiwode, "Guns"

The last sentence tells us that the point of the incident was the grandfather's turning away. But this sentence merely implies the real point of the paragraph: the grandfather's turning away made the writer recognize himself as a killer.

Also implied rather than stated is the main point of an ironic passage. In "Why I Want a Wife," Judy Syfers nowhere states her main point openly; you have to figure out what it is. The same is true of Twain's "Advice to Youth" (exercise 2, p. 205). While Twain seems to be saying that young people should be obedient, respectful, and nonviolent, he is ironically showing the difference between the way people are normally told to behave and the way they actually do.

In an extended piece of writing, the main point of the whole may not be immediately apparent. That is, a point developed in the early paragraphs may lead up to another, more important point. Consider this essay:

Walls and Barriers

My father's reaction to the bank building at 43rd Street and Fifth Avenue in New York City was immediate and definite: "You won't catch me putting my money in *there!*" he declared. "Not in that glass box!"

Of course, my father is a gentleman of the old school, a member of the generation to whom a good deal of modern architecture is unnerving; but I suspect—I more than suspect, I am convinced—that his negative response was not so much to the architecture as to a violation of his concept of the nature of money.

In his generation money was thought of as a tangible commodity—bullion, bank notes, coins—that could be hefted, carried, or stolen. Consequently, to attract the custom of a sensible man, a bank had to have heavy walls, barred windows, and bronze doors, to affirm the fact, however untrue, that money would be safe inside. If a building's design made it appear impregnable, the institution was necessarily sound, and the meaning of the heavy wall as an architectural symbol dwelt in the prevailing attitude toward money, rather than in any aesthetic theory.

But that attitude toward money has of course changed. Excepting pocket money, cash of any kind is now rarely used; money as a tangible commodity has largely been replaced by credit: a bookkeeping-banking matter. A deficit economy, accompanied by huge expansion, has led us to think of money as a product of the creative imagination. The banker no longer offers us a *safe;* he offers us a *service*—a service in which the most valuable elements are dash and a creative flair for the invention of large numbers. It is in no way surprising, in view of this change in attitude, that we are witnessing the disappearance of the heavy-walled bank. The Manufacturers Trust, which my father distrusted so heartily, is a great cubical cage of glass whose brilliantly lighted interior challenges even the brightness of a sunny day, while the door to the vault, far from being secluded and guarded, is set out as a window display.

Just as the older bank asserted its invulnerability, this bank *by its architecture* boasts of its imaginative powers. From this point of view it is hard to say where architecture ends and human assertion begins. In fact, there is no such division; the two are one and the same.

It is in the understanding of architecture as a medium for the expression of human attitudes, prejudices, taboos, and ideals that the new architectural criticism departs from classical aesthetics. The latter relied upon pure proportion, composition, etc., as bases for artistic judgment. In the age of sociology and psychology, walls are not simply walls but physical symbols of the barriers in men's minds.

In a primitive society, for example, men pictured the world as large, fearsome, hostile, and beyond human control. Therefore they built heavy walls of huge boulders, behind which they could feel themselves to be in a delimited space that was controllable and safe; these heavy walls expressed man's fear of the outer world and his need to find protection, however illusory. It might be argued that the undeveloped technology of the period precluded the construction of more delicate walls. This is of course true. Still, it was not technology, but a fearful attitude toward the world, which made people want to build walls in the first place. The greater the fear, the heavier the wall, until in the tombs of ancient kings we find structures that are practically all wall, the fear of dissolution being the ultimate fear.

And then there is the question of privacy—for it *has* become questionable. In some Mediterranean cultures it was not so much the world of nature that was feared, but the world of men. Men were dirty, prying, vile, and dangerous. One went about, if one could afford it, in guarded litters; women went about heavily veiled, if they went about at all. One's house was surrounded by a wall, and the rooms faced not out, but in, toward a patio, expressing the prevalent conviction that the beauties and values of life were to be found by looking inward, and by engaging in the intimate activities of a personal as against a public life. The rich intricacies of the decorative arts of the period, as well as its contemplative philosophies, are as illustrative of this attitude as the walls themselves.

We feel different today. For one thing, we place greater reliance upon the control of human hostility, not so much by physical barriers, as by the conventions of law and social practice—as well as the availability of motorized police. We do not cherish privacy as much as did our ancestors. We are proud to have our women seen and admired, and the same goes for our homes. We do not seek solitude; in fact, if we find ourselves alone for once, we flick a switch and invite the whole world in through the television screen. Small wonder, then, that the heavy surrounding wall is obsolete, and we build, instead, membranes of thin sheet metal or glass.

The principal function of today's wall is to separate possibly undesirable outside air from the controlled conditions of temperature and humidity which we have created inside. Glass may accomplish this function, though there are apparently a good many people who still have qualms about eating, sleeping, and dressing under conditions of high visibility; they demand walls that will at least give them a sense of adequate screening. But these shy ones are a vanishing breed. The Philip Johnson house in Connecticut, which is much admired and widely imitated, has glass walls all the way around, and the only real privacy is to be found in the bathroom, the toilet taboo being still unbroken, at least in Connecticut.

To repeat, it is not our advanced technology, but our changing conceptions of ourselves in relation to the world that determine how we shall build our walls. The glass wall expresses man's conviction that he can and does master nature and society. The "open plan" and the unobstructed view are consistent with his faith in the eventual solution of all problems through the expanding efforts of science. This is perhaps why it is the most "advanced" and "forward-looking" among us who live and work in glass houses. Even the fear of the cast stone has been analyzed out of us.

—Eugene Raskin

This essay begins by talking about banks, and the main point of the first four paragraphs is that since tangible money has been largely replaced by credit, the banker now offers not a heavy-walled safe, but a bright, open, inviting service. This point is a kind of landing place to which the first three paragraphs lead, step by step:

1. My father won't put his money in a glass-walled bank.
2. A glass-walled bank violates his concept of money.
3. People of his generation think of money as a tangible commodity that must be heavily protected.
4. However, since tangible money has been largely replaced by credit, the banker now offers not a heavy-walled safe, but a bright, open, inviting service.

The fourth point is the main point of the first four paragraphs, but not of the whole essay. In the fifth paragraph, the point about bank design gives way to a more general point about architecture as a whole, which is the subject of the rest of the essay. The contrast between old banks and new ones illustrates the contrast between traditional and modern architecture, and that contrast in turn supports the main point of the whole essay: architecture reflects the way we think about our relation to the outside world.

EXERCISE 3   Identifying the Main Point

In each of the following passages, one sentence expresses the main point. Identify that sentence.

1. The history of Florida is measured in freezes. Severe ones, for example, occurred in 1747, 1766, and 1774. The freeze of February, 1835, was probably the worst one in the state's history. But, because more growers were affected, the Great Freeze of 1895 seems to enjoy the same sort of status in Florida that the Blizzard of '88 once held in the North. Temperatures on the Ridge on February 8, 1895, went into the teens for much of the night. It is said that some orange growers, on being told what was happening out in the groves, got up from their dinner tables and left the state. In the morning, it was apparent that the Florida citrus industry had been virtually wiped out.   —John McPhee, *Oranges*

2. In early human history a Stone Age, a Bronze Age, or an Iron Age came into unhurried gestation and endured for centuries or even millennia; and as one technology gradually displaced or merged with another, the changes wrought in any single lifetime were easily absorbed, if noticed at all. But a transformation has come about in our own time. A centenarian born in 1879 has seen, in the years of his own life, scientific and technological advances more sweeping and radical than those that took place in all the accumulated past. He has witnessed—and felt the personal impact of—the Age of Electricity, the Automobile Age, the Aviation Age, the Electronic Age, the Atomic Age, the Space Age, and the Computer Age, to name but a few of the "ages" that have been crowding in upon us at such an unprecedented rate, sometimes arriving virtually side by side. Let us use the shortcut designation the "Age of Science" to encompass them all.
   —Albert Rosenfeld, "How Anxious Should Science Make Us?"

EXERCISE 4   Identifying the Main Point

Reread the passage on college standards given in exercise 1, pp. 200–202, and identify the main point of the selection.

10.2C   Summarizing

Summarizing a piece of writing is a good way to test and show your understanding of it. How you summarize will partly depend on whether you are dealing with a narrative or with an essay.

   The summary of a narrative or a drama is usually called a plot summary; it may be sequential or comprehensive. A **sequential** plot summary follows the order in which the main events of a narrative or drama are presented in the original work. A sequential plot summary of *Moby-Dick,* for instance, would begin as follows:

> Bored with his life on land, a young schoolteacher who calls himself Ishmael decides to go to sea on a whaling ship. He travels to New Bedford, where he meets and strikes up a friendship with a harpooner named Queequeg. Then the two men go to Nantucket and sign on board a ship named the *Pequod.* . . .

Like all summaries, this one reduces each event to its bare essentials. It says that Ishmael meets Queequeg, for instance, but does not mention the startling conditions under which they meet. And because this is a sequential plot summary, it starts with chapter 1 and follows the order of the original in retelling the events.

But that is not always the order that best expresses what happens. Instead of starting with the first chapter of a book or the first scene of a play, you can start with a **comprehensive** statement about the chief action of the book or play, and then give the chain of events making up that action:

> *Moby-Dick* is the story of Ahab's relentless quest for revenge against a white whale that has taken his leg and that eventually takes his life. Ahab is the captain of a whaling ship named the *Pequod,* and the story of his quest is told by one of the seamen who serve on his ship—a man who calls himself Ishmael. Bored with his life on land, Ishmael decides to go to sea on a whaling voyage, so he signs on the *Pequod* along with a new-found friend named Queequeg. Shortly after the ship embarks, Ahab announces that the sole purpose of the voyage is to catch and kill Moby-Dick, the great white whale that has cut off Ahab's leg. . . .

A comprehensive summary such as this gives a clearer account of the book as a whole than a sequential summary does. While a sequential summary simply recounts one event after another without saying which is the most important, a comprehensive summary immediately identifies the central action to which all other actions must be referred.

The summary of an essay should begin by stating the main point of the essay as a whole, and then proceed to the chief supporting points—all of the points used to explain or prove the main point. Here, for instance, is a summary of Eugene Raskin's "Walls and Barriers" (pp. 208–10):

> Architecture reveals the way we think about our relation to the outside world. While the heavy walls of traditional architecture express a fear of that world, the glass walls of modern architecture express confidence that human beings can master the outside world and eventually solve all of its problems.

This summary begins with the main point of the whole essay, and the second sentence states the chief supporting point. In the essay itself, the author uses banks and houses to show the difference between traditional and modern architecture, but such examples don't belong in a summary, which should consist of general facts and ideas, not specific illustrations. And this summary does not set down the main point of each paragraph in the essay; it simply goes to the final paragraph, which clearly states the essay's main point. The final paragraph of an essay, in fact, is often the best place to look for such a statement.

EXERCISE 5 Summarizing

Summarize the passage on college standards given in exercise 1, pp. 200–202.

10.2D Paraphrasing

Paraphrasing is restating a short passage in your own words. It enables you to discuss texts without quoting every word of them and thus to avoid interrupting your essay with long quotations. If you plan to analyze a particular passage in detail, you should quote it in full. But if you simply want to convey the essential point of the passage, you can paraphrase all or part of it. Consider these two ways of treating a passage in Thoreau's *Walden:*

1. According to Thoreau, the Kouroo artist spent hundreds of years making a perfect staff because, "having considered that in an imperfect work time is an ingredient, but into a perfect work time does not enter, he said to himself, 'It shall be perfect in all respects, though I should do nothing else in my life.' "

2. According to Thoreau, the Kouroo artist spent hundreds of years making a perfect staff because he believed that time had nothing to do with perfection, and he was willing to spend his whole life pursuing it.

While the quotation makes an awkward bulge in the writer's sentence, the paraphrase fits nicely. Slightly compressing the original, it clearly expresses Thoreau's essential point.

EXERCISE 6 Paraphrasing

Restate each of the following passages in one sentence, using your own words:

1. "Most people who bother with the matter at all would admit that the English language is in a bad way, but it is generally assumed that we cannot by conscious action do anything about it." —George Orwell

2. "Today it is not unusual for a student, even if he works part time at college and full time during the summer, to accrue $5,000 in loans after four years—loans that he must start to repay one year after graduation."
                                                              —William Zinsser

3. "A good city street neighborhood achieves a marvel of balance between its people's determination to have essential privacy and their simultaneous wishes for differing degrees of contact, enjoyment, or help from people around."
                                                              —Jane Jacobs

---

10.2E   Judging the Supporting Points in an Essay

To summarize an essay, you must be able to identify its main point and its chief supporting points. To analyze an essay, you must also be able to judge the relevance and strength of each supporting point. You should therefore try to answer these questions:

1. Are the supporting points facts or opinions? A fact is a statement that can be indisputably verified. An opinion is a statement that may be impossible to verify absolutely but can be supported by facts— and usually needs such support in order to make an impression on the reader.

In the passage in exercise 1, pp. 200–202, Alston Chase expresses an opinion when he says that "America's colleges and universities have grievously failed to maintain minimum academic standards." He supports this opinion with statements we can take as facts—such as the statement that "many colleges delete from a student's transcript any failing grade." This statement does not prove absolutely that Chase's opinion is true, but it helps to show that his opinion is probably true. Anyone who wishes to combat that opinion will have to show that Chase's supporting statements (facts) are false, that he has ignored an opposing point (see pp. 133–36, or that his reasoning is faulty (see section 7.5, pp. 127–32).

Since an opinion cannot stand on its own feet, you should take a hard look at what is said to support it. Sometimes there is no supporting statement at all, and sometimes the supporting statement turns out to be nothing but another opinion. When a writer says that "young people no longer work seriously" to persuade us that the nation is declining, the supporting statement is mere opinion. It cannot be verified until we know who the "young people" are, what their "work" is, and how to measure their seriousness. When a writer says that there is life outside the solar system, that too is an opinion; it remains to be verified—though it may one day become an established fact. (The established fact that the earth is round was once merely the opinion of daring thinkers.) Likewise, when a writer says that the United States must spend more on weapons because Russia is "winning the arms race," that too is opinion; it cannot be verified until we agree on what "winning" means here. Does it mean producing more nuclear weapons than the other nation, or producing more conventional weapons, or developing better antimissile missiles? Vague opinions must be made specific before they can be adequately supported by facts, and no opinion can serve by itself to support another opinion.

Between fact and opinion stands another kind of statement: the questionable claim. Suppose you read that there are eight million rats in New York City. This looks like a statement that can be checked and verified—a fact. But who can actually count the number of rats in New York? Contrary to popular belief, numbers have no special authority over words. The figures a writer cites are only as reliable as the methods used to get them.

Questionable assertions take a variety of other forms, and no definition of them can replace common sense and healthy skepticism. In general, you should read with a question mark between you and the page. Be on the watch for deceptive exaggeration, "figures" that come out of thin air, and editorial opinion masquerading as reportorial fact ("The president has lost the confidence of the American people"). Life is too short for you to check out every unsupported claim or surprising new "fact" for yourself; usually you must trust the writer. But you can reasonably ask that a writer earn your trust—by respecting the difference between fact and opinion.

2. Are the supporting points relevant to the main point? A main point "supported" by irrelevant points is like a house at number 32 Main Street supported by a foundation laid at number 31. Consider this passage:

> It would be foolish and dangerous for the United States to make any further agreement with Russia that would limit the production or deployment of strategic weapons. Russia is a communist country that tyrannizes her citizens. She crushes personal initiative. She demands unquestioning obedience to the Communist party line. She persecutes any who disagree. Some of her most brilliant writers have been subjected to prolonged imprisonment and even torture, and most of her citizens are virtual prisoners all of the time, forbidden to leave the country. The U.S. should have nothing whatsoever to do with such a ruthlessly totalitarian regime.

The first sentence states the writer's main point, and the rest of the sentences are offered to support it. But they fail to support it because they are beside the point. Even if we accept as matters of common belief the statements made about Russia's treatment of her citizens, Russia's domestic policies are not clearly relevant to the arms race, any more than American domestic policies are. In a persuasive argument against an arms-limitation agreement, the main point would have to be supported by relevant supporting points—such as the fact that the agreement fails to provide for U.S. inspection of Soviet weapons factories.

3. Are there enough supporting points? In the paragraph on barriers (p. 206), Desmond Morris's main point is that "people feel safer behind some kind of physical barrier," and he supports this point by describing what a child does when confronted by a stranger. Can you see what is missing? Clearly, Morris does not adequately support his point about "people" by simply describing the actions of a "tiny child." But Morris's paragraph on the child is merely the opening of a chapter in which he describes the barrier signals that grownups use, the subtle movements and postures with which adults continue to shield themselves in unfamiliar company. By citing specific examples of adult as well as child behavior, Morris convincingly supports his point in the chapter as a whole.

Supporting points, then, should cover a representative sample of the people or objects that the main point refers to. If a writer wants to show that blacks have become increasingly successful in American politics, his or her argument need not cite examples from all fifty states, but it should certainly cite examples from more than one state, and from states in different parts of the country. The more varied the examples are, the more convincing the argument will be.

4. Has the writer considered opposing points? To be wholly convincing, an argument must recognize the major points that can be set against it. (See section 7.7, "Reckoning with the Opposition," pp. 133–36.) When you read a completely one-sided essay on a subject you know has at least two sides, you may be sure that the argument is slanted.

EXERCISE 7   **Analyzing a Paragraph**

Read the following paragraph and answer these questions: (1) What is the main point? (2) What are the supporting points? (3) Are any of the supporting points not strictly relevant to the main point? (4) Which are the facts and which are the opinions?

> Today Japan is the world's foremost economic power. Last year the Japanese manufactured one and a half times as much per capita as Americans. While for the first time in decades our exports of industrial goods fell behind our imports, Japan exported $75 bil-
> 5 lion more of industrial goods than it imported. Japan's investment rate, as well as its GNP growth rate, is more than twice ours and its research and development efforts are growing much more rapidly

than our own. Its workers, contrary to our old stereotype, are effectively better paid than our own. And its performance in educat-
10 ing the population, minimizing disparities of income, reducing the crime rate, and increasing the length of human life is substantially ahead of America's. These differences will have far more profound consequences than we have begun to imagine.

—Ezra Vogel, "The Miracle of Japan:
How the Post-War Was Won"

EXERCISE 8   Analyzing and Judging an Argument

Analyze and judge Carl Becker's argument about history (pp. 197–98) or Eugene Raskin's argument about modern architecture (pp. 208–10).

EXERCISE 9   Using Facts in an Argument

Explain whether or not the facts stated by Alston Chase (exercise 1, pp. 200–202) could be used to support a positive conclusion about the state of American colleges.

10.2F   Writing an Interpretive Essay

To interpret a piece of writing is to explain what it means. Though interpretation calls for many of the analytical skills we have discussed above, it commonly aims not so much to evaluate as to elucidate, not so much to judge the effectiveness of arguments as to reveal the significance of works that do not usually make overt arguments: works of literature.

The interpretation of poetry, drama, and literary prose requires a number of specialized skills that we do not have space to explain in this book. But essentially, interpretive writing aims to construct an argument *about* the meaning of a literary work, to show that the work as a whole or some element of it—a character, a theme, a recurrent image, a scene, or a chapter—has a particular meaning. Here, for instance, is an interpretive essay written by a college freshman:

Thoreau's Treatment of Time in *Walden*

Henry David Thoreau's *Walden* is an account of the author's attempt to remove himself from society and live a life of self-sufficiency at Walden Pond. Yet strangely enough, Thoreau seems highly preoccupied with one of the very things that dominate the society he has left behind: time. If he is truly independent of society, if he has really forsaken the world of clock-watching businessmen and wage-earners, why is he so concerned with measuring time? Why does he have so much to say about it? The answer, I think, is that Thoreau measures his life at Walden not by clock time but by nature's time: not in hours and minutes but in mornings, evenings, seasons, deaths, and births.

Thoreau is sufficiently free from conventional notions of time that he can imagine a life without any time at all. He illustrates such a life with the story of the Kouroo artist who set out to make the perfect staff, and who devoted hundreds of years to the project because he believed that time had nothing to do with perfection, and he was willing to spend his whole life pursuing it. "As he made no compromise with Time," says Thoreau, "Time kept out of his way, and only sighed at a distance because he [Time] could not overcome him" (216). This story represents the ideal state that Thoreau would like to achieve. For him, the ultimate achievement would be to make time stand still.

But Thoreau knew that time could not be stopped. At Walden, therefore, he decided to regulate his life not by the clock time that mechanically runs society but by the natural cycles that govern every living thing on earth, and even the earth itself. The morning of each new day at Walden marks the beginning of a new life, just as spring marks the awakening of the pond from its long winter's death. Thoreau measured his life at Walden by these natural patterns of cyclic renewal. Though he actually spent two years at Walden Pond, he compressed the story of his sojourn into just one complete cycle that began with the building of his house in the spring and ended—after summer and fall and the chill of winter—with the glorious return of spring. "As every season seems best to us in its turn," he writes, "so the coming in of spring is like the creation of Cosmos out of Chaos and the realization of the Golden Age" (207). The calendar might have said that he was one or two years older, but Thoreau felt reborn when spring returned.

In Thoreau's concept of time, hours and minutes give way to the immeasurable rhythms of nature and life itself. He ends *Walden* with the story of the bug that suddenly emerged from the wood of a table. Many years before, its egg had been deposited in the tree from which the table was made; one day it gnawed its way out, "hatched perchance by the heat of an urn" (221). With no knowledge of how many years it had been buried and no desire to find out, it simply appeared because it had reached at last the peak of its life-cycle. Likewise, Thoreau urges us to disregard the years in which we have imprisoned ourselves and to stop measuring our existence by the clock and calendar. Instead, he shows us how to measure existence by the number of times we experience a renewal of our lives.

Works Cited

Thoreau, Henry David. Walden. Ed. Owen Thomas. New York: Norton, 1966.

The writer begins by stating a question in the introductory paragraph. If Thoreau seeks independence from society, why is he so preoccupied with the typically social activity of measuring time? The answer to this question becomes the thesis of the essay: Thoreau measures time not by mechanical but by natural means, by the cycles of days and seasons.

To develop this thesis, the writer first cites Thoreau's story of the Kouroo artist. Though this story represents an impossible ideal, it clearly shows what Thoreau is striving for: a freedom from ordinary, conventional notions of time. Having made that point, the author then shows how Thoreau found a freedom of his own in the cycle of seasons, and how he was reborn in the spring. Finally, the story of the bug exemplifies the kind of renewal that triumphs over time. Thus it enables the author to reaffirm his thesis.

This analysis of *Walden* also illustrates a good way of organizing an interpretive essay. The author begins with a specific topic (Thoreau's concept of time), defines a problem (the conflict between a desire for freedom and a preoccupation with time), and then proposes a solution in the form of a thesis to be developed. To develop the thesis, he writes three paragraphs on three specific things from the text: the story of the artist, the passage on spring, and the story of the bug. In each of these paragraphs he quotes from *Walden* but only enough to make his points. He uses paraphrase to keep down the amount of material quoted and thus to keep the reader's eye on the line of interpretation he develops.

A brief interpretive essay such as this should be sharply focused. It should concentrate on a definite topic and make specific references to the work interpreted. In the essay above, the author cites three different parts of *Walden*. If he had set out to analyze Thoreau's experience with planting beans, he could have worked with just one chapter, "The Bean-field." But in either case, the author should connect his topic to specific passages from the work being interpreted.

EXERCISE 10   Introducing an Interpretive Essay

Following the model shown above, write the introductory paragraph for an interpretive essay on any work chosen by you or your teacher. Your paragraph should (1) identify a topic, (2) define a problem, and (3) propose a solution in the form of a thesis to be developed.

EXERCISE 11   Writing an Interpretive Essay

Using the thesis generated for the previous exercise, write an interpretive essay in which you specifically refer to at least three passages from the work you have chosen. Include at least three quotations from the work.

10.3 Imitative Response—Reading for Style

Reading is to writing what hearing is to talking. Just as you cannot learn to talk without hearing other people speak, so you cannot learn to write without reading what others have written, without seeing and absorbing the huge variety of ways in which sentences, paragraphs, essays, stories, and poems have been put together. No guidelines for good writing can ever take the place of good writing itself, used as a model. If you like tennis, you don't watch John McEnroe play Jimmy Connors just to find out what the final score will be. You watch the game to see how McEnroe serves and Connors returns, to study the lobs, drop shots, passing shots, forehands, backhands, overhead smashes, and putaways, to see why one man finally wins and the other loses. In the same way, you should read good writing for more than its content. You should watch the way good writers make their points.

Style is often thought to be a mysterious ingredient. But the more you study the styles of good writers, the more tangible style becomes. Compare these two paragraphs:

> It is surprising, perhaps even embarrassing, to consider the ways in which ants resemble human beings. Fungi, for example, are grown by ants, and in this respect the ants are like human farmers. Furthermore, aphids are raised by ants, just as pigs are raised by farmers. Other activities include fighting in large numbers, just as human armies fight. Also, chemical sprays are sometimes used in those battles to disturb and confuse enemies. In addition, ants are taken to work for other ants as slaves. Moreover, in families of weaver ants, the larvae, or "children," are used for work; they are held like shuttles to spin out the thread with which leaves are sewn together for fungus gardens. Finally, information is continually passed back and forth among ants. Altogether, they do a considerable number of things that human beings do.

> Ants are so much like human beings as to be an embarrassment. They farm fungi, raise aphids as livestock, launch armies into wars, use chemical sprays to alarm and confuse enemies, capture slaves. The families of weaver ants engage in child labor, holding their larvae like shuttles to spin out the thread that sews the leaves together for their fungus gardens. They exchange information ceaselessly. They do everything but watch television.
>
> —Lewis Thomas, *Lives of a Cell*

These two paragraphs say essentially the same thing, but their styles are drastically different. The first is plodding, wordy, and ponderous; the second sprints. What makes it do so?

Part of the answer is compression. Instead of zigzagging around the main point ("It is surprising, perhaps even embarrassing, to consider the ways . . .”), Thomas goes directly to it: “Ants are so much like human beings as to be an embarrassment.” And what the second sentence of the first paragraph takes seventeen words to say, Thomas says in three: “They farm fungi.” Thomas achieves this compression largely by avoiding the passive verbs that clutter the first version and by using active verbs that bring the ants to life: they *farm, launch, use, capture, engage, exchange*—in sum, do everything that humans do.

Thomas startles us when he says that ants do everything but watch television. Of course he is exaggerating. He doesn't expect us to believe that ants drill oil wells, write novels, or play basketball. But he does expect us to make the implied comparison with human beings, many of whom do little *but* watch television. What he mischievously implies is that ants are much more lively and interesting than we are.

In writing, as in any other art, you learn by studying and imitating styles you admire. If you read a sentence or a paragraph that excites you, make it your own. Write it down or memorize it. Then quote it when you get the chance, or imitate its style in a sentence of your own.

Conscious and formal imitation of a writer with a distinctive style can be an excellent exercise. Start by reading aloud to yourself this passage from Mark Twain's *Autobiography:*

> As I have said, I spent some part of every year at the farm until I was twelve or thirteen years old. The life which I led there with my cousins was full of charm and so is the memory of it yet. I can call back the solemn twilight and the mystery of the deep woods, the earthy smells, the faint odors of the wild flowers, the sheen of rain-washed foliage, the rattling clatter of drops when the wind shook the trees, the far-off hammering of woodpeckers and the muffled drumming of wood-pheasants in the remoteness of the forest, the snapshot glimpses of disturbed wild creatures scurrying through the grass—I can call it all back and make it as real as it ever was, and as blessed. I can call back the prairie, and its loneliness and peace, and a vast hawk hanging motionless in the sky with his wings spread wide and the blue of the vault showing through the fringe of their end-feathers. I can see the woods in their autumn dress, the oaks purple, the hickories washed with gold, the maples and the sumachs luminous with crimson fires, and I can hear the rustle made by the fallen leaves as we plowed through them. I can see the blue clusters of wild grapes hanging amongst the foliage of the saplings, and I remember the taste of them and the smell. I know how the wild blackberries looked and how they tasted; and the same with the pawpaws, the hazelnuts, and the persimmons; and I can feel the thumping rain upon my head of hickory-nuts and walnuts when we were out in the frosty dawn to

scramble for them with the pigs, and the gusts of wind loosed them and sent them down.

You may not think you could ever write like this. But you can—right now. In your own descriptive writing you can immediately use the two simple techniques illustrated here: starting with a memory statement (*I can call back, I can see*), and filling each sentence with specific memories—sights, sounds, smells, and feelings.

Here, for instance, is a description of working on an asparagus farm written by a student who was deliberately imitating Twain:

> I can still remember changing pipe in nothing but gym shorts and tennis shoes, with swarms of bees humming all around me in the fern and never once was I stung. I remember disturbing countless quail and pheasants, and once in a while catching a brief glimpse of a coyote or jackrabbit. I remember freezing hands in early spring, when frost covered the pipes in the early morning, and burning hands in late summer, when a line had lain in the hot sun for a day or so. I know the sweet taste of grapes liberated from the next field, and the bitter taste of raw potato from another neighboring unit. I know how to grab a handful of wheat and rub off the chaff, leaving only the crunchy grain, and how good it tastes after a hard day's work. I can call back the ringing in my ears after driving a tractor all day, nonstop, and how good it would have felt to have had some earplugs. I remember the shimmering sun baking us to a golden brown as we lay snoozing on the ground after the pipes were changed, and how once in a while the boss would find us in that position. He never appreciated our attitude towards work.

Though you can easily recognize Twain's two basic techniques, you can also see that this is creative imitation. The student does not copy Twain's words. Rather he uses Twain's techniques to summon up personal memories, to generate a description of his own experience.

A passage of any length can be a model for you to imitate. Here, for instance, is a single long sentence:

> For four years this lovely college life lasted, and I simply survived in a happy somnambulistic state, blowsy, disheveled, dropping hairpins, tennis balls, and notebooks wherever I went, drinking tea with Dr. Lily Campbell and the professors, lapping up talk of books and history, drinking tea with classmates and Elizabeth Boynton, the librarian, having dated or nearly dated with the two M's on either side of me, Macon and Morgan, having dates with Leonard Keller, who was working out campus thefts and misdemeanors with the first lie detector, falling asleep in all afternoon lectures, late for every appointment, smiling sheepishly on the rare occasions when I arrived in class on time, and, always and ever, dreaming.
>
> —Agnes De Mille, *Dance to the Piper*

The writer begins with two simple statements: *For four years this lovely college life lasted, and I simply survived in a happy somnambulistic state.* Then she adds a string of adjectives and modifying phrases: *blowsy, disheveled, dropping hairpins, drinking tea, falling asleep, late for every appointment, smiling sheepishly.* This type of sentence is open-ended: once you have started it off with a statement or two, you can go on adding adjectives and modifiers as they come to mind.

Exercise 12   Imitating the Style of a Sentence

Imitating Agnes De Mille, describe your four years of high school in a single sentence. You can start the sentence with just one simple statement if you wish.

Exercise 13   Imitating the Style of a Passage

Drawing on your own memories of a specific period or experience in your life, write an imitation of Twain's passage. Begin at least one of your sentences with *I can still see,* at least one with *I can still hear,* and at least one with *I can still feel.*

Exercise 14   Explaining and Imitating the Style of a Passage

Copy out a brief passage by any writer whose work you admire, and then (1) explain why you admire its style, and (2) imitate its style in a passage of your own.

II

WRITING
SENTENCES

11

THE SIMPLE SENTENCE
Basic Parts

The sentence is a fundamentally human creation. Like the human beings who write them, sentences come in a seemingly endless variety of shapes and sizes: some stretch out for line upon line; others stop short after two or three words. Yet the sentence has a basic structure, just as the human body does. Despite the variety in the human race, there are certain things we can say about all human bodies, or about *the* human body, the structure that all of us share as long as we live. And despite the variety in sentences, there are certain things we can say about the structure of *the* sentence, the structure that most of us use whenever we write.

How much do you need to know about this structure in order to write well? Certainly you don't need to know everything, and many of the essentials you know already. Whether or not you can define any grammatical terms, the very fact that you can speak the English language means that you already know a good deal about the structure of the English sentence. But to improve the construction of your own sentences, you may need to know more. If your teacher says that one of your sentences is incorrect because you have tried to make a modifier do the work of a subject, you need to know what that means before you can rewrite the sentence. And if your teacher says that you overuse the passive voice, you need to know the difference between that and the active voice before you can use the active to invigorate your style. The aim of this chapter, then, is to explain the terms you will need to know in order to make your sentences both grammatically correct and rhetorically effective.

11.1 The Subject and the Predicate

A sentence normally has a subject and a predicate. The **subject** is the word or word group that tells who or what performs or undergoes the action named by the verb or experiences the condition named. The **predicate** is the word or word group that normally follows the subject and tells what it does, has, or is, what is done to it, or where it is. Consider the following examples:

SUBJECT	PREDICATE
Helen	is laughing
The movie	starts at eight.
The children	have a new toy.
This blade	is sharp.
Two tenants	have been evicted.
The milk	is in the refrigerator.

11.2 Sentences and Clauses

Every sentence normally has at least one combination of a subject (s) and predicate (P); such a combination is called a **clause**. But a sentence may have more than one clause:

CLAUSE 1: If the Oilers / win the Superbowl,

CLAUSE 2: I / will collect twenty bucks from my roommate,

CLAUSE 3: who / is betting against them.

In later chapters, we will consider sentences like this—sentences with two or more clauses. In this chapter, we consider chiefly the one-clause sentence (known as the **simple sentence**) because all other sentences are founded on its structure.

11.3 Writing the Predicate—The Role of Verbs

The predicate always includes a verb, and the verb is one of three types—linking, intransitive, or transitive.

11.3A Linking Verbs

A **linking verb** is followed by a word or word group that identifies, describes, or classifies the subject:

Whales *are* mammals.
Caterpillars *become* butterflies.
Stephen Sondheim *is* a songwriter.

Susan *felt* sleepy.
Aspirin *tastes* bitter.
The alligator *looked* hungry.

The most widely used linking verb is a form of *be,* such as *is, are, was,* or *were.* Other linking verbs include *seem, become, feel, sound,* and *taste.*

A word or phrase that follows a linking verb is called a **subject complement** because it completes the meaning initiated by the subject and the linking verb. If the subject complement is a noun, such as *mammals* or *butterflies,* it is called a **predicate noun.** If the subject complement is an adjective, such as *sleepy* or *bitter,* it is called a **predicate adjective.** (For more on nouns, see section 11.4; for more on adjectives, see section 12.2.)

11.3B   Intransitive Verbs

An **intransitive verb** names an action that has no direct impact on anyone or anything named in the predicate:

Frank *scowled.*
Gail *won* easily.
Children *giggle.*
Whales *sing.*
Frank *disappeared* after the party.

11.3C   Transitive Verbs and Direct Objects

A **transitive verb** names an action that directly affects a person or thing mentioned in the predicate. The word or word group naming this person or thing is the **direct object** (DO) of the verb.

DO
Hurricane Ethel *hit* Charleston.

Any verb followed by a direct object is transitive, and the direct object may be either a single word or a group of words:

	DO
Janet *drove*	the big yellow school bus.
David *writes*	songs about unemployed steelworkers.
Harry *gives*	lectures on acid rain.
Gamblers *lose*	money.
Keith *made*	a necklace.
Ellen *packed*	her suitcase.
The professor *gave*	a makeup exam.
Gail *won*	the marathon.

Some verbs can be transitive or intransitive. Compare these two sentences:

DO
TRANSITIVE: Gail *won* the marathon.
INTRANSITIVE: Gail *won* easily.

11.3D Transitive Verbs and Indirect Objects

Some transitive verbs can have two objects: a direct object, as already shown, and an **indirect object** (IO), which comes between the verb and the direct object:

IO   DO
Keith made *Janet* a necklace.
IO   DO
The professor gave *me* a makeup exam.

You can also write the sentences this way:

DO
Keith made a necklace for Janet.

DO
The professor gave a makeup exam to me.

If you want to stress the one *for* or *to* whom something was done, you can use a phrase: Keith made a necklace for *Janet.* But the use of an indirect object lets you highlight the direct object by putting it last: Keith made Janet *a necklace.* This arrangement also tightens the sentence by cutting out *for.* Verbs that give you this option include *make, give, send, offer, show, write,* and *tell.*

11.3E Transitive Verbs and Object Complements

Another kind of transitive verb usually calls for the use of an **object complement** (OC), a word or word group that immediately follows a direct object and identifies or describes it:

DO   OC
Stafford considers Alice *the best runner on the team.*
DO   OC
Critics thought the lyrics *meaningless.*

DO   OC
Employers found North *lazy.*
DO OC
We named the puppy *Fern.*

Object complements follow such verbs as *name, elect, appoint, think, consider, judge, find* (in the sense of "judge"), and *make* (as in "What *makes* some people stars?").

11.3F Active and Passive Voice

A transitive verb can be in either the active or the passive voice. A verb is in the **active voice** when the subject performs the action named by the verb:

> Bees *make* honey.

A verb is in the **passive voice** when the subject undergoes the action named by the verb:

> Honey *is made* by bees.

The performer of the action—the agent—can be specified in a *by* phrase after the verb. But the agent need not be specified:

> Four presidents *have been assassinated.*

To keep your writing vigorous, use the active voice unless you have good reason for the passive. (See chapter 22, pp. 391–99, for a full discussion of voice.)

11.3G Verb Phrases

Predicates often contain a **verb phrase,** which consists of two or more verbs—a base verb and at least one "helping" verb called an **auxiliary:**

	AUX	BASE VERB
Gail	*can*	*win.*
Gail	*did*	*win.*
Gail	*could have*	*lost.*

As these examples show, auxiliaries indicate such things as time, capability, and possibility. Other auxiliaries are *is, are, was, were, has, had, do, does, may, might, would,* and *should.*

In many questions the sentence begins with an auxiliary:

> *Can* Gail *win?*
> *Did* Gail *win?*
> *Could* Gail *have lost?*

(For a full discussion of verbs, see chapters 19–23.)

11.3H   Summary—The Chief Sentence Types

Following are the chief sentence types.

1. Subject + linking verb + subject complement

| Whales | are | mammals. (predicate noun) |
| Whales | are | huge. (predicate adjective) |

2. Subject + intransitive verb

Whales   sing.

3. Subject + transitive verb + direct object

ACTIVE VOICE
The whale   rammed   the ship.

4. Subject + transitive verb + agent

PASSIVE VOICE
The ship   was rammed   by the whale.

5. Subject + transitive verb + indirect object + direct object

The company   offered   me   a job.

6. Subject + transitive verb + direct object + object complement

The jury   found   him   guilty.

11.4 Writing the Subject

The subject of a simple sentence can be a noun, a noun phrase, a pronoun, or a verbal noun. We consider each in turn.

1. A **noun** is a word naming one or more persons, creatures, places, things, activities, conditions, or ideas:

> *Children* thrive on loving care.
> *Deer* run gracefully.
> *Freedom* entails responsibility.
> *Termites* eat wood.

2. A **noun phrase** is a group of words consisting of a main noun (MN) and the words that describe, limit, or qualify it:

> MN
> *The price of gold* has dropped.
>
> MN
> *Long-standing arguments* can be difficult to settle.
>
> MN
> *The sound of snoring in the audience* distracted the performers.
>
> MN
> *Patrons with passes* may enter the museum.

3. A **pronoun** (PR) is a word that takes the place of a noun (N):

> N   PR
> Bush frowned. *He* didn't like the question.

> N   PR
> Jennifer was stranded. *She* needed a ride.

> N   PR
> Traffic moved briskly at first. Then *it* slowed to a crawl.

(For a full discussion of pronouns, see chapter 18.)

4. A **verbal noun** is a word or phrase formed from a verb and used as a noun:

> *Hunting* can be dangerous.
> *Splitting logs* takes muscle.
> *Sky diving in cloudy weather* is risky.
> *To err* is human.
> *To see Julia again* excited him.

As the examples show, verbal nouns enable you to treat an action as if it were a thing, and thus to get more action into your sentence. There are two types: the **gerund,** which ends in *-ing,* and the **infinitive,** which is usually marked by *to.* Each can be followed by other words making up a phrase.

Verbal nouns may also serve as predicate nouns (PN) and direct objects (DO):

>   PN
> Their ambition was *to fly.*
>   PN
> Her hobby is *collecting stamps.*
>   DO
> Few enjoy *my singing.*
>   DO
> Gourmands love *to eat.*

11.5 Putting Subjects after the Verb

The subject of a declarative sentence—a sentence that makes a statement—usually precedes the verb. But the subject follows the verb in sentences like these:

> There was *water* in the basement.
> It is hard *to read small print.*

In these sentences *there* and *it* serve as introductory words or **expletives.**

The subject also follows the verb when the word order is inverted:

> "Watch closely," said *the magician.*
> In the middle of the room stood a *striking bronze nude.*

Except in the identifying tags used with quotations, as in the first example, the inversion of subject-verb order gives special prominence to the subject, as in the second example. You should therefore use inversion sparingly—and only when you want this special effect.

In questions the subject follows the auxiliary verb, so that the predicate is divided:

P   S   P
Will / *the Red Sox* / ever win a World Series?

11.6 Using Modifiers

A **modifier** is a word, phrase, or clause that describes, limits, or qualifies another word or word group. In *The price of gold has dropped,* the word *The* and the phrase *of gold* are both modifiers of *price* and are part of the subject. In each of the following sentences, the italicized word modifies the verb or verb phrase:

> Butch *greedily* gobbled the doughnut.
> Cynthia locked the door *immediately.*
> Frank disappeared *suddenly.*
> *Everywhere* we saw devastation.

Since modifiers include even such words as *the* and *a,* nearly all sentences have at least one, and most sentences have them in both the subject and the predicate. In the following examples the modifiers are italicized:

S   P
The boy *inside the closet* / was yelling *desperately.*

S   P
The heavy packing case / fell *to the floor.*

S   P
The clumsy workmen / dropped *the heavy* crate *to the floor.*

S   P
Raised in Digby, Nova Scotia, David / *sometimes* writes songs *about
fishermen.*

S   P
Shivering in the icy wind, Steve / pounded *the heavy oak* door *of the
old house.*

P   S   P
How often does / smoking / cause cancer?

These sentences show how modifiers can enrich and vivify your sentences. (For a full discussion of modifiers, see chapter 12.)

EXERCISE 1 **Composing—Recognizing Subjects and Predicates**

In each of the following sentences, identify the subject and the predicate. Then write a new sentence that follows the form of the original.

EXAMPLE
Foam from the liquid soap covered the plastic surface.

Foam from the liquid soap^{S} / covered the plastic surface.^{P}

Smoke from the burning schoolhouse / blackened the midday sky.

1. The hills across the valley of the Ebro were long and white.
   —Ernest Hemingway

2. Will the Protestants of Northern Ireland make peace with the Catholics?

3. Man without writing cannot long retain his history in his head.
   —Loren Eiseley

4. At once a black fin slit the pink cloud on the water, shearing it in two.
   —Annie Dillard

5. Outside literature, the main motive for writing is to describe the world.
   —Northrop Frye

6. Winning the marathon in the 1984 Olympics made Joan Benoit famous overnight.

EXERCISE 2   Sentence Expanding with Modifiers

Expand each of the following sentences by adding modifiers to both the subject and the predicate.

EXAMPLE
I fidgeted.
EXPANDED: Sitting in the back row, I fidgeted restlessly during the long lecture.

1. Sylvester (a cat) hissed.
2. Birds sang.
3. John grinned.
4. Boys shouted.
5. Claude mumbled.

11.7 Using Compound Phrases

You can develop a simple sentence by turning any part of it into a **compound phrase.** A compound phrase joins words or phrases to show one of the following things:

1. Addition

> The quarterback was smart.
> The quarterback was fast.
> COMBINED: The quarterback was *smart and fast.*

The dancer was lean.
The dancer was acrobatic.
The dancer was bold.
COMBINED: The dancer was *lean, acrobatic, and bold.*

Squirrels scampered among the trees.
Chipmunks scampered among the trees.
Field mice scampered among the trees.
COMBINED: *Squirrels, chipmunks, and field mice* scampered among the trees.

Ants crawled over the floor.
Ants crawled up the wall.
Ants crawled onto the counter.
Ants crawled into the honey pot.
COMBINED: Ants crawled *over the floor, up the wall, onto the counter, and into the honey pot.*

McGreavy took the ball from center.
He stepped back.
He looked coolly for his receiver.
He threw a bullet pass right over the middle of the line.
COMBINED: McGreavy *took the ball from center, stepped back, looked coolly for his receiver, and threw a bullet pass right over the middle of the line.*

2. Contrast

The deer was dying.
But he was not yet dead.
COMBINED: The deer was *dying but not yet dead.*

3. Choice

The government must reduce its spending.
Or it must raise taxes.
COMBINED: The government must *either reduce its spending or raise taxes.*

The parts of a compound phrase should normally be joined by one of the means listed here.

1. One or more conjunctions, such as *and, yet, or, but,* or *nor:*

He has neither charm *nor* talent.
She won the point *but* lost the game.
Phil was overweight *and* nervous.
Many students need loans *or* grants to meet their expenses.

2. A comma:

The fat, sleek walrus slipped into the icy water.

3. A comma plus a conjunction:

The dancer was lean, acrobatic, *and* bold.

When a compound phrase has three or more items, you normally need a comma plus a conjunction between the last two.

4. A pair of correlatives, such as *both . . . and* or *either . . . or:*

> *Both* England *and* Russia fought Germany in World War II.
> Motorists must *either* curb their demand for gas *or* face the prospect of gas rationing.

Among other correlatives are *not only . . . but also, whether . . . or,* and *neither . . . nor.* (For more on correlatives, see pp. 283–84.)

EXERCISE 3 **Sentence Combining with Compound Phrases**

Combine the sentences in each of the following sets by using compound phrases.

EXAMPLE
Martha is a tennis player.
Martha is a gymnast.
Martha is a member of the swimming team.
COMBINED: Martha is a tennis player, a gymnast, and a member of the swimming team.

1. Proud nations have gradually fallen into the dust.
   Great civilizations have gradually fallen into the dust.

2. The painting was savage.
   The painting was sensuous.
   The painting was brilliant.

3. The dog leaped.
   The dog yelped.
   The dog ran.

4. The Vietnam War cost millions of dollars.
   It took thousands of American lives.
   It left behind a legacy of national guilt.

5. The policeman whistled.
   He signaled me to stop.
   He·strode grimly to the car.
   He asked me to get out.
   He demanded to see my driver's permit.

6. We looked under the sofa.
   We looked over the bookcase.
   We looked in the closet.
   We looked behind the television set.

7. He saw the truck coming out of the fog.
   He could not avoid hitting it.

8. The president must use his power.
   Otherwise he must lose it.

9. She spent the summer in Newport.
   She spent the winter in Haiti.
   She spent the rest of the year in debt.

10. He walked slowly
    He walked awkwardly.
    He walked timidly.

EXERCISE 4   Sentence Expanding with Compounds

Expand each of the sentences that you wrote for exercise 2 by using compounds wherever possible.

EXAMPLE
Sitting in the back row, I fidgeted restlessly during the long lecture.
EXPANDED: Sitting in the back row, Craig and I yawned and fidgeted restlessly during the long lecture.

EXERCISE 5   Adding Subjects, Objects, and Modifiers

Add a subject and direct object to each of the following verbs to make a simple sentence. Also add any modifiers that come to mind.

EXAMPLE
rode
After seeing all the sights of Ottawa, Midge rode a train to Montreal.

1. clutched
2. tackled
3. created
4. stung
5. splashed

11.8 Revising Mixed Constructions   *mixed*

A mixed construction is a sentence in which a modifier takes the place of the subject. Consider the following examples:

s?
1. *Exiled from their homeland and persecuted in a foreign land /
   p
   is a plight shared by both Jews and blacks in America.

The would-be subject of this sentence is *Exiled from their homeland and persecuted in a foreign land*. But this group of words cannot serve as the subject because it is not a noun of any kind. It is a **modifying phrase.** To correct a sentence like this, you must furnish some kind of noun as the subject:

MODIFYING PHRASE
REVISED: Exiled from their homeland and persecuted in a foreign

land, Jews and blacks in America / share a common plight.

Now the would-be subject is made to modify the true subject—*Jews and blacks in America.*

2. *In jumping up and down on the stands / nearly broke them.

Once again, the sentence begins with a modifying phrase, which cannot serve by itself as a subject. To correct the sentence, you must furnish a new noun as the subject:

REVISED: In jumping up and down on the stands, the crowd / nearly broke them.

Or, by dropping *In,* you can turn the modifying phrase into a verbal noun:

REVISED: Jumping up and down on the stands / nearly broke them.

3. *Alone in the dark, narrow street / frightened him.

As before, the modifying phrase must be made to modify a noun or must itself become a noun:

REVISED: Alone in the dark, narrow street, he / was frightened.

REVISED: To be alone in the dark, narrow street / frightened him.

REVISED: Being alone in the dark, narrow street / frightened him.

EXERCISE 6   Revising Mixed Constructions

In each of the following, a modifier is misused as the subject of a sentence. Change the wording to correct the mistake.

EXAMPLE
*Raised in Wyoming has made Polly love the West.
REVISED: Raised in Wyoming, Polly loves the West.

1. By wearing sneakers in subzero weather froze John's toes.
2. Confident in her ability to understand physics prompted Joan to major in engineering.
3. On hearing grunting noises in the underbrush frightened the campers.
4. Victorious in his first three races encouraged Ted to dream of a gold medal.

5. Since he had never used a word processor before made him feel nervous.

11.9 Revising Faulty Predication *pred*

Faulty predication is misconnecting the basic parts of a sentence. There are three main kinds of misconnection.

1. Misconnecting of subject and active verb:

> *The Placement Office showed me how to write a résumé.

In this sentence, an abstract, impersonal thing is said to perform the kind of action that can be accomplished only by human beings. To correct a misconnection of this kind, replace the subject with the kind of agent that *can* perform the action named by the verb:

> REVISED: The Director of the Placement Office showed me how to write a résumé.

2. Misconnecting of verb and direct object:

> *The head of the shipbuilding company congratulated the achievement of the workers.

Here the main verb requires a human being or at least a living creature for an object. An *achievement* cannot be congratulated. To correct the error, change the verb or the object so that the two things fit together:

> REVISED: The head of the shipbuilding company congratulated the workers on their achievement. [or] The head of the shipbuilding company praised the achievement of the workers.

3. Misconnecting of subject and predicate noun:

> a. *Another kind of flying is a glider.

This type of sentence declares equivalence between an activity (flying) and an object (a glider). But an activity and an object are not equivalent. To correct the sentence, you must make the two items equivalent in form:

> REVISED: Another kind of flying is gliding. (two activities)
> [or]   Another type of aircraft is a glider. (two objects)

> b. *The reason for the evacuation of the building was because a bomb threat had been made.

This sentence tries to say that a *reason* is *because*. Those two words seem to go together, but they are not equivalent; *reason* is a noun, and *because* is not. To correct the sentence, use *that* instead of *because:*

> REVISED: The reason for the evacuation of the building was that a bomb threat had been made.

Or you could recast the sentence:

> The building was evacuated because of a bomb threat.

EXERCISE 7   Recognizing Correct Predication

Each of the following consists of two sentences with linking verbs. In one sentence the predication is correct; in the other it is faulty. Copy out the sentence with correct predication, and underline the two equivalent words or word groups.

EXAMPLE
(a) Another kind of flying is gliding.
(b) Another kind of flying is a glider.
a. Another kind of flying is gliding.

1. (a) Running a political campaign is where you have to sell personality.
   (b) Running a political campaign is a process of selling a personality.
2. (a) The main fault of Claghorn's speeches was the offense they gave to voters over sixty.
   (b) The main fault of Claghorn's speeches was how they offended voters over sixty.
3. (a) Sean's greatest achievement was when he predicted the scores of ten straight games correctly.
   (b) Sean's greatest achievement was predicting the scores of ten straight games correctly.
4. (a) An effective way to promote self-confidence in children is to encourage them to do things for themselves.
   (b) An effective way to promote self-confidence in children is doing things for themselves.
5. (a) A funny moment in the show is when the villain falls into a pile of wet cement.
   (b) A funny moment in the show is the villain falling into a pile of wet cement.
6. (a) The reason for the lawsuit was because the paper had published a lie.
   (b) The reason for the lawsuit was that the paper had published a lie.
7. (a) A picnic is when you eat outdoors.
   (b) A picnic is an outdoor meal.
8. (a) One unanswered question is "Who wrote the play?"
   (b) One unanswered question is the author of the play.

Revising Faulty Predication   241

9. (a) One of the most dramatic elements in the act is when Sarah asks Matthew: "What is more important to you—money or honor?"
   (b) One of the most dramatic moments in the act is when Sarah asks Matthew: "What is more important to you—money or honor?"

EXERCISE 8   Composing: Using Correct Predication

Each of the following consists of one whole sentence and the first part of another. Complete the second sentence with a phrase like the one italicized in the first.

> EXAMPLE
> Religion is *the opium of the people.* —Karl Marx.
> Television is <u>the junk food of the mind.</u>

1. The best way to shed weight is *to change your eating habits.*
   The quickest way to lose money is _____ .
2. My father's favorite summertime activity is *barbecuing steak.*
   My own favorite summertime activity is _____ .
3. My father's favorite wintertime activity is *watching hockey on TV.*
   My own favorite wintertime activity is _____ .
4. A graduating high school senior is *a nervous diver standing on a very high board.*
   A first-term college freshman is _____ .
5. To play football for Vince Lombardi was *to become part of a goal-scoring machine.*
   To run a marathon is _____ .
6. The big car has lately become *a big headache.*
   The small car has lately become _____ .

11.10 Revising Misused Gerunds   *mg*

Normally a noun or pronoun used before a gerund should be in the possessive case. Otherwise the gerund is misused.

> *Jake winning surprised everyone.
> REVISED: Jake's winning surprised everyone.
> *Everyone was surprised by him winning.
> REVISED: Everyone was surprised by his winning.

In sentences like these, you need the possessive to indicate that what concerns you is not the noun or pronoun—*Jake* or *him*—but the action "possessed" by the noun: *Jake's* winning or *his* winning. When the gerund is followed by a noun, you can clarify the meaning by using *of:*

> Jake's winning of the marathon surprised everyone.
> Everyone was surprised by his winning of the marathon.

EXERCISE 9 Revising Misused Gerunds

Revise each of the following sentences in which the writer fails to use the possessive case with a noun or pronoun followed by a gerund. If a sentence is correct as it stands, write *Correct*.

EXAMPLE
Helen shouting startled me.
REVISED: Helen's shouting startled me.

1. Jan resented him seizing the initiative in her project.
2. Alan denying the accusation convinced no one.
3. Davy Crockett defending the Alamo is one of the greatest feats in American history.
4. Vivian yawned; she already knew all about his winning of the election.
5. From Tom wrecking my car to Barbara ditching me, this semester has been a disaster.
6. William gobbling his food annoyed his mother.
7. The Voyager transmitting pictures all the way from Saturn to earth was a technological triumph.

12

MODIFIERS

12.1

In chapter 11 we cite modifiers as important elements in the simple sentence or any type of clause. Because of their importance and variety, they require a closer look. In this chapter we consider modifying words and phrases. We treat modifying clauses in chapter 15.

12.1 What Modifiers Do

A **modifier** is a word or word group that describes, limits, or qualifies another word or word group in a sentence. Consider what modifiers can do for this sentence:

> The balloons rose.

This is a bare-bones sentence. It has a subject *(balloons)* and a predicate *(rose)*, but no modifiers (except *The*), no words to tell us what the balloons looked like or how they rose. Modifiers can show the reader the size, color, and shape of a thing, or the way an action is performed. Thus they can help to make a sentence vivid, specific, emphatic, and lively:

> The balloons rose *slowly, big, red, and round, bobbing and weaving toward the fluffy white clouds.*

Modifiers also let you add information without adding more sentences. If you had to start a new sentence for every new piece of detail, you would soon begin to sound monotonous:

The balloons rose.
They rose *slowly*.
They were *big*.
They were *red*.
They were *round*.

Instead of serving up information in bite-size pieces like these, you can arrange the pieces in one simple sentence, putting each piece where it belongs:

The *big, red, round* balloons rose *slowly*.

There is often more than one place in a sentence where a modifier can go. You can add the word *slowly* to either end of a base sentence, or you can drop it into the middle:

The balloons rose *slowly*.
Slowly the balloons rose.
The balloons *slowly* rose.

12.2 Using Adjectives and Adjective Phrases

1. Adjectives are words that modify a noun, specifying such things as how many, what kind, and which one:

Complex problems require *careful* study.

Adjectives usually precede their nouns. But an adjective that modifies the subject of a sentence can appear in the predicate after a linking verb:

[s] The kick / [p] was *good*.

In addition, you can place adjectives after their nouns for dramatic effect:

The prosecutor, *intense and aggressive*, jabbed his forefinger at the witness.

Note the pair of commas.

2. Adjective phrases begin with a preposition—a word like *with*, *under*, *by*, *in*, *of*, or *at*. An adjective phrase usually tells more about a noun than a single adjective can:

She wore a *valuable* bracelet. [adjective]
She wore a bracelet *with emeralds, rubies, and sapphires.* [adjective phrase]
She grew up in a *large* house. [adjective]
She grew up in a house *with twenty-five rooms.* [adjective phrase]

Like a single adjective, an adjective phrase that modifies the subject of a sentence can appear in the predicate after a linking verb:

[s] The city / [P] was *in debt*.

Here are further examples:

It was Seymour, *with a bottle*.
Twenty-dollar bills sprouted from the pockets *of his coat*.
The grin *on his face* lit up the street.
The gleam *in his eye* was triumphant.
His day *at the racetrack* had made him rich.

Since adjective phrases contain nouns, you can add adjectives and other adjective phrases to them:

It was Seymour, *with a big bottle*.
It was Seymour, *with a big bottle of champagne*.
It was Seymour, *with a big bottle of champagne in his hand*.
Twenty-dollar bills sprouted from the pockets *of his red plaid coat*.

Like other modifiers, two or more adjective phrases can be made into a compound:

It was Seymour, *with a big bottle of champagne in his hand, a mile-wide grin on his fat, jolly face, and a triumphant gleam in his eye*.

Adjective phrases generally follow the noun or pronoun they modify.

12.3 Using and Overusing Nouns as Adjectives

A noun used before another noun often serves as an adjective. Like an adjective, it modifies the word that comes next:

Cars may not travel in the *bus* lane.
A *stone* wall surrounded the farm.
An orthopedist is a *bone* doctor.

It is usually all right to use a single noun in place of an adjective, but you should avoid overusing nouns in this way. Too many nouns run together make a sentence confusing:

The fund drive completion target date postponement gave the finance committee extension time to raise contributions.

In this sentence, the nouns are simply thrown together, and the reader is left to figure out how they relate to one another. To clarify the sentence, turn some of the nouns into ordinary adjectives or adjective phrases:

The postponement of the target date for completion of the fund drive gave the finance committee additional time to raise contributions.

12.4 Using Adverbs and Adverb Phrases

An **adverb** is a word that tells such things as how, when, where, why, and for what purpose. It can be used—

1. To modify a verb:

The balloons rose *slowly*.

2. To modify an adjective:

The bolt was *dangerously* loose.

3. To modify another adverb:

Light travels *amazingly* fast.

4. To modify a whole sentence:

Unfortunately, [the bolt was loose].

To form most adverbs, you add *-ly* to an adjective. Thus *quick* becomes *quickly*, and *gruff* becomes *gruffly*. Exceptions are as follows.

1. A few words (such as *fast, far, well,* and *little*) keep the same form when they turn from adjectives into adverbs:

We made a *fast* stop. [adjective]
We stopped *fast*. [adverb]

2. Adjectives ending in *-y* must be made to end in *-ily* when they become adverbs:

A *lucky* guess saved me. [adjective]
Luckily, I knew the answer. [adverb]

3. Adjectives ending in *-ly* do not change their endings when they become adverbs:

A *deadly* blow struck him. [adjective]
He looked *deadly* pale. [adverb]

4. Some adverbs—such as *never, soon,* and *always*—are not based on adjectives at all and have their own special forms.

An **adverb phrase** is a group of words that begins with a preposition—a word such as *at, with, in,* or *like*—and works like an adverb, telling how, when, or where:

At noon the whistle blew.
A gunman lurked *behind the door.*
Holmes used his right fist *like a sledgehammer.*

Using Adverbs and Adverb Phrases   **247**

Joan gasped, wide-eyed and red *to the roots of her hair.*
He spoke haltingly *at first.*
During the flight the bolt became loose.

EXERCISE 1   **Sentence Combining with Adjectives and Adverbs**

Combine the sentences in each of the following sets by using the first sentence as a base and adding modifiers (shown in italics) from the others. Combine the sentences of each set in at least two different ways. Then, if you prefer one of the combinations, put a check next to it.

EXAMPLE
The balloons hung.
They were *in the air.*
They were *big.*
They were *red.*
They were *round.*
They were *like apples.*
The apples were *oversized.*
The apples were *enormously* so.
COMBINATION 1: The balloons hung in the air, big, red, and round, like enormously oversized apples.
COMBINATION 2: Big, red, and round, the balloons hung in the air like enormously oversized apples.

1. The trumpeter blew.
   He was *fat.*
   He was *sweaty.*
   He was *red.*
   The redness was *in his face.*
   He blew *stridently.*
   He was *like an archangel.*
   The archangel was *mad.*
   The archangel was *hopelessly* so.
   The archangel was *drunken.*
   The archangel was *outrageously* so.

2. The president spoke.
   His speech was *in a certain kind of voice.*
   The voice was *low.*
   It was *chillingly* so.
   He was *stiff.*
   He was *somber.*
   He was *grim.*
   The grimness was *at the mouth.*
   He was *like a captain.*
   The captain was *in charge of a ship.*
   The ship was *sinking.*
   It was doing that *steadily.*

3. Ellen stood.
   She did so *during most of the evening.*
   She did so *elegantly.*

She was *against a column.*
The column was *fluted.*
The column was *white.*
The column was *on the terrace.*
The terrace was *flagstone.*

12.5 Misusing Adjectives as Adverbs

When the adjective form differs from the adverb form, do not use the first in place of the second. In conversation you might say that a car *stopped quick* or that its driver *talked gruff,* but in writing—especially formal writing—you should say that the car *stopped quickly* and that the driver *talked gruffly.* Most adverbs require the *-ly* ending. Unless you are quite sure that a particular word does not require this ending when used as an adverb, see your dictionary before leaving the *-ly* off. On *good* and *well, bad* and *badly, poor* and *poorly,* see the Glossary of Usage, beginning on p. 575.

12.6 Forming and Using Comparatives and Superlatives

The comparative lets you compare one person or thing with another; the superlative lets you compare one person or thing with all others in a group of three or more:

> Jake is *tall.*
> Jake is *taller* than Steve. [comparative]
> Jake is the *tallest* man on the team. [superlative]

12.6A Comparatives

When you add *-er* to some adjectives, you make them comparative. A **comparative adjective** starts a comparison between two different things or sets of things. Normally the comparisons must be completed by *than* plus a noun or noun equivalent:

> Dolphins are *smarter* than sharks.
> Skiing is *riskier* than skating.

With a long adjective, you form the comparative by using *more* rather than *-er:*

> Are women *more observant* than men?

You can use *less* with an adjective of any length:

> Are the Soviets any *less hostile* now than they were a year ago?

To form a **comparative adverb,** use *more* before an adverb ending in *-ly;* otherwise, add *-er:*

> The north star shines *more brightly* than any other star.
> Nothing moves *faster* than light.

Use *less* before any adverb:

> Wood heats *less expensively* than oil.

(For more on comparisons, see section 15.12.)

12.6B Superlatives

When you add *-est* to some adjectives, you make them superlative. A **superlative adjective** normally compares one thing with all others in its class:

> St. Augustine, Florida, is the *oldest* city in the U.S.
> The blue whale is the *largest* of all living creatures.

With a long adjective, you form the superlative by using *most* rather than *-est:*

> Forest Lawn Memorial Park in Los Angeles has been called "the *most cheerful* graveyard in the world."

You can use *least* with an adjective of any length:

> According to the *Guinness Book of World Records,* the *least successful* author in the world is William A. Gold, who in eighteen years of writing earned only fifty cents.

Normally, you also use *most* or *least* to form a **superlative adverb:**

> The *most lavishly* decorated float in the whole parade came last.
> Of all grammatical forms, the superlative adverb is perhaps the one *least commonly* used.

12.6C Special Forms

Some modifiers have special forms for the comparative and superlative:

	POSITIVE	COMPARATIVE	SUPERLATIVE
good well	[adjective] [adverb]	better	best
bad badly	[adjective] [adverb]	worse	worst
little	[adjective and adverb, for quantity]	less	least

	POSITIVE	COMPARATIVE	SUPERLATIVE
much	[adjective and adverb]	more	most
far	[adjective and adverb]	farther	farthest

12.7 Misusing Comparatives and Superlatives

Do not use *-er* and *more* or *-est* and *most* at the same time:

*Anthracite is more harder than bituminous coal.
REVISED: Anthracite is harder than bituminous coal.
*Mount Everest is the most highest peak in the world.
REVISED: Mount Everest is the highest peak in the world.

12.8 Using Appositives

An **appositive** is a noun or noun phrase that identifies another noun or noun phrase, or a pronoun. Professional writers use appositives to create sentences like these:

Graduation, *the hush-hush magic time of frills and gifts and congratulations and diplomas,* was finished for me before my name was called.
—Maya Angelou
Brian Mulroney, *head of the Progressive Conservatives,* became Prime Minister of Canada in 1984.
Michelle bought a new toy, *a Triumph Spitfire.*
Could I, *a knock-kneed beginner,* ever hope to ski down that icy slope without breaking a leg?

12.8A Placing Appositives

An appositive is usually placed right after the word or phrase it identifies. But it may sometimes come just before:

A chronic complainer, he was never satisfied.

12.8B Punctuating Appositives

Most appositives are set off by commas, as in all of the examples above. But you can set off an appositive with dashes if you want to emphasize it, and you should use dashes if the appositive consists of three or more nouns in a series:

Ninety-foot statues of three Confederate leaders—Jefferson Davis, Robert E. Lee, and Stonewall Jackson—have been carved in the face of Stone Mountain in Georgia.

Use no commas when the appositive identifies the noun just before it and the noun is not preceded by *a* or *the:*

> My sister *Kate* wants to become a television newscaster.
> Reporters questioned city employee *Frank Roberts* about the fire.
> (COMPARE: Reporters questioned a city employee, Frank Roberts, about the fire.)
> Film producer *Brenda Budget* intends to make a movie about the last woman on earth.

EXERCISE 2 Sentence Combining with Appositives

Combine the sentences in each of the following pairs by turning the second sentence into an appositive.

EXAMPLE
Could I ever hope to ski down that icy slope without breaking a leg?
I was a knock-kneed beginner.
COMBINED: Could I, a knock-kneed beginner, ever hope to ski down that icy slope without breaking a leg?

1. Mount Everest was first conquered in 1953 by two members of a British expedition.
   Mount Everest is the highest mountain in the world.

2. One of the two was Edmund Hillary.
   He was a New Zealander.

3. The other was Tenzing Norkay.
   He was a Nepalese guide.

4. Hillary and Colonel John Hunt were knighted for their achievement.
   Hunt was the leader of the expedition.

5. Could I ever get to the summit of Everest?
   I am a weekend backpacker.

6. She stole the show.
   She was a born actress.

12.9 Using Participles and Participle Phrases

A **participle** is a word formed from a verb and used to modify a noun; it can enrich any sentence with descriptive detail:

> The *sobbing* child stared at the *broken* fire engine.

A **participle phrase** is a group of words based on a participle:

> Her father, *taking her in his arms*, promised to fix it.

Participles may be present, past, or perfect:

1. The **present participle,** formed by the addition of *-ing* to the bare form of the verb, describes a noun as *acting:*

A *rolling* stone gathers no moss.
The *dancing* couples attracted attention.
Policemen watch for *speeding* motorists.
The athletes entered the stadium with *flaming* torches.

A present participle can take a direct object and can also be modified. The group of words thus formed is a participle phrase:

Sullivan stood up on the chair, *furiously shouting insults at the speaker.*
Planning every minute of the journey, she studied maps and tourist guides.
The prospector stared in disbelief at the gold dust *shining brightly in his hand.*

2. The **past participle,** commonly formed by the addition of *-d* or *-ed* to the bare form of the verb, describes a noun as *acted upon:*

A *sculpted* figure graced the entrance to the museum.
He took the *baked* lobster from the oven.

Past participles can be modified by adverbs and adverb phrases—especially *by* phrases:

A figure *sculpted by Alberto Giacometti* graced the entrance to the museum.
My grandfather gave me a whalebone figure *carved by a sailor before the Civil War.*
Politicians *influenced by flattery* talk of victory at receptions *given by self-serving backers.*

In the last sentence, the past participle *(given)* ends in *-n* because it is formed from an irregular verb, *give.* The past participles of other irregular verbs have various other forms, such as *seen, bought, flung,* and *bred.* (For the past participles of commonly used irregular verbs, see the list on pp. 375–79.)

3. The **perfect participle,** which is formed with *having,* describes an action that has been completed before the action named by the verb:

Having led his country for many years, Trudeau decided to retire from politics.

12.9A   Punctuating Participles

Punctuate participles and participle phrases as follows:

1. Normally, use one or more commas to set off a participle or participle phrase from the word or phrase it modifies:

Stalking her prey noiselessly, the cat crept up to the mouse.
The mouse, *frightened,* darted off into a hole.
The cat squealed, *clawing the hole in vain.*

2. Don't use commas to set off a single participle when it is part of a noun phrase or when it immediately follows a verb:

> A *raging* wind fanned the flames.
> The *exhausted* fighter sank to his knees.
> Let *sleeping* dogs lie.
> Steve walked *muttering* out of the room.

3. Don't use commas to set off a participle phrase when it restricts —that is, limits—the meaning of the word or phrase it modifies:

> Students *majoring in economics* must take at least one course in statistics.

(For more on restrictive modifiers, see 26.6.)

12.10 Misforming the Past Participle

The past participle is misformed in these sentences:

> *A lock door makes me curious.
> *For lunch I had steak and toss salad.
> *Prejudice persons see no difference between one Chicano and another.
> *I use to play basketball every week.

If you write this way, it is probably because you speak this way, not pronouncing the final -*d* or -*ed* when they are needed. You are most likely to do this when the special ending does not add an extra syllable. It's not hard to pronounce the special endings of past participles such as *bolted* and *wasted,* because in each of them the special ending makes an extra syllable. But it is hard to hit the special endings of words such as *locked, tossed, prejudiced,* and *used* because in each of them the special ending simply extends a syllable that is already there. If you can train yourself to accentuate those endings when you speak, you will also learn to write them in sentences such as these:

> REVISED: A locked door makes me curious.
> REVISED: For lunch I had steak and tossed salad.
> REVISED: Prejudiced persons see no difference between one Chicano and another.
> REVISED: I used to play basketball every week.

EXERCISE 3 Sentence Combining with Participles

Combine the sentences in each of the following sets by using the first sentence as a base and turning each of the others into a modifying participle or participle phrase. Combine the sentences of each set in at least two different ways. Then, if you prefer one of the combinations, put a check next to it.

EXAMPLE
Ruth doubled over.
She was laughing uncontrollably.
She was laughing at the sight of Frank.
Frank was wearing a bright red wig.
COMBINATION 1: Ruth doubled over, laughing uncontrollably at the sight of Frank wearing a bright red wig.
COMBINATION 2: Laughing uncontrollably at the sight of Frank wearing a bright red wig, Ruth doubled over.

1. The man looked at the sky.
   The man was startled.

2. The baby amused onlookers.
   The baby was laughing.

3. Corporal Grey stared straight ahead during inspection.
   Corporal Grey was trained to show no emotion.

4. The spaniel hid under the big easy chair.
   The spaniel was frightened by crashes of thunder.
   The crashes of thunder were resounding above the cabin.

5. The apartment building will house tenants.
   The apartment building is now being constructed on Ocean Drive.
   The tenants will be earning under fifteen thousand dollars a year.

6. At the track we watched a driver.
   The driver was practicing starts in a new car.
   The car was designed by Fenmore Wheel.

7. I could not get out of my chair.
   I had eaten five éclairs.
   The éclairs were filled with custard.
   The éclairs were coated with Danish chocolate.

8. The combination included a manager, a team of veterans, and a rookie.
   The combination was a winning one.
   The manager was jesting.
   The veterans were aiming for their first pennant.
   The rookie was yearning to make his name.

EXERCISE 4   Sentence Combining with Various Modifiers

Combine the sentences in each of the following sets by using the first sentence as a base and adding modifiers from the others. Some modifiers may have to be combined with each other before they can be joined to the base sentence. Combine the sentences of each set in at least two different ways. Then, if you prefer one of the combinations, put a check next to it.

EXAMPLE
The bird sailed.
He did so for hours.
He was searching the grasses.

The grasses were blanched.
The grasses were below him.
He was searching with his eyes.
The eyes were telescopic.
He was gaining height.
He was gaining it against the wind.
He was descending in swoops.
The swoops were mile-long.
The swoops were gently declining.

—Deliberately altered from a sentence by
Walter Van Tilburg Clark

COMBINATION 1: The bird sailed for hours, searching the blanched grasses below him with his telescopic eyes, gaining height against the wind, descending in mile-long, gently declining swoops.

COMBINATION 2: Searching the blanched grasses below him with his telescopic eyes, gaining height against the wind, descending in mile-long, gently declining swoops, the bird sailed for hours.

1. Wally sang.
   He was soulful.
   He was swaying.
   He was sensuous.
   He was dressed in a skinsuit.
   The skinsuit was glittering.
   The skinsuit was white.
   The skinsuit was satin.
   He was stroking his guitar.
   The guitar was electric.
   He stroked with fingers.
   The fingers were long.
   The fingers were pink.
   The fingers were nimble.
   The fingers were well manicured.

2. The quarterback lay.
   He was on the yard line.
   It was the fortieth.
   He was panting.
   He was still clutching the ball.
   He was nearly smothered.
   The smothering was done by the linebackers.
   There were two linebackers.
   They were burly.
   They were sprawled.
   They were on top of him.

EXERCISE 5   Sentence Expanding with Modifiers

Expand each of the following sentences by adding as many modifiers as possible. Let your imagination go.

1. The gorilla roared.
2. The flames crackled.
3. The clown danced.
4. The rock-climber slipped.
5. The building shook.

(Keep the sentences you write for this exercise. You will need them again for exercise 12.)

12.11 Using Infinitives and Infinitive Phrases

Infinitives and infinitive phrases can modify nouns, adjectives, and verbs.

1. The **infinitive,** usually made by placing *to* before the bare form of the verb, can be used—

    a. To modify a noun:

        Civilization has never eradicated the urge *to hunt.*

    b. To modify an adjective:

        After years away from the bullring, the legendary El Cordobes was eager *to return.*

    c. To modify a participle:

        Goaded *to strike,* the beast charged.

    d. To modify a verb:

        Chester plays *to win.*

An infinitive modifying a verb usually expresses purpose. You can emphasize the purpose by putting *in order* before the infinitive, as in "Some men will do anything *in order to win.*" (To use infinitives as verbal nouns, see p. 233.)

2. Infinitives can be modified by adverbs and adverb phrases, and some can take direct objects. The group of words thus formed is an **infinitive phrase:**

    To write effectively, you must know something about sentence structure.
    On August 27, 1966, Sir Francis Chichester set out *to sail a 53-foot boat singlehandedly around the world.*
    Jan shuffled off, dismayed *to find the old house empty.*
    Madame Curie did many experiments *to prove the existence of radium.*

3. Infinitives with *have* and *have been* plus a past participle identify an action or condition completed before another one:

The work to be done that morning seemed enormous. Sandra was glad *to have slept* a full eight hours the night before. But she was annoyed *to have been told* nothing of this work earlier.

Exercise 6   Supplying Infinitives

Complete each of the following sentences with a suitable infinitive or infinitive phrase.

Example
The sheer will <u>to live</u> brought him through the operation.

1. A starving prisoner will do almost anything _____.
2. Man's desire _____ has already taken him to the moon, and may someday take him beyond the solar system.
3. The cheerleader jumped a good three feet off the ground, overjoyed _____.
4. After thirty-six hours of practically nonstop driving, I was desperate _____.
5. Columbus sailed west _____.
6. _____, Brent stopped eating rich desserts.

12.12   Avoiding the Split Infinitive

When one or more adverbs are wedged between *to* and the rest of an infinitive, the infinitive is said to be **split:**

> Detectives needed special equipment *to thoroughly and accurately investigate the mystery.*

This sentence is weakened by the cumbersome splitting. The adverbs should go at the end of the infinitive phrase:

> Detectives needed special equipment *to investigate the mystery thoroughly and accurately.*

Sometimes an infinitive may be split by a one-word modifier that would be awkward in any other position:

> The mayors convened in order to *fully* explore and discuss the problems of managing large cities.

A construction of this type is acceptable nowadays to most readers. But unless you are sure there is no other suitable place in the sentence for the adverb or adverb phrase, do not split the infinitive with it.

Exercise 7   Revising Split Infinitives

Each of the following contains a split infinitive. If you consider the construction cumbersome, revise the word order to get rid of the split. If you find the split necessary, write *Acceptable.*

EXAMPLE
He was sorry to have rudely answered.
REVISED: He was sorry to have answered rudely.

1. Betty ran seventy miles a week for six weeks to diligently prepare for the Labor Day marathon.
2. The prosecutor sought to decisively establish the guilt of the defendant.
3. The pilot exercised all of his skill to gently land the large airplane on the icy runway.
4. In order for us to never lose hope of finding a cure, we must remember that few today die of tuberculosis or suffer from polio.
5. He is sorry to have not finished his report by the deadline.

12.13 Using Absolute Phrases

An **absolute phrase** is a modifier usually made from a noun or noun phrase and a participle. It modifies the whole of the base sentence to which it is attached:

> Donna laughed.
> Her eyes were flashing.
> COMBINED: Donna laughed, *her eyes flashing.* [or] *Eyes flashing,* Donna laughed.

The participle in an absolute phrase can be expanded into a participle phrase:

> Donna laughed, *eyes flashing with mischief.*

You can also make an absolute phrase with certain other combinations.

1. Noun and adverb:

> *Head down,* the bull charged straight at the man.

2. Noun and adverb phrase:

> *Nose in the air,* she walked right past me.

3. Noun and adjective:

> *Eyes bright,* Peg shot up her hand.

4. Noun and adjective phrase:

> *Eyes bright as new pennies,* Peg shot up her hand.

You can form compounds with absolute phrases, and you can use them in succession:

> *Eyes bright and flashing with mischief,* Donna laughed.
> The Texan turned to the nearest gatepost and climbed to the top

of it, *his alternate thighs thick and bulging in the tight jeans, the butt of his pistol catching and losing the sun in pearly gleams.*

—William Faulkner

The skaters are quick-silvering around the frosty rink, *the girls gliding and spinning, the boys swooping, their arms flailing like wings.*

—College student

He stood at the top of the stairs and watched me, *I waiting for him to call me up, he hesitating to come down, his lips nervous with the suggestion of a smile, mine asking whether the smile meant come, or go away.*

—College student

As the examples show, you can place absolute phrases at the beginning of a sentence or at the end. You can also put them in the middle:

Peg, *eyes bright as new pennies,* shot up her hand.

Use the position you consider best.

Exercise 8   Sentence Combining

Combine the sentences in each of the following sets by using the first sentence as a base and turning the others into absolute phrases.

Example
Donna laughed.
Her eyes were flashing.
Combined: Donna laughed, her eyes flashing. [or] Eyes flashing, Donna laughed.

1. Finch dozed.
   His chin was on his chest.

2. I gripped the wheel of the skidding car.
   My knuckles were white.
   My hair was standing on end.
   My stomach was heaving.

3. Janet rode the big wave.
   Her shoulders were hunched.
   Her hair was streaming in the wind.
   Her toes were curled over the edge of the board.

4. Traffic inched along.
   Horns were honking.
   Truck drivers were yelling.
   Policemen were whistling and flailing their arms.

5. Reese studied the board.
   His forehead was wrinkled.
   His mouth was pursed.
   His watch was ticking.

12.14 Placing Modifiers

One of the hardest things about writing an effective sentence is that unless you can plan it out completely in your head beforehand, you may not know at once the best way to arrange all of its parts. You know by habit, of course, that an adjective usually comes before the noun it modifies. You don't write *leaves green* or *fumes smelly* or *brass hot;* you write *green leaves, smelly fumes,* and *hot brass.* But the placing of other modifiers—especially modifying phrases—may call for some thought. Often, in fact, you will not be able to decide where to put a particular modifier until *after* you have written out the whole sentence in which it appears.

While you are writing a sentence, therefore, don't worry about where to place the modifiers. Just start with the base sentence and put the modifiers at the end, simply to get them down on paper. Thus, instead of having to plan out the whole sentence in advance, you can make it up as you write, adding modifiers as you think of them, using one modifier to lead you to another. Consider the way this sentence grows:

> Mary traveled.

Where from?

> Mary traveled *from Denver.*

Where to?

> Mary traveled *from Denver to San Francisco.*

How?

> Mary traveled *from Denver to San Francisco by hitchhiking.*

Did she hitchhike all the way?

> Mary traveled *from Denver to San Francisco by hitchhiking to the house of a friend in Salt Lake City.*

And how did she finish the trip?

> Mary traveled *from Denver to San Francisco by hitchhiking to the house of a friend in Salt Lake City and then borrowing his motorcycle to make the rest of the trip.*

Now, having written your base sentence and added as many modifiers as you want, you can think about where to place those modifiers. You may decide, for instance, that you want to put most of them up front instead of at the end. In that case, bracket the words you want to move and use an arrow to show where they are to go:

> Mary traveled from Denver to San Francisco [by hitchhiking to the house of a friend in Salt Lake City and then borrowing his motorcycle to make the rest of the trip.]

When you rewrite the sentence, it will look like this:

> By hitchhiking to the house of a friend in Salt Lake City and then borrowing his motorcycle to make the rest of the trip, Mary traveled from Denver to San Francisco.

Do you like this version better than the other? That's the kind of question you will have to answer for yourself. If you want to state a simple point and then develop it, you will lead with that point and put the modifiers after it; you will first say where Mary went and then explain how she got there. But if you want to create suspense, if you want the reader to wait for a main point that is delivered at the end, you will put all or most of your modifiers first. You will make the reader travel to the end of the sentence to discover Mary's destination.

So what does placing modifiers really mean in practice? Do you have to rearrange the words of every sentence just as soon as you've written it? No, you don't. *But you do have to develop the habit of considering various possibilities.* Good writers know that almost every sentence can be arranged in more than one way. As you develop your writing skill, you will learn how to place modifying phrases while you are composing a sentence instead of after you have completed it. But the longer and more complicated your sentences become, the more carefully you must consider how to arrange them. And the more you consciously study the art of placing your modifiers, the better you will write.

Placing a modifier well means not only creating a particular effect but also connecting the modifier to its **headword**—the word or phrase it modifies. If the modifier doesn't clearly point to its headword, it is *misplaced;* if it can't point to a headword because the headword is completely missing from the sentence, the modifier *dangles.* These problems are discussed in the following sections.

12.15 Misplaced Modifiers   *mm*

A **misplaced modifier** is one that does not clearly point to its headword—the word or phrase it modifies:

> 1. *The sheriff was looking for a middle-aged woman with a little Scotch terrier beside her driving a dark green Buick sedan.

This sentence seems to say that the Scotch terrier was doing the driving. To get the dog out of the driver's seat, put the modifying phrase right after its headword—*woman:*

> REVISED: The sheriff was looking for a middle-aged woman driving a dark green Buick sedan with a little Scotch terrier beside her.

2. *The College Librarian announced that all fines on overdue books will be doubled yesterday.

This sentence seems to put the future into yesterday, or yesterday into the future. Either way it makes no sense. To get *yesterday* back into the past, put it right after its headword—*announced:*

> REVISED: The College Librarian announced yesterday that all fines on overdue books will be doubled.

3. *I asked her for a light while waiting for the train to start a conversation.

This sentence seems to conjure up a talking train. To indicate clearly who is doing the talking, put the modifying phrase *(to start a conversation)* just before its headword, which in this case is *I asked her for a light:*

> REVISED: To start a conversation, I asked her for a light while waiting for the train.

EXERCISE 9   Correcting Misplaced Modifiers

Revise each of the following sentences that includes a misplaced modifier. If a sentence is correct, write *Correct.*

EXAMPLE
An article describes the way skunks eat in *Time* magazine.
REVISED: An article in *Time* magazine describes the way skunks eat.

1. We watched the gulls flying over the windswept waves and barren rocks with the aid of powerful binoculars.
2. Despite her inexperience and small size, Coach Jette has said that Sarah Wingate is the best goalie in the league.
3. When visiting the zoo, children should not put their hands between the bars of cages.
4. The detective advised the suspect of his right to consult a lawyer before booking him.
5. Circling steadily overhead, Seymour lay in a hammock and watched the vultures.
6. Today women have more opportunities for a challenging position than their grandmothers did in business and the professions.
7. The pair of antique candlesticks attracted the admiring glances of many visitors shining brightly on the table.
8. He begged the terrorists to spare his daughter's life tearfully.
9. She walked to the store with her dog whistling "Summertime."
10. Nancy carefully unwrapped the small package filled with eagerness, curiosity, and excitement.

12.16 Squinting Modifiers *sm*

A **squinting modifier** is one placed where it could modify either of two possible headwords. It squints at the words on either side of it instead of looking clearly in one direction:

>*The street vendor she saw on her way to school occasionally sold wild mushrooms.

Did she see the vendor ocasionally, or did he sell wild mushrooms occasionally? To make the meaning of the sentence unambiguously clear, you must clearly connect the modifier with one headword *or* the other:

>REVISED: The street vendor she occasionally saw on her way to school sold wild mushrooms. [or] The street vendor she saw on her way to school sold wild mushrooms occasionally.

12.17 Misplacing Restricters *mr*

A restricter is a one-word modifier that restricts the meaning of another word or a group of words. Restricters include *almost, only, merely, nearly, scarcely, simply, even, exactly, just,* and *hardly.* Usually a restricter modifies the word or phrase that immediately follows it. When you use a restricter, therefore, you must normally place it just before the word or phrase that you want it to modify.

To see what the placement of a restricter does, compare these sentences:

>*Only* The Fabulous Fork serves brunch on Sundays.
>The Fabulous Fork serves *only* brunch on Sundays.
>The Fabulous Fork serves brunch *only* on Sundays.

In each of these sentences, the writer controls the meaning by placing *only* just before the word or phrase it is meant to modify. But if you place *only* carelessly, the result will be a confusing sentence:

>*The Fabulous Fork *only* serves brunch on Sundays.

Is brunch the only meal it serves on Sundays, or is Sunday the only day on which it serves brunch? The sentence is ambiguous. If you read it in an advertisement, you would have to call the restaurant to find out for sure whether or not it served dinner on Sunday. To make the meaning of this sentence plain, the writer must put *only* just before the word or phrase it is meant to modify, as shown above in the second and third examples.

One other revision is possible. If you want to make *only* modify *on Sundays* and you want to make absolutely sure that it doesn't squint (see 12.16) toward *brunch,* put it at the end of the sentence:

REVISED: The Fabulous Fork serves brunch on Sundays *only*.

A restricter placed at the end of a sentence modifies the word or phrase just before it.

Now see what happens when *almost* is carelessly placed:

*On the fifth race, Arturo *almost* won five hundred dollars.

If Arturo *almost won* five hundred dollars, he may not have won anything at all. As every gambler knows, nobody makes money by *almost* winning. But if the writer means that Arturo won just a little less than five hundred dollars, *almost* belongs just before *five:*

REVISED: On the fifth race, Arturo won *almost* five hundred dollars.

EXERCISE 10 Placing Restricters Clearly

In each of the following sentences, place the parenthesized restricter so that it clearly modifies the underlined word or phrase.

EXAMPLE
The child wanted *one serving* of grits. (just)
REVISED: The child wanted just one serving of grits.

The two men caught *fifteen pounds* of bass between them. (almost)
Twenty visitors slipped on the freshly waxed floors. (nearly)
Joe could not answer *one* question on the test. (even)
They have painted *the living room*. (just)
Maggie jogs *on the track*. (only)

EXERCISE 11 Placing Modifiers

Each of the following sentences is accompanied by a phrase. Use the phrase as a modifier in the sentence and then underline the word or phrase that you want it to modify.

EXAMPLE
The MP announced that he would not run for reelection.
in North York
The MP *announced* in North York that he would not run for reelection [or] The MP announced that he would not *run for reelection* in North York.

1. The emerald belongs to a family of minerals.
   known as beryl
2. The emerald gets its color from chromium.
   distinctively bright green
3. The emerald was known not only for its beauty but also for its supposed power to cure eye ailments.
   in ancient times

4. Flawless emeralds of good color and size bring higher prices than dia-
   monds.
   of equal weight.
5. Emeralds are among the most precious of all stones.
   now chiefly mined in Colombia
6. Children may use the pool from ten o'clock to noon.
   only
7. Marianne showed her grandchildren the house where she was born.
   last week
8. The coach said that she was planning to quit her job at the end of the
   season.
   on Wednesday

EXERCISE 12   Correcting Misplaced Modifiers

Look at the sentences with added modifiers that you wrote for exercise 5,
pp. 257–58. If any of the modifiers you added do not clearly refer to their
headwords, revise the sentences in which they appear.

12.18 Dangling Modifiers   *dg*

A modifier dangles when its headword is missing. Since a modifier
always needs a headword, it will attach itself to a false one if the
true one is not in the sentence. The result is a sentence like this:

> *Running up the first long hill, my nose began to drip.

This sentence seems to say that a nose was running up the hill.
Since *Running up the first long hill* is a modifier, we expect to see its
headword immediately after it, to find out *who* was running. Instead,
what turns up in the headword slot is *my nose,* and there is nothing
else in the sentence that could do the running. The opening phrase,
therefore, is a *dangling modifier.* It has nothing to support it.

A dangling modifier results from the miscombination of two sentences. In this case they are:

> I was running up the first long hill.
> My nose began to drip.

These two sentences have different subjects: *I* and *my nose.* When
you combine two sentences like these by making one of them modify the other, you must normally keep both of their subjects:

> While I was running up the first long hill, my nose began to drip.

This combination turns the first sentence into a subordinate clause.
(For a full discussion of subordinate clauses, see chapter 15.) When
you combine two sentences, you can normally drop the subject of
one only if it is the same as the subject of the other:

I was running up the first long hill
I felt my nose dripping.
COMBINED: While running up the first long hill, I felt my nose dripping.

Here both subjects are the same—*I* and *I*—so the writer can drop one of them. The *I* that is left identifies the runner and thus serves as the headword of *Running up the first long hill.*

Now consider this sentence:

*After doing my homework, the dog was fed.

And any dog who can do your homework for you certainly deserves his food! But unless the dog is unusually clever, this sentence too contains a dangling modifier. You can eliminate it by saying who actually did the homework:

REVISED: After I did my homework, the dog was fed.

But this revision still doesn't tell us who fed the dog. It fails to do so because *The dog was fed* is in the passive voice and does not mention the agent—the one *by whom* the dog was fed. That agent should be named:

Then the dog was fed by me.

Once you've named the agent, you can turn this sentence from the passive to the active voice:

Then I fed the dog.

Now you can write:

After I did my homework, I fed the dog.

Or you can drop the first *I:*

After doing my homework, I fed the dog.

To correct dangling modifiers, you may often need to change a sentence from the passive to the active voice. For a full discussion of voice, see chapter 22.

Here is one more example:

*Based on the gradual decline in College Board scores over the past twenty years, American high school education is less effective than it used to be.

This is a miscombination of two sentences:

American high school education is less effective than it used to be. This conclusion is based on the gradual decline of College Board scores over the past twenty years.

So how can you combine these two sentences and not leave *Based* dangling? Our advice is to kick the *Based* habit altogether. To combine sentences like these, use *shows that, indicates that,* or *leads to the conclusion that:*

> The gradual decline of College Board scores over the past twenty years indicates that American high school education is less effective than it used to be.

EXERCISE 13   Avoiding Dangling Modifiers

Each of the following consists of two sentences, one with a dangling modifier and the other correct. Say which sentence you think is clearer—and why.

EXAMPLE
(a) While waiting for a bus, a passing car splashed mud all over my skirt.
(b) While I was waiting for a bus, a passing car splashed mud all over my skirt.
Sentence b tells plainly who was waiting for a bus. In sentence a, *While waiting for a bus* is a dangling modifier, with no headword to support it; we are not clearly told who was waiting.

1. (a) By exploring this problem thoroughly, a solution will hopefully be found.
   (b) By exploring this problem thoroughly, I hope to find a solution.
2. (a) By being overtaxed, the government of California goaded property owners into rebellion.
   (b) By overtaxing property owners, the government of California goaded them into rebellion.
3. (a) While walking to my chemistry final, a dog nipped my leg.
   (b) While I was walking to my chemistry final, a dog nipped my leg.
4. (a) In studying the stars, we must calculate the time which their light takes to reach us.
   (b) In studying the stars, the time which their light takes to reach us must be calculated.

EXERCISE 14   Correcting Dangling Modifiers

Revise each of the following sentences that includes a dangling modifier. Either supply a headword as best you can, or reconstruct the whole sentence. If a sentence is correct as it stands, write *Correct.*

EXAMPLE
After considering the offer carefully, it was refused.
REVISED: After considering the offer carefully, I refused it.

1. Peering into the fog, only a dim blue light shone in the distance.
2. Dancing to an old Beatles record, the thought of John Lennon's death suddenly ran through my mind.
3. The canoe tipped over while stepping into it.
4. After skipping lunch, I ate a big dinner.

5. Making our way slowly along the winding and bumpy road, a place to eat was finally found.
6. Insisting on her right to be heard, the microphone was seized.
7. Based on the growing number of women in all fields, women have more opportunities than ever before.
8. Looking first of all at the plot, it seems contrived.

Exercise 15   Sentence Combining

Combine the sentences in each of the following pairs by using the italicized words in one sentence as a modifier in the other.

Example
I was *painting our house last summer.*
I fell off a ladder and broke my arm.
Combined: While painting our house last summer, I fell off a ladder and broke my arm.

1. I was *chopping wood last summer.*
I cut my foot.

2. Harriet was *eager to see the sun rise.*
She got up at 5:30 a.m.

3. The boats were loaded with refugees.
The refugees had been *driven out to sea by the Malaysians.*

4. The child stood mute.
The child was *too frightened to utter a sound.*

5. The plane dropped.
Its engines were *failing.*

Exercise 16   Composing with Modifiers

Each of the following is a phrase that can serve as a modifier. Write a suitable base sentence for each modifier, and attach the modifier to it.

Example
upon hearing the news
Upon hearing the news, he let out a whoop.

1. after waiting at the hot, dusty, deserted gas station for an hour and a half
2. sounding the hours with solemn tones
3. ignoring the No Parking sign
4. bringing him down with a flying tackle
5. trying to change the tire with nothing but a jack and a pair of pliers

Exercise 17   Revising a Passage with Misused Modifiers

Revise the following passage by correcting all misused modifiers.

The *New York Times Magazine* often publishes striking advertisements. One example is an ad for Movado watches, which are made

in Switzerland from a recent issue of the magazine. Standing in the center of a large, ten-by-fifteen-inch page with pitch-black fur, the
5   ad shows a cat focusing its bright golden eyes on a fishbowl filled with sand, water, and white coral. But the fishbowl contains no fish. Resting among the pieces of coral, it only contains two Movado watches. Below the fishbowl are a brief description of the watches and the words "Movado, a century of Swiss Watchcraft" printed in
10 large white letters.

The ad designer has created an eerie effect by almost covering half the page in black, hiding the body of the cat in darkness, and only showing its head in a dim glow of light. Looking down at the fishbowl, the watches are being eyed as if they were fish. But the
15 watches also look like the cat. Set in a gold case, one has a black face, while the other has a gold face set in a black case. Thus both watches match the colors of the cat's eyes and fur.

The ad succeeds because it catches the reader's attention. Leafing through the magazine, the mysterious looking cat will strike the
20 average reader, and, submerged in a fishbowl, he or she will carefully examine the watches. The combination of gold and black under water will make them look like treasures discovered at the bottom of the sea.

13

COORDINATION 1
Compound Sentences

To coordinate two or more parts of a sentence is to give them the same rank and role by making them grammatically similar. As we have noted in section 11.9, you can coordinate words or phrases to make a compound phrase. In this chapter we show how you can coordinate simple sentences to make a compound sentence. The very fact that several ideas and actions of roughly equal weight are joined in one sentence indicates a connection among them, and the use of one conjunction rather than another shows just what the connection is. Further, when some sentences are compound and others are not, the variety of sentence length and structure helps to keep alive the reader's attention.

13.1 Making Compound Sentences

A **compound sentence** consists of two or more simple sentences joined together on the same level. When a simple sentence is thus joined to another simple sentence, each is called an **independent clause** because each could stand by itself as a complete sentence:

SIMPLE SENTENCES

S   P
Art / is long.

S   P
Life / is short.

COMPOUND SENTENCE

INDEPENDENT CLAUSE   INDEPENDENT CLAUSE
[s] Art / [P] is long,   but   [s] life / [P] is short.

SIMPLE SENTENCES

S　　　　　　　　　　　　　　　　P
The sentencing of criminals　/　often ignites controversy.

S　　　　　　　　　P
The death sentence　/　sometimes causes a furor.

COMPOUND SENTENCE

INDEPENDENT CLAUSE
[s] The sentencing of criminals　/　[P] often ignites controversy

and

INDEPENDENT CLAUSE
[s] the death sentence　/　[P] sometimes causes a furor.

In each of these examples, the compound sentence preserves the whole of each simple sentence in an independent clause.

You can join the independent clauses of a compound sentence in one of three ways: with a conjunction, a conjunctive adverb, or a semicolon.

13.2 Compounding with Conjunctions

Confunctions include the set of words commonly known as "A. B. Fonsy": *and, but, for, or, nor, so,* and *yet.* They can show any one of the following relations between words, phrases, and clauses:

1. Addition, shown by *and:*

> The whistle blew, *and* the big train chugged out of the station.

2. Addition of a negative point, shown by *nor:*

> Many of the settlers had never farmed before, *nor* were they ready for the brutal Saskatchewan winters.

3. Contrast, shown by *but* or *yet:*

> We are all in the gutter, *but* some of us are looking at the stars.
> —Oscar Wilde

4. Logical consequence, shown by *for* or *so:*

> My father never attended the military parades in the city, *for* he hated war.
> During World War II, Americans of Japanese descent were suspected of disloyalty, *so* they were placed in detention camps.

For introduces a reason; *so* introduces a consequence.

5. Choice, shown by *or:*

Nelson could keep his ships near England, *or* he could order them out against the French in Egypt.

13.2A Punctuation with Conjunctions

A conjunction used between clauses normally needs a comma just before it, as shown by all of the examples above. But there are two exceptions.

1. You can omit the comma when the clauses are particularly short:

Many are called but few are chosen.

2. You can replace the comma with a semicolon when there are commas elsewhere in the sentence:

On the morning of June 28, 1969, the weather finally cleared; but the climbers, wearied by their efforts of the previous days, could not attempt the summit.

You can use a comma without a conjunction when there are more than two clauses, but you should normally use a conjunction between the last two:

The sun shone, a stiff breeze ruffled the bay, the sails bellied out, and the bow cut the water like a knife.

13.3 Overusing *and*

Use *and* sparingly in compound sentences. A series of clauses strung together by *and* can become boring:

I was born in Illinois, and the first big city I ever saw was Chicago, and was I ever excited! I went there with my father and mother, and we stayed in a big hotel on the Loop, and I saw lots of interesting sights. We spent a whole day just walking around the city, and I got a stiff neck from looking up at the skyscrapers, and my feet got sore too from walking down so many streets. I was glad to go back to the hotel and take a long soak in the Jacuzzi.

To break the monotony of compounding with *and,* substitute other linking words—or other constructions:

Since I was born in Illinois, the first big city I ever saw was Chicago. Was I ever excited! My father and mother took me to a big hotel on the Loop. On the day after our arrival, we spent eight hours just walking around the city to see the sights. It was exhausting. In fact, I got a stiff neck from looking up at all the skyscrapers, and sore feet from walking down so many streets. I couldn't wait to take a long soak in the Jacuzzi at our hotel.

(For alternatives to the overuse of *and* constructions, see the chapter on subordination, chapter 15.)

13.4 Compounding with the Semicolon

A semicolon alone can join two independent clauses when the relation between them is obvious:

> Some books are undeservedly forgotten; none are undeservedly remembered.   —W. H. Auden
> The house was empty; everyone had gone.

But to specify a relation between the clauses, you will need a semicolon plus a conjunctive adverb, as explained in the next section.

13.5 Compounding with Conjunctive Adverbs

A **conjunctive adverb**—sometimes called a **sentence adverb**—is a word or phrase that shows a relation between the clauses it joins, as a conjunction does. But a conjunctive adverb is usually weightier and more emphatic than a conjunction:

> The Iron Duke had complete confidence in his soldiers' training and valor; *furthermore,* he considered his battle plan a work of genius.
> Chamberlain made an ill-considered peace treaty with Hitler after the German invasion of Czechoslovakia; *as a result,* England stood idly by during the German invasion of Poland.

13.5A What Conjunctive Adverbs Show

Like conjunctions, conjunctive adverbs specify a relation between one clause and another. Each indicates one of the relations listed here.

1. <u>Addition,</u> shown by *besides, furthermore, moreover,* or *in addition:*

> The Iron Duke had complete confidence in his soldiers' training and valor; *furthermore,* he considered his battle plan a work of genius.

2. <u>Likeness,</u> shown by *likewise, similarly,* or *in the same way:*

> Many young Englishmen condemned the English war against France in the 1790s; *likewise* many young Americans condemned the American war against North Vietnam in the 1960s.

3. <u>Contrast,</u> shown by *however, nevertheless, still, nonetheless, conversely, otherwise, instead, in contrast,* or *on the other hand:*

Einstein's theory of relativity was largely the product of speculation; experiments made within the past fifty years, *however,* have confirmed many of its basic points.

4. Cause and effect, shown by *accordingly, consequently, hence, therefore, as a result,* or *for this reason:*

Chamberlain made an ill-considered peace treaty with Hitler after the German invasion of Czechoslovakia; *as a result,* England stood idly by during the German invasion of Poland.

5. A means-and-end relation, shown by *thus, thereby, by this means,* or *in this manner:*

John F. Kennedy swept the 1960 presidential primaries; *thus* he cleared the way for his nomination at the Democratic convention.

Do not use *thus* to mean "therefore" or "for this reason."

6. Reinforcement, shown by *for example, for instance, in fact, in particular,* or *indeed:*

Public transportation will also be vastly improved; a high-speed train, *for instance,* will take passengers from Montreal to Toronto in less than two hours.
The repeal of the Stamp Act delighted the colonists; for a time, *in fact,* they actually regarded King George as the champion of their rights.

7. Time, shown by words like *meanwhile, then, subsequently, afterward, earlier,* and *later:*

First the tree must be cut into logs; *then* the logs must be split.

13.5B Punctuation with Conjunctive Adverbs

A conjunctive adverb normally takes punctuation on either side of it. The punctuation depends on where the conjunctive adverb is used.

1. When used between two independent clauses, the conjunctive adverb is normally preceded by a semicolon and followed by a comma:

Penthouse magazine decided to publish pictures of Miss America in the nude; *as a result,* she was made to give up her title.

2. Some conjunctive adverbs (including *thus, then, in fact, still, otherwise,* and *hence*) may be used to begin a clause with no comma after them:

The rise of the dollar against foreign currencies drives up the price of our exports; *thus* we lose customers abroad.

Compounding with Conjunctive Adverbs 275

The cat walked stealthily up to her prey; *then* she pounced.
She had hoped to win; *in fact* she triumphed.

3. When used *within* the second clause, the conjunctive adverb is normally set off by commas:

Jesse Jackson did not get the nomination; he managed, *however,* to make himself a potent force within the Democratic party.

4. Besides those mentioned above in 2, some conjunctive adverbs (including *therefore, nevertheless, nonetheless, otherwise,* and *instead*) may be used without commas when they are placed just before the main verb in a verb phrase. Compare these sentences:

The Northrop Corporation developed the F-20 Tigershark without supervision from the Pentagon; the Air Force, *therefore,* has opposed buying the plane.
The Northrop Corporation developed the F-20 Tigershark without supervision from the Pentagon; the Air Force has *therefore* opposed buying the plane.

13.6 Joining Independent Clauses—A Summary

The independent clauses (IC) of a compound sentence must normally be joined in one of the following three ways:

1. ___IC___ ; ___IC___ .
2. ___IC___ , conjunction ___IC___ .
3. ___IC___ ; conjunctive adverb, ___IC___ .
   (placement optional)

In general, use a semicolon alone when the relation between the clauses is obvious. Use a conjunction when you want to make the relation explicitly clear. Use a conjunctive adverb when you want to state the relation more precisely or more emphatically than a conjunction usually can. (On the sequence of tenses in compound sentences, see section 21.2)

EXERCISE 1 **Sentence Combining to Make Compound Sentences**

Using a semicolon, a conjunction, or a conjunctive adverb, combine the sentences in each of the following sets into a single sentence. Then in parentheses state the relationship that your combination shows.

EXAMPLE
We are all in the gutter.
Some of us are looking at the stars.
COMBINED: We are all in the gutter, but some of us are looking at the stars. (contrast)

1. A college education may lead to a well-paying job.
   It cannot guarantee success.

2. Many students do little or no writing in high school.
   They must learn to write in college.

3. Every New Year's Day I make a set of resolutions.
   I have never managed to keep any of them.

4. On its very first voyage, the "unsinkable" *Titanic* hit an iceberg.
   It sank.

5. James Joyce was a painstaking writer.
   He once spent half a day on the composition of a single sentence.

6. President Carter brought the leaders of Israel and Egypt together at Camp David.
   He helped to negotiate a peace treaty between the two countries.

7. The discovery of gold in California created the gold rush.
   The discovery of oil in Alaska created an oil rush.

8. The safety of nuclear power plants can never be absolutely guaranteed.
   Many people demand a shutdown of all existing plants and a halt to the building of new ones.

9. The shutdown of all nuclear power plants would be a serious step.
   Nuclear power is a major source of our energy.

10. You can take a leisurely five days to cross the Atlantic by ship.
    You can cross it in three hours by supersonic plane.

11. There may be more oil within the shale of the Rocky Mountains than in all of Saudi Arabia.
    Extracting the oil from the shale is difficult and expensive.

12. The brakes failed.
    The car skidded out of control
    A brick wall loomed up suddenly before us.
    Then we crashed.

13.7 Comma Splices *cs*

The **comma splice,** also called the "comma fault," is the error of joing two independent clauses—two possible sentences—with nothing but a comma:

*She wore huge dark glasses, no one recognized her.

This sentence consists of two statements that are related but nonetheless distinct. Each of them could stand by itself as a sentence. If you read the whole sentence aloud, you will probably hear your voice drop with the word *glasses,* which ends the first of the two sentences.

When you use the comma to join or splice two distinct statements, you are probably trying to keep two related thoughts together in one sentence. But the comma alone cannot do that for you. You should therefore do one of three things:

1. Put a conjunction after the comma:

> She wore huge dark glasses, so no one recognized her.

2. Replace the comma with a semicolon:

> She wore huge dark glasses; no one recognized her.

3. Replace the comma with a period, making two sentences:

> She wore huge dark glasses. No one recognized her.

Sometimes a comma splice occurs when the second clause in a sentence begins with a conjunctive adverb:

> *Most working people get at least one raise a year, nevertheless, inflation often leaves them with no increase in buying power.

Nevertheless is a conjunctive adverb, and a conjunctive adverb used between two clauses must be preceded by a semicolon:

> Most working people get at least one raise a year; nevertheless, inflation often leaves them with no increase in buying power.

Alternatively, you can use a period, making two sentences:

> Most working people get at least one raise a year. Nevertheless, inflation often leaves them with no increase in buying power.

EXERCISE 2   Correcting Comma Splices

Each of the following contains a comma splice. Correct it.

> EXAMPLE
> The holiday pleased the children, they welcomed the chance to play in the snow.
> REVISED: The holiday pleased the children; they welcomed the chance to play in the snow.

1. On moonlit nights some animals serenade all listeners, others scurry about looking for mates.
2. Cigarette smoking is no longer widely accepted, on the contrary, smokers have become an embattled minority.
3. The original settlers were short and dark, in contrast, the new colonists tend to be tall and fair.
4. Thoreau went to the woods in order to simplify his life, he also wanted to live close to nature.
5. Fairy tales end with the hero and heroine living happily together ever after, *A Doll's House* ends with the heroine leaving her husband.
6. A sense of humor is like fresh tonic water, it keeps bubbling to the surface.

7. Before the battle the king's forces had nine cannons, the peasants had none.
8. The high cost of gas makes life in the suburbs expensive, therefore some people are moving back to the cities.
9. To prevent another four-term presidency like that of Franklin D. Roosevelt, the law permits the president to succeed himself just once, nevertheless, no president is guaranteed reelection.
10. The price of serious illness has risen drastically in recent years, for example, some hospital rooms now cost over a hundred dollars a day.

13.8 Run-on (Fused) Sentences *run-on*

A **run-on sentence** joins two independent clauses—two possible sentences—with no punctuation or conjunction between them:

> *Emily listened to the lobster boats chugging out to sea from the cove she watched the gulls sailing overhead.

Here the first independent clause simply pushes into the second one. We cannot even tell for sure where the first one ends. Is its last word *sea* or *cove?*

You make this error when your thoughts come in a rush, outrunning your hand. You are most likely to find the error by reading your sentences aloud, listening for the drop in your voice to tell you where one statement (or independent clause) ends and another begins. When you find that point and see no punctuation to mark it, do one of three things:

1. Use a comma and a conjunction between the two clauses:

> Emily listened to the lobster boats chugging out to sea from the cove, and she watched the gulls sailing overhead.

2. Put a semicolon at the end of the first clause, in this case after *cove:*

> Emily listened to the lobster boats chugging out to sea from the cove; she watched the gulls sailing overhead.

3. Put a period at the end of the first clause. You will then have two sentences.

EXERCISE 3   Correcting Comma Splices and Run-on (Fused) Sentences

In some of the following, the punctuation is faulty. Correct any mistakes you find, adding words where necessary. If a sentence is correct as it stands, write *Correct.*

EXAMPLE
Cloudy days tend to make us gloomy, sunny days, in contrast, make us cheerful.

REVISED: Cloudy days tend to make us gloomy; sunny days, in contrast, make us cheerful.

1. Prejudice is like the bottom of a Coke bottle it shows you the world in a distorted light.
2. In the last act the collapse of Lady Macbeth is quite unexpected, earlier in the play she seemed to have almost superhuman strength.
3. On other long walks I had sometimes lost my way without feeling worried this time I panicked.
4. Scientists have sought the secret of hibernation in the endocrine glands; these are reduced in size during the winter sleep.
5. The new president was supported by the peasants he was distrusted by the wealthy landowners.
6. John is short and silent his roommate is tall and talkative.
7. Reckless drivers should be severely penalized in fact they should lose their driver's permits for at least six months.
8. Most fraternities include only students of a certain type and social category, thus fraternities reinforce social barriers.
9. Macaulay was a child prodigy by the age of ten he was writing a world history.
10. Before Columbus, the Central American Mayans developed a remarkable civilization, they built elaborate temples, devised a highly accurate calendar, and invented a form of writing.

14

COORDINATION 2
Parallel Construction

14.1 Why Choose Parallelism?

Parallel construction, also called "parallelism," enhances the coordination of words, phrases, or statements in a sentence by making them grammatically parallel: noun lined up with noun, verb with verb, phrase with phrase. Parallelism can lend clarity, elegance, and symmetry to what you say. For example:

> I came;
> I saw;
> I conquered.
> —Julius Caesar

Caesar uses three simple verbs to list the things he did.

> In many ways writing is the act of saying *I*,
> of imposing oneself upon other
> people,
> of saying *listen to me,*
> *see it my way,*
> *change your mind.*
> —Joan Didion

To reinforce her point about the assertiveness of writing, Didion uses three phrases starting with *of* and three imperatives.

> To be or not to be: that is the question.
> —William Shakespeare

The choice Hamlet contemplates is memorably clear because the phrase *to be* is grammatically parallel with the phrase *not to be.*

281

> It is better to break sod as a serf than to lord it over all the ex-
> hausted dead.　　　　—Homer, translated by Robert Fitzgerald

Here the phrase *to break sod* is grammatically parallel with the phrase
to lord it, and the parallel structure sharpens the comparison between life and death.

> Each must live within the isolation of his own senses, dreams and
> memories; each must die his own death.　　　—Ralph Ellison

The theme of man's loneliness is emphasized by the repetition of
each must and *his own* as well as by the series of nouns: *senses, dreams,
memories,* and *death.*

> Most of the floggings and lynchings occur at harvest time, when
> fruit hangs heavy and ripe, when the leaves are red and gold, when
> nuts fall from the trees, when the earth offers its best.
> 　　　　　　　　　　　　　　　　　　　—Richard Wright

Wright's sentence swells, but he keeps it under firm control by repeating the word *when,* thereby lining up the clauses that follow the
opening clause about floggings and lynchings. Layer on layer, Wright
builds his sentence to the final irony of the last clause—*when the
earth offers its best.*

You can do similar things in your own writing if you follow the
basic guidelines presented here.

14.2 Writing Parallel Constructions

When you have two or more items in a list, a series, a contrast, a
choice, a statement of equivalence, a formal definition, a statement
of evaluation, or a comparison, put all of the items into the same
grammatical form:

1. List

> I have nothing to offer but *blood, toil, tears,* and *sweat.* [four nouns]
> 　　　　　　　　　　　　　　　　　　　—Winston Churchill

2. Series

> Let every nation know, whether it wishes us well or ill, that we shall
> *pay any price, bear any burden, meet any hardship, support any friend,
> oppose any foe* to assure the survival and the success of liberty. [five
> verb-object combinations]　　　　　　　　　—John F. Kennedy

3. Contrast

> On all these shores there are echoes of past and future: of the flow
> of time, *obliterating* yet *containing* all that has gone before. [two
> participles]　　　　　　　　　　　　　　　　　—Rachel Carson

4. Series plus contrast

> Rather than *love*, than *money*, than *fame*, give me *truth*. [four nouns]
> —Henry David Thoreau

5. Choice

> *We must indeed all hang together*, or most assuredly, *we shall all hang separately*. [two clauses] —Benjamin Franklin

6. Statement of equivalence

> *An empty house* is *a lonely place*. [two noun phrases]
> *What I want to do* may not be *what I can do*. [two noun clauses]

7. Classification / definition

> *Robotics* is *the study of robots designed to work like human beings*. [a noun and a noun phrase]

8. Statement of evaluation

> *The first violinist* is *the most important member* of a symphony orchestra. [two noun phrases]

9. Comparison

> *A living dog* is better than *a dead lion*. [two noun phrases]
> —Ecclesiastes
> *Crawling down* a mountain is sometimes harder than *climbing up*. [two participle phrases]

14.3 Using Correlatives with Parallelism

When using a pair of correlatives, be sure that the word or word group following the first member of the pair is parallel with the word or word group following the second. The principal correlatives are *both . . . and, not only . . . but also, either . . . or, neither . . . nor,* and *whether . . . or:*

> She not only *got the job* but also *won a promotion* after just three months. [two verb-object combinations]
> Before the Polish strikes of 1980, both *the Hungarians* and *the Czechs* tried in vain to defy Soviet authority. [two noun phrases]
> Sheila was sure to be either *at the office* or *on her way*. [two adverb phrases]

EXERCISE 1   Recognizing Parallel Elements

Each of the following sentences contains a parallel construction. Write down the parallel elements.

EXAMPLE
Crawling down a mountain is sometimes harder than climbing up.
Crawling down, climbing up

1. For me, slipping on a piece of ice is as easy as falling off a log.
2. The more I read about tax reform, the less I understand about it.
3. The new method of photographing copies is less expensive than the old one.
4. We must either get control of inflation or lose control of the economy.
5. They were weak in numbers but strong in pride.
6. What is written without effort is in general read without pleasure.
   —Samuel Johnson
7. We must walk consciously only part way toward our goal, and then leap in the dark to our success. —Emerson
8. The cosmic ulcer comes not from great concerns but from little irritations. —Steinbeck

14.4 Revising Faulty Parallelism

When two or more parts of a sentence are parallel in meaning, you should coordinate them fully by making them parallel in form. If you don't, your sentence will be marred by **faulty parallelism.** Here are some examples of this error and of ways to correct it.

> 1. *The Allies decided to invade Italy and then that they would launch a massive assault on the Normandy coast.

The two Allied decisions can and should be stated in parallel form, but they aren't. The infinitive phrase beginning with *to invade* does not line up with the clause beginning with *that they would launch.*

> REVISED: The Allies decided *to invade Italy* and then *to launch a massive assault on the Normandy coast.*

> 2. *I like swimming, skiing, and to play ice hockey.

This sentence is awkward because *swimming* and *skiing*, both gerunds, do not line up with *to play ice hockey*, an infinitive phrase.

> REVISED: I like to *swim, ski,* and *play ice hockey.* [or] I like *swimming, skiing,* and *playing ice hockey.*

> 3. Chemistry used to be taught here from a textbook; now the lab method is followed.

> REVISED: *Chemistry* used to be *taught* here *from a textbook;* now *it* is *taught in the lab.*

> 4. The Dean can force a student to attend class but not think.

Repetition of *to* will make the sentence clearer:

REVISED: The Dean can force a student *to attend class* but not *to think.*

5. Centuries ago many people believed that the earth was flat and one could fall off the edge of it.

Repetition of *that* will clarify the sentence:

REVISED: Centuries ago many people believed *that* the earth was flat and *that* one could fall off the edge of it.

6. Either we must make nuclear power safe or stop using it altogether.

The sentence will be better if its correlatives *(either . . . or)* are immediately followed by grammatically parallel items:

REVISED: We must either *make* nuclear power safe or *stop* using it altogether. [or] Either *we must make* nuclear power safe or *we must stop* using it altogether.

EXERCISE 2   Recognizing Correct Parallel Construction

Each of the following consists of two sentences, one with correct parallel construction and the other with faulty parallelism. Write down the letter of the sentence with correct parallel construction.

1. (a) Skateboarding is both exciting and there is danger in it too.
   (b) Skateboarding is both exciting and dangerous.
2. (a) The detective stories of Max Brand are not so hard-boiled as Mickey Spillane.
   (b) The detective stories of Max Brand are not so hard-boiled as those of Mickey Spillane.
3. (a) The sentence is difficult to understand not because the vocabulary is technical but because the syntax is faulty.
   (b) The sentence is difficult to understand not because of the technical vocabulary but because the syntax is faulty.
4. (a) The actor was not only stunned by the noise of booing but also by the sight of flying tomatoes.
   (b) The actor was stunned not only by the noise of booing but also by the sight of flying tomatoes.
5. (a) Marian could not decide whether she should start college right after high school or to get a job first.
   (b) Marian could not decide whether to start college right after high school or to get a job first.

EXERCISE 3   Correcting Faulty Parallelism

Revise each of the following sentences that is marred by faulty parallelism. If a sentence is correct as it stands, write *Correct.*

EXAMPLE

You can improve your performance if you master the fundamentals and by training diligently.

REVISED: You can improve your performance by mastering the fundamentals and by training diligently.

1. The captain ordered his men to dig foxholes, to post sentries, and their weapons were to be cleaned before dark.
2. Smoking cigarettes can be as dangerous as to play Russian roulette.
3. Some writers care only about wealth and becoming famous.
4. The more David says about the pleasures of popcorn, the more I want to stuff his mouth with bubble gum.
   Rooming with Fred was like if you shared a telephone booth with a hippopotamus.

EXERCISE 4   Sentence Combining

Combine the sentences in each of the following sets by means of coordination and parallel construction. Change the wording where necessary.

EXAMPLE

The old Chevy pickup had three major defects.
The brakes were bad.
There was a crack in the windshield.
Sometimes the starter failed to work.

COMBINED: The old Chevy pickup had three major defects: bad brakes, a cracked windshield, and an unreliable starter.

1. Professor Harvey made two main points.
   He said that modern painting is essentially personal.
   He saw impersonality as the essence of modern architecture.

2. In the summer I especially like three things.
   I like to swim.
   I like to read science fiction.
   I like lying in the sun.

3. Not only may the study of literature help you to understand other people.
   You may also be helped to understand yourself.

4. Most writers hate neglect.
   They love to be acclaimed.

5. Summer was at an end.
   Another school year began.

EXERCISE 5   Using Correlatives in Parallel Constructions

Rewrite the following sentences by adding the correlatives given within parentheses and, where necessary, changing the wording.

EXAMPLE
The winner was lucky; on the other hand, he might have been clever.
(either . . . or)   .
WITH CORRELATIVES: Either the winner was lucky, or he was clever. [or]
The winner was either lucky or clever.

1. Sterling Rose is rich and powerful. (both . . . and)
2. My wallet was not on top of the bureau, and it was not in my tan slacks. (neither . . . nor)
3. Blake likes the idea of working in Japan, and he wants to move there at once. (not only . . . but also)
4. We haven't decided what to do: we may stay put, or we may move to a larger apartment near the university. (whether . . . or)
5. The new explosive is not dangerous to use, and it's not difficult to make. (neither . . . nor)

EXERCISES 6   Sentence Combining

Combine the sentences in each of the following sets into a single compound sentence, using compound phrases if necessary. Be careful to join all items in your compounds correctly, and use parallel construction where possible.

EXAMPLE
Black people in America have been neglected for years.
Black people in America have been underestimated for years.
Their recent accomplishments in a variety of fields have made "black power" a reality.
Their recent accomplishments in a variety of fields have made black pride possible.
COMBINED: Black people in America have been neglected and underestimated for years, but their recent accomplishments in a variety of fields have made "black power" real and black pride possible.

1. The hero in early cowboy movies was modest.
   He was reticent.
   He was shy with pretty women.
   He rode hard.
   He shot straight.
   He survived a hundred dangers.
   He always overcame the villain.

2. Much of the land was arid.
   Much of the land was filled with rocks.
   There was barrenness.
   The Moabites loved their homeland.
   The Moabites fought to keep their homeland.

3. People in the Northeast can spend more money on gasoline.
   They can spend more money on heating oil.
   They have alternatives.

They can organize car pools.
They can put more insulation in the walls of their houses.

4. Some theories about humor are interesting.
These theories are also surprising.
An example is George Orwell's theory.
According to Orwell, "a joke worth laughing at always has an idea behind it, and usually a subversive idea."

5. According to Marcel Pagnol, the cause of laughter is the same in all times.
According to Pagnol, the cause of laughter is the same in all countries.
Laughers feel momentarily superior to others.
Their laughter is "a song of triumph."

15

SUBORDINATION
Complex Sentences

15.1 What Subordination Does

Subordination enables you to show the relative importance of the parts of a sentence. To use **subordination** is to make one or more parts of a sentence depend on the part that is most important to you.

Suppose you want to describe what a dog did on a particular night, and you want your description to include the following points:

> The dog lived next door.
> The dog was scrawny.
> The dog barked.
> The dog was old.
> The dog howled.
> The dog kept me awake.
> I was awake all night.

What is the best way to arrange these isolated facts in a sentence? Part of the answer is to coordinate facts that belong on the same level. You can readily see that *scrawny* and *old* go together, and so do *barked* and *howled*. So here is one way of combining those sentences:

> The dog was scrawny and old, and he lived next door; he barked and howled and kept me awake all night.

Coordination has clearly begun the work of arranging the facts about the dog; it has brought some order and continuity to a collection of separate statements. Yet the sentence lacks something. It trots along without a jump or a leap. It never gets off the ground because it never tells us which of the many facts about the dog is most important to the writer.

Which *is* the most important? Only you as the writer can decide—in light of the context for which you are writing the sentence. If you are writing an essay on the people next door, the most important fact about the dog is that it belonged to them; if you are writing about yourself, the most important fact is that the dog kept you awake. Whichever the case, you can emphasize the key fact by subordinating all others to it.

You can begin with the simplest kind of subordination: using a word or phrase as the **modifier** of another word or phrase. For example, you can use *scrawny, old, next door,* and *all night* as modifiers without changing their form, and you can use *barked* and *howled* as modifiers when their endings are changed to *-ing*. The result will be a sentence like one of these:

> Barking and howling, the scrawny old dog next door kept me awake all night.
> The scrawny old dog next door kept me awake all night by barking and howling.

Both of these sentences are designed to emphasize one key statement: *the dog kept me awake.* All the other statements about the dog have been turned into modifiers of *dog* or *kept me awake,* and thus everything else has been subordinated to the one key statement.

But suppose you want to stress the link between your wakefulness and the noise of the dog. Here is a way of doing so:

> What kept me awake all night was the barking and howling of the scrawny old dog next door.

The subject of this sentence is *What kept me awake all night.* The verb *was* links the subject to *the barking and howling,* and *dog* is merely part of the attached modifier—*of the scrawny old dog.* So this construction makes the sound of the dog more important than the dog itself. The infernal racket is what you remember most vividly from that sleepless night.

Now suppose you want to emphasize the fact that the dog lived next door. Here is a way of doing so:

> The dog *that kept me awake all night with its barking and howling* lived next door.

The entire group of italicized words modifies *dog.* So all the other facts about the dog are now subordinated to the fact that it lived next door.

Finally, suppose you want to subordinate that and all the other facts about the dog to a brand-new fact. Suppose you mainly want to tell what happened to you *as a result* of that sleepless night. Then you might write a sentence like this:

> Because the barking and howling of the scrawny old dog next door had kept me awake all night, I fell asleep in the middle of the chemistry final.

This sentence subordinates all the facts about the dog to the fact that you fell asleep.

Whether you want to stress this fact in your sentence will depend on what you want to emphasize in the paragraph containing the sentence. For different contexts, a sentence should be written to emphasize different things. Consider these paragraphs:

> For me, the one big problem with dogs is noise. On the night before I had to take a final exam in chemistry, "man's best friend" turned out to be my worst enemy. I got to bed at eleven, but I didn't sleep a wink. *What kept me awake all night was the barking and howling of the scrawny old dog next door.*

> The Bible tells us all to love our neighbors, but I have always had trouble even liking most of mine. When I was about six years old, I climbed over the fence in our backyard, wandered into Mr. O'Reilly's flower garden, and sat down in the middle of some big yellow daffodils. Mr. O'Reilly came up from behind and whacked me so hard I can still feel it now. We've moved a few times since then, but I have yet to find neighbors that I love. On the contrary, many of the things I don't love seem to come from across a fence. In El Paso, for instance, *a scrawny old dog that kept me awake all night with its barking and howling lived next door.*

> In the chemistry course I managed to do just about everything wrong. To begin with, I bought a used textbook at a bargain price, and then found out that I was supposed to buy the new edition. Trying to get along instead with the old one, I almost always wound up reading the wrong pages for the assignment and giving the wrong answers to quiz questions. I did no better with beakers and test tubes; the only thing my experiments showed is that I could have blown up the lab. But the worst came last. *Because the barking and howling of the scrawny old dog next door had kept me awake all night, I fell asleep in the middle of the final.*

The sentence about the dog is written three different ways to emphasize three different things: the noise it made, the fact that it lived next door, and the fact that something happened because of its noise. In each case, the methods of subordination make the sentence fit the particular context for which it is written. The three ways of writing the sentence illustrate three different kinds of subordinate clauses; we consider these in the next sections.

15.2 What Subordinate Clauses Are

A **subordinate clause,** also called a "dependent clause," is a group
of words that has its own subject and predicate but cannot stand
alone as a simple sentence. It must be included in or connected to
an **independent clause**—one that can stand by itself as a sentence:

SUBORDINATE CLAUSE   INDEPENDENT CLAUSE
1. Before he spoke to reporters, he conferred with his advisers.

INDEPENDENT CLAUSE   SUBORDINATE CLAUSE
2. Medical researchers have long   that takes thousands of lives each
been seeking a cure for a dis-   year.
ease

INDEPENDENT   SUBORDINATE   SUBORDINATE
CLAUSE   CLAUSE   CLAUSE
3. Keene was tac-   as he threw the pass   that might have
kled   saved the game.

A sentence containing one independent clause and at least one subordinate clause is called **complex.** Complex sentences are made
with various kinds of subordinate clauses, and this chapter will explain how to use each kind. (On the sequence of tenses in complex
sentences, see section 21.3.)

15.3 Using Adjective (Relative) Clauses

An **adjective clause,** sometimes called a "relative clause," normally
begins with a relative pronoun—*which, that, who, whom,* and *whose.*
The relative pronoun relates the clause to its **antecedent,** which is
normally the noun or noun phrase preceding the clause:

The dog *that* kept me awake all night lived next door.

An adjective clause usually says more about its antecedent than a
single adjective can. Compare these two sentences:

Medical researchers have long been seeking a cure for a *fatal* disease.
Medical researchers have long been seeking a cure for a disease
that takes thousands of lives every year.

The adjective clause tells more about the extent and effect of the
disease than the one word *fatal* does.

An adjective clause also enables you to subordinate one set of
facts to another set. See how these two sentences can be combined:

Amelia Earhart disappeared in 1937 during a round-the-world trip.
She set new speed records for long-distance flying in the 1930s.

COMBINATION 1: Amelia Earhart, *who set new speed records for long-distance flying in the 1930s,* disappeared in 1937 during a round-the-world trip.

COMBINATION 2: Amelia Earhart, *who disappeared in 1937 during a round-the-world trip,* set new speed records for long-distance flying in the 1930s.

Combination 1 subordinates Earhart's record-setting to her disappearance; combination 2 subordinates her disappearance to her record-setting. In each combination, the subordinating word *who* marks the clause that the writer thinks less important.

15.4 Relative Pronouns and Antecedents

Normally an adjective clause is introduced by a **relative pronoun**—*which, that, who, whom,* or *whose.* The one you choose depends chiefly on the antecedent.

1. Use *who, whom, whose,* or *that* when the antecedent is one or more persons:

> A cynic is a man *who* knows the price of everything and the value of nothing. —Oscar Wilde
> Millard Fillmore, *whom* almost nobody remembers, was president of the United States from 1848 to 1852.
> Writers *whose* books turn into movies may suddenly find themselves rich.
> Pedestrians *that* ignore traffic lights are living dangerously.

The relative pronouns *who, whom,* and *whose* have **case endings** that depend on what the pronoun does in the clause it introduces. (For a full discussion of case endings, see section 18.11.)

2. Use *which* or *that* when the antecedent is one or more things:

> These are the times *that* try men's souls. —Thomas Paine
> A team of shipwreck hunters recently found the wreck of the *S.S. Leopoldville, which* was sunk by a German torpedo on Christmas Eve 1944.
> We must preserve the freedom for *which* our ancestors fought.

3. Use *which* when the antecedent is an entire clause—but only when nothing else can be mistaken for the antecedent:

> Tim cackled maliciously, *which* infuriated Paul.

For more on this use of *which,* see section 20.4B.

4. You may use *whose* with any antecedent to avoid writing *of which:*

The children worked in a schoolroom *whose* windows were never opened. (COMPARE: The children worked in a schoolroom *of which* the windows never opened.)

5. Do not use *that* to introduce a nonrestrictive clause (section 15.6) after any antecedent:

> *The world's greatest jumpers include Carl Lewis, *that* has cleared nearly twenty-nine feet.
> REVISED: The world's greatest jumpers include Carl Lewis, *who* has cleared nearly twenty-nine feet.
> *The Verrazano-Narrows Bridge, *that* links Brooklyn to Staten Island in New York City, has the longest suspension span in the world.
> REVISED: The Verrazano-Narrows Bridge, *which* links Brooklyn to Staten Island in New York City, has the longest suspension span in the world.

6. You may use *where* or *when* as a relative pronoun when the antecedent is a place or a time:

> That morning we drove to the town of Appomatox Court House, Virginia, *where* Lee surrendered to Grant at the end of the Civil War.
> Her favorite season was spring, *when* the earth seemed born again.

15.5 Placing the Adjective Clause

Place the adjective clause so that the reader can clearly see its connection to the antecedent of the relative pronoun. Observe the following guidelines.

1. Whenever possible, place the adjective clause immediately after the antecedent of the relative pronoun:

> Students *who cheat* poison the atmosphere of the college.
> Newhouse made a proposal *that nobody else liked.*

When the relative pronoun follows its antecedent immediately, the reader can see at once what the antecedent is.

2. If you separate the relative pronoun and its antecedent, do not put between the two any word or phrase that could be mistaken for the antecedent:

> *Mothers of small children who work must juggle conflicting responsibilities.

The antecedent of *who* is *mothers,* but because *children* comes just before *who,* the relative clause seems to refer to working children instead of working mothers. Unfortunately, it is sometimes impossible to correct this error by simply placing the relative clause right after the antecedent:

*Mothers who work of small children must juggle conflicting responsibilities.

The problem here is that a modifying clause (*who work*) and a modifying phrase (*of small children*) are each fighting for a place beside *mothers,* and neither one can give way without producing confusion or just plain nonsense. To solve the problem, you can do either one of two things:

a. Turn both modifiers into relative clauses:

Mothers who work and who have small children must juggle conflicting responsibilities.

b. Turn the relative clause into a participle, which can be placed before the word *Mothers:*

Working mothers of small children must juggle conflicting responsibilities.

3. A word or phrase that *cannot* be mistaken for the antecedent may be used between the antecedent and the relative pronoun:

The Braille system was invented by Louis Braille, a teacher of the blind who was himself blind from the age of three.

The phrase *of the blind* comes between *who* and its antecedent, *teacher,* but none of the words in this phrase can be mistaken for the antecedent.

4. If the adjective clause is long, try to move the antecedent to the end of the main clause so as to avoid an awkward interruption.
Consider the problem of combining these sentences:

Leonardo da Vinci painted the *Mona Lisa.*
He painted it about 1504 in Florence.
Da Vinci's knowledge of sculpture, painting, architecture, engineering, and science made him the intellectual wonder of his time.

If you care more about the *Mona Lisa* than about da Vinci's other accomplishments, you will want to subordinate the third sentence to the first two. The problem is how to do it—how to get an adjective clause right after *da Vinci,* which comes at the beginning of the first sentence. Here is one way:

Leonardo da Vinci, *whose* knowledge of sculpture, painting, architecture, engineering, and science made him the intellectual wonder of his time, painted the *Mona Lisa* about 1504 in Florence.

This is clear but cumbersome. It puts the relative pronoun right after its antecedent, but drives an enormous wedge between the subject and verb of the main clause, between *da Vinci* and *painted.*

You can make a smoother sentence by changing the verb in the main clause from the active to the passive voice:

> The *Mona Lisa* was painted about 1504 in Florence by Leonardo da Vinci, whose knowledge of sculpture, painting, architecture, engineering, and science made him the intellectual wonder of his time.

This change brings the parts of the main clause together and moves *da Vinci* from the beginning of the clause to the end, where it can still be immediately followed by *whose*. Note too that in order to get *da Vinci* at the very end of the opening clause, you have to put *about 1504* and *in Florence* right after the verb. (For more on this use of the passive voice, see pp. 395–96.)

EXERCISE 1 Placing Adjective Clauses

To each of the sentences add the adjective clause written within parentheses. Reword the sentence if necessary so as to connect the clause clearly to the italicized item.

> EXAMPLE
> Psychologists have been examining the *drawings* of children. (that depict an atomic explosion)
> NEW SENTENCE: Psychologists have been examining children's drawings that depict an atomic explosion.

1. Workmen are cleaning a *statue* in the park. (designed by Phidias Gold)
2. At the end of the tour, visitors are conducted to the *chapel* of the castle. (, where three kings were crowned in the sixteenth century)
3. University officials will honor *Maggie Smith* with a parade and a banquet on Arbor Day. (, who has planted over one hundred trees to beautify the campus,)
4. The senator discussed *a bill* with reporters. (that would establish a nationwide drinking age of twenty-one)
5. *Parents* of college-bound children must make sacrifices. (who have moderate incomes)

15.6 Adjective Clauses and Commas

Use commas to set off an adjective clause when and only when it is **nonrestrictive.**

A nonrestrictive adjective clause does not identify the antecedent but simply gives information about it.

> Phineas Q. Gradgrind, *who earned a cumulative grade-point average of 3.9999,* was graduated with highest honors.

This adjective clause does not identify the antecedent, Phineas Q. Gradgrind. The proper name by itself identifies the individual; the clause provides supplementary information about him. Without the adjective clause, some details would be lacking, but we would still know exactly who had earned highest honors:

> Phineas Q. Gradgrind was graduated with highest honors.

Do *not* use commas to set off an adjective clause when it is **restrictive**—that is, when it does identify the antecedent:

> Any student *who earns a cumulative grade-point average of 3.7 or more* will be graduated with highest honors.

This adjective clause restricts the meaning of the antecedent, *Any student*. Without the clause, the sentence would say something quite different:

> Any student will be graduated with highest honors.

Since a restrictive clause is essential to the meaning of the antecedent and of the sentence as a whole, it must not be set off or cut off from that antecedent by commas.

15.7 Overusing Adjective Clauses

Do not use adjective clauses starting with phrases like *who is* and *which are* when you don't really need them. Sometimes the modifying can be done by a phrase alone:

> Amelia Earhart, *who was born in 1898,* was the first woman to fly the Atlantic.
> REVISED: Amelia Earhart, *born in 1898,* was the first woman to fly the Atlantic.

> Some of the compact cars *which are sold by American companies* are manufactured in Japan.
> REVISED: Some of the compact cars *sold by American companies* are manufactured in Japan.

> Joseph P. Kennedy, *who was the father of President John F. Kennedy,* was a financial wizard.
> REVISED: Joseph P. Kennedy, *father of President John F. Kennedy,* was a financial wizard.

In the last sentence you don't even need *the* before *father*.

EXERCISE 2 Sentence Combining with Adjective Clauses

Combine the sentences in each of the following pairs by turning one sentence into an adjective clause and using it in the other. Then underline the adjective clause and in parentheses state whether it is restrictive or nonrestrictive.

EXAMPLE
Students of a certain kind will be expelled.
These students cheat.
COMBINED: Students <u>who cheat</u> will be expelled. (restrictive)

1. Charles Gates Dawes wrote a hit song during his student days at Yale.
He later became vice-president of the United States under Calvin Coolidge.

2. Women of a certain kind are a vanishing breed.
These women just want to be housewives.

3. Helen Keller lost her sight and hearing in infancy.
She nevertheless became a celebrated writer, lecturer, and scholar.

4. I wanted to buy a car of a certain kind.
This car would last at least as long as the payments on it.

5. Colombia supplies the world with coffee and emeralds.
It is also a leading source of the cocaine and marijuana smuggled into the United States.

6. It is often hard to find a certain kind of negotiator.
Both sides will trust this negotiator.

7. Students of a certain kind are becoming rare.
Their parents can afford the total cost of a college education.

8. The president's special emissary was sent to the Middle East for a purpose.
He did not achieve the purpose.

EXERCISE 3   Sentence Combining with Adjective Clauses

Combine the sentences in each of the following sets by using one or more adjective clauses. Where possible, avoid clauses using the verb *be*—that is, starting with *who is, which are,* and the like. Combine the sentences of each set in at least two different ways. Then, if you prefer one of the combinations, put a check next to it.

EXAMPLE
Ronald Reagan won the presidency by a landslide in 1980.
Reagan made his name in the movies.
Then he became governor of California.

COMBINATION 1: Ronald Reagan, who won the presidency by a landslide in 1980, made his name in the movies and then became governor of California.

COMBINATION 2: Ronald Reagan, who made his name in the movies and then became governor of California, won the presidency by a landslide in 1980.

1. A fundamental belief guided the founding fathers.
According to this belief, all men are created equal.

2. In 1848 men rushed to California.
   The men hoped to get rich quickly.
   Gold had just been discovered in California.

3. Pierre Charles L'Enfant laid out plans for the nation's capital in 1791.
   L'Enfant was a French architect.
   He had volunteered for service in the Continental Army.
   He had won the admiration of Washington for his heroism as an officer of engineers.

4. Space satellites are seeking the answer to a question.
   The space satellites are headed out beyond the solar system.
   The question has fascinated man for centuries.

5. Charlie Brown seems destined to remain forever a lovably bumbling little boy.
   He has been a national celebrity since the early fifties.
   That was when Charles M. Schulz invented him.

15.8 Using Adverb Clauses

An adverb clause begins with a subordinator—a word like *when, because, if,* and *although.* Modifying a word, phrase, or clause, it tells such things as why, when, how, and under what condition. Normally it tells more about what it modifies than an adverb does. Compare these sentences:

> *Suddenly,* she hit the brakes.
> *As the deer leaped onto the road,* she hit the brakes.

An adverb clause also enables you to subordinate one point in a sentence to the main one. Consider this sentence:

> ADVERB CLAUSE   INDEPENDENT CLAUSE
> As he was being tackled, / he threw the ball.

In this sentence the main point is that the player threw the ball; the subordinate point is that he was being tackled at the same time. The sentence is designed to fit into a particular kind of story, probably one in which the pass won the game:

> The line wavered, and Keene knew it would break in seconds. But he dropped back, dancing around until he spotted a receiver. *As he was being tackled, he threw the ball.* Polanski made a leaping catch at the twenty-five-yard line, came down running, zigzagged past the Iowa safety, and crossed the goal line. The crowd went wild.

But what if the story is different? Suppose the most important thing is not the pass but the tackle?

> Keene looked desperately for a receiver, sensing the seconds ticking away. Suddenly his blocking broke down and he was sur-

rounded. *As he threw the ball, he was being tackled.* The pass went nearly straight up, then fell to earth behind him. The game was over.

Now the sentence highlights the tackle. In the structure of the sentence, as in the situation it describes, the tackle is more important than the pass that failed because of it. Once again, the adverb clause lets you indicate which of two actions is more important.

15.9 Choosing Subordinators

As noted earlier, an adverb clause starts with a **subordinator,** a word or phrase that subordinates the clause to whatever it modifies. A subordinator can be used to signal one of the following relations:

1. Time

> The factory closed *when* the owner died.
> *Until* the power lines were restored, we had to read at night by candlelight.

You can also signal time with *after, as soon as, as long as, before, ever since, as,* and *while.*

2. Causality

> Kate was happy *because* she had just won her first case.
> *Since* I had no money, I walked all the way home.

3. Concession and contrast

> Money cannot make you happy, *though* it can keep you comfortable.

The clause begun by *though* concedes a point that contrasts with the main point: money cannot make you happy. If you attach *though* to the other clause, you can reverse the emphasis of the sentence:

> *Though* money cannot make you happy, it can keep you comfortable.

You can also signal concession and contrast with *although, even though,* and *whereas:*

> *Although* the mosquitoes were out in force, we spent an enjoyable hour fishing before sundown.
> In my new car, I am averaging over thirty-five miles per gallon of gas, *whereas* I got only twenty in my old one.

While can signal concession and contrast as well as time:

While Marian sang, Zachary played the piano. [time]
While Finnegan himself never ran for any office, he managed many successful campaigns. [concession and contrast]

4. Condition

If battery-powered cars become popular, the price of gas will drop.
He ran *as if* he had a broken leg.

You can also signal condition with *provided that, unless,* and *as though.* (For more on conditional clauses, see section 23.6.)

5. Purpose

I worked in a department store for a year *so that* I could earn money for college.

You can also signal purpose with *in order that* and *lest.*

6. Place

Where federal funds go, federal regulations go with them.

7. Result

We are *so* accustomed to adopting a mask before others *that* we end by being unable to recognize ourselves.   —William Hazlitt

Here *so* and *that* are separated. You can also use them together:

She fixed the clock *so that* it worked.

8. General possibility

Whatever the president wants, Congress has a will of its own.

You can also signal general possibility with *whenever, wherever, whoever, whichever,* and *however:*

I can't pronounce the name *however* it is spelled.

9. Comparison

The river is cleaner now *than* it was two years ago.

The clause begun by *than* completes the comparison initiated by *cleaner.* (For more on writing comparisons, see section 15.12.)

15.10 Placing Adverb Clauses

An adverb clause normally follows the word or phrase it modifies. But when it modifies a main clause, it can go either before or after that clause. To be clear-cut and straightforward, lead with your main clause and let the adverb clause follow:

The colonel ordered an investigation as soon as he heard the complaint of the enlisted men.
I worked in a department store for a year so that I could earn money for college.

That kind of order has a brisk, no-nonsense effect, and you will seldom go wrong with it. But it is not always the best order. To create suspense, or to build up to your main point, put the adverb clause at the beginning and save the main clause for the end. Consider these two versions of a sentence spoken by Winston Churchill in 1941, when the Germans had occupied most of Europe and were threatening to invade England:

> We shall not flag or fail even though large tracts of Europe and many old and famous states have fallen or may fall into the grip of the Gestapo and all the odious apparatus of Nazi rule.

> Even though large tracts of Europe and many old and famous states have fallen or may fall into the grip of the Gestapo and all the odious apparatus of Nazi rule, we shall not flag or fail.

There is nothing grammatically wrong with the first sentence, which starts with a main clause and finishes with a long adverb clause. But this sentence has all the fire of a wet match. Because the crucial words *we shall not flag or fail* come first, they are virtually smothered by what follows them. By the time we reach the end of the sentence we may even have forgotten its main point. The arrangement of the second sentence—the one Churchill actually wrote—guarantees that we will remember. Precisely because we are made to wait until the end of the sentence for the main clause, it now strikes with telling effect.

15.11 Punctuating Adverb Clauses

Introductory adverb clauses are followed by a comma:

> *Even though I kicked and pounded on the door,* the storekeeper would not open it.
> *When the gate opened,* the bull charged into the ring.

Ordinarily, an adverb clause coming at the end of a sentence is not preceded by a comma:

> The bull charged into the ring *when the gate opened.*
> A wall collapsed *because the foundation was poorly constructed.*

If the adverb clause at the end of a sentence is nonrestrictive—not essential to the meaning of the sentence—a comma may precede it:

> We planted the trees in the fall of 1984, *just after we bought the house.*

EXERCISE 4   Sentence Combining with Adverb Clauses

Combine the sentences in each of the following pairs by turning one sentence into an adverb clause and attaching it to the other. Be sure to begin the adverb clause with a suitable subordinator, and in parentheses state the relation that the subordinator shows.

EXAMPLE
I see roses.
Then my nose starts to itch.
COMBINED: Whenever I see roses, my nose starts to itch. (time)

1. I had studied my notes for hours.
   I could not remember a thing.

2. The bell in the steeple tolled midnight.
   A shrouded figure appeared at the entrance to the cemetery.

3. Scientists will continue to investigate the universe.
   They may never discover life on another planet.

4. Assume that commercial airlines will offer regular flights to the moon by the year 2000.
   The moon may become the new playground of the super-rich.

5. The Canadian Pacific railway was completed in 1885.
   Thousands of homesteaders from Europe and eastern Canada streamed west.

6. Many young wives are postponing motherhood indefinitely.
   Babies interfere with career plans.

7. I ran all the way to school in a downpour.
   I was drenched.

8. Tickets to professional football games get steadily more expensive.
   Each year the players demand higher salaries.

9. Wigglesworth lost the election.
   She had pledged to cut property taxes in half.

10. One clown took a huge, ungainly swing at the other and wound up punching himself in the nose.
    The children burst out laughing.

15.12   Using Adverb Clauses in Comparisons

You may sometimes need an adverb clause to make a comparison complete.

1. Use a full adverb clause to complete a comparison unless the comparison will be clear without one:

Most Americans are probably tested more *than they are taught.*
—Thomas C. Wheeler
The river is as clean now *as it was two years ago.*

In each of these sentences, you need a full clause to complete the comparison. See what happens, for instance, if you leave out *it was* in the second one:

*The river is as clean now as two years ago.

This sentence confuses the reader by comparing a river with two years.

2. You may omit certain words from the adverb clause when the comparison is perfectly clear without them:

Many forces have contributed to the decline of American students' writing ability, but none has been more effective *than the widespread use of multiple choice tests.* —Thomas C. Wheeler.

Here the writer does not need to say *than the widespread use of multiple choice tests has been* because the second *has been* would simply repeat the first. In the following sentences, the parenthesized words may likewise be omitted:

The new exhaust system emits less sulphur dioxide *than the original system (did).*
The new method of photographing a manuscript is not so [or "not as"] costly *as the old method (was).*
Some writers think more about plot *than (they do) about characters.*

3. Do not omit any word that is needed to make the comparison clear. Consider this example:

Roger moves faster *than any other player on the team (does).*

Does may be omitted, but if Roger himself is a player on the team, the word *other* is essential. If you merely compare him with *any player,* you are comparing him with himself as well as with others, and doing that makes no sense.

Tokyo's population is larger *than New York's (is).*

The *is* may be omitted, but the *-'s* on *New York* is essential. Without it the sentence is comparing a population to a city. You could also write:

Tokyo's population is larger *than that of New York.*

4. You need not complete a comparison that can be easily completed by the reader:

Ever since I started jogging every day, I have felt better.

You don't need to state the obvious: *better than I felt before I started jogging.*

EXERCISE 5   **Correcting Faulty Comparisons**

Each of the following sentences makes a comparison. Revise any sentence in which the comparison is not clear and complete. If a sentence is correct as it stands, write *Correct*.

> EXAMPLE
> The river is as clean now as two years ago.
> REVISED: The river is as clean now as it was two years ago.

1. Gas and oil cost much more now than ten years ago.
2. Hardwoods such as maple and oak burn more slowly.
3. Jack tackles harder than anyone on the team. [Jack is a member of the team.]
4. The old house on the bay looks just as good as it did five years ago.
5. Some students care more about grades than learning.
6. Many teachers talk more than listen.
7. In 1970, Mexico's recorded murder rate was higher than any other country in the world.

15.13 Using Noun Clauses

A **noun clause** is a clause used as a noun within a sentence. It begins with a word such as *whoever, whichever, whatever, that, who, what, how, why, when,* or *where.* A noun clause can serve as subject, object, or predicate noun.

1. Noun clause as subject

> *What Sylvia did* amazed me.
> *What kept me awake all night* was the barking and howling of the scrawny old dog.
> *Whoever wins the nomination* will be running against a popular incumbent.

2. Noun clause as object

> I feared *(that) we would never get out alive.*†
> Many voters will support *whoever‡ promises lower taxes.*
> The police have not discovered *how the prisoner escaped.*
> No one knows for certain *whether (or not) the strange and moody explorer was murdered on his last trip to the Arctic.*
> A prize will be given to *whoever solves the riddle.*
> We will plug the leaks with *whatever is handy.*

†Parenthesized words in these sentences are optional.
‡On the difference between *whoever* and *whomever*, see section 18.11.

My sister says *that the early bird gets indigestion along with the worm.*
Alexandra wondered *what marriage would do to her.*

The last two examples illustrate the use of noun clauses in the indirect reporting of discourse. (For a full discussion of indirect reporting, see chapter 24.)

3. Noun clause as predicate noun

My only hope was *that the ski patrol would rescue us.*
A fascinating question is *how Stonehenge was built.*
A computer with the brain of a genius is *what I need right now.*
The next candidate will be *whomover the party bosses select.*
The most puzzling mystery of all is *why she abdicated at the height of her power.*

4. The noun clause in a paragraph

Now consider an example of a noun clause used effectively at the end of a paragraph written to refute the idea that gunslinging is the essence of Americanism:

Such a definition of Americanism would come as a stark surprise to the men who were most directly involved in the making of the national undertaking that carries the name of the United States. For the one word that best expresses their purpose and their aspirations in founding this country is *law*. The U.S. Constitution is nothing if it is not a monument to law. It holds that anyone who takes the law into his own hands is to be treated as a criminal. It is based on the assumption that even the best men become dangerous when they substitute force for law. Gunslingers . . . are precisely what the founding fathers wanted to protect the American people against. —Norman Cousins, "In Praise of Famous Men"

The *what* construction lets you put a key word or phrase just where you want it to stress its importance.

EXERCISE 6   Using Noun Clauses

Underline the noun clause(s) in each of the following. Then write a sentence of your own that resembles the form of the given one.

EXAMPLE
Whoever climbs all the way up a mountain knows the thrill of reaching the top.
Whoever completes a difficult task enjoys a sense of achievement.

1. Experts doubt that the climbers reached the summit without oxygen masks.
2. I have sometimes wondered how automatic elevators respond to conflicting signals.
3. What solves one problem often causes another.

4. No one knows whether there is intelligent life on another planet.
5. One argument for destroying the infected trees is that the blight may be contagious.
6. It soon became evident that the witness was lying.
7. Whatever is hard to learn may prove easy to remember.
8. Whoever goes into politics will soon discover that nothing will please all of the voters all of the time.

15.14 Using Two or More Subordinate Clauses

A sentence can have more than one subordinate clause.

1. Two or more subordinate clauses may be directly attached to an independent clause:

ADVERB CLAUSE	INDEPENDENT CLAUSE	ADJECTIVE CLAUSE
Before an applicant can have an interview,	he or she must fill out a questionnaire	that would baffle an Einstein.

2. One subordinate clause may modify something in another:

ADVERB CLAUSE	ADJECTIVE CLAUSE	INDEPENDENT CLAUSE
As Keene threw the pass	that might have won the game,	he was tackled.

3. If a noun clause is used, it may fit within another clause:

NOUN CLAUSE AS SUBJECT	PREDICATE	ADJECTIVE CLAUSE
How the robbers opened the safe	is a question	that no one has answered.

ADVERB CLAUSE	INDEPENDENT CLAUSE	WITH NOUN CLAUSE AS OBJECT
When interest rates rise,	many would-be buyers decide	that the cost of financing the purchase of a home would be excessive.

A mastery of these and other combinations will enable you to discuss a wide variety of topics clearly and effectively.

EXERCISE 7 Sentence Combining: Review of Subordination

Combine the sentences in each of the following sets by using at least two of the three different kinds of subordinate clauses—noun clauses, adjective clauses, and adverb clauses. Then in parentheses state which kinds of clauses you have used; if one of them is an adverb clause, state also what relation it shows. Note that the sentences of each set may be combined in more than one way.

15.14

EXAMPLE
Frank Waters was a powerful man.
He could not lift the big stove.
It weighed over four hundred pounds.
COMBINED: Though Frank Waters was a powerful man, he could not lift the big stove, which weighed over four hundred pounds. (adverb clause of contrast, adjective clause)

1. The Sioux Indians settled down near the Black Hills.
   The Black Hills were invaded by white men.
   The white men were searching for gold.

2. A U.S. treaty forbade white men to enter the Black Hills.
   Army cavalrymen entered the Black Hills in 1874 under General George Custer.
   Custer had led the slaughter of the Southern Cheyenne in 1868.

3. Red Cloud led the Sioux.
   Red Cloud denounced Custer's invasion.
   The invasion violated the treaty.

4. I had not seen the movie.
   Everyone else was talking about it.
   I felt left out of the conversation.

5. Suppose my rich uncle dies and leaves me all his money.
   I will buy a Rolls-Royce Silver Cloud.
   I can drive around in a certain style.
   Such a style will suit me.

16

COORDINATION AND SUBORDINATION

16.1 Using Coordination and Subordination Together

Using coordination and subordination together, you can arrange all the parts of a sentence according to their relative importance. Almost every sentence calls for some subordination, some indication that one part is more important than another. But in some sentences you also need to put two or more parts on the same level of importance; you need to coordinate as well as subordinate. For example:

1. I remember Mr. Spingold.
2. He was short.
3. He was fat.
4. He always carried a black umbrella.
5. He always predicted rain.
   COMBINED: I remember Mr. Spingold, short and fat, who always carried a black umbrella and who always predicted rain.

The combined sentence is the product of coordination and subordination. Sentence 1 becomes the main clause. Sentences 2 and 3 turn into adjectives modifying *Mr. Spingold;* they are subordinated to *Mr. Spingold* and coordinated with each other in a compound phrase. Sentences 4 and 5 turn into adjective clauses modifying *Mr. Spingold,* the antecedent of both *who's,* so they too are subordinated to *Mr. Spingold* and coordinated with each other.

This example shows how coordination and subordination work together in a sentence with just one main clause. But they can also work together in a sentence with two or more main clauses. For example:

1. No one had the guts to raise a riot.
2. But suppose a European woman went through the bazaars alone.
3. Somebody would probably spit betel juice over her dress.
   COMBINED: No one had the guts to raise a riot, but if a European woman went through the bazaars alone somebody would probably spit betel juice over her dress. —George Orwell

In the combined sentence, both sentence 1 and sentence 3 have become main clauses; they are on the same level of importance, coordinated with each other and joined by *but*. The result is a compound sentence. Within it, sentence 2 becomes a subordinate clause. The word *if* subordinates it to the main clause that used to be sentence 3.

When you can manipulate entire clauses in this way, you have the power to express a highly complicated idea in a single sentence. Here is another example:

> Thus the essence of freedom of opinion is not in mere toleration as such, but in the debate which toleration provides; it is not in the venting of opinion, but in the confrontation of opinion.
> —Walter Lippmann

Lippmann reinforces the coordination between two main clauses by using parallel construction, with a total of four *in* phrases. At the same time, the sentence is enriched and varied by the adjective clause *which toleration provides;* it modifies *debate,* explaining what makes the debate possible. Here is one more example:

> Galileo and Shakespeare, who were born in the same year, grew into greatness in the same age; when Galileo was looking through his telescope at the moon, Shakespeare was writing *The Tempest* and all Europe was in ferment, from Johannes Kepler to Peter Paul Rubens, and from the first table of logarithms by John Napier to the Authorized Version of the Bible. —Jacob Bronowski

Here again coordination and subordination are skillfully used. The sentence conveys a powerful sense of simultaneous action, of many things happening at once. The ferment Bronowski talks about is packed into the very structure of his sentence, yet coordination and subordination work together to keep that ferment under control.

EXERCISE 1   Sentence Combining

This exercise tests your ability to use coordination and subordination together. If you feel uncertain about how to use coordination and subordination separately, review chapters 13, 14, and 15 before you begin this exercise. Using coordination and subordination together, make one sentence from each of the following sets of sentences. Include all the information given, but feel free to change the wording or arrangement of the sentences. Combine the sentences of each set in at least two different ways. Then, if you prefer one of the combinations, put a check next to it.

EXAMPLE
The snow melts in the spring.
The dirt roads in the region turn into muddy streams.
Certain people live in isolated houses.
Those people use old footpaths to reach Bridgeton.
Bridgeton has two grocery stores.
It has one gas pump.
COMBINATION 1: The snow melts in the spring, so the dirt roads in the region turn into muddy streams; certain people live in isolated houses, and those people use old footpaths to reach Bridgeton, which has two grocery stores and one gas pump.
COMBINATION 2: When the snow melts in the spring, the dirt roads in the region turn into muddy streams, so people who live in isolated houses use old footpaths to reach Bridgeton, which has two grocery stores and one gas pump.

1. He seldom got angry.
   His opponents often misrepresented the facts.
   He believed something about reason.
   Reason alone had power, in his view, to win an argument.

2. Only a few men and women remember the famine of 1943.
   Many recall certain celebrations.
   Those celebrations marked the coming of peace in 1952.

3. At graduation the seniors are happy.
   They have earned their diplomas.
   They are also sad.
   They are leaving friends.
   They may never see the friends again.

4. The treasurer of the company proposed something.
   Suppose the company made a profit.
   Every employee would get a pay raise.
   Suppose the company took a loss.
   Every employee would get a pay cut.

5. Charleston, South Carolina, sits at the mouths of two rivers.
   The rivers empty into the Atlantic.
   The people of Charleston like to say something about their city.
   Charleston is a certain kind of place, in their opinion.
   Two rivers meet in that place to form an ocean.

6. The governor admitted something.
   The admission was public.
   He was an alcoholic.
   He offended some of his supporters.

Using Coordination and Subordination Together **311**

He got many letters.
The letters were sympathetic.
The letters were from certain people.
Those people admired his willingness to speak out.
He spoke on a personal problem.
He spoke honestly.
He spoke openly.

7. Ralph is the leader of the boys.
   Ralph summons the boys to meetings in a certain way.
   He blows into a shell.
   The shell is called a conch.
   The conch is a large shell.
   The conch emits a loud noise at a certain time.
   Someone blows air into it.
   The boys respond to the sound for a certain reason.
   The conch is a symbol of authority.
   It is also a symbol of order.

8. Jack's followers attack Piggy one night.
   They want Piggy's glasses.
   The glasses are partly broken.
   They want the glasses for a purpose.
   They want to start a fire.
   They use the lenses.
   The lenses concentrate the sun's rays on firewood.

9. Jack and his followers like to hunt pigs.
   The pigs run wild on the island.
   The pigs hide in the thick undergrowth.
   Jack and his followers like to hunt them for two reasons.
   They enjoy eating meat.
   They enjoy hunting.
   The hunting is exciting.
   The hunting is especially exciting at the end.
   They kill the pig then.

10. The ending of *Lord of the Flies* is ironical.
    The young boys are saved by a strong naval officer.
    The naval officer scolds the boys.
    The boys look like savages.
    The boys have been fighting amongst themselves.
    The naval officer, however, has been fighting too.
    He has come ashore from a warship.
    The warship seeks to sink enemy warships and their crews.

EXERCISE 2   Writing One-Sentence Summaries

This exercise tests your ability to compress as well as combine a set of
sentences by means of coordination and subordination. Using either one
or both, write a one-sentence summary of each of the following passages.

EXAMPLE
More than ever before in American politics, language is used not as an instrument for forming and expressing thought. It is used to prevent, confuse and conceal thinking. Members of each branch and agency of government at every level, representing every hue of political opinion, habitually speak a language of nonresponsibility.
—Richard Gambino, "Through the Dark, Glassily"
ONE-SENTENCE SUMMARY: More than ever before, American politicians and government workers use language not to express thought but to prevent, confuse, and conceal it; they speak a language of nonresponsibility.

1. The average person has many worries, but there is one thing he does not generally worry about. He does not worry that somewhere, without his knowledge, a secret tribunal is about to order him seized, drugged, and imprisoned without the right of appeal. Indeed, anyone who worries overmuch about such a thing, and expresses that worry repeatedly and forcefully enough, would probably be classified as a paranoid schizophrenic.
—Hendrik Hertzberg and David C. K. McClelland, "Paranoia"

2. Of all things banish the egotism out of your conversation, and never think of entertaining people with your own personal concerns or private affairs; though they are interesting to you, they are tedious and impertinent to everybody else; besides that, one cannot keep one's own private affairs too secret.   —Lord Chesterfield, in a letter to his son
[Summarize Chesterfield's long sentence in a sentence of not over twenty words.]

3. Nevertheless a prince should not be too ready to listen to tale-bearers nor to act on suspicion, nor should he allow himself to be easily frightened. He should proceed with a mixture of prudence and humanity in such a way as not to be made incautious by overconfidence nor yet intolerable by excessive mistrust.   —Niccolo Machiavelli, *The Prince*

4. The need of securing success at the *outset* is imperative. Failure at first is apt to damp the energy of all future attempts, whereas past experiences of success nerve one to future vigor. Goethe said to a man who consulted him about an enterprise but mistrusted his own powers: "Ach! you need only blow on your hands!" And the remark illustrates the effect on Goethe's spirits of his own habitually successful career.
—William James, "Habit"

5. In this century there have been several extremely popular plays which are based on the notion that love, and goodwill—but especially Love—will overcome all difficulties, and bridge all chasms of social or cultural difference. Such a play was the immensely successful *Abie's Irish Rose*, in which Love overcame the gulf between Catholicism and Judaism. A more recent example was the play called *A Majority of One*, in which a Jewish lady of no particular culture but a rich folk-wisdom discovered that she and a Japanese gentleman of substantial wealth and rather advanced

culture were soul-mates. These plays succeed because people wish that the ideas they put forward were true. They are wish-fulfilments. They are, in fact, dreams which millions of by no means simple people cherish in their inmost hearts.　　　　—Robertson Davies, "Jung and the Theatre"

6. To lie habitually, as a way of life, is to lose contact with the unconscious. It is like taking sleeping pills, which confer sleep but blot out dreaming. The unconscious wants truth. It ceases to speak to those who want something else more than truth.

　　　　—Adrienne Rich, "Women and Honor: Some Notes on Lying"

16.2 Untangling Sentences　*tgl*

It is sometimes hard to put several ideas into a single sentence without getting them tangled up in the process. Consider this sentence:

> *Due to the progress in military weaponry over the years, there has been an increased passivity in mankind that such advancements bring as wars are easier to fight resulting in a total loss of honor in fighting.

This sentence cannot be understood as it stands. If you come across such a sentence in your own writing, you should first of all break it up:

1. There has been progress in military weaponry over the years.
2. There has been increased passivity in mankind.
3. Such advancements bring passivity.
4. The passivity is due to the progress.
5. Wars are easier to fight.
6. This results in a total loss of honor in fighting.

Once you have broken up the sentence into single ideas, you can use coordination and subordination to put them back together clearly:

> Since progress in military weaponry over the years has made mankind more passive and wars easier to fight, there has been a total loss of honor in fighting. [or] Since progress in military weaponry over the years has made mankind more passive and wars easier to fight, fighting has lost all honor.

The original sentence is thus untangled, and its meaning brought to light. If you find a tangled sentence in your own writing, or if your teacher points one out to you, treat it as shown here. Take it apart so that you can see its individual points; then put it back together.

Exercise 3 Sentence Untangling—A Challenge

This may well be the toughest exercise in the book. All of the following sentences were written by students who had a lot to say but who got into a tangle when they tried to say it. So you will probably have trouble even figuring out what the writers meant. But we're asking you to do just that—and more. We're asking you to untangle each sentence in the same way we untangled the sentence about weaponry in the preceding discussion. First, cut up each tangled sentence into a series of short, simple sentences; second, using coordination, subordination, or both, recombine these into one long sentence that makes sense. If you can untangle even half of the following sentences to your own satisfaction, you'll be doing very well.

1. As a youth Moses led a secure life because of the pharaoh's daughter's adoption of him, but one day he rashly murdered an Egyptian overseer, forcing him to flee from Egypt and change his life-style.
2. The author of "The Cold Equations" is saying, in effect, that the main difference of life on the frontier for the people living there is their lives are ruled by laws of nature rather than rules that people make.
3. For fifty years the people prospered under his rule; then feeling a personal responsibility for the welfare of his subjects and their safety, the old king fought another monster which he was severely injured and soon died.
4. If something in one of your paragraphs is marked as being "wrong," one possibility is the teacher making a mistake, not you, although the possibility is seldom admitted, teachers being mostly sure they are always right.
5. Since he spent so much time outdoors in nature which he loved so much, there was no reason to try and prevent it from entering his cabin, and he symbolized a doormat as a mistake of avoiding the sight of natural things like leaves and soil like his neighbors did.
6. The bean field made him self-sufficient, which was one of his beliefs, and he could also see it as an extension of himself, through the bean field, into nature in returning to a natural state.
7. The difference between Florida driving and New England driving is winter and having all the salt on the roads and the icy surfaces causing rusting and sometimes accidents.
8. With language human beings can express their emotions in and thoughts in two ways, depending on how language is used, whether spoken or written.

Exercise 4 Untangling Your Own Sentences

Pick a tangled sentence of your own from one of your essays or from the one-sentence summaries you wrote for exercise 2. Break the sentence into a set of short, simple sentences. Then recombine them so as to express your meaning clearly.

EXAMPLE

Language is not used more than ever before to express thought but to conceal thinking at every level by American politicians and government workers.

Language is not used to express thought.

It is used to conceal thinking at every level of the government.

This is true now more than ever before.

American politicians and government workers use language this way.

REVISED: More than ever before, government workers and American politicians at every level use language not to express thought but to conceal it.

17

COMPLETE SENTENCES AND SENTENCE FRAGMENTS

Good writers usually make their sentences complete. They do so because complete sentences convey or help to convey what most readers expect to find in writing: organized expression. Sentence fragments often do just the opposite. Unless skillfully used, they give the impression that the writer's thoughts are incomplete or disorganized.

To make all of your sentences complete or even to use sentence fragments skillfully, you must know the difference between a complete sentence and a sentence fragment. This chapter explains the characteristics of sentence fragments, the risks of using them, and the ways of turning them into complete sentences.

17.1 What Is a Sentence Fragment?

A sentence fragment is a part of a sentence punctuated as if it were a whole one. Here are some examples:

1. Then went to bed.†
2. Charlie Chaplin.
3. To keep litterbugs from spoiling the beaches.
4. Because it gives you a superstar smile.
5. But always meeting ourselves.
6. Showing an ability to think quickly in tight spots.

†Normally in this book nonstandard constructions used for illustration are marked with a star. However, in this chapter sentence fragments are not starred because, as the text points out, they may be acceptable under certain special circumstances.

Each of these examples *looks* like a sentence. Each begins with a capital letter and ends with a period, and each gives information. But none of them is complete. Fragment 1 lacks a subject; it could be turned into a sentence like *Then I went to bed.* Fragment 2 lacks a predicate; it could be turned into something like *Charlie Chaplin was the great tramp comedian of silent films.* Many of the other examples appear to have been cut off by their punctuation from their rightful place in a sentence. Thus Fragment 3 might be part of a sentence like this: *The selectmen in Wellfleet have been discussing ways to keep litterbugs from spoiling the beaches.*

17.2 What's Wrong with Sentence Fragments?

Rightly or wrongly, sentence fragments turn up often in both speech and writing. In conversation we use and hear them all the time. Fragment 2, for instance, could be the spoken answer to a spoken question, such as *Who was the great tramp comedian of silent films?* We also use fragments in informal letters—letters written to a reader who knows the writer well. Fragment 1, in fact, comes from a letter sent by J. R. R. Tolkien to his son Christopher—a letter in which he wrote:

> Spent part of day (and night) struggling with chapter. Gollum is playing up well on his return. A beautiful night with high moon. About 2 A.M. I was in the warm silver-lit garden, wishing we two could go for a walk. Then went to bed.

This passage contains several fragments, but the reader for whom it was written certainly had no trouble understanding it. Because Christopher knew the letter was from his father, he could take it for granted that the subject of *Spent* and *went* was *I*.

Sentence fragments appear not only in conversation and informal letters but also in print. Consider these passages:

> Buy Dazzle toothpaste. Today. Because it gives you a superstar smile.   —Advertising copy

> Every life is many days, day after day. We walk through ourselves, meeting robbers, ghosts, giants, old men, young men, wives, widows, brothers-in-love. But always meeting ourselves.
>
>   —James Joyce

Each of these has one or more sentence fragments, but no problems result; the meaning of each fragment is perfectly clear in its context. In fact, these fragments serve to emphasize points that might not have been made so effectively with complete sentences.

So why should you not feel free to use sentence fragments in your own essays? The answer is that until you learn how to use them sparingly and strategically, your writing will look disorganized. Consider the two sentence fragments in this piece of student writing:

> In conclusion I feel Falstaff proves to be a most likable and interesting character. Showing an ability to think quickly in tight spots. But above all he lends a comical light to the play. Which I feel makes it all the more enjoyable.

This passage is not much longer than the one by Joyce, but it is harder to read. Joyce's passage has just one fragment, and coming as it does at the end, after a long, abundantly complete sentence, the four-word tailpiece snaps the reader to attention. But the student's two fragments are simply distracting. Alternating with sentences of about equal length, they seem improvised and arbitrary—as if the writer could only now and then form a complete thought.

Though sentence fragments can sometimes enhance a passage, they are just as likely to break it into disconnected pieces. For that reason, they are generally not accepted in college essays, and you should avoid them. If you do use a sentence fragment, be sure that the surrounding text reveals your ability to write complete sentences, and be prepared to say why you have written the fragment.

17.3 Spotting and Revising Sentence Fragments *frag*

To correct sentence fragments, you have to be able to spot them. How can you tell whether a particular word group is a sentence fragment? Here are some useful questions to ask if you aren't sure.

1. Does the "sentence" sound like a sentence?

Before you submit your essay, read the whole thing aloud, exaggerating the fall of your voice whenever you come to a period. Often when you read a sentence fragment, the sound of your voice contrasting with the sense of your words will tell you that something is missing from the "sentence" you have just read.

2. Does the "sentence" have a subject and a predicate?

A sentence has both a subject and a predicate; a word group lacking either one is a sentence fragment. (If you aren't sure you can identify subject and predicate, see chapter 11.) Consider these examples:

> P
> a. Entertained tens of thousands with an outdoor concert every Fourth of July.

This word group has no subject; we are not told who did the entertaining. To make a complete sentence, you must supply a subject:

> ᔆ   ᴾ
> Arthur Fiedler / entertained tens of thousands with an outdoor concert every Fourth of July.

> ᔆ
> b. All of the officials with jobs at the Kennedy Space Center.

This word group has no verb; it could be a subject lacking a predicate—in which case you must supply one:

> ᔆ   ᴾ
> All of the officials with jobs at the Kennedy Space Center / were worried about the fall of Skylab.

Or perhaps this word group is meant to be not a subject but part of a predicate. Then you must supply both a subject and a verb:

> ᔆ   ᴾ
> The director / summoned all of the officials with jobs at the Kennedy Space Center.

> c. With a panoramic view of the Rockies.

Here both subject and predicate are missing; the word group is a prepositional phrase. In such a case, you can often find what the phrase modifies in the sentence just before the fragment:

> ᔆ   ᴾ
> They / went to a ski lodge. With a panoramic view of the Rockies.

To fix a fragment of this type, combine it with the preceding sentence:

> ᔆ   ᴾ
> They / went to a ski lodge with a panoramic view of the Rockies.

> d. After inventing the telephone.

As before, both subject and predicate are missing. *Inventing*, a participle, cannot be the verb of a sentence; it is a modifier of some missing word or phrase. Again, in such a case the missing word is often found in the sentence just before or after the fragment:

> ᔆ   ᴾ
> After inventing the telephone. Alexander Graham Bell / turned his attention to the phonograph.

To fix a fragment of this type, combine it with the adjacent sentence:

> ᔆ   ᴾ
> After inventing the telephone, Alexander Graham Bell / turned his attention to the phonograph.

3. If the "sentence" has both a subject and a predicate, does it start with a subordinator?

> Because political success often calls for compromise.

This word group is a clause, for it has its own subject and predicate. In conversation it could be the answer to a question:

> Why is it hard to find perfect consistency in a politician? Because political success often calls for compromise.

In conversation we often answer a *Why* question with a *Because* statement. *Because* is a subordinator. It makes the whole clause subordinate, and in formal written English a subordinate clause cannot stand alone. Directly or indirectly, it must be connected to a main clause:

> Perfect consistency in a politician is rare because political success often calls for compromise. [or] Because political success often calls for compromise, perfect consistency in a politician is rare.

Subordinators include such words as *since, because, although, when, if,* and *after.*

4. If the "sentence" has both a subject and a predicate, does it start with a relative pronoun, such as *who* or *which?*

> Which can fly from New York to London in three hours.

This word group is an adjective clause beginning with a relative pronoun, *which.* A clause of this type belongs inside a sentence and just after the word or phrase to which it refers:

> The British and French together developed a supersonic plane called the Concorde, which can fly from New York to London in three hours.

5. Does the "sentence" consist of a noun followed by an adjective clause?

> The Ohio senator who sought the Republican presidential nomination in 1952.

The word group is incomplete, with "The Ohio senator" left up in the air. The entire word group has been cut off from its sentence:

> General Dwight D. Eisenhower easily beat Robert A. Taft, the Ohio senator who sought the Republican presidential nomination in 1952. [or] Robert A. Taft, the Ohio senator who sought the Republican presidential nomination in 1952, was beaten by General Dwight D. Eisenhower.

EXERCISE 1   Recognizing Sentence Fragments

Identify each of the following word groups as either a sentence or a sentence fragment.

1. The gunman stood behind the gatehouse at the main entrance to the palace.
2. Forgot to put a stamp on the envelope.
3. But the Egyptians rejected the proposal when it was first made.
4. To make abortion once again illegal throughout the United States.
5. The people who want to abolish all nuclear power plants.
6. I had no time to correct the essay before submitting it.
7. After crawling for three hours in pitch darkness.
8. Under the welcome mat at the front door.
9. Which goes a hundred miles on a gallon of gas.
10. Whenever I see a thick, juicy steak sizzling on a barbecue.

17.4 Avoiding Sentence Fragments

To avoid fragments, you need to know how they happen. Here are some common ways.

1. The writer breaks up a single sentence by using a period where there should be either a comma or no punctuation at all:

> On Halloween night some years ago, a full-grown man with a sick sense of humor disguised himself as a ghost. *So that he could terrify little children.*

Because *So that* is a subordinator, the italicized word group is a fragment—cut off by a period from the sentence about the man in disguise. Such an error can easily occur if you finish a sentence and then decide to expand it. To add the fragment to the sentence, change the period before it to a comma or simply remove the period, and write the first word without a capital letter:

> On Halloween night some years ago, a full-grown man with a sick sense of humor disguised himself as a ghost so that he could terrify little children.

Now look at this passage:

> I cut my hand on the first day of the trip while trying to open a can of spaghetti. *With a hatchet.*

A period cuts off the phrase *With a hatchet* from the clause about cutting the hand. Perhaps the writer was trying for an effect—a kind of verbal double take—but the result is still a fragment. It would be better to write:

> I cut my hand on the first day of the trip while trying to open a can of spaghetti with a hatchet.

2. The writer skips the subject in the belief that a previous sentence has already provided it:

> Lancelot won fame as a knight because of his prowess in battle. *Defeated the other great warriors in the kingdom.* —College freshman

This passage appeared in an examination bluebook, and the writer may have been pressed for time. In any case, he forgot to provide a subject for the second word group. If you budget your time for a writing assignment so that you can reread what you have written before turning it in, you will probably be able to catch any error of this type and correct it by supplying the missing subject:

> Lancelot won fame as a knight because of his prowess in battle. He defeated the other great warriors in the kingdom.

3. The writer omits the verb and instead provides it in the next sentence:

> *Staying up all night to finish a paper.* That left me red-eyed in the morning.

The first word group is a subject without a predicate. Perhaps the writer began with one idea about how to write the sentence, and then switched to another idea without revising what was already on paper. There are two ways of eliminating the fragment. You can combine it with the sentence that comes next:

> Staying up all night to finish a paper left me red-eyed in the morning.

Or you can rewrite it as a separate sentence:

> I stayed up all night to finish a paper. That left me red-eyed in the morning.

4. The writer skips both subject and predicate in providing an example to illustrate a point just made:

> Voters can sometimes defy expectations. *As in the presidential election of 1948.*

The second word group is a modifier unattached to either a subject or a predicate. The writer thinks of the second word group as an extension of the first, but the two are in fact separated by a period. To revise a fragment of this kind, you can combine it with the sentence before it:

> Voters can sometimes defy expectations, as in the presidential election of 1948.

Or you can attach the fragment to a new sentence:

In the presidential election of 1948, for example, voters gave Harry S. Truman a victory over the highly favored Thomas E. Dewey.

Exercise 2   Eliminating Sentence Fragments

Each of the following consists of a sentence and a sentence fragment—not necessarily in that order. Make whatever changes are necessary to eliminate the fragment.

EXAMPLE

I cut my hand on the first day of the trip while trying to open a can of spaghetti. With a hatchet.

REVISED: I cut my hand on the first day of the trip while trying to open a can of spaghetti with a hatchet.

1. The farmers welcomed the evening breeze. Because they had sweltered all day.
2. When the temperature falls below zero and a north wind blows across the pasture. A pair of long johns will keep you warm.
3. To keep the cabin from slipping into the pond. We had to put a jack under the front porch and raise the frame eight inches.
4. I followed the buck for three tough miles. Running hard to keep up with him.
5. After a long search I found the ignition key. In a little box magnetically attached to the inside of the front bumper.
6. Gathering your own firewood takes plenty of hard work. But saves you money.
7. One reason for this punishment could have been the people's sullen behavior. Their constant complaining about their burdens.
8. Some dream of leaving the city and finding better conditions in the country. Such as uncrowded neighborhoods, peaceful streets, and clean air.
9. The Canadian people should develop their country's natural resources. In order to be free of foreign domination.
10. Carts were handy for pioneers winding their way over mountains. Whereas families crossing the Great Plains needed wagons.
11. According to one historian, Julius Caesar suffered from dizzy spells. Even fell to the ground sometimes.
12. A construction crew has started work on the foundation of the new library. Which will be paid for by donations from the alumni.
13. The sight of approximately five hundred people waiting to enter the store. It made the manager beam with pride.
14. The affluent nations are not meeting their obligations to the millions living in the Third World. And suffering from malnutrition, inadequate health programs, and widespread unemployment.
15. Astronomers at the Mount Flume observatory have been disappointed by the performance of the new telescope. Supposed to have been the most powerful of its kind.

EXERCISE 3   **Eliminating Sentence Fragments**

The following paragraph is a rewritten version of a paragraph in Erich Fromm's *The Heart of Man*. In rewriting Fromm's paragraph, we have deliberately introduced several sentence fragments. Make whatever changes are necessary to remove them.

EXAMPLE
line 2: manipulated so

     In a bureaucratically organized and centralized industrialism, tastes are manipulated. So that people consume maximally and in predictable and profitable directions. Their intelligence and character become standardized. By the ever increasing role of tests which
5 select the mediocre and unadventurous. In preference to the original and daring. Indeed, the bureaucratic-industrial civilization which has been victorious in Europe and North America has created a new type of man; he can be described as the *organizational man.* As the *automaton man,* and as *homo consumens.* He is, in addition, *homo*
10 *mechanicus;* by this I mean a gadget man. Deeply attracted by all that is mechanical. And inclined against that which is alive. It is true that man's biological and physiological equipment provides him with such strong sexual impulses. That even *homo mechanicus* still has sexual desires and looks for women. But there is no doubt that the
15 gadget man's interest in women is diminishing. A *New Yorker* cartoon pointed to this very amusingly; a salesgirl trying to sell a certain brand of perfume to a young female customer recommends it by remarking: "It smells like a new sportscar." Indeed, any observer of male behavior today will confirm that this cartoon is more
20 than a clever joke. There are apparently a great number of men. Who are more interested in sports cars, television and radio sets, space travel, and any number of gadgets. Than they are in women, love, nature, food; who are more stimulated by the manipulation of nonorganic, mechanical things than by life.

EXERCISE 4   **Eliminating Sentence Fragments**

The following paragraphs are rewritten versions of paragraphs originally written by Mark Bartlett. In the rewriting, we have created several sentence fragments. Make whatever changes are necessary to remove them.

     Most of the people who eat at a fast-food restaurant like McDonald's fall into one of four subgroups. The regulars, the families, the groups of kids, and the travelers. The members of these groups differ. In their liking of the food, their appearance, and
5 their actions in the restaurant.
     The person who goes regularly to McDonald's is different from the others. In that he actually enjoys the food. While ordering his usual meal. He converses briefly with the clerk. He then walks slowly to the seat. Where he always sits. He eats his food deliberately.

Avoiding Sentence Fragments   **325**

10 Placing the french fries one by one into his mouth and relishing each sip of the milkshake. He doesn't talk to other customers. His meal is an opportunity. To enjoy a tasty bite and to relax after a strenuous day on the job. When he has finished his meal. He crumples the empty styrofoam container. Which held his food. Drops it
15 in the trash barrel and leaves with his appetite satisfied. He waves to the clerk. As he pushes open the door.

. . . Among the kids who go to McDonald's are the members of a birthday party. They are usually about seven years old. One mother supervises the eight or nine children. Who all think that the Golden
20 Arches is the best place to have a party. They sit at a table. While the mother orders nine identical meals. As they wait. The kids play with straws. Blowing them through the air and shooting the wrappers at each other. When the food is brought to the table. There is a big argument over who gets what. Even though the orders are
25 basically the same. Each complains that he has fewer french fries than the others have. None of them, however, is able to finish his portion. During the meal they talk loudly despite the mother's efforts to control the volume. And stare at nearby adults. Who wish the kids had sat someplace else. Or in the parking lot. After the
30 kids leave the restaurant. Everybody is happy. The mother especially.

18

USING PRONOUNS

A **pronoun** is a word that commonly takes the place of a noun or noun phrase:

> Brenda thought that she had passed the exam.
> The old man smiled as he listened to the band.

She takes the place of *Brenda,* a noun; *he* takes the place of *the old man,* a noun phrase. Pronouns thus eliminate the need for awkward repetition. Without them, you would have to write sentences like these:

> Brenda thought that Brenda had passed the exam.
> The old man smiled as the old man listened to the band.

A pronoun can also take the place of a whole clause or a sentence:

> On June 28, 1914, the archduke of Austria was assassinated by Serbian nationalists. That precipitated World War I.

That in the second sentence refers to the whole of the first.

18.1 Using Pronouns with Antecedents

The word or word group that a pronoun refers to is called its **antecedent.** "Antecedent" means "going before," and this term is used because the antecedent usually goes before the pronoun that refers to it:

> Brenda thought that she had passed the exam.
> The old man smiled as he listened to the band.

To build city districts that are custom-made for crime is idiotic. Yet that is what we do. —Jane Jacobs

In the third example, the antecedent of the first *that* is *city districts*. The antecedent of the second *that* is a whole word group: *To build city districts that are custom-made for crime.*

In spite of its name, the antecedent sometimes goes after the pronoun that refers to it:

By the time he was three, Coleridge could read a chapter of the Bible.

In spite of its name, the antecedent sometimes goes after the pronoun.

EXERCISE 1 **Recognizing Pronouns and Antecedents**

Each of the following includes one or more pronouns. Write down each pronoun and its antecedent, using an arrow to identify the antecedent.

EXAMPLE
Sharon was surprised to find a frog in her mailbox.
her ⟶ Sharon

1. One of Jeff's hobbies is restoring old cars. He is now working on a 1955 Thunderbird that his father bought in Indianapolis.
2. Senator Black has assured his closest associates he will confer with them before deciding whether or not to seek reelection. Concerned about his failing health, they hope he will retire.
3. The children felt uneasy when the waiter served them cold bean soup. This was something that they had never seen before, and they were suspicious. It looked strange in the small bowls.
4. In the midst of the argument Sally said that she had never lost her temper. This amazed Mick, who saw her turning purple even as she said it.
5 When several children in the audience shouted that the magician was hiding something, she invited two of them to join her on the stage so that they could observe the next trick at close range.

18.2 Using Pronouns without Antecedents

Some pronouns have no antecedent, and others may sometimes be used without one.

1. Indefinite pronouns have no antecedents. Compare these two sentences:

Ellen said that she wanted privacy.
Everyone needs some privacy.

She is a **definite** pronoun. It refers to a particular person, and its meaning is clear only if its antecedent has been provided—that is, if the person has already been identified. But *Everyone* is an **indefinite** pronoun. Because it refers to someone unspecified, it has no antecedent. Other widely used indefinite pronouns include *everybody, one, no one, each, many,* and *some.* (For a complete list, see p. 338.) Note that an indefinite pronoun can *serve* as the antecedent for another pronoun:

One of the birds had broken its beak.

2. The pronouns *I* and *you* normally have no antecedent because they are understood to refer to the writer and the reader or to the speaker and the listener.

3. A definite pronoun needs no antecedent when it is immediately followed by a relative pronoun, such as *who:*

> Those who cannot remember the past are condemned to repeat it.
> —George Santayana

Those has no antecedent; it is explained by what comes after it rather than by what comes before.

4. The pronoun *we* sometimes appears without an antecedent, for example in newspaper editorials, where the writer clearly speaks for a group of people. But do not use *we* when you mean simply *I.* That is a privilege limited to royalty and the pope. If you use *we,* you should let your reader know just whom *we* refers to. That is what we have done on the title page of this book.

18.3 Using Pronouns Clearly

The meaning of a definite pronoun is clear when readers can identify the antecedent with certainty:

> The selectmen recommend a tax on public parking. They believe it would give the city approximately $10,000 annually.

The antecedent of each pronoun is obvious. *They* clearly stands for *The selectmen,* and *it* stands for *a tax on public parking.*

> People who saw the Tall Ships sail up the Hudson River in 1976 will long remember the experience. It gave them a handsome image of a bygone era.

Again, the antecedent of each pronoun is obvious. *Who* clearly refers to *People; It* refers to *the experience; them* refers to *People who saw the Tall Ships.*

18.4 Avoiding Unclear Reference with Pronouns *pr ref*

The meaning of a definite pronoun is unclear when readers cannot identify the antecedent with certainty. The chief obstacles to clear reference are as follows.

18.4A Ambiguity

Do not use a pronoun for which there is more than one possible antecedent:

> 1. *After my mother called Christina three times, she finally came downstairs.

Does *she* refer to *my mother* or to *Christina?* The reader cannot tell. The simplest way to eliminate the ambiguity is to replace the pronoun with a noun:

> REVISED: After my mother called Christina three times, Christina finally came downstairs.

But to avoid repeating the noun, you can put the pronoun before it:

> REVISED: After my mother called her three times, Christina finally came downstairs.

> 2. It is not so easy for women to enter career fields as it is for men. *They find it harder to get career jobs and keep them.

The reader might eventually figure out that *They* probably refers to *women,* but with *men* sitting just before the pronoun, it could refer to either one. The best way to get rid of the ambiguity here is to repeat the noun:

> REVISED: It is not so easy for women to enter career fields as it is for men. Women find it harder to get career jobs and keep them.

18.4B Broad Reference

Do not use *that, this, which,* or *it* to refer to a whole statement that contains one or more possible antecedents within it:

> 1. *The senator opposes the bottle bill, which rankles many of his constituents.

Are they rankled by the bill or by the senator's opposition to it? *Which* could refer to either—to the whole statement (*The senator opposes the bottle bill)* or to the noun phrase contained within it *(the bottle bill)*. If you make this kind of error, you may need to reconstruct the sentence:

REVISED: The senator's opposition to the bottle bill rankles many of his constituents.

2. Some people insist that a woman should have a career, while others say that she belongs in the home. This is unfair.

What is unfair? *This* could refer to the whole sentence that precedes it, to the first half, or to the second. To correct this kind of error, the writer needs to state explicitly the meaning of *this*.

REVISED: This contradictory set of demands is unfair.

18.4C   Muffled Reference

Do not use a pronoun to refer to something merely implied by what precedes it.

1. A recent editorial contained an attack on the medical profession. The writer accused them of charging excessively high fees.

Who is meant by *them?* From the phrase *medical profession* you may guess that the writer is referring to doctors. But the word *doctors* does not appear. Before using *them*, the writer should clearly establish its antecedent:

A recent editorial contained an attack on hospital administrators and doctors. The writer accused them of charging excessively high fees.

2. *Lincoln spoke immortal words at Gettysburg, but most of the large crowd gathered there couldn't hear it.

What couldn't they hear? The writer is thinking of Lincoln's address, of course, but the word *address* is missing. It must be inserted:

REVISED: Lincoln gave an immortal address at Gettysburg, but most of the large crowd gathered there couldn't hear it. [or] Lincoln spoke immortal words at Gettysburg, but most of the large crowd gathered there couldn't hear his address. [or: . . . couldn't hear them.]

3. *Only in the manager's office did she feel comfortable.

The writer wants *she* to refer to *the manager,* but since *the manager* is just part of a phrase about an office, we have trouble seeing *the manager* as an antecedent. We are led to think, in fact, that *she* must be someone other than the manager.

To correct this kind of error, put the pronoun before its antecedent (as above in section 18.4A) or rearrange the word order in the sentence:

> REVISED: Only in her office did the manager feel comfortable. [or] The manager felt comfortable only in her office.

18.4D   Free-Floating *they* and *it*

Do not use *they* or *it* as pronouns without definite antecedents:

> 1. *In the first part of the movie, it shows clouds billowing like waves.

What shows clouds? The pronoun *it* has no antecedent. The writer is probably thinking of the *it* that simply fills out a sentence such as *It was cloudy,* meaning *There were clouds.* That kind of *it* is called an expletive, and it needs no antecedent. But when *it* is a pronoun, as in *it shows clouds,* it needs an antecedent. If you can't readily figure out a way to furnish one, your best bet is to reconstruct the sentence:

> REVISED: The first part of the movie shows clouds billowing like waves.

> 2. *In high school they made me take three years of algebra.

The word *they* needs an antecedent, even though in conversation it is often used without one. Two ways of revising are possible. One is to replace the pronoun with a noun:

> REVISED: In high school the authorities made me take three years of algebra.

But this sounds stiff. Since the important thing here is not who made the writer take algebra but simply *that* he was made to take it, this sentence would go better in the passive voice:

> REVISED: In high school I was made to take three years of algebra. [or] In high school I had to take three years of algebra.

(For more on the passive voice, see chapter 22.)

18.4E Indefinite *you*

Do not use *you, your,* or *yourself* to mean anything but your reader. Though professional writers sometimes use *you* to mean "people in general," you will increase the precision of your sentences if you use *you* for your reader alone. Compare these three sentences:

1. You can teach pigeons to play Ping-Pong rather quickly by rewarding every gesture they make that moves them toward success in the game and by refusing to reward those gestures that you want to efface. —Wayne Booth

2. You didn't have microphones in Lincoln's day.

3. To make your pole snap upward, you curl upside-down in midair.

In sentence 1, Wayne Booth speaks directly to the reader, and it is therefore quite correct for him to use *you*. In sentence 2, *you* cannot possibly refer to any reader now living; *You didn't have microphones in Lincoln's day* really means *There were no microphones in Lincoln's day*. In sentence 3, *you* cannot refer to any reader who is not a pole-vaulter, even though the sentence is clearly meant to explain pole-vaulting to those who know little or nothing about it and probably do not own poles. The word *you,* therefore, should be replaced:

REVISED: To make the pole snap upward, the vaulter curls upside-down in midair.

4. One of Orwell's contradictions is the unperson, a man who existed once, but doesn't anymore, so he never existed. But by defining someone as an unperson, you are saying that he once existed.

In this case, the best way to eliminate the faulty *you* is to reconstruct the whole sentence:

REVISED: But to define someone as an unperson is to say that he once existed.

18.4F Remote Reference

Do not put the pronoun so far from the antecedent that readers cannot find their way from one to the other.

Bankers have said that another increase in the prime lending rate during the current quarter would seriously hurt their major customers: homeowners, small business personnel, and self-employed

Avoiding Unclear Reference with Pronouns   **333**

contractors using heavy equipment. It would keep all of these borrowers from getting needed capital.

The definite pronoun *It* is so far from its antecedent that we cannot readily put the two together. To clarify the second sentence, the writer should repeat the antecedent:

Such an increase would keep all of these borrowers from getting needed capital.

EXERCISE 2   Supplying Pronouns

Complete each of the following with one or more pronouns referring to the word or phrase shown in italics.

EXAMPLE
Harriet viewed *her car* with disgust. Noticeably rusty, it looked out of place between the new Cadillac and the gleaming Lincoln Continental.

1. After hearing *Roger* praise the appearance of the ugliest statue in the museum, Wanda was tempted to turn her back on _____ and leave.
2. Today, *the dollar* buys about one-fifth of what _____ bought forty years ago.
3. The patient's back was covered with *sores*. According to his doctor, _____ might have been caused by malnutrition.
4. The police said they have found no evidence to suggest *the door* was forced open. _____ bore no marks of rough handling.
5. *Warts* are wonderful structures. _____ can appear overnight on any part of the skin, like mushrooms on a damp lawn, full grown and splendid in the complexity of _____ architecture.

— Lewis Thomas, with words deliberately omitted

EXERCISE 3   Correcting Unclear Pronouns

In each of the following, the italicized pronoun has been used confusingly. Briefly diagnose what is wrong and then provide a cure.

EXAMPLE
The boy and the old man both knew that *he* had not much longer to live.
DIAGNOSIS: *He* is ambiguous; it can refer to either the boy or the old man.
CURE: The boy and the old man both knew that the old man had not much longer to live. [The ambiguous pronoun is simply replaced by its antecedent.]

1. The tracker fired at the cave from which the cry had come. He was directly on target, for *it* struck Coyotito in the head.
2. Hanging on a wall to the right of the entrance was a huge map showing the floor plan of the modern edifice. *It* was painted in six different colors.
3. Johnny kept throwing his cup to the floor. Finally, his mother decided to break him of *it*.

4. The job was tough. *They* made me work seventy-two hours a week.
5. The new robots work twenty-four hours a day without making a mistake, whereas human workers normally operate on eight-hour shifts and make mistakes periodically. Thus *they* have substantially increased production.
6. The detective studied the manuscript with the aid of a powerful magnifying glass. Then he put *it* in his pocket and left.
7. George Orwell's *1984* contains vivid descriptions of the way political prisoners are tortured in a police state. Officials put *you* in a special room and confront *you* with what *you* fear most of all.
8. According to some observers, whenever science experiments with genetic engineering *they* run the risk of creating a monster.
9. During any of the ice ages, *you* perished unless *you* had the strength and the will to adapt to new environments.
10. The president supports the proposal, *which* has provoked a storm of criticism.

18.5 Making Antecedents and Pronouns Agree in Gender   *pr agr/g*

Whenever possible, pronouns should agree with their antecedents in gender.

18.5A   Pronouns with Antecedents of Specified Gender

In English, gender affects only the singular definite pronoun, which is masculine (for example, *he*), feminine *(she)*, or neuter *(it)*, depending on the gender of its antecedent. Consider this passage:

> The men of our civilization have stripped themselves of the fineries of the earth so that they might work more freely to plunder the universe for treasures to deck my lady in. New raw materials, new processes, new machines are all brought into her service. My lady must therefore be the chief spender as well as the chief symbol of spending ability and monetary success. While her mate toils in his factory, she totters about the smartest streets and plushiest hotels with his fortune upon her back and bosom, fingers and wrists, continuing that essential expenditure in his house which is her frame and her setting, enjoying that silken idleness which is the necessary condition of maintaining her mate's prestige and her qualification to demonstrate it.   —Germaine Greer, *The Female Eunuch*

The feminine pronouns *her* and *she* refer to *my lady,* a woman; the masculine pronoun *his* refers to *her mate,* a man; the neuter pronoun *it* refers to a thing, *her mate's prestige.* The distinctions among *his* and *her, she* and *it,* help to make the meaning of the passage clear.

18.5B Nonsexist Pronouns with Antecedents of Unspecified Gender

When the antecedent of a pronoun is clearly singular and masculine, you use *he, his,* or *him;* when the antecedent is clearly singular and feminine, you use *she* or *her.* But what do you use when the gender of the antecedent is not clear—when it could be either masculine or feminine? What do you do with words like *everyone, student, doctor,* and *lawyer?* Not long ago, it was considered all right to say:

> Everyone has his own story to tell.
> A doctor needs years of training before he is fully qualified to operate.

But sentences like these are unfair to women. Saying *his* or *he* seems to imply that *Everyone* is exclusively male or that all doctors are men. To be fair to women, you must recognize that words like *everyone* usually refer to both sexes. Here is one way of using pronouns fairly:

> Everyone has his or her own problems.
> A doctor needs years of training before he or she is fully qualified to operate.

This double-pronoun construction is now widely used. But there is a problem with it. If repeated, the double pronouns soon become tedious and distracting:

> A doctor needs years of training before he or she is fully qualified to operate on his or her patients by himself or herself.

One alternative to *he or she* is *s/he.* But *s/he* cannot be read aloud, and even if it could be, it could not take the place of *his or her.* Another alternative is *he/she, her/his,* and *himself/herself,* but repetition of these soon becomes just as tedious as the repetition of a phrase like *he or she.* Still another alternative is the following:

> *Everyone has their own story to tell.

Their can refer to both women and men, so its use eliminates the need for *his or her;* the problem is that *their* is plural, and does not match *Everyone,* which should be treated as singular in formal writing. When the antecedent is a specific word, such as *doctor,* the mismatch becomes even more glaring:

> *A doctor needs years of training before they are fully qualified to operate.

Fortunately, there are better ways of avoiding sexism in the use of pronouns. One way is to make the antecedent plural, so that it does match the plural pronoun:

Doctors need years of training before they are fully qualified to operate.

Another way is to avoid specifically masculine and feminine pronouns altogether—when you can:

To become fully qualified to operate, a doctor needs years of training.
Everyone has a story to tell.
Everyone has personal problems.

18.6 Making Antecedents and Pronouns Agree in Number

Whenever possible, pronouns should agree with their antecedents in number.

An antecedent is singular if it refers to one person or thing, and plural if it refers to more than one. A singular antecedent calls for a singular pronoun; a plural antecedent calls for a plural pronoun:

The boy saw that he had cut his hand.

The Edmonton Oilers believed that they could win the Stanley Cup in 1984, and they did.

18.7 Pronouns and Antecedents—Resolving Problems in Number *pr agr/n*

Some antecedents can be problem cases—hard to classify as either singular or plural. Observe the following guidelines.

1. Two or more nouns or pronouns joined by *and* are usually plural:

Orville and Wilbur Wright are best known for their invention of the airplane.
He and I left our coats in the hall.

Nouns joined by *and* are singular only if they refer to one person or thing:

The chief cook and bottle-washer demanded his pay.

2. When two nouns are joined by *or* or *nor*, the pronoun normally agrees with the second:

Squirrels or a chipmunk has left its tracks in the new-fallen snow.
Neither Pierre LaCroix nor his boldest followers wanted to expose themselves to danger.

Its matches *chipmunk*, and *themselves* matches *his boldest followers.*

3. A noun or pronoun followed by a prepositional phrase is treated as if it stood by itself:

> In 1980 the United States, together with Canada and several other countries, kept its athletes from participating in the Moscow Olympics.

The antecedent of *its* is simply *United States*. Unlike the conjunction *and*, a phrase like *together with* or *along with* does not make a compound antecedent. The antecedent is what comes before the phrase.

> The leader of the strikers said that he would get them a new package of benefits.

The pronoun *he* agrees with *leader*, just as if *of the strikers* was omitted and *leader* stood by itself. The antecedent of *them* is *strikers*.

4. Collective nouns can be either singular or plural, depending on the context:

> The team chooses its captain in the spring.

Since the captain is a symbol of unity, the writer treats *The team* as singular, using the singular pronoun *its*.

> The audience shouted and stamped their feet.

Since each person in the audience was acting independently, the writer treats *The audience* as plural, using the plural pronoun *their*.

5. Some indefinite pronouns are singular, some are plural, and some can be either singular or plural:

ALWAYS SINGULAR

anybody	either	one
anyone	neither	another
anything		
each	nobody	somebody
each one	none	someone
	no one	something
everybody	nothing	
everyone		whatever
everything		whichever
		whoever

ALWAYS PLURAL

both	few	others	several

SOMETIMES SINGULAR AND SOMETIMES PLURAL

all	many	some
any	most	

As this list indicates, *each* is always singular:

> Each of the men brought his own tools.

Here the pronoun *his* is singular because its antecedent is the singular pronoun *each*. But when *each* immediately follows a plural noun, the pronoun after *each* must be plural also:

> The men each brought their own tools.

The antecedent of *their* is *men,* not *each.*

Though some writers treat *everybody* and *everyone* as plural, we recommend that you treat them as singular, or simply avoid using them as antecedents:

> Everyone in the cast had to furnish his or her own costume.
> The cast members each had to furnish their own costumes.

The number of a pronoun in the third group depends on the number of the word or phrase to which it refers:

> Some of the salad dressing left *its* mark on my shirt.
>
> Some of the students earn *their* tuition by working part time.
>
> Many of the customers do not pay *their* bills on time.
>
> Many a man owes *his* success to *his* first wife, and *his* second wife to *his* success. —Sean Connery

6. The number of a relative pronoun depends on the number of its antecedent:

> Marcia is one of those independent women who want to work for *themselves.*
>
> Marilyn is the only one of the graduating women who wants to start *her* own business.

EXERCISE 4   Recognizing Correct Pronoun Agreement

Each of the following consists of two sentences. In one sentence the number of each pronoun matches that of its antecedent; in the other there is a faulty shift in number. Say which sentence is correct—and why.

> EXAMPLE
> (a) The neighbor's dogs or a racoon had left its tracks on the freshly painted deck.
> (b) The neighbor's dog or a racoon had left their tracks on the freshly painted deck.
> Sentence *a* is correct because the singular pronoun *its* matches the singular noun *racoon*—which is the second of two antecedents joined by *or.*

1. (a) Steve liked playing hockey, but not the warm-ups they had to do before a game.
   (b) Steve liked playing hockey, but not the warm-ups he had to do before a game.
2. (a) Gritch, together with many of his fiercest followers, wanted to vent their rage in a ferocious counterattack.
   (b) Gritch, together with many of his fiercest followers, wanted to vent his range in a ferocious counterattack.
3. (a) As the ambulance sped off with the injured man, the crowd broke up and shuffled back to their cars.
   (b) As the ambulance sped off with the injured man, the crowd broke up and shuffled back to its cars.
4. (a) Neither of the two men has openly declared their candidacy.
   (b) Neither of the two men has openly declared his candidacy.
5. (a) Everyone carried their own provisions.
   (b) Everyone carried his or her own provisions.
6. (a) Twenty years ago, a woman who kept her own name after marriage was hardly considered married at all.
   (b) Twenty years ago, a woman who kept their own name after marriage was hardly considered married at all.
7. (a) Groucho is the only one of the Marx brothers who went from fame in the movies to a television show of their own.
   (b) Groucho is the only one of the Marx brothers who went from fame in the movies to a television show of his own.
8. (a) As usual, the orchestra will give their final performance of the year on December 30.
   (b) As usual, the orchestra will give its final performance of the year on December 30.
9. (a) No one on the girls' soccer teams has received their game jersey yet.
   (b) No one on the girls' soccer teams has received her game jersey yet.
10. (a) He is one of those rugged individualists who wants to build his own home.
    (b) He is one of those rugged individualists who want to build their own home.

18.8 Avoiding Faulty Shifts in Pronoun Reference *pr shift*

In paragraphs as well as sentences, pronouns referring to the same antecedent should be consistent in number and person. To make them consistent, observe the following guidelines.

1. Do not use *they, them,* or *their* with a singular antecedent:

> *No one should be forced into a career that they believe is not right for them.

The plural pronouns *they* and *them* are inconsistent in number with the singular antecedent *one*. To correct a sentence of this kind, make the antecedent plural or the pronouns singular:

> REVISED: People should not be forced into careers that they believe are not right for them. [or] No one should be forced into a career that he or she believes is not right for him or her.

To avoid the awkwardness of the final *him or her,* you could change the wording at the end:

> REVISED: No one should be forced into a career that he or she does not want.

(For more on making pronouns and antecedents consistent in number, see above, section 18.7.)

2. Do not shift the reference of a pronoun from one grammatical *person* to another:

> a. *Women are losing as much to our leaders as we are to some men. —female student

To move from *women* to *we* and *our* is to make an awkward shift in grammatical person. By itself, *Women* is a third-person term and requires a third-person pronoun such as *they*. But *our* and *we* are first-person pronouns denoting a group to which the writer herself belongs. To make the pronouns consistent, the writer can do one of two things.

Turn *women* into a first-person term:

> REVISED: We women are losing as much to our leaders as we are to some men.

Change the first-person pronouns to third-person:

> REVISED: Women are losing as much to their leaders as they are to some men.

> b. *When one is alone, one is free to do whatever you want without worrying what somebody else might say or think.

Here the writer uses second-person pronouns *(you, yourself)* with a third-person antecedent—the indefinite pronoun *one*. There are two ways of revising the sentence:

> REVISED: When one is alone, one is free to do whatever one wants without worrying what somebody else might say or think.
> REVISED: When you are alone, you are free to do whatever you want without worrying about what somebody else might say or think.

If you are more comfortable with *you* than with *one*, feel free to use *you*—provided it refers only to your reader and provided you use it consistently. Do not mix it with *one* or any other third-person pronoun.

EXERCISE 5   **Selecting Pronouns**

In each of the following, choose a pronoun that agrees in gender and number with its antecedent.

EXAMPLE
The children like their new toys.

1. No one on the Dallas Cowboys is likely to forget _____ first championship game.
2. Several members of the audience showed _____ disapproval of the performance by booing.
3. Betty is the only one in the college's four sororities to complain about the dullness of _____ social life.
4. Neither of the boys wanted to lose _____ place in line.
5. Even after weeks of rehearsal, some of the actors forgot _____ lines on opening night.

EXERCISE 6   **Revising a Passage with Inconsistent Pronoun Usage**

Each of the following passages is marred by shifts in the number and person of pronouns referring to the same antecedent. Make these pronouns consistent in number and person.

1. The job of being a counselor in a girls' summer camp is not an easy one. You have to meet your responsibilities twenty-four hours a day, and all are important. Because of the demands on us, we sometimes become tired and even cross. At these times everybody wants a break—a chance to go someplace else and relax. In a well-run camp you can do this; the director gives everybody a day off. After that we resume our duties with a cheerful, positive attitude.
2. Our body language often expresses our emotions. Through gestures, posture, facial expressions, and other visible signs, we indicate our feelings. If you are elated, for example, you tend to speak with more tonal fluctuations and with more arm movement than when a person is depressed. In a good mood, our eyes sparkle, our posture is erect, and you smile a lot. When someone is angry, their body language tells the tale. Our faces scowl, our jaws are clenched, one's gestures look aggressive, and sparks flash from your eyes.

18.9 Pronoun Case Forms

The form of a pronoun referring to a person depends partly on its **case**—that is, on the role it plays in a sentence. An essay about

Michael Jackson, for instance, might include the following statements:

> *He* has sold millions of records.
> Teenagers love *him*.
> *His* voice excites them.

The pronouns *He, him,* and *His* all have the same antecedent, Michael Jackson. They are different because they play different roles in the three different sentences. The first one is in the **subject case** because it serves as the subject of the verb phrase *has sold*. The second is in the **object case** because it serves as object of the verb *love*. And the third is in the **possessive case** because it indicates possession.

You may wonder why we need to bother with pronoun case forms at all. After all, you could say, no one has any trouble understanding what is meant by statements like *Him and me have been friends for years*. If case forms don't affect the meaning of what we say or write, who needs them?

The answer is simple. Besides the fact that most readers will expect you to use case forms correctly, the misuse of case forms *can* muddy the stream of communication. Compare these two passages:

1. The Kiowas are a summer people; them abide the cold and keep to them, but when the season turns and the land becomes warm and vital them cannot hold still; an old love of going returns upon them. The aged visitors who came to me grandmother's house when me was a child were made of lean and leather, and them bore them upright. Them wore great black hats and bright ample shirts that shook in the wind. Them rubbed fat upon them hair and wound them braids with strips of colored cloth.

2. The Kiowas are a summer people; they abide the cold and keep to themselves, but when the season turns and the land becomes warm and vital they cannot hold still; an old love of going returns upon them. The aged visitors who came to my grandmother's house when I was a child were made of lean and leather, and they bore themselves upright. They wore great black hats and bright ample shirts that shook in the wind. They rubbed fat upon their hair and wound their braids with strips of colored cloth.
   —N. Scott Momaday, *The Way to Rainy Mountain*

The second passage differs from the first not just in grammatical correctness, but also in clarity and sharpness of effect. Writing that makes no distinction between one case form and another is bothersome at best, and confusing at worst. A string of words like *them bore them upright* makes no sense.

What Momaday actually wrote, however, shows what case forms can do for a piece of writing. The difference between one case form and another enables him to distinguish between what the Kiowas do (*they* abide the cold), what they experience (an old love of going returns upon *them*), what they possess (*their* hair and *their* braids), and how they wish to appear (*they* bore *themselves* upright). Case forms play a crucial role in generating a precision that would be lost without them.

For this reason, a firm understanding of case forms and of how to use them is indispensable to anyone who hopes to write well. This section explains both the forms and their uses.

18.9A   Table of Pronoun Case Forms

Following are the case forms for all pronouns:

CASE FORMS OF PRONOUNS
PERSONAL PRONOUNS

	I	*He*	*She*	*It*	*We*	*You*	*They*
Subject case	I	he	she	it	we	you	they
Object case	me	him	her	it	us	you	them
Possessive case	my, mine	his	her, hers	its	our, ours	your, yours	their, theirs
Reflexive / emphatic case	myself	him-self	her-self	itself	our-selves	yourself, your-selves	them-selves

PRONOUNS USED IN QUESTIONS AND ADJECTIVE CLAUSES

	Who	*Whoever*
Subject case	who	whoever
Object case	whom	whomever
Possessive case	whose	

18.10   Using Pronoun Case

18.10A   Subject Case

Use the subject case when the pronoun is the subject of a verb:

> When Adam and Eve were accused of eating the forbidden fruit, *they* each excused themselves; *he* blamed Eve for tempting him, and *she* blamed the serpent for tempting her.

18.10B Object Case

1. Use the object case when the pronoun is the direct or indirect object of a verb:

> Rolls-Royces are so expensive that only millionaires can afford *them*.
> After several weeks of silence, Janet finally sent *us* a postcard.
> The earliest thing I can remember is the day that my father took my sister and *me* to the circus.

2. Use the object case when the pronoun is the object of a preposition, a word such as *to, against,* or *for:*

> When John F. Kennedy was assassinated, people from all over the world paid tribute to *him*.
> In the final match, Taylor and Nielsen played against Grogan and *me*.
> Delighted with the nomination of Ferraro, many women worked hard for *her* and Mondale.

3. Use the object case when the pronoun comes immediately before an infinitive:

> The teacher asked *me* to recite the Gettysburg Address in front of the whole school.
> The coach told Rosenberg and *me* to run eight laps before practice began.
> Just to be sure, he watched *us* run.

18.10C Possessive Case

1. Use the possessive case of the pronoun to indicate ownership of an object or close connection with it:

> Jill's trip went smoothly until she reached Santa Fe, where a crash wrecked *her* motorcycle and broke *her* leg in three places.
> On summer nights everyone sat outside, we on *our* front porch and the neighbors on *theirs*.
> The house is *mine*, but the car is *yours*, and the furniture is *hers*.

2. Use the possessive case of the pronoun before a gerund—an *-ing* word used as the name of an action:

> Because I had already studied calculus in high school, the math department approved *my* taking of advanced calculus.

Do not write **approved me taking*. Use the object case only if the pronoun is an object and the *-ing* word is a participle modifying it:

> She caught *me* taking a piece of cake.

For more on this point, see section 11.10.

18.10D   Reflexive/Emphatic Case

Use the reflexive/emphatic case of the pronoun either to indicate an action affecting the one who performs it or to indicate emphasis:

> While sharpening a knife, the butcher cut *himself*.
> I groaned when I saw *myself* in the mirror.
> The Alaskans *themselves* had mixed feelings about the new pipeline.
> The governor *herself* was opposed to the bill.

EXERCISE 7   Choosing Case Forms

Choose the correct form for the pronoun or pronouns in each of the following sentences, and explain the reason for each choice.

> EXAMPLE
> The coach watched Rosenberg and (I, me) run.
> *Me* (object case) is correct because the pronoun is the direct object of the verb *watched*.

1. (Me, My) father wants (me, my) to become an engineer.
2. Ruth's favorite sport is tennis; (my, mine) is hockey.
3. (Me, My) mother was smart; whenever (she, her) had just one chocolate bar to split between (me, my) sister and (I, me), she asked (I, me) to cut the candy in half and gave (me, my) sister first choice.
4. The Israelis believe that (they, their) country will always be subject to attack.
5. (She, Her) and (I, me) always get into arguments about politics.
6. Harrigan wanted to run the club like a marine platoon. He hated (me, my) raising of objections.
7. The teacher asked Harriet and (I, me) to give a report on Greenland.
8. An experienced stuntman can fall down a whole flight of stairs without hurting (him, himself).
9. What did you think of (him, his) getting a perfect score on the biology final?
10. (Them, they) and (them, their) enemies live in a state of barely controlled rage.

18.11 Using *who, whom, whose, whoever,* and *whomever*

The form you need depends on which part the pronoun plays in the sentence or clause that contains it. Observe the following guidelines.

1. Use *who* or *whoever* whenever the pronoun is a subject:

> *Who* knows anyone else perfectly?
> I can't remember *who* wrote *The Grapes of Wrath*.
> Spectators applauded all of the runners *who* finished the race.
> Tickets were given away to *whoever* wanted them.

Each of the italicized pronouns is in the subject case because each is the subject of a verb: *who knows, who wrote, who finished, whoever wanted.* No matter what words come before it, a pronoun that serves as the subject of a verb is always in the subject case.

2. Use *whom* or *whomever* when the pronoun is an object:

> *Whom* can we trust?
> Never seek to know for *whom* the bell tolls.　　　—John Donne
> I didn't know *whom* to ask.
> Some voters will support *whomever* the party nominates.
> Behind the counter stood a woman *whom* I instantly recognized.

A sentence like this last one can be tightened by the omission of *whom:*

> Behind the counter stood a woman I instantly recognized.

And if you find *whomever* stiff, you can replace it with *anyone:*

> Some voters will support *anyone* the party nominates.

3. Use *whose* whenever the pronoun is a possessor:

> *Whose* right is greater—the mother's or the unborn child's?
> The colt *whose* picked skeleton lay out there was mine.
> 　　　　　　　　　　　　　　　　　　—Wallace Stegner

18.12　Misusing Pronoun Case Forms　*pr ca*

To avoid misusing the case forms of pronouns, observe the following guidelines.

1. Do not use different case forms for pronouns linked by *and:*

> a. *Her and I went swimming every day.

Her is in the object case; *I* is in the subject case. Since they are linked by *and,* both should be in the same case. To see which case that should be, test each pronoun by itself:

> I went swimming every day.
> *Her went swimming every day.

I works; *Her* doesn't. So *Her* should be put in the subject case, *She:*

> REVISED: She and I went swimming every day.

Both pronouns belong in the subject case because both together make up the subject of *went.*

> b. *He and myself took turns driving.

He is in the subject case; *myself* is in the reflexive case. To see which case both should be, test them individually:

> *Myself took turns driving.
> He took turns driving.

He works; *Myself* doesn't. Both should be in the subject case because both together make up the compound subject of *took:*

> REVISED: He and I took turns driving.

> c. *The coach asked her and I to stay after practice.

> TEST: The coach asked her to stay after practice.
> *The coach asked I to stay after practice.

Her works; *I* doesn't. Both should be in the object case because both together make up the object of *asked:*

> REVISED: The coach asked her and me to stay after practice.

> d. *Jake told Alice that the profits would be split between her and I.

Test this one by reversing the pronouns:

> *Jake told Alice that the profits would be split between I and her.

I doesn't work because it's the object of *between,* a preposition, and the object of a preposition must be in the object case:

> REVISED: Jake told Alice that the profits would be split between her and me.

2. Do not use *me, him, myself, himself, herself,* or *themselves* as the subject of a verb:

> a. *Me and Sally waited three hours for the bus.

Test the pronoun by itself:

> *Me waited three hours for the bus.

If *Me* doesn't work by itself, it can't work as part of the compound. Here the compound it's part of is the subject of the verb *waited.* So *me* has to be put into the subject case, and for the sake of politeness it should follow *Sally:*

> REVISED: Sally and I waited three hours for the bus.

> b. *Herself and Frank danced for an hour.

> TEST: *Herself danced for an hour.

Herself doesn't work because it's a pronoun in the reflexive case being used as the subject of *danced*. A pronoun serving as a subject, or as part of a compound subject, must be in the subject case:

REVISED: She and Frank danced for an hour.

3. Do not use *myself, himself, herself,* or *themselves* as the object of a verb unless the object and subject refer to the same person:

*The coach told Frannie and myself to swim twenty laps.
TEST: *The coach told myself to swim twenty laps.

Myself doesn't work because it's being used as an object but does not refer to the same person as the subject. Unless the subject and object refer to the same person, the object of a verb must be in the object case:

REVISED: The coach told Frannie and me to swim twenty laps.

4. Do not use *I, he, she, we,* or *they* as the object of a verb or the object of a preposition:

*My uncle always brought presents for my sister and I.
TEST: *My uncle always brought presents for I.

I doesn't work because it's a pronoun in the subject case being used as the object of the preposition *for.* The object of a preposition must be in the object case:

REVISED: My uncle always brought presents for my sister and me.

5. Do not use the object case after *than* or *as* when the first term of the comparison is a subject:

a. *Pete dribbles faster than me.

To test this kind of sentence, complete the comparison:

*Pete dribbles faster than me dribble.

You see at once that *me* has to be in the subject case because it's the subject of an implied verb:

REVISED: Pete dribbles faster than I (dribble).

b. *Once Ferraro became Mondale's running mate, no other woman in American politics got so much attention as her.

TEST: *. . . no other woman in American politics got so much attention as her got.
REVISED: . . . no other woman in American politics got so much attention as she (got).

c. *The judges considered Roberta better than I.

Test by completing the comparison:

> *The judges considered Roberta better than they considered I.
> REVISED: The judges considered Roberta better than (they considered) me.

Here the first term of the comparison, *Roberta,* is the object of the verb *considered.* So the pronoun after *than* must be in the object case.

6. Do not use the forms **hisself,* **theirself,* or **theirselves* under any conditions in Standard English. **Hisself* is a misspelling of *himself;* **theirself* and **theirselves* are misspellings of *themselves.*

7. Do not confuse *its* and *it's* or *their, there,* and *they're.* If you are unsure about which of these words to use in a sentence, look them up in the Glossary of Usage, pp. 588 and 597.

EXERCISE 8   **Correcting Mistakes in Case**

Each of the following sentences may contain one or more mistakes in case. Correct every mistake you find by writing the correct form of the pronoun. If a sentence is correct as it stands, write *Correct.*

> EXAMPLE
> The argument between Paul and I is unimportant.
> REVISED: The argument between Paul and me is unimportant.

1. My uncle and me go hunting in the mountains every fall.
2. There are two sets of keys on the table—mine and yours.
3. Fortunately, a member of the ski patrol found Jan and myself before dark.
4. Jack hisself told my roommate and I not to bother clearing up after me and him completed our experiment.
5. Roger asked if he could go rock climbing with Peter and I.
6. Meg wondered who to see.
7. The ball hit the ground right between Sheehan and I.
8. Me and Sam are cousins.
9. Glenda is the world's greatest chatterbox; nobody talks faster than her.
10. From who did the message come?

19

SUBJECT-
VERB AGREEMENT

19.1 What is Agreement?

To say that a verb **agrees** in form with its subject is to say that a verb has more than one form, and that each form matches up with a particular kind of subject. Here are three parallel sets of examples based on a verb in the common present tense:

	STANDARD ENGLISH	FRENCH	SPANISH
Singular	I live	je vis	(yo)† vivo
	you live	tu vis	(tú) vives
	he lives	il vit	(él) vive
	she lives	elle vit	(ella) vive
Plural	we live	nous vivons	vivimos
	you live	vous vivez	vivis
	they live	ils vivent [masc.]	(ellos) viven [masc.]
		elles viven [fem.]	(ellas) viven [fem.]

†In Spanish, when the subject is a pronoun, it is sometimes omitted.

In this example, Spanish has six different verb forms, French has five, and Standard English has just two: *live* and *lives.*

To use any of these languages correctly, you must put the correct verb form with each subject. To write Standard English correctly, you need to know which form goes with each subject, where to find the subject in a clause, and whether the subject is singular or plural. We consider each of these matters in turn.

sv agr   19.2 Making Verbs Agree with Subjects   *sv agr*

In most cases, the subject affects the form of the verb only when the verb is in the present tense. Except for the verb *be* (see section 19.3) and for subjunctive verb forms (see sections 23.4 and 23.5), the rules of agreement in the present tense are as follows.

1. When the subject is a singular noun or third-person singular pronoun (such as *he* or *she*), add *s* or *-es* to the bare form of the verb:

> Peggy *wants* to study economics.
> She *works* at the bank.
> It *serves* over two thousand depositors.
> Each of them *holds* a passbook.
> Marvin Megabucks *owns* the bank.
> He *polishes* his Jaguar once a week.

2. For the verb *have,* the correct form with a singular noun or third-person singular pronoun is *has:*

> The scorpion *has* a venomous sting in its tail.
> Everyone *has* moments of self-doubt.
> The bank *has closed* for the holidays.

3. When the subject is NOT a singular noun or third-person singular pronoun, use the bare form of the verb:

> Economists *study* the fluctuation of prices.
> O. Henry's stories often *have* surprise endings.
> I *have worked* on a tobacco farm.
> Reporters and novelists both *write* for a living.
> I *do* very little work on Sundays.

4. Whatever the subject, do not add *-s* or *-es* to a verb accompanied by an auxiliary, such as *does, can,* or *may:*

> Does he *play* the sax?
> Can she *sing?*
> He can *run.*
> She may *dance.*
> The plane should *fly.*

5. Do not add *-s* or *-es* to the infinitive—whether or not it has *to* before it:

> Gail expects Jack to *wash* the dishes. [infinitive with *to*]
> Gail makes Jack *wash* the dishes. [infinitive without *to*]

Do not write **Gail makes Jack washes the dishes.*

19.3 Making the Verb *be* Agree with Subjects

1. When *be* is a main verb, its forms are as follows:

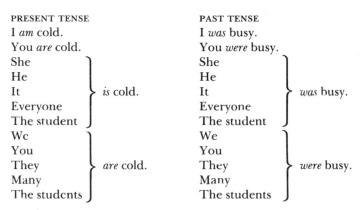

PRESENT TENSE | PAST TENSE
I *am* cold. | I *was* busy.
You *are* cold. | You *were* busy.
She / He / It / Everyone / The student ⎱ *is* cold. | She / He / It / Everyone / The student ⎱ *was* busy.
We / You / They / Many / The students ⎱ *are* cold. | We / You / They / Many / The students ⎱ *were* busy.

2. When *be* is an auxiliary, its form depends on the subject, just as when *be* is a main verb:

> I *am confused* by tax forms.
> The building *is painted* every two years.
> Supposedly, prisoners of war *are protected* by the Geneva Convention.
> Jane *is learning* to speak Russian.
> Several doctors *are attending* the meeting.
> Last night I *was awakened* by a scream.
> My roommates *were awakened* too.
> Architects *were examining* a house erected in 1703.
> One architect *was explaining* its construction.
> Naomi *was completing* an experiment in physics.
> Each of the diamonds *was shining*.

19.4 Avoiding Dialectal Mistakes in Agreement

The rules of agreement in Standard English differ from the rules of agreement in regional and ethnic dialects. To write Standard English correctly, observe the following guidelines.

1. Do not use the bare form of the verb with third-person singular nouns and pronouns in the present tense:

> *My brother *work* for the post office.
> *He *live* with a couple of his friends.

In writing Standard English, you must add *-s* or *-es* to a present-tense verb with a third-person singular subject:

> My brother *works* for the post office.
> He *lives* with a couple of his friends.

2. Do not add *-s* or *-es* to a verb used with *I, you,* or any plural subject:

> *I *needs* a job.
> *Politicians *loves* to make promises.
> *They *wants* votes.

In Standard English, all verbs except *be* take the bare form whenever the subject is *I, you,* or a plural noun of any kind:

> I *need* a job.
> Politicians *love* to make promises.
> They *want* votes.

3. Do not use *be* with any subject in the present indicative:

> *I *be* taking calculus this semester.
> *Veronica *be* my best friend.

Standard English requires different forms of the verb *be* with different subjects, as already shown:

> I *am* taking calculus this semester.
> Veronica *is* my best friend.

4. Do not use *been* right after any subject:

> *Everybody *been* hurt by the layoffs.
> *My parents *been* separated for two years.

In writing Standard English, you must use *has* before *been* with third-person singular subjects, and *have* before *been* with all other subjects:

> Everybody *has been* hurt by the layoffs.
> My parents *have been* separated for two years.

EXERCISE 1   **Using Correct Verb Forms**

For each verb in parentheses, write down a verb form that agrees with the subject. The correct form will sometimes be the same as the one in parentheses.

> EXAMPLE
> A nice cold drink (taste) good on a hot day.
> tastes

1. Whenever Frank (sing), Ellen (dance).
2. Whenever Ellen (hear) Frank (sing), she (dance).
3. Many men (fix) cars for a living; Jack (fix) bicycles.
4. Can he (reach) Indianapolis by six?
5. If he (catch) the 4:05 bus, he can (reach) Indianapolis by six.
6. I (have) three courses this term; she (have) four.
7. They (have) failed the courses; he (have) passed.

8. The workers (be) angry; the manager (be) frightened.
9. The workers (be) complaining; the manager (be) refusing to listen.
10. While they (was *or* were) throwing rocks at his office window, he (was *or* were) escaping by the back door.
11. Most people (do)n't work on Sundays, but Father Francis (do).
12. Money (do)n't grow on trees.
13. Everybody (have) to sleep sometime.
14. The sight of elephants (excite) young children.
15. Harold Grey, along with his two brothers, (be) helping to (build) a barn.
16. No one in the audience (want) to be bored.
17. Both freshmen and sophomores can (register) this week.
18. Neither my roommates nor Bob Black (have) found a summer job.

19.5 Finding the Subject

To make a verb form agree with the subject of the verb, you must know where to find the subject. This is easy to do when the subject comes right before the verb, as it does in many sentences:

> s
> Alan Paton / has written movingly about life in South Africa.

> s
> Many readers / consider *Cry, the Beloved Country* a classic.

> s
> The theme of the novel / is an ancient one, the struggle between people who hate and people who love.

However, a subject sometimes follows its verb, as in the kinds of sentences listed next.

1. Sentences starting with *There* or *Here:*

> s
> There was once / a thriving civilization in the jungles of the Yucatan.

> s
> Here comes / trouble.

> s
> There were / three accidents during the race.

In sentences of this pattern, *There* and *Here* are always introductory words, never subjects.

2. Sentences with inverted word order:

> s
> Visible alongside millions of U.S. roadways is / evidence of widespread littering.

For this example, the customary word order would be:

Evidence of widespread littering / is visible alongside millions of
U.S. roadways.

3. Some questions:

Does / the course in astronomy / require homework?

Have / recent decisions of the Supreme Court / clarified
matters?

EXERCISE 2 Recognizing Subjects and Verbs

Write down the complete subject and the verb of each of the following
sentences.

EXAMPLE
During the rainy season few farmers labor in the fields.
SUBJECT: few farmers
VERB: labor

1. Darwin, on the other hand, extended his revolution in thought consistently throughout the entire animal kingdom.   —Stephen Jay Gould
2. Here live descendants of the once mighty Puritans.
3. Despite the months of heavy shelling, a wild rose has blossomed in a small opening between the walls of the fort.
4. Sometimes there is no utterance so loud as silence.
5. During the past fifteen years, however, challenges to Darwin's focus on individuals have sparked some lively debates among evolutionists.
                                                    —Stephen Jay Gould
6. Disappearing into the hugeness of system is not unattractive.
                                                    —Richard Hugo
7. With single-syllable words we can show rigidity, honesty, toughness, relentlessness, the world of harm unvarnished.   —Richard Hugo
8. Behind the company's present fiscal policies lies a record of broken agreements and inept management.
9. Both the unemployment rate and the inflation rate are determined by the total level of spending on the goods and services produced by the economy.   —Edwin Mansfield
10. How does monetary policy affect our national output and the price level?   —Edwin Mansfield

19.6 Recognizing the Number of the Subject

To make a verb agree with the subject, you must know whether the subject is singular or plural. Observe the following guidelines for various kinds of subjects.

19.6A Nouns Meaning One Thing

A noun meaning one thing is always singular, even if it ends in *-s:*

The *boy* delivers newspapers every day.

The *lens* was cracked.

The *news* is created largely by those who report it.

The Grapes of Wrath was written by John Steinbeck.

19.6B Nouns Meaning More Than One Thing

A noun meaning more than one thing is always plural. Most plural nouns end in *-s* or *-es*, but some nouns form the plural by changing their spelling in other ways:

The *lenses* were cracked.

The *boys* deliver newspapers every day.

His *teeth* were crooked.

Women deserve to be paid as much as *men* are.

The *data* transmitted from space tell us many new things about the solar system.

If you don't know how to spell the plural of a particular word, see your dictionary. (For more on the word *data,* see the Glossary of Usage, p. 583).

19.6C Pronouns Fixed in Number

Though some pronouns are variable in number (see section 19.6K below), most pronouns are fixed in number. They include the following:

ALWAYS SINGULAR

he	each	one
she	each one	another
it	everybody	somebody
this	everyone	someone
that	everything	something
anybody	either	whatever
anyone	neither	whichever
anything		whoever
	nobody	
	none	
	no one	
	nothing	

ALWAYS PLURAL

we	these	both	few
they	those	others	several

19.6D Verbal Nouns and Noun Clauses

Verbal nouns and noun clauses are always singular:

> *Reassembling the broken pieces of a china bowl* takes steady hands and patience.
> *To raise two million dollars for the hospital* is our goal.
> *What Cliff wanted* was a job.

19.6E Nouns Linked to Other Nouns by the Verb *be*

When a noun or pronoun is linked to another noun or pronoun by the verb *be*, the verb agrees with what comes before it, no matter what comes after it:

> *Newspapers* are his business.
> His *business* is newspapers.
> *They* are a team.
> Winston was terrified by just one thing. *It* was rats.
> *It* has been many years since man first landed on the moon.

19.6F Modified Nouns and Pronouns

Except as noted below at 19.6K, the number of a modified noun or pronoun depends on the noun (N) or pronoun (PR) itself—not on any of the modifiers (M) attached to it:

> M N   M
> *A ship carrying hundreds of tourists* enters the harbor every Friday.
> M   N   M
> *The girls that Benson coaches* swim fifty laps every day.
> PR   M
> *Each of the candidates* has taken a different position.
> M   N   M
> *Big cities each* have their own special problems.
> M   N   M
> *The leader of the abolitionists* was John Brown.
> M   N   M
> *The leaders of the expedition* were Meriwether Lewis and William Clark.
> PR   M
> *Neither of the finalists* was well known before the start of the tournament.

N   M
Edmund, together with Goneril and Regan, meets disgrace and death at the end of the play.

M   N   M
Many scientists, but not Agassiz, were eventually persuaded by Darwin's arguments.

19.6G Compounds Made with *and*

1. Compound subjects made with *and* are plural when they are used before the verb and refer to more than one thing:

> *The lion and the tiger* belong to the cat family.

2. When a compound subject made with *and* follows the verb, the verb agrees with the first item in the compound:

> There was *a desk and three chairs* in the room.
> At the entrance stand *two marble pillars and a statue of Napoleon.*
> Where was *the boat and the sailors?*

3. A compound subject made with *and* and referring to only one thing is always singular:

> *The founder and first president of the college* was Eleazor Wheelock.
> *Ham and eggs* is one of my favorite dishes.

19.6H Items Joined by *or, either . . . or,* etc.

When items are joined by *or, either . . . or, neither . . . nor, not . . . but,* or *not only . . . but also,* the verb agrees with the item just before it:

> *Neither steel nor glass* cuts a diamond.
> *Not a new machine but new workers* are needed for the job.
> *Either several cars or one big bus* transports the team.

19.6I Nouns Spelled the Same Way in Singular and Plural

A noun spelled the same way in the singular and the plural depends for its number on the way it is used:

> *A deer* was nibbling the lettuce.
> *Two deer* were standing in the middle of the road.
> *One means* of campaigning is direct mail.
> *Two other means* are TV advertising and mass rallies.

Recognizing the Number of the Subject **359**

19.6J   Collective Nouns and Nouns of Measurement

Collective nouns and nouns of measurement are singular when they refer to a unit, and plural when they refer to the individuals or elements of a unit:

> To an actor, *the audience* is a big dark animal waiting to be fed.
> *The audience* were coughing and shuffling their feet.
> *Ten miles* was the length of the race.
> *Miles of railroad track* in America need repair.
> *Half of the cake* was eaten.
> *Half of the jewels* were stolen.
> *Statistics* is the study and analysis of numerical information about the world.
> *Recent statistics* show a marked decline in the U.S. birthrate during the past twenty years.

19.6K   Pronouns Variable in Number

The pronouns *all, any, many, more, most, some, who, that,* and *which* are variable in number. The number of such a pronoun depends on the number of the word or phrase to which it refers:

> Most of the sand *is* washed by the tide.
>
> Most of the sandpipers *are* white.
>
> All of the money *was* gone.
>
> All of the ships *were* lost.
>
> Some of the oil *has* been cleaned up.
>
> Some of the problems *have* been solved.
>
> A woman who *wants* complete financial independence starts her own business.
>
> Women who *want* complete financial independence start their own businesses.
>
> Titan is one of the fifteen known satellites that *revolve* around Saturn.
>
> Titan is the only one of those satellites that *has* an atmosphere.

Many is singular only when used with *a:*

> Many of the men *underestimate* women.
>
> Many a man *underestimates* women.

19.6L   Subjects Beginning with *every*

When a subject begins with *every*, treat it as singular:

> *Every cat and dog in the neighborhood* was fighting.

19.6M   The Word *number* as Subject

The word *number* is singular when it follows *the*, plural when it follows *a:*

> *The number of applications* was huge.
> *A number of women* now hold full-time jobs.

19.6N   Foreign Words and Expressions

When the subject is a foreign word or expression, use a dictionary to find out whether it is singular or plural:

> The *coup d'etat* just completed has caught diplomats by surprise.
> The *Carbonari* of the early nineteenth century were members of a secret political organization in Italy.

EXERCISE 3   Recognizing Number

Write down the complete subject of the italicized verb in each of the following sentences. Then say whether the subject is treated as singular or as plural—and why.

EXAMPLE
Most of the pies *were* stale.
Most of the pies
The subject is treated as plural because the number of *Most* depends on the number of the word it refers to—*pies.*

1. The team *practices* six days a week.
2. Some of the coloring *looks* unfinished.
3. Billions *are* needed by undeveloped nations.
4. Fifty dollars *was* a lot to pay for a sun visor.
5. The public *are* welcome at all of the meetings.
6. People who *live* in glass houses may have a heating problem.
7. None of the furniture *was* in place for the grand opening.
8. George is the only one of the hikers who *has* climbed above twenty thousand feet.
9. The crowd *was* noisy before the game.
10. Bert likes to spend his vacation in an old mining town that *defies* description.

EXERCISE 4 Supplying Correct Verb Forms

Use each of the following nouns and pronouns as the subject in a pair of sentences. In the first sentence, treat the noun or pronoun as singular; in the second, treat it as plural.

EXAMPLE
some
Some of the oil was cleaned up before it reached the beaches.
Some of the traffic problems have been solved.

1. sheep
2. most
3. dollars
4. half
5. who

EXERCISE 5 Choosing Correct Verb Forms

In some of the following sentences, the subject is singular; in some it is plural. Write down the subject of each sentence, and choose the verb form that agrees with it.

EXAMPLE
One of the candidates (was, were) a seventy-five-year-old woman.
SUBJECT: One
VERB: was

1. The only thing he loved (was, were) the cheers of the audience.
2. Two hundred dollars (was, were) all I could pay for the car.
3. Mumps (is, are) painful to many adults.
4. Neither the Arab nations nor Israel (wants, want) yet another all-out war.
5. There (was, were) thirteen colonies when America declared its independence of Great Britain.
6. The cargo on the boat (was, were) bananas.
7. There (is, are) mounds of dirt in the backyard.
8. Many a prisoner (has, have) tried to escape.
9. Neither a pile of sandbags nor a heavy-duty pump (has, have) prevented water from seeping into the basement.
10. Directly above the lamps (is, are) a charcoal drawing of two soldiers slumped over their rifles.

EXERCISE 6 Correcting Faulty Agreement

In some of the following sentences, the verb does not agree with its subject. Correct every verb you consider wrong and then explain the correction. If a sentence is correct as it stands, write *Correct.*

EXAMPLE
One of the insurance agents are a graduate of my university.
The verb should be *is* because the subject is *One,* a singular pronoun.

1. The members of the transportation committee have agreed on a solution to the parking problem on Main Street.
2. There has been many thunderstorms this summer.
3. A lawyer for the insurance company is reviewing my case.
4. Each of the spectators are bringing a pair of field glasses.
5. *Twenty Thousand Leagues under the Sea* have thrilled thousands of readers.
6. A number of bird watchers is gathering at Stony Point this Sunday.
7. Both the players and the owners want to negotiate new contracts.
8. Two-thirds of the room have been painted.
9. No one in the two buildings was injured in the fire.
10. Does everybody in the four towns want a fair?
11. Ten cents are little to pay for a large glass of cold lemonade.
12. Half of the apartments in the building is without heat.
13. Half of the furniture in the office was rented.
14. Physics are an important course for engineering students.
15. An additional means of support need to be found.

EXERCISE 7 Correcting Faulty Agreement

This exercise will give you practice in dealing with subject-verb agreement in an extended passage. In the following paragraphs from Juanita H. Williams's *Psychology of Women,* we have deliberately inserted some errors in agreement. We hope you can spot and correct them.

EXAMPLE
lines 3–4: efficiency and level . . . are usually measured

Cognition is the process by which the individual acquires knowledge about an object or an event. It includes perceiving, recognizing, judging, and sensing—the ways of knowing. The efficiency and level of the acquisition of knowledge is usually measured in older
5 children and adults by the use of tests which requires language. Studies of infant cognition, of what and how babies "know," have begun to appear only in the last decade, with the development of new techniques which provides insights into what and how babies learn.
10 In spite of the persistent belief that babies differ along sex lines— for example, that girl babies vocalize more and boy babies are more active—sex differences in cognitive functions in the first two years of life has not been demonstrated (Maccoby and Jacklin, 1974). Measurements of intellectual ability, learning, and memory does
15 not differ on the average for boys and girls. However, patterns of performances are different for the two sexes, as are the consistency (thus the predictability) of the measures as the infants get older. A

longitudinal study of 180 white, first-born infants, 91 boys and 89
girls, each of whom were tested in the laboratory at four, eight,
20 thirteen, and twenty-seven months, offers some evidence concern-
ing these patterns (Kagan, 1971). One of the behaviors for which
different patterns were observed for boys and girls were vocaliza-
tion, the infant's response when aroused or excited by an unusual
or discrepant stimulus.

20

VERBS
Tense

If English is your native language, you probably have a good working knowledge of tenses. You know how to describe what someone or something did in the past, is doing in the present, or will do in the future. But you may not know just how to describe an action that doesn't fall neatly into one time slot. For instance, how do you describe the action of a character in a novel or a play? How do you describe an action that started in the past but is still going on now? How do you write about an action that will be completed at some time in the future? This chapter is chiefly meant to answer questions like those.

The chapter is limited to verbs in the indicative mood (the mood of fact or matters close to the fact) and in the active voice (in which the subject performs the action, as in "Harry *drives* an old jalopy"). For a full discussion of mood, see chapter 23; for a full discussion of voice, see chapter 22.

20.1 Tense and Time

The **tense** of a verb helps to indicate the time of an action or condition:

> PAST: The sun *rose* at 6:03 this morning.
> PRESENT: As I *write* these words, the sun *is setting*.
> FUTURE: The sun *will rise* tomorrow at 6:04.

But tense is not the same as time. A verb in the present tense, for instance, may be used in a statement about the future:

The bus *leaves* tomorrow at 7:30 A.M.

As in this example, the time of an action or state is often indicated by a word or phrase like *tomorrow, next week,* or *last week.*

20.2 Forming the Tenses *tf*

20.2A Forming the Principal Parts of Verbs

The tenses of all but a few verbs are made from the four **principal parts:** the present (also called the "bare" form), the present participle, the past, and the past participle. The principal parts of most verbs are formed as shown here, with *-ing* or *-ed* added to the bare form as indicated. Such verbs are called **regular.**

PRESENT (BARE FORM)	PRESENT PARTICIPLE	PAST	PAST PARTICIPLE
cook	cook*ing*	cook*ed*	cook*ed*
lift	lift*ing*	lift*ed*	lift*ed*
polish	polish*ing*	polish*ed*	polish*ed*

Verbs with some principal parts formed in other ways are called **irregular.** Here are some examples:

eat	eating	ate	eaten
write	writing	wrote	written
go	going	went	gone
speak	speaking	spoke	spoken

(For the principal parts of commonly used irregular verbs, see section 20.11.)

20.2B Forming the Present

With most subjects, the form of a verb in the present tense is simply the bare form:

Seasoned traders *drive* hard bargains.
I *polish* my shoes every day.

But after a singular noun or a third-person singular pronoun, such as *she, it, this, each,* or *everyone,* you must add *-s* or *-es* to the bare form of the verb:

Helen *drives* a cab.
She *polishes* it once a week.

(For more on this point, see sections 19.1–19.4.)

20.2C   Forming the Past

The past tense of regular verbs is formed by the addition of -*d* or -*ed* to the bare form:

> Helen *liked* her work.
> She *polished* her cab regularly.

(For the past tense of commonly used irregular verbs, see section 20.11.)

20.2D   Forming Tenses with Auxiliaries

Besides the present and the past, there are four other tenses. You form these by using certain auxiliary verbs, such as *will, has,* and *had:*

	REGULAR VERB	IRREGULAR VERB
FUTURE:	She will work.	She will speak.
PRESENT PERFECT:	She has worked.	She has spoken.
PAST PERFECT:	She had worked.	She had spoken.
FUTURE PERFECT:	She will have worked.	She will have spoken.

20.2E   Forming the Progressive

The **common** forms discussed so far indicate a momentary, habitual, or completed action. The **progressive** forms indicate that the action named by the verb is viewed as continuing. Here are three examples:

> PRESENT: The president *is speaking* now.
> PRESENT PERFECT: You *have been speaking* for twenty minutes.
> PAST: You *were talking* while Professor Grant lectured.

The progressive consists of some form of the auxiliary *be* followed by a present participle—a verb with -*ing* on the end. For guidance in using both the progressive forms and the common forms, see section 21.3.

20.2F   Using *do* as an Auxiliary

As we have seen, *have* is used in forming the perfect tense, and *be* in forming the progressive. The third auxiliary is *do,* used in forming some negatives, some questions, and emphatic statements:

> I *do* not understand the question.
> *Do* you eat raw fish?

Peter *does* enjoy fishing.
She certainly *did* sing well, *didn't* she?

EXERCISE 1   Writing Principal Parts

For each of the following sentences write out the principal parts of the italicized verb, listing in sequence the present, the present participle, the past, and the past participle. Whenever you are unsure of a form, refer to your dictionary or to the list of irregular verbs in section 20.11.

EXAMPLE
The concert *begins* at 8 P.M.
begin, beginning, began, begun

1. The sun *rose* at 6:32 this morning.
2. Your spaghetti sauce always *smells* good.
3. The mayor *laid* the cornerstone for the new town hall.
4. Some tourists *lie* on the beach for hours. [For a full discussion of the verbs *lie* and *lay,* see the Glossary of Usage.]
5. *Have* you ever *flown* in a balloon?
6. Old age *is creeping* up on us.
7. She never *finished* her painting of Mount Flume.
8. *Did* you *break* your watch?
9. Bob *has been visiting* his grandparents.
10. *Do* you *swim* every day?

20.3   Using the Present

1. Use the <u>common present</u>—

  a. To report what a person or thing does regularly:

    I *run* two miles every day.
    Leaves *change* color in autumn.

  b. To state a fact or widely held belief:

    Water *freezes* at 32° F.
    Opposites *attract.*

  c. To describe characters, events, or other matters in an aesthetic work, such as a painting, a piece of music, a work of literature, a movie, or a television show:

    In *Jaws,* a man-eating shark *attacks* and *terrifies* swimmers until he is finally killed.

  d. To describe an opinion or idea:

    In the Marxist vision of history, the ruling classes ceaselessly *oppress* the working class.

e. To say what a writer or a creative artist does in his or her work:

20.4

> Shakespeare *exposes* the ruinous effects of "vaulting ambition" in many of his plays.
> In *The Wealth of Nations* (1776), Adam Smith *argues* that an "invisible hand" regulates individual enterprise for the good of society as a whole.
> In his famous Fifth Symphony, Beethoven *reveals* the power and fury of his imagination.

f. To indicate that a condition or situation is likely to last:

> My sister *loves* chocolate ice cream.

g. To describe a future action that is definitely predictable:

> The sun *rises* tomorrow at 6:04.

h. To report a statement of lasting significance:

> "All art," *says* Oscar Wilde, "is quite useless."

2. Use the <u>present progressive</u>—

a. To indicate that an action or state is occurring at the time of the writing:

> The sun *is setting* now, and the birches *are bending* in the wind.

b. To indicate that an action is in progress—even though it may not be taking place at the exact moment of the writing:

> Suburban life *is losing* its appeal. Many young couples *are moving* out of the suburbs and into the cities.

20.4 Using the Present Perfect

1. Use the <u>common present perfect</u>—

a. To report a past action or state that touches in some way on the present:

> I *have* just *finished* reading *Gone with the Wind.*
> A presidential commission *has* already *investigated* the causes of one nuclear accident.

The words *just* and *already* are often used with the present perfect.

b. To report an action or state begun in the past but extending into the present:

> Engineers *have begun* to explore the possibility of harnessing the tides.

Since the invention of the automobile, traffic accidents *have taken* many thousands of lives.

c. To report an action performed at some unspecified time in the past:

Have you ever *seen* the Statue of Liberty?

2. Use the <u>progressive</u> form of the <u>present perfect</u> when you want to emphasize the continuity of an action from the past into the present, and the likelihood of its continuing into the future:

Some man-made satellites *have been traveling* through space for years.
The cost of medical care *has been growing* at a staggering rate.

20.5 Using the Past

1. Use the <u>common past</u>—

a. To report an action or state definitely completed in the past:

Thomas Edison *invented* the phonograph in 1877.
The city *became* calm after the cease-fire.

b. To report actions repeated in the past but no longer occurring at the time of the writing:

The family always *went* to church on Sundays.

2. Use the <u>past progressive</u>—

a. To emphasize the continuity of a past action:

His insults *were becoming* unbearable.

b. To say that one action was being performed when another occurred:

I *was pouring* a glass of water when the pitcher suddenly cracked.

20.6 Using the Past Perfect

1. Use the <u>common past perfect</u>—

a. To say that an action or state was completed by a specified time in the past:

By noon we *had gathered* three hundred bushels.

b. To indicate that one past action or state was completed by the time another past action or state occurred:

By the time Hitler sent reinforcements, the Allies *had* already *taken* much of France.
I suddenly realized that I *had left* my keys at home.

c. To report an unfulfilled hope or intention:

> Mary *had planned* to travel as far as Denver, but her money ran out while she was still in Chicago.

2. Use the <u>progressive</u> form of the <u>past perfect</u> to say that the first of two past actions or states went on until the second occurred:

> Before Gloria entered Mark's life, he *had been spending* most of his time with books.

20.7 Using the Future

There are many ways to say that something will happen in the future. Here are some examples:

> We are seeing Harold Murphy in the morning.
> We are to see Harold Murphy in the morning.
> We are going to see Harold Murphy in the morning.
> We expect to see Harold Murphy in the morning.
> We have a date to see Harold Murphy in the morning.
> We shall see Harold Murphy in the morning.
> We will be seeing Harold Murphy in the morning.

Each of the constructions illustrated here can be used to indicate future action. But in the discussion that follows, we use only the verb forms that serve this purpose alone.

1. Use the <u>common future</u>—

a. To report a future event or state that will occur regardless of human intent:

> The sun *will rise* at 6:35 tomorrow morning.
> I *will be* nineteen on my next birthday.

b. To indicate willingness or determination to do something:

> The president has declared that he *will veto* the bill.

c. To report what will happen under certain conditions:

> If you get up early enough, you *will see* the sunrise.

d. To indicate future probability:

> The cost of a college education *will increase.*

In the preceding examples, the auxiliary *will* is used. Years ago, *will* was used only with *you, they, he, she, it,* and noun subjects, and *shall* was used with *I* and *we* to express the simple future. When *will* was used with *I* and *we,* it signified the speaker's (or writer's) determination: "We will stop the enemy." The use of *shall* with *you, they, he, she, it,* or a noun subject had the same function: "You shall pay the tax." But in current usage *shall* and *will* mean about the same thing, and most writers use *will* with all subjects to express the simple future. Some writers substitute *shall*, again with all subjects, to express determination or certainty: "We shall overcome."

2. Use the future progressive—

a. To say that an action or state will be continuing for a period of time in the future:

Economists *will be* closely *watching* fluctuations in the price of gold.

b. To say what the subject will be doing at a given time in the future:

Next summer I *will be teaching* tennis.

20.8 Using the Future Perfect

1. Use the common future perfect—

a. To say that an action or state will be completed by a specified time in the future:

At the rate I'm living, I *will have spent* all my summer earnings by the end of October.

b. To say that an action or state will be completed by the time something else happens:

By the time an efficient engine is produced, we *will have exhausted* our supplies of fuel.

2. Use the progressive form of the future perfect to say that an activity or state will continue until a specified time in the future:

By 1990 the *Pioneer 10* probe *will have been traveling* through space for more than fifteen years.

20.9 Misusing Tenses *mt*

1. Do not use the present progressive to describe what someone or something does regularly:

*Usually my day *is starting* at 7:00 A.M.
REVISED: Usually my day *starts* at 7:00 A.M.

2. Do not use the past tense to describe the action of a novel, play, film, or any other aesthetic work:

*In the first chapter, Gabriel *saw* the beautiful Bathsheba, but she *did* not see him.

REVISED: In the first chapter, Gabriel *sees* the beautiful Bathsheba, but she *does* not see him.

3. Do not use the past tense to say that one action was completed by the time another occurred:

> *By the time the game ended, many of the spectators *left*.
> REVISED: By the time the game ended, many of the spectators *had* left.

20.10 Managing Tense and Time with Participles and Infinitives

Participles and infinitives have two tenses: the present and the perfect. The present consists of the present participle or the infinitive by itself. The perfect participle consists of *having* and the past participle; the perfect infinitive requires *have* between *to* and the past participle.

1. Use the present tense when the action or state named by the participle or infinitive occurs at or after the time of the main verb:

> We spend hours in conference with individual students, hours *meeting* together and with counselors, *trying* to teach ourselves how to teach and *asking* ourselves what we ought to be teaching.
> —Adrienne Rich
> The speaker used the chalkboard *to outline* his main points.
> Many undergraduates take biology *to prepare* for medical school.
> By sunset the trapped animal had ceased *to struggle*.

2. Use the perfect tense when the action or state named by the participle or infinitive occurred before the time of the main verb:

> *Having lost* his cargo during the hurricane, the captain faced bankruptcy when his vessel finally reached port.
> Several reporters are sorry *to have missed* the president's impromptu press conference.

EXERCISE 2 Using Tenses

This exercise tests your ability to use the various tenses treated in this chapter. Each of the following consists of a pair of sentences, one complete and one with a verb omitted but the bare form supplied in parentheses. For each pair, complete the second sentence by using the parenthesized verb in the same tense and form as the italicized verb in the first sentence. Then make up a new sentence in which you use another verb in the same tense and form.

t

EXAMPLE

Four quarts *make* a gallon.

The earth _____ on its axis. (rotate)

The earth <u>rotates</u> on its axis.

Water freezes at 32° F.

1. She *was standing* on the corner when a passing truck splashed mud on her brand-new jeans.
   She _____ an operation when the lights failed. (perform)
2. By the time he reached the store, looters *had taken* everything of value.
   By the time I found the cheese, the mice _____ most of it. (eat)
3. White paper exposed to light for a long time *will turn* yellow.
   Fish left unrefrigerated for more than a day or two _____
   . (rot)
4. In recent years, many women *have been demanding* rights equal to those of men.
   Some men _____ women's demands. (resist)
5. In the final episode of the novel, the hero *risks* his life in a blizzard.
   In the last scene of the movie, the great ship _____.
   (sink)
6. We always *spent* Thanksgiving Day with my grandmother.
   Every Saturday I _____ stickball in a vacant lot behind the supermarket. (play)
7. By the end of the day we *had cut* five cords of wood.
   By the end of the sixties, the United States _____ a man on the moon. (put)
8. In 1894 Hugh Duffy *set* the all-time major-league batting record with an average of .438.
   During a career of more than sixteen seasons, he _____ almost six hundred bases. (steal)
9. For years we *have dumped* chemical wastes into our rivers, lakes, and oceans.
   We _____ many of our waterways. (pollute)
10. Frank *has* just *returned* from Quebec.
    Vivian _____ just _____ for Winnipeg. (leave)
11. Normally, heat *stimulates* molecular movement.
    Normally, cold _____ molecular movement. (reduce)
12. Before she broke her leg, she *had been running* fifty miles a week.
    Before I gave up cigarettes, I _____ two packs a day. (smoke)
13. *Having fixed* the generator, the repairman packed his tools and left the engine room.
    _____ the race, she collapsed with exhaustion. (won)
14. By Sunday night I *will have finished* the assignment.
    By graduation I _____ eight chemistry courses. (take)
15. In the mind of the liberal, the federal government *saves* us all from poverty and prejudice.
    In the mind of the conservative, the federal government _____ free enterprise. (suffocate)

20.11 Forming the Principal Parts of Commonly Used Irregular Verbs

Following is a partial list of irregular verbs, those with special forms for the past, the past participle, or both. When more than one form is shown, the first is more commonly used. For verbs not listed here, see your dictionary.

PRESENT (BARE FORM)	PRESENT PARTICIPLE	PAST	PAST PARTICIPLE
arise	arising	arose	arisen
awake	awaking	awoke, awaked	awoke, awaked, awoken
be †	being	was/were	been
bear [bring forth]	bearing	bore	born, borne
bear [carry]	bearing	bore	borne
beat	beating	beat	beaten, beat
begin	beginning	began	begun
bend	bending	bent	bent
bet	betting	bet, betted	bet
bid [command]	bidding	bade	bid, bidden
bid [offer to pay]	bidding	bid	bid
bind	binding	bound	bound
bite	biting	bit	bitten
bleed	bleeding	bled	bled
blend	blending	blended, blent	blended, blent
blow	blowing	blew	blown
break	breaking	broke	broken
breed	breeding	bred	bred
bring	bringing	brought	brought
build	building	built	built
burn	burning	burned, burnt	burned, burnt
burst	bursting	burst	burst
buy	buying	bought	bought
cast	casting	cast	cast
catch	catching	caught	caught
choose	choosing	chose	chosen
cling	clinging	clung	clung
clothe	clothing	clothed, clad	clothed, clad
come	coming	came	come
cost	costing	cost	cost
creep	creeping	crept	crept
crow	crowing	crowed, crew	crowed
cut	cutting	cut	cut

† In this case the bare form (*be*) is not the same as the present (*am, is, are*).

Forming the Principal Parts of Irregular Verbs 375

PRESENT (BARE FORM)	PRESENT PARTICIPLE	PAST	PAST PARTICIPLE
deal	dealing	dealt	dealt
dig	digging	dug	dug
dive	diving	dived, dove	dived
do	doing	did	done
draw	drawing	drew	drawn
drink	drinking	drank	drunk, drunken
drive	driving	drove	driven
eat	eating	ate	eaten
fall	falling	fell	fallen
feed	feeding	fed	fed
feel	feeling	felt	felt
fight	fighting	fought	fought
find	finding	found	found
fling	flinging	flung	flung
fly	flying	flew	flown
forbid	forbidding	forbade, forbad	forbidden, forbid
forget	forgetting	forgot	forgotten, forgot
freeze	freezing	froze	frozen
get	getting	got	got, gotten
give	giving	gave	given
go	going	went	gone
grind	grinding	ground	ground
grow	growing	grew	grown
hang [execute]	hanging	hanged	hanged
hang [suspend]	hanging	hung	hung
have	having	had	had
hear	hearing	heard	heard
heave	heaving	heaved, hove	heaved, hove
hide	hiding	hid	hidden, hid
hit	hitting	hit	hit
hold	holding	held	held
hurt	hurting	hurt	hurt
keep	keeping	kept	kept
kneel	kneeling	knelt, kneeled	knelt, kneeled
knit	knitting	knitted, knit	knitted, knit
know	knowing	knew	known
lay	laying	laid	laid
lead	leading	led	led

PRESENT (BARE FORM)	PRESENT PARTICIPLE	PAST	PAST PARTICIPLE
lean	leaning	leaned, leant	leaned, leant
leap	leaping	leaped, leapt	leaped, leapt
learn	learning	learned, learnt	learned, learnt
leave	leaving	left	left
lend	lending	lent	lent
let	letting	let	let
lie [recline]	lying	lay	lain
lie [tell a falsehood]	lying	lied	lied
light	lighting	lighted, lit	lighted, lit
lose	losing	lost	lost
make	making	made	made
mean	meaning	meant	meant
meet	meeting	met	met
mow	mowing	mowed	mowed, mown
pay	paying	paid	paid
plead	pleading	pleaded, pled	pleaded, pled
prove	proving	proved	proved, proven
put	putting	put	put
quit	quitting	quit, quitted	quit, quitted
read	reading	read	read
rend	rending	rent	rent
rid	ridding	rid, ridded	rid, ridded
ride	riding	rode	ridden
ring	ringing	rang	rung
rise	rising	rose	risen
run	running	ran	run
saw	sawing	sawed	sawed, sawn
say	saying	said	said
see	seeing	saw	seen
seek	seeking	sought	sought
sell	selling	sold	sold
send	sending	sent	sent
sew	sewing	sewed	sewed, sewn
shake	shaking	shook	shaken
shave	shaving	shaved	shaved, shaven
shed	shedding	shed	shed
shine	shining	shone	shone
shoe	shoeing	shod, shoed	shod, shoed
show	showing	showed	shown, showed
shred	shredding	shredded, shred	shredded, shred

PRESENT (BARE FORM)	PRESENT PARTICIPLE	PAST	PAST PARTICIPLE
shrink	shrinking	shrank, shrunk	shrunk, shrunken
shoot	shooting	shot	shot
shut	shutting	shut	shut
sing	singing	sang	sung
sink	sinking	sank, sunk	sunk, sunken
sit	sitting	sat	sat
slay	slaying	slew	slain
sleep	sleeping	slept	slept
slide	sliding	slid	slid
sling	slinging	slung	slung
slink	slinking	slunk	slunk
slit	slitting	slit	slit
smell	smelling	smelled, smelt	smelled, smelt
sow	sowing	sowed	sown, sowed
speak	speaking	spoke	spoken
speed	speeding	sped, speeded	sped, speeded
spin	spinning	spun, span	spun
spit	spitting	spit, spat	spit, spat
split	splitting	split	split
spoil	spoiling	spoiled, spoilt	spoiled, spoilt
spread	spreading	spread	spread
spring	springing	sprang	sprung
stand	standing	stood	stood
steal	stealing	stole	stolen
stick	sticking	stuck	stuck
sting	stinging	stung	stung
stink	stinking	stank, stunk	stunk
stride	striding	strode	stridden
strike	striking	struck	struck, stricken
string	stringing	strung	strung
strive	striving	strove	striven
swear	swearing	swore	sworn
sweat	sweating	sweat, sweated	sweat, sweated
sweep	sweeping	swept	swept
swell	swelling	swelled	swelled, swollen
swim	swimming	swam	swum
swing	swinging	swung	swung
take	taking	took	taken
teach	teaching	taught	taught
tear	tearing	tore	torn
tell	telling	told	told
think	thinking	thought	thought
throw	throwing	threw	thrown
thrust	thrusting	thrust	thrust

PRESENT (BARE FORM)	PRESENT PARTICIPLE	PAST	PAST PARTICIPLE
toss	tossing	tossed, tost	tossed, tost
tread	treading	trod	trodden, trod
wake	waking	woke, waked	woke, waked, woken
wear	wearing	wore	worn
weave	weaving	wove	woven
wed	wedding	wed, wedded	wed, wedded
weep	weeping	wept	wept
wet	wetting	wet, wetted	wet, wetted
win	winning	won	won
wind	winding	wound	wound
work	working	worked, wrought	worked, wrought
wring	wringing	wrung	wrung
write	writing	wrote	written

21

VERBS
Sequence of Tenses

21.1 Understanding Sequence of Tenses

When a passage has more than one verb, the relation between the tenses of the verbs is called the **sequence of tenses.** Various sequences are possible.

When all the verbs in a sentence describe actions or states that occur at or about the same time, their tenses should be the same:

> Whenever the alarm clock *rings,* I *yawn, stretch,* and *roll* over for another fifteen minutes of sleep. [all present tense]
> The batter *cocked* his arms, *stepped* into the pitch, and *took* a round-house swing. [all past tense]
> My parents *will pay* for my tuition, but I *will pay* for all my other college expenses. [both future tense]

But of course actions do not always happen at the same time, even if they are described in the same sentence. A sentence may describe actions that happen at different times, and it will then have verbs in different tenses. In other words, the tense in the sentence will shift:

> Beth *had been working* on the research project for almost three years before she *made* the first discovery. [past perfect and past]
> The coach *says* that we *will have* a winning season. [present and future]
> The Lakers *won* in overtime; they always *play* well under pressure. [past and present]

In the rest of this chapter, we discuss some of the common sequences and the principal ways in which writers sometimes go wrong when using sequences within sentences and paragraphs.

21.2 Sequences in Compound Sentences

A compound sentence consists of two or more independent clauses. Since the clauses are independent, the tenses of the verbs in those clauses may be entirely independent of each other:

> In the past, most consumers *wanted* big cars, but now they *want* small cars. [past and present tense]
> The accident *broke* her spinal column; as a result, she *will* never *walk* again. [past and future tense]

21.3 Sequences in Complex Sentences

A complex sentence consists of one independent clause and at least one subordinate clause (see chapter 15). In this kind of sentence, the tense of the subordinate verb depends on the tense of the main verb (the verb in the independent clause). Common sequences are as follows.

21.3A   Main Verb in the Present

When the main verb is in the **present tense,** the subordinate verb is commonly in the present also:

MAIN VERB	SUBORDINATE VERB PRESENT
Some Americans *are* so poor	that they *suffer* from malnutrition.
	PRESENT
Monetarists *think*	that federal interference with the economy *does* more harm than good.

The subordinate verb is in the present perfect or the past only when it refers to action that occurred before the time of the main verb:

MAIN VERB	SUBORDINATE VERB
	PRESENT PERFECT
Most children *learn* to talk	after they *have learned* to walk.
	PAST
Greg *likes* to boast about the marlin	that he *caught* last summer.

The subordinate verb is in the future when it refers to action in the future:

MAIN VERB	SUBORDINATE VERB
	FUTURE
Astronomers *predict*	that the sun *will die* in about ten billion years.

21.3B   Main Verb in the Present Perfect

When the main verb is in the **present perfect tense,** the subordinate verb is normally in the past tense:

MAIN VERB	SUBORDINATE VERB
	PAST
Scientists *have studied* the rings of Saturn	ever since Galileo *discovered* them.

21.3C   Main Verb in the Past

When the main verb is in the **past tense,** the subordinate verb is normally in the past or past perfect tense. (For an exception, in the indirect reporting of discourse, see section 24.2.) An auxiliary verb in the subordinate clause should also be in the past tense, taking a form like *was, were, had, did, could, might, should, used to,* or *would:*

MAIN VERB	SUBORDINATE VERB
	PAST
Centuries ago most people *believed*	that the sun *revolved* around the earth
	PAST
Stacy *thought*	that she *could win* the match
	PAST PERFECT
	even though she *had lost* the first set.
	PAST
In 1969 the Cuyahoga River in Cleveland *was* so full of wastes	that it *caught* fire.
	PAST PERFECT
After the presidential election of 1948, some newspapers mistakenly *reported*	that Dewey *had beaten* Truman.

21.3D Main Verb in the Past Perfect

When the main verb is in the past perfect tense, the subordinate verb is normally in the past:

SUBORDINATE VERB PAST	MAIN VERB
By the time the fire engine *arrived,*	the blaze *had* already *gutted* the house.

21.3E Main Verb Indicating Future

When the main verb refers to action in the future, the subordinate verb is normally in the present or the present perfect tense—but not in the future tense:

MAIN VERB	SUBORDINATE VERB PRESENT
I *start* [or *will start*] my summer job	just as soon as I *finish* my final exams.
	PRESENT PERFECT
I *start* [or *will start*] my summer job	just as soon as I *have finished* my final exams.

Do not write:

*I *start* [or *will start*] my summer job just as soon as I *will finish* my final exams.

21.3F Main Verb in the Future Perfect

When the main verb is in the future perfect tense, the subordinate verb is normally in the present or present perfect tense—but not in the future tense:

MAIN VERB	SUBORDINATE VERB PRESENT
Workmen *will have completed* their repairs	by the time the airport *is* reopened.
SUBORDINATE VERB PRESENT PERFECT	MAIN VERB
Before a new SALT agreement *has been* signed,	the United States and Russia *will have spent* billions on the development of new weapons systems.

Sequences in Complex Sentences **383**

eq

21.4

EXERCISE 1 Using Tenses

Complete each of the following sentences by inserting, in a suitable tense, the appropriate form of each verb shown in parentheses.

> EXAMPLE
> Brenda cheered when she _____ the news. (hear)
> Brenda cheered when she <u>heard</u> the news.

1. Keynesian economists believe that federal action often _____ to stabilize the economy. (help)
2. Conservatives think that the welfare system _____ millions of dollars. (waste)
3. In the summer of 1980, Polish workers went on strike so that they _____ the right to run their own unions. (can win)
4. At the start of the race, Fran wondered if she _____ the turn where the snow _____ during the night. (can make, freeze)
5. The director interviewed over two hundred applicants before she _____ one of them. (choose)
6. When I _____ college, I will go to law school. (finish)
7. By the time I saw the ad, the company _____ someone else. (hire)
8. In the seventy-five years since the Wright brothers _____ the airplane, it has drastically changed the way we live. (invent)

EXERCISE 2 Transforming Tenses

This exercise should help you understand how the tense of a subordinate verb is related to the tense of the main verb. In each of the following, change the main verb to the past tense if it is in the present, and to the present tense if it is in the past. Then make whatever other tense changes have become necessary.

> EXAMPLE
> We want to take a walk before it starts raining.
> TRANSFORMED: We wanted to take a walk before it started raining.

1. The officer manager was looking for a machine that would print fifty copies a minute.
2. The ducks circle above the pond until all humans have left the area.
3. The children hope they can see the circus at least once before it leaves town.
4. When the stock market crashes, millions of workers lose their jobs.
5. Most students did not start learning a foreign language until after they had finished grade school.

21.4 Using Sequences in Paragraphs

A single sentence can often include more than one verb and more than one tense. A paragraph normally includes many verbs and often several different tenses. But you should shift tenses in a paragraph only when you have good reason for doing so.

A well-written paragraph is usually dominated by just one tense. Consider the following examples:

1. Before I set my world record, I was a great fan of *The Guinness Book of World Records* and read each new edition from cover to cover. I liked knowing and being able to tell others that the world's chug-a-lug champ consumed 2.58 pints of beer in 10 seconds, that the world's lightest adult person weighed only 13 pounds, that the largest vocabulary for a talking bird was 531 words, spoken by a brown-beaked budgerigar named Sparky. There is, of course, only a fine line between admiration and envy, and for awhile I had been secretly desiring to be in that book myself—to astonish others just as I had been astonished. But it seemed hopeless. How could a nervous college sophomore, an anonymous bookworm, perform any of those wonderful feats? The open-throat technique necessary for chug-a-lugging was incomprehensible to my trachea—and I thought my head alone must weigh close to 13 pounds.

   —William Allen, "How to Set a World Record"

The author is describing a past condition, so the dominant tense here is the simple past. That is the tense, for example, of *was, read, liked, consumed, weighed,* and *seemed.* About the middle of the paragraph the author shifts out of the simple past, saying that there *is* a fine line between admiration and envy, and that he *had been* secretly *desiring* to be in the *Guinness* book. He has good reasons for both of these shifts: *is* describes a general truth and *had been desiring* describes a condition that existed before the simple past, before the time described in the rest of the paragraph. Then the author returns to the simple past with *seemed, was,* and *thought.*

Now consider this paragraph:

2. February 2, 1975. Wasps begin to appear in country houses about now, and even in some suburban houses. One sees them dart uncertainly about, hears them buzz and bang on window panes, and one wonders where they came from. They probably came from the attic, where they spent the early part of the winter hibernating. Now, with longer hours of daylight, the wasps begin to rouse and start exploring.

   —Hal Borland, "Those Attic Wasps"

This passage describes not a past condition but a recurrent one—something that happens every year. The dominant tense of the verbs, therefore, is the present: *begin, sees, hears, wonders, begin, start.* Since the presence of the wasps calls for some explanation, the writer shifts tense in the middle of the paragraph to tell us where they *came* from and where they *spent* the early part of the winter. But in the final sentence, *Now* brings us back to the present, and the verbs of this sentence, *begin* and *start,* are in the present tense.

> 3. As a first gain from the sale of the heroin, the simple motorbikes on which Wyatt and Billy were riding at the start of the picture are replaced by a pair of the biggest, flashiest, most expensive motorcycles ever to fill the male American heart with envy. It is on these splendid vehicles—Fonda-Wyatt's is decorated with a splash of American flag—that the two men now begin their beautiful journey from California to near New Orleans, where their trip will be suddenly and violently cut off.
> —Diana Trilling, *"Easy Rider* and Its Critics"

Since this passage tells what happened at a certain point in a film, the prevailing tense of the verbs is the present: *are replaced, is, is decorated,* and *begin.* But the first sentence compares the motorcycles which are seen "now" with the motorbikes on which Wyatt and Billy *were riding* earlier, and the end of the second sentence anticipates what *will* happen later in the film. Normally, the present tense should predominate when you describe an aesthetic work of any kind, such as a film, a play, a symphony, a painting, a photograph, a recording, or a piece of sculpture.

> 4. Commercial banks have two primary functions. First, banks hold demand deposits and permit checks to be drawn on these deposits. This function is familiar to practically everyone. Most people have a checking account in some commercial bank, and draw checks on this account. Second, banks lend money to industrialists, merchants, homeowners, and other individuals and firms. At one time or another, you will probably apply for a loan to finance some project for your business or home. Indeed, it is quite possible that some of the costs of your college education are being covered by a loan to you or your parents from a commercial bank.
> —Edwin Mansfield, *Economics: Principles, Problems, Decisions*

The author is explaining what banks regularly do. So here again the predominant tense of the verbs is present: *have, hold, permit, is, have, draw, lend, is, are being covered.* The writer departs from the present just once—to say what business you will probably do with a bank in the future.

21.5 Correcting Faulty Tense Shifts in Sentences
t shift

The shift of tenses in a sentence is faulty when the tense of any verb differs without good reason from the tense of the one before it, or when the tense of a subordinate verb is inconsistent with the tense of the main verb. Consider the following examples:

1. *The novel *describes* the adventures of two immigrant families who *enter* the United States at New York, *withstand* the stresses of culture shock, and *traveled* to the Dakota Territory to make their fortune.

The shift to the past *(traveled)* is faulty. The time of the action should be reported in the present—the tense of the main verb *(describes)* and of the other subordinate verbs:

The novel *describes* the adventures of two immigrant families who *enter* the United States at New York, *withstand* the stresses of culture shock, and *travel* to the Dakota Territory to make their fortune.

2. *General Lee *informed* his staff that he *would* not *order* a retreat unless General Stuart *advises* him to.

The shift to the present *(advises)* is faulty. All of the actions reported in the sentence occurred at about the same time in the past—the time of the main verb *(informed)*. So the past tense should be used throughout:

General Lee *informed* his staff that he *would* not *order* a retreat unless General Stuart *advised* him to.

3. *Marthe *likes* to display the miniature spoons she *had collected* since her marriage to an antique dealer.

A subordinate verb in the past perfect *(had collected)* is inconsistent with a main verb in the present *(likes)*. In this sentence the tense of the subordinate verb should be present perfect:

Marthe *likes* to display the miniature spoons she *has collected* since her marriage to an antique dealer.

EXERCISE 3   Correcting Faulty Shifts in a Sentence

In some of the following sentences, the tense of one or more verbs does not properly correspond to the tense of the italicized verb. Correct those sentences. If a sentence is correct as it stands, write *Correct*.

EXAMPLE
A roll of thunder *announced* the coming of the storm; then drops of rain begin to pelt the earth.
REVISED: A roll of thunder announced the coming of the storm; then drops of rain began to pelt the earth.

1. Filters *are being installed* in water systems that had been threatened by pollutants from industrial wastes.

2. Many Canadians who speak only English *enroll* in French courses to become bilingual.

3. My grandfather always *tooted* the horn of his Model A as he drives past the police station.

4. Caroline *is* excited; she had just received a fellowship which enables her to do research in chemistry.

5. When the rain came, the streets *are flooded.*

6. Every Saturday morning, the station *broadcasted* music that listeners have requested.

7. The circulation of the regional newspaper *has been climbing* ever since the editors begin printing feature stories about local characters.

8. In "The Tell-Tale Heart," Edgar Allan Poe *creates* suspense until it was almost unbearable in the final scene.

9. The appearance of gray streaks in the paint *stumped* the chemist; he has no idea what causes them.

10. Magicians *delight* us partly because they seemed superior to the laws of nature.

21.6 Correcting Faulty Tense Shifts in Paragraphs ¶ *t shift*

The shift of tenses in a paragraph is faulty when the tense of any verb differs without good reason from the dominant tense of the paragraph. Consider two examples, the first a commentary on *Green Mansions,* a novel by W. H. Hudson:

1. [1] On his return to the once peaceful woods, Abel is horrified to learn that his beloved Rima has been slain by savages. [2] Rage and grief swell within him as Kua-kó tells how Rima was forced to seek refuge in a lofty tree and how the tree became a trap when the savages sent searing flames and choking smoke high into the branches. [3] As Abel hears of her final cry—"Abel! Abel!"—and fatal plunge to earth, he fought against a wild impulse to leap upon the triumphant Indian and tear his heart out.

Since this is a description of a literary work, the dominant tense is the present *(swell, tells,* and *hears).* There is one shift to the present perfect *(has been slain* in sentence 1) and four shifts to the past *(was forced, became,* and *sent* in sentence 2, and *fought* in sentence 3). The shifts in sentences 1 and 2 are correct; the shift in sentence 3 is not. In sentence 1, *has been slain* tells what happened before Abel is horrified to learn about it. In sentence 2, the past-tense verbs describe what happened shortly before Kua-kó *tells* about it. But in sentence 3, the verb *fought* tells what Abel does just at the time that he *hears* of Rima's death. *Fought* should therefore be *fights.*

2. [1] Computer buffs who use their expertise to tamper with computers owned by others are known as "hackers." [2] After gaining access to someone else's system either by stealing the password or by breaking through the computer's defenses, they cause all kinds of mischief. [3] Recently, in Wisconsin, a group of seventeen-year-olds gained access to a large medical center's computer. [4] They damage some important medical records stored in the files. [5] The group, unaware of the medical computer's particular system, destroyed records that were, literally, of life and death importance to the patients. [6] Cases like this one proved that we must somehow prevent "hackers" from using their skills at the expense of others.   —Matthew Schuster

The dominant tense is the present. In sentence 3 the shift to the past tense is justified; the writer is citing something that happened in the past. For this reason the tense of the verb in sentence 4 should be *damaged*. In sentence 6, where the writer resumes the discussion of the problem today, *proved* is incorrect; the tense should be present, *prove*, or present perfect, *have proved*.

EXERCISE 4   Correcting Faulty Tense Shifts in a Paragraph

Each of the following paragraphs is a rewritten version of a paragraph from the source cited after it. In rewriting each paragraph, we have deliberately introduced one or more faulty shifts in tense. Correct them.

EXAMPLE
line 3; manfully thrashes

1.   However violent his acts, Kong remains a gentleman. Whenever a fresh boa constrictor threatens Fay, Kong first sees that the lady is safely parked, then manfully thrashed her attacker. (And she, the ingrate, runs away every time his back was turned.) Atop
5 the Empire State Building, ignoring his pursuers, Kong places Fay on a ledge as tenderly as if she were a dozen eggs. He fondled her, then turned to face the Army Air Force. And Kong is perhaps the most disinterested lover since Cyrano: his attentions to the lady were utterly without hope of reward. After all, between a five-foot
10 blonde and a fifty-foot ape, love can hardly be more than an intellectual flirtation. His forced exit from his jungle, in chains, results directly from his single-minded pursuit of Fay. He smashes a Broadway theater when the notion entered his dull brain that the flashbulbs of photographers somehow endanger the lady. His per-
15 ilous shinnying up a skyscraper to have plucked Fay from her boudoir is an act of the kindliest of hearts. He was impossible to discourage even though the love of his life can't lay eyes on him without shrieking murder.
                    —Deliberately altered from X. J. Kennedy,
                                    "Who Killed King Kong?"

2.   To understand Marx, we need to know something about the times in which he lived. The period was characterized by revolutionary pressures against the ruling classes. In most of the countries of Europe, there was little democracy, as we know it. The masses
5   participated little, if at all, in the world of political affairs, and very fully in the world of drudgery. For example, at one factory in Manchester, England, in 1862, people work an average of 80 hours per week. For these long hours of toil, the workers generally receive small wages. They often can do little more than feed and
10 clothe themselves. Given these circumstances, it is little wonder that revolutionary pressures were manifest.

—Deliberately altered from Edwin Mansfield,
Economics: Principles, Problems, Decisions

3.   Since graduating from college, Susan has held a variety of political jobs. Her warm, friendly manner, together with her capacity for hard work, makes her an ideal employee. Three years ago, she managed the reelection campaign of a New England governor.
5   She has to talk with people in all parts of the state, trying to build support. Soon after the election, which turns out successfully for the governor, Susan goes to Washington, D.C., to work for a senator. She had a high-paying position; but, being more interested in working creatively than in making money, she soon resigned, pro-
10 claiming, "Never have so many people done so little work for so much money." Because she has had so much experience, finding a new job was easy. She becomes an adviser to the New England Governors' Conference on Energy.

—Deliberately altered from Mark Bartlett, "A Political Woman"

22

VERBS
Active and Passive Voice

22.1 What Voice Is

The word "voice" generally refers to the sound of someone speaking. But as applied to sentences, "voice" has to do with verbs. When the subject of a verb acts, the verb is in the **active voice;** when the subject is acted upon, the verb is in the **passive voice.**

The active voice stresses the activity of the subject and helps to make a sentence direct, concise, and vigorous:

> Babe Ruth *hit* sixty home runs in one season.
> Each man *kills* the thing he *loves*. —Oscar Wilde

The passive voice presents the subject as receiver of an action:

> The barn *was struck* by a bolt of lightning.
> In Moulmein, in Lower Burma, I *was hated* by large numbers of people—the only time in my life that I have been important enough for this to happen to me. —George Orwell

22.2 Forming the Active and the Passive Voice

22.2A   Forming the Active Voice

Clauses with transitive verbs in the active voice have three main parts, usually in the following order—subject, verb, direct object:

SUBJECT	VERB	DIRECT OBJECT
She	was chewing	gum.
We	love	liberty.

22.2B   Changing from Active to Passive

You can change a verb from active to passive only if it has a direct object (DO). Consider the following examples

S   ACTIVE   DO
1. *Heavy waves* pounded the seacoast.
S   PASSIVE   AGENT
The seacoast was pounded *by heavy waves.*

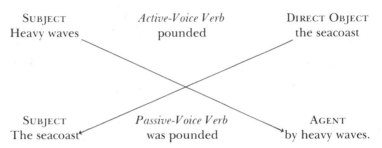

In the passive version, the direct object of *pounded* becomes the subject of *was pounded:* it is acted upon. The subject of *pounded* becomes the agent of *was pounded*—the thing *by which* the action was performed.

Consider two more examples:

S   ACTIVE   DO
2. *Babe Ruth* hit sixty homeruns in one season.
S   PASSIVE   AGENT
Sixty homeruns were hit *by Babe Ruth* in one season.

3. After the tanker capsized in the hurricane, *heavy waves covered*
                ACTIVE   DO
with oil slick pounded the rocky New England seacoast.

After the tanker capsized in the hurricane, the rocky New En-
        S   PASSIVE   AGENT
gland seacoast was pounded *by heavy waves covered with oil slick.*

22.2C   Changing from Passive to Active

To change a verb from the passive to the active voice, turn the subject of the passive verb into the direct object of the active one:

S   PASSIVE   AGENT
1. *Pearl Harbor* was bombed by the Japanese.
S   ACTIVE   DO
The Japanese bombed *Pearl Harbor.*

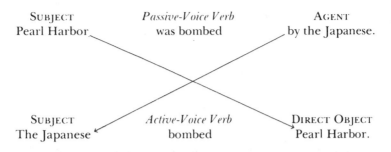

SUBJECT	*Passive-Voice Verb*	AGENT
Pearl Harbor	was bombed	by the Japanese.

SUBJECT	*Active-Voice Verb*	DIRECT OBJECT
The Japanese	bombed	Pearl Harbor.

The agent of the passive verb becomes the subject of the active one. Here are two more examples:

2. *The barn* was struck by a bolt of lightning.
   A bolt of lightning struck *the barn*.

3. *The house* is being painted by my sister and me.
   My sister and I are painting *the house*.

If the passive version does not include the agent, you must either keep the passive or supply the agent yourself before changing to the active.

> The city of Washington was planned in 1791. [passive, no agent]
> The city of Washington was planned in 1791 by Pierre Charles L'Enfant. [passive, agent supplied]
> Pierre Charles L'Enfant planned the city of Washington in 1791. [active]

EXERCISE 1 Transforming Verbs—From Active to Passive

Change the main verb in each of the following sentences from active to passive, and rearrange the other words as necessary.

EXAMPLE
Heavy waves covered with oil slick pounded the rocky New England seacoast.
TRANSFORMED: The rocky New England seacoast was pounded by heavy waves covered with oil slick.

1. Leonardo da Vinci painted the *Mona Lisa*.
2. People found traces of the oil spill as far away as Newfoundland.
3. In years to come, unmanned space satellites will explore planets beyond the solar system.
4. Voters elected Ronald Reagan president of the United States in 1980.
5. Her colored shawl, which caught in the wheel of a moving car, strangled the famous dancer.
6. Thomas Jefferson, who later became president of the United States, wrote the Declaration of Independence.

Forming the Active and the Passive Voice **393**

7. The Revenue Act of 1978 made important changes in the tax law.
8. Some people built the pyramids at Teotihuacán, Mexico, during the second and third centuries A.D.
9. Some people sharply attacked Lincoln for his opposition to slavery.
10. Father Robert I. Charlesbois, a forty-eight-year-old Catholic priest from Gary, Indiana, with twelve years of experience in the Vietnam war zone, organized a secret mission to help thousands of starving Cambodians in the summer of 1979.

EXERCISE 2 Transforming Verbs—From Passive to Active

Change the verb or verbs in each of the following sentences from passive to active, and rearrange the other words as necessary:

EXAMPLE
On December 7, 1941, Pearl Harbor, an American base in the Hawaiian Islands, was bombed without warning by the Japanese.
TRANSFORMED: On December 7, 1941, the Japanese without warning bombed Pearl Harbor, an American base in the Hawaiian Islands.

1. Swimming is taught by Roberta.
2. Permanent settlements in the new land were never established by the Vikings.
3. A solution to the problems of inflation and high unemployment is being urgently sought by the president.
4. No bribes are taken by Death.
5. A novel about the stormy years of the French Revolution was written by Charles Dickens.
6. Weekly meetings are held by the company commander so that the questions of the recruits can be answered by him.
7. No tales are told by dead men.
8. A play about the hardships which were suffered by her during a canoe trip down the Amazon River in 1972 has been written by Jane Stowe.
9. In every work of genius our own rejected thoughts are recognized by us.

22.3 Choosing the Active Voice

To make your writing forceful, direct, and concise, you should use the active voice frequently. If you have done the preceding exercise, you have seen what happens to a sentence when the verb is changed from passive to active:

> Swimming is taught by Roberta. [passive]
> Roberta teaches swimming. [active]

The active version ditches the excess verbal baggage—*is* and *by*. Also, because it makes *Roberta* the subject, the active version makes her more important and stresses her activity. To a great extent, the life and energy of your writing will depend on what the subjects of your sentences do.

Steady use of the active voice can also enhance the unity and coherence of your paragraphs. Compare the following passages.

1. At the sound of a bell, the huge red building was entered by me along with hundreds of others. Just inside the entrance, instructions were being yelled at us by an old lady who looked mean. My lunchbox was clutched, and a crowd of six-year-olds was followed down a long hallway, up some steps, and down another corridor. Mrs. Nearing's room was being looked for by us. I knew our destination had been reached when I was greeted by a tall woman. Her black hair was piled on top of her head. I was asked my name. Then a sticky tag was pressed to my chest. My name was printed on the tag. Inside the room several other six-year-olds could be seen. Some looked big. Finally the classroom door was closed, and a loud bang was made in the process. The small pane of glass near the top was prevented from shattering by a network of wires. To my imagination, they looked like the bars in a prison. I was back in school.

2. At the sound of a bell, I entered the huge red building along with hundreds of others. Just inside the entrance, a mean-looking old lady was yelling instructions. Clutching my lunchbox, I followed a crowd of six-year-olds down a long hallway, up some steps, and down another corridor. We were looking for Mrs. Nearing's room. I knew we had reached our destination when I was greeted by a tall woman with black hair piled on top of her head. She asked my name, wrote it on a tag, and stuck the tag on my chest. Several other six-year-olds were standing in the room, some of them big-looking. Finally, Mrs. Nearing closed the classroom door with a bang. A network of wires prevented the small pane of glass near the top from shattering. To my imagination, the wires resembled prison bars. I was back in school.

In the first passage, passive verbs predominate, and since almost every sentence has a different subject, the writing is not only tedious but unfocused. In the second passage, the predominantly active verbs keep the focus on what various people did: what *I* did, what *we* did, and what *the teachers* did. The result is livelier prose.

22.4 Choosing the Passive

Since overuse of the passive is one of the chief obstacles to good writing, you should use the active voice as much as possible. But just as a good driver knows when to shift into reverse, a good writer knows when to shift into the passive. Use the passive under the following conditions.

1. Use the passive when you want to keep the focus on someone or something important that is acted upon:

> a. John F. Kennedy *was assassinated* on November 22, 1963.

> b. On August 13, 1927, while driving on the Promenade des Anglais at Nice, Isadora Duncan met her death. She *was strangled* by her colored shawl, which became tangled in the wheel of the automobile. —Janet Flanner

Here the writer shifts from the active *(met)* in the first sentence to the passive *(was strangled)* in the second sentence. The shift from active to passive enables the writer to keep the focus on a subject who is shown first acting, and then acted upon.

> c. Frederick Douglass learned to read while he *was owned* by Mr. and Mrs. Ault of Baltimore.

Here the writer moves from active to passive in one sentence. The shift keeps the focus on Douglass, who is shown at once acting (he *learned*) and acted upon (he *was owned*).

> d. If our heads swim occasionally, if we grow giddy with change, is it any wonder? We are urged to take our rightful place in the world of affairs. We are also commanded to stay at home and mind the hearth. We are lauded for our stamina and pitied for our lack of it. If we run to large families, we are told we are overpopulating the earth. If we are childless, we are damned for not fulfilling our functions. We are goaded into jobs and careers, then warned that our competition with men is unsettling both sexes. —Phyllis McGinley, "The Honor of Being a Woman"

The consistent use of the passive here helps the writer to keep the focus on women as acted upon, relentlessly subjected to pressures and demands. They *are urged, are damned, are goaded,* and so on.

2. Use the passive when you do not know or do not care to say who or what performed the action shown by the verb:

> Traces of the oil spill *were found* as far away as Newfoundland.
> The pyramids at Teotihuacán, Mexico, *were built* during the second and third centuries A.D.

3. Use the passive when you want to put the person or thing acting at the end of a clause, where you can easily attach a long modifier:

> A secret mission to help thousands of starving Cambodians *was organized* in the summer of 1979 by Father Robert I. Charlesbois, a forty-eight-year-old Catholic priest from Gary, Indiana, with twelve years of experience in the Vietnam war zone.

EXERCISE 3   Choosing the Appropriate Voice

Select five sentences from exercise 1, and five from exercise 2. Indicate for each whether the passive or active version is better, and explain the reason for your choice.

> EXAMPLE
> In exercise 1, sentence 10, the passive version is better because it puts the agent, Father Robert L. Charlesbois, at the end of the clause, where the long modifier can easily follow without awkwardly separating the subject and verb.

22.5 Misusing the Passive   *pass*

Do not switch from active to passive in midsentence or midparagraph without a good reason:

> Usually I run two miles in the morning, but that morning it *was decided* that a four-mile run *should be taken.*

The passive voice turns the second part of the sentence into a pretzel, and since there is no *by* phrase, we can't be sure just who made the decision. Keep the active voice as long as the person or thing you are writing about is acting rather than acted upon:

> Usually I run two miles in the morning, but that morning I decided to run four.

The active voice makes the sentence snap into shape. You should switch to the passive only if the person or thing you are writing about is acted upon:

> Usually I run two miles in the morning, but that morning I *was kept* in bed by the flu.

EXERCISE 4   Revising Faulty Shifts in Voice

Rewrite any of the following sentences in which you find the passive voice misused. If the passive voice is justified, write *Acceptable.*

> EXAMPLE
> Every year we cut a Christmas tree in the woods, and it is decorated by us on December 24.
> REVISED: Every year we cut a Christmas tree in the woods and decorate it on December 24.

1. My mother always insists that before we hang any ornaments on the branches, the tree should be placed upright in its stand.
2. One of Mrs. Green's best qualities was her sensitivity to my needs. Whenever I had baseball practice, for example, she let me out early so that the field could be reached on time.

3. All of this planning took time, but an enjoyable trip was assured by it.
4. At the start of the story, the doctor enters the house knowing that a throat culture has to be obtained from a frightened girl.
5. The father displays an old-fashioned courtesy when an attempt to stand up and greet the doctor is made by him while holding the sick child.
6. Adequate shelter from the cold was badly needed, yet we did nothing to obtain it.
7. Through experience I have learned that sleeping on hard ground is uncomfortable at best, so for the journey an air mattress was added that could be inflated for sleeping and deflated for easy storage.
8. While walking among the trees bordering on the meadow, we played hide-and-seek with the dogs, and then an effort to catch them before the pond could be reached by them was made.
9. Just as the soprano reached the highest note in the aria, she was hit by a tomato.
10. After I had run ten miles, a severe pain in my chest was felt.

EXERCISE 5 Sentence Combining

Following is a group of simple sentences, some with verbs in the active voice, others with verbs in the passive. Make one continuous passage out of these sentences by combining some of them and changing the voice of the verbs where necessary.

EXAMPLE
1. As prime minister of England from 1940 to 1945, Churchill led his country through World War II.
2. But immediately after the war people voted him out of office.
3. Later his position as prime minister was regained by him.
4. That office was left by him in 1955.
5. Great popularity for the rest of his life was enjoyed by him.
6. He died in 1965.
7. People acclaimed him as a national hero.

COMBINED: As prime minister of England from 1940 to 1945, Churchill led his country through World War II, but immediately after the war he was voted out of office. Later he regained his position as prime minister. After he left that office in 1955, he enjoyed great popularity for the rest of his life, and when he died in 1965, he was acclaimed as a national hero.

1. The political structure of modern China was largely created by Mao Zedong.
2. Mao led the Chinese Communist revolution.
3. The theory behind it was formulated by him.
4. China was virtually ruled by him from 1949 to his death in 1976.
5. Mao worked for revolution throughout much of his early life.
6. In 1911 the Nationalist armed forces of Hunan Province were joined by him in their revolt against the Manchu dynasty.
7. He was then eighteen.
8. In 1921 he helped to found the Chinese Communist party.

9. In the spring of 1928, the Fourth Chinese Red Army was organized by him and a fellow revolutionary named Zhu De.
10. In 1934–35, he and Zhu De led a six-thousand-mile march of Chinese Communist forces to northwest China.
11. There a new base of operations was established by the two leaders.
12. The new base was established against the Kuomintang.
13. That was the Nationalist political organization.
14. Generalissimo Chiang Kai-shek headed it.
15. Mao and Chiang joined forces during World War II in order to fight their common enemy, the Japanese.
16. But in the summer of 1946 a full-scale civil war against the Nationalists was resumed by Mao.
17. Mao's forces won the war in three years.
18. On September 21, 1949, the establishment of the People's Republic of China was proclaimed by Mao.
19. A succession of increasingly powerful posts was then assumed by him.
20. The posts included chairmanship of the Government Council, chairmanship of the Republic, and, most important, chairmanship of the Chinese Communist party.
21. In effect, China was ruled by Mao for nearly thirty years.
22. For better or worse, a lasting change in that country was made by Mao.
23. People will long remember him as one of the most important revolutionaries of the twentieth century.

23

VERBS
Mood

23.1 What Mood Is

The **mood** of a verb or verb phrase indicates your attitude toward a particular statement as you are making it. Do you think of it as a statement of fact? Then you will use the indicative mood. Do you think of it as a command? Then you will use the imperative. Do you think of it as a wish, a recommendation, or a hypothetical condition? Then you will use the subjunctive.

The mood of a verb is sometimes shown by a special form or an auxiliary. We treat each mood in turn.

23.2 Using the Indicative

The **indicative** mood is for statements of actuality or strong probability:

> Brian Mulroney *became* prime minister of Canada in 1984.
> The spine-tailed swift *flies* faster than any other bird in the world.

Use *do, does,* or *did* with the indicative for emphasis:

> Fred is no Olympic star, but he *does run* ten miles a day.
> Small cars are often short on leg room, but they *do save* gas.
> The blizzard of '78 was not the worst in history, but it *did paralyze* Boston for several days.

23.3 Using the Imperative

The **imperative** mood is for commands and requests made directly:

1. Use the bare form of the verb for commands addressed entirely to others:

> *Vote* for Mulroney.
> *Fight* pollution.
> *Be* yourself.
> Kindly *send* me your latest catalog.

2. When a command or suggestion includes yourself as well as others, use *let us* or *let's* before the bare form of the verb:

> *Let us negotiate* our differences in a spirit of mutual trust and respect.
> *Let's cooperate.*

23.4 Using the Subjunctive—Modal Auxiliaries

The **subjunctive** mood is for statements of hypothetical conditions or of wishes, recommendations, requirements, or suggestions. To express the subjunctive, you often need one of the modal auxiliaries, which include *can, could, may, might, must, ought, should,* and *would.* Use them as follows.

1. Use can to express

> CAPABILITY: *Can* the Israelis and the Palestinians ever make peace?
> PERMISSION: Why *can't* Americans visit Cuba?

In formal writing, permission is normally signified by *may* rather than *can,* which is reserved for capability. But *can* may be used informally to express permission and is actually better than *may* in requests for permission involving the negative. The only alternative to *can't* in such questions is the awkward term *mayn't.*

2. Use could to express

> THE OBJECT OF A WISH: I wish I *could* climb Mount Everest.
> A CONDITION: If the United States and the Soviet Union *could* set aside their antagonism once every four years, the Olympics would be truly international.
> A DISTINCT POSSIBILITY: A major earthquake *could* strike California within the next ten years.

On the distinction between *would* and *could* in statements of wishing, see number 8 below.

3. Use may to express

A MILD POSSIBILITY: The next president of the United States *may* be a woman.

PERMISSION: Students who cannot afford tuition *may* apply for loans.

4. Use <u>might</u> to express

A REMOTE POSSIBILITY: Biogenetic experiments *might* produce some horribly dangerous new form of life.

THE RESULT OF A CONTRARY-TO-FACT CONDITION: If the Soviets had participated in the 1984 Olympics, they *might* have won several gold medals.

5. Use <u>ought</u> to express

STRONG RECOMMENDATION: The Pentagon *ought* to eliminate waste in defense spending.

LIKELIHOOD: The new museum *ought* to be ready by next fall.

Ought is normally followed by the infinitive.

6. Use <u>must</u> to express

AN ABSOLUTE OBLIGATION: Firemen *must* be ready for action at any hour of the day or night.

A FIRM CONCLUSION: William Bligh, who with eighteen other men and scant provisions sailed a small boat nearly four thousand miles, *must* have been an extraordinary seaman.

7. Use <u>should</u> to express

ADVICE: Students who hope to get into medical school *should* take biology.

EXPECTATION: By the year 2025, the population of the world *should* exceed eight billion.

8. Use <u>would</u> to express

THE RESULT OF A CONDITION OR EVENT: If a one-kiloton neutron bomb were exploded a few hundred feet over the earth, it *would* instantly kill everyone within a radius of three hundred yards.

THE OBJECT OF A WISH: Some people wish the federal government *would* support them for the rest of their lives.

Both *would* and *could* may be used to express the object of a wish. But *I wish you could go* means *I wish you were able to go; I wish you would go* means *I wish you were willing to go.*

23.4A Misusing Modal Auxiliaries

Do not put two or more modal auxiliaries together:

*He might could win the race.

REVISED: He might win the race. [or] He could win the race.

EXERCISE 1   **Supplying Modal Auxiliaries**

Complete each of the following sentences with a suitable modal auxiliary. Then in parentheses identify the meaning it expresses.

EXAMPLE
Students who hope to get into medical school _____ take biology.
Students who hope to get into medical school <u>should</u> take biology. (recommendation)

1. In the volcanic world of the Middle East, open warfare _____ erupt at any time.
2. After weeks of training with the barbells, Doug White _____ lift 350 pounds.
3. To become an actor, you _____ learn how to manage your body as well as your voice.
4. If I _____ speak Italian, I would spend the summer in Rome.
5. To help the poor effectively, we _____ understand the causes of poverty.
6. If there were no limit on the supply of money in our economy, the dollar _____ soon lose all its value.
7. I _____ leave the hospital for the weekend; the doctor has just given me permission.
8. Because of all that Harry has done for us over the years, we _____ hold a banquet in his honor and give him a gold watch.
9. Soldiers on guard duty near the border _____ be alert at all times; we _____ predict when the attack will come.
10. The flower you reported seeing _____ have been a daisy or an aster.

23.5 Using the Subjunctive—Special Verb Forms

The subjunctive mood is sometimes indicated by a special verb form instead of by a modal auxiliary.

1. The <u>present subjunctive</u> is the same in form as the bare form (<u>infinitive form</u>) of the verb. Use it to express a hope, a requirement, a recommendation, or a suggestion:

INDICATIVE	SUBJUNCTIVE
God *has* mercy on us.	God *have* mercy on us!
The queen *lives*.	Long *live* the queen!
A premed student normally *takes* biology.	The college requires that every student *take* freshman English.
The trustees' meetings *are* closed.	The students demand that those meetings *be* open.

The present subjunctive of the verb *be* is *be* with every subject.

2. The <u>past subjunctive</u> is the same in form as the common past, except that the past subjunctive of *be* is *were* with every subject. Use the past subjunctive to express a wish for something in the present:

INDICATIVE (FACT)	SUBJUNCTIVE (WISH)
I *have* five dollars.	I wish (that) I *had* a million dollars.
I *am* a pauper.	I wish (that) I *were a millionaire.*
I *am taking* Math 36.	I wish (that) I *were taking* Math 23.
I *live* in Ontario.	I wish (that) I *lived* in Alberta.

3. The past perfect subjunctive is the same in form as the common past perfect. Use it to express a wish for something in the past:

INDICATIVE (FACT)	SUBJUNCTIVE (WISH)
I *saw* the second half of the game.	I wish (that) I *had seen* the first. [or] I wished (that) I *had seen* the first.
I *was* there for the second half.	I wish (that) I *had been* there for the first.

EXERCISE 2   Using Subjunctive Verb Forms

Complete each of the following sentences by inserting the appropriate form of the verb shown in parentheses. The appropriate form will sometimes be the same as the one in parentheses.

> **EXAMPLE**
> I saw the second half of the game, but I wish I _____ all of it.
> (see)
> I saw the second half of the game, but I wish I <u>had seen</u> all of it.

1. I took History 34 last term, but I wish that I _____ History 32. (take)
2. Some students demand that the university _____ all of its stocks in companies that do business in South Africa. (sell)
3. Since Sally is the best player on the team, the other players insist that she _____ the captain. (be)
4. The Social Security system requires that every worker _____ a fixed percentage of his or her earnings to a government-sponsored retirement fund. (contribute)
5. Sal felt out of place at the meeting and wished that he _____ someplace else. (be)
6. Since the old ambulance was no longer reliable, the townspeople voted to recommend that the fire department _____ a new one. (buy)

23.6 Forming and Using Conditional Sentences

A conditional sentence normally consists of an *if* clause, which states a condition, and a result clause, which states the result of that condition. The mood of the verb in the *if* clause depends on the likelihood of the condition.

23.6A   The Possible Condition

If the condition is likely or even barely possible, the mood is indicative:

> [condition] If wages *are* increased, [result] prices will rise.

An increase in wages is more than likely, so the mood is indicative; the verb is *are*.

23.6B   The Impossible or Contrary-to-Fact Condition

If the condition is impossible or contrary to fact, the mood of the verb in the *if* clause is subjunctive, and the result clause usually includes a modal auxiliary, such as *would* or *might*. The tense of the verb in the *if* clause depends on the tense of the condition.

1. A condition contrary to present fact should be stated in the past subjunctive:

> If the federal government *spent* no more than it collected, interest rates would plunge.
> If I *were* a millionaire, I would buy an airplane.
> Carl Lewis runs as if he *were* jet-propelled.

The expression *as if* always signals a condition contrary to fact. Some writers now use *was* instead of *were* in sentences like the second and third, but in formal writing you should use *were*.

2. A condition contrary to past fact should be stated in the past perfect subjunctive:

> After the fight, the former champion looked as if he *had been put through a meat grinder*.
> If Montcalm *had defeated* Wolfe in 1759, the Canadian province of Quebec might now belong to France.
> If the Watergate scandal *had not occurred,* Gerald Ford might never have become president of the United States.

23.6C   Misusing *would have* in Conditional Clauses

Do not use *would have* to express a condition of any kind:

> *If I *would have* attended the meeting, I would have attacked the proposal.

Use *would have* only to express the *result* of a condition:

> REVISED: If I had attended the meeting, I *would have* attacked the proposal.

EXERCISE 3   **Supplying Verbs**

Using the facts in brackets as a guide, complete each of the following sentences by supplying a suitable verb or verb phrase.

EXAMPLE

If the Soviet Union and its allies _____ the 1984 Olympics, American athletes might not have won so many medals. [The Soviet Union and its allies did not attend the 1984 Olympics.]

If the Soviet Union and its allies <u>had attended</u> the 1984 Olympics, American athletes might not have won so many medals.

1. If high-speed trains _____ all major cities in the United States, Americans could travel much more often without their cars. [High-speed trains serve hardly any cities in the United States.]
2. If my father _____ five hundred shares of IBM in 1950, he would be a millionaire today. [Alas, my father never bought any shares of IBM.]
3. If the prime rate _____, unemployment may go up also. [The prime rate goes up and down regularly.]
4. After winning the match, Joan felt as if she _____ the world. [She did not actually conquer the world.]
5. If the Continental Army _____ to the British at Yorktown, George Washington might never have become president of the United States. [The Continental Army did not lose to the British at Yorktown.]

EXERCISE 4   **Supplying Verbs**

For each of the blanks in the following passage, supply a suitable verb or verb phrase.

EXAMPLE
line 1: were

Many student wish that the Thanksgiving recess _____ one week long, or that the fall term _____ completely before Thanksgiving, so that they could stay home between Thanksgiving and Christmas. But the students have not asked for either of those things. They
5 have asked only that the Thanksgiving recess _____ on the Wednesday before Thanksgiving. If the recess _____ on Wednesday, students would have one full day to travel home before Thanksgiving Day itself. Many students need that time. If every student _____ rich, he or she could fly home in an hour or two.
10 But most students are not rich.

24

DIRECT AND INDIRECT REPORTING OF DISCOURSE

Any statement, whether spoken or written, can be reported directly —by quotation of the actual words. Or it can be reported indirectly—by a paraphrase of those words. In this chapter we explain when and how to use each method of reporting discourse. (For special instruction on how to quote or paraphrase source material in a research paper, see sections 33.11–12.)

24.1 Direct Reporting of Statements

Use direct reporting when the exact words of the original statement are memorable or otherwise important:

> "The vilest abortionist," writes Shaw, "is he who attempts to mould a child's character."
> There are five strong stresses in Robert Frost's line, "Something there is that doesn't love a wall."

24.1A Using Quotation Marks

Here is a statement that might be made in a conversation or a letter:

> You should go to law school.

To report this statement directly, you must keep the words exactly as they are and enclose them in quotation marks:

> "You should go to law school."

By using quotation marks you tell the reader that the words were originally spoken or written by someone else. But in addition, you should normally say who that someone is, and explain the reference of any pronouns in the quotation, such as *You* in the example. So a quotation often needs an explanatory tag:

> "You should go to law school," said the judge to his daughter.

(For a full discussion of how to punctuate quotations, see chapter 29, pp. 443–50.)

24.1B   Using Tenses in Tags

Since no statement can be reported until after it has been made, you should normally use the past tense for the verb in the tag:

> "I want to go to law school," she *said.*
> In 1782 Thomas Jefferson *wrote:* "There must doubtless be an unhappy influence on the manners of our people produced by the existence of slavery among us."

But use the present when you are quoting a statement of lasting significance or a statement made by a literary character:

> "In every work of genius," *observes* Emerson, "we recognize our own rejected thoughts."
> In the first chapter of *Huckleberry Finn,* Huck *says,* "I don't take no stock in dead people."

24.1C   Quoting Extended Dialogue

In reporting an exchange between two speakers, you should first indicate clearly who is speaking and in what order. You can then omit tags until the dialogue ends or is interrupted. The speakers' remarks should be set off from each other with double quotation marks, and you should normally begin a new paragraph whenever one speaker gives way to another:

> "Our market surveys indicate," Hurts said, "that there are also a lot of kids who claim their parents don't listen to them. If they could rent a gun, they feel they could arrive at an understanding with their folks in no time."
>
> "There's no end to the business," I said. "How would you charge for Hurts Rent-A-Gun?"
>
> "There would be hourly rates, day rates, and weekly rates, plus ten cents for each bullet fired. Our guns would be the latest models, and we would guarantee clean barrels and the latest safety devices. If a gun malfunctions through no fault of the user, we will give him another gun absolutely free. . . ."

"Why didn't you start this before?"
"We wanted to see what happened with the gun-control legislation. . . ." —Art Buchwald, "Hurts Rent-A-Gun"

24.1D Quoting Several Lines of Prose or Poetry

When you quote more than four lines of prose or two lines of poetry, you should indent instead of using quotation marks, as described in "Quoting Long Prose Passages," p. 446.

24.2 Indirect Reporting of Statements

Use indirect reporting when the exact words of the original statement are less important than their content:

> The new governor says he will cut property taxes.

When a statement is reported indirectly, no quotation marks are used:

> ORIGINAL STATEMENT: I want you to get a good education.
> DIRECT REPORT (QUOTATION): My father said to me, "I want you to get a good education."
> INDIRECT REPORT: My father said that he wanted me to get a good education.

As this example shows, an indirect report does the following:

1. It refers to the speaker or writer.

2. It often puts *that* just before the reported statement. But *that* may be omitted:

> My father said he wanted me to get a college education.

3. It changes the pronouns in the reported statement where necessary. In this example, *I* becomes *he,* and *you* becomes *me.*

4. It may change the tense of the verb in the reported statement. If the introductory verb in is the past tense, the verb in the reported statement may be in the past tense also—even if the verb in the original was not. Thus, after *My father said, I want you* may become *he wanted me.* But if the original statement was recently made or has lasting significance, the original tense may be kept in the reported statement:

> My father said that he wants me to get a good education.
> Ben Franklin once said that the sting of a reproach is the truth of it.

EXERCISE 1   **Transforming Reports of Statements**

Each of the following consists of a statement, with the speaker and listener identified in brackets. Write a direct and an indirect report of the statement. Then put a check next to the version you think is more suitable, and say why you prefer it.

EXAMPLE
You will have to take a breath test. [*Speaker:* the policeman; *listener:* me]
DIRECT: "You will have to take a breath test," said the policeman.
✔ INDIRECT: The policeman said that I would have to take a breath test.
The content is more important than the exact words.

1. You will have to earn your own spending money. [*Speaker:* my father; *listener,* me]
2. I do not mind lying, but I hate inaccuracy. [*Writer:* Samuel Butler]
3. I will pay you $3.50 an hour. [*Speaker:* the manager; *listener:* me]
4. You have been baptized in fire and blood and have come out steel. [*Speaker:* General Patton; *listeners:* the battle survivors]
5. Nothing in education is so astonishing as the amount of ignorance it accumulates in the form of inert facts. [*Writer:* Henry Adams]
6. Fanaticism consists in redoubling your efforts when you have forgotten your aim. [*Writer:* George Santayana]

24.3 Direct Reporting of Questions

To report a question directly, you normally use a verb of asking in the past tense:

> The Sphinx asked, "What walks on four legs in the morning, two legs at noon, and three legs in the evening?"
> "Have you thought about college?" my father asked.

Use the present tense when you are reporting a question of standing importance or a question asked by a literary character:

> The consumer advocate asks, "How can we have safe and effective products without government regulations?"
> The businessman asks, "How can we have free enterprise with government interference?"
> When Tom Sawyer proposes to form a gang that will rob and kill people, Huck says, "Must we always kill the people?"

24.4 Indirect Reporting of Questions

In many respects the indirect reporting of questions resembles the indirect reporting of statements. But to report a question indirectly, you must normally introduce it with a verb of asking and a word like *who, what, whether, how, when, where, why,* or *if:*

> ORIGINAL QUESTION: Do you want to go to law school?
> INDIRECT REPORT: My father asked me if I wanted to go to law school.

As this example shows, you must change the word order and the wording of the question: *Do you want* becomes *if I wanted.* Also, the question mark at the end of the original question becomes a period.

As in the direct reporting of questions, use the present tense for the introductory verb when reporting a question of continuing importance or a question asked by a literary character:

> The consumer advocate asks how we can have safe and effective products without government regulation.
> The businessman asks how we can have free enterprise with government interference.
> When Tom Sawyer proposes to form a gang that will rob and kill people, Huck asks whether they must always kill the people.

After a past-tense verb of asking, you must normally use the past tense in the reported question. But you may use the present tense if the reported question is essentially timeless:

> The Sphinx asked what walks on four legs in the morning, two legs at noon, and three legs in the evening.

24.5 Confusing the Direct and Indirect Reporting of Questions

Do not confuse the direct and indirect reporting of questions:

> *The customer sat down at the counter and asked did we have any scruples?

This sentence begins as a statement and ends as a question. When you report a question, you must decide whether to do so directly or indirectly. The **direct report** of a question repeats its actual words and ends in a question mark:

> REVISED: The customer sat down at the counter and asked, "Do you have any scruples?"

The **indirect report** of a question states that a question has been asked. The statement must introduce the question with a word such as *if* or *whether* and must end with a period:

> REVISED: The customer sat down at the counter and asked if we had any scruples.

EXERCISE 2   Transforming Reports of Questions

Each of the following sentences contains either a direct or an indirect question. If the question is direct, make it indirect; if it is indirect, make it direct. Then say which version you think is more suitable, and why you prefer it.

EXAMPLE
"Do you plan to seek reelection, Ms. Greene?" a reporter for Channel 31 asked.

TRANSFORMED: A reporter for Channel 31 asked Ms. Greene whether she was planning to seek reelection.

The indirect question is preferable because the content is more important than the exact words.

1. The waitress asked us, "What would you like?"
2. Many economists are asking themselves how the rate of inflation can keep rising during a period of high unemployment.
3. At one point in *Leaves of Grass,* Whitman asks us, "What do you suppose will satisfy the soul, except to walk free and own no superior?"
4. Early in *The Republic* one of Socrates' friends asks him if he wants to prove that justice is always better than injustice.
5. "But how shall we expect charity towards others, when we are uncharitable to ourselves?" asks Sir Thomas Browne.
6. One citizen asked the selectmen how they proposed to pay for the new addition to the high school.
7. "Do you expect to increase the tax on personal property?" she asked the selectmen.

25

INVIGORATING YOUR STYLE

Nearly all of the chapters in parts I and II of this book aim to help you improve your style: to write not just correctly but cogently, to shape your sentences with coordination and subordination, to enhance them with parallel structure, to enrich them with modifiers, and to perfect them with well-chosen words. In this chapter, we focus specifically on what you can do to invigorate your style.

Good writing exudes vitality. It not only sidesteps awkwardness, obscurity, and grammatical error; it also expresses a mind continually at work, a mind seeking, discovering, wondering, prodding, provoking, asserting. Whatever else it does, good writing keeps the reader awake.

Unfortunately, much of what gets written seems designed to put readers asleep. Too many people write the way they jog, never changing the pace or skipping a beat, never leaping, zigzagging, or stopping to scratch the reader's mind. Does this mean that in order to be lively, you have to write like an acrobat? No, it doesn't. Different subjects call for different styles, and you shouldn't write about a problem in economics or history the same way you would write about a beach party or a New Year's Day parade. In most college writing you are expected to sound thoughtful and judicious. But no reader wants you to sound dull. To enliven your writing on any subject, here are five specific things you can do.

25.1 Vary Your Sentences

Vary the length and construction of your sentences. Nothing animates prose like variety, and the sentence is infinitely variable. It can stop short after a couple of words. Or it can stretch luxuriously, reaching up over hills of thought and down into valleys of speculation, glancing to this side and that, moving along for as long as the writer cares to keep it going. You can vary its structure as well as its length. You can make it passive or active; you can arrange and rearrange its parts. Opening with a modifier, as we do in this sentence, you can hold your subject back. Or you can start with your subject and thus sound forthright and decisive. In structure and length as well as in meaning, English sentences admit of infinite variety.

How can you get some of that variety into your writing? Take a hard look at one of your paragraphs—or at a whole essay. Do all of your sentences sound about the same? If most are short and simple, combine some of them to make longer ones. If most are lengthened out with modifiers and dependent clauses, break some of them up. Be bold. Be unpredictable. Use a short sentence to set off a long one, a simple structure to set off a complicated one. Do anything to break the monotony of assembly-line sentences.

To see what you can do with a variety of sentences, consider this passage:

> I toss restlessly in bed, unable to relax. I remember that I forgot to take the telephone off the hook; I don't want anyone to wake me early Saturday morning. I pick up the receiver and stuff it in a drawer under my undershirts. After twenty more sleepless minutes, I draw a hot bath and ease into its relaxing warmth. Foam from the liquid soap covers the water's surface. After ten minutes of soaking and a slow towel-dry, I fall into bed and sleep. It is dawn.   —Bill Bradley, *Life on the Run*

Though Bradley often uses the pronoun *I,* no two of these sentences are alike. They range in length from twenty-two words to three; they range in structure from simple to complex; and they show how the same subject *(I)* can be moved around, taking the lead in the first three sentences and then following the modifier in the fourth *(After twenty more sleepless minutes, I draw a hot bath and ease into its relaxing warmth.)* Finally, the ending of the paragraph shows what a very short sentence can do when it follows a long one.

Now consider this passage:

> This looking business is risky. Once I stood on nearby Purgatory Mountain, watching through binoculars the great autumn hawk migration below, until I discovered that I was in danger of joining the hawks on a vertical migration of my own. I was used to binoculars, but not, apparently, to balancing on humped rocks while looking through them. I reeled.
> —Annie Dillard, "Pilgrim at Tinker Creek"

Dillard varies the length of her sentences even more than Bradley does. She moves from five to thirty-five words, then down to just two at the end. To express the dizzying exhilaration she felt while looking down on hawks from the peak of a mountain, she writes the simplest possible sentence: *I reeled.* A succession of such sentences would soon become monotonous. But when a very short sentence follows one or more long ones, it can strike like a dart.

EXERCISE 1   Using Short Sentences after Long Ones

Add a suitable two-word sentence to each of the following entries.

EXAMPLE
Crossing the goal after a spectacular display of broken-field running, the halfback waved to the thousands of spectators in the stands. *They roared.*

1. Whenever I am asked to sit absolutely still and keep perfectly quiet, something awkward happens.
2. After cursing all automobile manufacturers for the stalling of his sedan on a deserted country road, Henry once again turned the ignition key. "This time," he muttered to himself, "the engine must turn over."
3. The two prisoners stared intently at the foreman of the jury. They felt sure his expression would reveal the verdict. If he frowned, they would be found guilty; if he smiled, they would be acquitted.
4. The startled customer could not believe his eyes as he stared at the lobster on his plate.
5. Concealing his nervousness behind a fixed smile, Jonathan approached Jennifer and asked her to dance.

25.2   Use Verbs of Action instead of *be*

Use verbs of action as much as possible. Verbs of action show the subject not just being something but doing something. At times, of course, you need to say what your subject *is* or *was* or *has been.* But verbs of action can often replace verbs of being:

> Sheila *was the winner of* the race.
> Sheila *won* the race.

> Mr. and Mrs. Ault of Baltimore *were once owners of* Frederick Douglass.
> Mr. and Mrs. Ault of Baltimore *once owned* Frederick Douglass.

> Frederick's desire to learn reading *would have been a shock to* other slaveholders.
> Frederick's desire to learn reading *would have shocked* other slaveholders.

Use Verbs of Action instead of be   415

It *was not a shock to* Mrs. Ault.
It *did not shock* Mrs. Ault.

Mr. Ault believed that learning *would be the ruin of* Frederick as a slave.
Mr. Ault believed that learning *would ruin* Frederick as a slave.

The first sentence in each pair tells what the subject was, would have been, or would be; the second sentence tells what the subject did, would have done, or would do. In each case the verb of action tightens and invigorates the sentence. So whenever you can turn a verb of being into a verb of action, do so.

25.3 Use the Active Voice More Often Than the Passive

Use the active voice as much as possible. Verbs that tell of a subject acting usually express more vitality than verbs that tell of a subject acted upon. While some sentences actually work better in the passive voice, overuse of the passive can paralyze your writing. This is a problem *to be seriously considered by anyone who has ever been asked* to write an essay in which a subject of some sort is *to be analyzed, to be explained, or to be commented upon by him or her.* That sentence shows what overuse of the passive will do to your sentences: it will make them wordy, stagnant, boring, dead. Whenever you start to use the passive, ask yourself whether the sentence might sound better in the active. Often it will.

(For a full discussion of the active and passive voice, see chapter 22.)

25.4 Ask Questions

Break the forward march of your statements with an occasional question. For example:

One technical definition of a system is as follows: a system is a structure of interacting, intercommunicating components that, as a group, act or operate individually and jointly to achieve a common goal through the concerted activity of the individual parts. That is, of course, a completely satisfactory definition of the earth, except maybe for that last part about a common goal. What on earth is *our* common goal? How did we ever get mixed up in a place like this?

This is the greatest discomfort for our species. Some of us simply write it off by announcing that our situation is ridiculous, that the whole place is ungovernable, and that our responsibilities are therefore to ourselves alone. And yet, there it is; we are components in a dense, fantastically complicated system of life, we are

enmeshed in the interliving, and we really don't know what we're
up to.   —Lewis Thomas, *The Medusa and the Snail*

Thomas doesn't pretend to have all the answers; what he does have
are questions about the common goal of mankind on earth. You
can ask questions too. Don't feel bound to make every sentence a
statement, to write as if you knew all there is to know about your
subject. Get your curiosity out front. Make it generate questions,
and get the questions into your writing. Questions let you speculate
out loud, let you wonder what other people are thinking—or may
have thought:

> He falls back upon the bed awkwardly. His stumps, unweighted
> by legs and feet, rise in the air, presenting themselves. I unwrap
> the bandages from the stumps, and begin to cut away the black
> scabs and the dead, glazed fat with scissors and forceps. A shard of
> white bone comes loose. I pick it away. I wash the wounds with
> disinfectant and redress the stumps. All this while, he does not speak.
> What is he thinking behind those lids that do not blink? Is he re-
> membering a time when he was whole? Does he dream of feet?
> —Richard Selzer, "The Discus Thrower"

Questions like these can draw the reader into the very heart of
your subject. And questions can do more than advertise your curiosity. They can also voice your conviction. In conversation you
sometimes ask a question that assumes a particular answer—don't
you? Such a question is called **rhetorical,** and you can use it in
writing as well as in speech. It will challenge your readers, prompt-
ing them either to agree with you or to explain to themselves why
they do not. And why shouldn't you challenge your readers now
and then?

25.5 Cut Any Words You Don't Need

To make your writing lively, make it lean. Cut away the verbal fat
that slows it down to a ponderous crawl. For a full discussion of
how to eliminate wordiness, see section 9.11.

EXERCISE 2   **Revising to Invigorate Style**

Doing this exercise requires knowledge of how to use coordination and
subordination in connecting sentences. If you don't yet know how to use
these methods, see chapter six.

Following are three sets of sentences. The first has been put together
for you as an example. Turn each of the other two sets into a short essay
in which you (1) vary sentence length and structure, (2) use verbs of action
as much as possible, and (3) ask at least one question. For a clear idea of
what is to be done, study the example carefully before you begin.

EXAMPLE
Mr. and Mrs. Ault were once owners of Frederick Douglass.
They were residents of Baltimore.
At this time Frederick learned to read.
He asked Mrs. Ault to help him learn.
He felt safe in doing so.
She thought of him more as a child than as a slave.
Those of course were not the only alternatives.
She could have seen him as a man.
But at least he was more in her eyes than a piece of property.
His request would have been a shock to other slaveholders.
They would have thrashed him just for making it.
But it was not a shock to Mrs. Ault.
She was willing to help.
Frederick learned the alphabet under her care.
He began to read simple verses in the Bible.
Then Mr. Ault intervened.
He forbade his wife to continue the lessons.
He believed that learning would be the ruin of Frederick as a slave.
But fortunately Frederick had learned enough to teach himself more.
Soon he became an excellent reader.

ESSAY: Frederick Douglass learned to read while he was owned by Mr. and Mrs. Ault of Baltimore. He felt safe in asking Mrs. Ault to help him learn, for she thought of him more as a child than as a slave. Those of course were not the only alternatives. Couldn't she have seen him as a man? But at least he meant more in her eyes than a piece of property. Though his request would have shocked other slaveholders, who would have thrashed him just for making it, it did not shock Mrs. Ault; she wanted to help him. Under her care Frederick learned the alphabet and began to read simple verses in the Bible. Then Mr. Ault intervened. He forbade his wife to continue the lessons because he believed that learning would ruin Frederick as a slave. But fortunately Frederick had learned enough to teach himself more, and he soon became an excellent reader.

SET A
1. Scott's mother took him to the Palace courtyard once a week.
2. They stayed there for half an hour.
3. They watched the Palace Guards.
4. Scott loved the Guards.
5. They each wore bright-red boots.
6. They each wore dark-blue stockings.
7. The stockings were knee-high.
8. They each wore white kilts.
9. They each wore a stiff white shirt.
10. The shirt had a closed collar.
11. They each wore a magnificent jacket.
12. The jacket was like a blazing fire.
13. It had silver sparkles.
14. It had shining gold epaulets.

15. It had red embroidery.
16. The whole uniform was topped by a black beret.
17. The black beret had a long tassle.
18. The tassle hung down below the jaw.
19. The guards marched in this uniform.
20. They marched back and forth across the Palace courtyard.
21. They were all over six feet tall.
22. They held their rifles firmly against their right shoulders.
23. No boy could watch all of this without wishing.
24. Scott wished something.
25. He could someday be with them.

SET B

1. He had been running on level ground for half an hour.
2. Then suddenly the hill was ahead of him.
3. It rose up.
4. It looked as steep as a wall.
5. He didn't know whether he could get up that wall without stopping.
6. But he would damn well try.
7. He breathed heavily.
8. He relaxed his arms and shoulders.
9. His stride was shortened.
10. He started landing on his toes instead of his heels.
11. Then his whole body was pushed forward into the hill.
12. There was a push back made by the hill.
13. He pumped his arms against the hill.
14. His knees rose upward one after the other.
15. They came up almost to his chest.
16. The balls of his feet bounded off the solid ground.
17. He was a watcher of the ground ahead.
18. He wanted to be sure of his footing.
19. He couldn't afford to slip on pine needles.
20. He couldn't afford to slide on a loose bit of stone.
21. He kept moving.
22. He took quick, deep breaths.
23. He lengthened his stride at a certain point.
24. He was nearing the top of the hill.
25. Finally the ground leveled off.
26. He could ease his pace.
27. He had reached the top.

III

PUNCTUATION AND MECHANICS

26

THE COMMA

The comma separates or sets off words and groups of words within sentences. This chapter explains how to use the comma correctly and how to avoid misusing it.

26.1 Using Commas with Conjunctions

Use a comma before a conjunction *(and, but, for, or, nor, so, yet)* linking two independent clauses:

> Canadians watch America closely, *but* most Americans know little about Canada.
> The prospectors hoped to find gold on the rocky slopes of the Sierra Madre, *so* they set out eagerly.
> The cowards never started on the long trek west, *and* the weak died along the way.

(For more on conjunctions, see sections 13.2 and 13.3.)

26.2 Misusing Commas with Conjunctions $\curvearrowright$ *conj*

1. Do not use a comma before a conjunction that links a pair of words or phrases:

> *He was genial, but shrewd.
> REVISED: He was genial but shrewd.
> *I phoned the store, and asked to speak with the manager.
> REVISED: I phoned the store and asked to speak with the manager.

2. Except as noted below, do not use a comma after a conjunction:

> *I could not find the light switch, *so,* I had to grope my way through the house.
> REVISED: I could not find the light switch, *so* I had to grope my way through the house.
> *Mr. Martin worked me hard. *But,* he never demanded more of me than of himself.
> REVISED: Mr. Martin worked me hard. *But* he never demanded more of me than of himself.

EXCEPTION: Use a pair of commas after a conjunction to set off a word, phrase, or clause:

> Mr. Martin worked me hard. But, I have to admit, he never demanded more of me than of himself.

(On misusing commas with *and* in a series of items, see 26.8.)

26.3 Misusing Commas between Independent Clauses—The Comma Splice ⊙ *cs*

Do not use a comma alone between two independent clauses:

> *The beams have rotted, they can no longer support the roof.

This sentence illustrates the error known as the comma splice. To correct the error, you must either replace the comma or add a conjunction:

> REVISED: The beams have rotted; they can no longer support the roof. [or] The beams have rotted, so they can no longer support the roof.

(For a full discussion of the comma splice, see section 13.7.)

EXERCISE 1   Using Commas with Conjunctions

Each of the following may require the addition or removal of a comma before a conjunction. Make any changes necessary. If an entry is correct as it stands, write *Correct.*

EXAMPLE
We can stop for the night in Moose Jaw or we can push on to Regina.
REVISED: We can stop for the night in Moose Jaw, or we can push on to Regina.

1. Grant may have lost the battle but he left the enemy weakened beyond recovery.
2. My grandfather never carried his gun into the woods above Southport for he loved the sight and sound of the wildlife there.

3. The captured sailors received no message from Admiral Walker nor had they expected to receive one.

4. The traditional approach to landscape painting bored him so he experimented with radically different methods of depicting light.
5. Columbus wanted to find a new way of reaching the Indies and he also hoped to prove a new theory about the shape of the earth.
6. Quarterbacks regularly pass the football and sometimes run with it.
7. Odysseus longs to return to his home on Ithaca but he does not reach the island for ten years.
8. The firemen felt helpless for they could do nothing to rescue the child.
9. Antarctica has always attracted scientists, for, its chief wealth is the gold of knowledge.
10. The collapse of the East Antarctic Ice Sheet could raise worldwide sea levels by twenty feet, so, scientists are studying the ice sheet closely.

26.4 Using Commas after Introductory Elements

1. Use a comma after an introductory clause, phrase, or word:

> Whenever it rains hard, the roof leaks.
> After the final concert of the season, the musicians celebrated with a party.
> To prepare for the bar exam, Jan attended a tutoring school after work.
> Encouraged by the applause, the pianist played an encore.
> Eyes flashing, Gretta stood up and denounced the speaker.
> Unfortunately, a blizzard closed the airport for two days.

2. Use a comma after a conjunctive adverb at the beginning of a sentence or clause:

> Labor unions no longer denounce the use of robots in manufacturing. Nevertheless, some of the problems caused by automation remain unsolved.
> Auto workers have stopped demanding big wage increases each year; on the other hand, they are asking for job security.

(For more on conjunctive adverbs, see section 13.5.)

EXCEPTION: You may sometimes omit the comma after an introductory adverb or short introductory phrase:

> Today students protest individually rather than in concert.
> —Caroline Bird

> Throughout the 1930s the number of addicts remained about the same in both England and the United States.   —Edward Bunker

EXERCISE 2 Using Commas after Introductory Elements

Each of the following may require a comma after an introductory element. Add a comma if needed. If the entry is correct as it stands, write *Correct*.

EXAMPLE
Furthermore an increase in property taxes would severely limit the number of young adults who could live in the area.
REVISED: Furthermore, an increase in property taxes would severely limit the number of young adults who could live in the area.

1. To cope with the heavy fogs many fishermen have installed radar equipment in their boats.
2. Nevertheless left-handed pitchers have an advantage over most left-handed batters.
3. Unable to think of a topic the student stared glumly at his pencil.
4. During the intermission following the second act the lead tenor collapsed in his dressing room.
5. Laughter is good for the soul; in addition it may also be good for the lungs.
6. On the other hand no one likes to get a zero after studying hard for five hours.
7. To avoid a catastrophe, we must negotiate with the Soviets.
8. Although there were three holes in the bottom of the canoe we started to paddle across the lake.

26.5 Using Commas with Nonrestrictive Elements

Use a comma or a pair of commas to set off **nonrestrictive** elements: words, phrases, and clauses that are not essential to the meaning of the sentences in which they appear:

Anyone *who publishes a book at the age of six* must be remarkable.
Dorothy Straight of Washington, D.C., *who published her first book at the age of six,* was a remarkable child.

In the first sentence, the *who* clause is essential to the meaning of the sentence because it restricts the meaning of *Anyone*. Without the clause the sentence would say something fundamentally different: *Anyone must be remarkable*. In the second sentence, the *who* clause is nonrestrictive because it does not restrict the meaning of *Dorothy Straight*. Without the clause, the sentence would be fundamentally unchanged: *Dorothy Straight of Washington, D.C., was a remarkable child*.

Now compare these two sentences:

At the microphone stood a man *wearing a green suit*. [restrictive]
At the microphone stood Willy, *wearing a green suit*. [nonrestrictive]

In the first sentence the italicized phrase is restrictive because it identifies *a man*. In the second sentence, the italicized phrase is nonrestrictive because the man has already been identified by his name. The phrase just adds further information about him.

The distinction between restrictive and nonrestrictive is commonly applied to adjective clauses (such as *who publishes a book at the age of six*) and adjective phrases (such as *wearing a green suit*). Broadly speaking, however, nonrestrictive elements include anything that *supplements* the basic meaning of the sentence, anything not essential to that meaning. Here are further examples:

> Running, *a good thing to be doing for its own sake,* has acquired the medicinal value formerly attributed to rare herbs from Indonesia.
> —Lewis Thomas
> At midnight, *long after the final out of the game,* the losing coach was still shaking his head in disbelief.
> The tour includes three days in Toronto, *which must be one of the cleanest cities in the world.*
> The Atomic Age began in 1945, *when the United States dropped two atomic bombs on Japan.*
> The surgeon, *her hands moving deftly,* probed the wound.
> Most of the toys were expensive; a rocket, *for instance,* carried a price tag of $75.50.
> Fearful, *not confident,* he embarked on his journey.
> By the time they reach adolescence, most girls, *unconsciously or not,* have learned enough about role definition to qualify for a master's degree.   —Betty Rollin
> In the seventh inning, *however,* the pitcher lost his control.
> The tornado left the town in ruins; a few buildings, *though,* still rose up out of the rubble.
> François Truffaut, *the film director,* died of cancer in 1984.

26.6 Misusing Commas with Restrictive Elements   (,) *res*

Do not use commas with restrictive elements: with words, phrases, or clauses essential to the meaning of the sentences in which they appear.

> *All entries, *postmarked later than July 1,* will be discounted.

The italicized phrase is restrictive because without it, the meaning of the sentence would be fundamentally changed. Such a phrase should not be set off by commas:

> REVISED: All entries *postmarked later than July 1* will be discounted.

In the following sentences, the italicized items are all restrictive:

> Volcanoes *pumping ash into the air* can add a streak of color to sunsets thousands of miles away.   —Thomas Powers
> Police arrested everyone *who was carrying a rifle.*
> The pie was so hot *that I burned my tongue with a bite of it.*
> The crowd stood up *when the band began playing the national anthem.*

No one *without a ticket* will be admitted.
Film director *François Truffaut* died of cancer in 1984.

A name that follows a common noun or noun phrase is restrictive and should not be set off by commas. But when the name comes first, the common noun that follows it is nonrestrictive and *should* be set off by commas, as shown in the last example of section 26.5.

EXERCISE 3   **Punctuating Restrictive and Nonrestrictive Elements**

Decide whether each of the italicized elements is restrictive or nonrestrictive, and add or remove commas where necessary. If a sentence is correct as it stands, write *Correct.*

EXAMPLES
All motorists, *who drive recklessly,* should have their licenses suspended for six months.
DECISION: restrictive
REVISED: All motorists who drive recklessly should have their licenses suspended for six months

Tom Wilson *looking sharp in a red blazer* led the singing.
DECISION: nonrestrictive
REVISED: Tom Wilson, looking sharp in a red blazer, led the singing.

1. Young couples *hoping to buy a house* are faced with high interest rates.
2. A man, *carrying a rifle,* walked into the restaurant.
3. Muriel had to jump from the sailboat to retrieve the rudder *which had slipped out of its bracket.*
4. At approximately 2:30 P.M. *when most inhabitants of the village were taking a siesta* firecrackers began popping in the square.
5. Motorists are required to replace every tire *with tread less than ³⁄₁₆ of an inch thick.*
6. Bathrobes with horizontal stripes should not be worn by men, *weighing over two hundred pounds.*
7. A free twenty-pound turkey will be given to every customer, *holding an orange ticket stub.*
8. A medal was awarded to the platoon leader by Colonel Grant *his regimental commander.*
9. If a nuclear war breaks out, the smoke from burning cities may block the light and heat of the sun, *until all living things die.*
10. No one wants roommates *that yodel all night.*
11. The runner-up stared at the silver trophy *his mouth twisting in a grotesque smile.*
12. The defense attorney *on the other hand* was a waspish man with an intimidating manner.
13. Motorists have been cautioned to avoid places *where flooding has been reported.*
14. Many in the village believe that the eerie moaning comes from the ghost of a woman *slain by pirates in the 1700s.*
15. The drivers have agreed to race again, *but only in dry weather.*

16. The old Stanton House *its golden dome glistening in the sunlight* attracts thousands of visitors every summer.

17. The courthouse *says the guidebook* is the only seventeenth-century building to be found in the city.

18. Napoleon's greatest mistake *according to some historians* was his decision to invade Russia.

19. The opera will be performed in January *not March*.

20. The mayor has come under attack from several quarters. Her associates *however* insist that she will seek reelection.

26.7 Using Commas with Coordinate Items in Series

1. Use commas to separate three or more coordinate items in a series:

> Sally, Beth, and Cathy were reading in the library.
> The cat awoke, stretched, and leaped from the chair.
> The sentry asked us who we were, where we had come from, why we had entered a restricted zone, and what we planned to do there.

Note that a comma precedes the *and* that links the final item to the others.

2. Use commas to separate two or more coordinate adjectives modifying the same noun:

> The man spoke in a low, mysterious voice.
> A big, old, dilapidated house stood on the corner.

When items in a series are long or internally punctuated, use semicolons between them. (See p. 435.)

26.8 Misusing Commas with Coordinate Items in a Series ⟨⁷⟩ *ser*

1. Do not use a comma to separate adjectives when they are not coordinate—that is, when they do not both modify the same noun:

> *His deep, blue eyes stared at me.
> REVISED: His deep blue eyes stared at me.

If you aren't sure whether the adjectives are coordinate, try reversing them. Coordinate adjectives can be reversed: A *low, mysterious* voice can become a *mysterious, low* voice. But *deep blue* eyes cannot become *blue deep* eyes.

2. Do not use a comma before *and* in a compound phrase with just two items:

*The man carried a blue suitcase, and a red umbrella.
REVISED: The man carried a blue suitcase and a red umbrella.

3. Do not use a comma between *and* and the last item in a series:

*The speaker coughed, studied his notes, and, frowned in dismay.
REVISED: The speaker coughed, studied his notes, and frowned in dismay.

EXERCISE 4 Using Commas with Items in a Series

Each of the following may require the addition or removal of a comma or commas. Make the necessary changes. If an entry is correct as it stands, write *Correct.*

EXAMPLE
Under the circumstances, only an intelligent discreet and experienced official should be assigned to the case.
REVISED: Under the circumstances, only an intelligent, discreet, and experienced official should be assigned to the case.

1. The motor coughed wheezed sputtered and died.
2. Strands of thick heavy rope were strewn about the freshly varnished desk of the venerable merchant ship.
3. Our guide was slow to rise in the morning slow to work during the day and quick to eat at night.
4. The carpenter's chest contained a tape measure two chisels some nails and a hammer.
5. The toilet kit contained a razor, and five Band-Aids.
6. Lumberjacks were felling trees, cutting them into logs, and, clearing underbrush.
7. Carefully expertly and patiently, he listened to the sound of the tumblers as he turned the combination lock.

26.9 Using Commas to Prevent a Misreading

Use a comma when you need one to prevent a misreading of your sentence:

*On the left walls of sheer ice rose over five thousand feet into the clouds.
REVISED: On the left, walls of sheer ice rose over five thousand feet into the clouds.

26.10 Using Commas with Dates, Addresses, Greetings, Names, and Large Numbers

1. Use commas to set off successive items in dates and addresses:

On the afternoon of July 1, 1963, the fighting began.
The return address on the letter was 23 Hockney Street, Lexington, Kentucky 40502.

2. Use commas to set off the name of someone directly addressed in a sentence:

> A few weeks ago, Mr. Taplow, I spoke to you on the telephone about the possibility of a summer job.

3. Use a comma after the greeting in a friendly or informal letter, and after the closing in a letter of any kind:

> Dear Mary,   Sincerely,
> Dear Uncle Paul,   Yours truly,

4. Use commas to set off titles or degrees after a person's name:

> Barbara Kane, M.D., delivered the commencement address.

But *Jr., Sr.,* and *III* may be written without commas:

> Sammy Davis Jr. started his singing career at age four.

5. Use a comma after the last part of a proper name when the last part comes first:

> Lunt, George D.

6. Use commas to mark groups of three digits in large numbers,

> Antarctica is 5,400,000 square miles of ice-covered land.

26.11 Misusing Commas with Addresses and Dates ⊘ *a/d*

1. Do not use a comma to separate the name of a month from the day:

> *October, 22   *15, May
> REVISED: October 22   REVISED: 15 May

2. Do not use a comma to separate a street number from the name of the street:

> *15, Amsterdam Avenue
> REVISED: 15 Amsterdam Avenue

3. Do not use a comma to separate the name of a state, province, or country from the zip code:

> *Lebanon, New Hampshire, 03766
> REVISED: Lebanon, New Hampshire 03766
> *Toronto, Canada, M5S 1A1
> REVISED: Toronto, Canada M5S 1A1

4. Do not use a comma to separate the name of the month from the year when the day is not given or comes before the month:

| *January, 1982 | *22 April, 1939 |
| REVISED: January 1982 | REVISED: 22 April 1939 |

⊙ *bp*

EXERCISE 5 Using Commas with Dates, Addresses, Greetings, Names, and Large Numbers

Each of the following may require the addition or removal of commas. Make the necessary changes. If an entry is correct as it stands, write *Correct*.

EXAMPLE
The convoy reached Brussels Belgium on November 8 1942.
REVISED: The convoy reached Brussels, Belgium, on November 8, 1942.

1. Mail should be forwarded to Ms. Jane Flynt 22 Wheeler Avenue Wiscutt Massachusetts, 08566.
2. A crowd gathered outside 10 Downing Street to catch a glimpse of the prime minister.
3. The fireworks display on July 4 may be viewed from the roof of the Marine Terminal at 55 Shore Drive Rockport Oregon.
4. Before the fireworks display on July, 4, there will be a total of ten picnics for over 15500 people.
5. Martin Smith M.D. and his wife arrived in Montreal Canada on March 3 1982 and departed for Mexico City on April 15.
6. A total of 1750325 people had contributed to the fund by January 15 1984.
7. On 8 March 1985 Henry Stimpson LL.D. lectured on three recent decisions of the Supreme Court.

26.12 Using Commas with Quotation Marks

For a full discussion of how to use commas with quotation marks, see section 29.3.

26.13 Misusing the Comma between Basic Parts of a Sentence ⊙ *bp*

1. Do not use a comma between a subject and its predicate:

> *Voters with no understanding of the issue, should learn the facts.
> REVISED: Voters with no understanding of the issue should learn the facts.

2. Do not use a comma between a verb and its object:

> *For dessert we all had, strawberry shortcake.
> REVISED: For dessert we all had strawberry shortcake.
> *I could not understand, why she refused to see me.
> REVISED: I could not understand why she refused to see me.

In the following passage from Peter M. Lincoln's "Documentary Wallpapers," we have deliberately introduced some errors in punctuation. Remove all misused commas, add any that are needed, and leave any that are correctly used.

Many early American homes, were decorated with block-printed wallpapers. Imported from England, and France, the papers made the arrival of ships from abroad an exciting event for Colonial homemakers. Merchants, looking for sales, advertised that paper-
5 ing was cheaper than whitewashing, and, they urged would-be customers to examine the endless variety of brightly colored patterns. Indeed by today's standards the colors in many Colonial papers seem vibrant, intense, and, even gaudy. One wonders whether the citizens of Boston Massachusetts and Providence Rhode Island,
10 yearned for bright reds, greens, and, blues because of the grey, New England winters.

The process of reproducing historic wallpapers, requires the finesse of a craftsman. To establish a particular paper's full pattern, the expert may have to fit together the fragments of surviving sam-
15 ples, which he finds in museums in the attics of old houses and even under layers of other papers. He determines the original hue of the colors in various ways: he runs chemical tests, or, he matches a fragment to a fresh original in some museum, even then he must be careful before proceeding to the next step printing the design.
20 As a final precaution therefore he makes, a blacklight examination knowing it may reveal otherwise indistinguishable elements of the pattern.

One of the leading experts in America is Dorothy Waterhouse cofounder of Waterhouse Hangings. She first became interested in
25 historic wallpapers in 1932 when she was restoring, an old house on Cape Cod Massachusetts. While stripping the walls in one room she got down to the eighth, and bottom layer of paper. She became very excited, she knew it had to be over 140 years old. That discovery was the first of many. Today she has a collection of some three
30 hundred historic wallpapers, all carefully stored in her Boston home.

27

THE SEMICOLON AND
THE COLON

27.1 Using the Semicolon   ;

1. Use a semicolon to join two independent clauses that are closely related in meaning:

> Insist on yourself; never imitate.   —Ralph Waldo Emerson
> During the summer the resort is crowded with tourists; during the winter only sea gulls perch on the benches or walk the beach.

2. Use a semicolon to join two independent clauses when the second begins with or includes a conjunctive adverb:

> Shakespeare's plays are nearly four hundred years old; nevertheless, they still speak to us.
> The voters have rejected a plan to widen Main Street; truckers, therefore, will have to find an alternate route through town.

(For more on semicolons and conjunctive adverbs, see section 13.5.)

3. Use a semicolon to separate independent clauses linked by a conjunction if commas appear in the clauses:

> By laughing at our faults, we can learn to acknowledge them graciously; and we can try to overcome them in a positive, even cheerful way, not grimly and disagreeably.

Instead of the semicolon here and in the preceding examples, you could use a period, making two sentences. But the semicolon allows you to keep closely related ideas in one sentence.

4. Use semicolons to emphasize the division between items in a se- |
ries when one or more of the items include commas:

> There were three new delegates at the meeting: Ms. Barbara Smith from Red Bank, New Jersey; Ms. Beth Waters from Pocumtuck, Massachusetts; and Mr. James Papson from Freeport, Maine.

27.2 Misusing the Semicolon ⊙

1. Do not use a semicolon between a phrase and the clause to which it belongs:

> *The climbers carried an extra nylon rope with them; to ensure their safe descent from the cliff.
> REVISED: The climbers carried an extra nylon rope with them to ensure their safe descent from the cliff.

2. Do not use a semicolon between a subordinate clause and the main clause:

> *Most of the crowd had left; before the concert ended.
> REVISED: Most of the crowd had left before the concert ended.

3. Do not use a semicolon to introduce a list:

> *The prophets denounced three types of wrongdoing; idolatry, injustice, and neglect of the needy.

Use a colon (as discussed in the next section) for this purpose:

> REVISED: The prophets denounced three types of wrongdoing: idolatry, injustice, and neglect of the needy.

EXERCISE 1   Using Semicolons

Each of the following requires the addition or removal of one or more semicolons. Make any necessary changes, adding other punctuation if appropriate.

> EXAMPLE
> Some people give others take.
> REVISED: Some people give; others take.

1. The company increased its sales by over 20 percent in the third and fourth quarters, however, the directors have voted not to declare a dividend.
2. Weary fire fighters see no way of extinguishing the flames; unless the strong winds subside.
3. The newcomers brought needed manpower and supplies to the small community, on the other hand, they also brought unwanted customs and ideas.

4. The Gateway Arch in St. Louis symbolizes the soaring aspirations of the pioneers; who ventured forth into unknown lands.
5. The old reception center lacks office space, a comfortable lounge, and adequate restrooms, nevertheless, many people like it.
6. During the first stage of the trip, tourists visit London, the capital of Great Britain, Paris, the capital of France, Madrid, the capital of Spain, and Rome, Italy, the oldest capital of them all.
7. Winter brings skiers to the region, summer brings mosquitoes.
8. A basketball team has five players; a center, two forwards, and two guards.
9. The sight of the statue with the torch of liberty caused many on the ship to weep, at last they were free.
10. A bull-master in government is like Tarzan in the jungle, swinging from office to office on vines of grandiloquent rhetoric, in contrast, the plain-talker is fed to the lions. —Sean Maloney

27.3 Using the Colon :

1. Use a colon to introduce a list coming at the end of a sentence:

Passengers may have one of four beverages: coffee, tea, milk, or soda.

2. Use a colon to introduce an example or an explanation related to something just mentioned:

The animals have a good many of our practical skills: some insects make pretty fair architects, and beavers know quite a lot about engineering. —Northrop Frye

3. Use a colon to introduce a quotation (usually of more than one line) in an essay:

In the opening sentence of his novel *Scaramouche,* Rafael Sabatini says of his hero: "He was born with the gift of laughter, and a sense that the world was mad."

4. Use a colon to follow the salutation in a formal letter:

Dear Mayor:
Dear Mr. Watson:
To Whom It May Concern:

5. Use a colon to separate hours from minutes when the time of day is shown in numerals:

8:40   6:30   11:15

27.4 Misusing the Colon ⊙

1. Do not use a colon after *such as, including,* or a form of the verb *be:*

> *On rainy days we played board games such as: Monopoly, Scrabble, and Trivial Pursuit.
> REVISED: On rainy days we played board games such as Monopoly, Scrabble, and Trivial Pursuit.
> *I woke up to find that someone had taken all of my valuables, including: my watch, my camera, my passport, and all of my money.
> REVISED: I woke up to find that someone had taken all of my valuables, including my watch, my camera, my passport, and all of my money.
> *In the kit were: soap, matches, an axe, and water.
> REVISED: In the kit were soap, matches, an axe, and water.

2. Do not use a colon between a verb and its object or between a preposition and its object:

> *In less than two minutes, the assailant knocked out: Bob, John, and Harold.
> REVISED: In less than two minutes, the assailant knocked out Bob, John, and Harold.
> *Before heading home, we stopped at: the supermarket, the hardware store, and the gas station.
> REVISED: Before heading home, we stopped at the supermarket, the hardware store, and the gas station.

EXERCISE 2   Using Colons

Each of the following requires the addition or removal of one or more colons. Make any necessary change.

EXAMPLE
The Council has received recommendations from: seniors, juniors, and freshmen.
REVISED: The Council has received recommendations from seniors, juniors, and freshmen.

1. The plane should arrive in Montreal at 4 30 P.M.
2. La Rochefoucauld punctures the illusions of many in a maxim about pity "We are all strong enough to endure the misfortunes of others."
3. On display were: a diamond necklace, a pair of gold earrings, a pin with four rubies, and a diamond engagement ring.
4. The 12 30 broadcast will offer music by the following composers Bach, Mozart, Debussy, and Copeland.
5. To Whom It May Concern We, the undersigned, hereby declare our unyielding support of the Union. Long may it stand!

EXERCISE 3   Using Semicolons and Colons

In the following passage from Ismene Phylactopoulou's "Greek Easter," we have deliberately removed some of the author's punctuation. Add a semicolon or a colon wherever necessary.

EXAMPLE
line 1: 10:00

The events on Good Friday are tragic. At 10 00 a grim-looking priest conducts a solemn service Christ is removed from the Cross and placed in a tomb. All work ceases flags fly at half mast. Soldiers carry their rifles reversed as they do during funeral processions.
5 Offices and shops close everyone goes to church. The church bells will toll all day long. After the service the young girls of the parish perform a bitter-sweet task they decorate the bier of Jesus with flowers from 11 00 to 1 00. By that time it is a mass of flowers.

Lunch consists of simple fare boiled lentils, which represent the
10 tears of the Virgin, and vinegar, which represents the vinegar given to Christ on the Cross.

On Friday evening the church is filled to overflowing. All in the city are present old men and women, officials, husbands and wives, children. The songs of mourning are lovely in their sadness for
15 example, in one of them Mary refers to her dead son as a child who was as sweet as spring. After the service, which usually ends at 9 00, a kind of funeral procession takes place. It follows a definite order first comes a band playing a funeral march next comes a priest carrying the Cross then comes the bier accompanied by girls in
20 white, the Boy Scouts, and a detachment of soldiers then come the other priests. The people follow, each carrying a brown candle. The gathering has spiritual meaning it is also deeply human.

28

END MARKS

The punctuation marks used to end sentences are the period, the question mark, and the exclamation point. The period is also used to mark the end of some abbreviations.

.

28.1 Using the Period .

Use a period—

1. To mark the end of a declarative sentence, a mild command, or an indirect question:

> The days are growing shorter, and the nights are becoming cool.
> On some highways in Germany there is no speed limit.
> Drivers choose their own speed.
> Please send me the report.
> The taxi driver asked us where we wanted to go.

When typing, skip two spaces after the period before beginning the next sentence.

2. To mark the end of some abbreviations:

Dr. Boyle	Mr. G. H. Johnson
500 Fifth Ave.	Mrs. L. S. Allingham
N.Y., N.Y.	Ms. N. A. Stephens
Kate Fansler, Ph.D.	3 P.M.
	350 B.C.

Generally, you don't need periods with acronyms (words formed from the initials of a multiword title), with capital-letter abbreviations of technical terms, or with abbreviated names of states, agencies, and organizations:

CBS	ROTC	IBM
NATO	TVA	IQ
FM	ID	KP
NY	CIA	VISTA
CA		

But you do need periods with B.C. and A.D., and with abbreviations standing for the names of political entities:

U.S.A.   U.K.   U.S.S.R.

For guidance, see your dictionary.

3. To mark letters or numerals used in vertical lists:

The handbook describes four kinds of cycles:

1. unicycles
2. bicycles
3. tricycles
4. motorcycles

If you give the information in a sentence, enclose the letters or numbers within parentheses and omit the periods:

The handbook has interesting descriptions of (1) unicycles, (2) bicycles, (3) tricycles, and (4) motorcycles.

28.2 Misusing the Period ⊙

1. In formal writing, do not use a period to separate the parts of a sentence. If you do, you will create a sentence fragment:

*Customers should be treated courteously. Even if they are rude.
REVISED: Customers should be treated courteously even if they are rude.

(For more on sentence fragments, see chapter 17.)

2. Do not use a period after another period or other end mark:

*We have ordered materials from Home Supplies Company, Inc..
REVISED: We have ordered materials from Home Supplies Company, Inc.
*Harry always used to ask, "Where's the fire?".
REVISED: Harry always used to ask, "Where's the fire?"

EXERCISE 1   Using Periods

Each of the following may require the addition or removal of one or more periods. Make any necessary change; also make any accompanying change in capitalization that may be required. If an entry is correct as it stands, write *Correct*.

EXAMPLE
Dr Brenda Lange is scheduled to present a paper on kinesics at Friday's meeting.
REVISED: Dr. Brenda Lange is scheduled to present a paper on kinesics at Friday's meeting.

1. Please remove all litter. Before leaving the picnic area
2. Mr and Mrs Frank I. Thomas will ask the mayor why the town has failed to install street lights in their neighborhood
3. No one wants to rent an apartment at 10 South Main Street. Because the incessant traffic is both noisy and dangerous
4. Delegates to the A.F.L.-C.I.O. convention in Chicago are asking when the secretary of labor will address them
5. I wonder how many peanut butter and jelly sandwiches are consumed in one day

28.3 Using the Question Mark ?

Use a question mark—

1. To mark the end of a direct question:

> Must the problems of the farmer be ignored?
> To what agency can the poor go for legal aid?

2. To indicate uncertainty within a statement:

> Some animal—a skunk?—is boring holes in the lawn at night.
> They must have paid a lot of money (fifty dollars?) for that meal.

28.4 Misusing the Question Mark (?)

Do not use a question mark at the end of an *indirect* question:

> *I wonder who wrote this song?
> REVISED: I wonder who wrote this song.

(For more on this point, see section 24.5.)

28.5 Using the Exclamation Point !

Use the exclamation point to mark the end of an exclamatory sentence, phrase, or word:

> Men are walking on the moon!
> What a spectacular view!
> Impossible!

28.6 Misusing the Exclamation Point $(!)$

Do not overuse exclamation points. Too many of them will dull your effect:

> *We finally got there! We thought we'd never make it!! But we were there at last!!!
> REVISED: We finally got there. We thought we'd never make it. But we were there at last!

EXERCISE 2   Using Question Marks and Exclamation Points

Each of the following may require a question mark or an exclamation point. Add any necessary punctuation. If an entry is correct as it stands, write *Correct.*

> EXAMPLE
> What is the weather forecast for Saturday
> REVISED: What is the weather forecast for Saturday?

1. A lion was loose in the park
2. One vehicle—was it a jeep—finished the whole three-thousand-mile course without a single breakdown.
3. What a shock
4. Customers often ask us where their typewriters can be repaired.
5. After giving me a written estimate for $175, why have you sent me a bill for $300

EXERCISE 3   Using Periods and Question Marks

Improve the punctuation in the following paragraph by adding a period or question mark wherever necessary; also make any accompanying change in capitalization that may be required. As you make these corrections, write out the entire paragraph.

> How do historians rate the contributions of Gen Gordon to his country their opinions differ some consider him a military genius, one of the greatest soldiers in British history others criticize him severely in their opinion C G Gordon, or "Chinese" Gordon as he was popularly known, acted impulsively he was rash he was dangerous he was not fit to hold a command did he seek death on Jan 26, 1885 historians give conflicting answers

29

QUOTATION MARKS
AND QUOTING

To quote is to repeat words written or spoken. In this chapter, we explain how to punctuate quotations clearly and correctly. We also explain how to use quotation marks for other purposes, such as punctuating certain titles.

29.1

29.1 Quoting Words, Phrases, and Short Passages of Prose

Use double quotation marks (" ") to enclose any words, phrases, or short passages quoted from speech, writing, or printed matter:

> After the murder of the old king in Shakespeare's *Macbeth,* Lady Macbeth imagines there is blood on her hand and cries, "Out, damned spot!"
> "An agnostic," writes Clarence Darrow, "is a doubter."
> At his press conference yesterday, the president said that his talk with the Soviet ambassador had been "fruitful."

In the last example, note how the quoted word fits into the writer's sentence structure. Here is another example:

> Smith writes that during his stay in London he was struck with "the beauty of the parks" and "the friendliness of the people."

(Quoted passages must normally be accompanied by identifying tags; see section 24.1A.)

29.2 Using Double and Single Quotation Marks

1. Use double quotation marks to enclose the words of speakers engaged in dialogue (conversation), and start a new paragraph each time the speaker changes:

> "How did the interview go?" Bob asked.
> "It's hard to say," said Helen. "At first I was nervous. Then I relaxed and spoke clearly. I even began to enjoy myself."
> "Well, it sounds as if you might get the job. If you do, let's celebrate."

2. Use single quotation marks (' ') to enclose a quotation within a quotation:

> At the beginning of the class, Professor Baker asked, "Where does Thoreau speak of 'quiet desperation' and what does he mean by this phrase?"

29.3 Using Quotation Marks with Other Punctuation

To punctuate quotations, you must often use quotation marks with other punctuation. Here are guidelines.

1. Use a comma or a colon to introduce a quotation:

> Frank said, "Let's buy some beer and a pizza."
> Carl Jung writes: "Ideas spring from something greater than the personal human being."

Most writers use a comma to introduce quoted speech, and a colon to introduce quoted writing. But you need neither a comma nor a colon to introduce a quoted word or phrase:

> The doctor said that Fenster "might not live."
> The president said the talks had been "encouraging."

2. Use a comma to mark the end of a quoted sentence that is followed by an identifying tag:

> "It's time to eat," said John.
> "I'm leaving tomorrow," said Nancy. "We can clean up when I get back."

But do not use the comma if the quoted sentence ends in a question mark or an exclamation point:

> "What's the evidence?" the scientist asks.
> "Get out!" he screamed.

As these examples show, even after a full stop the tag begins with a lower-case letter, not a capital.

3. Use a pair of commas to set off a tag that interrupts a quoted sentence, whether spoken or written:

> "I have noticed," Benwick Branch declared, "that no one else arrives at work on time."
> "Ideas," writes Carl Jung, "spring from something greater than the personal human being."

The second part of the quotation does not begin with a capital letter because it does not begin a new sentence. It completes the sentence that was interrupted by the tag.

4. Use a period to mark the end of a quoted statement that is not followed by a tag:

> John said, "I'm hungry."

5. When you use a comma or a period at the end of a quotation, put it *inside* the closing quotation mark:

> Though Thoreau wrote that most men "lead lives of quiet desperation," much of his book about Walden Pond expresses joy.
> One of the astronauts said, "The earth looked unbelievably beautiful from the spaceship."

6. When you use a semicolon or a colon at the end of a quotation, put it *outside* the closing quotation mark:

> The senator announced, "I will not seek reelection"; then he left the room.
> The new contract has "new benefits for women": payment for overtime, maternity leave, and seniority privileges.

7. When you use a question mark or an exclamation point at the end of a quotation, put it inside the closing quotation mark only if it belongs to the quotation; otherwise, put it outside:

> Who wrote, "What's in a name?"
> A new idea about the universe always prompts the scientist to ask, "What's the evidence for it?"
> Should the United States support Latin American governments that it considers "moderately repressive"?
> Suddenly he screamed, "Get out!"
> Yet the congressman simply dismissed the charge as "unimportant"!

Wherever you put the question mark or the exclamation point, do not use a period with it.

8. When *that* introduces a quotation, use no comma after it and no capital to start the quotation unless it begins with a proper name:

> Carl Jung writes that "ideas spring from something greater than the personal human being."

29.4 Quoting Long Prose Passages

To quote more than four lines of prose, use indentation instead of quotation marks. Introduce the quotation with a colon, double-space the quoted matter, and indent it ten spaces from the left margin of your own text:

```
Thoreau exhibits this strength of will in "Civil

Disobedience":

                I was not born to be forced.  I will

                breathe after my own fashion.  Let us see

                who is the strongest.  What force has a

                multitude?  They only can force me who obey a

                higher law than I.  They force me to become

                like themselves.  I do not hear of men being

                forced to live this way or that by masses of

                men.  What sort of life were that to live?

                When I meet a government which says to me,

                "Your money or your life," why should I be in

                haste to give it my money?
```

As the example shows, you should preserve any quotation marks and underlinings that appear within the quoted matter.

29.5 Quoting Two or More Paragraphs

When quoting two or more paragraphs, indent the left margin of the quoted matter ten spaces from the left margin of your own text, and indent the first line of each quoted paragraph three additional spaces:

```
At the end of his Inaugural Address, John F. Kennedy

declared:

                   And so, my fellow Americans: ask not what

                your country can do for you--ask what you can

                do for your country.
```

```
My fellow citizens of the world: ask not

what America will do for you, but what

together we can do for the freedom of man.

    Finally, whether you are citizens of

America or citizens of the world, ask of us

here the same high standards of strength and

sacrifice which we ask of you.  With a good

conscience our only sure reward, with history

the final judge of our deeds, let us go forth

to lead the land we love, asking His blessing

and His help, but knowing that here on earth

God's work must truly be our own.
```

29.6 Quoting Poetry

1. If you quote more than a single line of poetry within a sentence you must show where one line ends and another begins. Use a slash (/), with a space on each side, to mark the division:

```
Dylan Thomas wrote:  "The force that through the

green fuse drives the flower / Drives my green

age."
```

2. To quote more than three lines of poetry, double-space them and indent each line ten spaces from the left margin:

```
William Blake's "The Tyger" begins with the lines:

        Tyger!  Tyger!  burning bright

        In the forests of the night,

        What immortal hand or eye

        Could frame thy fearful symmetry?
```

If the lines are long, you may indent fewer than ten spaces. If a single line is long, let it run to the right-hand margin and put the overflow under the right-hand side:

Ruefully alluding to his own ill-fated marriage,

Byron rhetorically asks,

>   But-OH! ye lords of ladies intellectual,
>
>   Inform us truly, have they not hen-peck´d you
>
>   all?

(For more on quoting poetry, see section 35.2, nos. 12–14.)

29.7 Using Quotation Marks with Titles

Use double or single quotation marks with certain titles, as explained in section 32.3.

29.8 Punctuating Definitions, Sayings, and Words with Special Meanings

1. Use double quotation marks to define words:

> *Disinterested* means "impartial," "unbiased," "objective." As a verb, *censure* means "find fault with," or "reprimand."

2. Use double quotation marks to set off familiar sayings:

> "Where's the beef?" became a political battle cry in the spring of 1984.

3. Use double quotation marks to set off common words and phrases that you don't take at face value:

> When a man and woman decide to live together without being married, are they "living in sin"?
> In what sense is the German Democratic Republic "democratic"?

But use underlining (as discussed in section 32.2) to set off a word you refer to as a word:

>   The word <u>freedom</u> means different things to
>
>   different people.

29.9 Misusing Quotation Marks

1. Do not use quotation marks in indirect discourse:

> *The foreman said that "her crew had finished ahead of schedule."
> Revised: The foreman said that her crew had finished ahead of schedule.
> *Clients are asking "when the rates will go down."

REVISED: Clients are asking when the rates will go down.

(For a full discussion of indirect discourse, see sections 24.2 and 24.4.)

2. Do not use quotation marks for emphasis. Quotation marks can actually weaken a statement. For example:

> Joe's restaurant serves "good" pie. [TRANSLATION: They say it's good, but I know better.]

EXERCISE 1 Punctuating Quotations, Titles, Definitions, and Sayings

Punctuate the quotations, titles, definitions, and sayings in the following sentences.

EXAMPLE
We are all strong enough wrote La Rochefoucauld to endure the misfortunes of others.
REVISED: "We are all strong enough," wrote La Rochefoucauld, "to endure the misfortunes of others."

1. What writer asked, Who has deceived thee so oft as thyself
2. The professor concluded her lecture by saying, I hope each of you will read a few poems by Hopkins, especially one called The Windhover
3. Then the singer said, I wish I could remember the name of the person who wrote Brother, Can You Spare a Dime
4. Did Ambrose Bierce define a bore as a person who talks when you wish him to listen
5. Alexander Pope wrote, True wit is nature to advantage dressed, What oft was thought, but ne'er so well expressed
6. The history of life on earth says Rachel Carson has been a history of interaction between living things and their surroundings.
7. *Continual* means going on with occasional slight interruptions. *Continuous* means going on with no interruption.
8. Two of Faulkner's best short stories are Barn Burning and Dry September.
9. One of my favorite lines in The Star Spangled Banner, said Sarah, is By the dawn's early light.
10. Perhaps the poet John Donne was right when he wrote: One short sleep past, we wake eternally / And Death shall be no more.
11. My roommate torments me by repeating trite sayings like better safe than sorry.

EXERCISE 2 Punctuating Dialogue

Punctuate the quotations in the following passage. As you add the punctuation, write out the entire passage.

> Everything in Texas is big said the Texan to the Alaskan.
> Tell me about it said the Alaskan.
> Well, for one thing the Texan said we have the biggest jackrabbits in the world and the biggest cowboy hats.

5 That's impressive said the visitor. Anything else?

The smallest of our ranches is larger than most states, and we serve the biggest mint julep in the entire South. It takes the average person an entire week to finish one the Texan said. What have you-all got in Alaska?

10 The Alaskan smiled. Then he said That must seem like a mighty big drink to you folks. He paused, shaking his head. But I guess you couldn't know any better he said if you haven't seen the icebergs in Alaska. We use them for ice cubes.

30

Other Punctuation Marks

30.1 Using the Dash —

1. Use a dash to introduce a word, phrase, or clause that summarizes the words preceding it:

> The strikers included plumbers, electricians, carpenters, truck drivers, miners—all kinds of workers.

2. Use a dash to set off an interruption that is closely relevant to the sentence but not grammatically part of it:

> Everyone looked shabby—to be anything else is an affront to humanity in Prague—but almost everybody was full of the kind of joyful anticipation you see in North America only on the faces of five-year-olds watching a magician.　　　　　—Peter Newman

Less relevant interruptions may be set off by parentheses (as discussed in section 30.3).

3. Use a dash or a pair of dashes to set off a series of items in apposition to a preceding noun:

> Three of the senators—Cranston, Hollis, and Glenn—were relatively unknown to voters in the state.

4. Use a dash in dialogue to indicate an unfinished remark:

> "You wouldn't dare to—" Mabel gasped in disbelief.
> "But I would," he said. "In fact, I—"
> "No!" she screamed.

When the dash is used to indicate an unfinished remark, it should be followed only by quotation marks, not by a comma or period.

5. If dashes set off a parenthetical remark that asks a question or makes an exclamation, put the question mark or the exclamation point before the second dash:

> If Mayor Grant decides to run for reelection—how did he ever get elected in the first place?—none of the party officials will support him.

Note that the comma ordinarily used after an introductory adverb clause *(If . . .)* is omitted because of the dashes.

6. In typing, make a dash with two hyphens (--) and leave no space on either side.

30.2 Misusing the Dash

The main misuse is overuse. Too many dashes can make your writing seem breathless or fragmented:

> Merryl's new designs looked stunning—do they ever look otherwise?—with their bold colors and daring lines. She was cheered by all of the regulars—the regular staff, that is—who work in the art department. One of them—I think it was Harry—did a cartwheel—what a surprise that was!—and then shrieked till he was blue in the face. I thought Merryl would die of blushing—she's really modest, you know.

EXERCISE 1   Using Dashes

Add a dash or a pair of dashes as needed in the following sentences.

> EXAMPLE
> When we arrived in Warner it's about fifteen miles west of Concord we had the fan belt adjusted.
> REVISED: When we arrived in Warner—it's about fifteen miles west of Concord—we had the fan belt adjusted.

1. Helen, Mary, Barbara, and Gretchen all of the old gang had returned for their twenty-fifth reunion.
2. "When I arrived at the accident, I found" Barney faltered, his eyes filling with tears.
3. The Sox ought to draft three pitchers Finney, Marcott, and Prince.
4. In the third race the filly Hardtack the program listed her as belonging to Cranberry Stables set a track record.
5. Tell the director the truth whatever you know to be the facts.

30.3 Using Parentheses ( )

1. Use parentheses to enclose words, phrases, or complete sentences that offer a side comment or help to clarify a point:

> During last month's meeting at City Hall, opponents of the proposed leash law (they are certainly a vocal group) dominated the discussion.

A parenthesized sentence that appears within another sentence does not need a capital or a period. But otherwise it needs both:

> A well-known sight to millions of immigrants was the Statue of Liberty, designed by the French sculptor Frédéric-Auguste Bartholdi. (He himself never immigrated to America.) The statue still stands on a small island in New York harbor.

The insertion of parentheses *within* a sentence does not change the punctuation of the sentence itself. The closing parenthesis should be followed by a comma only if the comma would have been required without the parentheses, as in this sentence:

> Among those attending the concert were Peter Mengis, Roberta Green (the composer), and Reginald Grant.

2. Use parentheses to enclose numerals or letters introducing the items of a list:

> One of the selectmen supports the proposed change in traffic patterns for three reasons: (1) more customers would be attracted to the shopping area, (2) the hospital zone would become quieter, and (3) fire engines would be able to move more quickly than they now can.

3. Use parentheses to enclose numerals clarifying or confirming a spelled-out number:

> The law permits individuals to give no more than one thousand dollars ($1,000.00) to any one candidate in a campaign.

Like material put between dashes, a parenthetical insertion interrupts the flow of a sentence. Parentheses make the interruption less emphatic than dashes do, but since they do in fact break up the sentence, you should use them sparingly.

EXERCISE 2   Using Parentheses

Add parentheses as needed in the following sentences. Provide other punctuation as required.

EXAMPLE
Last night we saw an excellent performance of *Antigone* the version by Jean Anouilh and we were reminded how easily tyrants justify their actions.

REVISED: Last night we saw an excellent performance of *Antigone* (the version by Jean Anouilh), and we were reminded how easily tyrants justify their actions.

1. During a visit to the fortress at Louisbourg a historic site in Nova Scotia we saw dwellings inhabited in the 1700s.
2. A local philanthropist has pledged fifty thousand dollars $50,000.00 to the restoration fund.
3. Historic Nantucket Island it was the site of a major whaling port in the nineteenth century attracts thousands of visitors every summer.
4 Fenwick offered several excuses to justify his absence from the final examination: 1 he was meditating at the time, 2 he had misplaced the schedule, 3 he wanted to write his mother, and 4 he had a doctor's appointment.

30.4 Using Brackets [ ]

1. Use brackets to insert a clarifying detail, comment, or correction of your own into a passage written by someone else:

> "DeCato's bid [$850] sounds reasonable to me," declared Robert Grant, chairman of the school board.
> "When we last see Lady Macbeth [in the sleepwalking scene], she is obviously distraught."
> "The Allied invasion of Brittany [Normandy] began on June 6, 1944."
> "Only three other senators were present to hear the speech—Senators Brown, Stilmore, and Wiggins. [In reality, Senator Stilmore was in a hospital.] To a man, they called it the most eloquent attack on slavery they had ever heard."

When a misspelling occurs in quoted material, the Latin word *sic* ("thus") may be used to call attention to it, or the correct spelling may be given within the brackets:

> "There were no pieces of strong [*sic*] around the boxes," one witness wrote. [or] "There were no pieces of strong [string] around the boxes," one witness wrote.

Typewriters do not normally include keys for brackets. You may either put the brackets in by hand or construct them using the slash and underlining keys: [   ]

2. Do not use brackets when inserting comments into your own writing. Use parentheses or dashes.

EXERCISE 3 Using Dashes, Parentheses, and Brackets

Each of the following requires dashes, parentheses, or brackets. Using the comment in brackets as a guide, add the appropriate punctuation.

Example
The asking price for the clock a whopping $500,000 has not de-
terred some collectors from attending the auction. [The explanatory phrase is relevant and important.]
Revised: The asking price for the clock—a whopping $500,000—
has not deterred some collectors from attending the auction.

1. The number of acres allotted to one family may not be less than
   twenty-five 25 nor more than fifty 50. [The numerals clarify the
   spelled-out numbers.]
2. The pioneers celebrated Thanksgiving in the new settlement the
   exact location is unknown and then returned to Springfield for
   the winter. [The aside is relatively unimportant to the discussion.]
3. They eloped to Paris is there any better city for lovers? and had
   five glorious days before emerging to pay the piper. [The question is closely relevant to the narrative.]
4. "This song, which was composed by Bailey in 1928 1930, reflects
   the influences of his five years in New Orleans." [The second
   date represents your correction of a mistake in a sentence written by someone else.]
5. "The most popular recording of the song featured Bix Dandy
   on the trumpit trumpet." [The second spelling represents your
   correction of a misspelling in a passage written by someone else.]
6. The neighborhood needs three things: 1 paved roads, 2 traffic
   lights at every major intersection, and 3 a committee consisting
   of homeowners who would welcome and orient newcomers. [The
   numerals introduce the items in a list.]

30.5 Using Ellipsis Dots · · ·

1. Use three spaced dots—

a. To signal the omission of a word or words from the middle of
   a quoted sentence:

> Thoreau wrote, "We must learn to reawaken and keep ourselves
> awake . . . by an infinite expectation of the dawn, which does not
> forsake us in our soundest sleep."

In all cases, the material left out should be nonessential to the
meaning of what is quoted. Here, for example, the words omitted
are "not by mechanical aids, but."

b. To signal hesitation or halting speech in dialogue:

> "I . . . don't know what to say," he whispered.

In typing, leave one space before the first dot, between each pair
of dots, and after the last one.

2. Use four spaced dots—

  a. To show that you are omitting the end of a quoted sentence:

> Thoreau wrote, "We must learn to reawaken and keep ourselves awake, not by mechanical aids, but by an infinite expectation of the dawn. . . ."

Like all periods, the fourth dot comes before the closing quotation mark. Normally you may cut off the end of a quoted sentence in this way only if what remains makes a complete sentence.

  b. To show that you have omitted one or more whole sentences:

> "In other words," as Percy Marks says, "the spirit of football is wrong. 'Win at any cost' is the slogan of most teams, and the methods used to win are often abominable. . . . In nearly every scrimmage the roughest kind of unsportsmanlike play is indulged in, and the broken arms and ankles are often intentional rather than accidental."

  c. Use an entire line of spaced dots to signal that a line (or more) of poetry has been omitted:

> In the beginning was the word, the word.
> . . . .
> And from the cloudy bases of the breath
> The word flowed up, translating to the heart
> First characters of birth and death.   —Dylan Thomas

EXERCISE 4   Quoting with Ellipses

Select a passage of expository prose in a book or magazine. In three separate quotations from it, use ellipsis dots to signal omissions of (1) part of the middle of a sentence, (2) the end of a sentence, and (3) a complete sentence or more. Be careful to avoid distorting the meaning and tone of the original passage. Also, be sure to space the dots properly.

30.6 Using the Slash   /

1. Use a slash, or virgule, to indicate alternative words:

> Every writer needs to know at least something about his/her audience.

Leave no space before or after a slash used in this way.

2. Use a slash to mark off lines of poetry when you run them on as if they were prose:

> Coleridge introduces the mariner in the very first stanza: "It is an ancient Mariner, / And he stoppeth one of three."

Leave one space before and after a slash used in this way.

3. Use a slash in typing a fraction that is not on one of your typewriter keys:

2 1/2   5 7/8   15/16

31

SPELLING

"I have no respect," said Thomas Jefferson, "for a man who can think of only one way to spell a word." Not many of us would ever have lost Jefferson's respect on this account. Is it *e* before *i* in *neither*, we ask ourselves, or *i* before *e*? How many *r*'s are there in *occurrence*? Is it *separate* or *seperate*? If you've puzzled over questions like these while writing, you're in distinguished company; some of our best writers—among them Stephen Crane and F. Scott Fitzgerald—have been notoriously bad spellers. They have struggled with a language in which the sound of a word frequently diverges from the way it is spelled, a language in which the same set of letters may be sounded several different ways in several different words. The letters *ough*, for instance, are sounded four different ways in the words *rough*, *through*, *bough*, and *thorough*. No wonder George Bernard Shaw could demonstrate the irrationality of English by spelling fish "ghoti." As Shaw noted, the *f* sound of *gh* in *rough*, the *i* sound of *o* in *women*, and the *sh* sound of *ti* in *diction* will together make a fish—or, he might have said, a very fishy word.

Yet in spite of all these difficulties, careful writers learn to spell their words correctly. They do so because they know that misspelled words can confuse as well as annoy the reader. The difference between *principle* and *principal*, for instance, is a difference in meaning as well as in spelling.

How can you learn to spell all of your words correctly? No one method will guarantee success, but the following methods may help.

31.1 Listing Your Spelling Demons

Keep an analytical list of your spelling demons—words you have trouble spelling. After an essay has been marked by your teacher, make a list of all the words you have misspelled in it. Beside each of the words, write out the correct spelling, as shown in your dictionary. (If you can't find the word in the dictionary, ask your teacher for help.) Then, beside the correct spelling of the word, write out the letter or letters involved in the error. Your list will look like this:

MISSPELLED	CORRECTLY SPELLED	ERROR
alot	a lot	al/a l
neather	neither	ea/ei
cuting	cutting	t/tt
goverment	government	er/ern
silense	silence	se/ce
defensable	defensible	able/ible
imovable	immovable	im/imm
famuos	famous	uo/ou
neet	neat	ee/ea
boxs	boxes	s/es

31.2 Learning How to Add Suffixes

Learn how to add suffixes—extra letters at the end of a word.

1. Change final *y* to *i*. If the *y* at the end of a word follows a consonant, change it to *i* before adding a suffix:

beauty + ful = beautiful
bury + ed = buried
tricky + est = trickiest
carry + es = carries

EXCEPTION: If the suffix is *-ing*, keep the *y:*

carry + ing = carrying
bury + ing = burying

2. Drop silent *e*. If a word ends in a silent (unpronounced) *e,* drop the *e* before adding *-able* or *-ing:*

love + able = lovable
care + ing = caring

If any other suffix is added, keep the *e:*

care = ful = careful

EXCEPTION: If the silent *e* follows *c* or *g*, keep the *e* before *-able:*

> change + able = changeable
> peace + able = peaceable

3. If the word ends in a single consonant after a single vowel *(forget)* and the accent is on the last syllable *(for get')* *double the consonant* before adding *-ing, -ed, -or,* or *-er:*

> for get' + ing = forgetting
> re fer' + ed = referred
> bet' + or = bettor
> win' + er = winner
> fit' + ed = fitted

If the accent is not on the last syllable of the word, do not double the consonant:

> ham' mer + ing = hammering
> clat' ter + ing = clattering

31.3 Learning When to Use *ie* and *ei*

Learn when to use *ie* and when to use *ei.* Some of the time, you can follow the rules of the jingle:

> Put *i* before *e*
> Except after *c*
> Or when pronounced *a*
> As in *neighbor* and *weigh*

Examples of *i* before *e* include *achieve, believe, grieve, relieve, grief,* and *niece.* Words with *ei* after *c* include *conceit, deceit, perceive,* and *receive.* Other words pronounced with an *a* sound as in *weigh* include *eight, sleigh,* and *vein.* Some words, however, have an *ei* combination that neither follows *c* nor is pronounced *a.* Examples are *either, neither, leisure, seize, weird, atheist,* and *sheik.*

31.4 Learning How to Add Prefixes

Learn how to add prefixes—extra letters at the beginning of a word. When adding a prefix, be careful to add all of its letters, and only those. Here are examples:

> dis + satisfaction = dissatisfaction
> mis + fire = misfire
> un + necessary = unnecessary
> pre + view = preview
> inter + relationship = interrelationship

To join a prefix to a capitalized word, you need a hyphen; see section 31.9, item 5.

31.5

EXERCISE 1   Adding Suffixes and Prefixes

Add each suffix or prefix as indicated.

EXAMPLE
Add the suffix *-ful* to *beauty.*
beautiful

1. Add the suffix *-able* to *forgive.*
2. Add the suffix *-ment* to *encourage.*
3. Add the suffix *-er* to *swim.*
4. Add the suffix *-ing* to *worry.*
5. Add the suffix *-ing* to *recede.*
6. Add the prefix *re-* to *enter.*
7. Add the prefix *un-* to *needed.*
8. Add the prefix *intra-* to *venous.*
9. Add the prefix *re-* to *examine.*
10. Add the prefix *anti-* to *ballistic.*

31.5 Recognizing Homonyms

1. Distinguish between homonyms—words that sound alike but have different meanings and different spellings. Examples are *bare* and *bear; brake* and *break; capital* and *capitol; cite, site,* and *sight; peace* and *piece; principal* and *principle; right, rite,* and *write.* Especially troublesome are *there, their,* and *they're; whose* and *who's;* and *its* and *it's.* For help in using these words, consult the Glossary of Usage (pp. 575–599) and a dictionary.

2. Distinguish between partial homonyms—words with syllables that sound alike but are spelled differently. "Seed" words, for instance, all have a syllable pronounced like *seed.* The group includes *supersede* (the only word ending in *-sede*); *exceed, proceed,* and *succeed* (the only words ending *-ceed*); *accede, antecede, cede, concede, intercede, precede, recede,* and *secede* (the only words ending in *-cede*).

Words ending in *-ance* and *-ence* often sound alike. One way to keep the spelling straight is to think of related words. To spell *dominance* correctly, think of dominate; to spell *existence,* think of existential; to spell *tolerance,* think of tolerate. A similar method can help you decide between *-able* and *-ible* endings. To spell *imaginable* correctly, think of imagination; to spell *incredible,* think of credit; to spell *irritable,* think of irritation; to spell *permissible,* think of permissive.

Unfortunately, this method does not work for all partial homo-

Recognizing Homonyms   **461**

nyms. To distinguish between tol*erate* and sep*arate,* for instance, you just have to remember that there's *a rat* in *separate.* And if you aren't sure how to spell a particular word, see your dictionary.

31.6 Pluralizing Simple Nouns

Learn how to pluralize simple nouns—nouns such as *hand* and *book* as distinct from compound nouns such as *handbook.* To be sure of the plurals with some nouns, you will need to see your dictionary. But the following guidelines will help.

1. Form the plural of most nouns by adding *s:*

> book, books; car, cars; spoon, spoons; rake, rakes; hand, hands

2. Form the plural of nouns ending in *ch, s, sh, x,* and *z* by adding *-es* (pronounced as a syllable):

> church, churches; porch, porches; watch, watches; Jones, Joneses
> glass, glasses; business, businesses; mess, messes
> bush, bushes; finish, finishes; flash, flashes
> box, boxes; fox, foxes; tax, taxes
> buzz, buzzes
> EXCEPTIONS: crisis, crises; basis, bases; ox, oxen

3. Form the plural of nouns ending in *fe* by changing the *f* to *v* before adding *-s:*

> wife, wives; life, lives; knife, knives
> EXCEPTION: cafe, cafes.

4. Form the plural of *some* nouns ending in *f* by changing the *f* to *v* and then adding *-es:*

> leaf, leaves; thief, thieves; elf, elves; self, selves.

But some nouns ending in *f* need only an *-s* to become plural:
>   chief, chiefs; belief, beliefs; roof, roofs; proof, proofs

5. Form the plural of *some* nouns ending in *o* by adding *-es:*

> hero, heroes; veto, vetoes; potato, potatoes; mosquito, mosquitoes

But some nouns ending in *o* need only an *-s* to become plural:

> piano, pianos; zero, zeros; banjo, banjos; tobacco, tobaccos

6. Form the plural of words ending in a consonant plus *y* by changing the *y* to *-ies:*

> vacancy, vacancies; authority, authorities; party, parties

Words ending in a vowel plus *y* need only an *-s* to become plural:

> boy, boys; day, days, attorney, attorneys; valley, valleys

7. Form the plural of some nouns in special ways:

> datum, data; medium, media; criterion, criteria; foot, feet; man, men; child, children; woman, women; tooth, teeth

8. Form the plural of numbers, capitalized letters, and many capitalized abbreviations by adding *s:*.

> the 1980s   by twos and threes   four Cs   three YMCAs

Note that the abbreviation has no periods. For abbreviations with periods, see the next entry.

9. Form the plural of lower-case letters and abbreviations that have periods by adding an apostrophe and *s:*

> three M.A.'s   two c.o.d.'s   six *s*'s and five *m*'s

10. Some nouns are spelled the same in the plural as in the singular:

> deer, deer; fish, fish; barracks, barracks

31.7 Pluralizing Compound Nouns

Learn how to pluralize compound nouns. Compound nouns are written as separate words (master chef), as words linked by a hyphen (self-esteem), or as one word (notebook). Here are guidelines for pluralizing each type:

1. If the compound is written as one word, pluralize the final word:

notebook	notebooks
bookshelf	bookshelves
blueberry	blueberries

EXCEPTION: passerby, passersby

2. If the compound is hyphenated or written as separate words, pluralize the major word:

mother-in-law	mothers-in-law
city-state	city-states
fellow employee	fellow employees
editor in chief	editors in chief

A few compounds have alternative plurals: *attorney general,* for instance, may be pluralized as *attorneys general* or *attorney generals.*

3. If the compound has no noun within it, pluralize the final word:

also-ran	also-rans
hand-me-down	hand-me-downs

4. If the compound ends in *-ful*, add *s:*

cupful   cupfuls
mouthful   mouthfuls

EXERCISE 2   **Forming Plurals**

Form the plural of every word listed.

EXAMPLE
peanut
peanuts

1. coat
2. box
3. tooth
4. majesty
5. valley
6. criterion
7. nephew
8. go-between
9. sister-in-law
10. commander in chief

31.8   Noting Words Frequently Misspelled

Identify the words in the following list that you never misspell. Then learn to master the others by the method recommended in section 31.1.

absence	adviser	anoint	associate
absorption	aerial	answer	athlete
abundant	affect	antiseptic	athletic
accessible	against	apology	author
accidentally	aggravate	apparatus	auxiliary
accommodate	aggressive	apparent	awful
accompanied	a lot	appear	
accomplish	all right	appearance	balloon
accuracy	almost	appetite	bargain
accustomed	already	appropriate	basically
achieve	although	argue	beginning
achievement	altogether	arguing	believe
acquire	always	argument	believed
across	amateur	arrangement	benefit
actually	among	article	benefited
address	analysis	ascend	boundary
admission	analyze	assailant	breath
adolescence	angel	assassinate	breathe
advice	annihilate	assistance	brilliant
advise	annual	assistant	bureaucracy

bureaucratic	conquer	different	every
burial	conscience	dilemma	exaggerate
buried	conscientious	dilettante	exaggeration
bury	conscious	dining	exceed
business	considerable	disagree	excel
busy	consistency	disappear	excellent
	consistent	disappoint	except
cafeteria	continually	disapproval	exceptional
calamity	continuous	disapprove	exercise
calculator	control	disastrous	exhausted
calendar	controlled	discipline	exhaustion
capital	convenience	discoveries	exhilaration
captain	conveniently	discriminate	existence
careful	conversation	discussion	expense
carrying	coolly	disease	experience
categorical	corporal	dissatisfaction	experiment
category	corroborate	dissatisfied	explanation
cede	council	dissection	extremely
ceiling	counsel	dissipate	
cemetery	countries	dissipation	familiar
certain	course	distinction	fascinate
changeable	courteous	divide	fascinating
characteristic	criticism	divine	February
characteristically	criticize	division	finally
chief	crowd	doctor	financial
choose	crystal	drunkenness	financier
choosing	curiosity		flourish
chose	cylinder	easily	forcibly
climbed		ecstasy	foreign
clothes	deceive	ecstatic	foresee
coarse	deception	efficiency	formally
column	decide	efficient	formerly
coming	decision	eight	forth
commercial	decisively	eighth	forty
commitment	definite	either	forward
committed	degree	eligible	fourth
committee	dependent	eliminate	friend
common	derelict	embarrassed	frightening
comparatively	descendant	embarrassment	fulfill
competent	describe	emphasis	fundamental
competition	desperate	emphasize	fundamentally
complement	dessert	enemies	further
compliment	destroy	enemy	
conceivable	determine	engineer	gardener
conceive	develop	environment	gauge
concentration	development	equipment	generally
concern	device	equipped	government
condemn	devise	especially	governor
connoisseur	difference	essential	grammar

grateful
grievous
guarantee
guard
guidance

handle
happily
harass
height
heroes
heroine
hideous
hoping
humorous
hurriedly
hurrying
hypocrisy
hypocrite

identification
identity
illogical
imaginary
imagination
imbecile
imitation
immediately
immigrant
incidentally
increase
incredible
independence
independent
indispensable
individual
inevitably
influential
initiate
inoculate
insistent
integration
intellectual
intelligence
intelligent
interest
interfere
interference

interpreted
invitation
irrelevant
irresistible
irritable
island
it's
its

jealous
judgment

kindergarten
knew
know
knowledge

laboratory
later
latter
led
leisure
length
lenient
library
license
lightning
likelihood
likely
literally
literary
literature
livelihood
loneliness
loose
lose
losing
loyally
loyalty
lying

magazine
maintenance
manageable
maneuver
marriage
married
mathematics

medicine
miniature
minor
minutes
mischief
mischievous
missile
misspelled
misspelling
morale
mournful
muscle
mysterious

naturally
necessary
necessity
neighbor
neither
newsstand
nickel
niece
ninety
ninth
noticeable
nuisance

obstacle
occasion
occasionally
occur
occurred
occurrence
o'clock
official
omission
omit
omitted
omniscient
opportune
opportunity
optimism
optimist
optimistic
ordinarily
origin
original
oscillate

paid
panicky
parallel
parallelism
particular
particularly
partner
pastime
peaceable
peculiar
peculiarity
perceive
perception
perform
performance
permanence
permanent
permissible
perseverance
persevere
persistent
personality
personally
personnel
perspiration
persuade
persuasion
pertain
physical
piece
plain
planning
playwright
pleasant
pleasure
poison
political
politician
pollution
populace
portrayal
possess
possession
possessive
possible
practical
practically
prairie

precede
preceding
predictable
prefer
preference
preferential
preferred
prejudice
preparation
prepare
presence
prevalent
primitive
principal
principle
privilege
probably
procedure
processor
proceed
professional
professor
profitable
projectile
prominent
pronunciation
proof
propeller
prophecy
prophesied
prophesy
prophet
prove
psychology
pursue
pursuit

quantity
quarter
quiet
quiz

realistically
realize
really
rebellion

recede
receipt
receive
recognize
recommend
referred
relieve
religious
remembrance
reminisce
repetition
representative
resemblance
resistance
respectability
restaurant
rhythm
rhythmical
ridiculous
roommate

sacrifice
sacrilegious
safety
satellite
satire
scarcely
scene
schedule
science
scientific
secretary
seize
seminar
sense
separate
sergeant
several
severely
shepherd
sheriff
shining
shoulder
signal
significance
significant

similar
similarity
simile
sincerely
sophomore
source
specimen
speech
sponsor
stationary
stationery
stopping
straight
strategic
strength
strenuous
stretch
striking
studying
succeed
successful
successfully
suddenness
summary
superintendent
supersede
suppress
surely
surprise
suspicion
syllable
symmetrical

tariff
technical
temperament
temperature
tendency
than
their
then
there
therefore
they're
thorough
through

title
together
toward
tragedy
transferred
tries
truly
twelfth
tyrannical
tyrannize
tyranny

unanimous
unconscious
undoubtedly
university
unnecessarily
unnecessary
until
unusual
using
usually

vacillate
vacuum
vengeance
versatile
vicious
village
villain

weapon
weather
Wednesday
weird
whereabouts
whether
whimsical
wholly
woman
women
wretched
writing
written

EXERCISE 3   Spotting and Correcting Misspellings

In the following passage by Andrew Evans, we have deliberately misspelled some words. Make the necessary corrections.

> Mr. Bunten's farm is sucessful largely because he has kept the size within reason and because he is a skilful farmer. His heard is relatively small, consistting of only thirty-five milkers plus thirty more cows, including the heifers. When most farmers in the reg-
> 5 gion expanded there operation after World War II by building expensive silos and milking systemes, Mr. Bunten kept his farm about the same size. Within a few years, many of his neighbors had gone into debt, and some had failed alltogether. It was a sad sceen for just about everybody.
> 10 We milk the cows in the mourning and at night. He gets up at 5:30, and I arive at 6 p.m. After geting down a dozen bales of hey, I dash around, feeding the cows and prepareing the milking machines. I literaly run to complete the chores in the shortest time posible. He never askes me to do them quickly; however, if I should
> 15 be moveing slowly, he'll say, "Geeze, boy, what took ya!" Usualy he doesn't have to say anything because he's the type of person one wants to please—some one on the go all the time. For a man of sixty-four he has unbeleivable endurence. Viewing his efforts as a challenge, I try to keep up and win his respect. Fortunetely, he
> 20 gives me the benifit of the doubt much of the time.

31.9 Using the Hyphen   -

1. Use a hyphen to divide a long word at the end of a line:

> The long black centipede walked across the sand with an enormous limp.

Normally you divide a word at the end of a syllable. But do not put syllables of one or two letters on either side of a hyphen, as * *i-tem* and * *end-ed.* If you aren't sure what the syllables of a word are, see your dictionary.

2. Use a hyphen to show that two or three words are being used as a single grammatical unit:

> The older citizens don't want a Johnny-come-lately for mayor.
> But they don't want a stick-in-the-mud either.

3. Use a hyphen to form certain compounds:

> Enrico Caruso was a world-famous tenor.
> The new translation of the Bible will be welcomed by all English-speaking peoples.
> I wouldn't touch a deal like that with a ten-foot pole.

As noted in section 31.7, not all compounds require a hyphen. Some are written as one word (notebook, bookshelf, storytelling), and some as two separate words (police officer, master chef). Whenever you are in doubt, check your dictionary.

4. Do not use a hyphen when an *-ly* adverb is part of the compound:

> Widely held misconceptions cannot be easily overturned.

Compounds using *well* drop the hyphen when the modifer follows the noun. Compare these two sentences:

> A well-known economist has warned against a tax cut.
> John Kenneth Galbraith is well known.

5. Use a hyphen to join a prefix to a capitalized word:

> un-American
> post-Renaissance

Do not use a hyphen when you join a prefix to an uncapitalized word:

> postwar
> deemphasize
> nonprofit

6. Use a hyphen in a number written as two words, provided it is below one hundred:

> Twenty-five applicants have requested interviews.
> Two-thirds of the trees had been cut.
> One-half of the design is complete.

Do not attach a hyphen to the word for any number over ninety-nine:

> Some suits now cost over three hundred dollars.
> Some of the new "economy" cars cost more than eight thousand dollars.
> Thirty-five thousand spectators watched the game.

Thirty-five, which is below one hundred, is hyphenated, but no hyphen is attached to *thousand*.

EXERCISE 4   **Using the Hyphen**

Each of the following may require the addition of one or more hyphens. Add one as needed. If an entry is correct as it stands, write *Correct*.

EXAMPLE
The running of high speed trains between major cities in America would definitely reduce traffic on major highways.

REVISED: The running of high-speed trains between major cities in America would definitely reduce traffic on major highways.

1. The long distance runners looked buoyant as they passed the fifteen mile mark.
2. A world renowned biologist representing the well known organization Food Now will present a report to an all Russian audience.
3. Rescue workers have removed three-quarters of the debris.
4. Fifty five of the survivors had been able to salvage only one quarter of their personal belongings.
5. The town is medium sized, with a population of forty six thousand.

31.10 Using the Apostrophe ✔

1. To form the possessive of singular nouns and abbreviations of singular items, use an apostrophe plus *s:*

> a girl's hat   Bill's car   the cow's tail   a team's mascot
> NATO's future   the C.O.'s orders   Dr. T.'s patients

If the singular noun ends in *s* (as in *James*), you may form the possessive by adding an apostrophe plus *s* (James's apartment) or by adding just the apostrophe (James' apartment). Custom calls for this latter form with Zeus, Moses, and Jesus: Zeus' thunderbolts, Moses' staff, Jesus' teachings.

2. To form the possessive of plural nouns ending in *s,* add just an apostrophe:

> players   players' uniforms
> animals   animals' eating habits
> the Joneses   the Joneses' car

3. To form the possessive of plural nouns not ending in *s,* add an apostrophe plus *s:*

> men   men's activities
> children   children's toys

4. To indicate that two people own something jointly, add an apostrophe, and *s* if necessary, to the second of the two nouns:

> Ann and James' apartment

To indicate that two people own two or more things separately, use the apostrophe, and *s* if necessary, with both of the nouns:

> Paul's and Edith's homes

5. To form the possessive with singular compound nouns, add an apostrophe plus *s* to the last word:

my sister-in-law's career   the editor in chief's policy

6. To form the possessive of certain indefinite pronouns, add an apostrophe plus *s:*

someone's coat   no one's fault   everybody else's jokes

With indefinite pronouns that do not take the apostrophe, form the possessive with *of:* the plans of most, the hopes of many, the cooking of few.

7. Use the possessive case with nouns or pronouns followed by gerunds:

Sarah's running   the crowd's cheering   the men's arguing
the Joneses' celebrating   her protesting   our laughing

(For more on this point, see section 11.5.)

8. Use an apostrophe, and *s* when necessary, in common phrases of time and measurement:

four o'clock   five dollars' worth
two weeks' notice   a day's work
our money's worth   a stone's throw

9. Use an apostrophe plus *s* to form the plural of lower-case letters, abbreviations containing periods, and words treated as words:

a's and *b*'s   three Ph.D.'s   five *but*'s

10. Use an apostrophe to mark the omission of a letter or letters in a contraction:

I have finished.   I've finished.
He is not here.   He isn't here.
This does not work.   This doesn't work.
They will not stop.   They won't stop.
You should have written.   You should've written.

11. Use an apostrophe to mark the omission of numbers in dates:

the election of '84   the hurricane of '36

31.11 Misusing the Apostrophe ⓥ

1. Do not use an apostrophe to form the plural of nouns:

*Five girl's went swimming.   REVISED: Five girls went swimming.
*Two houses' need paint.   REVISED: Two houses need paint.

2. Do not use an apostrophe with the possessive forms of the personal pronouns:

*This is our thermos; that one is their's.
REVISED: This is our thermos; that one is theirs.
*Ben's notes are incomplete; your's are thorough.
REVISED: Ben's notes are incomplete; yours are thorough.

3. Do not confuse the possessive pronoun *its* with the contraction *it's.* Use *its* as you use *his;* use *it's* as you use *he's.*

his success	he's successful
its success	it's successful

4. Do not confuse the possessive *whose* with the contraction *who's:*

Whose notebook is this?
No one knows whose painting this is.
Who's going to the concert?
No one has heard of the pianist who's scheduled to play.

5. Do not use the apostrophe and *s* to form a possessive when the construction would be cumbersome:

WEAK: Questions about the candidate's husband's financial dealings hurt her campaign.
REVISED: Questions about the financial dealings of the candidate's husband hurt her campaign.

EXERCISE 5   Using the Apostrophe

Improve the punctuation in the following passage by adding or removing an apostrophe wherever necessary. As you make these corrections, write out the entire passage.

Everyones talking about Frank Smiths novel. Its plot seems to be based on something that happened to him during his freshman year. Its weird to read about characters youve seen in class or in the students lounge. I dont think there are many of his classmate's
5 who wont be annoyed when they discover theyve been depicted as thugs' and moron's. Its as if Frank thought that his experiences were the same as everyones—Johns, Marys, and Jims. That kind of thinking can be overlooked in someone whos in his early teen's, but it isnt all right for someone in his twenties'.

32

MECHANICS

Mechanics are conventional rules such as the one requiring capitalization for the first word of a sentence. You need to follow the conventions so that your writing will look the way formal writing is expected to look.

32.1 Using Capital Letters   *cap*

1. Capitalize the first word of a sentence:

> The quick brown fox jumped over the lazy dog.
> Where do bears hibernate in the winter?

Here and elsewhere in the chapter, to *capitalize* a word means to capitalize its first letter.

2. Capitalize proper nouns and proper adjectives. Unlike a common noun, which names a *class* of objects, a proper noun names a *particular* person, place, thing, or event. Proper adjectives are based on common nouns. Here are examples:

COMMON NOUNS	PROPER NOUNS	PROPER ADJECTIVES
country	Canada	Canadian
person	Jefferson	Jeffersonian
university	University of Miami	
state	Texas	Texan
river	Mississippi River	
lake	Lake Erie	
revolution	the French Revolution	

473

COMMON NOUNS	PROPER NOUNS
war	World War I
party	the Communist Party
east (direction)	the East (particular region)
library	Library of Congress
corporation	the Rand Corporation
economics	Economics 101
month	January
day	Wednesday

Do not capitalize words such as *a* and *the* when used with proper nouns, and do not capitalize the names of the seasons (fall, winter, spring, summer).

3. Capitalize a personal title when it is used before a name or when it denotes a particular position of high rank.

the president	President Eisenhower
	the President of the United States
	the Pope
the senator	Senator Helms
the queen	Queen Elizabeth
	the Queen of England
the professor	Professor Harvey
the mayor	Mayor Bradley

4. Capitalize a term denoting kinship when it is used before a name:

my aunt   Aunt Sally
his uncle   his Uncle Bob
her cousin   her Cousin Michael

5. Capitalize titles as explained in section 32.3.

6. Always capitalize the pronoun *I:*

When I heard the news, I laughed.

EXERCISE 1   Using Capitals

Improve each of the following by capitalizing where necessary.

1. multinational corporations have invested millions to extract minerals from the jungles along the amazon river in south america.
2. bruce jenner competed for the united states in the 1976 olympic games, which were held in montreal.
3. "i can't find my philosophy book," said frank. "has anyone seen it?"
4. lake george is one of the most popular vacation spots in the northeast. it has been praised in many poems, like the one that begins, "i love thy scented shores."

5. after graduation sally and sandy plan to work at the general motors plant in pontiac, michigan.
6. If you like stories about spies, you will enjoy *a spy in winter* by michael hastings.
7. A very different sort of book is *structure and history in greek mythology and ritual* by walter burkert.

32.2 Using Underlining *und*

Most of this book is set in ordinary type (known as "roman"), but you've no doubt already noticed that we have been using *italic type* for distinction and emphasis *(this is an example of italic type)*. You may need to use italics in your own writing, but if you are using a pen or pencil or a standard typewriter, you cannot readily produce words in italic lettering. You can, however, represent italics by underlining

1. Use underlining to emphasize a word or phrase in a statement:

> There are <u>just</u> laws and there are <u>unjust</u> laws.
>
> --Martin Luther King, Jr.

2. Use underlining to identify a letter or a word treated as a word:

> The word <u>suspense</u> has three <u>s</u>´s.
>
> The poet uses <u>eyes</u> twice in the first stanza and
>
> once in the second.

3. Use underlining to identify a foreign word or phrase not yet absorbed into English:

> <u>au courant</u>   <u>Angst</u>   <u>Bildungsroman</u>   <u>carpe diem</u>

4. Use underlining to identify the name of a ship, an airplane, or the like:

> <u>Queen Elizabeth II</u> [ship]
>
> <u>Spirit of St. Louis</u> [airplane]
>
> <u>Apollo 2</u> [spaceship]

5. Use underlining for titles as explained in section 32.3.

EXERCISE 2   Using Underlining

Each of the following may require the addition or removal of underlining. Make any necessary change. If an entry is correct as it stands, write *Correct.*

Using Underlining   **475**

1. They named their motorboat The Linda Ronstadt.

2. I can never remember how to spell harassment.

3. After their <u>yoga</u> and <u>karate</u> classes, Carol and Alex always went out for a <u>pizza</u>.

4. A drink known as a <u>frappe</u> in one part of the country may be called a <u>cabinet</u>, a frost, or a <u>milk shake</u> in another.

5. The English word mother derives from the Middle English word moder and is akin to the Latin word mater.

32.3 Titles *title*

1. Capitalize the first and last word of a title, whatever they are, and all the words in between except articles (such as *a* and *the)*, prepositions (such as *for, among,* and *to)*, and conjunctions (such as *and, but,* and *or):*

<u>Zen and the Art of Motorcycle Maintenance</u> [book]

"Ode on a Grecian Urn" [poem]

"What Americans Stand For" [essay]

<u>Death of a Salesman</u> [play]

2. Use underlining for the title of a book, scholarly journal, magazine, newspaper, government report, play, musical, opera or other long musical composition, film, television show, radio program, or long poem:

<u>The Grapes of Wrath</u> [book]

<u>The Collected Poems of Dylan Thomas</u> [book]

<u>The American Scholar</u> [journal]

<u>Newsweek</u> [magazine]

<u>New York Times</u> [newspaper]

<u>Uniform Crime Reports for the United States</u> [government publication]

<u>Hamlet</u> [play]

<u>Oklahoma</u> [musical]

<u>The Barber of Seville</u> [opera]

<u>Scheherazade</u> [orchestral suite]

<u>Star Wars</u> [film]

<u>All in the Family</u> [television show]

<u>Morning Pro Musica</u> [radio program]

<u>Song of Myself</u> [long poem]

3. Use double quotation marks for the title of an article in a magazine or newspaper, and for the title of an essay, short story, short poem, song or other short musical composition, speech, or chapter in a book:

"Seal Hunting in Alaska" [magazine article]

"The Hot Seat" [newspaper column]

"Bullfighting in Hemingway's Fiction" [essay]

"The Tell-Tale Heart" [short story]

"Mending Wall" [short poem]

"Born in the U.S.A." [song]

"The American Scholar" [speech]

"Winning the West" [chapter in a book]

4. Use single quotation marks to enclose a title requiring quotation marks when it is part of another title requiring quotation marks or is mentioned within a quotation:

"Fences and Neighbors in Frost's 'Mending Wall'"
  [title of an essay on the poem]

"Frost's 'Mending Wall,'" said Professor Ainsley,

"is a gently disarming poem."

5. Do not use both underlining and quotation marks in a title unless the title itself includes one or the other:

"Experience" [essay]

Gone with the Wind [novel]

"On Sitting Down to Read King Lear Again" [poem]

6. Do not use italics or quotation marks in a title of your own unless it includes a reference to another title:

What to Do with Nuclear Waste

Bull-fighting in Hemingway´s The Sun Also Rises

Art and Sex in Pope´s "Rape of the Lock"

EXERCISE 3 **Writing Titles**

Each of the following titles requires capitalization and may also require underlining or quotation marks. Make the necessary changes.

1. carmen [opera]
2. politics and leadership [speech]
3. my old kentucky home [song]
4. washington post [newspaper]
5. what freud forgot [essay]
6. 60 minutes [television show]
7. the will of zeus [history book]
8. john brown's body [long poem]
9. the mismatch between school and children [editorial]
10. natural history [magazine]
11. solutions to the energy problem [your report]
12. the role of fate in shakespeare's romeo and juliet [your essay]
13. imagery in the battle hymn of the republic [your essay]
14. barefoot in the park [play]

32.4 Using Abbreviations *ab*

Abbreviations occur often in informal writing, but in formal writing you should use them less often. We suggest you follow these guidelines.

1. Abbreviate most titles accompanying a name:

Mrs. James Low	Dr. Martha Peters.
Mr. Peter Smith	Robert Greene, Jr.
Ms. Elizabeth Fish	Susan Flagg, D.D.
BUT: Miss Jenny Lind	Joseph Stevens, M.D.

But use the full titles when referring to religious, governmental, and military leaders:

the Reverend Leonard Flischer
Senator Nancy Kassebaum
the Honorable Mario Cuomo, governor of New York
General George C. Marshall

2. Abbreviate terms that help to specify a date or a time of day:

350 B.C.   8:30 A.M.
A.D. 1776   2:15 P.M.

Note that A.D. precedes the date.

3. Abbreviate the name of a state, a province, or a country when it forms part of an address:

Austin, TX   Galway, Ire.
Long Beach, CA   Sherbrooke, Que.
Plains, GA   Montreal, Can.
Miami, FL   Manchester, Eng.
Washington, DC   Naples, It.

Abbreviate names of U.S. states and the District of Columbia with just two capital letters and no periods, as shown at left. Abbreviate names of foreign provinces and countries as shown at right.

4. You may use abbreviations in referring to well-known firms and other organizations:

NBC   YMCA
IBM   NAACP

5. If an abbreviation comes at the end of a declarative sentence, use the period marking the abbreviation as the period for the sentence:

The rocket was launched at 11:30 P.M.

If an abbreviation ends a question, add a question mark:

Was the rocket launched at 11:30 P.M.?

32.5 Misusing Abbreviations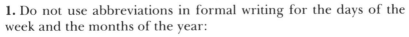

1. Do not use abbreviations in formal writing for the days of the week and the months of the year:

Sunday   August
Saturday   December

2. Do not use abbreviations in formal writing for the names of most geographical entities when they are not part of an address:

New England	Great Britain	Mulberry Street
Mississippi	the Snake River	Lake Avenue
Canada	the Rocky Mountains	

Many writers now use *U.S.* and *U.S.S.R.* You may also use *Mt.* before the name of a mountain, as in *Mt. McKinley,* and *St.* in the name of a place, as in *St. Louis.*

3. In formal writing do not use abbreviations for the names of academic subjects and the subdivisions of books:

Old English poetry	biology
French 205	chapter 10
European history	page 45

4. Do not use abbreviations for units of measurement (such as size and weight) unless the accompanying amounts are given in numerals:

> The new guard is six feet seven inches tall.
> This box must weigh over fifty pounds.
> A 50 lb. bag of fertilizer costs $24.50.
> The first three runners finished the race in under four minutes.

5. Do not use any abbreviation that is not widely known without first explaining its meaning:

> *The MISAA was passed in 1978.
> REVISED: The Middle Income Student Assistance Act (MISAA) was passed in 1978.

After you have explained its meaning, you may use the abbreviation on its own. But beware of crowding too many abbreviations into a sentence or passage. If you don't keep them under control, your reader may end up drowning in alphabet soup:

> *In 1971 Congress established the BEOG program, and the EOGs were renamed SEOGs.
> REVISED: In 1972 Congress established the Basic Educational Opportunity Grant (BEOG) program, and the Educational Opportunity Grants (EOG) were renamed Supplemental Educational Opportunity Grants (SEOG).

If you aren't sure how to abbreviate a particular term, see your dictionary or ask your instructor. If you don't know whether you should abbreviate a term at all, don't. In formal writing, most terms should be spelled out in full.

32.6 Using Numbers *num*

When you refer to a number, you have to decide whether to use a figure or to spell it out as a word. In much scientific and technical writing, figures predominate; in magazines and books of general interest, words are common, though figures are also used. In this section, we offer guidelines for nontechnical writing.

1. Spell out a number when it begins a sentence:

Eighty-five dignitaries attended the opening ceremony.
Five orchestras performed.

Rearrange the sentence if spelling out the number would require three or more words:

The opening ceremony was attended by 1,250 dignitaries.

2. Spell out a number that can be written in one or two words, except as noted in item 4, below:

A batter is out after three strikes.
The firemen worked without relief for twenty-two hours.
The stadium can hold eighty thousand spectators.

3. Use numerals if spelling out a number would require more than two words:

She has a herd of 350 cows.
The stadium can hold 85,600 spectators.

4. Use numerals for addresses, dates, exact times of day, exact sums of money, exact measurements such as miles per hour, scores of games, mathematical ratios, fractions, and page numbers:

22 East Main Street   65 mph
October 7, 1981   by a score of 5 to 4
44 B.C.   a ratio of 2 to 1
11:15 A.M.   5⅞
$4.36   page 102
3.5 million

However, when a time of day or a sum of money is given as a round figure, spell it out:

Uncle Ben always gets up at six.
He used to earn two dollars for ten hours of work.
With ten cents in his pocket, anything seemed possible.

5. Be consistent within a piece of writing. Use either words *or* figures but not both:

*In the fifth inning, the Sox scored 5 runs on four hits, three walks, and 1 error.
REVISED: In the fifth inning, the Sox scored five runs on four hits, three walks, and one error.

*As a result of the government's relocation program, seventy-six families have left the valley, 115 families have entered it, and 203 have stayed put.

REVISED: As a result of the government's relocation program, 76 families have left the valley, 115 families have entered it, and 203 have stayed put.

EXERCISE 4 Using Abbreviations and Numbers

Each of the following may include incorrectly written abbreviations and numbers. Make any necessary changes. If an entry is correct as it stands, write *Correct*.

1. "Why," said the White Queen to Alice, "sometimes I've believed as many as 6 impossible things before breakfast."

    —Adapted from Lewis Carroll

2. We plan to spend part of our vacation on a Miss. Riv. steamboat and the rest in the Adirondack Mts.

3. For my psych homework I have to review pages eighteen and 38.

4. 2 students were elected to the presidential search committee, which also included Doctor Laura Freeman, the Rev. David Proctor, and Professor Ann Kaufman, Doctor of Philosophy.

5. The Young Women's Christian Association will hold an art fair on Mon., Jul. twenty-third, beginning at ten-fifteen A.M.

6. In this town, if you exceed the speed limit of 30 mph, you will be fined fifty dollars.

7. The Star Trek Convention attracted a crowd of 25 hundred fans.

8. If we split the costs by a ratio of three to one, my contribution will be seven hundred dollars and seventy-two cents.

9. Ms. Emily Sutherland will speak tonight on behalf of ERA.

10. He has four hundred and twenty matchboxes in his collection.

11. Playing for forty-five minutes, Larry Bird scored thirty-three points and had 10 rebounds and 12 assists.

12. Over two hundred and fifty thousand spectators watched 5,000 soldiers parade up Kingston Avenue on Saturday.

IV

THE
RESEARCH
PAPER

33

PREPARING THE
RESEARCH PAPER

Writing a library research paper is much like writing an ordinary essay. Both kinds of writing involve many of the same basic steps: choosing a topic, asking questions to define and develop it, gauging the audience, getting raw material to work with, outlining the paper, writing it, and revising it. What makes a research paper different is that much of your raw material comes not from your own head but from printed sources, chiefly books and periodicals. Collecting raw material—by reading and taking notes—corresponds to the process of prewriting an ordinary essay.

A research paper may belong to one of two basic types. It may be a **survey** of facts and opinions available on a given topic, or an **analytical argument** that uses those facts and opinions to prove a thesis. Your instructor may tell you which kind of paper you are expected to write. If not, you yourself should eventually choose between surveying and arguing. You will then have a definite way of managing your sources.

In a survey-type research paper, you gather facts and a variety of opinions on a given topic. You make little attempt to interpret or evaluate what your sources say, or to prove a particular point. Instead, through quotation, summary, and paraphrase, you try to provide a representative sampling of facts and opinions, a noncommittal report on your topic. You explain the pros and cons of various positions, but you don't side definitely with any one of them. (For a sample of a survey-type research paper, see Appendix 1, section A1.6.)

In an argumentative research paper, you do considerably more.

You do not simply quote, paraphrase, and summarize. You interpret, question, compare, and judge the statements you cite. You explain why one opinion is sound and another is not, why one fact is relevant and another is not, why one writer is correct and another is mistaken. Your purpose may vary with your topic; you may seek to explain a situation, to recommend a course of action, to reveal the solution to a problem, or to present and defend a particular interpretation of a historical event or a work of art. But whether the topic is space travel or Shakespeare's *Hamlet,* an argumentative research paper deals actively with the statements it cites. It makes them work together in an argument that you create—an argument that leads to a conclusion of your own. (For a sample argumentative research paper, see chapter 37.)

What follows will help you write either a survey-type research paper or an argumentative one. Whichever you choose, we have designed this chapter as a succession of steps to guide you systematically through the whole process of preparation. But you may well find, as you work your way into your topic and discover its potentialities, that you can't take the steps exactly in order. You may want to read a particular source even before you know what other sources there are, or you may want to double back in order to push forward, rethinking and redefining your topic long after you have chosen it. So you should feel free to take the steps of this chapter in the order that best suits your needs and to make your own path toward an understanding of your topic.

33.1 Choosing a Topic

Choosing a topic for a research paper is in some ways like choosing a topic for an ordinary essay. But there are some differences. As you weigh your topic, ask yourself these questions.

1. Do you really want to know more about this topic? Research on any subject will keep you busy for weeks. You will do it well only if you expect to learn something interesting or important in the process.

2. Are you likely to find many sources of information on this topic? You cannot write a research paper without consulting a variety of sources. If only one source, or none at all, is readily available, you should rethink your topic or choose another. You should also be wary of topics that have just appeared in the news and are therefore likely to change their shape even as you try to write about them. You need not avoid subjects like solar power or population control or the Equal Rights Amendment—all of which are continually in the news—but you should hesitate to write about the latest earthquake or the latest cult. If you want a contemporary topic, choose one that has been around long enough to generate substantial articles and books.

3. Can you cut the topic down to manageable size? Be reasonable and realistic about what you can do in a period of two to four weeks. If your topic is "The Causes of the American Revolution," you will scarcely have time to make a list of books on your subject, let alone read and analyze them. Find something specific, such as "The Harassment of Loyalists after Watertown" or "The Role of Patrick Henry in the American Revolution."

4. What questions can you ask about the topic itself? Questions help you get the topic down to manageable size, discover its possibilities, and find the goal of your research—the specific problem you want to investigate. Suppose you want to write about the problem of financing a college education—a topic not only current but also directly linked to the lives of most college students. You could ask at least two or three pointed questions: How much does educational opportunity depend on financial status? Are middle-income families actually being squeezed by a system that favors low-income students? Is financial aid going to the students who need it most? Bart Naylor asked himself these questions as he started work on the research paper that appears on pp. 561–72. From time to time in this chapter and the next, we will see how he came to focus on one of these questions during the course of his research and how he found and used the sources that went into his paper.

EXERCISE 1 **Writing Questions about Various Topics**

Choose five of the following topics, and write two questions on each of them. Make the questions as pointed and specific as possible.

1. Solar energy
2. Viking explorations in North America
3. Censorship
4. Libel
5. French separatism in Quebec
6. Prayer in the public schools
7. Divorce
8. Sexual abuse of children
9. Oil spills
10. Balloon flight
11. Acid rain
12. Prohibition
13. The circus in America
14. The plight of the American farmer
15. The political career of Pierre Trudeau

33.2

EXERCISE 2   **Writing Questions about One Topic**

Think of a research topic that interests you, or take a topic you have been assigned, and write at least three specific questions about it.

33.2 Using the Library—The Reference Section

The task of preparing a research paper will sooner or later take you into the library. Though a library can be a bewildering place, any good library is staffed with people ready and willing to help you find your way around. If your library offers an orientation tour or a self-guided tour, you should of course take it as soon as you can. But whether or not you take a tour, the best place to start your systematic preparation for a research paper is the reference section, where you will find reference works of all kinds: encyclopedias, indexes, bibliographies, atlases, and dictionaries. Whatever your subject may be, a reference book will usually give you either direct information or leads to other sources, or both. In the reference section, you will also find the reference librarian, who will do everything possible to help you find what you need for your research.

Because working your way through the reference section takes time, you may want to turn right now to section 33.3, where we explain how to search the library catalogs for books on your topic. In the subject catalog (as explained in section 33.3), you may well find just the book you need to introduce you to your topic and to further sources on it. But for leads to articles on your topic as well as for a systematic overview of it, you need the reference section. Going there first will not only improve the quality of your research; it may actually save you time.

The reference works you are likely to find in the reference section include the following:

33.2A   General Encyclopedias

These give you an overview of virtually any subject in language that a nonspecialist can understand, and many encyclopedia articles end with a short list of books recommended for further reading on the subject. General encyclopedias include the thirty-volume *New Encyclopaedia Britannica* (1974), the thirty-volume *Americana* (revised annually), and the one-volume *New Columbia* (1975).

33.2B   Specialized Reference Works

These cover subjects in particular fields, such as art, education, history, literature, and psychology. To find the reference work for your subject, ask the reference librarian or see the *Guide to Reference Books* compiled by Eugene P. Sheehy (1976, with two supplements to date), which lists specialized guides to research in all fields. Here is a small, illustrative sample of them:

> *Encyclopedia of World Art* (1959–83)
> *Dictionary of Economics and Business,* by Harold Sloan and Arnold Zurcher (1970)
> *The Encyclopedia of Education* (1971)
> *International Encyclopedia of the Film* (1972)
> *An Encyclopaedia of World History,* ed. William L. Langer (1972)
> *New Grove Dictionary of Music and Musicians,* ed. Stanley Sadie (1980)
> *The Encyclopedia of Philosophy,* ed. Paul Edwards (1973)
> *Encyclopedia of Religion and Ethics,* ed. James Hastings (1955–58)
> *McGraw-Hill Encyclopedia of Science & Technology* (1982, with yearbooks since then)
> *International Encyclopedia of the Social Sciences,* ed. David L. Sills (1968–)

The articles in these books will tell you a good deal more about your topic than you will find in a general encyclopedia. At the start of his research, Bart Naylor—the author of the research paper on pp. 561–72—found two articles on student aid in volume 8 of *The Encyclopedia of Education:* "Scholarships, Fellowships, and Loans" on pages 18–23, and "Student Aid, Federal" on pages 505–24. Together, these two articles helped to give him a general grasp of his topic.

EXERCISE 3   Using Encyclopedias

Read an article in a standard encyclopedia about the research topic you chose for exercise 2, and jot down any questions this article raises for you. Then find a specialized encyclopedia that contains an article on your topic. Explain how the second article differs from the first and whether or not the second answered all of the questions raised by the first.

33.2C   Compilations of Facts and Statistics

These include the following:

1. *Facts on File* (1904–), described by the publisher as a "weekly news digest with cumulative index," provides up-to-date summaries of current events, with names, dates, and places.

2. *Statistical Abstract of the United States,* published annually by the U.S. Bureau of the Census, offers statistics on many subjects.

EXERCISE 4   Finding Facts and Statistics

Assume that you want to do research on oil spills at sea. Choose a six-month period taken from the past year, and from *Facts on File* and *Statis-*

tical Abstract of the United States see what you can learn about oil spills during this period.

33.2D Biographical Guides

These give brief accounts of notable figures, sometimes with bibliographies. They include the following:

1. *Chamber's Biographical Dictionary* (1968) covers figures in all historical periods and all parts of the world.

2. Volumes such as *Who's Who* cover living persons. Besides *Who's Who in the World* (1976), there are national volumes such as *Who's Who in America* and volumes devoted to special categories such as black Americans and American women.

3. The *Dictionary of American Biography* (1928–) covers deceased Americans, and the *Dictionary of National Biography* (1885–) covers deceased Britons. The *Dictionary of American Negro Biography* (1982) covers deceased black Americans.

4. The *Biography Index* directs you to books and magazine articles about various figures.

EXERCISE 5 Using Biographical Reference Works

If your topic concerns a particular person, consult one or more of the biographical dictionaries or *Who's Who* volumes mentioned above. Jot down at least two questions about the person, and then consult the *Biography Index* for the titles of two recent books or articles on your subject.

33.2E Guides to Books

Besides the *Guide to Reference Books* mentioned above in section 33.2B, these include the following:

1. The *Cumulative Book Index* (1898–) lists by author, title, and subject all books published in the United States from 1898 to the present.

2. The *Subject Guide to Books in Print* tells you what hardbound *and* paperbound books on your topic are currently in print. (If you have any trouble finding a book on your topic in the *Subject Guide*, see below, section 33.3A [pp. 498–99].) This guide does not list any out-of-print books that may be important for your topic, and your library may not have all the books it does list. Nevertheless, it does provide up-to-date information about the latest books on your topic. Here, for instance, is a segment of the listings that Bart Naylor found under "Student Aid" in the 1983–84 edition:

STUDENT AID
see also Scholarships; Student Employment
Barger, Harold & Barger, Gwyneth. College on Credit:
A History of United Student Aid Funds, 1960-
1980. LC 81-6537. 122p. 1981. 8.50 (ISBN 0-
915145-20-0). Hackett Pub.
Carley, V. A. Student Aid in the Secondary Schools of
the United States. LC 77-176626. (Columbia
University. Teachers College. Contributions to
Education: No. 594). Repr. of 1933 ed. 17.50
(ISBN 0-404-55594-2). AMS Pr.
Chronicle Guidance Publications. Chronicle Student
Aid Annual, 1983. rev. ed. 395p. 1983. pap. 14.50
(ISBN 0-912578-56-4). Chron Guide.
Davis, Jerry S. & Van Dusen, William D. Guide to the
Literature of Student Financial Aid. 1978. pap.
7.00 (ISBN 0-87447-053-6, 238620) College Bd.
Fenske, Robert H. & Huff, Robert P. Handbook of
Student Financial Aid: Programs, Procedures &
Policies. LC 83-11336. (Higher Education Ser.).
1983. text ed. write for info. (ISBN 0-87589-571-
9). Jossey-Bass.

Not every item in this list interested Bart. Since he had already decided to write about financial aid for college students, he knew that he could safely ignore the Carley book. But the first item on the list looked promising, and so did the fourth and fifth. The fifth, in fact, seemed the most promising of all, since it had just been published and Bart wanted up-to-date information on student aid. So he did what you should do whenever you find a reference to a source that may be useful; he made a note of its author (in this case two authors) and title. (If you want to know right now how to fill out a source card completely, see section 33.5, "Keeping Track of Your Sources.")

3. The *Book Review Digest* summarizes book reviews under the name of the author, and will tell you what you can learn from a book and how good it is. If, for instance, you were thinking about a paper on evolution and wanted to know something about *The Dragons of Eden*, by Carl Sagan (1977), here is a sample of what the *Digest* would tell you:

SAGAN, CARL. The dragons of Eden; speculations on the evolution of human intelligence. 263p il $8.95 '77 Random House

153 Intellect. Brain. Genetics
ISBN 0-394-41045-9   LC 76-53472

In this study of human intellect "Sagan is principally preoccupied with the neocortex, with its left hemisphere, responsible for language and logic, a right hemisphere in charge of intuition and spatial dimension, and a corpus callosum that mediates and synthesizes the two. The book [also offers] . . . an examination of myths, of dreams and dreaming, of left-handedness versus right-handedness, of the moment when abortion crosses the boundary that divides the possibly humane from the possibly criminal, of the teaching of chimpanzees to communicate. [Sagan] writes of the future of computers and the likelihood that someday science will find it possible to apply by computer technology 'eyeglasses to the mind.'" (Atlantic) Bibliography. Index.

Reviewed by S. C. Reingold
America 137:319 N 4 '77 1100w

"What happens when an astronomer and space scientist turns inward to an exploration of the

human brain? If the man is Sagan, he writes a
rational, elegant, and witty book. . . . The second
chapter is, as he acknowledges, difficult for even
an initiated layman. . . . [But] after that, the
going is illuminating and 'frequently delightful.
. . . No doubt some scientists will quarrel or
quibble over some of Sagan's speculations. Many
others will surely squirm with envy that one of
their number can combine such clarity and charm
of prose with a considerable measure of humility."
Robert Manning

Atlantic 240:91 Ag '77 360w

Choice 14:1386 D '77 180w

"Like many non-specialist popularizers of psychology, Sagan overestimates our physiological
knowledge and underestimates our psychological
knowledge. . . . Though he knows how profoundly
science can change our picture of the world, [he]
seems not to realize that the psychological shift
in outlook promises to be deeper, broader, and at
times more difficult to accept than the Copernican
and Darwinian ones were. Once again, people are
to confront a science that challenges their ego-
centricity. . . . The intensity of their resistance
is already apparent. . . . None of this surfaces
in, or even ripples the surface of, Professor
Sagan's book. He is asking his readers to change
their minds about almost nothing, though doing
so with grace, humor, and style." R. J. Herrn-
stein

Commentary 64:66 Ag '77 2500w

Reviewed by M. C. Coombs
Library J 102:1198 My 15 '77 130w

All of these reviews appeared in 1977, the same year as the book.
But some book reviews do not appear until the year after a book is
published, so you should check the *Digest* for both years. Also, since
the *Digest* favors books of general interest over academic and specialized works, it may not contain any reviews of a book in the latter
category.

4. The *Book Review Index* and *Current Review Citations* (which ended
in 1982) will tell you where to find reviews of the books you're
interested in, though they don't print digests of the reviews themselves. Also, you can learn about reviews of scholarly books—which
are usually not covered by the *Book Review Digest*—in three other
sources: the *Combined Retrospective Index to Book Reviews in Scholarly
Journals, 1886–1974*, and the book review sections of the *Humanities Index* and *Social Sciences Index*. But if the title and date of a particular book make it seem promising, you may simply want to get
the book itself rather than tracking down reviews of it first.

5. The *RIE (Resources in Education)* summarizes virtually all books
on educational topics. See p. 496.

EXERCISE 6   Using Book Reviews

Using the *Book Review Digest* and the *Book Review Index*, investigate reviews
of *Time on the Cross*, a book about slavery written by Robert William Fogel
and Stanley L. Engerman and published in 1974. What impression of the
book do you get from the reviews?

33.2F Guides to Articles in Books

The *Essay and General Literature Index* lists the titles and authors of articles collected in books. Though it does not list articles from highly specialized books, it does cover a wide range of topics. If you wanted sources on the revolution in Nicaragua, for instance, looking up "Nicaragua" in the *Essay and General Literature Index* for 1983 would lead you to this:

> **Nicaragua**
>
> **Foreign relations—United States**
>
> Gorostiaga, X. Dilemmas of the Nicaraguan Revolution. *In* The Future of Central America, ed. by R. R. Fagen and O. Pellicer p47-66

To make a note on this source, record the author and title of the article as well as the title of the book in which it appears: *The Future of Central America.* You will need the title to locate the book in the library catalogue.

EXERCISE 7   **Making a Note on an Article in a Book**

Using the *Essay and General Literature Index,* find an article in a book that might prove useful for research on your topic. Then make a note of the article, being sure to record not only its author and title but also the title of the book.

33.2G General Indexes to Periodicals

These include the following:

1. The *Reader's Guide to Periodical Literature,* issued every month and cumulated quarterly as well annually, is an author-and-subject index to articles of general (rather than scholarly) interest published in over a hundred American magazines. When Bart Naylor looked up "Student Aid" in the August 1984 issue of the *Guide,* here is what he found:

> **Student aid**
> *See also*
> Scholarships and fellowships
> Student Loan Marketing Association
> Civil rights v. freedom [Supreme Court decision in Grove City College Title IX sex discrimination case] *Natl Rev* 36:19 Ap 20 '84
> A double-edged decision by the Court on Grove City College [Title IX sex discrimination case] *Christ Today* 28:70-2 Ap 6 '84
> Financing higher education for low-income students. K. G. Ryder. il *USA Today* 112:53-4 My '84

Graduate education in America [address, February 14,
1984] J. Brademas. *Vital Speeches Day* 50:373-7 Ap
1 '84
How to pay for the Ivy League. R. Kaldenbach. por
Newsweek 103:16 Ap 23 '84
New ways to pay for college. G. Hechinger. il *Glamour*
82:348+ Ap '84
Rep. Stokes urges loans for black health students. por
Jet 66:23 My 7 '84

To identify and locate any of these sources, you have to know
how to decipher the entries. First, the words *See also* direct you to
other headings in the *Guide* that might give you other useful sources.
Then comes the first source under this heading: an article entitled
"Civil Rights versus Freedom," which appeared in the April 20,
1984 issue of the *National Review*, volume 36, page 19. (If the name
of the periodical is abbreviated, as in this case, the list of abbreviations at the beginning of the *Reader's Guide* will tell you what *Natl
Rev* stands for.) Finally, the bracketed words after the title tell you
what the article is about when the title itself doesn't tell you enough.

In this list Bart Naylor found an item that not only caught his
eye but also helped him to narrow his topic. Looking at the third
item (in which "il," by the way, means "illustrated"), he began to
think that he might focus on the special problems of low-income
students. In any case, he could see at once that Ryder's article would
help him find the answer to one of the questions he had already
asked himself: Is financial aid going to the students who need it
most? Once again, therefore, he made a note of the item, jotting
down not only the author's name and title of the article, but also—
just as importantly—the facts on where it appeared: *USA Today*,
volume 112, pages 53–54, issue of May 1984. He would need this
information to find the article.

2. The *Magazine Index* lists chiefly by subject matter articles from
over four hundred magazines. It's a microtext made to be used
with a special viewer. The reference librarian will tell you if your
library has one and where to find it.

3. The *New York Times Index* lists selected articles published in the
Times from 1851–1912, and all articles published in the *Times*
thereafter. Issued twice a month with quarterly cumulations and
then bound into annual volumes, this index is a prime source of
up-to-date information.

33.2H Specialized Indexes to Periodicals

These list articles in one or more more specified fields. Here is a
small selection:

1. The *Environment Index* lists articles as well as books and technical reports under subject headings such as "Oil Spills." Many of the articles are briefly summarized in a companion volume, *Environment Abstracts.*

2. The *General Science Index* lists articles under subject headings in fields such as astronomy, botany, genetics, mathematics, physics, and oceanography.

3. The *Humanities Index* lists articles by author and subject in fields such as archaeology, folklore, history, language, literature, the performing arts, and philosophy.

4. The *MLA International Bibliography,* published annually, is an author-and-subject index to books as well as articles on modern languages, literatures, folklore, and linguistics. Until 1981, the "subjects" covered are usually the names of literary authors—such as Shakespeare, Hemingway, and Virginia Woolf—on whom scholarly articles have been written. But since 1981, the bibliography has also included "topics" in the usual sense, such as "women in fiction."

5. The *Social Sciences Index* lists articles by author and subject in fields such as anthropology, economics, law, criminology, medical science, political science, and sociology.

6. The *Public Affairs Information Service (PAIS)* covers articles on public affairs and public policy as well as government documents and books.

EXERCISE 8   Making Notes on Articles in Periodicals

Using a general or specialized index to periodicals, find out about two articles on your topic and make a note on each. Be sure to note the name and date of the periodical in which each article appears.

33.2I   Government Publications

The United States government produces a vast amount of printed matter on a wide range of subjects. Here is a sample of the guides to this material:

1. The *ASI (American Statistics Index)* consists of two volumes, *Index* and *Abstracts.* The first is a subject index to statistical documents produced by hundreds of government offices; the second describes the documents more fully.

2. The *CIS,* published by the Congressional Information Service, also consists of two volumes, *Index* and *Abstracts.* It indexes the working papers of Congress, including reports, documents, and other special publications of nearly three hundred House, Senate, and joint committees and subcommittees.

3. The *Monthly Catalog of United States Government Publications*, indexed semiannually, lists government publications by author, title, and subject matter.

4. *Resources in Education (RIE)*, issued monthly and indexed semiannually by the Educational Resources Information Center (ERIC), lists books, pamphlets, and conference papers on educational topics under subject headings, author, and title, and also *summarizes* every document it lists. Though *RIE* does not list journal articles on education, you will find these in the *Current Index to Journals in Education (CIJE)*, also produced by ERIC. Since these two sources together treat virtually all publications dealing with educational topics, they are indispensable to anyone working on a topic in the field of education.

The reference librarian who told Bart Naylor about this source advised him first to check the *Thesaurus* of subject headings for *RIE* listings. There Bart found that for items on "Student Aid" he should look under "Student Financial Aid." A check of that heading in the semiannual index for January to June 1984 turned up a very promising item numbered ED (ERIC Document) 234 734. To locate the summary of this item, he simply checked the ED numbers on the backs of the monthly issues of *RIE* for the first half of 1984. What he found in the February 1984 issue was this:

ED 234 734   HE 016 695
Access and Choice: Equitable Financing of Post-
   secondary Education. Report No. 7.   — **Publisher**
National Commission on Student Financial Assist-◄
   ance, Washington, DC.
Spons Agency—Congress of the U.S., Washington,
   D.C.   **Summaries of**
Pub Date—Jul 83   **related docu-**
Note—186p.; For related documents, see ED 228 ◄   **ments can be**
   926-975, HE 016 690-694, and HE 016 697.   **found under**
Pub Type— Reports - Evaluative (142)   **this number.**
EDRS Price - MF01/PC08 Plus Postage.
Descriptors—*Access to Education, College
   Choice, College Students, Cooperative Educa-
   tion, Credit (Finance), *Educational Equity (Fi-
   nance), Eligibility, Enrollment Trends, Federal
   Aid, *Financial Policy, Inflation (Economics),
   Low Income Groups, Operating Expenses, Post-
   secondary Education, Program Costs, Public Poli-
   cy, Student Employment, *Student Financial Aid,
   *Student Loan Programs   **Subject head-**
Identifiers—*Guaranteed Student Loan Program,   **ings under**
   *National Comm on Student Financial Assistance   **which related**
   Current federal student financial assistance pro-   **documents**
   grams are described, and their impact on access to   **can be found**
   and choice of postsecondary education are assessed.
   In addition, recommendations and policy options
   for promoting educational opportunity are offered.
   Findings of the following eight studies are analyzed:
   (1) changes in college attendance and student aid
   for 1969, 1974, and 1981; (2) the effects of inflation

"EDRS Price" indicates that the document is published on ERIC microfiche.

on student aid policy; work patterns of full-time college students in 1974 and 1981; (3) a national assessment of cooperative education; (4) the effects of phasing out social security student benefits; (5) the cost to borrowers of participating in the Guaranteed Student Loan program (GSL); (6) the cost and flows of capital in the GSL program; (7) restrictions imposed on GSL borrowing by guaranty agencies, lenders, and state secondary markets; (8) and contradictions of federal public assistance and college opportunity policies. In addition, testimonies from hearings on student financial assistance are presented. The difficulties that low income students encounter in obtaining a college education are addressed. Appendices include a paper on the eighth study listed above; a summary and commentary on the third study listed above; a discussion of income-contingent proposals; and an index of self-help effort required to pay for college. (SW) ◄——

Since Bart was investigating the problems of low-income students, this sentence told him that here was a source definitely worth looking at.

ED 234 735   HE 016 706
Bok, Derek
Beyond the Ivory Tower. Social Responsibilities of the Modern University.
Report No.—ISBN-0-674-06899-8
Pub Date—82
Note—318p.
Available from—Harvard University Press, Cambridge, MA 02168 ($15.95).
Pub Type— Books (010) — Opinion Papers (120)
Document Not Available from EDRS.
Descriptors—Academic Freedom, Access to Education, *College Role, Developing Nations, *Educational Responsibility, Equal Education, Ethics, *Higher Education, Institutional Autonomy, Moral Development, Public Policy, Racial Relations, *School Community Relationship, *Social Responsibility, Student Development, Technical Assistance, Technological Advancement
    The university's many social and ethical responsibilities are examined in this book by the president of Harvard University. After a discussion of the traditional values of academic freedom, institutional autonomy, and political neutrality, ways that the university's desire for autonomy can be reconciled with the legitimate demands of state and society are suggested. Proposals are offered for using the university's academic resources to address the specific problems of racial inequality, the decline of ethical standards, the need for technological innovation, the risks of scientific research, and the desire for economic development in the Third World. Sugggestions that the university attack social injustice through such nonacademic means as voting stock, boycotting companies, and taking formal stands on controversial issues are assessed. The ramifications of each side of these issues are considered, and solutions are suggested that allow the university to serve society while continuing its primary mission of teaching and research. The book is divided into three main sections: Basic Academic Values; Academic Responses to Social Problems; and Addressing Social Problems by Nonacademic Means. (LB)

Some items listed in *RIE* (such as the second one here) are books and articles you can find on the shelves of your college library. But since the first document summarized is on ERIC microfiche, Bart had to go to the microtext section of the library. There he asked for the document by its ED number, and read it on a microfiche machine, making notes as he did so. (If your library has a microtext copier, you can copy any pages you wish for a small fee.)

EXERCISE 9   Making Notes on Government Publications

Using any of the works listed above, find two sources on your topic (books, reports, or articles) and make a note on each. Be sure to record whatever information you need to find the source, including ERIC ED numbers where necessary.

33.3 Finding Books—The On-Line Catalog and the Card Catalog

If you have done some work in the reference section, you now have not only an overview of your topic but also a list of books and articles on it. But you don't yet know how many of those sources your library has. To find that out and then locate the books themselves, you need to consult one or more catalogs. This section explains how to find books through the catalog; section 33.4 explains how to find articles.

33.3A   Finding Subject Headings for Your Topic

Unless you already know from your work in the reference room exactly what books you want, you should first look up your topic in the *Library of Congress Subject Headings.* Since library catalogs (whether on-line or on cards) use these subject headings, this volume will tell you which headings to check for your topic, and which ones aren't worth checking. When Bart Naylor looked up "student aid" in the volume, part of what he found was this:

Student aid   *(Indirect)*
　　sa Scholarships
　　　　Student employment
　　　　Student financial aid administration
　　　　Student loan funds
　　xx College costs
　　　　Personnel service in education
　　　　Students
　　— Law and legislation   *(Indirect)*
　　　　x Scholarships—Law and legislation
　　　　　　Student loan funds—Law and
　　　　　　　legislation
Student aspirations   *(Indirect)*
　　x Aspirations, Student
　　　　Educational aspirations
　　　　Student plans
　　xx Level of aspiration
Student assistants in libraries
　　See Student library assistants
Student attitudes
　　See Students—Attitudes

Student bar associations *(Indirect)*
 x Law student associations
 xx Bar associations
  Law—Study and teaching
  Law schools
  Law students
Student cheating
 See Cheating (Education)

The boldfaced phrase at the top indicates that "student aid" is a recognized subject heading.† Under "student aid" the symbol *sa* ("see also") points to four related headings that may lead to sources not cataloged under the main heading. The symbol *xx* designates broader headings, such as "college costs" that also may lead to further useful sources. Finally, the symbol *x* designates headings not used by the Library of Congress, and therefore not worth checking.

33.3B Using the On-Line Catalog

The on-line catalog is a computerized file of a library's holdings. No such catalog is likely to be complete for some years to come, but if your library has begun to compile one, it's the best place to start your search for the books you need. (If your library doesn't have an on-line catalog, skip this section and go on now to section 33.3C on p. 500.) To use the on-line catalog, ask any librarian for the location of the nearest terminal and follow the instructions listed beside it. You can then call up a specific book by author or title, or ask the computer to search its file for books on a given topic. Since no two computer systems are exactly alike, we can't tell you exactly what your library's system will do, but we can tell you what Bart Naylor got from the on-line catalog in his library. Knowing that "student aid" was a recognized subject heading, he asked the computer to tell him what books the library had on that topic. The computer promptly came up with twenty-one items, which he could scan by simply pressing the "Return" key from time to time. Here is a partial list of the items that came up on the screen:

```
Citation  4
LO   Baker LB-2340-146
TI   The impact of *student* financial *aid* on institutions /.
IM   San Francisco : Jossey-Bass, 1980.

Citation  6
LO   Baker LB-2336-069
AU   Cox, Claire.
TI   How to beat the high cost of college.
IM   [New York] Bernard Geis Associates; 1964.
```

†The word *Indirect* means that subheadings under "Student Aid" may include references to student aid in various countries, so that if you wanted to know about student aid in England, for instance, you would learn about it indirectly here, and not directly under the heading "England."

Finding Books—The On-Line Catalog and the Card Catalog **499**

```
Citation  13
LO   Baker  LB-2371-B727
AU   Breneman,  David  W.
TI   Graduate school adjustments to the  "New Depression" in higher
     education.
IM   Washington,  National Board on Graduate Education, 1975.

Citation  14
LO   Baker LB-2833-U5
AU   United States.   General Accounting Office.
TI   Supply and demand conditions for teachers and implications for Federal
     programs,  Office of Education,  Department of Health,  Education, and
     Welfare.
IM   [Washington]  1974.

Citation  15
LO   Baker  LB-2337.  5-N47-P39
TI   Paying for college, financing education at nine private institutions.
IM   Hanover,  N.H.  Distributed for the Sloan Study Consortium by the
     University Press of New England,  1974.
```

The first line in each citation locates (LO) the book by giving the name of the library (in this case "Baker") and the library call number. The second line gives the author (AU) unless—as in the case of citation 4—the book is a collection of articles written by various hands. The third line gives the title (TI); the fourth gives the imprint (IM) or name of the publisher.

Looking at these citations, Bart could see that not all of them would be helpful. Since his topic concerned college students, he knew that he could safely ignore books about graduate school (no. 13) and teachers (no. 14). He also wondered about item 6: would a book over twenty years old help him to define the problems currently faced by college students? Since it might be useful for the purpose of comparing present costs with previous costs, he made a note of it, jotting down the library call number along with the author and title. Bart could also see that items 4 and 15 would be particularly useful to him, so he jotted them down too. (The asterisks in the title of item 4 highlight the search words "student aid" and thus mark this book as one of particular interest to the searcher.)

33.3C   Using the Card Catalog

The on-line catalog may eventually displace the card catalog, but for the next few years at least, the card catalog will remain essential to anyone who wants to know what a particular library has on a given topic. One thing Bart discovered when he scanned the twenty-one citations on the computer screen is that they did not include Fenske and Huff's *Handbook of Student Financial Aid*—a book that any computer worth its bytes should certainly have turned up in a search for items on "student aid." Did this mean that his library didn't have the book? Only the card catalog could tell him, and only the card catalog could tell him what other library books on his topic the computer might not yet have on file.

The card catalog tells you about *all* the books in the library. Each book is listed in three ways: by author, by title, and by subject. Usually the author cards, title cards, and subject cards are alphabetized together; in some libraries, the subject cards are separate. If you don't know where to find a particular card, ask a librarian to help you.

If you know the author of the book you want, check the author card. That will give you the title and a good deal more. By looking up *Fenske, Robert H.* in the card catalog, Bart found this:

Library call number indicates where you can find the book

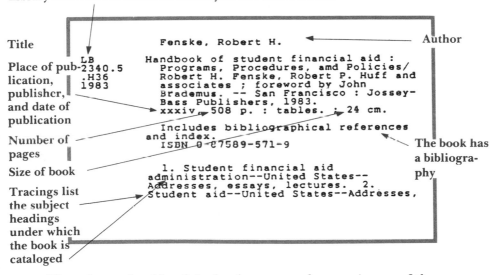

If you know the title of the book you want but aren't sure of the author, check the title card.

If you have only a subject, check the subject card.

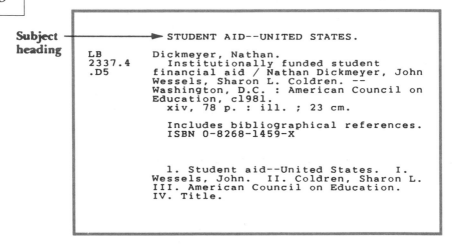

Subject
heading → STUDENT AID--UNITED STATES.

```
LB          Dickmeyer, Nathan.
2337.4        Institutionally funded student
.D5         financial aid / Nathan Dickmeyer, John
            Wessels, Sharon L. Coldren. --
            Washington, D.C. : American Council on
            Education, c1981.
              xiv, 78 p. : ill. ; 23 cm.

              Includes bibliographical references.
              ISBN 0-8268-1459-X


              1. Student aid--United States.   I.
            Wessels, John.   II. Coldren, Sharon L.
            III. American Council on Education.
            IV. Title.
```

Subject cards tell what books a library has on a subject. But you may not readily find your subject among the headings in the card catalog. For instance, if your research topic is "Blacks in Business," you have to know that until 1976 the subject heading for books on blacks was "Negroes" and that the subject heading for books on American blacks now is "Afro-Americans." If you are doing research on computers, you may have to look under "Electronic Calculating Machines." These are the kinds of things you can learn from the *Library of Congress Subject Headings* mentioned earlier. But once again, if you can't readily find the subject heading for your topic, ask the reference librarian to help you.

If a card has tracings, check them for possible leads. Tracings tell you what subjects to look for in the library catalog in order to find more books on your topic. When Bart checked the author card for the Fenske book, he noted the tracing "Student Aid—United States." Checking the subject cards under this heading, he found the Dickmeyer book—and a number of others.

Or take another example. After reading Herman Melville's *Moby-Dick,* a student wanted to find out about whaling in nineteenth-century America. Checking the subject cards for "Whaling," she found one for *Yankee Whalers in the South Seas,* by A. B. C. Whipple. The second tracing on this card was "Voyages and travels." On checking through the cards with this subject heading, she found one for the book *Whale Hunt,* by Nelson Cole Haley, a harpooner. Here was a book by someone with firsthand experience of whaling—an ideal source for anyone interested in that topic.

33.3D   Getting Books Your Library Doesn't Have

33.5

If you can't find a particular book in the card catalog but would like to use it in your research, ask to see the person in charge of interlibrary loan. Provided you can wait at least a week for the book, your library may be able to borrow it for you from another library.

33.4 Finding Articles

The reference works described above in sections 33.2F–H will tell you about articles on your topic. Once you know what those articles are, you need to locate each of them in your library.

If the article appears in a book of articles or essays, find the call number of the book by looking up its title in the card catalog.

If the article appears in a periodical, ask the reference librarian where to find it. Some libraries list all periodicals under their titles (like book titles) in the card catalog; others list periodicals in a separate file, often called a "serials list." If the article you want is more than a year old, it may be in a bound volume with a library call number, and you can locate the volume just as you locate a book. If the article is less than a year old, you will probably find the issue that contains it in the periodical section of your library, where printed instructions or the person in charge will tell you where to locate the issue.

Since it always takes time for new issues to be bound at the end of each year, the issue you want may be neither on the shelf nor in the periodical room, but at the bindery. If you can't find the issue you want, ask the person in charge of the periodical section when and where it will be available.

33.5 Keeping Track of Your Sources

As you learn about sources from various reference books, you should jot down names of authors, titles, and other information (such as names and dates of periodicals) so that you can find the sources in your college library. You can make these notes in any form you wish, so long as you get the essential information you need. But the best way to keep track of your sources—especially when you start using the card catalog—is to fill out a 3-by-5-inch card on each source you plan to read. The card should have all the information you need to find the source in the library and then to cite it in your paper. Here, for instance, are source cards for three different kinds of publications.

33.5A   Source Card for a Book

a
> LB 2340. 5
> , H36
> 1983

b
> Fenske, Robert H., Robert P. Huff and
> Associates

c
> <u>Handbook of Student Financial Aid:</u>
> <u>Programs, Procedures, and Policies</u>

d
> Bibliography

e
> San Francisco: Jossey-Bass, 1983

This source card provides the following information:

    a. The library call number at upper left. This enables you to locate the book in the stacks, or to fill out a call slip for the librarian at the circulation desk.

    b. Author's name, last name first. If there is more than one author, the names of those after the first one go in normal order, and if the authors include "associates," you should note that too.

    c. Title and subtitle. To distinguish books from articles, underline book titles.

    d. Bibliography. If the book has a bibliography, you should note that because it can lead you to further sources.

    e. Place of publication, publisher, and date of publication. You'll need all three when you cite the book in your paper, and you must often consider the date of a book when you use material from it. (A book about college costs published in 1964, for instance, hardly carries the same weight as a book on this topic published in 1983.) If the book is a reprint, you should note both the date of the reprint and the date of original publication.

33.5B   Source Card for an Article

If the periodical containing the article has a call number, put that number in the upper left (a); if not, just make a note of the periodical's location, such as "per rm Row G" (row G of periodical room), or just "per rm." You also need the author's name (b) if the article is signed, and the title of the article in quotation marks to distina   *L11. 144*

b   *Ryder, K. G.*

c   *"Financing Higher Education for Low-Income Students"*

d   *USA Today 112: 53-54 May '84*

guish it from a book title (c). At the bottom goes the name of the periodical, the volume number, issue number (if given), page numbers, and date (d).

If the article appears within a book, record the call number and publishing information on the book in the way shown above (at no. 1).

33.5C   Source Card for a Document from an Information Service

a   *National Commission on Student Financial Assistance*

b   *Access and Choice: Equitable Financing of Postsecondary Education*

c   *Rept. 7*

d   *ERIC, 1983. ED 234 734*

Besides the author (a) and title (b), a source card on a document from an information service must include the report number (C), if any, plus the name of the service and the document number (d).

33.5D   Checking Your Source Card against the Source

Once you actually do get hold of a particular source, make sure that the information on your source card is accurate and complete. Do as follows:

1. If the book has more than one author listed on the title page, get all of the names.

2. If it's an edited book, get the editor's name.

3. If it's part of a series, get the name of the series and its number in the series.

4. If it's an article, get the numbers of the first and last pages, the numbers of the volume and issue (if given), and the date.

5. If it's a document from an information service, check the author, title, and document numbers against the data on your source card.

Checking all this information now can save you trouble later, when you may not have the source in hand but will have to cite it fully and accurately.

EXERCISE 10   **Making Source Cards**

Using the card catalog and the list of serials, get the call numbers of one book and of one periodical containing an article that you would like to use in your research. Fill out a card for each source as shown above.

33.6 Using Microtexts

Because of storage problems, libraries have increased their use of microtexts—printed material photographically reduced in size and readable only with the aid of mechanical viewers. The two most common forms are microfilm (on reels) and microfiche (in which the images are placed in rows on cards). On general principles you should probably familiarize yourself with your library's supply of microtexts and with the procedures for viewing them. Some excellent sources, such as complete files of major newspapers, may be available only in this form.

EXERCISE 11   **Finding Microtext Sources**

Find out whether any promising sources on your topic are printed on microfilm or microfiche. Make a list of at least three such sources.

33.7 Choosing Which Sources to Consult

As you work your way through reference books and catalogs, you will probably find more sources than you can manage in the time you have. You should therefore look for the following:

1. Works with obvious relevance to your topic. A title such as *Handbook of Student Financial Aid* clearly promises a book important to anyone doing research on the financing of a college education. Likewise, a title such as *Whale Hunt* should capture the interest of anyone working on the topic of whaling. But if your topic is exploration, you should ignore a book such as Nelson Cole Haley's *Whale Hunt*—even though it is cataloged under the subject heading "Voyages and travels." Whaling and exploration are two different things, and the slim chance that Haley might have something to say about exploration doesn't really justify a search for his book.

2. Works published recently. Most of the time you can safely assume that recently published works give you up-to-date information, which is valuable not just for current topics but for topics concerned with the past. A recent book on the American Revolution, for instance, may be more reliable and more informative than one published in 1862 or even 1962. Furthermore, a recent book will usually cite most or all of the important books on its subject that came before it.

How recent is "recent"? That depends on the field. If you are writing about computers or energy sources or television or the exploration of outer space, you will want books published within the past five or ten years because these are technological fields, and technology changes fast. But if your topic is in a slower-moving field, such as history or psychology, you can regard anything published since 1970 as relatively recent.

3. Classics. Some books stay alive long after they are published. Classics include not just enduringly great works of poetry, fiction, and drama, but also nonfiction works of lasting importance in various fields: in political theory, Alexis de Tocqueville's *Democracy in America* (1835); in biology, Charles Darwin's *Origin of Species* (1859); in psychology, Sigmund Freud's *Interpretation of Dreams* (1900); in physics, Albert Einstein's *Relativity* (1916); in economics, John Maynard Keynes's *General Theory of Employment, Interest, and Money* (1936). Unfortunately, the card catalog won't tell you whether a particular book is a classic in its field. But if you start your research by reading an overview of your topic, or a recent book on it, you are almost certain to find out what the classics in the field are.

4. Primary and Secondary Sources. *Primary* means "first," and a primary source is one on which later, or secondary, sources are based. Depending on the subject, primary sources may be more or less valuable than secondary ones.

There are two kinds of primary sources: informational and authorial. An *informational* primary source is any firsthand account of an experience or discovery—an Arctic explorer's diary of an expedition, a scientist's report on the results of an experiment, a news story on a disaster written by someone who has seen it. *Authorial* primary sources are the writings of the individual you are studying. If you are investigating the life, works, or theories of a particular person, anything written by that person is a primary source for your purposes; anything written about that person's writings is a secondary source.

You need not always draw a line between primary and secondary sources, nor should you always feel obliged to start with primary ones. If you are investigating a particular author or thinker, you should normally start by reading at least some of what he or she has written and then see what has been written about that person's works. But if you are seeking information of an impersonal kind, you do best to start with secondary sources and let them lead you to the primary ones. Secondary sources are further than primary sources from what they describe, but for that very reason, they may give you a more detached, objective point of view.

5. Books with bibliographies. As already noted above, the catalog card tells you whether the book has a bibliography—a list of related books and articles. Because it focuses on a given topic, a bibliography can save you time—especially if it appears in a recent book.

Some bibliographies are annotated, supplying descriptions and evaluations of the works they list. And in place of a list, you will often find bibliographical notes—that is, a succession of paragraphs about various books. Here, for instance, is just one of the notes to be found in the bibliographical section of *Handbook of Student Financial Aid:*

Franklin, P. *Beyond Student Financial Aid: Issues and Options for Strengthening Support Service Programs Under Title IV of the Higher Education Act.* New York: College Entrance Examination Board, 1980. Franklin argues that student financial aid is not enough to equalize opportunity for postsecondary education; federal support service programs, Talent Search, Upward Bound, and Special Services for Disadvantaged Students (known as the "Trio" programs), as well as the more recent Educational Information Centers, are critical to the achievement of this goal. The heart of this publication is Chapter 3, which assesses issues and options that span the Title IV support service programs. These involve (1) level of authorization, (2) interprogram overlap and duplication, (3) interprogram integration and/or coordination, and (4) student eligibility. The final chapter contains program-by-program recommendations intended to help clarify the purpose and scope of Trio programs and enhance their respective operations. This publication is an illuminating discussion of the policy options for the "other" provision of Title IV.

EXERCISE 12   Using a Bibliography

In the card catalog under a subject heading that interests you, find the title of a book with a bibliography. Then get the book, consult the bibliography, and write down the four sources you would most want to read if you were doing a research paper on the subject.

33.8 Examining Your Sources

When you have gathered the sources you plan to use, you are ready to examine them. As you read, of course, you will probably learn about other sources, and you should keep a record of these for later investigation. But your chief task now is to examine the materials you have on hand. Here are some suggestions about how to do so.

1. Organize your reading time. List in order of importance the books and articles you plan to consult, and set up a reading schedule. Plan to finish all your reading and note-taking a week before the paper is due. After you have done your reading and note-taking, you will need time to assimilate your sources, to make coherent sense out of them.

2. Read selectively. You can often get what you want from a source without reading all of it. Since you may have to consult many sources in a very short time, you should learn to read them selectively.

If your source is a book, read the preface to get an idea of its scope and purpose. Then scan the table of contents and the index for specific discussions of your topic. Then read any promising sections, watching for important facts and interpretations and taking notes.

3. Read responsibly. Respect the context of what you quote. Reading selectively doesn't mean reading carelessly or lifting statements out of context. To understand what you are quoting and to judge it adequately, you may have to read a good part of the section or chapter in which it appears—enough, at least, to familiarize yourself with the context.

4. Read critically. Critical reading is more important for an analytical research paper than for a survey, but in either case, you need to decide whether what you are reading is worth citing at all. Beyond that, you need to decide how reliable its evidence and arguments are. If the writer gives opinions without facts to support them, or makes statements of "fact" without citing sources, you should be suspicious.

33.9 Taking Notes

You can take notes on your sources in a variety of ways: by writing on index cards, legal pads, or loose sheets; by photocopying the pages you need; or by typing them out with a word processor so they can be called up and inserted where you need them. One of the best as well as one of the simplest ways of taking notes is with a stack of index cards. Putting each note on a separate card considerably simplifies the task of *arranging* your notes when you start to organize your paper.

We therefore suggest that you use one whole card (4-by-6 or 5-by-7 inches) for each quotation, paraphrase, or summary. The larger size makes it easy to keep note cards separate from source cards and leaves room for comments of your own. (If a note is long, continue it on a second card, which can be stapled to the first.) At the end of each note, write the author's last name, the first important word of the title, and the page number(s) of the material you have used. (See the example on p. 511.)

33.10 Summarizing and Paraphrasing

MIDDLE-INCOME STUDENT AID

The Middle Income Student Assistance Act of 1978 (MISAA) provided federal funds to help middle-income families with the rising college costs.

Gladieux, "Future" 402

Fine — but are low-income students still getting the help they need?

You will need some quotations in your paper, but if you use too many, the reader may lose track of what you yourself are saying. As you take notes, therefore, you should feel free to summarize and paraphrase your sources, compressing them and putting them into your own words. Summarizing a passage or section of a source is a particularly good way of making sure you understand it.

Take for example one of the note cards that Bart Naylor wrote for his paper on student aid—the card shown on the bottom of page 510.

This note derives from a passage on page 402 of an essay by Lawrence Gladieux titled "Future Directions of Student Aid"—an essay appearing on pages 399–433 in the *Handbook* by Fenske and others already cited. Before writing the note, Bart filled out a source card on Gladieux—the card shown below.

Since he already had a source card on the Fenske book, this is all he needed for an essay included in the book. So long as you fill out a source card on every author you use, the only citation you normally need on a note is the name of the author and the page number(s) of the material you're using. (You need a title on the note only if you are using more than one work by an author.)

To see just how Bart has used the Gladieux material, compare his note with what Gladieux actually wrote:

By the mid-1970s, then, a battery of aid programs was in place designed to equalize opportunity for higher education, programs generally targeted (especially the federal ones) on low-income students. But pressure had begun to mount for broadening the base of eligibility—for some kind of response to a perceived "middle-income squeeze" in financing college costs. To reduce the pressure,

33.10

Summarizing and Paraphrasing **511**

the Carter administration went along with a legislative package, the Middle Income Student Assistance Act, to liberalize eligibility for basic grants and open subsidized, guaranteed loans to any student regardless of income or need.

Bart's note does three things with Gladieux's passage:

1. It gives the passage a subject heading that will help Bart decide how to use this note in his paper. When Bart starts writing, he can readily see that this note will fit into his opening discussion of aid for middle-income students.

2. The note catches the essential point of the passage in just one sentence. You can often summarize a writer's words in less time than it would take you to copy all of them out (or even find your way to a Xerox machine), and when you summarize a passage, you are getting a firm grip on its meaning. Notice, by the way, that even though the summary takes just one sentence, it includes the full name of the Middle Income Student Assistance Act as well as its initials in parentheses.

3. The note records Bart's reaction. So even while taking notes, he was beginning to write his paper.

As you summarize or paraphrase, you should of course quote particular words or phrases that seem important. Compare the following passage from Kenneth G. Ryder's article (cited above, p. 505) with Bart Naylor's note on it:

THE PASSAGE: Our data show that low-income and minority students have been particularly hurt by reductions in student financial assistance. This has occurred because funding for Pell grants has been disproportionately lower than funding for the Guaranteed Student Loan (GSL) program.

THE NOTE:

> LOANS vs. GRANTS
>
> Low-income students have been "particularly hurt" by cuts in aid because Pell Grants funding has been "disproportionately lower" than funding for Guaranteed Student Loans.   Ryder, "Financing" 53
>
> _____
>
> Loans vs. grants — a key distinction

In this compressed version of Ryder's statement, Bart quotes only what is most important to him, and the quoted phrases become parts of Bart's own sentence. Once again, Bart is starting to work *on* his sources even at the note-taking stage.

EXERCISE 13 Note-taking

For a source that interests you, make a 3-by-5-inch source card. Then read a passage of at least one paragraph in length and summarize it on one side of a 4-by-6-inch note card, adding your own comment or question. Be sure the note card has a subject heading, the author's last name, the first important word of the title, and the page(s) used.

33.11 Quoting from Sources

You should quote rather than summarize a statement when it precisely and concisely expresses one of the author's fundamental views, when its language is notably vivid or eloquent, or when you expect to analyze it in detail. The note shown here, for instance, quotes a key statement about distortion in dreams from Sigmund Freud's *The Complete Introductory Lectures on Psychoanalysis,* translated and edited by James Strachey (New York: Norton, 1966).

> DISTORTION — CENSORSHIP
>
> "For the time being let us hold fast to this: dream-distortion is a result of the censorship which is exercised by recognized purposes of the ego against wishful impulses in any way objectionable that stir within us at night-time during our sleep."
>
> Freud, Complete 147
>
> Was Freud dogmatic about his theories? He sounds like it.

In quoting, observe the following guidelines:

1. Quote accurately. Be careful to avoid mistakes of any kind. After copying a passage, always proofread your version, comparing it with the original.

2. Use quotation marks to indicate the beginning and the end of quoted material. You must always distinguish between quotation and paraphrase on the card.

3. Use ellipsis dots (. . .) to indicate that you have deliberately omitted words in writing out the quotation. Be careful not to make an omission that distorts the original. You may leave out words only when they are not essential to the meaning of what you quote.

> ORIGINS
>
> "One cannot afford to be naive in dealing with dreams. They originate in a spirit that is not quite human, but is rather a breath of nature. . . . If we want to characterize this spirit, we shall certainly get closer to it in the sphere of ancient mythologies, or the fables of the primeval forest, than in the consciousness of modern man."
>
> Jung, "Approaching" 52
>
> So dreaming is a kind of myth-making?

Compare the quotation on the note card above with the complete passage in Carl Jung's "Approaching the Unconscious," *Man and His Symbols,* ed. Jung and M.-L. von Franz (Garden City, NY: Doubleday, 1964):

> One cannot afford to be naive in dealing with dreams. They originate in a spirit that is not quite human, but is rather a breath of nature—a spirit of the beautiful and generous as well as of the cruel goddess. If we want to characterize this spirit, we shall certainly get closer to it in the sphere of ancient mythologies, or the fables of the primeval forest, than in the consciousness of modern man.

The researcher uses three ellipsis dots to indicate that the last part of the second sentence has been omitted; the fourth dot is a period. If the words before the omission did not make a complete sentence, the researcher would use just the three ellipsis dots and then finish the quotation: "One cannot . . . be naive in dealing with dreams."

What the researcher has omitted in this note is not essential to the meaning of the passage quoted. But see what happens to the passage when a quotation does leave out something essential:

> One cannot afford to be naive in dealing with dreams. They originate in a spirit that is not quite human, but is rather a breath of nature. . . . If we want to characterize this spirit, we shall certainly get closer to it . . . in the consciousness of modern man.

Jung is now made to say just the opposite of what he actually said. This is the worst possible way of quoting a source.

4. Use brackets to mark explanatory words added within a quotation. The note below derives from Erich Fromm's *The Forgotten Language* (New York: Rinehart, 1951). The brackets in the note indicate an insertion made by the note-taker to indicate who *He* is. The first set of ellipsis dots marks the omission of a whole sentence; the second set marks an omission within a sentence.

FUNCTIONS

"Not only do insights into our relations to others or theirs to us, value judgments and predictions occur in our dreams, but also intellectual operations superior to those in the waking state. . . . The best known example of this kind of dream is the one of the discoverer of the Benzine ring. He [Friedrich Kekule] had been searching for the chemical formula for Benzine . . . and one night the correct formula stood before his eyes in a dream. He was fortunate enough to remember it after he awoke."

Fromm, *Forgotten* 45

So one function of dreams is problem solving.

EXERCISE 14 Quoting a Source

On a note card quote a statement from one of your sources, being sure to use quotation marks. Then check your version against the original, word for word.

EXERCISE 15 Using Ellipsis Dots

In one of your sources find a passage of four or five sentences from which words could be omitted without distortion of the original. Write a version in which you use ellipsis dots twice.

EXERCISE 16 Summarizing and Quoting

Make a note that includes both summary of a source and quotation from it.

33.12 Formulating Your Thesis

By the time you have finished your research, you will have a substantial pile of note cards—perhaps thirty or more. The first step in turning the notes into a paper is to sort them according to their headings. When Bart was taking notes for his paper, he was seeking answers to the questions mentioned earlier in section 33.1, p. 487: questions about the link between financial status and educational opportunity. In reviewing the notes he had taken, Bart saw that they could be sorted into three piles: one for the problems of middle-income students, one for the problems of low-income students, and one for possible solutions to the problems of both.

Once you have sorted the cards, you should reread them, one pile at a time. As you read, you may find that some cards are in the wrong pile, or that some of them belong in a whole new category, or that one of the piles is too big and needs to be broken up into smaller categories. Whatever you do, you will find that the process of sorting note cards is the beginning of thinking your way into the organization of the paper.

If you plan to write an argumentative paper, you should also be thinking now about what your thesis will be. Rereading the cards gives you a concentrated review of all your research, and thus prepares you to decide or discover what basic question you will try to answer. As Bart reread his cards, as he compared the problems of middle-income students with those of low-income students, he found himself drawn to the latter. He asked himself whether middle-income students were in fact getting squeezed as hard as low-income students, what special problems low-income students faced, and how those problems could be solved. The basic question toward which all these questions finally led was this: Is college possible for truly needy students? This question in turn led to a tentative answer, a tentative statement of thesis: The present system fails to give truly needy students a fair chance for higher education.

To formulate a thesis such as this is to take a major step forward in the organization of your paper. If you are writing a survey rather than an analytical argument, you can work without a thesis, but in either case, the right question can help to give all of your notes a coherent shape and purpose. When Erica Berl was preparing her research paper on working women (pp. 631–39), she asked herself how any working mother could reconcile the demands of a job with the responsibilities of child-rearing. That one question generated her expository survey of possible answers—of options for the working mother.

With the basic question in mind, you should look for relations among your notes. You should try to see how one idea reinforces, qualifies, or contradicts another. You must be patient at this point; you must be willing sometimes to stare at a particular note for five or ten minutes, wondering what to do with it. This is the seminal moment of organization, the moment when you begin to see how various individual notes can be made to work together.

33.13 Filling Gaps in Your Research

While you are rereading and sorting your notes, or even after you have decided what kind of paper you will write and what its thesis will be, you may discover that you need to know more about one or two things. You may suddenly discover that you have failed to consult an important source—one that several of your sources often refer to—or have failed to answer an important question. While sorting his own notes, Bart Naylor realized that he had failed to consider the problem of keeping needy students in college once they got there. Looking again at the Fenske *Handbook,* he found a reference to A. W. Astin's *Preventing Students from Dropping Out* (1975). That book filled a definite gap in his research.

34

WRITING THE
RESEARCH PAPER

34.1 In every writing project there comes a time when you must shift from exploring your subject and gathering materials about it to writing a full first draft. For the research paper, this time comes when you are reasonably sure that there are no major gaps in your reading, and when you begin to find patterns of thought or argument as you sort through your note cards. For many writers, the logical next step is to make an outline.

34.1 Making an Outline

The outline of your research paper will grow directly from the arrangement of your note cards. If you have sorted them carefully, you have established the main subject headings of your paper, and the notes themselves, of course, contain the material you will consider under those headings. You must now decide the order in which you will arrange the headings and the order in which, under each heading, you will present your materials. Most importantly, as we have said already in section 33.12, you need a framing question or a thesis. If you plan to write a survey-type research paper, you need a question that will frame or define the survey—such as the question of how working mothers can reconcile their conflicting obligations (see p. 527). If you plan to write an argumentative research paper, you need a thesis, a statement you will defend.

In Part I of this book, we said that the thesis of an ordinary essay is something you often discover as you write, something that emerges from material you yourself have generated or improvised. The thesis of a research paper emerges differently. It comes from the study of your notes. As your notes help you answer the questions with which you set out and at the same time help you choose the basic question you will pursue, this question in turn should lead you to an answer, to a statement, to the contention you will substantiate from your notes. In Bart's case, a basic question about truly needy students led to a thesis about why they were not getting a fair chance for higher education.

Once Bart had formulated his thesis, he could devise an order in which to present the main headings of his topic. To defend his thesis effectively, he knew that he would first have to discuss the financial problems faced by college-bound students from middle-income families. Then he would have to show why low-income students were suffering even more and what specific problems were impeding or even blocking their access to higher education. Finally, having analyzed the problems, he could end by recommending specific solutions.

When you have decided on the order of your main heads and have laid out your note cards, you can outline your research paper. Since you have the material of the paper before you, you don't need a preliminary session of freewriting. And since you have on the cards virtually all of the points you will cover in your paper, you may find that a standard vertical list will serve you better than a tree diagram. (For a full discussion of vertical lists and tree diagrams, see pp. 31–35.) In any case, here is the outline Bart made for his research paper on student aid. Since he knew what he wanted to say, he wrote in full sentences:

THESIS: Though many students from middle-income families must struggle to meet college costs, low-income students suffer even more because of the ways in which colleges and federal agencies distribute aid, advertise it, analyze students' needs, and "package" the aid provided.

    I. College costs often exceed what middle-income families can comfortably afford.
   II. But low-income students face greater obstacles to higher education than middle-income students do.
     A. Federal programs now work to the disadvantage of low-income students.
       1. With funding for grants "disproportionately lower" than funding for loans, fear of heavy debt makes low-income students unwilling to borrow.
       2. The half-cost rule hurts low-income students more than it helps middle-income students.
       3. Besides cutbacks in federal aid to education, cutbacks and

restrictions in other federal programs also penalize low-income students.

   B. Colleges are generally neglecting low-income students.
      1. Better-off students are squeezing out low-income students even at public and community colleges.
      2. Competing for students from middle-income families, some colleges are granting aid to students who don't truly need it.
      3. The gap between the cost of college and the value of aid—including aid from the college itself—forces low-income students into overdemanding combinations of work and study.

III. Without spending substantially more, colleges and federal agencies can and should give low-income students a better chance.
   A. The federal government should eliminate the half-cost rule in the distribution of Pell Grants.
   B. The Department of Education should advertise its aid programs more effectively.
   C. Colleges and federal agencies alike should analyze every student's needs more rigorously.
   D. They should also increase the value of grants in packages of aid designed for low-income students.

IV. CONCLUSION: All of these steps can help to insure that truly needy students get the educational opportunities they deserve.

A full-sentence outline allows you to see exactly where you are headed from the beginning of the paper to the end. As an ordered structure of assertions that work together to support the thesis, this kind of outline plainly defines the writer's argumentative strategy.

34.2 Managing Your Sources as You Write

34.2A Citing Sources in the First Draft

In the final draft of your paper, you may be asked to use one of the methods explained below (see chapter 35, p. 530) to cite your sources. But in writing the first draft, you can cite them simply by putting the following items in parentheses after each use of a source:

   1. author's last name
   2. first important word of title
   3. page number(s) of material used

These three items—along with your source card—will provide all the information you will need for each citation in your first draft. Item 1 will identify the source card for you; item 2 will prevent confusion in case you end up citing two or more sources by one author; and item 3 will give you the page number(s). To illustrate, here is a passage from the first draft of Bart's paper:

> Why does this disproportion hit low-income students harder than others? If loans will serve them just as well, as Hartman indicates (Hartman, *Credit* 3–4), why do they depend more heavily on grants? The simple answer is that loans frighten them. Their reluctance to borrow, says Arthur Hauptman, springs from "deep-seated fears about excessive repayment burdens" (Hauptman, "Shaping" 70).

Use the last name of the first author on your source card if there are two authors or more, and the full name of a corporate author such as "Bureau of Labor Statistics." If your source is anonymous, give just the title word and page numbers.

34.2B Introducing Your Sources

Whenever you use a source in any way, you should introduce it smoothly, either naming the author or clearly indicating that you are about to use a source. If you begin summarizing or paraphrasing without referring to the author, the reader has no way of knowing where your comment ends and your source material begins. Compare these two passages:

> Besides getting less than their fair share of grants, low-income students have also been hurt by cutbacks in other programs. Since 1981, the federal government has been gradually eliminating the student benefits provided by Old Age Survivors Disability Insurance (Ryder, "Financing" 54).

> Besides getting less than their fair share of grants, low-income students have also been hurt by cutbacks in other programs. Ryder points out that since 1981, the federal government has been gradually eliminating the student benefits provided by Old Age Survivors Disability Insurance (Ryder, "Financing" 54).

In the first passage, the reader has no way of knowing just where the writer's use of Ryder begins. In the second, the writer clearly indicates the beginning as well as the end of that use.

Quotation marks indicate the boundary between your own words and those of your source, but you can mark the boundary still more clearly by identifying your source at once. Compare these two passages:

> The mind in sleep is often more creative than the mind in waking hours. "Not only do insights . . . , value judgments and predictions occur in our dreams, but also intellectual operations superior to those in the waking state" (Fromm, *Forgotten* 45).

> The mind in sleep is often more creative than it is in waking hours, Erich Fromm writes: "Not only do insights . . . , value judgments

and predictions occur in our dreams, but also intellectual operations superior to those in the waking state" (Fromm, *Forgotten* 45).

In the first version, the quotation marks indicate that the second sentence is a quotation, but the reader doesn't learn who wrote these words until the end of the passage. In the second version the reader learns the author's name at once. If you were the reader, which would you prefer?

Here are other examples of how to introduce a source.

> According to Fromm, dreams involve "intellectual operations superior to those in the waking state" (Fromm, *Forgotten* 45).

> Freud believed that a dream was always the fulfillment of a wish (Freud, *Interpretation* 154).

> Recent studies cast serious doubt on the Jungian theory that children's dreams are full of frightening archetypes and primitive myths. After five years of research, David Foulkes has reported as follows:
>> At no age was the typical child's REM [rapid eye movement] dream particularly frightening or overwhelming. Little direct evidence could be found, at any age, for a preemptive role of primitive impulses or fantasies in the organization of children's dreams. Little or no evidence could be found, at any age, for the hypothesis that children's dreams bring them into contact with a symbolically complex world of archetypal, primitive myths. (Foulkes, "Dreams" 81)

In each of these examples, the writer introduces a source by naming the author. Because the quotation in the last example is long, it is set off by indentation rather than enclosed in quotation marks. (For more on this point, see section 29.4, p. 446).

34.2C   Plagiarism

Plagiarism is the dishonest act of presenting the words or thoughts of another writer as if they were your own. You commit plagiarism whenever you use a source *in any way* without indicating that you have used it. If you quote anything at all, even a phrase, you must put quotation marks around it or set it off from your text; if you summarize or paraphrase an author's words, you must clearly indicate where the summary or paraphrase begins and ends; if you use an author's idea, you must say that you are doing so. In every instance, you must also formally acknowledge the written source from which you took the material.

You may use a source without formal acknowledgment only when you refer to a specific phrase, statement, or passage that you have used and acknowledged earlier in the same paper. But when you use new material from a source already cited, you must make a new acknowledgment.

We have explained above how to use sources honestly, how to draw the line between what is your own and what you have taken from others. Now here are examples of various kinds of plagiarism. In each instance, the source is a passage from p. 102 of E. R. Dodds's *The Greeks and the Irrational* (Berkeley, 1951; rpt. Boston: Beacon, 1957). First, here is the original note, copied accurately from the book:

FUNCTIONS OF DREAMS: FANTASY

"If the working world has certain advantages of solidity and continuity, its social opportunities are terribly restricted. In it we meet, as a rule, only the neighbors, whereas the dream world offers the chance of intercourse, however fugitive, with our distant friends, our dead, and our gods. For normal men it is the sole experience in which they escape the offensive and incomprehensible bondage of time and space."

Dodds, Greeks 102

Fantasy — an obvious function, but nicely described.

And here are five ways of plagiarizing this source.

1. Word-for-word continuous copying without quotation marks or mention of the author's name:

Dreams help us satisfy another important psychic need—our need to vary our social life. This need is regularly thwarted in our waking moments. If the waking world has certain advantages of solidity and continuity, its social opportunities are terribly restricted. In it we meet, as a rule, only the neighbors, whereas the dream world offers us the chance of intercourse, however fugitive, with our distant friends. We awaken from such encounters feeling refreshed, the dream having liberated us from the here and now. . . .

2. Copying many words and phrases without quotation marks or mention of the author's name:

Dreams help us satisfy another psychic need—our need to vary our social life. In the waking world our social opportunities, for example, are terribly restricted. As a rule, we usually encounter only the neighbors. In the dream world, on the other hand, we have the chance of meeting our distant friends. For most of us it is the sole experience in which we escape the bondage of time and space. . . .

3. Copying an occasional key word or phrase without quotation marks or mention of the author's name:

> Dreams help us satisfy another psychic need—our need to vary our social life. During our waking hours our social opportunities are terribly restricted. We see only the people next door and our business associates. In contrast, whenever we dream, we can see our distant friends. Even though the encounter is brief, we awaken refreshed, having freed ourselves from the bondage of the here and now. . . .

4. Paraphrasing without mention of the author's name:

> Dreams help us satisfy another important psychic need—our need to vary our social life. When awake, we are creatures of this time and this place. Those we meet are usually those we live near and work with. When dreaming, on the other hand, we can meet far-off friends. We awaken refreshed by our flight from the here and now. . . .

5. Taking the author's idea without acknowledging the source:

> Dreams help us to satisfy another important psychic need—the need for a change. They liberate us from the here and now, taking us out of the world we normally live in. . . .

A final note: if there is anything about plagiarism you do not understand, *ask your teacher*.

EXERCISE 1 Recognizing Plagiarism

Pick out the sentences, phrases, and key words that were taken from Dodds in examples 1–3.

EXERCISE 2 Recognizing Plagiarism

Read this two-paragraph passage. Then read the summary that follows, and indicate whether any part of the summary—aside from the word "motifs"—should be in quotation marks.

> And, speaking more generally, it is plain foolishness to believe in ready-made systematic guides to dream interpretation, as if one could simply buy a reference book and look up a particular symbol. No dream symbol can be separated from the individual who dreams
> 5 it, and there is no definite or straightforward interpretation of any dream. Each individual varies so much in the way that his unconscious complements or compensates his conscious mind that it is impossible to be sure how far dreams and their symbols can be classified at all.

10 It is true that there are dreams and single symbols (I should prefer to call them "motifs") that are typical and often occur. Among such motifs are falling, flying, being persecuted by dangerous animals or hostile men, being insufficiently or absurdly clothed in public places, being in a hurry or lost in a milling crowd, fighting with
15 useless weapons or being wholly defenseless, running hard yet getting nowhere. A typical infantile motif is the dream of growing infinitely small or infinitely big, or being transformed from one to the other—as you find it, for instance, in Lewis Carroll's *Alice in Wonderland*. But I must stress again that these are motifs that must
20 be considered in the context of the dream itself, not as self-explanatory ciphers.

—Carl G. Jung, "Approaching the Unconscious," *Man and His Symbols*, ed. Jung and M.-L. von Franz (Garden City, NY: Doubleday, 1964), 53.

SUMMARY: According to Carl G. Jung in "Approaching the Unconscious," it would be just plain foolishness for anyone to think he or she could interpret dreams reliably by buying a ready-made reference book. No such guide has value because it is impossible to separate a dream symbol from the person who dreams it, and the unconscious of everyone is unique. Jung does admit that certain dreams and symbols come often to many. Calling these "motifs," he lists several, including falling, fighting with useless weapons, and running hard yet getting nowhere. But he emphasizes that even the motifs cannot be understood properly unless considered in the context of each dream itself.

34.3 Composing the Paper as a Whole

Composing a research paper is in many ways like writing an ordinary essay. With raw material on your note cards and an outline at hand, you need to turn the material into a coherent survey of a topic or an analytical argument about it. You need to introduce your survey or argument, to develop it with the aid of your notes, and to conclude it. Beyond these general requirements, the writing of a research paper makes its own special demands. To help you meet them we make these suggestions:

1. Introduce the paper by clearly announcing its topic and thesis, or its topic and framing question. Once you have studied your notes, sorted them under headings, decided whether you are going to write an argumentative paper or a survey, formulated a thesis or a framing question, and outlined your paper, you should know essentially what your paper is going to do. If the outline is not quite firm as you start to write, you don't have to write the introduction first. You can write it after you've written the rest of the paper—when you know exactly what you're introducing. But whenever you write it, the introduction should clearly establish the topic of your paper and its thesis or its framing question.

Like any good introduction, the introduction to a research paper should also take account of the reader. If the paper is to be argumentative, the introduction should start by describing the views that the paper will challenge. Here, for instance, is the two-paragraph introduction to Bart Naylor's paper:

> Today few families or students can readily afford a college education. Twenty years ago, the average annual cost of attending a publicly supported college was $2,000 (Cox 16).† In 1982–83, the average was $4,388 at a public institution and $7,475 at a private one (*College Cost Book* 56–57), with some private colleges costing over twice that much. These price tags make it difficult for all but upper-income parents to put their children through college. Though the Middle Income Student Assistance Act of 1978 (MISAA) provided federal funds to help middle-income families with rising costs (Gladieux 402), the net costs continue to rise beyond what middle-income parents can comfortably afford, especially when they have more than one child to put through college. As a result, spokesmen for the middle class have been once again pointing with resentment at the size of federal programs designed to help the poor, once again complaining that middle-income students are being squeezed out of college, and once again demanding that the high cost of college tuition be offset by tax credits (Hearn 8–9).
>
> Middle-income families unquestionably have cause to complain and to demand relief from the strain that college puts on their budgets. But their complaints and demands miss a crucial point. Students from low-income families are not getting more federal aid than students from middle-income families are. They are getting less. Furthermore, while no clear evidence indicates that middle-income students are actually being squeezed out of college (Hearn 8), low-income students definitely are. Their access to higher education is seriously impeded by the ways in which colleges and federal agencies distribute aid, advertise it, analyze students' needs, and "package" the aid provided.

This introduction begins by describing the view that the writer will go on to oppose: the belief that federal laws and aid programs favor low-income students at the expense of middle-income students. Only after considering this view and the problems of middle-income students does the writer turn to low-income students and announce the thesis of his argument.

The introduction to a survey-type research paper leads up to a framing question rather than a thesis, but it can appeal to the reader

---

† For guidance on the parenthetical style of documentation illustrated here, see chapter 35 (pp. 530–57). For the complete text of Bart's paper, see chapter 37 (pp. 560–72).

by describing general attitudes before focusing on a specific problem. Consider the introduction to Erica Berl's paper, "Options for the Working Mother" (starting on p. 631):

> Everyone knows that women are no longer staying at home. They have gone out into the world of work, filling not only such traditionally feminine roles as secretary and clerk, but also such typically masculine roles as lawyer, doctor, stockbroker, business executive, governor, United States senator, and even candidate for the vice presidency. But statistics show that a growing percentage of working women are mothers of preschool children. While less than a third of these mothers held jobs outside the home in 1970, the figure rose to nearly a half by 1978 and is expected to keep on rising into the 1990s.† A crucial question of our time, therefore, is how these women can reconcile the demands of a career with the responsibilities of child-rearing.

Beginning with general observations about working women, this introduction moves to the particular problems faced by working mothers. The question raised by its final sentence identifies a conflict and thus clearly introduces a survey of possible solutions.

2. Make your sources work together. Writing the main part of a research paper is largely a process of weaving your sources into a coherent whole. You are responsible for showing your reader the relations among your sources, for explaining what they signify when taken together.

The trouble with many student research papers is that they are not much more than collections of quoted passages. It is tempting to quote at length, for long quotations fill up the page and save you the trouble of filling it with your own words. But you will not get much credit for a paper full of long quotations. You are much more likely to get a question from your instructor about what you have to say for yourself.

Whenever you quote anything, therefore, ask yourself why you are quoting it. Quote only as much as you need to make your point, and no more. Bear in mind that quoting a word or phrase is a way of emphasizing it—provided it is quoted all by itself. If you want to stress the point that low-income students have been "particularly hurt" by cuts in aid, the quotation marks do the emphasizing for you. But you will lose that emphasis if the phrase is buried in a quotation several sentences long.

In general, your commentary on anything you quote should be at least as long as the quotation itself. If a lengthy passage is impor-

---

† The source of this information is given in a note to the complete text of Erica's paper, which appears in Appendix 1.6 (pp. 631–39). For guidance on documenting with notes, see A1.1–5 (starting on p. 619).

tant enough to be quoted in full, you ought to have something important to say about it. If you don't have much to say about a passage, don't quote it at length, or at all. A long quotation followed by a single sentence of commentary usually tells the reader that the writer is dozing his or her way through the paper.

Remember, too, that quoting is not the only way of using the material in your notes. If you have summarized and paraphrased some of your material while taking notes on it, you already have in hand alternatives to quotation, restatements of your sources in your own words. You will find that when you use summaries instead of lengthy quotations, you can wield your sources much more effectively, that you can make them talk to each other instead of just stolidly filling up a page. Consider this passage from Bart's paper:

> Whatever the future brings, the cuts already made in grants and benefits have clearly begun to take their toll. While studies made in the late 1970s indicated that students considering college were not "primarily" influenced by their parents' ability to pay (Hearn 2), more recent evidence indicates that low-income students are gradually disappearing from colleges of all kinds. A study of enrollment at private colleges in the academic years from 1979–80 to 1981–82 showed a 39 percent drop in students with family incomes of $24,000 or less (Magarrel 1). Furthermore, though Green credits federal aid with getting minority students into public colleges (25), their numbers are falling even at community colleges, which, says Astin, "represent the bottom of the institutional hierarchy within public systems," and which have traditionally had a "disproportionate share" of minority students (*Minorities* 141). Robert G. Templin, Jr., Dean of Instruction at Piedmont Community College in Virginia, says that better-off students are "squeezing out the poor, disadvantaged, and minority students who once called the community college theirs" (quoted Watkins 1).

The writer cites five different sources in this paragraph, but he makes them work together by contrast, subordination, and reinforcement. He contrasts Hearn's point with Magarrel's, subordinating the first to the second, and he then leads up to a telling quotation that reinforces Magarrel's point as well as the main point of the paragraph. The use of brief summaries and short quotations instead of long ones allows him to keep the cited material under control from beginning to end, making it serve his argumentative purpose. (The word "quoted" in the final parentheses indicates that Templin's statement has been quoted in Watkins's article.)

3. End an argumentative paper by reaffirming your thesis and stating its implications. Here is the concluding paragraph of Bart Naylor's paper on needy students:

The widespread notion that low-income students have been reaping educational aid at the expense of middle- and upper-income students is a dangerous misconception. It thrives only because the political influence of higher income groups has diverted attention from the formidable problems that low-income students face. While many middle-income students have legitimate claims to aid, the needs of poorer students are still more pressing. Those students will not be helped by tuition tax credits, which, says Hearn, are "in no way tied to the need of individual families or targeted to specific populations" (8). To enhance the educational opportunities of low-income students, the Department of Education should eliminate the half-cost rule in the distribution of Pell Grants, and together with institutions, it should advertise educational aid more effectively, analyze the needs of all students more rigorously, and give first priority to grants in packages of aid designed for low-income students. All of these steps can help to insure that truly needy students who are capable of college work will get the chance to tackle it.

This concluding paragraph restates the thesis introduced at the beginning of the paper. But after reaffirming the point that low-income students have greater needs than middle-income students do, it ends by recapitulating what has grown out of the thesis: a set of recommendations.

4. End a survey-type research paper by summarizing its findings and stating its implications. Here is the concluding paragraph of Erica's paper on working mothers:

It takes a gift for organization to manage both a job and a family. But given the variety of ways in which the demands of each can be met, a woman no longer needs to feel that she must sacrifice one for the other, must abandon her family for the sake of her job or give up her job for the sake of her family. Working women who happen to be mothers have made themselves an indispensable part of the workforce, and in time, the working mother may become as familiar on the American scene as the working father.

Noting "the variety of ways" in which a working mother can meet her conflicting obligations, Erica neatly sums up her survey. Then she states its implications: women are no longer bound to choose between motherhood and a career.

35

DOCUMENTING THE RESEARCH PAPER

35.1

In the final draft of your research paper, you must clearly identify all the sources you have quoted from, summarized, or paraphrased. For this purpose you will need a style of documentation.

35.1 Styles of Documentation

You can document your sources in one of two ways: (1) by parenthetical references within the paper and a list of works cited at the end, or (2) by numbered notes and a bibliography. This chapter explains the MLA style of parenthetical citation, which is commonly used in research papers on literature, philosophy, art, and other humanistic subjects. If your instructor expects you to cite your sources with notes, turn to Appendix 1. For brief comment on the APA style of parenthetical citation, which is commonly used in papers on history, psychology, and other social sciences, see Appendix 2. If you are writing a research paper on a scientific subject, you may be asked to follow the guidance provided by one of the style manuals listed here under specific subjects:

BIOLOGY

> Council of Biology Editors. Style Manual Committee. *Council of Biology Editors Style Manual: A Guide for Authors, Editors, and Publishers in the Biological Sciences.* 5th ed. Bethesda: Council of Biology Editors, 1983.

CHEMISTRY

> American Chemical Society. *Handbook for Authors of Papers in American Chemical Society Publications.* Washington: American Chemical Soc. 1978.

GEOLOGY

United States Geological Survey. *Suggestions to Authors of the Reports of the United States Geological Survey.* 6th ed. Washington: GPO, 1978.

LINGUISTICS

Linguistic Society of America. *L.S.A. Bulletin,* Dec. issue, annually.

MATHEMATICS

American Mathematical Society. *A Manual for Authors of Mathematical Papers.* 7th ed. Providence: American Mathematical Soc., 1980.

MEDICINE

International Steering Committee of Medical Editors. "Uniform Requirements for Manuscripts Submitted to Biomedical Journals." *Annals of Internal Medicine* 90 (Jan. 1979): 95–99.

PHYSICS

American Institute of Physics. Publications Board. *Style Manual for Guidance in the Preparation of Papers.* 3rd ed. New York: American Inst. of Physics, 1978.

35.2 Citing with Parentheses—The MLA Style

The MLA style of parenthetical citation has been recommended for papers on literature and other humanistic subjects by the Modern Language Association (MLA)—a professional organization of over twenty-five thousand teachers of English and other languages. Complete information on the MLA style appears in the second edition of the *MLA Handbook for Writers of Research Papers,* by Joseph Gibaldi and Walter S. Achtert (New York: Modern Language Association, 1984). In what follows here, we try to explain briefly how to use the MLA style with the kinds of sources you are likely to cite in a research paper written for a college course. Each source cited parenthetically in this section is also shown as it would appear in the list of Works Cited at the end of the paper—an alphabetical list of all the works you have cited. We explain how to write this list in section 35.4.

1. Material introduced without the author's name

When citing the source of material you have introduced without using the author's name, give the author's last name and the pagination—the page number or numbers—within parentheses:

In the early sixties, the average annual cost of
attending a publicly supported college was $2,000
(Cox 16).

For guidance on punctuating parenthetical citations, see section 35.3.

Works Cited

Cox, Claire. How to Beat the High Cost of College.

New York: Bernard Geis Associates, 1964.

2. Material introduced with the author's name

If you use the author's name to introduce the material cited, give
only the pagination:

Ryder points out that colleges now face a "rapid
decline in the number of 18-24 year olds from
middle-income families and a relative increase in
the number of 18-24 year olds from low-income
families" (54).

Works Cited

Ryder, Kenneth G. "Financing Higher Education for
Low-Income Students." USA Today May 1984: 53-
54.

3. Citing more than one work by an author

If you cite in your paper more than one work by an author, give a
short form of the title—along with the pagination—each time you
cite that author:

Community colleges, says Astin, have traditionally
had a "disproportionate share" of minority
students (Minorities 141).

On-campus work of up to twenty-five hours a week,
says Astin, can give students a sense of involve-

ment and help them persevere in their studies

(<u>Preventing</u> 63).

If you introduce the cited material without using the author's name, put that in parentheses just before the title, with a comma and a space dividing the two:

Modern dream researchers now accept the principle

that dreams express "profound aspects of person-

ality" (Foulkes, <u>Sleep</u> 184). But investigation

has shown that young children's dreams are in

general "rather simple and unemotional" (Foulkes,

"Dreams" 78).

Works Cited

Astin, A. W. <u>Minorities in American Higher Educa-</u>

<u>tion: Recent Trends, Current Prospects,</u>

<u>and Recommendations</u>. San Francisco: Jossey-

Bass, 1982.

---. <u>Preventing Students from Dropping Out</u>. San

Francisco: Jossey-Bass, 1975.

Foulkes, David. "Dreams of Innocence."

<u>Psychology Today</u> Dec. 1978: 78-88.

<u>The Psychology of Sleep</u>. New York: Scribner's,

1966.

4. A work with two or three authors

If you cite a work with two or three authors, give all of their last names either in your text or in parentheses:

According to Dickmeyer, Wessels, and Coldren,

commuting students are often poorer than residents

and are generally forced to take on more outside

work (13).

or

One study found that commuting students are often poorer than residents and are generally forced to take on more outside work (Dickmeyer, Wessels, and Coldren 13).

Works Cited

Dickmeyer, Nathan, John Wessels, and Sharon L. Coldren. <u>Institutionally Funded Student Financial Aid</u>. Washington: American Council on Education, 1981.

5. A work with an editor

Mrs. Hurstwood, Dreiser says, "was a cold, self-centered woman, with many a thought of her own which never found expression, not even by so much as the glint of an eye" (104).

Cite the author—not the editor—of the material you are using. Cite the editor only if you are using material written by him or her:

Kenneth Lynn writes: "In the slow, measured manner of Hurstwood´s preparation for suicide, Dreiser reveals to us the essential dignity as well as the tragedy of man" (xvi).

Works Cited

Dreiser, Theodore. <u>Sister Carrie</u>. Ed. Kenneth S. Lynn. New York: Rinehart, 1959.

Lynn, Kenneth. Introduction. Dreiser v-xvi.

(For an explanation of the reference to "Dreiser v–xvi," see section 35.4, item 2, p. 547.)

6. A work with more than three authors or editors

If you cite a work with more than three authors or editors, give the last name of the first author listed plus "et al.," which stands for "et alia," meaning "and others":

```
Some critics argue that content cannot be

separated from form.  "A change in one," they say,

"is a change in the other" (Eastman et al. 1207).
```

Works Cited

```
Eastman, Arthur M., et al., eds.  The Norton

    Reader: An Anthology of Expository Prose.  6th

    ed.  New York: Norton, 1984.
```

7. A work with a corporate author

A work by a corporate author must be cited by the author's full name. If possible, use the name to introduce the material cited:

```
In addition, the National Commission on Student

Financial Assistance says that the federal

government actually discourages low-income

students from going to college.  When they enroll,

says the Commission, it reduces or eliminates

benefits to them and their families from programs

such as Medicaid, Food Stamps, and Public Housing

(4, 11).
```

If the name is long (as corporate names often are), using it to introduce the material spares you the awkwardness of a long parenthesis. But if you do cite the long name parenthetically, try to get it at the end of a sentence:

```
But these programs now serve only about 3 percent

of students eligible for them (National Commission

on Student Financial Assistance 76).
```

Works Cited

```
National Commission on Student Financial

    Assistance.  Access and Choice: Equitable
```

Financing of Postsecondary Education.

Rept. 7. ERIC, 1983. ED 234 734.

8. A work in more than one volume

"Having witnessed the corruption of the English

government at first hand," Smith writes, the

colonists who had visited England "were determined

to preserve America from exploitation and repres-

sion" (1: 151).

Here a colon separates the number of the volume (1) from the number of the page (151).

Works Cited

Smith, Page. A New Age Now Begins. 2 vols.

New York: McGraw-Hill, 1976.

9. An anonymous work

If the work is anonymous, cite it by its full title or, if the title is long, by its first words:

In 1982-83, the average was $4,388 a year at a

public institution and $7,475 at a private one

(College Cost Book, 56-57), with some private

colleges costing twice that much.

Works Cited

College Cost Book, 1982-83. New York:

College Entrance Examination Board, 1983.

10. Material quoted by your source

If the material you are using was quoted by your source from some other source, use the word "quoted" before the name of your source:

Robert G. Templin, Jr., Dean of Instruction at

Piedmont Community College in Virginia, says that

better-off students are "squeezing out the poor,

disadvantaged, and minority students who once called the community college theirs" (quoted Watkins 1).

Works Cited

Watkins, Beverly T. "2-Year Colleges Told They´re Becoming Institutions for Middle-Class Students." <u>Chronicle of Higher Education</u> 11 Apr. 1984: 1.

11. A play with act, scene, and line numbers

In Shakespeare´s <u>Romeo and Juliet</u>, Romeo sees Juliet as "the sun" of his universe (2.2.3).

Plays with act-scene divisions and numbered lines should be cited by those divisions, not by page numbers. Arabic numerals divided by unspaced periods designate the act, scene, and line number(s) in that order. If your instructor asks you to use roman numerals in citing plays, use upper case for the act, lower case for the scene, and arabic numeral(s) for the line number(s):

Shakespeare's Romeo sees Juliet as "the sun" of his universe (<u>Romeo and Juliet</u>, II.ii.3).

You should normally give the title as well as the author of a literary work you cite. But if you cite it repeatedly, you don't need to repeat the author and title each time. After the first reference, just give the relevant numbers:

Juliet speaks of Romeo as "the god of my idolatry" (2.2.114).

Works Cited

Shakespeare, William. <u>Romeo and Juliet</u>. Ed. John E. Hankins. Baltimore: Penguin, 1970.

12. A poem with numbered lines but without sections

A poem with numbered lines should always be cited by the lines, not by page numbers:

In Robert Frost´s "Death of the Hired Man," one
character speaks of home as "the place where, when
you have to go there / They have to take you in"
(lines 118-19).

Since "1." and "11." can too easily be mistaken for the numbers one
and eleven, use the whole word "line" or "lines." Once you've established that the parenthesized numerals mean line numbers rather
than page numbers, just give the numbers:

But his wife calls home "something you somehow
haven´t to deserve" (120).

Works Cited

Frost, Robert.   "The Death of the Hired Man."

The Poetry of Robert Frost.   Ed. Edward

Connery Lathem.   New York: Holt, 1969.   34-40.

13. A poem with sections and numbered lines

When Milton´s Satan first sees Adam and Eve in
their bliss, he cries out, "O Hell! what do mine
eyes with grief behold!" (Paradise Lost 4.353).

If the poem is divided into sections ("books," cantos, or parts) that
each start at line 1, give in order the section number and the line
number(s), using arabic numerals for both. If the lines are numbered continuously through all the parts, give just the line numbers:

At the end of part 4 of Coleridge´s "Rime of the
Ancient Mariner," the mariner says that when he
looked upon the watersnakes, a "spring of love"
gushed from his heart (line 284).

Works Cited

Coleridge, S. T.   "The Rime of the Ancient
Mariner." The Norton Anthology of
English Literature.   Ed. M. H. Abrams

```
    et al.  2 vols.  New York: Norton, 1962.

    2: 181-97.
```

Milton, John. <u>Paradise Lost</u>. Ed. Scott

    Elledge. New York: Norton, 1975.

14. A poem without numbered lines

A poem without numbered lines may be cited by its title alone:

```
In "Cape Breton," Bishop speaks of mist hanging in

thin layers "like rotting snow-ice sucked away /

almost to spirit."
```

Works Cited

Bishop, Elizabeth. "Cape Breton." <u>The Complete

    Poems</u>. New York: Farrar, 1969. 75-77.

15. The Bible

```
When Jacob dreams, he hears the voice of God

promising to give him and his descendants "the

land whereon thou liest" (Genesis 28.12-13).
```

Cite biblical passages by giving the name of the biblical book (without underlining or quotation marks) followed by the chapter and verse numbers. You need not include the Bible in your list of Works Cited.

16. Nonprint sources

Cite films, recordings, radio and television programs, computer software programs, machine-readable documents, performances, and works of art by the title or the name(s) of the person(s) chiefly responsible for the work cited, or both. Give pagination only for machine-readable documents:

Film

```
In Atlantic City, Guare exposes the tawdriness,

ruthlessness, and brutality that undermine the

would-be revival of a fabled sea resort.
```

Recording

Frost's own reading of "Birches" fully exploits the resonance of its language.

Computer program

Computer programs such as Wayne Holder's The Word Plus allow the writer to see exactly which of the words in a computerized text may be misspelled.

Television program

"The Enlightened Machine" graphically revealed just what happens to the brain during an epileptic seizure.

Machine readable document from an information service

"For the most part," writes one observer, "the practice of reading for errors is based on the assumption that all errors can be classified" (Heffernan 4).

Work of art

The vortex that became Turner's trademark first appeared in his Snow Storm: Hannibal and His Army Crossing the Alps.

Performance

A recent performance of Shakespeare's Much Ado about Nothing once again demonstrated how much his language can achieve theatrically without the aid of elaborate sets.

Works Cited

"The Enlightened Machine." The Brain. Narr. George Page. PBS. WETK, Burlington, VT. 10 Oct. 1984.

Frost, Robert. "Birches." <u>Robert Frost Reads</u>
    <u>His Poetry</u>. Caedmon, TC 1060, 1956.

Guare, John, screenwriter. <u>Atlantic City</u>. Dir.
    Louis Malle. With Burt Lancaster, Kate Reid,
    and Susan Sarandon. Paramount, 1980.

Heffernan, James A. W. <u>Getting the Red Out: Grading</u>
    <u>without Degrading</u>. ERIC, 1983. ED 229 788.

Holder, Wayne. <u>The Word Plus</u>. Computer Software.
    Oasis Systems, 1982. CP/M 2.2, disk.

Shakespeare, William. <u>Much Ado about Nothing</u>.
    Dir. Terry Hands. With Derek Jacobi, Sinead
    Cusack, and the Royal Shakespeare Company.
    Gershwin Theatre, New York. 19 October 1984

Turner, J. M. W. <u>Snow Storm: Hannibal and His</u>
    <u>Army Crossing the Alps</u> (1812). The Tate
    Gallery, London.

35.3 Placing and Punctuating Parenthetical Citations

1. Placing parenthetical citations

Place the parenthetical citation at the end of the material taken from a particular source, whether or not the end of the material coincides with the end of a sentence:

Twenty years ago, the average annual cost of
attending a publicly supported college was $2,000
(Cox 16).

Though the Middle Income Student Assistance Act
of 1978 (MISAA) provided federal funds to help
middle-income families with rising college costs

(Gladieux 402), the net costs continue to rise beyond what middle income parents can comfortably afford.

In each case, the parenthetical citation marks the end of the material that comes from the source cited.

Works Cited

Cox, Claire. How to Beat the High Cost of College. New York: Bernard Geis Associates, 1964.

Gladieux, Lawrence E. "Future Directions of Student Aid." Handbook of Student Financial Aid. Ed. Robert H. Fenske et al. San Francisco: Jossey-Bass, 1983.

2. Punctuation within parenthetical citations

Within parenthetical citations, punctuate as follows.

a. Use a comma and a space—

To separate the name of an author from a title:

(Astin, Preventing 63)

To indicate that your material comes from nonconsecutive pages.

(Hartman 6, 24)

Use a space but no comma between the author's name and the pagination or between the title and the pagination.

b. Use a semicolon and a space between two different sources cited within the same parentheses:

(Hartman 6; Astin, Minorities 141)

c. Use unspaced periods between the divisions of a play, a long poem, or a chapter of the Bible:

(Macbeth 5.5.23-28)

(Paradise Lost 4.353)

(Genesis 28.12-13)

d. Use a colon and a space between the number of a volume (in a multivolume work) and the pagination:

35.3

(Smith 1: 151)

Works Cited

Astin, A. W. <u>Preventing Students from Dropping Out</u>. San Francisco: Jossey-Bass, 1975.

Hartman, Robert W. <u>Credit for College: Public Policy for Student Loans</u>. New York: McGraw-Hill, 1971.

Milton, John. <u>Paradise Lost</u>. Ed. Scott Elledge. New York: Norton, 1975.

Shakespeare, William. <u>Romeo and Juliet</u>. Ed. John E. Hankins. Baltimore: Penguin, 1960.

Smith, Page. <u>A New Age Now Begins</u>. 2 vols. New York: McGraw-Hill, 1976.

3. Citing material that is not indented from your text

To cite the source of material that is not indented from your own text, start the parenthetical citation just one space after the material used. Except for closing quotation marks, no punctuation of any kind should come between the material used and the opening parenthesis. Periods, commas, and semicolons go *after* the closing parenthesis:

Furthermore, though Green credits federal aid with getting minority students into public colleges (25), their numbers are falling even at community colleges, which, says Astin, "represent the bottom of the institutional hierarchy within public systems" (<u>Minorities</u> 141).

A major modern theorist has defined dreams as "the essential message carriers from the instinctive to the rational parts of the human mind" (Jung 52); if this is true, dreams may tell us things we could not learn by any other means.

Works Cited

Astin, A. W. Minorities in American Higher Education: Recent Trends, Current Prospects, and Recommendations. San Francisco: Jossey-Bass, 1982.

Green, K. C. Access and Opportunity: Government Support for Minority Participation in Higher Education. Washington: American Association for Higher Education, 1982.

Jung, Carl G. "Approaching the Unconscious." Man and His Symbols. Eds. Carl G. Jung and M.-L. von Franz. Garden City, NY: Doubleday, 1964. 18-103

4. Citing material that is indented from your text

To cite the source of quoted prose that has been set off from your own text by indentation, put the citation two spaces *after* the final punctuation mark:

In A Room of One's Own, Virginia Woolf goes on to speak about women in literature and history:

> A very queer, composite being thus emerges.
> Imaginatively she is of the highest importance; practically she is completely insignificant. She pervades poetry from cover
> to cover; she is all but absent from history.
> She dominates the lives of kings and conquerors
> in fiction; in fact she was the slave of any

```
boy whose parents forced a ring upon her

finger. Some of the most inspired words,

some of the most profound thoughts in

literature fall from her lips. . . . (60)
```

To cite the source of quoted poetry that has been set off from your text, put the parenthetical citation at the right-hand end of the last line or—if it won't fit there—at the right-hand end of the next line:

```
Questioning his own dissatisfaction with the mountains of

New Hampshire, Frost writes:

    How, to my sorrow, how have I attained

    A height from which to look down critical

    On mountains?  What has given me assurance

    To say what height becomes New Hampshire mountains,

    Or any mountains?   ("New Hampshire," lines 313-17)
```

Works Cited

```
Frost, Robert.  "New Hampshire."  The Poetry

     of Robert Frost.  Ed. Edward Connery Lathem.

     New York: Holt, 1969.  159-72.

Woolf, Virginia.  A Room of One's Own.  New

     York: Fountain, 1929.
```

35.4 Writing the List of Works Cited—The MLA Style

If you use the MLA parenthetical style, you must provide a list of Works Cited at the end of your paper: an alphabetical list of all the works you have cited—and only those you have cited. Start the list on a separate sheet and arrange the entries alphabetically according to the authors' last names or—where you have no author's name—by the first significant word in the title. Where you include several works by one author, list these alphabetically by title, and

35.4 instead of repeating the author's name, use three hyphens followed by a period, as shown by the sample below.

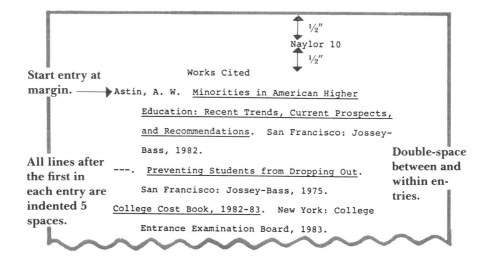

1. A book with one author

```
Hartman, Robert.  Credit for College: Public

     Policy for Student Loans.  New York: McGraw-

     Hill, 1971.
```

    a. Author and title: Give the author's name inverted, a period, two spaces, the complete title—including subtitle, if any— underlined, another period, and two spaces. (On the capitalization of titles, see section 32.3.)

    b. Place of publication: When more than one place is printed on the title page, give just the first. If the city or town of publication may be unfamiliar to your reader or mistaken for some other place, add an abbreviated form of the name of the state, province, or country:

```
Lawrence, KS

Manchester, Eng.

Sherbrooke, Que.

Long Beach, CA
```

(On the capitalizing of abbreviated place names, see section 32.4.)

c. Publisher: Use the short form of a well-known publisher such as McGraw-Hill (for McGraw-Hill Book Company) or St. Martin's (for St. Martin's Press). But include the initials U and P (without periods) in the name of any university press:

```
Clawson, Marion.  America's Land and Its Uses.

     Baltimore: Johns Hopkins UP, 1972.

McGann, Jerome J.  The Romantic Ideology: A

     Critical Investigation.  Chicago: U of

     Chicago P, 1983.
```

d. Date of publication: Look for this date on the copyright page, which is on the other side of the title page. If you find more than one copyright date, give the latest one, but ignore the dates of printings or "impressions" made after that date. If you find no date of publication, write "n.d." If the book is a reprint, see item 11 below.

2. A book with one author and an editor

```
Dreiser, Theodore.  Sister Carrie.  Ed. Kenneth

     S. Lynn.  New York: Rinehart, 1959.
```

Put the author's name first when you are citing the author's text. To cite material written by the editor, put the editor's name first, then the title of his or her material (capitalized but not underlined), and, at the end, the pagination of the material:

```
Lynn, Kenneth.  Introduction.  Sister Carrie.

     By Theodore Dreiser.  New York: Rinehart,

     1959.  v-viii.
```

If you are citing both the author's text and the editor's material, list the book under both names, using the author's name for cross-reference:

```
Dreiser, Theodore.  Sister Carrie.  Ed. Kenneth S.

     Lynn.  New York: Rinehart, 1959.

Lynn, Kenneth S.  Introduction.  Dreiser v-xvi.
```

3. A second or later edition

```
Ornstein, Robert E.  The Psychology of Conscious-

     ness.  2nd ed.  New York: Harcourt, 1977.
```

The abbreviation "2nd ed." means "second edition." Other abbreviations commonly used for second or later editions are "Rev." for "revised" and "Enl." for "Enlarged."

4. A book with two or three authors

Give the authors' names in the order you find them on the title page, and invert only the first name.

> Dickmeyer, Nathan, John Wessels, and Sharon L.
>
> Coldren. Institutionally Funded Student
>
> Financial Aid. Washington: American Council
>
> on Education, 1981.

5. A book with more than three authors or editors

Give the name of the first author listed on the title page and "et al.," which stands for *et alia*—"and others."

> Fenske, Robert H., et al. Handbook of Student
>
> Financial Aid: Programs, Procedures, and
>
> Policies. San Francisco: Jossey-Bass, 1983.

6. A book with a corporate author

> Sloan Study Consortium. Paying for College:
>
> Financing Education at Nine Private Institution
>
> Hanover, NH: UP of New England, 1974.

7. A work in more than one volume

> Smith, Page. A New Age Now Begins. 2 vols. New
>
> York: McGraw-Hill, 1976.

8. A book in a numbered series

> Henry, Joe B., ed. The Impact of Student Financial
>
> Aid on Institutions. New Directions for
>
> Institutional Research 25. San Francisco:
>
> Jossey-Bass, 1980.

The title of a book in a series is followed by the name of the series and the number of the book. Capitalize the name of the series but use no underlining or quotation marks with it.

9. A work from a collection of works by one author

Give first the title of the work in quotation marks, then the underlined title of the book it appears in. At the end go the page numbers.

> Frost, Robert. "The Death of the Hired Man." The
>
>   Poetry of Robert Frost. Ed. Edward Connery
>
>   Lathem. New York: Holt, 1969. 34-40.
>
> Thomas, Lewis. "The Long Habit." The Lives of
>
>   a Cell: Notes of a Biology Watcher. New
>
>   York: Viking, 1974. 47-52.
>
> Hemingway, Ernest. "The Short Happy Life of
>
>   Francis Macomber." The Short Stories of
>
>   Ernest Hemingway. New York: Scribner´s,
>
>   1938. 3-37.

10. A work from a collection of works by various authors

> Dimock, George E., Jr. "The Name of Odysseus."
>
>   Essays on The Odyssey: Selected Modern
>
>   Criticism. Ed. Charles Taylor. Bloomington:
>
>   Indiana UP, 1963. 54-72.
>
> Coleridge, Samuel T. "The Rime of the Ancient
>
>   Mariner." The Norton Anthology of English
>
>   Literature. Ed. M. H. Abrams et al. 2 vols.
>
>   New York: Norton, 1962. 2: 181-97.

If you are citing two or more works from a collection of works by various authors, list the collection by the name of its editor and use that for cross-reference:

> Hauptman, Arthur M. "Shaping Alternative Loan
>
>   Programs." Kramer 69-82.
>
> Kramer, Martin, ed. Meeting Student Aid Needs
>
>   in a Period of Retrenchment. New Directions

for Higher Education 40. San Francisco:

Jossey-Bass, 1982.

11. A reprint

Weston, Jessie L. <u>From Ritual to Romance</u>. 1920.

Garden City: Anchor-Doubleday, 1957.

The date of original publication follows the title; the date of the reprint follows the name of the publisher.

12. A translation

Flaubert, Gustave. <u>Madame Bovary</u>. Trans. Francis

Steegmüller. New York: Random House, 1957.

Use this form to cite the source of material from the primary author's text. To cite the source of material from the translator's introduction or notes, put the translator's name before the title and the primary author's name after it:

Steegmüller, Francis. Translator's Introduction.

<u>Madame Bovary</u>. By Gustave Flaubert.

New York: Random House, 1957.

If you use material from both the author's text and the translator's introduction, list both names and use the author's name for cross-reference:

Flaubert, Gustave. <u>Madame Bovary</u>. Trans. Francis

Steegmüller. New York: Random House, 1957.

Steegmüller, Francis. Translator´s Introduction.

Flaubert v-xv.

13. An anonymous book

<u>College Cost Book, 1982-83</u>. New York: College

Entrance Examination Board, 1983.

14. An article in an reference book

In citing articles from familiar reference works, give just the name(s) of the author(s), the title of the article, the title of the book, and the year of the edition. If the articles are alphabetically arranged, you don't need volume or page numbers:

Spilhaus, Athelstan, and Jane J. Stein. "Pollu-

tion Control." Encyclopaedia Britannica:

Macropaedia. 1974 ed.

Kilma, Edward S. "Phonetics." Funk & Wagnalls

New Encyclopedia. 1973 ed.

The initials usually given at the end of the article will lead you to
the name(s) of the author(s) in a reference list commonly given at
the beginning of the book. If the article is unsigned, start with its
title:

"Pollution." The Columbia Encyclopedia. 1963 ed.

If the edition is numbered, give the edition number before the
year(s) of publication.

"Graham, Martha." Who´s Who of American Women.

13th ed. 1983-84.

If the book is specialized or has appeared in only one or two editions, give full information about its publication:

Weinberg, Kurt. "Romanticism." Princeton Encyclo-

pedia of Poetry and Poetics. Eds. Alex

Preminger, Frank J. Warnke, and O. B.

Hardison, Jr. Enl. ed. Princeton: Princeton

UP, 1974.

15. An article in a journal with continuous pagination

Delbruck, Max. "Mind from Matter?" The American

Scholar 47 (1978): 339-53.

Use this form when the pagination is continuous throughout a volume—that is, for instance, when the first issue ends at page 230
and the second one starts at page 231. Give the volume number in
arabic (not roman) numerals, the year of issue in parentheses, a
colon, a space, and the page numbers.

16. An article in a journal without continuous pagination

Posen, I. Sheldon, and Joseph Sciorra. "Brook-

lyn´s Dancing Tower." Natural History

92.6 (1983): 30-37.

Use this form when the pagination is not continuous—that is, when every issue starts at page 1. Here you need the volume number *and* the issue number with an unspaced period between the two.

17. An article in a periodical published monthly, weekly, or daily

> Stein, Jane. "The Bioethicists: Facing Matters
>
> of Life and Death." <u>Smithsonian</u> Jan. 1979:
>
> 107-15.
>
> Strout, Richard L. "Another Bicentennial."
>
> <u>Christian Science Monitor</u> 10 Nov. 1978: 27.

To cite any periodical published monthly, weekly, or daily, give just the date right after the name of the periodical, with no punctuation between the two. Abbreviate the name of the month (except for May, June, and July), and put the day of the month first when the day is cited. If the article you cite appears on nonconsecutive pages— starting on page 1, for instance, and continuing on page 11—cite just the starting page with a plus sign right after it:

> Watkins, Beverly T. "2-Year Colleges Told They´re
>
> Becoming Institutions for Middle-Class Stu-
>
> dents." <u>Chronicle of Higher Education</u>
>
> 11 April 1984: 1+.

18. An unsigned article

When the article is unsigned, the entry begins with the title:

> "The Vietnam War: The Executioner." <u>Newsweek</u>
>
> 13 Nov. 1978: 70.

19. A newspaper

> Martin, Douglas. "Mulroney Says Canada Seeks
>
> ´True Partnership´ with U.S." <u>New York</u>
>
> <u>Times</u> 6 Nov. 1984: A16.

If the paper is divided into lettered sections (A, B., C, etc.) that each start from page 1, give the section letter before the page number, as shown above. If the sections are numbered, cite them this way:

```
Brody, Jane E.   "Multiple Cancers Termed on
      Increase."   New York Times 10 Oct. 1976:
      sec. 1: 37.
```

20. An editorial

```
"How to End Watergate."   Editorial.   New York
      Times 10 Jan. 1979: A22.
```

You should identify an editorial as such to distinguish it from a news report.

21. A government publication

```
U.S. Bureau of Labor Statistics.   Women in
      the Labor Force: Some New Data Series.
      Rept. 575.   Washington: GPO, 1979.
```

"GPO" is a standard abbreviation for "Government Printing Office." "Rept." stands for "Report."

22. A personal letter to the researcher

```
Achtert, Walter S.   Letter to the author.   2 Nov.
      1984.
```

23. A document from an information service

```
National Commission on Student Financial Assis-
      tance.   Access and Choice: Equitable Financ-
      ing of Postsecondary Education.   Rept. 7.
      ERIC, 1983.   ED 234 734.
```

The initials ERIC stand for Educational Resources Information Center. The initials are followed by a comma, the date of issue, a period, two spaces, and the ERIC document number. But if the source originates from a publisher other than ERIC, give the original publisher's name and publishing date before the ERIC number:

```
Franklin, P.   Beyond Student Financial Aid:
      Issues and Options for Strengthening Support
      Service Programs under Title IV of the
```

Higher Education Act. Washington: College

 Entrance Examination Board, 1980. ERIC ED

 185 913.

24. Computer software

 Holder, Wayne. _The Word Plus_. Computer Soft-

 ware. Oasis Systems, 1982. CP/M 2.2, disk.

Give the name of the program writer if known, the program title underlined, the words "Computer Software" without quotation marks or underlinings, the name of the distributor, and the year of distribution. Then add any other pertinent information about the computer or operating system for which the program is designed (such as CP / M 2.2), and the form of the program, whether cartridge, cassette, or disk.

25. A television program

 "The Enlightened Machine." _The Brain_. Narr.

 George Page. PBS. WETK, Burlington, VT. 10

 Oct. 1984.

Give the title of the episode (if known) in quotation marks, the title of the program underlined, and the name(s) of those chiefly responsible for it. Then give the network (such as PBS or CBS), the local station, the city and state, and the date of broadcast. In citing the broadcast of a play or musical work, such as an opera, give the title, then the author or composer, then the names of the principals, with broadcast information at the end:

 La Forza del Destino. By Guiseppe Verdi.

 With Leontyne Price, Isola Jones, Guiseppe

 Giacomini, and Leo Nucci. Cond. James Levine.

 Metropolitan Opera Orch. PBS. NHPTV, Durham,

 NH. 31 Oct. 1984.

26. A recording

Start with the name of the performer, composer, or conductor, or with the title of the work performed—whichever is most important to your discussion. End with the manufacturer, the catalog number, and (if known) the date of issue:

Frost, Robert. "The Road Not Taken." Robert
    Frost Reads His Poetry. Caedmon, TC 1060,
    1956.

Der Rosenkavalier. By Richard Strauss. With
    Elisabeth Schwarzkopf, Christa Ludwig, Teresa
    Stich-Randall, and Otto Edelmann. Cond.
    Herbert von Karajan. London Philharmonia
    Orchestra and Chorus. Angel Album, 3563 D/L,
    1957.

27. A film

Way Down East. Dir. D. W. Griffith. With
    Lillian Gish, Creighton Hale, and Burr
    McIntosh. D. W. Griffith, Inc., 1920.

If you are concerned with a particular individual, begin with his or her name:

Guare, John, screenwriter. Atlantic City.
    Dir. Louis Malle. With Burt Lancaster, Kate
    Reid, and Susan Sarandon. Paramount, 1980.

28. A live performance

Shakespeare, William. Much Ado about Nothing.
    Dir. Terry Hands. With Derek Jacobi and
    Sinead Cusack. Gershwin Theatre, New York.
    19 October 1984.

29. A work of art

Give the artist, the title, and, in parentheses, the date if knowr Then give the name and place of the institution where the work is located.

Turner, J. M. W. Snow Storm: Hannibal and His
    Army Crossing the Alps (1812). The Tate
    Gallery, London.

30. An interview

```
Hoisington, Harland W., Jr.  Director of Financial

     Aid at Dartmouth College.  Personal Interview.

3 May 1985.
```

If the interview has been published or broadcast, give the relevant information in the form appropriate for the source:

```
Gordon, Suzanne.  Interview.  All Things Con-

     sidered.  Natl. Public Radio.  WNYC, New York.

1 June 1983.

Kundera, Milan.  Interview.  New York Times

     18 Jan. 1982: sec. 3: 13+.
```

EXERCISE 1   Citing with Parentheses—MLA Style

Take the information given on each source, and use it to write two entries in the MLA style: a parenthetical citation as it would look in the text, and the entry as it would appear in a list of Works Cited.

EXAMPLE

The source is a book by Paul Fussell entitled *The Great War and Modern Memory*. It was published by the Oxford University Press in 1975. The first place of publication listed is New York. Your reference is to material on pages 96 and 97. In the text you introduce the material without mentioning Fussell's name. You are using no other book by him.

PARENTHETICAL CITATION

```
(Fussell 96-97)
```

IN WORKS CITED

```
Fussell, Paul.  The Great War and Modern

     Memory.  NY: Oxford UP, 1975.
```

1. The source is a book by Gordon A. Craig entitled *The Germans*. It was published by G. P. Putnam's Sons in 1982. The place of publication is listed as New York. Your reference is to material on pages 121, 122, and 123. In the text you introduce the material in a sentence in which you mention Craig by name. In your paper you are using another book by Craig entitled *The Politics of the Prussian Army, 1640–1945*.

2. The source is a book by Joseph Conrad entitled *Lord Jim*. It was edited by Thomas C. Moser and published by W. W. Norton & Company, Inc. in 1968. The place of publication is listed as New York. Your reference,

a direct quotation, is to something the editor states on page vi, and you mention him by name when introducing the quotation. You are using no other work edited or written by Moser.

3. The source is a book written by two scholars—Milton Meltzer and Walter Harding. Its title is *A Thoreau Profile,* and it was published in 1962 by Thomas C. Crowell Company. The place of publication listed is New York. Your reference is to something the authors say on page 301 about a portrait of Thoreau, but you do not mention the authors by name. This is the only book of theirs you are using.

4. The source is an essay by Stuart Levine entitled "Emerson and Modern Social Concepts." The essay is one of several essays by different authors in a book entitled *Emerson: Prospect and and Retrospect.* The essay appears on pages 155 through 178 of the book. The editor of the book is Joel Porte. The book is number 10 in a series named Harvard English Studies. The book was published in 1982 by the Harvard University Press. The places of publication listed are Cambridge, Massachusetts, and London, England, in that order. Your reference is to the entire essay by Levine, and you mention him by name in the text.

5. The source is an article by George F. Kennan entitled "America's Unstable Soviet Policy." It appears on pages 71 through 80 of *The Atlantic Monthly,* a monthly magazine published by The Atlantic Monthly Company. The place of publication is Boston, MA. Kennans' article is printed in the November 1982 issue. You quote two sentences on page 79, but do not mention Kennan. You are using another work by him, *The Nuclear Delusion.*

6. The source is Victor Hugo's *Les Misérables* in the translation by Norman Denny. The edition is in two volumes, each with its own pagination; that is, each begins with a page 1. The edition was first published by the Folio Press in 1976; then by Penguin Books in 1980. The place of publication of the Penguin edition, which is the one you are using, is listed as Harmondsworth, Middlesex, England. Your reference is to an episode Hugo presents on pages 210 through 214 of volume 2. You name Hugo in the text when making the reference.

7. The source is an editorial printed on page 15 of *The Christian Science Monitor* dated November 9, 1984. The editorial is unsigned; its title is "Polling Power." You give the name of the newspaper when introducing the source.

8. The source is a recording of a poem as read by the author, T. S. Eliot. The title of the poem is "The Love Song of J. Alfred Prufrock." It is one of several poems on a record entitled *T. S. Eliot Reading [Poems and Choruses].* The manufacturer is Caedmon Records, Inc., of New York City. The catalog number is TC 1045. A note on the record states that the recording was made in 1955. Your reference is to Eliot's portrayal of Prufrock in the entire poem. You mention Eliot by name in your text, and you also mention the title of the recorded poem.

36

PREPARING THE FINAL COPY OF THE RESEARCH PAPER

<table><tr><td>36</td></tr></table>

Following are generally accepted requirements for the final copy of a research paper. If your teacher has special requirements, you should of course follow those. But otherwise, we suggest you do as follows:

1. Type with fresh black ribbon on white, twenty-pound 8½-by-11-inch paper. If you have typed on erasable paper or fanfold computer paper, make a photocopy on uncoated paper and submit that. Always keep a copy of what you have submitted.

2. Use double-spacing throughout, and leave one-inch margins all around the text (top, bottom, and both sides).

3. Type on one side of the paper only.

4. Indent the first word of a paragraph five spaces from the left margin and every line of a set-off quotation ten spaces from the left margin.

5. If your instructor requires a title page, follow the second format shown in section 5.7, p. 77. If your instructor also wishes an outline, follow the format shown on pp. 519–20 and put the outline between the title page and the first page of your paper.

6. If your instructor does not require a title page, follow the first format shown on p. 77, putting on the first page your name, your instructor's name, the course number, the date and the title of your paper. Do not underline the title or put it in quotation marks.

7. On each page after the first, give your last name and the page number at upper right, as shown on p. 78.

Research paper: format with title on first page of text

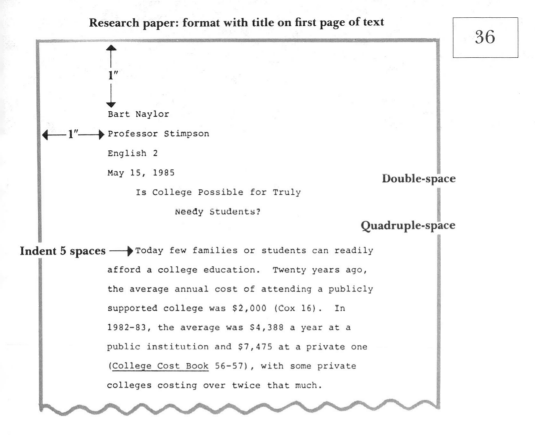

1"

Bart Naylor

←—1"—→ Professor Stimpson

English 2

May 15, 1985

Is College Possible for Truly

Needy Students?

Double-space

Quadruple-space

Indent 5 spaces —→ Today few families or students can readily

afford a college education. Twenty years ago,

the average annual cost of attending a publicly

supported college was $2,000 (Cox 16). In

1982-83, the average was $4,388 a year at a

public institution and $7,475 at a private one

(College Cost Book 56-57), with some private

colleges costing over twice that much.

Research paper: second and succeeding pages of text

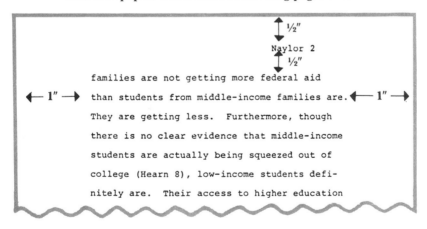

½"

Naylor 2

½"

families are not getting more federal aid

←—1"—→ than students from middle-income families are. ←—1"—→

They are getting less. Furthermore, though

there is no clear evidence that middle-income

students are actually being squeezed out of

college (Hearn 8), low-income students defi-

nitely are. Their access to higher education

37

SAMPLE ARGUMENTATIVE RESEARCH PAPER WITH MLA PARENTHETICAL STYLE

<table>
<tr><td>37</td><td>The following research paper is argumentative. (On the distinction between argumentative and survey-type research papers, see section 33.1.) The sources in this paper have been cited in the MLA parenthetical style, with a list of Works Cited at the end.</td></tr>
</table>

Bart Naylor

Professor Stimpson

English 2

May 15, 1985

Is College Possible for Truly

Needy Students?

Today few families or students can readily afford a college
education. Twenty years ago, the average annual cost of
attending a publicly supported college was $2,000 (Cox 16). In
1982-83, the average was $4,388 a year at a public institution
and $7,475 at a private one (College Cost Book 56-57), with some
private colleges costing over twice that much. These price tags
make it difficult for all but upper-income parents to put their
children through college. Though the Middle Income Student
Assistance Act of 1978 (MISAA) provided federal funds to help
middle-income families with rising college costs (Gladieux 402),
the net costs continue to rise beyond what middle-income parents
can comfortably afford, especially when they have more than one
child to put through college. As a result, spokesmen for the
middle class have been once again pointing with resentment at the
size of federal programs designed to help the poor, once again
complaining that middle-income students are being squeezed out of
college, and once again demanding that the high cost of college
tuition be offset by tax credits (Hearn 8-9).

Middle-income families unquestionably have cause to complain

The writer concedes that middle-income students have a problem financing their college educations.

and to demand relief from the strain that college puts on their budgets. But their complaints and demands miss a crucial point. Students from low-income families are not getting more federal aid than students from middle-income families are. They are getting less. Furthermore, though there is no clear evidence that middle-income students are actually being squeezed out of college (Hearn 8), low-income students definitely are. Their access to higher education is seriously impeded by the ways in which colleges and federal agencies distribute aid, advertise it, analyze students´ needs, and "package" the aid provided.

The present system of providing aid favors middle- and upper-income students much more than it did ten years ago. Since 1974, inflation has substantially increased the number of low-income families needing help with college bills. Yet when a congressionally sponsored research team compared recipients of federal aid in 1974 with those in 1981, it found that higher-income students gained more from the changes legislated between those years than lower-income students did. From 1974 to 1981, the percentage of aid recipients from low-income families-- especially from families with incomes under $7,500 a year-- dropped. At the same time, the number of aid recipients from families with incomes over $20,000 (in 1981 dollars) doubled. Furthermore, the researchers found that the value of awards made to students from low-income families generally declined while the value of awards made to better-off students generally rose (National Commission 26).

Much of this inequity results from the government´s decision to reduce the percentage of educational aid that is offered in

The writer presents his thesis: low-income students face special obstacles to higher education.

The writer explains the obstacles created by federal policies.

Naylor 3

the form of grants. Primarily, the Department of Education helps college students in two ways: through the Pell Grant program, which makes direct grants to needy students, and the Guaranteed Student Loan Program, which insures loans made by private lenders to college students who qualify for them and which also subsidizes a low interest rate on those loans (St. John and Byce 24). But according to Kenneth Ryder, low-income students have been "particularly hurt" by cuts in aid because Pell Grant funding has been "disproportionately lower" than funding for Guaranteed Student Loans (53). Why should this disproportion hit low-income students harder than others? If loans will serve them just as well, as Hartman indicates (3-4), why should they depend more heavily on grants? The simple answer is that loans frighten them. Their reluctance to borrow, says Arthur Hauptman, springs from "deep-seated fears about excessive repayment burdens" (70).

Whether or not they can overcome those fears, low-income students are clearly penalized by the half-cost rule: the provision that no Pell Grant may exceed half the cost of a student's college education. Hearn notes that the rule was designed to help private institutions by reducing the difference between the cost of attending one of them and the cost of attending a public institution, which is usually less expensive (5). But the half-cost rule hurts more than it helps. According to Hearn, it promotes enrollment at private institutions "probably only minimally" while it seriously burdens "self-supporting students and students with annual family incomes under $6,000.00"--the very students who "comprise the core of the

target population for the Basic Grant program" (6). Studies
cited by Hearn show that since these students normally attend
low-cost public institutions, the half-cost rule usually leaves
them with less than they would receive without it (6). Thus it
increases the amount they must borrow or earn.

Besides getting less than their fair share of grants, low-
income students have also been hurt by cutbacks in other federal
programs. Ryder points out that since 1981, the federal
government has been gradually eliminating the student benefits
provided by Old Age Survivors Disability Insurance, and that
according to the General Accounting Office, an increase of nearly
one billion dollars in the Pell Grant program would have been
required just to make up for the benefits lost (54). In
addition, the National Commission on Student Financial Assistance
says that the federal government actually discourages low-income
students from going to college. When they enroll, says the
Commission, it reduces or eliminates benefits to them and their
families from programs such as Medicaid, Food Stamps, and Public
Housing (4, 11).

As if all these obstacles to college for low-income students
were not enough, Donna Engelgau reports that further reductions
in aid to education and particularly in the Pell Grant program
lie ahead (20). But whatever the future brings, the cuts already
made in grants and benefits provided to low-income students have
clearly begun to take their toll. While studies made in the late
1970s indicated that students considering college were not
"primarily" influenced by their parents' ability to pay (Hearn
2), more recent evidence indicates that low-income students are

The writer explains the effect of these obstacles: low-income students are getting squeezed out of college.

Naylor 5

gradually disappearing from colleges of all kinds. A study of enrollment at private colleges in the academic years from 1979-80 to 1981-82 showed a 39 percent drop in students with family incomes of $24,000 or less (Magarrel 1). Furthermore, though Green credits federal aid with getting minority students into public colleges (25), their numbers are falling even at community colleges, which, says Astin, "represent the bottom of the institutional hierarchy within public systems," and which have traditionally had a "disproportionate share" of minority students (Minorities 141). Robert G. Templin, Jr., Dean of Instruction at Piedmont Community College in Virginia, says that better-off students are "squeezing out the poor, disadvantaged, and minority students who once called the community college theirs" (quoted Watkins 1).

These developments do not come from reductions in federal aid alone. Much of the responsibility for the present plight of low-income students belongs to colleges. Though some colleges still preserve what the Sloan Consortium calls "a vital commitment to equal access without regard to economic background" (6), many institutions are simply competing with each other for the best qualified students, offering them aid even when they may not need it or when it simply enables their parents to avoid making any financial sacrifice on their behalf. According to Chester Finn, Professor of Education and Public Policy at Vanderbilt University, "the higher education industry has become a collection of highly competitive vendors," and aid is "just another economic lure" (Madison B1). Since the granting of aid

The writer explains the obstacles created by college policies.

Naylor 6

to students who don´t truly need it inevitably reduces the aid available for those who do, this kind of competition all too often pushes low-income students right out of the game.

They are not, of course, the only ones hurt by recent cuts in aid to education. According to the United States Students Association, students in general are facing record levels of "unmet need": the difference between the total cost of attending college and the total value of their grants, institutional loans, parental contributions, personal earnings, and what they can spare from personal assets (Engelgau 20). But some students are better equipped than others to meet this "unmet need." A study of Boston College made in 1979 showed that resident students there met it chiefly by taking out guaranteed insured loans, by getting more help from their parents, or by digging deeper into their own assets. But since commuting students are often poorer than residents and usually lack these options, they are generally forced to take on more outside work: a course of action that threatens their chances for academic success and eventually their chances of staying in college (Dickmeyer, Wessels, and Coldren 13). Thus the widening gap between the cost of college and the value of aid hurts low-income students more than any others.

What can we do for these students? The most obvious answer is to increase federal aid to higher education, or at least to stop any further reductions in such aid. But even with little or no increase in funding, colleges and federal agencies can enhance educational opportunity for low-income students by changing the ways in which they operate.

First of all, the federal government should eliminate the

The writer now makes four specific proposals designed to improve educational opportunity for low-income students.

half-cost rule in the distribution of Pell Grants. Though the
maximum amount of each grant would remain unchanged, the
percentage of this amount awarded in particular cases would
depend on individual need rather than on an arbitrary formula.
Hearn admits that dropping the rule would mean spending more
money--an estimated 250 million dollars a year (5-6). But this
expense would be justified by what Hearn calls its "major
effect": reducing the amounts that low-income students at low-
tuition institutions would have to borrow and earn (6).

Whether or not more money can be spent in this way, the
Department of Education can and should advertise its aid programs
more effectively. When low-income students look for aid at
present, they are more likely to see a smoke screen of
complications than a window of opportunity. Dan Hall, Dean of
Admissions and Aid at the University of Chicago, says that the
continuing news of actual or rumored reductions in federal aid,
the lengthening delays in the announcement of college-based
awards, and the complexities of application procedures and
eligibility requirements all combine to make low-income students
feel beaten before they start (National Commission 77). Many of
the problems they face in applying to college and staying there
have been solved by the so-called TRIO programs, which--says
Franklin--are designed to seek out low-income students, steer
them into college,and improve their chances of finishing once
they start (2-3). But these programs now serve only about 3
percent of students eligible for them (National Commission 76).
In view of this fact, the Department of Education should heed the

advice of Hearn, who urges that full information about federal
aid for higher education be given to high school students in the
tenth grade, when they are most likely to decide whether or not
they will go to college at all (4).

Third, colleges and federal agencies alike must improve the
rigor and precision with which they analyze a student's financial
needs. Low-income students will get their fair share of support
only if all students applying for aid are required to say exactly
what their personal income and assets are and exactly how much
help they expect to receive from their parents or any other
relatives. "Undoubtedly," says Lawrence Gladieux, "some well-off
students have established self-supporting status under government
rules by artificially claiming that they are financially
independent of their parents, thereby increasing the aid they
might receive" (421). Besides, according to Harland Hoisington,
Director of Financial Aid at Dartmouth College, the nationally
distributed form now used to analyze a student's needs does not
even ask what grandparents or other relatives may be contributing
to his or her education. Aid administrators have a right to this
information. They should not only refine the methods used to
determine whether or not a student is self-supporting, as Kramer
suggests (3); they should also ask all applicants to reveal all
their sources of support. Only then can aid go to those who
truly need it.

Meeting the needs of low-income students not only takes a
rigorous approach to the needs of their better-off classmates.
It also takes a special way of "packaging" the grants, loans, and
jobs that together enable low-income students to get through

Naylor 9

college. A certain amount of employment can be good for them: on-campus work of up to twenty-five hours a week, says Astin, can give students a sense of involvement and thus help them persevere in their studies (Preventing 63). But as I have already noted, too much employment can hamper their academic progress, and heavy loans can intimidate them. Those who design packages of aid for low-income students, therefore, should give first priority to grants.

The widespread notion that low-income students have been reaping educational aid at the expense of middle- and upper-income students is a dangerous misconception. It thrives only because the political influence of the higher-income groups has diverted attention from the formidable problems that low-income students face. While many middle-income students have legitimate claims to aid, the needs of poorer students are still more pressing. Those students will not be helped by tuition tax credits, which, says Hearn, are "in no way tied to the need of individual families or targeted to specific populations" (8). To enhance the educational opportunities of low-income students, the Department of Education should eliminate the half-cost rule in the distribution of Pell Grants, and together with institutions, it should advertise educational aid more effectively, analyze the needs of all students more rigorously, and give first priority to grants in packages of aid designed for low-income students. All of these steps can help to insure that truly needy students who are capable of college work will get the chance to tackle it.

The writer concludes by affirming the special problems faced by low-income students and summarizing his solutions.

Works Cited

Astin, A. W. Minorities in American Higher Education: Recent
     Trends, Current Prospects, and Recommendations. San
     Francisco: Jossey-Bass, 1982.

---. Preventing Students from Dropping Out. San Francisco:
     Jossey-Bass, 1975.

College Cost Book, 1982-83. New York: College Entrance
     Examination Board, 1983.

Cox, Claire. How to Beat the High Cost of College. New York:
     Bernard Geis Associates, 1964.

Dickmeyer, Nathan, John Wessels, and Sharon L. Coldren.
     Institutionally Funded Student Financial Aid. Washington:
     American Council on Education, 1981.

Engelgau, Donna. "Education Groups Assail Reagan's Budget, Charge
     It's $5.7 Billion Shy of 1980 Level." Chronicle of Higher
     Education 9 May 1984: 20.

Fenske, Robert H., et al. Handbook of Student Financial Aid:
     Programs, Procedures, and Policies. San Francisco:
     Jossey-Bass, 1983.

Franklin, P. Beyond Student Financial Aid: Issues and Options
     for Strengthening Support Service Programs under Title IV of
     the Higher Education Act. Washington: College Entrance
     Examination Board, 1980. ERIC ED 185 913.

Gladieux, Lawrence E. "Future Directions of Student Aid."
     Fenske 399-433. Green, K. C. Access and Opportunity:

Naylor 11

Government Support for Minority Participation in Higher
    Education. Washington: American Association for Higher
    Education, 1982.

Hartman, Robert W. Credit for College: Public Policy for
    Student Loans. New York: McGraw-Hill, 1971.

Hauptman, Arthur M. "Shaping Alternative Loan Programs."
    Kramer 69-82.

Hearn, James C. "Effects on Enrollment of Changes in Student Aid
    Policies and Programs." The Impact of Student Financial
    Aid on Institutions. New Directions for Institutional
    Research 25. Ed. Joe B. Henry. San Francisco: Jossey-Bass,
    1980. 1-14.

Hoisington, Harland W., Jr., Director of Financial Aid at
    Dartmouth College. Personal interview. 3 May 1985.

Kramer, Martin, ed. Meeting Student Aid Needs in a Period of
    Retrenchment. New Directions for Higher Education 40.
    San Francisco: Jossey-Bass, 1982.

Magarrel, Jack. "Number of Low-Income Students Drops 39 Percent
    at Private Colleges." Chronicle of Higher Education
    1 Sept. 1982: 1+.

Madison, Mary. "Colleges Will Seek Students." The Peninsula
    Times Tribune 8 June 1984: B1+.

National Commission on Student Financial Assistance. Access
    and Choice: Equitable Financing of Postsecondary
    Education. Rept. 7. ERIC, 1983. ED 234 734.

Ryder, Kenneth G. "Financing Higher Education for Low-Income
    Students." USA Today May 1984: 53-54.

St. John, Edward P., and Charles Byce. "The Changing Federal

Role in Student Financial Aid." Kramer 21-40.

Sloan Study Consortium. <u>Paying for College: Financing</u>
<u>Education at Nine Private Institutions</u>. Hanover, NH: UP
of New England, 1974.

Watkins, Beverly T. "2-Year Colleges Told They´re Becoming
Institutions for Middle-Class Students." <u>Chronicle of</u>
<u>Higher Education</u> 11 Apr. 1984: 1+.

GLOSSARIES

GLOSSARY OF USAGE

a, an

Use *a* before a word starting with a consonant, and *an* before a word starting with a vowel.

A fool and his money are soon parted.

An empty bag cannot stand upright.   —Ben Franklin

accept, except

Accept means "receive" or "agree to."

Medical schools accept less than half the students who apply.

As a preposition, *except* means "other than."

I can resist anything except temptation.   —Oscar Wilde

As a verb, *except* means "exclude," "omit," "leave out."

If you except Eisenhower, no U.S. president since Roosevelt has served a full two terms in office.

A.D., B.C.

A.D. stands for *anno Domini*, "in the year of our Lord." It designates the period since the birth of Christ, and precedes the year number.

The emperor Claudius began the Roman conquest of England in A.D. 43.

B.C. designates the period before the birth of Christ, and follows the year number. For this period, the lower the number, the more recent the year.

Alexander the Great ruled Macedonia from 336 B.C. to his death in 323.

advice, advise

Advice is a noun meaning "guidance."

When a man is too old to give bad examples, he gives good advice.   —La Rochefoucauld

Advise is a verb meaning "counsel," "give advice to," "recommend," or "notify."

Shortly before the stock market crash of 1929, Bernard Baruch advised investors to buy bonds.

affect, effect

Affect means "change," "disturb," or "influence."

The rising cost of gas has drastically affected the automobile industry.

It can also mean "feign" or "pretend to feel."

She knew exactly what was in the package, but she affected surprise when she opened it.

As a verb, *effect* means "bring about," "accomplish," or "perform."

With dazzling skill, the gymnast effected a triple somersault.

As a noun, *effect* means "result" or "impact."

His appeal for mercy had no effect on the judge.

afraid   *See* frightened.

aggravate, irritate

Aggravate means "make worse."

The recent bombing of a school bus has aggravated racial hostilities.

Irritate means "annoy" or "bring discomfort to."

His tuneless whistling began to irritate me.

all   *See* almost.

all ready, already

Use *all ready* when *all* refers to things or people.

At noon the runners were all ready to start. [The meaning is that *all* of the runners were *ready*.]

Use *already* to mean "by this time" or "by that time."

I reached the halfway mark, but the front-runners had already crossed the finish line.

all right, *alright

All right means "completely correct," "safe and sound," or "satisfactory."

My answers on the quiz were all right. [The meaning is that *all* of the answers were *right*.]

The car was demolished, but aside from a muscle bruise in my shoulder and a few minor cuts, I was all right.

In formal writing, do not use *all right* to mean "satisfactorily" or "well."

*In spite of a bruised shoulder, Ashe played all right.

REVISED: In spite of a bruised shoulder, Ashe played well.

In formal writing, do not use *all right* before a noun to mean "very good" or "excellent."

*The Casio calculator is an all right electronic device.

REVISED: The Casio calculator is an excellent electronic device.

Do not use **alright* anywhere; it is a misspelling of *all right*.

all together altogether

Use *all together* when *all* refers to things or people.

The demonstrators stood all together at the gate of the nuclear power plant.

Use *altogether* to mean "entirely" or "wholly."

> Never put off till tomorrow what you can avoid altogether.
> (Preston's Axiom)

allude, refer

Allude means "call attention indirectly."

> When the speaker mentioned the "Watergate scandal," he alluded to a chain of events that led to the resignation of President Richard Nixon.

Refer means "call attention directly."

> In the Declaration of Independence, Jefferson refers many times to England's mistreatment of the American colonies.

allusion, delusion, illusion

An *allusion* is an indirect reference.

> Prufrock's vision of his own head "brought in upon a platter" is an allusion to John the Baptist, whose head was presented that way to Salome, Herod's daughter.

A *delusion* is a false opinion or belief, especially one that springs from self-deception or madness.

> A megalomaniac suffers from the delusion that he or she is fabulously rich and powerful.

An *illusion* is a false impression, especially one that springs from false perception (an optical illusion, for example) or from wishful thinking.

> The sight of palm trees on the horizon proved to be an illusion.

> The so-called "free gifts" offered in advertisements feed the illusion that you can get something for nothing.

almost, most, mostly, all, *most all

Almost means "nearly."

> By the time we reached the gas station, the tank was almost empty.

> Almost all the Republicans support the proposed amendment.

As an adjective or noun, *most* means "the greater part (of)" or "the majority (of)."

> Most birds migrate in the fall and spring.

> Most of the land has become a dust bowl.

As an adverb, *most* designates the superlative form of long adjectives and adverbs.

> Truman thought MacArthur the most egotistical man he ever knew.

Mostly means "chiefly," "primarily."

> Milk is mostly water.

All means "the whole amount," "the total number of," or "entirely."

> All art is useless.   —Oscar Wilde

> The manufacturer has recalled all (of) the new models.

> The new buildings are all finished.

In formal writing, do not use *most all. Use *almost all* or *most*.

> *Most all of the plants looked healthy, but two of the roses were dying.

REVISED: Almost all of the plants looked healthy, but two of the roses were dying.

*Most all of the refugees suffered from malnutrition.

REVISED: Most of the refugees suffered from malnutrition.

a lot, *alot   *See* lots of.

already   *See* all ready.

***alright**   *See* all right.

altogether   *See* all together.

alumnus, alumni; alumna, alumnae

Use *alumnus* for one male graduate of a school, college, or university, and *alumni* for two or more male graduates or for a predominantly male group of graduates.

Dartmouth alumni are extraordinarily loyal to their college.

Use *alumna* for one female graduate, and *alumnae* for two or more female graduates or for a predominantly female group of graduates.

Vassar's alumnae include Mary McCarthy and Meryl Streep.

If you can't cope with all those Latin endings, use *graduate* for an individual of either sex, and just remember that *alumni* designates a male group, *alumnae* a female group. Do not refer to any one person of either sex as an *alumni*.

*He is an alumni of Florida State.

REVISED: He is an alumnus [*or* a graduate] of Florida State.

among, between

Use *among* with three or more persons, things, or groups.

There is no honor among thieves.

In general, use *between* with two persons, two things, or two groups.

Political freedom in America means the right to choose between a Democrat and a Republican.

amoral, immoral

Amoral means "without morals or a code of behavior," "beyond or outside the moral sphere."

Rich, riotous, and totally amoral, he lived for nothing but excitement and pleasure.

Immoral means "wicked."

The Roman emperor Nero was so immoral that he once kicked a pregnant woman to death.

amount, number

Use *amount* when discussing uncountable things.

No one knows the amount of damage that a nuclear war would do.

Use *number* when discussing countable things or persons.

The store offered a prize to anyone who could guess the number of marbles in a large glass jug.

anyone, any one

Anyone is an indefinite pronoun (like *everyone, everybody*).

Anyone who hates dogs and children can't be all bad.

—W. C. Fields

Any one means "any one of many."

>I felt wretched; I could not answer any one of the questions on the test.

apt *See* likely.

as, as if, like

>Use *as* or *as if* as a subordinator to introduce a clause.

>>As I walked up the driveway, a huge dog suddenly leaped out at me.

>>Susan looked as if she had just seen a ghost.

>Use *like* as a preposition meaning "similar to."

>>At first glance the organism looks like an amoeba.

>Do not use *like* to mean "as if," "as," or "that."

>>*Pat looked like he had just won the sweepstakes.

>>REVISED: Pat looked as if he had just won the sweepstakes.

>>*The hinge didn't work like the instructions said it would.

>>REVISED: The hinge didn't work as the instructions said it would.

>>*I felt like he resented me.

>>REVISED: I felt that he resented me.

assure, ensure, insure

>*Assure* means "state with confidence to."

>>The builders of the *Titanic* assured everyone that it could not sink.

>*Ensure* means "make sure" or "guarantee."

>>There is no way to ensure that every provision of the treaty will be honored.

>*Insure* means "make a contract for payment in the event of specified loss, damage, injury, or death."

>>I insured the package for fifty dollars.

awfully *See* very.

bad, badly

>*Bad* is an adjective meaning "not good," "sick," or "sorry."

>>We paid a lot for the meal, but it was bad.

>>In spite of the medicine, I still felt bad.

>>She felt bad about losing the ring.

>*Badly* is an adverb meaning "not well."

>>Anything that begins well ends badly. (Pudder's Law)

>Used with *want* or *need, badly* means "very much."

>>The fans badly wanted a victory.

>Do not use *bad* as an adverb.

>>*We played bad during the first half of the game.

>>REVISED: We played badly during the first half of the game.

B.C. *See* A.D.

because, since, *being that

>Use *since* and *because* to introduce clauses. Do not use **being that*.

>>Since fossil fuels are becoming scarce, scientists are working to develop synthetic forms of energy.

>>The soldiers could not advance because they had run out of ammunition.

because of *See* due to.

***being that** *See* because.

beside, besides

>*Beside* means "next to."

>>A little restaurant stood beside the wharf.

>As a preposition, *besides* means "in addition to."

>>Besides working with the sun and the wind, engineers are seeking to harness the power of tides.

>As a conjunctive adverb, *besides* means "moreover" or "also."

>>Randy's notion of bliss was a night at the disco, but discos made me dizzy; besides, Randy stepped on my toes whenever we danced.

between *See* among.

can hardly, *can't hardly*

>*Can hardly* means virtually the same thing as *cannot* or *can't*. Do not use **can't hardly*.

>>*We can't hardly bomb Moscow without getting bombed in return.

>>REVISED: We can hardly bomb Moscow without getting bombed in return.

capital, capitol

>*Capital* means the seat of government of a country or state, the type of letter used at the beginning of a sentence, or a stock of accumulated wealth.

>>Paris is the capital of France.

>>This sentence begins with a capital *T*.

>>What does capital consist of? It consists of money and commodities.   —Karl Marx

>*Capitol* means the building that houses the state or federal legislature. Remember that the *o* in *capitol* is like the *o* in the dome of a capitol.

>>The new governor delivered his first official speech from the steps of the capitol.

censor, censure

>As a verb, *censor* means "expurgate."

>>Television networks usually censor X-rated movies before broadcasting them.

>As a noun, *censor* means "one who censors."

>>Censors cut the best part of the film.

>As a verb, *censure* means "find fault with" or "reprimand."

>>In the 1950s, Senator Joseph McCarthy was censured for publicly questioning the integrity of President Eisenhower.

>As a noun, *censure* means "disapproval" or "blame."

>>Ridicule often hurts more than censure.

childish, childlike

>*Childish* means "disagreeably like a child."

>>The childish whining of a chronic complainer soon becomes an unbearable bore.

Childlike means "agreeably like a child."

> Picasso's brilliant canvases express his childlike love of color.

cite *See* sight.

compare, comparison, contrast

Compare means "bring together in order to note similarities and differences."

> In *A Stillness at Appomattox*, Bruce Catton compares Lee and Grant not only to show the difference between a Virginia aristocrat and a rough-hewn frontiersman but also to show what these two men had in common.

Use *compare to* to stress similarities.

> Lewis Thomas compares human societies to ant colonies, noting that individuals in each of these groups sometimes work together as if they were parts of a single organism.

Use *compare with* to stress differences.

> Compared with Texas, Rhode Island is a postage stamp.

Comparison means "act of comparing."

> Catton's comparison of Lee and Grant shows the difference between the South and the frontier.

> In comparison with Texas, Rhode Island is a postage stamp.

As a transitive verb, *contrast* means "bring together to show differences."

> In *Huckleberry Finn*, Twain contrasts the peaceful, easy flow of life on the river with the tense and violent atmosphere of life on shore.

As an intransitive verb, *contrast* means "show one or more differences."

> In *Huckleberry Finn*, the peaceful flow of life on the river contrasts vividly with the violent atmosphere of life on shore.

As a noun, *contrast* means "striking difference."

> To drive across America is to feel the contrast between the level plains of the Midwest and the towering peaks of the Rockies.

complement, compliment

As a verb, *complement* means "bring to perfect completion."

> A red silk scarf complemented her white dress.

As a noun, *complement* means "something that makes a whole when combined with something else" or "the total number of persons needed in a group or team."

> Experience is the complement of learning.

> Without a full complement of volunteers, a small-town fire department cannot do its job.

As a verb, *compliment* means "praise."

> The teacher complimented me on my handwriting but complained about everything else.

As a noun, *compliment* means "expression of praise."

> Cheryl's compliment made my day.

conscience, conscious

Conscience is a noun meaning "inner guide or voice in matters of right and wrong."

> A pacifist will not fight in any war because his or her conscience says that all killing is wrong.

Conscious is an adjective meaning "aware" or "able to perceive."

> Conscious of something on my leg, I looked down to see a cockroach crawling over my knee.

> I was conscious during the whole operation.

consul   *See* council.

continual, continuous

Continual means "going on with occasional slight interruptions."

> I grew up next to an airport. What I remember most from my childhood is the continual roaring of jet planes.

Continuous means "going on with no interruption."

> In some factories the assembly line never stops; production is continuous.

contrast   *See* compare.

council, counsel, consul

Council means "group of persons who discuss and decide certain matters."

> The city council often disagrees with the mayor.

As a verb, *counsel* means "advise."

> President John F. Kennedy was badly counseled when he approved the American attack on Cuba at the Bay of Pigs.

As a noun, *counsel* means "advice" or "lawyer."

> Camp counselors tend to give orders more often than counsel.

> When the prosecution showed a picture of the victim's mangled corpse, the defense counsel vigorously objected.

A *consul* is a government official working in a foreign country to protect the interests of his or her country's citizens there.

> If you lose your passport in a foreign country, you will need to see the American consul there.

credible, credulous

Credible means "believable."

> A skillful liar can often sound highly credible.

Credulous means "overly ready to believe."

> Some people are credulous enough to believe anything they read in a newspaper.

See also incredible, incredulous.

criterion, criteria

A *criterion* is a standard by which someone or something is judged.

> In works of art, the only criterion of lasting value is lasting fame.

Criteria is the plural of *criterion*.

> What criteria influence voters in judging a presidential candidate?

data

> *Data* is the plural of the Latin *datum* (literally, "given"), meaning "something given"—that is, a piece of information. *Data* should be treated as plural.
>
>> The data transmitted by space satellites tell us much more about distant planets than we have ever known before.

delusion   *See* allusion.

different from, *different than

> In formal writing do not use *than* after *different.* Use *from.*
>
>> An adult's idea of a good time is often very different from a child's.

differ from, differ with

> *Differ from* means "be unlike."
>
>> Black English differs from Standard English not only in its sounds but also in its structure.   —Dorothy Z. Seymour
>
> *Differ with* means "disagree with."
>
>> Jung differed with Freud on the importance of the sex drive.

disinterested, uninterested

> *Disinterested* means "impartial," "unbiased," "objective."
>
>> Lawyers respect Judge Brown for his disinterested handling of controversial cases.
>
> *Uninterested* means "indifferent," "not interested."
>
>> Some people are so uninterested in politics that they do not even bother to vote.

due to, because of

> *Due to* is adjectival and means "resulting from" or "the result of."
>
>> Home-insurance policies sometimes fail to cover losses due to "acts of God," such as hurricanes and tornadoes.
>>
>> The senator's failure to win reelection was largely due to his lackluster campaigning.
>
> *Because of* is adverbial and means "as a result of."
>
>> Fighting persists in Northern Ireland because of animosities nearly three hundred years old.
>
> Do not use *due to* to mean *because of.*
>
>> *Due to a sprained ankle I had to drop out of the race.
>>
>> REVISED: Because of a sprained ankle I had to drop out of the race.

effect   *See* affect.

emigrate   *See* immigrate.

eminent, imminent, immanent

> *Eminent* means "distinguished," "prominent."
>
>> An eminent biologist has recently redefined the concept of evolution.
>
> *Imminent* means "about to happen."
>
>> The leaden air and the black, heavy clouds told us that a thunderstorm was imminent.
>
> *Immanent* means "inherent," "existing within."
>
>> Pantheists believe that God is immanent in all things.

ensure   *See* assure.

envelop, envelope

EnVELop (second syllable accented) is a verb meaning "cover" or "enclose."

Fog seemed to envelop the whole city.

ENvelope (first syllable accented) is a noun meaning "container used for mailing."

The small white envelope contained a big check.

*etc., et al.

The abbreviation **etc.* stands for *et cetera,* "and other things." You should avoid it in formal writing. Instead, use *and so on,* or tell what the other things are.

*Before setting out that morning, I put on my hat, mittens, etc.

REVISED: Before setting out that morning, I put on my hat, mittens, scarf, and boots.

The abbreviation *et al.* stands for *et alia,* "and others." Use it only in a footnote or bibliography when citing a book written by three or more authors.

Maynard Mack et al., eds., *World Masterpieces,* 3rd ed. (New York: Norton, 1973) 73–74.

everyday, every day

Everyday means "ordinary" or "regular."

The governor has a common touch; even in public speeches he likes to use everyday words.

Every day means "daily."

While in training, Mary Thomas commonly runs at least ten miles every day.

except *See* accept.

factor

Factor means "contributing element" or "partial cause." It can be used effectively, but far too often it simply clutters and obscures the sentence in which it appears. In general, you should avoid it.

One factor in the decay of the cities is the movement of middle-class to the suburbs.

REVISED: One reason for the decay of the cities is the movement of middle-class families to the suburbs.

farther, further

Farther means "a greater distance."

The trail went farther into the bush than the hunter had expected.

As an adjective, *further* means "more."

After high school, how many students really need further education?

As a conjunctive adverb, *further* means "besides."

Lincoln disliked slavery; further, he abhorred secession.

As a transitive verb, *further* means "promote" or "advance."

How much has the federal government done to further the development of solar energy?

fatal, fateful

Fatal means "sure to cause death" or "resulting in death."

Even a small dose of cyanide is fatal.

In a fruitless and fatal attempt to save the manuscript which he had spent ten years to produce, the novelist rushed back into the burning house.

Fateful means "momentous in effect," and can be used whether the outcome is good or bad.

In the end, Eisenhower made the fateful decision to land the Allies at Normandy.

few, little, less

Use *few* or *fewer* with countable nouns.

Few pianists even try to play the eerie music of George Crumb.

Use *little* (in the sense of "not much") or *less* with uncountable nouns.

A little honey on your hands can be a big sticky nuisance.

In spite of his grandiloquent title, the vice-president of the United States often has less power than a congressman.

former, formerly, formally

As an adjective, *former* means "previous."

When we moved in, the apartment was a mess. The former tenants had never even bothered to throw out the garbage.

As a noun, *former* refers to the first of two persons or things mentioned previously.

Muhammad Ali first fought Leon Spinks in February 1978. At the time, the former was an international celebrity, while the latter was a twenty-four-year-old unknown.

Formerly means "at an earlier time."

Most of the men in the tribe were formerly hunters, not farmers.

Formally means "in a formal or ceremonious manner."

The president is elected in November, but he does not formally take office until the following January.

frightened, afraid

Frightened is followed by *at* or *by*.

Many people are frightened at the thought of dying.

As I walked down the deserted road I was frightened by a snarling wolfhound.

Afraid is followed by *of*.

Afraid of heights, Sylvia would not go near the edge of the cliff.

fun

Use *fun* as a noun, but not (in formal writing) as an adjective before a noun.

As soon as Mark arrived, the fun began.

*We spent a fun afternoon at the zoo.

REVISED: We spent an enjoyable afternoon at the zoo.

further *See* farther.

good, well

Use *good* as an adjective, but not as an adverb.

The proposal to rebuild the chapel sounded good to many in the congregation.

> *She ran good for the first twenty miles, but then she collapsed.
>
> REVISED: She ran well for the first twenty miles, but then she collapsed.

Use *well* as an adverb when you mean "in an effective manner" or "ably."

> Fenneman did so well in practice that the coach decided to put him in the starting lineup for the opening game.

Use *well* as an adjective when you mean "in good health."

> My grandfather hasn't looked well since his operation.

*got to *See* has to.

hanged, hung

Hanged means "executed by hanging."

> The prisoner was hanged at dawn.

Hung means "suspended" or "held oneself up."

> I hung my coat on the back of the door and sat down.
>
> I hung on the side of the cliff, frantically seeking a foothold.

Do not use *hung* to mean "executed by hanging."

> *They hung the prisoner at dawn.
>
> REVISED: They hanged the prisoner at dawn.

has to, have to, *got to

In formal writing, do not use **got to* to denote an obligation. Use *have to, has to,* or *must.*

> *Anyone who wants to win the nomination has got to run in the primaries.
>
> REVISED: Anyone who wants to win the nomination has to run in the primaries.

hopefully

Use *hopefully* to modify a verb.

> As the ice-cream truck approached, the children looked hopefully at their parents. [*Hopefully* modifies *looked,* telling how the children looked.]

Do not use *hopefully* when you mean "I hope that," "we hope that," or the like.

> *Hopefully, the company will make a profit in the final quarter.
>
> REVISED: The stockholders hope that the company will make a profit in the final quarter.

human, humane

Human means "pertaining to human beings."

> To err is human.

Humane means "merciful," "kindhearted," or "considerate."

> To forgive is both divine and humane.

illusion *See* allusion.

immanent, imminent *See* eminent.

immigrate, emigrate

Immigrate means "enter a country in order to live there permanently."

> Professor Korowitz immigrated to the United States in 1955.

Emigrate means "leave one country in order to live in another."

> My great-great-grandfather emigrated from Ireland in 1848.

immoral *See* amoral.

imply, infer

Imply means "suggest" or "hint at something."

> The manager implied that I could not be trusted with the job.

Infer means "reach a conclusion on the basis of evidence"; it is often used with *from*.

> From the manager's letter I inferred that my chances were nil.

in, into, in to

Use *in* when referring to a direction, location, or position.

> Easterners used to think that everyone in the West was a cowboy.

Use *into* to mean movement toward the inside.

> Before he started drilling, the dentist shot Novocain into my gum.

Use *in to* when the two words have separate functions.

> The museum was open, so I walked in to look at the paintings.

incredible, incredulous

Incredible means "not believable."

> Since unmanned exploration of Mars has revealed no signs of life there, the idea that "Martians" could invade the earth is now incredible.

In formal writing, do not use *incredible* to mean "amazingly bad," "compelling," "brilliant," or "extraordinary." In speech, you can indicate the meaning of *incredible* by the way you say it, but in writing, this word may be ambiguous and confusing.

> *Marian gave an incredible performance. [The reader has no way of knowing whether the performance was not believable, amazingly good, or amazingly bad.]
>
> REVISED: Marian gave a brilliant performance.

Incredulous means "unbelieving" or "skeptical."

> When Columbus argued that his ship would not fall off the edge of the earth, many of his hearers were incredulous, for they believed the earth was flat.

infer *See* imply.

inferior to, *inferior than

Always use *to* after *inferior*. Do not use *than*.

> *America once led the world in its technology, but now many of its products—including the automobile—are inferior than those made elsewhere.
>
> REVISED: America once led the world in its technology, but now many of its products—including the automobile—are inferior to those made elsewhere.

insure *See* assure.

***irregardless** *See* regardless.

irritate   *See* aggravate.

its, it's

> *Its* is the possessive form of *it*.
>
>> We liked the house because of its appearance, its location, and its price.
>
> *It's* means "it is."
>
>> It's a pity that we seldom see ourselves as others see us.

kind of, sort of

> In formal writing, do not use *kind of* or *sort of* to mean "somewhat" or "rather."
>
>> *When I got off the roller coaster, I felt sort of sick.
>>
>> REVISED: When I got off the roller coaster, I felt rather sick.

later, latter

> Use *later* when referring to time.
>
>> Russia developed the atomic bomb later than the United States did.
>>
>> During our century, aerospace technology has progressed with astounding speed. In 1903 the Wright brothers invented the first successful airplane; sixty-six years later, America put a man on the moon.
>
> Use *latter* when referring to the second of two persons or things mentioned previously.
>
>> Muhammed Ali first fought Leon Spinks in February 1978. At the time, the former was an international celebrity, while the latter was a twenty-four-year-old unknown.

lay   *See* lie.

lead, led

> *Lead* (rhymes with *seed*) is the present-tense and infinitive form of the verb meaning "cause," "guide," or "direct."
>
>> Deficit spending leads to inflation.
>>
>> An effective president must be able to lead Congress without bullying it.
>
> *Led* is the past-tense form and past participle of *lead*.
>
>> During the Civil War, General Robert E. Lee led the Confederate forces.
>>
>> Some buyers are led astray by simple-minded slogans.

learn, teach

> *Learn* means "gain knowledge, information, or skill."
>
> *Teach* means "give lessons or instructions."
>
>> If you want to know how well you have learned something, teach it to someone else.

leave, let

> *Leave* means "go away from" or "put in a place."
>
>> I had to leave the house at 6:00 A.M. in order to catch the bus.
>>
>> Just as I got to the bus station, I suddenly realized that I had left my suitcase at home.
>
> *Let* means "permit," "allow."
>
>> Some colleges let students take courses by mail.

led *See* lead.

less *See* few.

let *See* leave.

let's, *let's us
> Use *let's* before a verb. Do not follow *let's* with *us;* that would mean "let us us."
>> *Let's us finish the job.
>>
>> Revised: Let's finish the job.

liable *See* likely.

lie, lay
> *Lie (lie, lying, lay, lain)* is an intransitive verb meaning "rest," "recline," or "stay."
>> I love to lie on the sand in the hot sun.
>>
>> Lying on the sand, I watched the clouds and listened to the pounding of the surf.
>>
>> After she lay in the sun for three hours, she looked like a boiled lobster.
>>
>> On April 26, 1952, workers digging peat near Grueballe, Denmark, found a well-preserved body that had lain in the bog for fifteen hundred years.
>
> *Lay (lay, laying, laid, laid)* is a transitive verb meaning "put in a certain position."
>> "Lay down your weapons," shouted the captain. "We have you surrounded."
>>
>> A good education lays the foundation for a good life.
>>
>> The workers were laying bricks when an earthquake struck.
>>
>> He laid the book on the counter and walked out of the library.
>>
>> The earthquake struck after the foundation had been laid.

like *See* as.

likely, apt, liable
> *Likely* indicates future probability.
>> As gas becomes scarcer and more expensive, battery-powered cars are likely to become popular.
>
> *Apt* indicates a usual or habitual tendency.
>> Most cars are apt to rust after two or three years.
>
> *Liable* indicates a risk or adverse possibility.
>> Cars left unlocked are liable to be stolen.

little *See* few.

loose, lose
> *Loose* (rhymes with *moose*) means "free" or "not securely tied or fastened."
>> The center grabbed the loose ball and ran for a touchdown.
>>
>> From the rattling of the door, I could tell that the catch was loose.
>
> *Lose* (sounds like *Lou's*) means "fail to keep" or "fail to win."
>> In some cultures, to lose face is to lose everything.
>>
>> The hard truth about sports is that whenever somebody wins, somebody else loses.

lots of, a lot of, *alot of

A *lot of* and *lots of* are colloquial and wordy. In formal writing, use *much* for "a great amount" and *many* for "a great number." Do not use *alot* anywhere; it is a misspelling of *a lot.*

> Lots of students come to college with no clear notion of what they want to do.
>
> BETTER: Many students come to college with no clear notion of what they want to do.

many, much, *muchly

Use *many* with countable nouns.

> Many hands make light work.

Use *much* with uncountable nouns.

> Much of the work has been done.

Use *much* or *very much*, not *muchly*, as an adverb.

> *The long sleep left me muchly refreshed.
>
> REVISED: The long sleep left me much [for "very much"] refreshed.

maybe, may be

Maybe means "perhaps."

> Maybe all cars will be electric by the year 2000.

May be is a verb phrase.

> Before the year 2000, the president of the United States may be a woman.

might have, *might of.

Use *might have*, not *might of.*

> *Oklahoma might of won the game if it had lasted just two minutes longer.
>
> REVISED: Oklahoma might have won the game if it had lasted just two minutes longer.

moral, morale

MORal (first syllable accented) is an adjective meaning "ethical" or "virtuous."

> To heed a cry for help is not a legal duty but a moral one.
>
> Piety and morality are two different things: a pious man can be immoral, and an impious man can be moral.

MoRALE (second syllable accented syllable accented) is a noun meaning "spirit," "attitude."

> Eisenhower's habit of mixing with his troops before a battle kept up their morale.

most, mostly, *most all   *See* almost.

much, *muchly   *See* many.

not very, none too, *not too

In formal writing, use *not very* or *none too* instead of *not too.*

> *Not too pleased with the dull and droning lecture, the students filled the air with catcalls, spitballs, and paper planes.
>
> REVISED: None too pleased with the dull and droning lecture, the students filled the air with catcalls, spitballs, and paper planes.

nowhere, *nowheres

Use *nowhere*, not *nowheres.*

    *The child was nowheres to be seen.

    REVISED: The child was nowhere to be seen.

number   *See* amount.

OK, O.K., okay

Avoid all three in formal writing. In business letters or informal writing, you can use *OK* as a noun meaning "endorsement" or "approval," or *okay* as a verb meaning "endorse," "approve."

    The stockholders have given their OK.

    Union negotiators have okayed the company's latest offer.

only

Place *only* carefully. It belongs immediately before the word, phrase, or clause it modifies.

    *At most colleges, students only get their diplomas if they have paid all their bills.

    REVISED: At most colleges, students get their diplomas only if they have paid all their bills.

    *Some busy executives only relax on Sundays.

    REVISED: Some busy executives relax only on Sundays.

ourselves, ourself

Use *ourselves*, not *ourself,* when the antecedent is plural.

    Nearly an hour after the front-runners had come in, Sally and I dragged ourselves across the finish line.

passed, past

Passed means "went by" or "threw."

    The idiot passed me on the inside lane.

    Conversation ground to a painful halt, and minutes passed like hours.

    Seymour passed to Winowski, but the ball was intercepted.

As a noun, *past* means "a certain previous time" or "all previous time."

    Prehistoric monuments like Stonehenge speak to us of a past that we can only speculate about.

As an adjective, *past* means "connected with a certain previous time" or "connected with all previous time."

    Past experience never tells us everything we want to know about the future.

As a preposition, *past* means "beyond."

    The space probe *Pioneer 10* will eventually travel past the limits of the solar system.

persecute, prosecute

Persecute means "pester" or "harass."

    As Nero persecuted the Christians, Hitler persecuted the Jews.

Prosecute means "bring charges against someone in a formal, legal way."

    Al Capone ran his criminal empire so shrewdly that authorities took years to prosecute him.

personal, personnel

PERsonal (first syllable accented) is an adjective meaning "private" or "individual."

> In writing or speaking, you can sometimes use a personal experience to illustrate a general point.

PersonNEL (last syllable accented) is a noun meaning "persons in a firm or a military group."

> If you want a job with a big company, you normally have to see the director of personnel.

phenomenon, phenomena

Phenomenon means "something perceived by the senses" or "something extraordinary."

> A rainbow is a phenomenon caused by the separation of sunlight into various colors as it passes through raindrops.
>
> Old Barney is a phenomenon. At eighty years of age he still swims five miles every day.

Phenomena is the plural of *phenomenon.*

> The Northern Lights are among the most impressive phenomena in nature.

poor, poorly

Use *poor* as an adjective.

> The poor man stood waiting in the rain.

Use *poorly* as an adverb.

> French ran the last mile poorly.

Do not use *poor* as an adverb:

> *The car starts poor in cold weather.
>
> REVISED: The car starts poorly in cold weather.

Do not use *poorly* as an adjective.

> *Heather looked poorly after the operation.
>
> REVISED: Heather looked poor after the operation.

precede, proceed, proceeds, proceedings, procedure

To *precede* is to come before or go before in place or time.

> A dead calm often precedes a hurricane.

To *proceed* is to move forward or go on.

> With the bridge washed out, the bus could not proceed, so we had to get out and take a ferry across the river.
>
> The bishop proceeded toward the cathedral.
>
> After the judge silenced the uproar, he told the prosecutor to proceed with her questioning.

Proceeds are funds generated by a business deal or a money-raising event.

> The proceeds of the auction went to buy new furniture for the Student Center.

Proceedings are formal actions, especially in an official meeting.

> During a trial, a court stenographer takes down every word of the proceedings for the record.

A *procedure* is a standardized way of doing something.

> Anyone who wants to run a meeting effectively should know the rules of parliamentary procedure.

principal, principle

As a noun, *principal* means "administrator" or "sum of money."

The school principal wanted all of us to think of him as a pal, but none of us did.

The interest on the principal came to $550 a year.

As an adjective, *principal* means "most important."

In most American households, television is the principal source of entertainment.

Principle means "rule of behavior," "basic truth," or "general law of nature."

Whenever we officially recognize a government that abuses its own citizens, we are tacitly accepting the principle that might makes right.

proceed *See* precede.

proceeds, proceedings, procedure *See* precede.

prosecute *See* persecute.

quote, quotation

Quote means "repeat the exact words of."

In his "Letter from Birmingham Jail," Martin Luther King, Jr., quotes Lincoln: "This nation cannot survive half slave and half free."

Do not use *quote* to mean "refer to" or "paraphrase the view of." Use *cite*.

In defense of his stand against segregation, King cites more than a dozen authorities, and he quotes Lincoln: "This nation cannot survive half slave and half free."

Do not use *quote* as a noun to mean "something quoted." Use *quotation*.

*A sermon usually begins with a quote from Scripture.

REVISED: A sermon usually begins with a quotation from Scripture.

Quotation means "something quoted," as in the preceding example. But you should not normally use it to mean something *you* are quoting.

*In a quotation on the very first page of the book, Holden expresses his opinion of Hollywood. "If there's one thing I hate," he says, "it's the movies." [Holden is not quoting anybody. He is speaking for himself.]

REVISED: In a statement on the very first page of the book, Holden expresses his opinion of Hollywood. "If there's one thing I hate," he says, "it's the movies.'

You can improve this passage even further by compressing the first sentence.

Holden states his opinion of Hollywood on the very first page of the book.

raise, rise

Raise (raise, raising, raised, raised) is a transitive verb—one followed by an object.

Moments before his hanging, Dandy Tom raised his hat to the ladies.

My grandmother has raised ten children.

Rise (rise, rising, rose, risen) is an intransitive verb—one that has no object.

Puffs of smoke rose skyward.

The farmhands rose at 5:00 A.M. Monday through Saturday.

Have you ever risen early enough to see the sun rise?

rational, rationale, rationalize

Rational means "able to reason," "sensible," or "logical."

Can a rational person ever commit suicide?

Is there such a thing as a rational argument for nuclear warfare?

Rationale means "justification," "explanation," or "underlying reason."

The rationale for the new bypass is that it will reduce the flow of traffic through the center of town.

Rationalize means "justify with one or more fake reasons."

He rationalized his extravagance by saying that he was only doing his part to keep money in circulation.

real, really

Real means "actual."

The unicorn is an imaginary beast, but it is made up of features taken from real ones.

Really means "actually."

Petrified wood looks like ordinary wood, but it is really stone.

In formal writing, do not use *real* to modify an adjective.

*In parts of the country synthetic fuels have met real strong resistance.

REVISED: In parts of the country synthetic fuels have met really strong resistance.

FURTHER REVISED: In parts of the country synthetic fuels have met strong resistance. [This version eliminates *really,* which—like *very*—often weakens rather than strengthens the word it modifies.]

reason . . . is that, *reason . . . is because

Use *reason* with *that,* not with *because,* or use *because* by itself.

*The reason many college freshmen have trouble with writing is because they did little or no writing in high school.

REVISED: The reason many college freshmen have trouble with writing is that they did little or no writing in high school. [or] Many college freshmen have trouble with writing because they did little or no writing in high school.

refer   *See* allude.

regardless, *irregardless

Use *regardless,* not *irregardless.*

*Irregardless of what happens to school systems and public services, some cities and towns have voted to cut property taxes substantially.

REVISED: Regardless of what happens to school systems and

public services, some cities and towns have voted to cut property taxes substantially.

respectively, respectfully, respectably

Respectively means "in turn" or "in the order presented."

The college presented honorary degrees to Harriet Brown and Emanuel Lee, who are, respectively, an Olympic medalist and a concert pianist.

Respectfully means "with respect."

Parents who speak respectfully to their children are most likely to end up with children who speak respectfully to them.

Respectably means "presentably" or "in a manner deserving respect."

She ran respectably but not quite successfully for the Senate.

rise   *See* raise.

set, sit

Set (set, setting, set, set) means "put" or "place."

I filled the kettle and set it on the range.

When daylight saving changes to standard time, I can never remember whether to set my watch forward or back.

Sit (sit, sitting, sat, sat) means "place oneself in a sitting position."

On clear summer nights I love to sit outside, listen to crickets, and look at the stars.

Grandfather sat in an easy chair and smoked his pipe.

sight, cite, site

As a verb, *sight* means "observe" or "perceive with the eyes."

After twenty days on the open sea the sailors sighted land.

As a noun, *sight* means "spectacle," "device for aiming," or "vision."

Some travelers care only for the sights of a foreign country; they have no interest in its people.

The deadliest weapon of all is a rifle with a telescopic sight.

Most of us take the gift of sight for granted; only the blind know how much it is worth.

Cite means "refer to," "mention as an example or piece of evidence."

Anyone opposed to nuclear power cites the case of Three Mile Island. But just how serious was the accident that occurred there?

As a verb, *site* means "locate" or "place at a certain point."

The architect sited the house on the side of a hill.

As a noun, *site* means "location" or "place," often the place where something has been or will be built.

The site of the long-gone Globe Theatre, where Shakespeare himself once trod the boards, is now occupied by a brewery.

since   *See* because.

sit   *See* set.

site   *See* sight.

so   *See* very.

sometimes, sometime

Sometimes means "occasionally."

Sometimes I lie awake at night and wonder what I will do with my life.

As an adjective, *sometime* means "former."

In the presidential campaigns of 1952 and 1956, Eisenhower twice defeated Adlai Stevenson, sometime governor of Illinois and later U.S. ambassador to the United Nations.

As an adverb, *sometime* means "at some point."

A slot machine addict invariably thinks that he or she will sometime hit the jackpot.

somewhere, *somewheres

Use *somewhere*, not **somewheres*.

*Somewheres in that pile of junk was a diamond necklace.

REVISED: Somewhere in that pile of junk was a diamond necklace.

sort of   *See* kind of.

stationary, stationery

Stationary means "not moving."

Before you can expect to hit a moving target, you need to practice with a stationary one.

Stationery means "writing paper," "writing materials."

Since my parents sent me off to college with a big box of personalized stationery, I guess I'd better write to them occasionally.

statue, statute

Statue means "sculpted figure."

The Statue of Liberty in New York harbor was given to America by France.

Statute means "law passed by a governing body."

Some people are upset by the new statute governing the registration of motorcycles.

Though the Supreme Court has ruled that abortion is legally permissible, some state legislatures have enacted statutes restricting the conditions under which it may be performed.

such a

Do not use *such a* as an intensifier unless you add a result clause beginning with *that*.

WEAK: The commencement speech was such a bore.

BETTER: The commencement speech was such a bore that I fell asleep after the first five minutes.

supposed to, *suppose to

Use *supposed to* when you mean "expected to" or "required to." Do not use **suppose to*.

*Truman was suppose to lose when he ran against Dewey, but he surprised almost everyone by winning.

REVISED: Truman was supposed to lose when he ran against Dewey, but he surprised almost everyone by winning.

*I was suppose to get up at 5:30 A.M., but I overslept.

REVISED: I was supposed to get up at 5:30 A.M., but I overslept.

teach *See* learn.

than, then

Use *than* when writing comparisons.

Many people spend money faster than they earn it.

Use *then* when referring to time.

Lightning flashed, thunder cracked, and then the rain began.

that, which, who

Use *which* or *that* as the pronoun when the antecedent is a thing.

There was nothing to drink but root beer, which I loathe.

Any restaurant that doesn't serve grits ought to be closed.

Use *who* as the pronoun when the antecedent is a person or persons.

I like people who can do things.

—R. W. Emerson

themselves, *theirselves, *theirself

Use *themselves,* not *theirselves or **theirself.*

*Fortunately, the children did not hurt theirselves when they fell out of the tree.

REVISED: Fortunately, the children did not hurt themselves when they fell out of the tree.

then *See* than.

there, their, they're

Use *there* to mean "in that place" or "to that place," and in the expressions *there is* and *there are.*

I have always wanted to see Las Vegas, but I have never been there.

There is nothing we can do to change the past, but there are many things we can do to improve the future.

There is and *there are* should be used sparingly, since most sentences are tighter and better without them.

We can do nothing to change the past, but many things to improve the future.

Use *their* as the possessive form of *they.*

The immigrants had to leave most of their possessions behind.

Use *they're* when you mean "they are."

I like cats because they're sleek, quiet, and sly.

thus, therefore, *thusly

Use *thus* to mean "in that manner" or "by this means." In formal writing, do not use **thusly.*

Carmichael bought a thousand shares of IBM when it was a brand-new company. Thus he became a millionaire.

Do not use *thus* to mean "therefore," "so," or "for this reason."

A heavy storm hit the mountain. *Thus the climbers had to take shelter.

REVISED: A heavy storm hit the mountain, so the climbers had to take shelter.

to, too, two

Use *to* when writing about place, direction, or position, and with infinitives.

We drove from Cleveland to Pittsburgh without stopping.

Like many before him, Fenwick was determined to write the great American novel.

Use *too* when you mean "also" or "excessively."

In spite of the cast on my foot, I too got up and danced.

Some poems are too confusing to be enjoyable.

Use *two* when you mean "one plus one."

In some mathematical systems, two and two do not make four.

try to, *try and

Use *try to,* not *try and.*

*Whenever I feel depressed, I try and lose myself in science fiction.

REVISED: Whenever I feel depressed, I try to lose myself in science fiction.

two   *See* to.

-type

Do not attach *-type* to the end of an adjective.

*He had a psychosomatic-type illness.

REVISED: He had a psychosomatic illness.

uninterested   *See* disinterested.

unique

Unique means "one of a kind."

Among pop singers of the fifties, Elvis Presley was unique.

Do not use *unique* to mean "remarkable," "unusual," or "striking."

*She wore a unique dress to the party.

REVISED: She wore a striking dress to the party.

used to, *use to

Write *used to,* not **use to,* when you mean "did regularly" or "was accustomed to."

*She use to run three miles every morning.

REVISED: She used to run three miles every morning.

very, awfully, so

Use *very* sparingly, if at all. It can weaken the effect of potent modifiers.

The very icy wind cut through me as I walked across the bridge.

BETTER: The icy wind cut through me as I walked across the bridge.

Do not use *awfully* to mean "very."

*We were awfully tired.

REVISED: We were very tired.

FURTHER REVISED: We were exhausted.

Do not use *so* as an intensifier unless you add a result clause beginning with *that*.

> *They were so happy.
>
> REVISED: They were so happy that they tossed their hats in the air.

wait for, wait on

> To *wait for* means "to stay until someone arrives, something is provided, or something happens."
>
> > The restaurant was so crowded that we had to wait half an hour for a table.
>
> To *wait on* means "to serve."
>
> > Monica waited on more than fifty people that night. When the restaurant closed, she could barely stand up.

way, ways

> Use *way*, not *ways*, when writing about distance.
>
> > *A short ways up the trail we found a dead rabbit.
> >
> > REVISED: A short way up the trail we found a dead rabbit.

well   *See* good

were, we're

> Use *were* as a verb or part of a verb phrase.
>
> > The soldiers were a sorry sight.
> >
> > They were trudging across a wheat field.
>
> Use *we're* when you mean "we are."
>
> > We're trying to build a telescope for the observatory.
> >
> > Most Americans have lost the urge to roam. With television scanning the world for us, we're a nation of sitters.

which, who   *See* that.

whose, who's

> *Whose* means "of whom."
>
> > Whose property has been destroyed?
>
> *Who's* means "who is."
>
> > Who's deceived by such claims?

would have, *would of

> Use *would have*, not **would of*.
>
> > *Churchill said that he would of made a pact with the devil himself to defeat Hitler.
> >
> > REVISED: Churchill said that he would have made a pact with the devil himself to defeat Hitler.
>
> *Have*, not *of*, is also customary after *may*, *might*, *must*, and *should*.

GLOSSARY OF TERMS

absolute phrase

A modifier usually made from a noun or noun phrase and a participle. It modifies the whole of the base sentence to which it is attached.

> *Teeth chattering*, we waited for hours in the bitter cold.
>
> Who is best for the job, *all things considered*?

active voice *See* voice.

adjective

A word that modifies a noun, specifying such things as how many, what kind, and which one.

> For a *small* crime, he was made to spend *seven* years in a *tiny* cell of the *old* prison.

adjective phrase

A phrase that modifies a noun.

> On the table was a bouquet *of red roses*.
>
> The man *in the center of the picture* has never been identified.

adjective (relative) clause

A subordinate clause that is used as an adjective within a sentence. It normally begins with a relative pronoun—a word that relates the clause to a preceding word or phrase.

> Pablo Picasso, *who learned to paint by the age of twelve*, worked at his art for nearly eighty years.

adverb

A word that modifies a verb, an adjective, another adverb, or a clause. It tells such things as how, when, where, why, and for what purpose. It often ends in *-ly*.

The cyclist breathed *heavily*.

She spoke *forcefully*.

Trains are *frequently* late.

adverb clause

A subordinate clause that is used as an adverb within a sentence. It commonly modifies another entire clause, but can also modify a word or phrase. It begins with a subordinator, a term like *before*, *because, when, since,* or *although.*

Because he faltered in the seventh inning, the pitcher was taken off the mound.

Smiling *when the guests arrived,* she was miserable *by the time they left.*

To cut all the grass *before the rains came,* I had to work fast.

adverb phrase

A phrase that modifies a verb, an adjective, another adverb, or a clause.

The fox jumped *over the hedge.*

Wary *at first,* he soon threw caution *to the winds.*

The Amazon runs *through some of the most densely vegetated land in the world.*

On the eve of the battle, the valley seemed peaceful.

agreement of pronoun and antecedent

Correspondence in gender and number between a pronoun and its antecedent.

Nellie Bly, the American journalist, was noted for *her* daring. [*Her* is feminine and singular.]

Ms. Sterns handed Mr. Nichols *his* briefcase. [*His* is masculine and singular.]

You can't tell a book by *its* cover. [*Its* is neuter and singular.]

The Andrews Sisters sang some of *their* best-known songs during World War II. [*Their* is plural and used for all genders.]

agreement of subject and verb

Correspondence in number between the form of a verb and its subject. In most cases, the subject affects the form of the verb only in the present tense; when the subject is a singular noun or a third-person singular pronoun, the present tense is made by the addition of *-s* or *-es* to the bare form.

Naomi *paints* houses.

He *fishes* every summer.

When the subject is not a singular noun or a third-person singular pronoun, the present tense is normally the same as the bare form.

I *paint* houses.

The men *fish* every summer.

The verb *be* has special forms in the present and the past, as shown on p. 353.

analogy

A noting of the similarities between two or more things of different classes. It is commonly used to clarify an abstract or specialized subject by linking it with something concrete, ordinary, and familiar.

> Electrical energy is like the force that travels through a row of falling dominoes.

antecedent

The word or word group that a pronoun refers to.

> *Oliver* said that he could eat a whole pizza. [*Oliver* is the antecedent of *he.*]
>
> *The police,* who have surrounded the building, expect to free the hostages tonight. [*The police* is the antecedent of *who.*]
>
> *A snake* sheds its skin several times a year. [*A snake* is the antecedent of *its.*]

appositive

A noun or noun phrase that is used to identify another noun or noun phrase, or a pronoun.

> The blackjack player, *an expert at counting cards in play,* was barred from the casino.
>
> He was denied his favorite foods—*ice cream, pizza, and peanut butter.*
>
> He and she—*brother and sister*—decided to run away from home together.

article

A short word commonly used before a noun or noun equivalent. The articles are *a, an,* and *the.*

> *The* bombing of *the* village provoked *a* storm of protest.

auxiliary (helping verb)

A verb used with a base verb to make a verb phrase.

> I *have* seen the Kennedy Library.
>
> It *was* designed by I. M. Pei.

bare form

The verb form used in the present tense with every subject except a singular noun and a third-person singular pronoun.

> When the children *laugh,* we *laugh* too.

base predicate   *See* predicate.

base sentence

A sentence without modifiers.

> Borg lost.
>
> McEnroe beat him.

base verb

The principal verb in a verb phrase made with an auxiliary.

> She has *earned* a promotion.
>
> He might *sell* the house.

case

The form that a noun or pronoun takes as determined by its role in a sentence. The **subject case** is used for a pronoun that is the subject of a verb.

> The dog was far from home, but *he* still wore a leather collar.

The **object case** is used for a pronoun that is the object of a verb or preposition, or that immediately precedes an infinitive.

I found *him* trailing a broken leash behind *him*.

I wanted *him* to come with *me*.

The possessive case of a noun or pronoun is used to indicate ownership of something or close connection with it.

The *dog's* hind feet were bleeding, and *his* coat was muddy.

The reflexive / emphatic case is used with pronouns to indicate a reflexive action—an action affecting the one who performs it. This case is also used for emphasis.

The dog had injured *himself;* I *myself* had seen him do so.

clause

A word group consisting of a subject and a predicate.

$\overset{\text{S}}{\text{We}}$ / $\overset{\text{P}}{\text{bought}}$ an old house. [one clause]

$\overset{\text{S}}{\text{After we}}$ / $\overset{\text{P}}{\text{bought}}$ the house, $\overset{\text{S}}{\text{we}}$ / $\overset{\text{P}}{\text{found}}$ a crack in the foundation. [two clauses]

$\overset{\text{S}}{\text{Furthermore, the roof}}$ / $\overset{\text{P}}{\text{leaked}}$, $\overset{\text{S}}{\text{the floors}}$ / $\overset{\text{P}}{\text{sagged}}$,

$\overset{\text{S}}{\text{and the furnace}}$ / $\overset{\text{P}}{\text{was}}$ out of order. [three clauses]

comma splice (comma fault)

The error of joining two independent clauses with nothing but a comma.

*Sir Richard Burton failed to trace the source of the Nile, John Hanning Speke discovered it in 1862.

REVISED: Sir Richard Burton failed to trace the source of the Nile; John Hanning Speke discovered it in 1862.

common and progressive forms

Tense forms of the verb. The **common form** indicates a momentary, habitual, or completed action.

She *cooks* on weekends.

He *cooked* dinner last night.

I *will cook* next month.

The **progressive form** indicates a continuing action.

Divers *are searching* for the sunken ship.

Was I *doing* it right?

We *will be seeing* you.

The progressive consists of some form of the auxiliary *be* followed by a present participle—a verb with *-ing* on the end.

comparative and superlative

Forms of the adjective and adverb. The **comparative** is used to compare one person, thing, or group with another person, thing, or group.

Los Angeles is *bigger* than Sacramento.

Cal was *more ambitious* than his classmates.

Sheila argued *more persuasively* than Tim did.

In general, women live *longer* than men.

The **superlative** is used to compare one person, thing, or group with all others in its class.

Joan's quilt was the *most colorful* one on display.

Whales are the *largest* of all mammals.

George was the *most eagerly* awaited bachelor at the party.

comparison

A noting of the similarities and differences—or just the similarities—between two or more things of the same class.

Like a tramp, a hobo is a homeless vagrant with little or no money; but unlike a tramp, a hobo will sometimes do odd jobs.

complete subject   *See* subject.

complex sentence

A sentence consisting of one independent clause and at least one subordinate clause. The independent clause in a complex sentence is usually called the main clause.

Although Frank pleaded with Ida [subordinate clause], she would not give him the money [main clause].

compound-complex sentence

A sentence consisting of two or more independent clauses and one or more subordinate clauses.

When I moved to Chicago [subordinate clause], I first applied for a job [main clause], and then I looked for an apartment [main clause].

compound phrase

Words or phrases joined by a conjunction, a comma, or both.

The plan was *simple but shrewd.*

We saw an *old, rough-skinned, enormous* elephant.

The kitten was *lively, friendly, and curious.*

You must *either pay your dues on time or turn in your membership card.*

compound sentence

A sentence consisting of two or more independent clauses.

Jill made the coffe, and Frank scrambled the eggs.

He practiced many hours each day, but he never learned to play the piano well.

conditional sentence

A sentence normally consisting of an *if* clause, which states a condition, and a result clause, which states the result of that condition.

If it rains on the Fourth of July, the fireworks will be canceled.

If Social Security were abolished, millions of retirees would be destitute.

conjunction (coordinating conjunction)

A word used to show a relation between words, phrases, or clauses.

The conjunctions are *and, yet, or, but, nor,* and—for joining clauses only—*for* and *so.*

The tablecloth was red, white, *and* blue.

Small *but* sturdy, the cabin had withstood many winters.

Al *and* Joan walked to the meeting, *for* they liked exercise.

conjunctive adverb

A word or phrase used to show a relation between clauses or sentences. Conjunctive adverbs include *nevertheless, as a result, therefore, however,* and *likewise.*

> The ship was supposed to be unsinkable; *nevertheless,* it did not survive its collision with an iceberg.
>
> The lawyer spoke for an hour; the jury, *however,* was unimpressed.

connotation and denotation

Connotation is the feeling, attitude, or set of associations that a word conveys. **Denotation** is the specific person, object, sensation, idea, action, or condition that a word signifies or names. *Home* connotes the warmth of familial affections; it denotes a place in which one or more persons or creatures live.

contrast

A noting of the differences between two or more things of the same class.

> Cross-country skis are thinner, lighter, and usually longer than downhill skis.

coordinating conjunction   *See* conjunction.

coordination

An arrangement that makes two or more parts of a sentence equal in grammatical rank.

> Martha *took the script* home and *read it* to her husband.
> *The fight ended,* and *the crowd dispersed.*
> A *porcupine* or a *racoon* had raided the garbage can.

correlatives

Words or phrases used in pairs to join words, phrases, or clauses. Correlatives include *both . . . and, not only . . . but also, either . . . or neither . . . nor,* and *whether . . . or*

> He was *both* rich *and* handsome.
> She *not only* got the part *but also* played it brilliantly.
> *Either* they would visit us, *or* we would visit them.

dangling modifier

A modifier without a headword—a word or phrase that it can modify.

> **Running angrily out the back way,* a couple of milk bottles were overturned.
>
> REVISED: Running angrily out the back way, he overturned a couple of milk bottles.

declarative sentence

A sentence that makes a statement and ends with a period.

> The earth orbits around the sun.
> Americans spend millions of dollars on Japanese products every year.

deductive argument

A type of argument in which a conclusion is drawn from one or more assumptions and one or more statements of fact.

definite pronoun   *See* pronoun.

denotation   *See* connotation and denotation.

dependent clause   *See* subordinate clause.

direct object   *See* object.

expletive

A word used before a linking verb that is followed by the subject.

There was no food in the house.
<small>s</small>

It was frightening to see the waters rise.
<small>s</small>

fallacy

An unsound or illogical way of arguing.

faulty parallelism

An error in which two or more parts of a sentence are parallel in meaning but not parallel in form.

*I want to learn how to write *with simplicity, clarity, and logically.*

REVISED: I want to learn how to write with simplicity, clarity, and logic.

faulty predication

Misconnecting the basic parts of a sentence.

*What surprised me was when she canceled the party.

REVISED: What surprised me was her cancellation of the party.

*The agency greeted me warmly.

REVISED: The manager of the agency greeted me warmly.

faulty tense shift

An unjustified shift from one tense to another, or an inconsistency between the tense of a subordinate verb and the tense of the main verb.

*I lit a candle, but the darkness *is* so thick I saw nothing.

REVISED: I lit a candle, but the darkness was so thick I saw nothing.

*Though he *blows* as hard as he could, the drummer drowned him out.

REVISED: Though he blew as hard as he could, the drummer drowned him out.

fragment *See* sentence fragment.

fused sentence *See* run-on sentence.

future perfect tense *See* tense.

future tense *See* tense.

gender

The form of a pronoun as determined by the sex of its antecedent, which may be masculine, feminine, or neuter.

Bill [antecedent] brought *his* fishing rod, and Sally [antecedent] brought *her* paints.

The sun [antecedent] shed *its* rays over the lake.

gerund

A verbal noun made with the present participle.

Gambling takes nerve.

Fawn hated *washing dishes.*

headword

A word or phrase modified by another word or phrase, or by a clause.

Running for the elevator, *Pritchett* nearly knocked over Mr. Givens. [*Pritchett* is the headword of *Running for the elevator.*]

I found *the dog* digging for bones in the town dump. [*The dog* is the headword of *digging for bones in the town dump.*]

The bullet that killed him came from a high-powered rifle. [*The bullet* is the headword of *that killed him.*]

helping verb   *See* auxiliary.

imperative mood   *See* mood.

indefinite pronoun   *See* pronoun.

independent clause

A clause that begins without a subordinator or a relative pronoun. Such a clause can stand by itself as a simple sentence.

The roof leaks.

It can be combined with one or more other independent clauses in a compound sentence.

The roof leaks, and the floor sags.

And it can serve as the main clause in a complex sentence.

Whenever it rains, the roof leaks.

indicative mood   *See* mood.

indirect object   *See* object.

inductive argument

A type of argument in which a conclusion is drawn from a set of examples.

infinitive

A form usually made by the placing of *to* before the bare form of a verb.

Some say that politicians are born *to run.*

The prisoners of war refused *to continue* their forced march.

After some verbs the *to* in the infinitive is omitted. Compare:

Jack wanted the little boy *to feed* the ducks.

Jack watched the little boy *feed* the ducks.

infinitive phrase

A phrase formed by an infinitive and its object, its modifiers, or both.

She hates *to see horror movies.*

It was beginning *to rain furiously.*

I hope *to find a job soon.*

interrogative pronoun   *See* pronoun.

interrogative sentence

A sentence that asks a question and ends with a question mark.

Do whales have lungs?

intransitive verb   *See* transitive and intransitive verbs.

irregular verb   *See* regular and irregular verbs.

limiter

An adverb that limits or restricts the meaning of the word immediately after it.

On the first day, we traveled *only* fifty miles.

Walking up the beach, I *almost* stepped on a crab.

Limiters include *almost, hardly, just, only,* and *nearly.* When used at the end of a sentence, a limiter restricts the meaning of the word just before it.

> Tickets were sold to adults *only.*

linking verb

A verb followed by a word or word group that identifies or describes the subject.

> This machine *is* a drill press.
> I *feel* good today.
> That perfume *smells* sweet.

main clause

The independent clause in a complex sentence.

> Since there was no food in the house, *we went to a restaurant.*

main verb

The verb of the independent clause in a complex sentence.

> I *cut* the grass before the storm came.
> Since the store was closed, we *drove* away.

metaphor and simile

A **metaphor** is a figure of speech in which two things of different classes are implicitly compared.

> Jane's outcry *scorched* him. [Her outcry is implicitly compared to fire.]
> The applause *intoxicated* her. [The applause is implicitly compared to liquor.]
> Only *the skeleton of the building* remained. [The framework of the building is implicitly compared to the skeleton of a body.]

A **simile** is a figure of speech in which two things of different classes are explicitly compared.

> His belly sagged over his belt *like a sack of cornmeal.*

misplaced modifier

A modifier that does not clearly point to its headword—the word or phrase it modifies.

> **Crawling slowly up the tree,* the elderly Mrs. Cartwright spotted a bright green worm.
> REVISED: The elderly Mrs. Cartwright spotted a bright green worm crawling slowly up the tree.

modal auxiliary

A helping verb that indicates the subjunctive mood.

> The children *should* be here on Father's Day this year.
> I'm not so sure that the average citizen *can* fight City Hall.

Besides *should* and *can,* the modal auxiliaries include *would, could, may, might, must,* and *ought.*

modifier

A word or word group that describes, limits, or qualifies another word or word group in a sentence

> Pat smiled *winningly.*
> I *rarely* travel *anymore.*

The big gray cat seized *the little* mouse *as it ran up the stairs.*
Polished to a high gloss, the mahogany table *immediately* drew *our* attention.

mood

The form of a verb that indicates the writer's attitude toward a particular statement as it is made. The **indicative** is the mood used in statements of actuality or strong probability.

He always *lingers* over his second cup of coffee.

We *will sleep* well tonight.

The **imperative** is the mood of commands and requests made directly.

Be quiet!

Please *go* away.

Let us pray.

Down, Fido!

The **subjunctive** is the mood used in statements of hypothetical conditions or of wishes, recommendations, requirements, or suggestions. Normally the subjunctive requires either a modal auxiliary or a subjunctive verb form.

I wish I *could* go. [wish with modal auxiliary]

I wish I *were* a rock star. [wish with subjunctive verb form]

Each member *must* pay her dues by December 1. [requirement with modal auxiliary]

The rules require that each member *pay* her dues by December 1. [requirement with subjunctive verb form]

nonrestrictive modifier   *See* restrictive and nonrestrictive modifiers.

noun

A word that names a person, creature, place, thing, activity, condition, or idea.

noun clause

A subordinate clause that is used as a noun within a sentence. It serves as subject, object, predicate noun, or object of a preposition.

Whoever contributed to the office party deserves many thanks.

I said *that I was hungry.*

You are *what you eat.*

He did not know *how to start the engine.*

noun equivalent

A verbal noun or a noun clause.

noun phrase

A phrase formed by a noun and its modifiers.

She floated happily on *a big, fat, black inner tube.*

The eighteenth-century building was declared a landmark last week.

number

The form of a word as determined by the number of persons or things it refers to. Most nouns and many pronouns may be singular or plural.

A *carpenter* [singular] works hard.

Carpenters [plural] work hard.

Jeff said that *he* [singular] would give the party.

All *his* [singular] friends said that *they* [plural] would come.

object

A word or word group naming a person or thing affected by the action that a verb, a participle, an infinitive, or a gerund specifies.

I hit *the ball.*

Sighting *the bear,* he started to aim *his rifle.*

Splitting *wood* is hard work.

A **direct object** names the person or thing directly affected by the action specified.

The accountant prepared *my tax return.*

An **indirect object** names the person or thing indirectly affected by the action specified.

I gave *Joe* a bit of advice.

She bought *her father* a shirt.

Objects also include any word or word group that immediately follows a preposition.

For *her,* the meeting was crucial.

I found the sponge under *the kitchen sink.*

object case

See case.

object complement

A word or word group that immediately follows a direct object and identifies or describes it.

I found the first chapter *fascinating.*

Many sportswriters consider Greg Louganis *the best diver in the world.*

parallel construction

The arrangement of two or more elements of a sentence in gramatically equivalent patterns: noun lined up with noun, verb with verb, phrase with phrase, and clause with clause.

Sink or swim, live or die, survive or perish, I give *my hand* and *my heart* to this vote. —Daniel Webster

We must *take the risk* or *lose our chance.*

participle

A term usually made by the addition of *-ing, -d,* or *-ed* to the bare form of a verb.

Present Participle:	calling	living	burning	lifting
Past Participle:	called	lived	burned	lifted

A **perfect participle** is made by the combination of *having* or *having been* with the past participle.

having called   having been lifted

participle phrase

A phrase formed by a participle and its object, its modifiers, or both. Usually it modifies a noun or pronoun:

Screaming the lyrics of its hit song, the rock group could hardly be heard above the cheers of the crowd.

Wearied after their long climb, the hikers were glad to stop and make camp.

She picked at the knot, *loosening it gradually.*

passive voice   *See* voice.

past participle   *See* participle.

past perfect tense   *See* tense.

past tense   *See* tense.

perfect participle   *See* participle.

person

In English grammar the term *person* designates the following system of classification.

	SINGULAR	PLURAL
first person	I, me, mine, my	we, us, ours, our
second person	you, yours, your	you, yours, your
third person	he, him, his	
	she, her, hers	they, them, theirs, their
	it, its	
	and singular nouns	*and* plural nouns

phrase

A word group that forms a unit but lacks a subject, a predicate, or both.

On his way to the elevator, Hawkins sneezed.

Encouraged by her friends, Helen bought the house.

A bright red kimono caught my eye.

possessive case   *See* case.

predicate

A word or word group that normally follows the subject of a sentence and tells what it does, has, or is, or what is done to it.

The strong man *can lift 450 pounds.*

The pastry chef *makes doughnuts, napoleons, and éclairs.*

Venice *is a golden city interlaced with canals.*

A **base predicate (simple predicate)** is a predicate without its modifiers.

Simon and Garfunkel *sang* for a crowd of almost half a million.

The little boys *threw snowballs* at all of the passing cars.

They *were* soon *punished.*

predicate adjective

An adjective or adjective phrase that follows a linking verb and describes the subject.

Velvet feels *soft.*

Henry seemed *upset by the vote.*

predicate noun

A noun or noun phrase that follows a linking verb and identifies the subject.

Bill Gorham is *treasurer.*

"Ma Bell" is *a nickname for AT&T.*

Time was our only *enemy*.

Children eventually become *adults*.

preposition

A word used to show the relationship of a noun, pronoun, or noun equivalent to another word or word group in a sentence.

The table was set *under* a tree.

Hounded *by* his creditors, he finally declared himself bankrupt.

Besides *under* and *by*, prepositions include *with, at, of, in,* and *on*.

prepositional phrase

A phrase that starts with a preposition. Phrases of this type are regularly used as adjectives or adverbs.

Helen admired women *with strong ambition*.

Have you ridden *on the Ferris wheel?*

present participle *See* participle.

present perfect tense *See* tense.

present tense *See* tense.

principal parts

The present, present participle, past, and past participle of a verb.

PRESENT (BARE FORM)	PRESENT PARTICIPLE	PAST	PAST PARTICIPLE
see	seeing	saw	seen
work	working	worked	worked

progressive form *See* common and progressive forms.

pronoun

A word that commonly takes the place of a noun or noun phrase. Pronouns may be definite or indefinite. A **definite pronoun** refers to an antecedent, a noun or noun phrase appearing before or shortly after the pronoun.

As soon as Grant [antecedent] saw the enemy, *he* ordered the men to fire.

Janis Joplin [antecedent] was only twenty-seven when *she* died.

Though *he* won the battle, Nelson [antecedent] did not live to savor the victory.

An **indefinite pronoun** refers to unspecified persons or things. It has no antecedent.

Everyone likes Marvin.

Anything you can do, I can do better.

Nobody around here ever tells me anything.

An *interrogative pronoun* introduces a question.

What did the policeman say?

Who is pitching for the Blue Jays tomorrow?

pronoun-antecedent agreement *See* agreement of pronoun and antecedent.

reflexive / emphatic case *See* case.

regular and irregular verbs

A **regular verb** is one for which the past and past participle are formed by the addition of *-d* or *-ed* to the present.

PRESENT (BARE FORM)	PAST	PAST PARTICIPLE
work	worked	worked
tickle	tickled	tickled
walk	walked	walked

An **irregular verb** is one for which the past, the past participle, or both are formed in other ways.

sew	sewed	sewn
have	had	had
eat	atc	eaten

relative clause   *See* adjective clause.

relative pronoun

A pronoun that introduccs an adjective clause.

> Women *who* like engineering are hard to find.
> Some companies now make furnaces *that* burn wood as well as oil.

The relative pronouns are *which, that, who, whom,* and *whose.*

restrictive and nonrestrictive modifiers

A **restrictive modifier** identifies or limits the meaning of its headword.

> All taxpayers *who fail to file their returns by April 15* will be fined.

A restrictive modifier is essential to the meaning of a sentence; without the modifier, the meaning of the preceding sentence would be fundamentally different.

> All taxpayers will be fined.

A **nonrestrictive modifier** does not identify or limit the meaning of its headword.

> Daphne, *who loves football,* cheered louder than anyone else.

A nonrestrictive modifier is not essential to the meaning of a sentence; without the modifier, the meaning of the preceding sentence remains basically the same.

> Daphne cheered louder than anyone else.

run-on sentence (fused sentence)

Two or more independent clauses run together with no punctuation or conjunction between them.

> *Mosquitoes arrived at dusk they whined about our ear as we huddled in our sleeping bags.
> REVISED: Mosquitoes arrived at dusk, and they whined about our ears as we huddled in our sleeping bags.

sentence

A word group containing at least one independent clause.

The telephone was ringing.

By the time I got out of the shower, the caller had hung up.

sentence fragment

A part of a sentence punctuated as if it were a whole one.

The plant drooped. *And died.*

I could not get into the house. *Because I had forgotten my key.*

sequence of tenses

The relation between the tenses of the verbs in a sentence that contains more than one verb, or in a passage of several sentences.

By the time I *arrived,* everyone else *had left.*

When the parade *goes* through town, all the townspeople *come* to see it.

simile   *See* metaphor and simile.

simple sentence

A sentence consisting of one independent clause.

The rat ate the cheese.

simple subject   *See* subject.

split infinitive

An infinitive in which one or more words are wedged between *to* and the verb.

The purchasing department is going *to carefully check* each new order.

BETTER: The purchasing department is going to check each new order carefully.

subject

A word or word group that tells who or what performs or undergoes the action named by a verb, or experiences the condition named by the verb.

Gossip amuses me.

Morgan hit one of Johnson's best pitches.

Piccadilly Circus is the Times Square of London.

Does *your allergy* cause a rash?

Jan and I were pelted by the rain.

There was *a snake* under the chair.

A **simple subject** is a subject without its modifiers.

The old dusty *volumes* fell to the floor.

A **complete subject** is a subject with its modifiers.

The old dusty volumes fell to the floor.

subject case   *See* case.

subject complement

A word or word group that immediately follows a linking verb and identifies or describes the subject:

Blue is *my favorite color.*

The house was *enormous.*

subject-verb agreement   *See* agreement of subject and verb.

subjunctive mood   *See* mood.

subordinate (dependent) clause

A clause that normally begins with a subordinator or a relative pronoun. Such a clause cannot stand alone as a sentence. It must be connected to or included in a main clause.

> *Because Mrs. Braithwaite was writing her memoirs,* she reviewed all her old diaries and correspondence.
>
> The essay *that won the prize* was written by a freshman.
>
> I didn't know *where she had left the key.*

subordinate verb

The verb of a subordinate clause in a complex sentence.

> I cut the grass before the storm *came.*
>
> Since the door *was* open, I walked in.

subordinating conjunction   *See* subordinator.

subordination

An arrangement that makes one or more parts of a sentence grammatically subordinate to another part.

> WITHOUT SUBORDINATION: The dog ate his dinner, and then he took a nap.
>
> WITH SUBORDINATION: After the dog ate his dinner, he took a nap.

subordinator (subordinating conjunction)

A word or phrase used to introduce an adverb clause.

> *Before* we left, I locked all the doors.

Besides *before,* subordinators include *because, after, since, while,* and *even though.*

tense

The form of a verb that helps to indicate the time of an action or condition.

> **Present:** I jump.
>
> **Past:** I jumped.
>
> **Future:** I will jump.
>
> **Present Perfect:** I have jumped.
>
> **Past Perfect:** I had jumped.
>
> **Future Perfect:** I will have jumped.

transitive and intransitive verbs

A **transitive verb** names an action that directly affects a person or thing specified in the predicate.

> He *struck* the gong.
>
> Water *erodes* even granite.
>
> Did you *mail* the letters?
>
> We *elected* Sloan.

An **intransitive verb** names an action that has no direct impact on anyone or anything specified in the predicate.

> Wilson *smiled* at the comedian's best efforts, but he did not *laugh.*

verb

A word or phrase naming an action done by or to a subject, a state of being experienced by a subject, or an occurrence.

> Cavanaugh *runs* every day.
>
> Pandas *eat* bamboo.

My aunt *has lived* in Chicago.

President Reagan *was reelected* by a landslide.

verbal noun

A word or phrase formed from a verb and used as a noun.

Hunting was once the sport of kings.

I want *to travel*.

Fixing bicycles keeps me busy.

To sacrifice his rook would have been Gilman's best move.

verb phrase

A phrase formed by two or more verbs—a base verb and at least one auxiliary.

Richard *may complete* his experiment by July.

Alison *would have come* earlier if you *had called* her.

voice

The aspect of a verb that indicates whether the subject acts or is acted upon. A verb is in the **active voice** when the subject performs the action named by the verb.

She *raised* her hand.

He *painted* the ceiling.

They *built* a house.

A verb is in the **passive voice** when the subject undergoes the action named by the verb.

I *was told* to do it that way.

The operation *was performed* by a famous surgeon,

Is this form *preferred*?

APPENDICES

APPENDIX

1

CITING WITH NOTES— MLA STYLE

Complete information on the MLA note style appears in the *MLA Handbook for Writers of Research Papers,* by Joseph Gibaldi and Walter B. Achtert (New York: Modern Language Association, 1984). In what follows here, we explain how to use the MLA note style with the kinds of sources you are likely to use in a research paper written for a college course.

A1.1   Writing Footnotes and Endnotes

To cite a source by means of a note, put a slightly raised number in your text and, at the foot of the page or on a page of endnotes, a corresponding number followed by your identification of the source. Since careful measurements are needed to fit footnotes on the bottom of a page, endnotes are much easier to use. But footnotes are easier for the reader to find. Ask your teacher which format you are expected to follow.

Whether you use footnotes or endnotes, you should number your notes consecutively throughout the paper. Do not start with number 1 on each new page of your text.

Put the note number at the end of the sentence or group of sentences in which you have used a source. Avoid the awkwardness of putting a number in the middle of a sentence:

> While Jung says that children's dreams are complex
> 2
> and frightening, Foulkes's research has led him
> to conclude that children's dreams are "rather
> 3
> simple and unemotional."

Every number you insert draws the reader away from your text to a note, and no reader wants to be interrupted in the middle of a sentence. If you

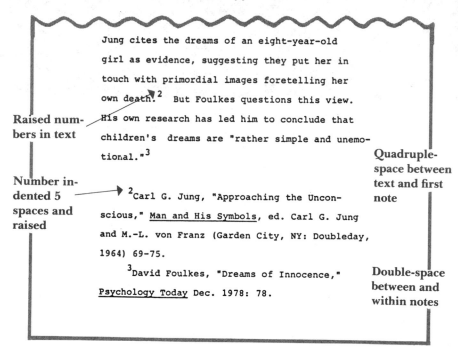

Jung cites the dreams of an eight-year-old
girl as evidence, suggesting they put her in
touch with primordial images foretelling her
own death.² But Foulkes questions this view.
His own research has led him to conclude that
children's dreams are "rather simple and unemotional."³

Raised numbers in text

Number indented 5 spaces and raised

²Carl G. Jung, "Approaching the Unconscious," Man and His Symbols, ed. Carl G. Jung
and M.-L. von Franz (Garden City, NY: Doubleday,
1964) 69-75.

³David Foulkes, "Dreams of Innocence,"
Psychology Today Dec. 1978: 78.

Quadruple-space between text and first note

Double-space between and within notes

refer to two or more sources in one sentence, use one number at the end
of the sentence and one note to identify them all; within the note, use a
semicolon between one reference and another:

While Jung says that children's dreams are complex
and frightening, Foulkes's research has led him to
conclude that children's dreams are "rather simple
and unemotional."²

²Carl G. Jung, "Approaching the Unconscious,"
Man and His Symbols, ed. Carl G. Jung and M.-L von
Franz (Garden City, NY: Doubleday, 1964) 69-75;
David Foulkes, "Dreams of Innocence," Psychology
Today Dec. 1978: 78.

A1.2 Writing Explanatory Notes

Besides documenting a source, a note can give an explanation that cannot
be easily fitted into the text:

Sample endnotes

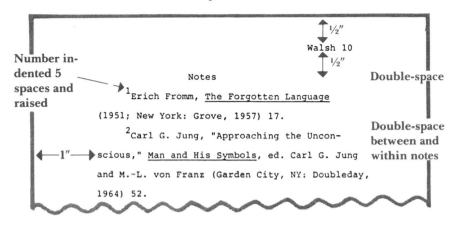

Psychologists disagree about the content and

significance of children's dreams.[1] Jung believed

that children's dreams could be rich, complex, and

[1]
    I refer to children old enough to talk about

their dreams. Though measurement of REM may tell

us how long and how often infants dream, we have

no way of knowing just what they dream about.

Explanatory notes are sometimes necessary, but before you write one, you should try to see whether you can fit the explanation into your text. Every note interrupts the reader, and the fewer the interruptions, the more readable your paper will be.

A1.3   Writing Notes—First and Later References

1. The first note for any source gives detailed information:

[1]
    Lawrence Durrell, <u>Bitter Lemons</u>

(New York: Dutton, 1957) 138-42.

The author's name in the normal order (surname last) is followed by a comma, the full title and subtitle (if any), the facts of publication in parentheses, the page numbers without p. or pp., and a period. The facts of publication include the place, the publisher, and the copyright date. Use a colon after the place and a comma after the publisher.

If the city or town is relatively unknown, give the state or country in abbreviated form (as in Long Beach, CA, and Sherbrooke, Que.). If more than one place of publication is listed on the title page, give just the first. Use the short form of a well-known publisher such as E. P. Dutton & Company, but after the name of any university press, use the initials UP without periods, as in Columbia UP (for Columbia University Press). If you find more than one copyright date, give the latest one, but ignore the dates of printings or "impressions" made after the latest copyright date.

2. Later references to a source normally include just the author's name, the page number(s), and a period:

> 2
> Durrell 197.

If you are citing more than one work by an author, use a short form of the title in references after the first:

> 8
> Durrell, <u>Bitter</u> 80.
> 9
> Durrell, <u>Reflections</u> 138-40.

The first reference to *Reflections* would give the full title: *Reflections on a Marine Venus*.

A1.4 Writing Notes for Various Sources

1. A book with one author

> 1
> Robert Hartman, <u>Credit for College:</u>
>
> <u>Public Policy for Student Loans</u> (New York:
>
> McGraw-Hill, 1971) 45.

2. A book with one author and an editor

> 2Theodore Dreiser, <u>Sister Carrie</u>, ed.,
>
> Kenneth S. Lynn (New York: Rinehart, 1959) 145.

Put the author's name first when you are citing the author's text. To cite material written by the editor, start with the editor's name and the uncapitalized title of the material.

> Kenneth S. Lynn, introduction, <u>Sister Carrie</u>,
>
> by Theodore Dreiser (New York: Rinehart, 1959) xvi.

3. A second or later edition

> 4
> Robert E. Ornstein, <u>The Psychology of</u>
>
> <u>Consciousness</u>, 2nd ed. (New York: Harcourt, 1977)
>
> 104-15.

The abbreviation "2nd ed." means "second edition."

4. A book with two or three authors

> 5
> Nathan Dickmeyer, John Wessels, and
> Sharon L. Coldren, <u>Institutionally Funded</u>
> <u>Student Financial Aid</u>, (Washington: American
> Council on Education, 1981) 8.

The name of each author is given in full in ordinary word order.

5. A book with more than three authors or editors

> 6
> Robert H. Fenske et al., eds., <u>Handbook of</u>
> <u>Student Financial Aid</u> (San Francisco: Jossey-Bass,
> 1983) 22.

When a book has more than three authors or editors, give the name of the first one listed and add the abbreviation "et al.," which means "and others."

6. A book with a corporate author

> 7
> Sloan Study Consortium, <u>Paying for College:</u>
> <u>Financing Education at Nine Private Institutions</u>
> (Hanover, NH: UP of New England, 1974) 30.

7. A work in more than one volume

> 8
> Page Smith, <u>A New Age Now Begins</u>,
> 2 vols. (New York: McGraw-Hill, 1976) 2: 15-25.

The number of volumes in the work follows the title, and the volume cited appears at the end, followed by a colon and the page numbers.

8. A book in a numbered series

> 9
> Joe B. Henry, ed., <u>The Impact of Student</u>
> <u>Financial Aid on Institutions</u>, New Directions for
> Institutional Research 25 (San Francisco: Jossey-
> Bass) 12-20.

The name of the series and the number of the book follow the title.

9. A work from a collection of works by one author

> 10
> Robert Frost, "The Death of the Hired Man,"
> <u>The Poetry of Robert Frost</u>, ed. Edward Connery
> Lathem (New York: Holt, 1969) 39-40.

¹¹
Lewis Thomas, "The Long Habit," <u>The</u>
<u>Lives of a Cell: Notes of a Biology Watcher</u>
(New York: Viking, 1974) 48.

¹²
Ernest Hemingway, "The Short Happy Life
of Francis Macomber," <u>The Short Stories of Ernest</u>
<u>Hemingway</u> (New York: Scribner's, 1938) 3-37.

10. A work from a collection of works by various authors

¹³
George E. Dimock, Jr., "The Names of
Odysseus," <u>Essays on</u> The Odyssey: <u>Selected</u>
<u>Modern Criticism</u>, ed. Charles Taylor (Bloomington:
Indiana UP, 1963) 54-72.

The title of a book contained *within* the title of another book is not underlined.

¹⁴
Samuel Taylor Coleridge, "The Rime of the
Ancient Mariner," <u>The Norton Anthology of English</u>
<u>Literature</u>, ed. M. H. Abrams et al., 2 vols. (New
York: Norton, 1962) 2: 181-97.

11. A reprint

¹⁵
Jessie L. Weston, <u>From Ritual to Romance</u>
(1920; Garden City, NY: Anchor-Doubleday, 1957)
32-45.

The date of the original publication comes first, followed by a semicolon. The date of the reprint follows the name of the publisher.

12. A translation

¹⁶
Gustave Flaubert, <u>Madame Bovary</u>, trans.
Francis Steegmüller (New York: Random House, 1957)
46-52.

Use this form to cite material from the author's text. To cite material from the translator's introduction or notes, put the translator's name before the title and the primary author's name after it:

```
              17
        Francis Steegmüller, trans., Madame
```

Bovary, by Gustave Flaubert (New York: Random

House, 1957) v-xv.

13. An anonymous book

```
        18
              College Cost Book, 1982-83 (New York:
```

College Entrance Examination Board, 1983) 23.

14. An article in a reference book

In citing articles from familiar reference works, give the name(s) of the author(s), the title of the article, the title of the book, and the year of the edition. If the articles are alphabetically arranged, you don't need volume or page numbers:

```
        19
              Athelstan Spilhaus and Jane J. Stein,
```

"Pollution Control," Encyclopaedia Britannica:

Macropaedia, 1974 ed.

```
        20
              Edward S. Kilma, "Phonetics," Funk &
```

Wagnalls New Encyclopedia, 1973 ed.

The initials usually given at the end of the article will lead you to the name(s) of the author(s) in a reference list commonly given at the beginning of the book. If the article is unsigned, start with its title:

```
        21
              "Pollution," The Columbia Encyclopedia,
```

1963 ed.

If the edition is numbered, give the edition number before the year(s) of publication:

```
        22
              "Martha Graham," Who's Who of American
```

Women, 13th ed., 1983-84.

If the book is specialized or has appeared in only one or two editions, give full information about its publication:

```
        23
              Kurt Weinberg, "Romanticism," Princeton
```

Encyclopedia of Poetry and Poetics, ed. Alex

Preminger, Frank J. Warnke, and O. B. Hardison,

Jr., enl. ed. (Princeton: Princeton UP, 1974).

Note that even here you need no page numbers so long as the article has been alphabetized.

15. An article in a journal with continuous pagination

> 24
> Max Delbruck, "Mind from Matter?" <u>The</u>
>
> <u>American Scholar</u> 47 (1978): 345.

Use this form when the pagination is continuous throughout a volume—that is, for instance, when the first issue ends at page 230 and the second one starts at 231. After the title of the journal, give the volume number in arabic numbers, a space, the year of issue within parentheses, a colon, a space, and the page number(s) of the reference.

16. An article in a journal without continuous pagination

> 25
> Sheldon I. Posen and Joseph Sciorra,
>
> "Brooklyn´s Dancing Tower," <u>Natural History</u> 92.6
>
> (1983): 30-37.

Use this form when the pagination is not continuous—that is, when every issue starts at page 1. After the title of the journal, give the volume number, a period, the issue number, a space, the year of issue within parentheses, a colon, a space, and the page number(s) of the reference.

17. An article in a periodical published monthly, weekly, or daily

> 26
> Jane Stein, The Bioethicists: Facing
>
> Matters of Life and Death," <u>Smithsonian</u> Jan.
>
> 1979: 107-09.

> 27
> Richard L. Strout, "Another Bicentennial,"
>
> <u>Christian Science Monitor</u> 10 Nov. 1978: 27.

To cite any magazine or newspaper published monthly, weekly, or daily, give the date after the name of the periodical with no punctuation between the two. Abbreviate the name of the month (except May, June, and July) and put the day of the month first when the day is given. Follow the year with a colon, a space, and the page(s) cited.

18. An unsigned article

> 28
> "The Vietnam War: The Executioner,"
>
> <u>Newsweek</u> 13 Nov. 1978: 70.

When the article is unsigned, begin the entry with the title.

19. A newspaper

²⁹Jane E. Brody, "Multiple Cancers Termed
on Increase," <u>New York Times</u> 10 Oct. 1976:
sec. 1: 37.

If the paper is divided into numbered sections each of which starts from page 1, you must give the section number before the page number, separating the two with a colon. If the article comes from a lettered section (A, B, C, etc.), cite it this way:

30
Douglas Martin, "Mulroney Says Canada
Seeks `True Partnership´ with U.S.," <u>New York</u>
<u>Times</u> 6 Nov. 1984: A16.

20. An editorial

31
"How to End Watergate," editorial,
<u>New York Times</u> 10 Jan. 1979, city ed.: A22.

You should identify an editorial as such to distinguish it from a news report. If the editorial is signed, begin the entry with the writer's name. Otherwise begin with the title of the article.

21. An interview

³²Harland W. Hoisington, Jr., Director
of Financial Aid at Dartmouth College, personal
interview, 3 May 1985.

22. A personal letter to the researcher

33
Walter S. Achtert, letter to the author, 2
Nov. 1984.

23. A government publication

34
United States, National Commission on
Student Financial Assistance, <u>Access and Choice:</u>
<u>Equitable Financing of Postsecondary Education,</u>
Rept. 7 (Washington: GPO, 1983) 10-15.

Identify the name of the country first, then the name of the agency. "Rept." stands for "Report." "GPO" is a standard abbreviation for "Government Printing Office."

24. A document from an information service

> 35
>   National Commission on Student Financial
>
> Assistance, <u>Access and Choice: Equitable Financing</u>
>
> <u>of Postsecondary Education</u>, Rept. 7. (ERIC, 1983)
>
> (ED 234 734).

The initials ERIC stand for Educational Resources Information Center. The initials are followed by a comma, the date of issue, and the ERIC document number. If the document was originally published by someone other than ERIC, cite the original publisher in the usual way before giving the ERIC data:

> 36
>   Paul Franklin, <u>Beyond Student Financial</u>
>
> <u>Aid: Issues and Options for Strengthening Support</u>
>
> <u>Service Programs under Title IV of the Higher</u>
>
> <u>Education Act</u> (Washington: College Entrance
>
> Examination Board, 1980) (ERIC ED 185 913).

25. Computer software

> 37
>   Wayne Holder, <u>The Word Plus</u>, computer
>
> software, Oasis Systems, 1982.

Give the name of the program writer if known, the program title underlined, the words "computer software" without quotation marks or underlinings, the name of the distributor, and the year of distribution.

26. A television program

> 38
>   "The Enlightened Machine," <u>The Brain</u>,
>
> narr. George Page, PBS, WETK, Burlington, VT, 10 Oct.
>
> 1984.

Give the title of the episode (if known) in quotation marks, the title of the program underlined, and the name(s) of those chiefly responsible for it. (In the example, "narr." stands for "the narrator.") Then give the network (such as PBS or CBS), the local station and city (plus state if necessary), and the date of the broadcast. In citing the broadcast of a play or musical work, such as an opera, give the author or composer, the title, then the names of the principals, with broadcast information at the end:

> 39
>   Giuseppe Verdi, <u>La Forza del Destino</u>,
>
> with Leontyne Price, Isola Jones, Giuseppe Giacomini,

and Leo Nucci, cond. James Levine, Metropolitan

Opera Orch., PBS, NHPTV, Durham, NH, 31 Oct. 1984.

27. A recording

40
    Robert Frost, "The Road Not Taken," <u>Robert

<u>Frost Reads His Poetry</u>, Caedmon, TC 1060, 1956.

41
    Richard Strauss, <u>Der Rosenkavalier</u>, with

Elisabeth Schwarzkopf, Christa Ludwig, Teresa

Stich-Randall, and Otto Edelmann, cond. Herbert

von Karajan, London Philharmonic Orchestra and

Chorus, Angel 3563 D/L, 1957.

Start with the name of the performer, composer, or conductor, or with the title of the work performed—whichever is most important to your discussion. Then give details of the work. End with the manufacturer, the catalog number, and (if known) the date of the issue.

28. A film

42
    <u>Way Down East</u>, dir. D. W. Griffith,

with Lillian Gish, Creighton Hale, and Burr McIntosh,

D. W. Griffith, Inc., 1920.

If your reference is to a particular individual involved in the film, begin with his or her name:

43
    John Guare, screenwriter, <u>Atlantic City</u>,

dir. Louis Malle, with Burt Lancaster, Kate

Reid, and Susan Sarandon, Paramount, 1980.

29. A live performance

44
    William Shakespeare, <u>Much Ado about

<u>Nothing</u>, dir. Terry Hands, with Derek Jacobi and

Sinead Cusack, Gershwin Theatre, New York, 19 Oct.
1984.

30. A work of art

45
    J. M. W. Turner, <u>Snow Storm: Hannibal

<u>and His Army Crossing the Alps</u> (1812), The Tate

Gallery, London.

Give the artist, the title, and within parentheses the date, if known. Then give the name and place of the institution where the work is located.

A1.5 Writing the Bibliography

The bibliography for a paper documented with notes in the MLA style should follow the general and specific rules given for the list of Works Cited on pp. 545–56.

EXERCISE 1 Citing with Notes—The MLA Style

Take the information given on each source in exercise 1, pp. 556–57, and use it to write two entries in the MLA note style: one on the source as it would appear in a note and the other on the source as it would appear in the bibliography.

EXAMPLE

IN A NOTE

        Paul Fussell, <u>The Great War and Modern Memory</u>

    (NY: Oxford UP, 1975) 96-97.

IN THE BIBLIOGRAPHY

    Fussell, Paul. <u>The Great War and Modern Memory</u>.

        NY: Oxford UP, 1975.

A1.6　Sample Survey-Type Research Paper with MLA Note Style

Erica Berl

Professor Stephen Jones

Sociology 101

November 10, 1985

Options for the Working Mother

　　Everyone knows that women are no longer staying at home.
They have gone out into the world of work, filling not only such
traditionally feminine roles as secretary and clerk, but also
such typically masculine roles as lawyer, doctor, stockbroker,
business executive, United States senator, and even candidate for
the vice presidency. At the same time, statistics show that a
growing percentage of working women are mothers of preschool
children. While less than a third of these mothers held jobs
outside the home in 1970, the figure rose to nearly a half by
1978 and is expected to keep on rising into the 1990s.[1] A crucial
question of our time, therefore, is how these women can reconcile
the demands of a career with the responsibilities of child-
rearing.

　　The cheapest solution to this problem is for the working
mother to find a relative willing to supervise her children while
she works. But aside from the children's father, who may not be
living with her and who in any case usually has a job of his own,
she may not have relatives near enough or free enough to serve as
babysitters. The children's grandparents, for instance, may live
beyond commuting distance, and even if they live nearby and are
willing to babysit regularly, they too may both be holding jobs

that make them unavailable during the day. In any case a census
taken in 1982 showed that less than half the working mothers of
young children had them supervised by a relative other than their
father.[2]

An obvious alternative to the babysitting relative is the
professional babysitter who can be hired to care for children
alone or in small groups, usually in the babysitter´s home. But
the major drawback here is that professional babysitters cost
money. Since a professional babysitter is running a business, he
or she must not only cover expenses but also make a profit, which
often means consuming a substantial portion of the working
mother´s paycheck.

The decreasing availability of relatives for babysitting and
the high cost of professional babysitters have together helped to
increase the use of preschools, where children are taught as well
as supervised. Kamerman reports that from 1967 to 1980,
kindergarten enrollment rose by about a third, and from 1969 to
1980, nursery school enrollment of three- and four-year-olds more
than doubled.[3] Kindergartens are especially attractive because 88
percent of them are public and therefore free. But kindergartens
do not take children under five, and only 34 percent of nursery
schools are public.[4] As a result, the only kind of preschool
available for most three- and four-year-olds is the private
nursery school, which charges fees that not all working mothers
can afford.

Another kind of preschooling, however, is absolutely free.
Federally funded Head Start centers are designed to help poor

women work so they can escape from their poverty and shed their
dependence on welfare.[5] In these centers, children of poor
parents get not only an education but also medical care, dental
care, and psychological counseling. Furthermore, under Title XX
of the Social Security Act of 1975, the number of these centers
has grown from about eight thousand in 1977 to over eleven
thousand in 1981, and in quality they usually surpass federal
guidelines.[6]

Nevertheless, besides the fact that funding for the Title XX
programs has recently been cut, Head Start centers do not help
working mothers of the vast middle class.[7] In fact, as Norgren
observes, none of the current federal programs is designed for
them.[8] So where can they find day care for their children? A
number of private centers have been established by churches,
settlement houses, social agencies, parent cooperatives,
hospitals, and universities. But Feinstein notes that because
these centers have to meet federal guidelines in order to be
licensed, they are costly to run and expensive to use.[9]

Given the cost of independent day-care centers, a growing
number of companies have established day-care centers of their
own. In 1982, the National Employer-Supported Child-Care Project
reported that 240 employers provided child-care facilities, which
was twice the number provided in 1978.[10] And to promote the
establishment of still more company-sponsored centers, the Reagan
administration has revised the tax code so that employers no
longer have to pay taxes on child-care benefits.

Though some companies have been slow to respond to such
inducements, many have taken decisive action. Business Week

reported recently that Corning Glass Wares bought a church across
the street from its main office in New York and turned it into a
day-care center where employees can leave their children for just
forty-three dollars a week per child, which covers only two-
thirds of the total operating cost.[11] Companies that subsidize
day care in this way often reap more than tax benefits.
According to Business Week, Intermedics Inc., which makes
pacemakers with the aid of a 70 percent female staff, established
a center where employees can leave their children for just
fifteen dollars a week per child--barely a fourth of the
operating cost. But since the center was established, employee
turnover has dropped by 23 percent and absenteeism has dropped by
fifteen thousand hours. As a result, productivity has increased
by quite enough to cover the cost of subsidizing the new
center.[12]

    Day-care centers in the workplace benefit employee and
employer alike. The mother who can take her child to work saves
the time that would otherwise be required to leave and pick the
child up elsewhere. Because she can easily see her child during
the day--on her lunch hour, for instance--and can easily get to
the child in case of emergency, she is free from worry. As a
result, she can concentrate better on her work, which benefits
her employer. In addition, Clarke-Stewart notes that because
day-care centers relieve the mother from the strain of caring for
her child all day long, they can also improve the "quality of
time" that mother and child spend together.[13]

    Another way in which companies are beginning to meet the

needs of working mothers is the system of flextime--an
alternative to the standard eight-hour day. Under flextime, the
employee must work for certain specified periods each day, such
as from 9:00 to 11:00 and from 2:00 to 4:00, but otherwise she
can choose her working hours to suit her convenience from one day
to the next. This gives the mother extra time when she needs it
in the morning, in the afternoon, or in the middle of the day.

Though companies rarely declare an official policy on
flextime, they have been led to see its advantages for them as
well as for working mothers. Business Week reported that
Elizabeth Carlson, manager of personnel systems and research at
Continental Illinois National Bank & Trust Company of Chicago,
left the bank because she was denied flextime there and went to
work for Bell and Howell, where she was granted it. When other
employees left the bank for the same reason, the bank stopped
fighting flextime and rehired Ms. Carlson on her own terms.[14]
Clearly, women are gaining new respect on the job, and employers
have begun to recognize the importance of meeting their needs.
Says Eugene Ricci, president of CIGNA Service Company: "You
don't voluntarily lose key people. Brains are hard to come
by."[15] Thus flextime may eventually win acceptance in the
business world at large. Lynette and Thomas Long note that while
it is now available in only 15 percent of private organizations
employing more than fifty people, three independent surveys have
found that a majority of respondents would welcome it.

For women who cannot work a full day, even on flextime
hours, the obvious alternative is a part-time job. Though many
women say that part-time work reduces their chances for

advancement, most of them agree that even part-time work is
better than none at all.[17]   And some women can do part of their
jobs at home. Randi Starr Savitzky, a production manager at
McDougal Littell & Company in Northbrook, Illinois, divides her
working day between the office and her own home, where she uses a
computer.[18]

    All of the options so far described are available to the
single mother--whether unmarried, divorced, or separated. Yet no
matter how the working mother arranges her schedule, she will
seldom if ever find that she can easily resolve the conflicts
involved in pursuing a career while raising one or more children
by herself. This is why the most valuable thing that a working
mother can have is a husband who not only lives with her but also
fully cooperates with her. If women are going to work outside
the home, men must be willing to share the jobs that have to be
done inside it, to help not just with weekend chores but also
with the daily tasks of washing dishes, washing clothes, mopping
floors, vacuuming rugs, making beds, and--most importantly--
looking after the children. This arrangement offers a bonus to
both partners, since Levine has found that "marriages in which
the parents share responsibilities equally tend to be the
happiest."[19]

    It takes a gift for organization to manage both a job and a
family. But given the variety of ways in which the demands of
each can be met, a woman no longer needs to feel that she must
sacrifice one for the other, must abandon her family for the sake
of her job or give up her job for the sake of her family.

Working women who happen to be mothers have made themselves an indispensable part of the work force, and in time, the working mother may become as familiar on the American scene as the working father.

Notes

[1]
      U.S. Bureau of Labor Statistics, <u>Women in the Labor</u>

<u>Force: Some New Data Series</u>, Rept. 575 (Washington: GPO, 1979) 1.
[2]
      U.S. Bureau of Census, <u>Child-Care Arrangements of</u>

<u>Working Mothers: June 1982</u> (Washington: GPO, 1983) 9-10.
[3]
      Sheila B. Kamerman, "Child-Care Services: A National

Picture," <u>Monthly Labor Review</u> 106.12 (1983): 36.
[4]
      Kamerman 37.
[5]
      Karen Wolk Feinstein, "Directions for Day Care,"

<u>Working Women and Families</u>, ed. Karen Wolk Feinstein

(Beverly Hills: Sage, 1979) 182.
[6]
      Kamerman 37.
[7]
      Kamerman 38.
[8]
      Jill Norgren, "In Search of a National Child-Care Policy:

Backgrounds and Prospects," <u>Women, Power, and Policy</u>, ed. Ellen

Boneparth (New York: Pergamon, 1982) 134.
[9]
      Feinstein 187.
[10]
       "Child Care Grows as a Benefit," <u>Business Week</u> 21

Dec. 81: 63.
[11]
       "Child Care Grows" 60.
[12]
       "Child Care Grows" 60.
[13]
       Alison Clarke-Stewart, <u>Child Care in the Family:</u>

<u>A Review of Research and Some Propositions for Policy</u>, A

Carnegie Council on Children Monograph (New York: Academic

Press, 1977) 111.
[14]
       "Working Around Motherhood," <u>Business Week</u>

24 May 1982: 108.

[15] "Companies Start to Meet Executive Mothers Halfway,"
<u>Business Week</u> 17 Oct. 1983: 191-95.

[16] Lynette and Thomas T. Long, <u>The Handbook for</u>
<u>Latchkey Children and Their Parents</u> (New York: Arbor House,
1983) 226.

[17] "Companies Start" 195.

[18] "Companies Start" 191.

[19] James A. Levine, <u>Who Will Raise the Children?</u>
(Philadelphia: Lippincott, 1976) 176.

Works Cited

"Child Care Grows as a Benefit." Business Week 21 Dec.
    1981: 60-63.

Clarke-Stewart, Alison. Child Care in the Family: A Review
    of Research and Some Propositions for Policy. A Carnegie
    Council on Children Monograph. New York: Academic Press, 1977.

"Companies Start to Meet Executive Mothers Halfway." Business
    Week 17 Oct. 1983: 191-95.

Feinstein, Karen Wolk. "Directions for Day Care." Working Women
    and Families. Ed. Karen Wolk Feinstein. Beverly Hills:
    Sage, 1979. 177-94.

Kamerman, Sheila B. "Child-Care Services: A National Picture."
    Monthly Labor Review 106.12 (1983): 35-39.

Levine, James A. Who Will Raise the Children? Philadelphia:
    Lippincott, 1976.

Long, Lynette, and Thomas T. Long. The Handbook for Latchkey
    Children and Their Parents. New York: Arbor House, 1983.

Norgren, Jill. "In Search of a National Child-Care Policy:
    Backgrounds and Prospects." Women, Power, and Policy. Ed.
    Ellen Boneparth. New York: Pergamon, 1982. 124-43.

U.S. Bureau of Census. Child-Care Arrangements of Working
    Mothers: June 1982. Washington: GPO, 1983.

U.S. Bureau of Labor Statistics. Women in the Labor Force:
    Some New Data Series. Rept. 575. Washington: GPO, 1979.

"Working Around Motherhood." Business Week 24 May 1982: 108.

APPENDIX

2

CITING WITH PARENTHESES—APA STYLE

The APA style of parenthetical citation is recommended by the American Psychological Association (APA) for research papers in the social sciences. Complete information on this style appears in the *Publication Manual of the American Psychological Association,* 3rd ed. (Washington: Psychological Association, 1983). Here we briefly explain how to use the APA style with some of the sources you are likely to cite in a research paper written for a college course. Each source cited parenthetically in this section is also shown as it would appear in the list of References at the end of the paper. We explain how to write this list in section A2.2.

A2.1 Writing APA Parenthetical Citations—A Few Examples

1. Material introduced without the author's name

When citing the source of material you have introduced without using the author's name, give in parentheses the author's last name, the year in which the source was published, and—where necessary—the pagination:

> Studies have found that "marriages in which the
>
> parents share responsibilities equally tend to be
>
> the happiest" (Levine, 1976, p. 176).

References

> Levine, J. A. (1976). <u>Who will raise the</u>
>
> <u>children?</u> Philadelphia: Lippincott.

2. Material introduced with the author's name

If you use the author's name to introduce the material cited, give only the date and the pagination in parentheses:

Kamerman (1983, p. 36) reports that from 1967 to 1980, kindergarten enrollment rose by about a third, and from 1969 to 1980, nursery school enrollment more than doubled.

References

Kamerman, S. B. (1983). Child-care services: A national picture. Monthly Labor Review, 106 (12), 35-39.

3. A work with more than one author

If you cite a work with two authors, give both names every time you cite it:

For all their efforts to generalize about child behavior, psychologists recognize that "no two children are exactly alike" (Gesell and Ilg, 1949, p. 68).

If the work has more than two authors, give all the names in the first citation only; in later citations give just the first author's name followed by "et al."

First Citation: Miller, Dellefield, and Musso (1980) have called for more effective advertising of financial aid programs.

Later Citation: Miller et al. (1980) have studied the institutional management of financial aid.

References

Gesell, A. & Ilg, F. L. (1949). Child development: An introduction to the study of human growth. New York: Harper.

Miller, S., Dellefield, W., & Musso, T. (1980). A guide to selected financial aid management practices. Washington, D.C.: U.S. Department

of Education.

A2.2 Writing the Reference List—APA Style

If you use the APA parenthetical style of citation, you must provide a list of references at the end of your paper: an alphabetical list of all the sources you have used, and only of those sources. Start the list on a separate sheet and arrange the entries alphabetically according to the authors' last names. If there are two or more works by one author, list them chronologically by date of publication. If the works were published in the same year, list them alphabetically by title and use the letters a, b, c, etc. after the year, as shown below.

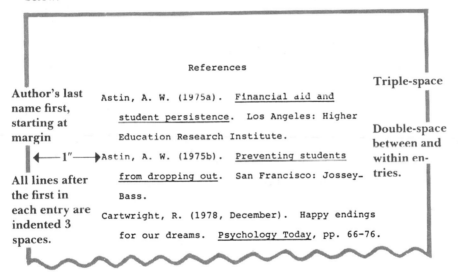

1. A book with one author

Erikson, E. H. (1964). Insight and responsibility:

Lectures on the ethical implications of

psychoanalytic insight. New York: Norton.

a. *Author and date.* The author's surname goes first. It is followed by a comma, a space, one or more spaced initials with periods, another space, the parenthesized date of publication, and another period.

b. *Title and subtitle.* Underline the whole title, but capitalize only the first words of the title and subtitle (if any), and put a period at the end.

c. *Place of publication.* Give just the first place if more than one is listed on the title page, and add the state, country, or province after the city or town of publication if it is not well known or might be confused with another, as in Long Beach, CA. Put a colon and a space after the place of publication.

d. *Publisher's name.* Use the short form for widely known publishers such as Norton (instead of W. W. Norton & Company, Inc.), but give the full names of associations and university presses.

2. A book with two or more authors

> Hall, C. S., & Nordby, V. J. (1972). The individual
>
> and his dreams. New York: New American Library.

Give the names of the authors in the order they assume on the title page, and invert all the names. Use a comma after each name up to the last, and an ampersand (&) just before that. No matter how many authors there are, give all of their names; do not use "et al."

3. A work with an editor

> El-Khawas, E. (Ed.) (1980). Special policy issues
>
> in management of student aid. Washington, DC:
>
> American Council on Education.

4. An article in a journal paginated by issue

> Kamerman, S. B. (1983). Child-care services: A
>
> national picture. Monthly Labor Review, 106
>
> (12), 35-39.

The title of an article is neither underlined nor enclosed in quotation marks, and the only words capitalized are the first words of the title and subtitle (if any), as well as any proper names. The volume number—in this case 106—is underlined and given right after the name of the journal. If each new issue of the journal starts from page 1, give the issue number in parentheses right after the volume number, then the pages—with no p. or pp. before them. (Use p. or pp. only in citing the pages of a newspaper or magazine, as in the Cartwright reference on p. 643.)

5. An article in a journal with continuous pagination

> Palvio, A. (1975). Perceptual comparisons through
>
> the mind's eye. Memory & Cognition, 3,
>
> 635-647.

Use this form when the pagination is continuous throughout a volume—that is, when the first issue ends, let us say, at page 230, and the second one starts at page 231. In a case like this, give just the volume number underlined, a comma, and then the page numbers.

APPENDIX
3

WRITING WITH A WORD PROCESSOR

About a hundred years ago, a new machine called the automobile began to leave the horse-drawn carriage in its dusty wake. Today the word processor is doing the same to the typewriter. If you have not already put your fingers to the keyboard of this computer-age marvel, you will almost certainly do so before you finish college. And once you start using a word processor, you will rapidly discover that it can save you a good deal of work.

This does not mean that you should scrap your typewriter at once. Until and unless you can afford a word processor of your own, a typewriter will continue to serve you well, especially since the average portable is not only cheaper to buy and maintain but also easier to carry around than most word processors and the printers that go with them. Some of the latest portable typewriters, in fact, are battery-powered machines no bigger than an ordinary loose-leaf notebook, and they come equipped with little screens that display the two or three words you have just typed, so that you can correct errors before the words reach the page. The average typewriter also produces better-looking print than the dot-matrix printer commonly used with word-processors. Only the more expensive "letter quality" printers produce words that look as if they had been typed.

But word processors do many things that typewriters cannot. Essentially, the word processor is an electronic scratch pad that can be wired to an electronic typist. Because it lets you do all of your writing and rewriting on a screen, it ensures that what comes out on paper is clean and tidy. It also ensures that after you have printed a piece of writing, you can call it up on the screen, make any further changes you wish, and then print the entire new version without having to retype it.

This brief chapter cannot possibly tell you everything you need to know about writing with a word processor. Instead, it simply aims to introduce you to word processing: to let you know generally what it can do for your writing—and what it can't.

A3.1 Learning to Use a Word Processor

Broadly speaking, word processors come in two different forms: self-contained microcomputers, which run all by themselves, and "dumb" terminals, which are run by the brain of the mainframe computer wired to them. A mainframe computer serves many terminals on a time-sharing basis, as if it were a superhuman teacher who could answer five different questions from five different students in just five seconds. It also runs one or more printers.

So which do you choose—a "dumb" terminal or your very own microcomputer? If you can afford a microcomputer and a printer to go with it, you might well consider spending the money. (You can find advice on specific brands in magazines such as *Consumer Reports, Byte,* and *PC World.*) You can then do your word processing in the privacy of your own room at any time you like, without ever having to wait for a terminal or for your turn in the time-sharing "line" when many other users are competing for the attention of the mainframe computer. But not many students can afford their own microcomputers. And even if you do have a personal computer, or access to one, certain kinds of information and programs you may need for your writing can be obtained only from large, institutional computers through public-access terminals. Sooner or later, therefore, you will probably want to learn how to write on such a terminal.

To do so, you must first find out where the writing terminals are at your college or university. Writing terminals differ, of course, from terminals that can be used only to call up information: information such as what your library has on a particular topic. But many institutions now keep writing terminals in a Computer Center, and your Department of English or Writing Center may have writing terminals of its own.

Once you have found a writing terminal, you must learn how to operate it. There are three ways of doing so: reading an instruction manual, hearing a lecture-demonstration, and sitting down before the terminal with a computer-wise friend beside you who is able and willing to answer all of your questions. This last way is the best of all. Since you cannot ask questions of a manual, and since you cannot learn how to use a computer without getting your fingers on the keyboard, nothing beats a "hands on" personal coaching session. If you can't arrange that, learn what you can from an introductory lecture-demonstration and from the manual for your particular terminal, and then feel free to ask questions of the person in charge of the writing terminals. It is his or her job to help you.

One way or another, you will soon enough learn the basics: how to sign on to the computer (normally by giving your student ID number and a password), how to call up a program that allows you to create a "file" for what you write, how to save what you write, and how to call it back up on the screen when you want to see it again. Since every screen editing program has its own peculiarities, this chapter cannot explain the particular program you will find on your institution's computer. But whatever the program, you should learn how to use it before you try to write an essay with it. Writing is hard enough by itself. If you are trying to write an essay and struggling to learn a screen-editing system at the same time, you may soon find yourself turning back to the typewriter—or to a plain old ball-point pen—in sheer desperation.

To forestall that desperation, we suggest you spend a few hours doing the following warm-up exercises:

1. Write out and then save a short passage taken from this book or any other printed source. In learning to write with a word processor, one of the first things you have to overcome is the fear that once your words have disappeared from the screen, you have lost them forever. You can master this fear by forming the habit of "saving" your words every time you write. So just to get started, write out and save a short passage taken from this book or any other printed source. Do not worry about errors; you can learn how to correct them later. Simply create a file called "save" and write out the passage as best you can. Then (1) save it, (2) exit from the program, (3) return to the program, and (4) call up the file containing the passage. If you can't get the passage back on the screen, ask the person supervising the terminals to help you. Once you have learned how to save material and call it back up again, repeat the process a few more times with other passages. You will thus gain confidence in your ability to save whatever you want, and to call it back whenever you need it.

2. Print out all the passages you have saved, and then use pen or pencil to correct the printout so that it perfectly matches the passages you have copied. In taking this step, you will of course be learning how to print a file—a simple matter of pressing a few buttons. But more importantly, you will start to form the crucially important habit of *printing at the end of every writing session.* There are three good reasons for doing so. First, printed words are often easier to read than words on a screen. Second, you'll be able to read them in the privacy and quiet of your own room—away from the noise and the crowds that all too often gather around computer terminals. Third, while a screen can show you just one or two paragraphs at a time, printed pages allow you to see the whole of your essay at once. For these reasons, you should print every one of your drafts—not just the final one.

You will start to discover the advantages of working with a printout when you compare your first one to the passages you have copied. In doing so, you will almost certainly find that you have made a number of typographical errors. Because the keys on a terminal keyboard are highly sensitive, it is easy to press the wrong ones and thus produce the wrong letters, even when you are simply copying a passage. Also, until you learn how to make corrections quickly with the screen editor, you will find it easier to make them first with pen or pencil on your printout. So you should carefully correct the printout before returning to the terminal and correcting what you see on the screen.

3. Using the screen editor, make the text on the screen match the corrected version of your printout. To guide you in making corrections, use only the corrected printout, not the passages you copied. You will thus gain practice in transferring corrections from a printout to the screen. To make the corrections required in this case, you will probably need to learn no more than a few simple operations, such as how to "delete" or erase single letters in misspelled words and how to replace them with other letters. Once again, ask the supervisor of the terminals for any help you may need with these procedures.

When you have transferred all the corrections to the screen, press the keys that will save the file, print it, and compare the new printout to the original passages. If you find any errors remaining, correct them with pen or pencil as before and repeat the process just described until the printout perfectly matches the passages in this book.

4. Using a new file, copy a different passage onto the screen and correct it thoroughly before printing. This exercise will give you practice in learning to spot errors on the screen. When you believe the text is perfectly correct, print it and compare the printout to the passage you copied. If you find any errors, correct them on the printout and then on the screen as in step 3.

5. Copy a passage of at least two paragraphs and then move parts of it around. To take full advantage of a word processor, you need to know not only how to change individual letters but also how to move parts of your writing around: to transpose letters and words, to move phrases from one end of a sentence to another, and even to move whole sentences and paragraphs. Most screen editing programs allow you to do all of these things, and thus give you enormous freedom to manipulate your written work.

Exercise this freedom on an extended passage copied from this book or any other printed source. Experiment with moving phrases, sentences, and entire paragraphs. If they look strange in their new positions (as they certainly should!), restore them to their old ones. In doing so, you will not only learn how to manipulate parts of a text on a screen; you will also see why one way of ordering sentences and paragraphs works better than another.

When you have learned and practiced all these procedures, you will be ready to use a word processor in writing essays of your own. You will of course have more technical details to learn—such as how to underline words and how to "format" a text for printing. But if you have followed the five suggestions given above, you should be ready to take full advantage of what can be done with a good screen-editing program.

A3.2 Writing and Rewriting with a Computerized Tutor

A good screen-editing program is just one of the ways in which a computer can help to improve your writing. Besides screen-editing, the world of computer research now offers a growing number of programs designed to stimulate writing, to help you develop your ideas, and to help you revise a completed draft. Some of these programs are designed to guide you all the way from pre-writing to final revision, while others aim simply to help you revise.

It is hard to assess all of these programs now because they are still being developed, tested, and improved. But for the time being, they seem to provide more help on revision than on generating an essay. While some programs can show you how to make an outline and can ask you certain questions about such things as your readership and your aims, these planning-aid programs are not yet equipped to *respond* specifically to the answers you provide. So just how effective they can be—or will be—remains to be seen.

On the other hand, computerized tutoring can offer quite specific help with revision. Various programs can check such things as your spelling, punctuation, style, sentence structure, and even—to some extent—your organization. But no computer program now known to us can actually correct your writing, or even positively identify more than a few kinds of errors. For the most part, revision-aid programs can tell you only where you *may* have grammatically erred or rhetorically faltered, and what you might do to improve your writing at that point. You alone must decide whether to make a particular revision, and just what it should be.

To illustrate more specifically what computerized tutoring can and cannot now do at the revising stage, here is a partial list of services currently available from some computer programs, and possibly available at your institution:†

1. Organizational analysis. The program prints the first and last sentence of each paragraph in your essay, and thus allows you to see—*perhaps*—whether or not the last sentence of each paragraph clinches the point introduced by the first one. Though the absence of any direct connection between the two is not necessarily a bad sign, a drastic difference between them indicates that the paragraph may lack unity, coherence, or both.

2. Measuring paragraph length. The program counts the words in each of your paragraphs and tells you whether any of them falls short of "average" length for good essays; you can thus see which of your paragraphs may need further development. You may find, of course, that you do not need a computer program to spot your skimpy paragraphs for you.

3. Identifying words and phrases that could be cut or changed. By asterisks, brackets, or some other form of highlighting, the program identifies the kinds of words and phrases that often weaken sentences. It identifies, for instance, all forms of the verb *to be,* and thus marks all uses of the passive voice (which requires the verb *to be*) as well as of phrases such as *there is, there are,* which frequently clutter sentences that would be better off without them. It can also identify any other words or phrases that are overused, vague, frequently misused, awkward, or undesirable for any reason—items such as *very, hopefully, interesting,* and *due to the fact that.* In some cases, the program suggests substitutes for the words and phrases thus identified.

---

† This account chiefly describes the present state (1985) of the UNIX Writer's Workbench Software, originated by Patricia S. Gingrich at Bell Laboratories and developed by Charles R. Smith and Kathleen E. Kiefer at Colorado State University.

4. Checking your spelling. The program checks each of your words against its own dictionary and marks any word it doesn't recognize. Because the computer's dictionary may not contain every word you might use and does not contain proper nouns, you can't assume that every word the computer marks is misspelled. Nor can you assume that every word the computer accepts is correctly spelled for its context, since the computer will always accept a word such as *peace*—even in a phrase such as *peace of pie. But the computer will catch many of your spelling errors, and with some programs you can ask the computer to give you all of the words in its dictionary that look like the one you may have misspelled—so that you can readily find the correct spelling of the word you want to use.

5. Checking punctuation. The program can now recognize certain kinds of obvious punctuation errors, such as missing capitals after periods. By the time you read this, it may be able to recognize comma splices and sentence fragments—parts of sentences punctuated as if they were whole ones.

6. Analyzing your sentences. The computer counts the number of words in each sentence, calculates the average length of your sentences, counts the number of short and long sentences (under and over set lengths), gives you a percentage for each sentence type (simple 48 percent, compound 12 percent, and so on), and thus indicates whether or not you may need more variety and complexity in the length and structure of your sentences.

The usefulness of computer programs offering services such as these is something you will finally have to judge for yourself. Some programs have already helped large numbers of students, and better programs are in the works. But it is just as risky to overestimate as to underestimate what computerized tutoring can do. It can help to develop your capacity to generate and revise essays, but it can never do the essential work of writing for you. It cannot choose your topic, develop it for you, reorganize a draft for you, or turn a weak sentence into a strong one. Even in the age of computers, the hardest tasks that writing involves must still be faced directly by the writer.

APPENDIX
4

BEYOND FRESHMAN ENGLISH
Writing Examinations, Applications, and Letters

Freshman composition is like a course in body building or modern dance. Just as either of those courses can develop your muscles, so a composition course can develop your powers of expression. But the long-range value of any such course depends on what you do after you take it. If you stop exercising your muscles after completing the body-building course, you may lose your new-found strength; if you stop writing after completing the composition course, you may lose your hard-earned facility with words. So you should keep on writing. If you do, you will find yourself increasingly able to face a variety of writing tasks: to write effective examination essays, business letters, job applications, and applications to postgraduate programs.

Anyone who writes well is likely to succeed in almost any writing task. But the requirements for various kinds of writing differ in some respects, and you should know what these differing requirements are. Also, you should know what good writing can do for you in the world beyond freshman composition. So this chapter aims to show you how to use your writing skills for a variety of purposes both in and out of the classroom.

A4.1 Writing Examination Essays

Obviously, the first thing you need in order to write a good examination essay is a knowledge of the subject on which you are being examined. But knowledge alone is not enough. In an examination essay, as in any other kind of essay, you must be able to organize what you are saying and point it toward a specific end. In this case, you must focus your knowledge on a particular question.

The best way to start writing a good examination essay, therefore, is to read the question carefully. On a final examination in a course on modern

American history, for example, students were asked to "show how Lyndon Johnson's policies in Vietnam grew out of the policies pursued by his predecessors from 1941 on." The question was quite pointed. It asked not for general impressions of the Vietnam War but for a specific analysis of the succession of policies that led America into it.

After reading the question, one student made a simple scratch outline inside the cover of his bluebook:

> CONTAINMENT
> 1. FDR, Truman—Vietnam and Korea
> 2. Ike—1954, SEATO, South Vietnam
> 3. JFK—military buildup
> Sum up Johnson's inheritance

With those few notes before him, the student then wrote the following essay:

> American involvement in the Vietnam War did not begin with Johnson, or even with Kennedy. Rather, it began during World War II and was developed considerably during the years of containment of the Truman administration. As Stephen Ambrose puts it in his book, the U.S. was paying up on an insurance policy on containment that began with the Truman doctrine (1947), was extended to Korea (1950), and was applied finally to Vietnam (1954).
>
> In 1941, Roosevelt supported the Vietnamese (specifically Ho Chi Minh), along with the French colonialists, against Japanese aggression. But after the Japanese were forced out, intense fighting broke out between the French and the Vietnamese, and in 1950 Truman signed a Mutual Defense Agreement with the French. From this point on, the U.S. had committed itself to support *anyone* against Ho Chi Minh and the communists of Hanoi. Truman was thus applying to Vietnam the containment policy he was also using in Korea. As in Korea, the U.S. aimed to halt the communism (in this case, of China) anywhere.
>
> The next rung in the American ladder of involvement came in 1954. The Vietnamese defeat of the French at Dien Bien Phu signalled the end of French involvement and the official beginning of American involvement. In September 1954 the Eisenhower administration formed the Southeast Asia Treaty Organization (SEATO) and committed the United States to the defense of South Vietnam as a bulwark against the expansion of Communist China.
>
> Kennedy inherited much of Eisenhower's policy toward Vietnam and added some of his own thinking, leaving Johnson an even larger legacy of involvement. While Kennedy did not commit troops, his military actions were significant. First, he increased dramatically (to 16,000) the number of American advisers in Vietnam. Second, he gave American air support to South Vietnam and allowed American advisers to shoot back if shot at. Third, he began military preparations within the Pentagon. As a result of all these actions, the first death of an American soldier occurred during Kennedy's first year in office, and American casualties increased considerably.
>
> When Kennedy was assassinated in 1963, Johnson inherited the Vietnam quagmire, and his inheritance was a rich one. From Roosevelt, he got the beginning of a U.S. role in Vietnam. From Truman, the policy of containment—the pledge to stop communist expansion at the hands of Ho Chi Minh. From Eisenhower he got an official commitment to the defense of

South Vietnam. And from Kennedy, finally, he got the beginnings of a substantial U.S. military involvement there.

So Johnson's decision to send troops to Vietnam in 1965 simply capitalized on the military preparations that Kennedy had made. Though Johnson imposed his own personality on Vietnam policy, he was strongly influenced by what Truman, Eisenhower, and Kennedy gave him: the need to succeed in Vietnam—militarily—along the lines of containment.

Like most examination essays, this one shows some signs of haste, such as the sentence fragment in the next to last paragraph. But no one taking a one- or two-hour exam has much time to worry about the finer points of diction and sentence structure. What we do find here are the three things essential to a good examination essay: (1) a response focused sharply and consistently on the question, (2) a substantial quantity of specific detail, and (3) strong organization.

From beginning to end, the author consistently focuses on the development of the policies Johnson inherited. In the opening paragraph, he introduces the key idea of containment; in the concluding paragraph, after summarizing what Johnson inherited from each of his predecessors, he reaffirms the influence of this idea. In between, he traces its evolution through a succession of stages, with one paragraph for each major stage: Truman's application of containment to Vietnam, Eisenhower's commitment of U.S. support to South Vietnam, and Kennedy's military actions there. Throughout the essay, the author keeps his eye on the task of answering the question: of explaining what Johnson received from his predecessors and how that inheritance shaped his actions in Vietnam.

Now consider what another student did with a question on a sociology exam. Asked to "define 'economic-opportunity structure' and describe its relation to the traditional nuclear family," the student wrote this:

The "economic-opportunity structure" (EOS) refers to the "working world" and is most often associated with the practical aspect of marriage. Traditionally, males have had superior access to this structure and still do today.

In the traditional nuclear family, the male is the mediator between the family and the EOS. Such a position gives him considerable "power" within the family unit. If members of a family are totally dependent on the man for economic survival, they must concede all power and authority to him. He is the "king of the family." He brings home the fruits of the EOS, the production (usually monetary), and the family consumes these products, investing in various material possessions which in turn give them social status and prestige.

The man's degree of success in the EOS highly affects his relation to his wife and family. In the traditional family, if the man fulfills his "duty" as chief economic supporter, the wife "rewards" him with more attention to his needs and to her traditional duties—keeping a house and raising children. The husband then rewards her in various ways, with a car of her own, perhaps, or a fur coat, or a bigger house. It's an ongoing cycle. The higher-status wives are also more likely to concede that the husband should have the "upper hand" in the marriage.

This whole cycle works in reverse in lower-status families where the husband is unsuccessful as a breadwinner, causing resentment among the wives and unwillingness to submit to his authority.

If the wife in the traditional nuclear family decides to enter the EOS, her commitment to a career is usually far less than that of her husband. Her primary duty is still to her family and husband. The husband remains chief economic provider. But the woman gains more marital power because now she actually brings income into the house. Her occupation gives her self-esteem, and the marriage moves toward an egalitarian relation.

All of these cases show how economic power outside the family affects the balance of power within it. A successful breadwinner is rewarded with attention; an unsuccessful one has to put up with resentment; and the status of a wife within the family improves when she takes a job. Thus the power of any one member of a nuclear family seems to depend a lot on his or her performance in the "economic-opportunity structure"—the working world.

The question calls for a definition of a phrase and an explanation of a relationship. The answer provides both. It defines the phrase and explains the relationship of the "EOS" to the traditional nuclear family, showing how the husband's power to make money affects his power within the family and how the status of the wife is affected by her decision to take a job. This essay has no introduction because it needs none; in effect, it is introduced by the question. But it does have a conclusion. Its final paragraph sums up its principal points, and its final sentence clearly states the essential point of the whole essay. (For more on conclusions, see section 3.6, pp. 44–46.)

To write a good examination essay, then, you should go directly to the point of the question. You should deal with the question as specifically as possible, and you should keep it continually in sight. Finally, you should end by summarizing your chief points and reaffirming the main point of the essay as a whole.

A4.2 Applying for Admission to a School of Business, Law, Medicine, or Graduate Study—The Personal Statement

Applying for admission takes more than simply filling out an application form. Most schools ask you to write a personal statement in which you explain why you plan to go into business, medicine, law, or an academic field. Your chances of getting admitted will of course depend considerably on your college grades, your letters of recommendation, and your performance on examinations like the LSAT. But a personal statement often tells more about you than anything else can. That is why it may well determine whether or not you are admitted to a particular school.

What kind of statement do admissions officers want? They want to know as specifically as possible what has led you to choose a particular career, what you hope to accomplish in it, and what you have already done to prepare yourself for it. The more specific you can be about your motivation, your experience, and your long-range plans, the more persuasive your statement will be. To see how this kind of information can be effectively presented, consider this statement made by an applicant to medical school:

A major turning point in my life occurred following my second year in college, when I was hired as a research assistant in pediatric hematology at the New England Medical Center. During the sixteen months I spent in Boston, I gained valuable insights into the practice of medicine and found that I had a special aptitude for research. I returned to college determined to become a doctor and quite motivated in my academic work.

At New England Medical Center I worked with very little supervision and was expected to be resourceful and creative in carrying out my lab responsibilities. I found that I had a talent for working out technical problems and the intellectual ability to design my own procedures. In addition to my laboratory work, I took the initiative to learn about the diseases seen by the department and about the treatment programs that were employed.

I learned a great deal about terminal illness through my job, and also through the death, from leukemia, of the young son of close friends of mine. During the last months of this child's life, I spent a considerable amount of time with his family, helping them to cope with their impending loss. I found I was able to offer types of support other friends and family members could not. I matured and grew from this experience. I learned that I could be open and responsive when faced with difficult and painful situations. I also realized that a need existed for people who could assist the terminally ill and their families.

In January 1979 I joined Hospice of Santa Cruz, where I was trained as a volunteer visitor and was assigned to the family of a man with stomach cancer. I feel that my involvement with the family is of benefit both to them and to me. I can support them by serving as a catalyst to get feelings expressed, and from them I am learning to be a compassionate listener. I am convinced my experience with Hospice will help me, as a medical worker, to be understanding and open in dealing with death.

My academic work during the past two years, has, for the most part, been of outstanding quality. I chose to complete a chemistry major, with emphasis in biochemistry, and will be graduating in December 1979. I have worked for the past year and a half on a senior research project in cryoenzymology. Laboratory work presents numerous technical and intellectual challenges, and I have become quite skilled and competent in approaching these problems. I have been attracted to research because it serves to ground the theory one learns in the classroom in practical day-to-day applications. Whereas I do not expect to pursue a career in research, my laboratory experience has given me a good perspective into the nature of scientific study, has helped me develop critical thinking skills, and has offered the pleasure and satisfaction that comes with the successful completion of a project.

This past academic year I have encountered for the first time the challenge of teaching. I have been a tutor for organic chemistry, introductory chemistry, and biochemistry. To be a good tutor one not only needs to have a solid command of the subject matter but must also look at the material from the student's perspective and seek creative methods to convey information in a way that can be grasped by the student. I have found that I can do this quite effectively, both at the very basic introductory level and at the more sophisticated level of biochemistry. Through tutoring I have discovered that I love teaching. I now realize that one of the compelling attractions that medicine offers me is the opportunity to be a teacher of all kinds of people, from patients to other physicians.

I am grateful to have had in these past five years a rich variety of experiences that have prepared me for the diversity I expect to encounter in a medical career. Research, teaching, the direct care of people who are sick, and encounters with death are all part of the practice of medicine. I have gained insights, limited though they may be, into all of these. As a result I am confident that I know what I will be facing as a doctor and that I have the skills and ability to be a creative and supportive physician.

This statement bristles with detail. It tells exactly how the writer discovered her interest in medicine and what she has already done to prepare herself for a career in it. By specifically describing her experiences in laboratory research, college courses, teaching, and working with the families of the terminally ill, she convincingly shows that she has both the ability and the sensitivity to make a career in medicine.

Furthermore, this statement is very well organized. Introduced with a paragraph on the particular experience that led the writer to a medical career, the statement concludes with a paragraph on the net effect of all her experiences. In between these two paragraphs, she tells in chronological order the story of her development, and each of her paragraphs is written to develop a point about what she learned. Altogether, it is not hard to see why she was admitted to medical school.

Obviously, this applicant had plenty of experience to write about. But if you take the time to recall the various kinds of work that you yourself have probably done, you may discover that you too have had a good deal of experience. In any case, the fact that you have had experience will not by itself make your statement effective. You have to organize your account of that experience, to present it in such a way that the reader can see how it led to a specific end. The statement just discussed is organized in exactly this way, clearly showing how the stages of the writer's experience led to her desire for admission to medical school. To see what a difference organization makes, compare her statement with one made by an applicant to a graduate school of business:

> Represented a Cable TV association in a twelve-million dollar public financing. Responsibilities included fostering a marketable image of our client and their objectives for the benefet of the underwriters and potential investors. This also involved making numerous decisions and analyses in regard to our interface with FCC requirements.
>
> The more significint factors impacting my long-range development from this experience include that I learned the coordination of financing needs and federal requirements. Throughly mastered quality control. Discovered how to identify areas of agreement and difference among the participants. Who eventually reached agreement through my involvement. Developed methods of meeting and turning around objections. And developed the ability to state my opinions in spite of intense pressure from various individules in a high-demand environment situation.

The writer has obviously had a good deal of experience in business, but he has failed to describe it effectively. First of all, he has confused a personal statement with a résumé (see below, section A4.3). In a résumé, statements about what the applicant has done sometimes start without a subject, so that instead of saying, "I represented X," the applicant might simply say, "Represented X." But a personal statement requires complete sentences. The lack of subjects in the first two sentences of the opening paragraph and the vagueness of *This* in the third sentence make the paragraph incoherent. Instead of an organized summary of the writer's experience, we get a string of disconnected remarks.

Second, the language is at once pretentious and sloppy. The writer uses pretentious jargon in phrases like *fostering a marketable image, in regard to our interface,* and *impacting my long-range development.* At the same time, he makes a number of spelling errors: *objctives* for *objectives, benifet* for *benefit, significint* for *significant,* and *individules* for *individuals.* In the second paragraph the writer claims to have *throughly mastered quality control,* but he has not yet mastered the spelling of *thoroughly.*

These two examples show what makes the difference between a bad statement and a good one, or—to put it bluntly—between rejection and acceptance. If you want to be rejected, put a lot of high-sounding words and phrases together without bothering to check your organization, sentence construction, or spelling, and without bothering to provide any clear and telling detail about what you have done. If you want to be accepted, write clearly, honestly, and specifically about your own experience and goals; take the time to see that your statement is well organized, that every sentence is complete and correct, and that every word is spelled right. Sloppy writing makes a bad impression; careful writing makes a good one. If you write carefully and explain specifically what has led you to choose a particular career, your statement will carry the kind of commitment and conviction that admissions officers want to see.

A4.3 Applying for a Job—The Résumé and the Covering Letter

The most important thing you need when applying for a job is a résumé—a list of your achievements and qualifications. The résumé should give all the essential facts about the position you seek, the date of your availability, your education, your work experience (with informative details), your extracurricular activities, and your special interests. You may include personal data, but you do not have to. The résumé should also list the names and addresses of your references—persons who can write to a prospective employer on your behalf; before listing their names, of course, you should get their permission to do so. The sample résumé on p. 658 shows the format we recommend.

The résumé alone, however, will seldom get you a job or even an interview. With the résumé you must send what a hiring officer expects to see first: a covering letter. Since the résumé will list all the essential facts about you, the covering letter may be brief. But it should nonetheless be carefully written. If the letter makes a bad first impression, you will have one strike against you even before your résumé is seen. With some company offices getting over a thousand applications a month, you need to give yourself the best possible chance, and your covering letter can make a difference in the way your résumé is read.

What do hiring officers want in a covering letter? They look for a capsule summary of the résumé itself, and also for the things that résumés don't often tell them: how much you know about the company you hope to work for, what kind of work you hope to do, where you want to work, and what special skills you may have that need to be emphasized. The résumé defines your past; the covering letter can define your future, indicating what you hope to do for the company if you are hired.

Sample résumé

```
                         Harold B. Rivers
                          44 Buell Street
                    Faribault, Minnesota 55021
                         (507) 555-6789
```

Job Objective
      Marketing or advertising trainee
      (Date available: July 1, 1986)

Education

1982-86
      Monmouth College, Monmouth, Illinois
      Degree: B.A. (expected in June 1986)
      Major: Business administration

1978-82
      Fairbault Senior High School, Faribault,
      Minnesota
      Academic degree

Work Experience

Summer 1985
      Acting Assistant Manager, Brown's
      Department Store, Faribault, Minnesota.
      Responsibilities included checking
      inventory, handling complaints, and
      processing special orders.

Summer 1984
      Salesclerk, Brown's Department Store,
      Faribault, Minnesota

Summers 1982
and 1983
      Waiter, The Village Pub, Northfield,
      Minnesota

Extracurricular
Activities
      Undergraduate Council, Monmouth College
      Debate Forum (President, 1981-82),
      Monmouth College
      Drama Club (President, 1977-78),
      Faribault Senior High School

Special Interests
      Photography, public speaking, drama

References
      For academic references:
          Office of Student Placement
          Monmouth College
          Monmouth, Illinois 61462

          Mr. George C. Hazen
          Manager, Brown's Department Store
          300 Main Street
          Faribault, Minnesota 55021

          Mrs. Nancy Wright
          Manager, The Village Pub
          24 Harris Street
          Northfield, Minnesota 55057

To see what a difference a covering letter can make, compare these two, both sent to the same company:

Dear Mr. ————:

In January, 1986, you were interviewing at the ———— College campus. I was schedule to see you but I had just accepted a position with ———— Stores and canceled my interview.

At the present time I am working as assistant buyer in Tulsa, Oklahoma. I have been commuting every two weeks to see my family in Chicago. I am seeking employment in the Chicago area.

Enclosed is my résumé for your consideration again. Thank you for your attention. I will look forward to hearing from you in the near future.

Sincerely,

Dear Mr. ————:

I am seeking a challenging position in marketing and consumer relations with a company in the Chicago area. I am particularly drawn to your firm because it is a utility, and utilities must maintain a proper balance between serving the public and protecting their own corporate interests. The challenge of maintaining this balance strongly appeals to me.

I have studied both marketing and consumer relations. At Monmouth College, from which I will shortly receive a B.A. in business administration, I took courses in such subjects as Consumer Attitudes, Marketing Strategies, and Principles of Retail Management.

Along with my education, I have had job experience which has given me frequent contact with the public. Working in a small business for two summers, I learned firsthand how to deal with consumers, and in the second summer I was promoted from salesclerk to acting assistant manager.

I hope you will review the attached résumé. Although a position in my field of interest may not be open at this time, I would appreciate your consideration for future management or marketing opportunities.

Yours truly,

These two letters make quite different impressions. The first writer opens by misspelling *scheduled* and by recalling that he once canceled an interview with the man to whom he is now writing for a job; the second writer opens with a clear-cut statement of his ambition. The first writer tells almost nothing about his interest in the company; the second tells exactly what makes the company appealing. The first writer asks to be hired because he wants to see more of his family; the second asks to be hired because his studies in marketing and consumer relations and his experience in selling will enable him to help the company. Which of these two applicants do you think the hiring officer will want to see?

If you can answer that question, you know the difference between a weak covering letter and a strong one. A weak letter speaks of what the company can do for the writer; a strong letter speaks of what the writer can do for the company. If your own covering letter can at least begin to indicate how your experience and qualifications will help the company, the hiring officer will probably read your résumé with more than usual interest.

(For the format of a covering letter, which is a kind of business letter, see the next section.)

A4.4 Writing a Business Letter—The Proper Format

The covering letter that accompanies a résumé is just one example of a business letter—a letter designed to initiate or transact business. Such a letter should be concise and forthright. In relatively short paragraphs it should accurately state all the information that the writer needs to convey.

The format of a business letter is shown on p. 661. For a business letter you normally use medium-weight typing paper of standard size (8½ by 11 inches). Center the letter as well as you can, leaving side margins of at least 1½ inches. Unless the body of the letter is extremely short, use single-spacing and block form; type the paragraphs without indentation, and separate one from the next by a double space. Also leave a double space between the inside address and the salutation, between the salutation and the body, and between the body and the complimentary close. Leave at least four spaces for your signature between the complimentary close and the typed name.

Fold the completed letter in two places—a third of the way down from the top and up from the bottom—and insert it in a business envelope (4⅛ by 9½ inches) addressed as shown on p. 661.

A4.5 Writing for Your Rights—The Letter of Protest

We live in a world of huge and increasingly impersonal corporations. Most of the bills and probably most of the letters you get come not from human beings but from machines. Bills are processed automatically; letters are clacked out by computers that know your address and your social-security number and have been taught to use your name in every other sentence, but nonetheless have not the faintest idea who you are or what your problems might be. How do you shout back at all this machinery? When you have a problem that can't be solved by a computerized explanation, how do you make yourself heard?

In a word, write. Do not accept the computerized explanation. Do not accept the words of a machine. If you think you have been overcharged or incorrectly billed or stuck with defective goods or shoddy service, don't keep silent. Fight back. Write a letter to the company or the institution, and demand to have your letter answered by a live human being. If the facts are on your side and you state them plainly, you may win your case without ever going to court or spending one cent for legal advice.

A friend of ours was billed $46.00 for an emergency service that he thought his medical insurance should cover. When the insurance company denied the claim, he phoned the company, got the name of the president, and wrote this letter directly to him:

> Dear Sir:
>   In connection with the enclosed bill for emergency-room service provided to my son Andrew on October 15, I write to ask an explanation for your company's refusal to pay for this service.
>   Your company's statement for October indicates that the charge for emergency-room service is not covered because "use of emergency room is covered when in connection with accident or minor surgery." Does this mean that use of the emergency room is covered *only* when in connection with

Format of a business letter

Return address { 14 Sunset Drive
Interlaken, N.J.   08074
October 1, 1985
← Date

Side address {
Mr. Roy A. Blodgett
Director, Research Division
Baker Games, Inc.
502 Broad Street
Buffalo, N.Y. 14216

Salutation → Dear Mr. Blodgett:

I am writing at the suggestion of Ms. Grace Smith, owner of the
Nifty Novelty Shop in Interlaken, N.J. She has carried your
games for more than fifteen years.

Ms. Smith thinks you would be interested in a game I have
invented. It resembles backgammon but requires the two players
to use mini-computers rather than dice when making a move. This
Body {
step reduces the element of chance and rewards the players´
skill. Friends tell me the game is more exciting than backgammon
or chess.

If you would like to see the game, I would be glad to give a
demonstration when you come to New York City for a meeting with
your buyers in the area. I can be reached at the following
number: 1-609-555-2468.

Complimentary close →
Sincerely yours,

Signature →
George A. Andrews

Typed name →
George A. Andrews

Format of a business envelope

George A. Andrews
14 Sunset Drive
Interlaken, N.J. 08074

Mr. Roy A. Blodgett
Director, Research Division
Baker Games, Inc.
502 Broad Street
Buffalo, N.Y. 14216

accident or minor surgery? Andrew had neither of these, but his condition was a genuine emergency, and I don't see why you refuse to cover treatment for it.

Andrew has asthma. He has long been treated for it by Dr. ———, who is an allergy specialist, but from time to time he has severe respiratory attacks that require emergency treatment—or rather, that require adrenalin, which is available *only* at the emergency room of ——— Hospital. If Andrew could have received adrenalin anywhere else, I could understand your denial of our claim, but so long as the hospital dispenses adrenalin *only* to emergency-room patients, we have to take him there. If we hadn't taken him there on October 15, he might have stopped breathing.

I can fully understand why you stop short of reimbursing all visits to the emergency room, since that would be an open invitation for your subscribers to use the emergency room for any and all ailments. But I believe you must distinguish between genuine emergencies and routine problems. I therefore expect your company to pay this particular bill in full.

Yours truly,

This letter got fast results. The president of the company referred it to the vice-president in charge of claims, and within a week the vice-president wrote to say that an asthma attack was indeed a genuine emergency, so the company would pay the bill in full. Thus the letter writer saved himself $46.00—not bad pay for the half hour he took to write the letter.

To see the effect that a letter of protest can have is to discover the power of the written word. Whether you realize it or not right now, the way you write can make a real difference in the life you lead after you have completed freshman English. In a composition course, you are writing for a grade. But when you write a statement for an admissions officer, you are writing for a place in a school, and getting that place may determine the rest of your career. When you write a letter of application to a hiring officer, you are writing for a job. And when you write a letter of protest, you are writing for your rights.

What writing ability finally gives you, then, is the power to express yourself on paper for any purpose you choose. The more you write, the better you will write; and the more kinds of writing you do, the more you will discover what writing can do for you. If you care about your writing, you will continue to refine and develop it long after the composition course is over. Very few things that college can give you will be more important to you afterward than the ability to put your thoughts and feelings into words.

Copyright acknowledgments *(continued from p. iv)*

Life: From "An Ugly New Footprint in the Sand" by A. B. C. Whipple. A. B. C. Whipple, *Life Magazine* © 1970 Time Inc. Reprinted by permission.

Little, Brown and Company: Alston Chase: from GROUP MEMORY by Alston Chase. Copyright © 1980 by Alston Chase. By permission of Little, Brown and Company, in association with The Atlantic Monthly Press.

McGraw-Hill: From *The Attack on Corporate America* by Bruce M. Johnson: Robert Thomas's essay "Is Corporate Executive Compensation Excessive?" Copyright © 1978. Reprinted by permission of McGraw-Hill Book Company.

New York Times: From "About Morris Heller" by Janet Heller. Copyright © 1976 by The New York Times Company. From "Double Vision" by Lynn Minton. Copyright © 1973 by The New York Times Company. Reprinted by permission.

W. W. Norton: From *Economics: Principles, Problems, Decisions* by Edwin Mansfield. From *Psychology of Women* by Juanita H. Williams. Reprinted by permission.

George S. Phylactopoulos: From "Greek Easter" by Ismene Phylactopoulos. Reprinted by permission.

Random House: From *The Immense Journey* by Loren Eiseley. Copyright 1946. From *The Autobiography of Malcolm X* by Malcolm X and Alex Haley, and copyright © 1965 by Alex Haley and Betty Shabazz. Reprinted by permission of Random House, Inc.

Straight Arrow Publishers: From "Memoirs of a Non-Prom Queen" by Ellen Willis from *Rolling Stone.* By Straight Arrow Publishers, Inc. © 1976. All Rights Reserved. Reprinted by permission.

Judy Syfers: From "Why I Want a Wife." Copyright © 1970 by Judy Syfers. Reprinted by permission.

Silver Burdett: © Silver Burdett Company, *Modern History* by Carl Becker and Kenneth S. Cooper. Used by permission (copyright 1958 & 1977).

H. W. Wilson: From *Readers' Guide to Periodical Literature.* Copyright © 1978, 1979 by The H. W. Wilson Company. Material reproduced by permission of the publisher.

INDEX

tense sequence in, 381
compound words, 463–64, 468–69
comprehensive summary, 212–13
compression, 220–21
conclusions:
    in arguments, 123
    course of action recommended
        in, 45
    in deduction, 122–23
    for essays, 44–46
    findings summarized in, 529
    paragraphs ended with, 165–66
    questions answered in, 45
    for research papers, 528–29
    thesis reaffirmed in, 44–46, 59,
        528–29
conditional sentences, 404–5, 604
conjunctions:
    commas with, 72–73, 273,
        423–24
    in compound phrases, 236–37
    in compound sentences, 272–73
    defined, 604
    semicolons with, 434
    in titles, 476
conjunctive (sentence) adverbs,
        274–76, 278
    commas with, 276, 425
    defined, 604–5
    semicolons with, 275, 434
connotation, 179–81
    defined, 179, 605
    editing for, 70
conscience, conscious, 581–82
continual, continuous, 582
continuity:
    defined, 56
    revising for, 58
contractions, 471
contrast:
    alternating structure for, 94–97
    block structure for, 94–97
    in compound phrases, 236
    with conjunctive adverbs,
        274–75
    defined, 605
    in exposition, 93–97
    in parallel constructions, 282–83
    subordinators used for, 300
    words defined by, 98

words indicative of, 158
coordination, 309–10
    defined, 605
    in parallel constructions, 69,
        281–88
    subordination combined with,
        289–90, 309–14
    untangling sentences with,
        314–16
correlatives:
    in compound phrases, 237
    defined, 605
    in parallel constructions, 283
council, counsel, consul, 582
countries, abbreviations for, 479
covering letters, 657, 659
    format for, 659
    résumés accompanied by, 657,
        659
credible, credulous, 582
criterion, criteria, 582
Cumulative Book Index, 490
Current Index to Journals in Education (CIJE), 196
Current Review Citations, 492

dangling modifiers, 266–69
    defined, 605
    editing for, 71
dashes, 451–52
    appositives set off by, 251, 451
    in dialogue, 451–52
    overuse of, 452
    phrases set off by, 451
data, 582–83
dates, 430–32
    abbreviations for, 479
    commas in, 430–32
    numbers in, 481
declarative sentences, 605
deduction, 120–22, 605
    fallacies in, 127–32
    induction combined with,
        123–25
    induction vs., 117–18
    persuasive, 121–22
    premises in, 120–22
    scientific, 120
    syllogisms in, 120–21

deduction *(continued)*
  valid vs. invalid conclusions in,
    122–23
definitions of words, 97–100, 448,
  449
  by analogy, 98
  by analysis, 98
  by comparison and contrast, 98
  dictionary as guide to, 174–78
  by etymology, 99–100, 177
  by example, 98–99
  for exposition, 97–100
  by function, 98
  by synonym, 98
degrees, punctuation of, 431
delusion, illusion, allusion, 577
denotation, 178–79
  defined, 178, 605
  dictionary as guide to, 178
  editing for, 70
dependent clauses, *see* subordinate
  clauses
description, 82–86
  analytical, 83
  defined, 82, 83
  evocative, 84
  as exposition, 89–91
  informative, 83
  narration combined with, 87–89
dialects, 353–54
dialogue:
  dashes in, 451–52
  ellipsis dots in, 455
  extended, 408–9
  paragraphing of, 444
  punctuation of, 444
diction, 170–74
  consistency in, 173–74
  defined, 170
  dictionary as guide to, 178
  editing for, 70
  high level of, 172
  low level of, 172
  middle level of, 171–72, 173
  mixed levels of, 172–73
  in tone, 54
  usage labels in, 176–77
dictionary, use of, 174–78
Dictionary of American Biography,
  490

different from, different than, 583
differ from, differ with, 583
direct objects:
  defined, 610
  faulty predication and, 240
  in infinitive phrases, 257
  noun clauses as, 305–6
  transitive verbs and, 229–30
direct reporting of discourse,
  407–12
  extended dialogue in, 408–9
  of poetry and prose, 409
  questions in, 410, 411
  quotation marks in, 407–8
  use of, 407
  verb tenses in, 408
discourse, spoken, 446–47, 448–49
disinterested, uninterested, 583
diversion, as analytical method,
  100–103
do, 367–68
documentation, styles of, 530–31
  see also citation
drama, 217
due to, because of, 583

each, 339
editing, 67–81
  to activate verbs, 68–69
  for choice of words, 70
  for grammer, 70–72
  for punctuation, 72–73
  revising vs., 47
  for rhetorical effectiveness,
    67–70
  for spelling, 73–75
  for wordiness, 69
  on word processor, 649–50
effect, affect, 576
ellipsis dots, 455–56
  in dialogue, 455
  for omissions in quotations,
    455–56, 514–15
eminent, imminent, immanent, 583
emotional persuasion, 112–14
emphasis, 154–57
  arrangement for, 156–57
  bold print for, 52
  exclamation points for, 52,
    441–42

with parentheses, 453
in parenthetical citations, 542
in quotations, 445
in sentence fragments, 322, 440
persecute, prosecute, 591
person, 611
personal, personnel, 591–92
personal statements, 654–57
  detail in, 656
  organization in, 656
  pretentious jargon in, 657
  purpose of, 654
  résumés vs., 656
persuasion, 55, 111–42
  in advertising, 111–12
  defined, 111
  emotional appeals in, 112–14,
    142–43
  see also argument
phenomenon, phenomena, 592
phrases:
  absolute, 259–60, 600
  adjective, 245–46, 600
  adverb, 247, 601
  compound, 235–38, 309, 604
  dashes in, 451
  defined, 611
  infinitive, 257, 258, 607
  modifying, 238–39
  noun, 232, 609
  participle, 252–55, 610–11
  prepositional, 193, 320, 612
  verb, 231, 616
plagiarism, 522–25
  acknowledgment of sources and,
    522–23
  copying key word or phrase, 524
  defined, 522
  paraphrasing without citation,
    524
  word-for-word copying, 523
plays, parenthetical citations for,
  537
plural forms:
  of abbreviations, 463, 471
  of nouns, 337, 357, 462–64
  of numbers, 463
  of pronouns, 338–39, 341
poetry, 217

parenthetical citations for,
  537–39
quoting from, 447–48, 456–57
poor, poorly, 592
possessive forms:
  of abbreviations, 470
  of nouns, 74, 470–71, 472
  of pronouns, 74, 343, 345,
    471–72
post hoc, ergo propter hoc argument,
  129
precede, proceed, proceeds, proceedings,
  procedure, 592
predicate adjectives, 229, 611
predicate nouns, 229
  defined, 611–12
  faulty predication and, 240
  noun clauses as, 306
predicates, 228
  defined, 611
  in sentence fragments, 319–20,
    323
predication, faulty, 240–42, 606
prefixes, 460–61, 469
premises, 120–22
prepositional phrases:
  defined, 612
  in sentence fragments, 310
  in wordiness, 193
prepositions:
  defined, 612
  in idioms, 187–88
  objects of, 345, 437
present perfect tense, 369–70, 382
present progressive tense, 369
present tense, 368–69, 381–82
pretentious words, 189, 657
pre-writing, 13–21
  analogies used in, 20–21
  asking questions in, 18–20
  for assigned topics, 16–17
  conflicts as stimulation for, 14,
    19–20
  inspiration and, 13
  methods of discovery in, 14–17
  nuggets in, 21
  reading for, 21
  soliciting reactions to, 20
  thesis in, 22

style invigorated by elimination of, 417
technique for elimination of, 191
word processing, 645–50
    editing programs in, 649–50
    for final copy, 75
    forms of instruction for, 646
    microcomputers vs. "dumb" terminals for, 646
    organizational analysis programs in, 649
    paragraph length programs in, 649
    printouts in, 647–48
    punctuation programs in, 650
    screen editing in, 646–47
    spelling programs in, 650
    typing vs., 645
    warm-up exercises for, 647–48
    writing stimulation programs in, 648–49
words, 170–95
    abstract vs. concrete, 70, 181–83
    argumentative, 132–33
    compound, 463–64, 468–69
    connotation of, 70, 179–81, 605
    definitions of, 97–100, 174–78, 448, 449
    denotations of, 70, 178–79, 605
    dictionaries and, 174–78
    diction level and, 170–74
    divided at end of line, 468
    editing for choice of, 70
    euphemisms, 70, 189–90
    forms of, 176
    general vs. specific, 70, 181–83

jargon, 70, 188–89
    pretentious, 189, 657
    related forms of, 177
    transitional, 158–59, 166
    usage labels for, 176
    see also language
Works Cited
    for APA style parenthetical citations, 643–44
    arrangement of, 545
    author's name in, 546, 548, 549
    collections of works in, 549–50
    information given in, 546–47
    information service documents in, 553–54
    interviews in, 556
    journal articles in, 551–52
    newspapers in, 552–53
    nonprint sources in, 554–56
    punctuation in, 545–46
    reference books in, 550–51
    translations in, 550
would have, would of, 599
writing:
    conscious learning in, 3
    descriptive, 82–86
    directed freewriting and, 22–25
    expository, 89–110
    narrative, 86–89
    pre-writing and, 13–21
    readers considered in, 35–38
    rhetoric in, 6–7
    as solitary act, 3–4
    talking vs., 3–4

you, your, yourself, 333